Communications
in Computer and Information Science 1738

More information about this series at https://link.springer.com/bookseries/7899

Vijayan Sugumaran · Divya Upadhyay ·
Shanu Sharma (Eds.)

Advancements in Interdisciplinary Research

First International Conference, AIR 2022
Prayagraj, India, May 6–7, 2022
Revised Selected Papers

 Springer

Editors
Vijayan Sugumaran ⓘ
Oakland University
Rochester, NY, USA

Divya Upadhyay ⓘ
ABES Engineering College
Ghaziabad, India

Shanu Sharma ⓘ
ABES Engineering College
Ghaziabad, India

ISSN 1865-0929   ISSN 1865-0937 (electronic)
Communications in Computer and Information Science
ISBN 978-3-031-23723-2   ISBN 978-3-031-23724-9 (eBook)
https://doi.org/10.1007/978-3-031-23724-9

This Springer imprint is published by the registered company Springer Nature Switzerland AG
The registered company address is: Gewerbestrasse 11, 6330 Cham, Switzerland

Preface

The International Conference on Advancements in Interdisciplinary Research (AIR 2022) was organized by the Department of Applied Mechanics, Motilal Nehru National Institute of Technology (MNNIT) Allahabad, Prayagraj, India and took place on May 6–7, 2022. The conference was proposed around the theme of a smart and sustainable Society.

The purpose of the conference was to raise participant awareness of the sustainability issues presented by technological advancement and how they affect both people's individual lives and society as a whole. Considered in its entirety, this conference offered precise and comprehensive insights into the development of sustainable technology in a variety of fields.

In addition, the goal of AIR 2022 was to offer a forum for debating the problems, concerns, and scientific discoveries in the multidisciplinary field of engineering. The main goal of holding this conference was to give researchers from various fields, including biomedicine, computer science, mechanical engineering, electronics, manufacturing, industry, and management, a single forum to discuss obstacles, trends, technologies, and opportunities for the development of a smart and sustainable society.

The conference was a two-day online gathering that featured keynote speeches by subject matter experts, roundtable discussions, and oral and poster presentations of new ideas and research. Innovative engineering solutions, emerging technologies, and challenges for a sustainable healthcare industry were the topics of the research findings covered during the conference. Different advances in robotics and automation engineering, and economic and environmentally sustainable smart cities were also discussed. The topics covered and presented during AIR 2022 represented a vast pool of research knowledge, resources, and expertise of the various research and technological communities from India and other countries such as USA, UK, Canada, and South Korea. Participants at AIR 2022 made a substantial contribution to our overall national development in the emerging fields of energy, artificial intelligence, IoT applications in agriculture, and healthcare systems.

Sustainable development is needed in the current scenarios and this has a significant impact on society worldwide. Automation and the creation of intelligent systems have opened up new opportunities for sustainable development in the modern era. The advancement of these intelligent systems offers chances to address problems that negatively impact our way of life. The environment, energy and natural resources, and society all face unprecedented challenges as a result of the rapid pace of global urbanization, urban growth, and rising urban population density.

On the other hand, the confluence of cutting-edge technologies like AIoT, Edge Computing, Fog Computing, Blockchain, and 5G has caused a significant transformation in the technology sector. In terms of digital transformation, blockchain and artificial intelligence of things (AIoT) technologies represent a stunning 21st-century revolution. While blockchain technology has the potential to offer an effective and safe method of controlling various operations, AIoT gives a platform for bringing intelligent automation to industries to regulate various processes. Several domains, including healthcare, agriculture, automation, governance, and others, are adopting these next-generation technologies in order to cut costs, improve efficiency, and increase productivity with the introduction of 5G and the power of remote data processing technologies like cloud and fog computing.

To bring a revolutionary change to automation industries, AIR 2022 invited authors involved in the design of Sustainable Computing Methods to present the remarkable power of next-generation technologies in transforming industries.

AIR 2022 received an overwhelming response through more than 250 submissions for the conference. A rigorous double-blind peer review process was adopted under the supervision of Program Committee members, and 49 regular papers and 12 short papers for oral presentation (not included in the conference proceeding) were selected by the committee in the field of Computer Science.

This conference proceedings presents technological advancements involving various transformative technologies. The major sections of the book are: Novel Technologies-Enabled Secured Privacy Models and Optimized Networking Infrastructures for Secure Industries, Developments Towards a Sustainable Healthcare Sector, Machine Learning and Deep Learning-Enabled Applications in Different Sectors, and Robotics and Computer Vision for Intelligent Automation in Industry. It also focuses on trending technologies-enabled frameworks and applications to solve real-life issues.

This proceedings is the result of advancements made in the creation of intelligent approaches with the assistance of numerous authors from across the world. We hope that readers will gain worthwhile knowledge from the book.

November 2022   Vijayan Sugumaran
                                                                        Divya Upadhyay
                                                                          Shanu Sharma

Organization

General Chair

Abhishek Kumar   Motilal Nehru National Institute of Technology, Prayagraj, Allahabad, India

Program Committee Chairs

Vijayan Sugumaran   Oakland University, USA
Divya Upadhyay   ABES Engineering College, Ghaziabad, India
Shanu Sharma   ABES Engineering College, Ghaziabad, India
Ashutosh Mishra   Motilal Nehru National Institute of Technology, Prayagraj, Allahabad, India
Abhishek Tiwari   Motilal Nehru National Institute of Technology, Prayagraj, Allahabad, India
Ravindra Kannojiya   Amity University Uttar Pradesh, India

Steering Committee

Farid Meziane   University of Derby, UK
Sunil Vadera   Salford University, UK
Matthias Volk   Otto-von-Guericke-University Magdeburg, Germany
Epaminondas Kapetanios   University of Hertfordshire, UK
Joerg Leukel   University of Hohenheim, Germany
Stefan Kirn   University of Hohenheim, Germany
Elisabeth Metais   Conservatoire National des Arts et Métiers (CNAM), Paris, France
Jordi Conesa Caralt   University of Catalonia, Barcelona, Spain
Ghassan Beydoun   University of Technology, Sydney, Australia
Veda C. Storey   Georgia State University, USA
Wynne Chin   University of Houston, USA
Aurona Gerber   University of Pretoria, South Africa
Daniel Staegemann   Otto-von-Guericke-University Magdeburg, Germany
Victoria Yoon   Virginia Commonwealth University, USA
Neil Y. Yen   University of Aizu, Japan

| Aaron French | Kennesaw State University, USA |
| Priya Ranjan | Bhubaneswar Institute of Technology, Odisha, India |

Program Committee

Alok Verma	Energy Research Institute, NTU, Singapore
Shalini Sharma	National Tsing Hua University, Taiwan
Geetika Jain	Keele University, UK
Meenal Chaudhari	North Carolina State University, USA
Kirti Seth	INHA University, Uzbekistan
Sunanda Sinha	MNIT Jaipur, India
R. Jayaganthan	Indian Institute of Technology Madras, India
Dharmendra Singh	IIT Roorkee, India
Santosh Kumar	IIT (BHU), India
K.K. Shukla	NIT Jamshedpur, India
B. N. Singh	IIT Kharagpur, India
P. Chellapandi	IIT Madras, India
M. Sai Baba	Ramaiah University of Applied Sciences, Bangalore, India
Anil Kumar Sharma	Jamia Millia Islamia, India
Dhiraj Mahajan	IIT Ropar, India
Jitendra Prasad	IIT Ropar, India
Chander Prakash	Lovely Professional University, India
Ravi Panwar	IIT Jabalpur, India

Additional Reviewers

Misha Kakkar	Ela Kumar
Saru Dhir	Deepak Mane
Pushpa Singh	Kishore Balasubramanian
Shilpi Sharma	Sanatan Ratna
Anil Kumar Dubey	D. Jeya Mala
Kimmi Verma	K. Saravanan
Deepti Agarwal	Govindha Rasu N.
Arashdeep Kaur	Gagan Gupta
P. Sriramalakshmi	Kulbir Singh
Manish Bhardwaj	Ashutosh Pratap Singh
Sailesh Iyer	R. P. Pandey
Sudhanshu Maurya	Lakshmi Kanthan Narayanan
Kanwalvir Singh Dhindsa	Madan Lal Yadav
Abhilasha Singh	T. Hema
Manish Kumar Ojha	Manish Kumar

Arvind Kumar
Sudhanshu Singh
Keshav Kaushik
Rahul Deo Sah
Laxmi Ahuja
Kiran Chaudhary
Nikhil Sharma
Nalini Shankarnarayanan
Kaushal Kishor
Shamik Tiwari
Deepa Jose
Megha Bhushan
Umesh Chandra Pati
Siddharth Gautam
Megha Gupta

Devendra Kumar Misra
Rajiv Ranjan
Amit Kumar Mishra
Ila Kaushik
Suman Lata
Pallavi Gupta
Monoj Kumar Sur
Pooja Singh
Anand Kumar Pandey
Saigeeta Priyadarshini
Hoor Fatima
Sumeet Kumar
Rohit Sachdeva
D. Loganathan
Ritu Gupta

Contents

Robotics and Computer Vision for Intelligent Automation in Industries

Trending Technological Frameworks and Applications Focusing Real Life Issues

Novel Technologies Enabled Secured Privacy Models and Optimized Networking Infrastructures Toward Secure Industries

Fast Phrased Search for Encrypted Cloud Storage

Lokesh Kumar$^{(\boxtimes)}$ (iD) and Sushil Kumar Sharma

Institute of Technology and Management, Aligarh, India
cslokesh92@gmail.com

Abstract. In the cloud computing world, access and storage of confidential and sensitive documents have been a challenge. Data Breach is one of the major concerns in the cloud-computing world. Secure access to the data is crucial in order to protect personal information. Usually, untrusted cloud providers after the encryption of files maintain the private keys with themselves instead of data owners, which leads to data leakage and no privacy to the users. Hence, there is a requirement to securely store data on public, private, or Hybrid clouds without any use of private keys. In this paper, the aim is to provide a technique which helps in the conjunctive key search of encrypted documents, with the help of Bloom filters, which is faster, scalable, secure, and does not require any private key storage. The cloud facility will only contain a list of bloom filters with the Bloom Filter Identification numbers (IDs), which aids in privacy of the user.

Keywords: Conjunctive keyword search · Phrase search · Privacy · Security · Encryption

1 Introduction

With the onset of the digital era, cloud technologies are being adopted as data is increasing day by day. With that comes the need for security and proper rules for privacy and proper administration of access. With recent events of digital warfare, the need for secure cloud storage is now more than ever. Current or traditional methods involve the encryption to be done at the cloud providers' end, and not at the user, causing privacy issues and data leaks as well. Therefore, there is a need for proper private encryption methods which can help users create their own keys without letting the cloud providers know about the encryption and the method used. Many researchers have been working in coming up with methods which involve the storage of private keys with the users itself, and not the cloud owners.

Up until now, the cloud owners used to encrypt the keys and the data and kept the private key in their domain, however that allowed attacks and criminal intent towards cloud owners, and the users did not have any privacy. Also, there is no technique available to audit data outsourcing.

One of the earliest work done in the aforementioned field was proposed by Boneh et al. [1]. The proposed scheme mentioned the use of public key encryption which will

© The Author(s), under exclusive license to Springer Nature Switzerland AG 2022
V. Sugumaran et al. (Eds.): AIR 2022, CCIS 1738, pp. 3–13, 2022.
https://doi.org/10.1007/978-3-031-23724-9_1

help the keyword search methods and still keep the data hidden. However, the data search issue with encryption was still an issue due the speed of extracting information. Waters et al. [2] provided some insights for the same, by focusing on a new approach of single keyword searches. However, single keyword searches cannot provide the depth of the search required in a big database management system, therefore, conjunctive keyword search was proposed, which can provide a search of multiple keywords and find the data most similar to it, [3, 4]. However, the solution was not efficient to perform the conjunctive keyword search, therefore other solutions were introduced such as the ranking of search results [5–9] and fuzzy keyword search. Now with advancements in technology, phrases are being searched instead of a number of keywords [10–13]. However, with such methods, their security of fetching data must be improved, therefore new advancements were required [14, 15].

The aim of this work is to provide advancements in the field of the conjunctive key search of encrypted documents, with the help of Bloom filters, which is faster, scalable, secure, and does not require any private key storage. The cloud facility will only contain a list of bloom filters with the Bloom Filter Identification numbers (IDs).

1.1 Bloom Filters

Bloom filters are space-efficient probabilistic data structures that are used to test if the lookup element is a member of the given set. The usage of bloom filters has been increased in the implementation of search queries in database management systems as it is very space efficient. Working of Bloom filters includes a set of Hash Functions n, Hn (x) where x is the lookup element. E.g.: x be the element "Cloud" and let there be four Hash Functions H0 H1 H2 H3. The output is {3, 10, 17,19}. Also, let us assume that the size of the Hash function is 20. Therefore, the status of the Bloom filter will be as follows:

Then at the time of searching, when we try to search the Keyword "Cloud". It will again find the hash set against four Hash functions i.e. {3,10,17,19}. And search if these indexes in our Bloom filter are set as 1. If these indexes are set as 1, we can safely say that elements exist.

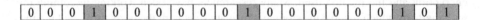

Bloom filter never gives false negatives, it always gives accuracy as 100%. However, there is an issue of False positives. For a given k hash functions and n bit terms and m be the size of the filter, the probability of false positives is approximately and the minimum false positive rate can be achieved when $k = (m/n) \ln 2$.

1.2 Inclusion Related Attack

In the scheme of encrypted cloud storage searching, the cloud service provider has access to three components: the encrypted files using symmetric encryption algorithm, the bloom filters associated with the encrypted files using their IDs and the searching mechanism.

Although the previous components do not contain any form of plain data, an attacker who has access to them can easily collect valuable information about users' data using N number of queries combined with some statistical information about files' content. The information leakage caused by these types of attacks would break the security of the entire scheme and hence they are known as Inclusion-related attacks. In the case of cloud services storing thousands of files over a period of time, there is a high probability that a set of keywords extracted from one file will have a strong correlation with other sets. For example, a new set could be almost a subset or superset of other sets.

Given that, observing the results of sending N queries will give information about the structure of the stored files, because highly correlated files will appear more frequently in the results. Moreover, this leakage could even be more severe if the attacker has access to a set of trapdoors, which will allow him to reveal information about the original content of the file (plain data from a set of keywords) and other correlated files.

However, the proposed searching mechanism utilizes bloom filters that map N number of queries to many sets of keywords which are shown in its false-positive rate. This mapping defends against inclusion-related attacks since different sets of keywords will have the same bits of bloom filter set to 1. Which will hide any correlations among the stored data as shown in Fig. 1.

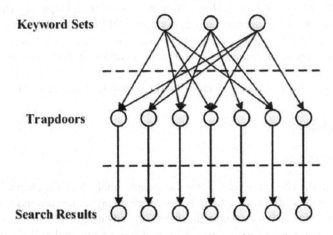

Fig. 1. Relation between results and set of keywords

Hence, there is a requirement to securely store data on public, private, or Hybrid clouds without any use of private keys.

In this paper, the aim is to provide a technique which helps in the conjunctive key search of encrypted documents, with the help of Bloom filters, which is faster, scalable, secure, and does not require any private key storage. The cloud facility will only contain a list of bloom filters with the Bloom Filter Identification numbers (IDs), which aids in privacy of the user.

With this study, the advantage would be the cloud facility will only contain a list of bloom filters with the Bloom Filter Identification numbers (IDs), which will make them faster, scalable, secure, and will not require any private key storage.

2   Literature Review

Work of Boneh et al. [1] proposed a very basic scheme of public key encryption, which allowed single keyword search on an encrypted keyword. Bilinear mapping was used in their study with user's identification.

Working with single keyword search was not enough, therefore conjunctive keyword search was introduced. The work of Ding et al. [3] improved upon the work of Boneh et al.'s [1] work, which was much easier to implement and produced less overhead than [1]'s work. However, for unstructured texts, it failed. Therefore the work of Kerschbaum et al. [4] provided some improvements in the field by working on searching for keywords in an unstructured manner, where positions of keywords are unknown. Another solution for the same was proposed by Wang et al. in [17] based on raking of the searched results. Their work mentions the usage of TFIDF (Term Frequency × Inverse Document Frequency) rule and the use of order preserving symmetric encryption.

However, the data search was not efficient on encrypted data. The first to work on the problem and provide a solution was Zittrower et al. [10] by using a keyword-to document index and a keyword location index. The pattern was recognized by the researchers that certain words are more common than others in every natural language. Therefore, to make this encryption more strong, conjunction was made in encrypted keywords, which added a number of false positives in query results, which masked the true search terms. And these false positives could easily be found by the user who encrypted it as some indicators are included in the index entries and also stored client-side. All of the tasks are performed on the client side, making it more secure for the user's privacy.

3   Methodology

3.1   Research Issues

It is clear from the above discussion that the security analysis of the channel is the key point where better analysis is required. Furthermore, many of the conventional schemes are slow in transformation domains. In general, the advantages of using a bloom filter are very high as it makes the system robust, scalable, secure, and will not require any private key storage.

3.2   Research Methodology

In the proposed scheme, there are 3 major roles: users, proxy server, and cloud storage server as shown in Fig. 2. Group of users of any organization that wishes to outsource their storage to the cloud. These users can have different privileged access to the resources as per the organization structure (administration wise such as standard users, head of the department, administrator, etc.). In this scheme, users can utilize the cloud service indirectly by accessing the local proxy server as they can upload/download files, remove files and search in the data stored in the cloud. The proxy server will have direct access to the cloud service API. It will forward all the operations which are needed to be done from the users to the cloud after processing them locally. The processing includes: checking user's credentials if it will grant him access to the requested operations.

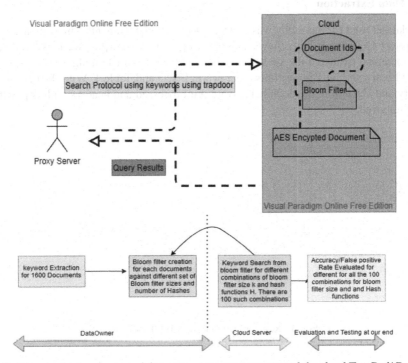

Fig. 2. Communication framework between users, proxy server and the cloud Test Bed/ Design

In case of uploading a new file, the proxy server will generate the encryption key from the given password then use the key to encrypt the file using the AES algorithm. Also, it will extract a set of keywords out of the file and generate a bloom filter. Finally, it will assign a new ID to the file and upload the encrypted file with the associated bloom filter to the cloud directly using its access token provided by the cloud service.

In case of searching in the data stored in the cloud, the proxy server will use hashing functions to generate the query sequence from the given keywords and will send it to the cloud. After receiving the response in the form of a list of IDs, the proxy server will match these IDs with the corresponding files name in its local database and forward the results to the user. If the user requests to download one of the files appearing in the result, the proxy server will download the encrypted file from the cloud storage, decrypted using the same key stored in the local database associated with the respected

ID, and send the decrypted file to the corresponding user. Cloud server will store the encrypted files along with their IDs, and will run the searching mechanism. Besides receiving uploading/downloading request from the proxy server, it will be receiving a query sequence which is a set of integers, this sequence will be used to perform AND operation on the stored bloom filters where the output will indicate the IDs of which files contains the data in respect to the current query. Later, these IDs will be sent back to the proxy server in order to show the final results to the corresponding user.

3.3 Data Extraction

The dataset used for this study was collected from 1600 documents which are available in Project Gutenberg: https://www.gutenberg.org/. In this corpus, we have read each document and extracted the keywords using a keyword extraction algorithm, using the spacy library and NLP algorithms as shown in Fig. 3 and Table 1. With the help of the library and algorithm, the documents were pre-processed and headers with copywrites were removed.

Fig. 3. Keyword extraction of 1600 documents

3.4 Implementation

All the 1600 Keywords were processed from the document in JSON format consisting of a Document ID, Document Name, and List of Keywords as presented in Fig. 4. This Payload will be further processed. After this, hash functions will be produced for different sets (from 1 to 10) for a list of keywords associated with each payload as presented in Fig. 5 and 6. The output of these hash functions will be mapped to our bloom filter of different sizes (from 100–1000). Therefore, one document with keywords there will be a total of 100 bloom filters with different combinations of hash functions and bloom filter size as presented in Fig. 7 and Table 2. Therefore, in total, we have 160000 bloom filters.

Table 1. Properties of the sample dataset

Sample Dataset	Properties
The average number of documents associated with a keyword: "Cloud", "Second", "Algorithm"	887
Total number of documents	1600
Total distinct keywords	310,000
The average number of keywords per document	10
Maximum number of keywords per document	50
The average number of distinct keywords per document	7
Maximum number of distinct keywords per document	20
The average number of times each keyword appears per document	5.5

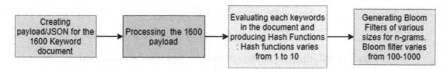

Fig. 4. Keyword extraction of 1600 documents

Table 2. Properties of Bloom Filter generated

Sample dataset	Properties
Number of hash functions	10
Range of hash functions	[1–10]
Number of bloom filter size	10
Range of bloom filter sizes	[100–1000]
Number of bloom filters for each document	100
Total number of bloom filters generated	160000
Average size of each folder	160 KB
Total size of 160000 Bloom filters	84.7 MB

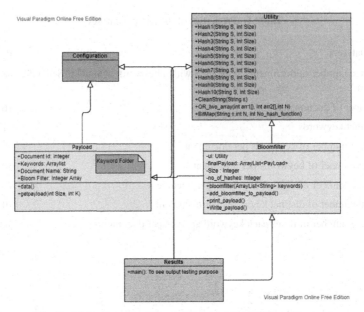

Fig. 5. UML diagram of the architecture that will be with cloud

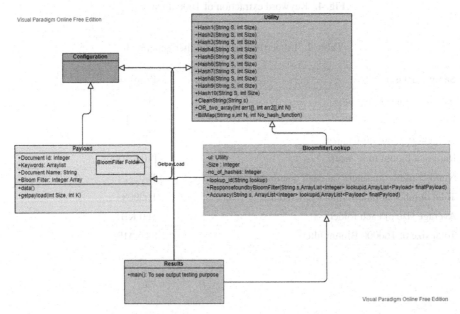

Fig. 6. UML diagram of the design that will be with user

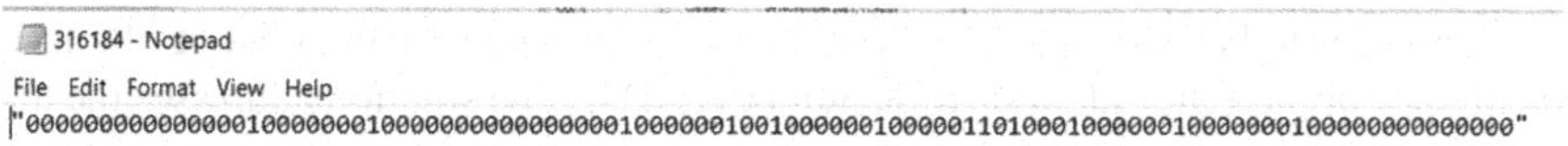

316184 - Notepad
File Edit Format View Help
"000000000000000100000001000000000000000010000001001000000100000110100010000000100000001000000000000000"

Fig. 7. Bloom filter sample for size = 100 and hash function = 1 for document 316184

4 Results

To present the results for the study we conducted, we have generated bloom filters of different sizes using a different number of hash functions for each one of the 1600 files. The specifications used for this experiment are mentioned below:

Bloom filter size range (m): from 200 bits to 1000 bits Number of hash functions (k): 2 to 10. Considering that in our setup the average number of keywords extracted from a single file is 10 keywords, the Bits per entry (m/n) parameter will vary between 10 and 100.

We plotted the false positive rate with respect to the size and number of hash functions used to generate each bloom filter as shown in Fig. 8. We can see that the false positive rate decreases while increasing the size of bloom filters and we will have the highest false-positive rate when more hash functions are used in smaller filter sizes.

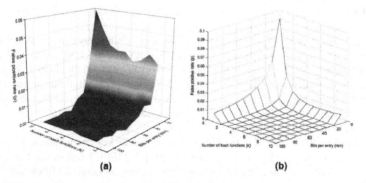

False positive rate (p)
Number of hash functions (k)
Bits per entry (m/n)
(a)
(b)

Fig. 8. (a) False-positive rate as a function of k and m/n in our experiment, (b) the false positive rate as in the experiment done by Poon et al. [1]

Figure 8 also shows that the false positive rate is stable and acceptable for any value of m/n > 40 which we should choose in practice since using larger sizes will only increase the storage overhead. However, in the experiments done by Poon et al. [1] the stable value of false-positive was for m/n > 10. Similarly using more than two hash functions will increase the computational overhead with no noticeable contribution to the false positive rate.

5 Conclusion

In this study, the aim was to work on the conjunctive key search of encrypted documents, with the help of Bloom filters, which is faster, scalable, secure, and does not require any private key storage. The cloud facility will only contain a list of bloom filters with the Bloom Filter Identification numbers (IDs). The solution addresses the high computational cost noted in [13] by reformulating phrase search as n-gram verification rather than a location search or a sequential chain verification. Unlike [10, 12, 13], our scheme consider only the existence of a phrase, omitting any information of its location. Unlike [11], our schemes do not require sequential verification, is parallelizable and has a practical storage requirement. Our approach is also the first to effectively allow phrase search to run independently without first performing a conjunctive keyword search to identify candidate documents. Considering that in our setup, the average number of keywords extracted from a single file is 10 keywords, the Bits per entry (m/n) parameter will vary between 10 and 100. We plotted the false positive rate with respect to the size and number of hash functions used to generate each bloom filter, and the false positive rate decreases while increasing the size of bloom filters and we will have the highest false-positive rate when more hash functions are used in smaller filter sizes. In this work, we have evaluated the false positive rate of searching schemes that utilize bloom filters, however, more analysis on both the computational efficiency and the storage efficiency is yet to be done. Which we are looking forward to doing in the future as a continuation of the current work.

References

1. Boneh, D., Di Crescenzo, G., Ostrovsky, R., Persiano, G.: Public key encryption with keyword search. In: Cachin, C., Camenisch, J.L. (eds.) EUROCRYPT 2004. LNCS, vol. 3027, pp. 506–522. Springer, Heidelberg (2004). https://doi.org/10.1007/978-3-540-24676-3_30
2. Waters B. R., Balfanz, D, Glenn Durfee, G., K. Smetters, D.K.: Building an encrypted and searchable audit log. In: Conference: Proceedings of the Network and Distributed System Security Symposium. NDSS, San Diego, California, USA (2004). https://www.cs.utexas.edu/~bwaters/publications/papers/audit_log.pdf
3. Ding, M., Gao, F., Jin, Z., Zhang, H.: An efficient public key encryption with conjunctive keyword search scheme based on pairings. In: 2012 3rd IEEE International Conference on Network Infrastructure and Digital Content (2012). https://doi.org/10.1109/icnidc.2012.6418809
4. Kerschbaum, F.: Secure conjunctive keyword searches for unstructured text. In: 2011 5th International Conference on Network and System Security (2011). https://doi.org/10.1109/icnss.2011.6060016
5. Hu, C., Liu, P.: Public key encryption with ranked multi-keyword search. In: 2013 5th International Conference on Intelligent Networking and Collaborative Systems (2013). https://doi.org/10.1109/incos.2013.24
6. Fu, Z., Sun, X., Linge, N., Zhou, L.: Achieving effective cloud search services: multi-keyword ranked search over encrypted cloud data supporting synonym query. IEEE Trans. Consum. Electron. **60**, 164–172 (2014). https://doi.org/10.1109/tce.2014.6780939
7. Clarke, C.L.A., Cormack, G.V., Tudhope, E.A.: Relevance ranking for one to three term queries. Inf. Process. Manage. **36**, 291–311 (2000). https://doi.org/10.1016/s0306-4573(99)00017-5
8. Tuo, H., Wenping, M.: An effective fuzzy keyword search scheme in cloud computing. In: 2013 5th International Conference on Intelligent Networking and Collaborative Systems (2013). https://doi.org/10.1109/incos.2013.150

9. Zheng, M., Zhou, H.: An efficient attack on a fuzzy keyword search scheme over encrypted data. In: 2013 IEEE 10th International Conference on High Performance Computing and Communications & 2013 IEEE International Conference on Embedded and Ubiquitous Computing (2013). https://doi.org/10.1109/hpcc.and.euc.2013.232

10. Zittrower, S., Zou, C.C.: Encrypted phrase searching in the cloud. In: 2012 IEEE Global Communications Conference (GLOBECOM), pp. 764–770 (2012). https://doi.org/10.1109/GLOCOM.2012.6503205.

11. Tang, Y., Gu, D., Ding, N., Lu, H.: Phrase search over encrypted data with symmetric encryption scheme. In: 2012 32nd International Conference on Distributed Computing Systems Workshops (2012). https://doi.org/10.1109/icdcsw.2012.89

12. Poon, H.T., Miri, A.: An efficient conjunctive keyword and phase search scheme for encrypted cloud storage systems. In: 2015 IEEE 8th International Conference on Cloud Computing (2015). https://doi.org/10.1109/cloud.2015.74

13. Poon, H.T., Miri, A.: A low storage phase search scheme based on bloom filters for encrypted cloud services. In: 2015 IEEE 2nd International Conference on Cyber Security and Cloud Computing (2015). https://doi.org/10.1109/cscloud.2015.30

14. Rhee, H.S., Jeong, I.R., Byun, J.W., Lee, D.H.: Difference set attacks on conjunctive keyword search schemes. In: Jonker, W., Petković, M. (eds.) SDM 2006. LNCS, vol. 4165, pp. 64–74. Springer, Heidelberg (2006). https://doi.org/10.1007/11844662_5

Secure Data Hiding and Extraction Using RSA Algorithm

Aminu Aminu Muazu[1,2]([✉]) [iD], Umar Danjuma Maiwada[1,2], Abubakar Rufa'i Garba[2],
Muhammad Garzali Qabasiyu[3], and Kamaluddeen Usman Danyaro[1] [iD]

[1] Department of Computer and Information Science, Universiti Teknologi PETRONAS, Perak,
Malaysia
{aminu.aminu,umar.danjuma}@umyu.edu.ng,
kamaluddeen.usman@utp.edu.my
[2] Computer Science Department, Faculty of Natural and Applied Sciences, Umaru Musa
Yar'adua University, Katsina, Nigeria
abubakar.rufai@umyu.edu.ng
[3] Department of Computer Studies, Hassan Usman Katsina Polytechnic, Katsina, Nigeria
garzaliqabasiyu@hukpoly.edu.ng

Abstract. Data hiding and extraction is an important aspect of information security because the data will be safer and more manageable. Data hiding technology that works well produces data that is efficient, secure, and simple to connect. The underlying communication network that enables the transport of sensitive data is insecure and unprotected. The fast rise of electronic methods of communication implies that information security has become a critical concern in the real world. As such, anyone with the necessary expertise and software may eavesdrop and intercept data transmissions, which can be extremely harmful and even life threatening in so many cases. Therefore, the research of this paper offers a software framework that allows users to create messages and hide them within image file documents that can be sent to a desired recipient. Moreover, we conducted an experiment with different data that guarantee the increase level of confidentiality of information exchange over the internet.

Keywords: Data hiding · RSA algorithm · Encryption · Decryption · Bit-plane

1 Introduction

In today's environment, information technology is the most important factor [1–3]. Based on this fact, computer applications are still being developed to better manage financial and personal data in a safe manner [4–7]. These data are incredibly valuable in every way, and we must protect them from illegal access. The process of preventing and detecting unwanted data, computer, or network usage is known as security [8]. Preventative measures assist us in preventing unauthorized users from gaining access to any component of the computer system [9]. Detection aids in determining whether someone attempted to break into the system, if they were successful, and what they did.

V. Sugumaran et al. (Eds.): AIR 2022, CCIS 1738, pp. 14–28, 2022.
https://doi.org/10.1007/978-3-031-23724-9_2

We may employ a variety of encryption approaches to attain that security. However, data encryption is no longer sufficient, and we must additionally safeguard the existence of data if we want to achieve good security [10, 11].

The Rivest-Shamir-Adleman (RSA) Algorithm becomes necessary at this point. However, we must keep in mind that neither cryptography nor the RSA method can guarantee entire security for data or information, thus we must use both approaches to obtain necessary security. There are a variety of ways to accomplish this, but we'll focus on techniques for modifying information in such a manner that the receiver can reverse the change and recover the original content [10, 12]. Although the RSA method is sometimes mistaken with cryptography, there are several significant and clear distinctions between the two. Because the cypher text is a scrambled output of the plaintext in cryptography, the attacker can predict that encryption has been conducted and so use decryption techniques to obtain the secret data in some scenarios, the RSA Algorithm is generally preferable over cryptography [12]. Furthermore, cryptographic approaches frequently necessitate a lot of computer power to execute encryption, which can be a big problem for small devices that don't have enough computing power [8]. To disguise the data in this paper, a bitmap (bmp) picture will be employed. The pixels will be used to insert data into the picture. The RSA technique may then be used to recover the concealed data inside the picture [8].

The remainder of the paper is structured as follows: Sect. 2 will discuss some related works, Sect. 3 to present the Image Data Hiding Algorithm for Donathan Hutchings, Sect. 4 contains the System Implementation Using RSA Algorithm, Sect. 5 gives the system evaluation, and the final Sect. 6 to conclude the paperwork.

2 Related Works

Kuo et al. has proposed a reversible adaptive data concealing technique which is a novel strategy based on the histogram and slope method that improves data concealing capacity while simultaneously increasing efficiency and maintaining image quality [13]. Ma et al. has another strategy which was introduced, they used a method called reversible data hiding (RDH). The space for data embedding is discovered in this method by examining the redundancy in the provided picture. Because of the storage capacity of secret data and the visual quality of embedded images, this approach is the finest of all the techniques in literature survey. In addition, when compared to other methods, this has a low computing complexity [14]. Xioatian et al. proposed another technique for partitioning an image into many encrypted shares to safeguard it [15]. When sufficient shares were obtained, the image can be losslessly retrieved. The study implements an image encryption algorithm using Shamir's secret sharing methods. Ref. [16] introduced a unique reversible data hiding in encrypted images (RDHEI) technique that synchronizes embedding and re-encryption and is well implemented by a data hider that uses a permutation ordered binary (POB) number system. This approach uses two peak locations for embedding, but it completely disregards the previous idea of a shifting process. The proposed method's superiority was confirmed by the experimental results.

Another high-capacity RDHEI technique based on multi-MSB (most significant bit) prediction and Huffman coding was introduced in ref. [17]. Initially, the multi-MSB of each pixel was adaptively anticipated and marked in the original image using

Huffman coding. The image was then encrypted using the stream cypher approach. Finally, utilizing multi-MSB replacement, the empty space was utilized to embed more data. The proposed approach achieved a higher embedding capacity, according to the experimental data.

In [12] a new hybrid approach combining RSA and steganography was introduced. The RSA technique was employed to encrypt and decode the secret file for image compression in the study. Furthermore, the two algorithms were used to compress images for both lossy and lossless compression techniques. This approach has a larger capacity, allowing the total message bits to be reduced by up to 25% of the original message bits. Achieving an average PSNR score of above 40db and SSIM nearest to the unit also demonstrates good stego-image quality.

It is more broadly concerned with establishing and analyzing protocols that are resistant to adversarial impact and are linked to various aspects of information security, including data secrecy, data integrity, authentication, and non-repudiation. However, the modern cryptography brings together mathematics, computer science, and electrical engineering. Cryptography applications include ATM cards, computer passwords, and electronic commerce. The usage of a key file, full-volume encryption, and plausible deniability are only a few of the features. The broad availability of software that performs these activities has significantly disadvantaged the area of digital forensics. Most of the open-source encryption software allows users to build virtual encrypted drives that can only be accessed with a certain key. These programs make data practically impossible to read without the required key by employing advanced encryption algorithms and techniques.

3   Image Data Hiding Algorithm for Donathan Hutchings

This algorithm embeds the text inside a graphic file and creates a key file to be used to read the message later.

Input: Image File, Secret_Message.

a. Determine the size of the Image File.
b. Determine the length of the Secret_Message.
c. Determine the offset to use when embedding the Secret_Message. //This gives a reliable starting position based on the sizes of the Image_File and Secret_Message.
d. Loop through the Image_File data and begin placing one Secret_Message byte at a time.
e. Make sure we are not at the end of the Secret_Message. //This keeps the loop above to continue swapping the Image_File byte with the Secret_Message byte.
f. Expand our key data array. //This array stores the locations of each Secret_Message byte.
g. Store the location of the whole Secret_Message byte.
h. Create a new Image_File with the Secret_Message inside.
i. Create the key file.

Output: Stego_Image.
Input: Stego_Image _File.
This algorithm reads the message stored in a graphics file.

a. Determine the size of the Image_File.
b. Determine the length of the Secret_Message.
c. Read the Image_File byte data into a byte array.
d. Read our message location data from the key file.
e. Loop through the Image_File data to find our message and construct our actual Secret_Message.
f. Get the message byte from the Image_File data.
g. Convert the byte data back to our original Secret_Message.

Output Secret_Message.

3.1 Implementation

The use case diagram depicts the system's users, its components, and the interactions that exist between them (Fig. 1 and Fig. 2).

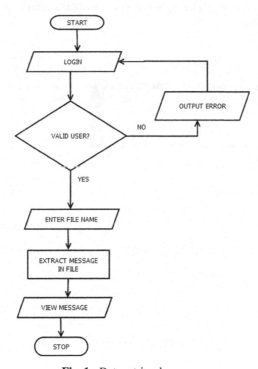

Fig. 1. Data retrieval process

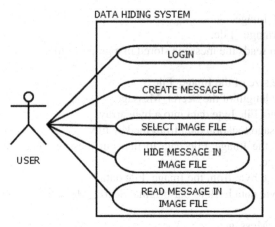

Fig. 2. Use case diagram

3.2 User Interface Design

When you launch the programme, the first interface that displays on the screen is illustrated is Fig. 3, Encrypt Image and Decrypt Image are the two-tab options for encryption and decryption, respectively. The right top panel displays image information such as size, height, and width.

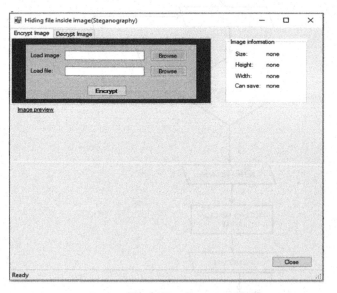

Fig. 3. Interface

3.3 Image Tab Encryption

The equation should be submitted in the equation editor and should be keyed in as below in editable text:

a. To encrypt an image, go to the encrypt image tab (Fig. 4).

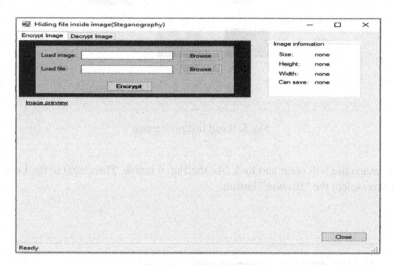

Fig. 4. Encryption tab

b. Click the "Browse" button next to the Load Image textbox to load an image. Select the Image file that you wish to use to hide your information and click the Open button in the file open dialogue box that appears (Fig. 5).

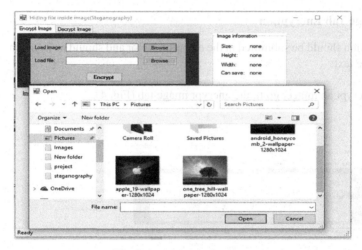

Fig. 5. Load Image interface

c. The image file will open and look like the Fig. 6 below. Then, next to the Load File textbox, select the "Browse" button.

Fig. 6. Load image preview

d. The file open dialogue box will appear once more; select any file you want to hide within the image and click the open button (Fig. 7).

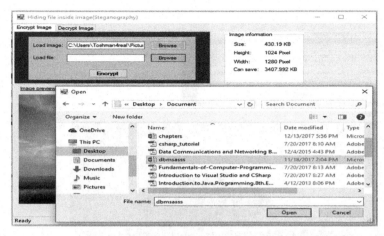

Fig. 7. Open file dialog for the encryption file

e. Encrypting the file is the next step. When you click the "Encrypt" button, a save dialogue box will appear, asking you to choose a location for the new image file and a name for it (Fig. 8 and Fig. 9).

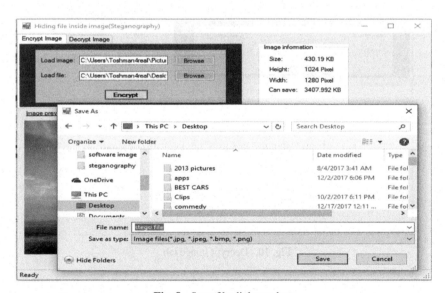

Fig. 8. Save file dialogue box

3.4 Image Tab Decryption

a. To decrypt an image, go to the decrypt image tab (Fig. 10).

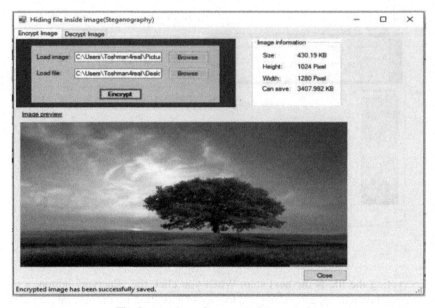

Fig. 9. Interface after successful encryption

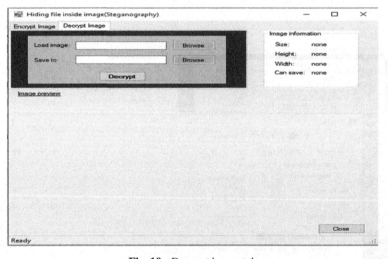

Fig. 10. Decrypt image tab

b. After that, click the "Browse" button to enter the Open file dialogue box, where you must select the image that is encrypted and contains concealed data. Click on the Open button after selecting the image file (Fig. 11).

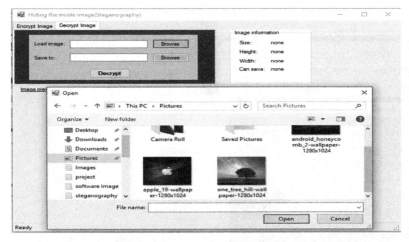

Fig. 11. Open encrypted file dialog box

c. The image file looked like the Fig. 12 below:

Fig. 12. Encrypted image file display

d. Now, next to the "Save file to" textbox, click "Browse" button. It will bring up a "Browse for Folder" dialogue box. It will prompt you to choose a path or folder to extract the hidden file from. Click the Ok button after selecting the folder (Fig. 13).

Fig. 13. Save file dialog box

e. Now, click the Decrypt button, which will decrypt the image and save the secret file to the specified folder. The status bar, which is located at the bottom of the screen, displays the message for successful decryption (Fig. 14).

Fig. 14. Interface after successful decryption

4   System Implementation Using RSA Algorithm

This system was implemented using a parallel approach strategy. We construct a basic system that implements the RSA Algorithm based on the algorithm. The system is known as the Data Hiding System (DHS). According to the system's framework, the first layer is for login purposes, and the second layer is for concealing, retrieving, and finally displaying concealed message file information interface. Below are the several user interfaces that make up the Data Hiding System (Fig. 15):

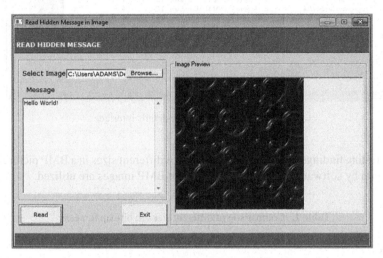

Fig. 15. Read hidden message interface

This form is used to decipher the secret message in the image. The user gets shown the hidden message in the picture file after selecting the image (Fig. 16).

This form is used to access the database of information about the hidden message pictures.

5   Evaluation

The equation should be submitted in the equation editor and should be keyed in as below in editable text:

The bitmap (BMP) format is the image file format utilized in this paper. Within the Microsoft Windows operating system, the BMP file format is used to store graphic files. BMP files are often uncompressed and hence big. The ease of use and widespread acceptance of BMP files in Windows programmes are two advantages of utilizing them. As a result, this picture type was chosen to be utilized in our paper. Because the BMP picture is quite huge in size, the pixels in the image are also relatively large. As a result, it has more room for binary codes to be encoded. In this new approach, we test various sizes of BMP pictures to observe the varied amounts of data being contained in the image, to improve the number of characters that may be hidden. Table 1 displays the

Fig. 16. View message file details interface

various testing findings as well as a comparison of different sizes in a BMP picture using steganography software. As cover pictures, these BMP images are utilized.

Table 1. Comparison of different sizes in bitmap images.

File sizes				
Cover image	Text file	Stego image	Hide message	Retrieve message
439 KB	4.01 KB	286 KB	Yes	Yes
439 KB	12.1 KB	286 KB	Yes	Yes
1.0 MB	10.4 KB	286 KB	Yes	Yes
1.0 MB	10.5 KB	286 KB	Yes	Yes
3.47 MB	12.1 KB	286 KB	Yes	Yes
3.47 MB	27.0 KB	286 KB	Yes	Yes
3.47 MB	54.1 KB	286 KB	Yes	Yes
6.74 MB	54.1 KB	286 KB	Yes	Yes
9.9 MB	334 KB	286 KB	Yes	Yes
9.9 MB	335 KB	286 KB	Yes	Yes

As a result of the new system's examination about various photos, we can infer that the method appears to downsize any size of bmp image from its original size to 286 KB, which greatly aids in data un-detection when sent over networks. The data concealment programme will hide the messages to be transmitted within an image file. This file may then be forwarded to the recipient by attaching it to the current message service. The receiver uses his copy of the data hiding software to read the concealed message in the image file after getting it as a mail attachment.

6 Conclusion

In this paper, a new system was created by utilizing Microsoft Visual Basic Programming Language and the Microsoft Access database to handle the system's data. Moreover, a suggested Data Hiding System's design was thoroughly explored, and the Donathan Hutchings technique was employed in implementation. The successful implementation of this paper ensures that the results of this research can be used by other researchers in the field of data information security; the benefits of the proposed strategies are illustrated through experimental data which increases the level of confidentiality of information exchange over the internet; access to information by malicious individuals such as hackers will no longer be possible because they will be unable to determine which form of media was used to hide the information; and government monitoring will no longer be possible because malicious individuals such as hackers will be unable to determine which form of media was used to hide the information. Therefore, the documentations in this paper are strongly suggested for comparable steganography data concealment studies. Finally, there were several suggestions made such as efforts to construct a steganography data concealment system in the future.

References

1. Aminu Muazu, A., Ismaila Audi, U.: Network configuration by utilizing cisco technologies with proper segmentation of broadcast domain in FNAS-UMYUK Nigeria. J. Netw. Secur. Data Min. 4(1), 1–13 (2021). https://doi.org/10.5281/zenodo.4776375
2. Maiwada, U.D., Muazu, A.A., Yakasai, I.K., Zakari, R.Y.: Identifying actual users in a web surfing session using tracing and tracking. JINAV: J. Inform. Vis. 1, 36–43 (2020). https://doi.org/10.35877/454ri.jinav174
3. Maiwada, U.D., Muazu, A.A., Yakasai, I.K.: Using LTE-sim in new hanover decision algorithm for 2-tier macrocell-femtocell LTE network. Int. J. Comput. Inform. Technol. (2279-0764) 9(4), 78–83 (2020). https://doi.org/10.24203/ijcit.v9i4.20
4. Muazu, A.A., Aminu, B., Kamal, A.: Design and implementation of android quiz app-in higher institution of learning: Umaru MUSA Yar'Auda University Katsina, Nigeria. In: AICTTRA 2018 Proceeding, pp. 67–71 (2018)
5. Alsewari, A.A., Mu'aza, A.A., Rassem, T.H., Tairan, N.M., Shah, H., Zamli, K.Z.: One-parameter-at-a-time combinatorial testing strategy based on harmony search algorithm OPAT-HS. Adv. Sci. Lett. 24(10), 7273–7277 (2018). https://doi.org/10.1166/asl.2018.12927
6. Muazu, A.A., Maiwada, U.D.: PWiseHA: application of harmony search algorithm for test suites generation using pairwise techniques. Int. J. Comput. Inform. Technol.(2279-0764) 9, 91–98 (2020). https://doi.org/10.24203/ijcit.v9i4.23
7. Muazu, A.A., Hashim, A.S., Sarlan, A.: Application and adjustment of "don't care" values in t-way testing techniques for generating an optimal test suite. J. Adv. Inform. Technol. 13, 347–357 (2022). https://doi.org/10.12720/jait.13.4.347-357
8. Arora, H., Soni, G.K., Kushwaha, R.K., Prasoon, P.: Digital image security based on the hybrid model of image hiding and encryption. In: 2021 6th International Conference on Communication and Electronics Systems (ICCES) (2021). https://doi.org/10.1109/icces51350.2021.9488973

9. Bandyopadhyay, S.K., Roy, S.: Information security through data encryption and data hiding. Int. J. Comput. Appl.. **4**, 32–35 (2010). https://doi.org/10.5120/874-1235

10. Berinato, S.: The Rise of Anti-Forensics | CSO Online, https://www.csoonline.com/article/2122329/the-rise-of-anti-forensics.html. Accessed 1 2022

11. Umar, D.M., Aminu, A.M., Nadzira, N.: The security paradigm that strikes a balance between a holistic security mechanism and the wsn's resource constraints. East Asian J. Multi. Res. **1**, 343–352 (2022). https://doi.org/10.55927/eajmr.v1i3.102

12. Wahab, O.F.A., Khalaf, A.A.M., Hussein, A.I., Hamed, H.F.A.: Hiding data using efficient combination of rsa cryptography, and compression steganography techniques. IEEE Access **9**, 31805–31815 (2021). https://doi.org/10.1109/access.2021.3060317

13. Kuo, W.-C., Lai, P.-Y., Wuu, L.-C.: Adaptive reversible data hiding based on histogram. In: 2010 10th International Conference on Intelligent Systems Design and Applications (2010). https://doi.org/10.1109/isda.2010.5687102

14. Ma, K., Zhang, W., Zhao, X., Yu, N., Li, F.: Reversible data hiding in encrypted images by reserving room before encryption. IEEE Trans. Inf. Forensics Secur. **8**, 553–562 (2013). https://doi.org/10.1109/tifs.2013.2248725

15. Wu, X., Weng, J., Yan, W.: Adopting secret sharing for reversible data hiding in encrypted images. Signal Process. **143**, 269–281 (2018). https://doi.org/10.1016/j.sigpro.2017.09.017

16. Ren, H., Niu, S., Wang, X.: Reversible data hiding in encrypted images using POB number system. IEEE Access **7**, 149527–149541 (2019). https://doi.org/10.1109/access.2019.2946929

17. Yin, Z., Xiang, Y., Zhang, X.: Reversible data hiding in encrypted images based on multi-MSB prediction and huffman coding. IEEE Trans. Multimedia **22**, 874–884 (2020). https://doi.org/10.1109/tmm.2019.2936314

Token Bases Valid and Secure Payment System Using SHA-256

Ravi Shankar Jha[1] (✉), Saleh Umar[2], Tokpe Kossi[2],
and Ouattara Mohamad Lamine[2]

[1] School of Computing, DIT University, Uttarakhand, India
ravishankarjha87@gmail.com

[2] Department Computer Science and Information Technology, Sharda University,
Greater Noida, India

Abstract. Every connected device must be safe, with no easily compromised card, account, or personal information secured to it, to address the growing security concerns for retailers, consumers, and financial institutions. As a result of that tokenization will be critical in the future of linked devices. Implementing the EMV mechanisms approach, which describes the adoption of payment tokens as a replacement for PANs and how security can be improved by limiting their use to a specific environment, is one way to handle this challenge. By using the approach to hide sensitive data and restrict access to it, this study influences the use of Network tokenization as an alternate strategy for guaranteeing data security in modern cloud computing systems The research also looked at Host Card Emulation (HCE) and Near Field Communication (NFC), which are all utilized in the transaction process to encrypt data from both sides Java Spring Boot and Angular JS were used for both the backend and frontend of the web services, and hash and salting algorithms were employed to ascertain the token value from the cardholder. Tokenization systems are easy to set up and may be used in a variety of ways in IT systems to maintain data security.

Keywords: Mobile payments · Euro-pay Master and Visa (EMV) · Near field communication (NFC) · Tokenization · User and device authentication · Host card emulation (HCE)

1 Introduction

Cloud computing has enticed modern businesses to use it since its inception, promising a plethora of benefits [1]. However, the new technology presents several challenges, including redesigning internal IT architecture and reengineering internal business processes to accommodate the new technology and maximize benefits, as well as identifying the necessary instruments to adequately protect the companies' data assets. Data security is the most significant impediment to cloud adoption, according to expert [2], and losing data security is one of the major downsides that halt cloud adoption. Mobile payment is a store value account system that functions as a digital replacement for a physical wallet.

V. Sugumaran et al. (Eds.): AIR 2022, CCIS 1738, pp. 29–38, 2022.
https://doi.org/10.1007/978-3-031-23724-9_3

When compared to other fields of research such as internet banking, mobile banking, or eCommerce [3]. Mobile payment is a relatively recent topic of study. Contactless smartphone transactions are the next generation of digital payments and purchases, and they're as safe and convenient as rap and vigor. Contactless mobile payment is a payment performed by tapping a mobile phone on a contactless reader at a checkout counter. Near Field Communication (NFC) and Euro-pay Master card and visa (EMV) are the technologies that enable this payment feasible, with the highest security attached.

In the payment ecosystem and EMV is a payment token that is a replacement value that replaces the main account number i.e. Personal Authentication Number (PAN). It's part of the payment chain, and submitting it in a transaction to the payment system will result in a payment. Depending on the usage case, a single PAN may be associated with numerous EMV Payment Tokens. Payment tokens can only be used on certain domains. A payment token, for example, may only be utilized within a certain merchant's e-commerce acceptance channel [2, 4]. They can be updated for a variety of reasons, including when a device is lost or stolen, or when other lifecycle events occur. Europay-Master and Verve create a technical foundation for generating, distributing, and maintaining payment tokens in the United States in a secure and interoperable manner around the world [5]. This technical framework must be compatible with existing payment infrastructure while also providing uniformity and ensuring a standard level of robust security.

2   Literature Work

The transition from magnetic stripe-based payment cards to EMV chip cards is an inescapable process that started about 22 years ago and could last another 25 years or longer. Euro pay (now part of MasterCard), MasterCard, and Visa pioneered this change, which became known as EMV [6, 7]. Due to the vulnerability of magnetic-stripe cards to fraudulent attacks such as counterfeiting (cloning cards by copying magnetic-stripe data), forging signatures, intercepting card data online, and a variety of other forms of attacks originating from lost or stolen cards, the switch to EMV chip cards were deemed necessary.

Payment tokenization solutions associated with the EMV Payment Tokenization Specification – Technical Framework v2.0 give options for issuers, merchants, acquirers, payment processors, and other stakeholders in the larger acceptance ecosystem to improve the security of digital payments [8]. These technologies provide the CIA triad confidentiality, integrity, and availability as well as authentication and nonrepudiation when it comes to data security [9, 10].

The NFC technology and ecosystem allow researchers to better grasp the present state of NFC research [11]. As well as the many operating modes of NFC in terms of availability, usability, and security. However, when comparing the performance of near field communication in a mobile payment service to that of a short messages-based solution, it is concluded that NFC technology is superior in terms of speed and ease when aspects such as communication setup and cost are ignored [12]. The user must purchase an empty NFC-Micro SD card and bring it to a human firm to have secret data and credit card information recorded on it in a Near Field Communication mobile payment via NFC-Micro SD technology project presented an Anonymous Proximity Mobile Payment model in which customers can choose how anonymous they want to be according to their personal preferences [13, 14]. Integration of an NFC-enabled mobile wallet with an NFC-enabled payment card, banking transactions used mobile wallets, and merchant payments using smart cards, but the usage of an NFC-enabled mobile wallet is pleasing for both types of transactions [15].

3   Methodology

In designing the web services Java Spring Boot and Angular JS for both the Backend and Frontend were used EMV mechanisms the security structure of the method contains significant capabilities and draw.io was also used to draw the flow chart as a tokenization-based service The use of a cloud-based secure element for payment transactions and user and device authentication called Host Card Emulation in the mobile part would provide complete knowledge about mobile payments for valid and secure transactions for the customers.

3.1   Proposed Tokenization Approach Security Framework

Tokenization security architecture, which combines tokenization with dynamic token issuance as well as user and device verification, will improve the security of HCE-based mobile payment transactions. A framework showing a Tokenization process (Fig. 1).

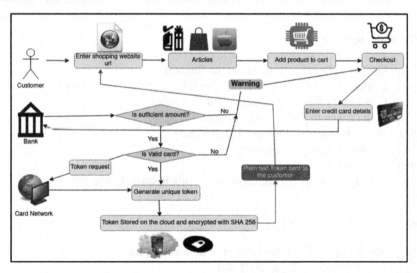

Fig. 1. Block diagram of Tokenization based transaction

The components involved in the Tokenization approach security framework are:

(a) Consumer: A customer is a person who needs to buy goods or services from the merchant with an NFC-enabled mobile phone.

(b) Merchant: A merchant is an entity that has goods or services to sell with an NFC reader.
(c) Issuer: The Issuer is the consumer's bank, which interrelates between the payment server and the customer. The issuer referred to as the Token service provider is responsible for carrying out the tokenization process.
(d) Acquirer: The Acquirer is the merchant's bank, which interrelates with the payment server and the merchant's POS.
(e) Payment service provider: The Payment service provider is an intermediary entity between the Acquirer and the Issuer, accountable for payment approval and payment.

When the customer wants to pay for their product, they hold their phone near an NFC-enabled POS terminal and select the debit or credit card that is stored on their phone. Furthermore, the customer is authenticated by a right thumb scan (biometric digital data), and the device is authenticated via IMEI, device ID, OS version, production details, and so on. The HCE enables contactless transactions between NFC-enabled devices [8, 16]. The issuer completes the tokenization process, which includes creating a token for the PAN, performing IVV, and assigning a level of assurance for the generated token, the issuer's cloud-based secure element sends the token to the merchant via the consumer machine; The payment network authenticates the token before sending it to the customer bank (issuer) [17]. The issuer de-tokenizes the transaction, mapping the token to the PAN, and then approves the transaction to the acquirer. The amount of the purchase will be credited to the acquirer and debited from the issuer, below is the transaction algorithm process.

Tokenization Algorithm process.

1. Step. Generate (Req);   // Generate the Request
2. Step. If (Req = = Authenticated)   ///Check Request Authentication {
3. Step. Generate (Token);   // Generate Token Value
4. Step. Map (Token to PAN); // Mapping of Token
5. Step. Store (Token); //   Saving Token Value}
6. Step. Return (Token);   //Returning Token
7. Step.   } else
8. Step.   (Req = = Fail);   // Authentication Fails Request Discarded

Pseudocode for De-tokenization process.

1. Step Get (Req);   // Get the Request of de-tokenization
2. Step. Get (Token);   // Getting Token
3. Step. Do   // Doing De-tokenization on the basis of Authorization {
4. Step. If (TokenRID = = Req && TokenID = = Token) // Token Request ID And
            {   // Token ID Validation
5. Step. Get (PAN); // Validating TokenID with PAN
         }Else
            {

6. Step. (Req = = Transaction Failed); // Validation Fail
      }
        }
7. Step. While (TokenRID = = True);

The proposed Transaction system is the combination of two algorithms first is for the generation of tokens for respective token requests. The request will successfully completed only when validation is done. If validation fails request will be discarded.

The second Algorithm for De-Tokenization with validation and authentication takes place. As marked in the proposed algorithm Getting a request for De-tokenization requested token validated with its request ID and with Token ID, if these two-parameter are not valid the whole process will be terminated here and transaction will fails and if the validation is complete and return true then de-tokenization will be done and validate the transaction.

Here in the result section, experimental results show how token-based transactions are more reliable and have the capability to provide a safe and secure transaction.

Valid Transaction: The Valid transaction and secured illustrates how an EMV payment is successful.

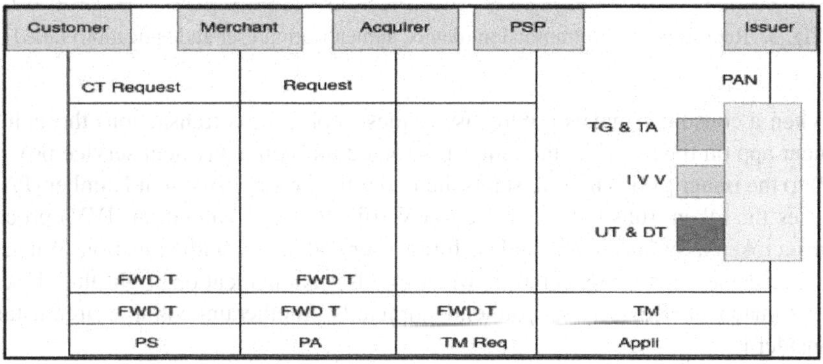

Fig. 2. Represent valid transaction (payment successful)

When a consumer makes a purchase request (contactless transaction) through a payment application on their device, the request is routed through a PSP (payment service provider) is a company that provides payment services to the government. Issuer. The Payment Service Provider sends issuer the Primary Account Number (PAN), produces a token, runs the Identification Verification and Validation (IVV) process, assigns a token assurance level, and performs user and device authentication. The PSP sends the token generated by the issuer to the consumer device [29, 37]. Through the merchant's Point-of-Sale (POS) device, the token is sent from the consumer device to the acquirer. The acquirer then transmits the token to the issuer via PSP for the match, and if the match is successful, the acquirer receives the token match answer and permission. The merchant's POS equipment receives payment acceptance approval from the acquirer, and the consumer device receives a final payment successful message. If the tokens do not match, the response and disapproval status are communicated to the acquirer, and the POS device shows a payment denied message, followed by a payment failure message on the consumer device.

Invalid Transaction: The invalid transaction illustrates the flow when a user and device authentication fails (Fig. 3).

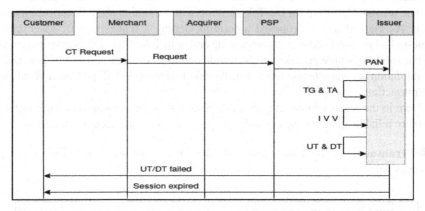

Fig. 3. Represent invalid transaction (device authentication/user authentication) failed

When a consumer makes a purchase request (contactless transaction) through the payment app on their device, the request is routed through a payment service provider (PSP) to the issuer [38]. The PSP sends the issuer the Primary Account Number (PAN), produces the token, runs the Identification Verification and Validation (IVV) process, assigns a token assurance level, and performs user and device authentication. When the consumer device is not registered or when the user authentication (right thumb scan) does not match, the Device/User Authentication fails. Another unfavorable circumstance to consider is:

- The Token is produced but has not reached the customer's device.
- The Token was created and received by the customer device, but not reached at POS.
- The Customer device accepts a token, but the token is not for the intended customer.

3.2   Comparison Between the Existing Payment and Our Proposed Work

Despite the different payment modes were already in existence in different parts of the globe, all the payment procedures are the same using debit or credit card to make transactions via Master Card, Rupay, Visa card, Discover and American Express card, etc., and each card defends on the security attached to it, in this paper we used two different algorithms to strategize our transaction payment with SHA-256 and SALT algorithm to validate the transaction either success of failure adding SHA-256 and SALT as an added security which is used in different ways in our work, therefore in this work we employed the two algorithms for security reason encryption algorithm which is one-way encryption for random input data and used to secure storage of passwords. Similarly, the generated transaction receipt will be displayed on both parts of the parties, the transaction activity of the success and failure of the merchant as well as the issuer's information should not be revealed.

Tokenization adds security, increases approval rates, and improves transaction administration, all of which improve the customer experience. To make online commerce more secure, a variety of digital commerce solutions have been offered. Next work should focus on data Encryption with fingerprint recognition which has not been conducted so far, for adding more security functionalities, a novel data encryption technique, is made up of a set of interconnected goods that share a common infrastructure. These scalability solutions use encryption, tokenization, data masking, and identity management to secure databases, files, and containers across hybrid multi-cloud systems, protecting assets in the cloud, virtual, big data, and on-premise environments.

4 Result and Discussion

The simulation work of the proposed solution shows that the ratio of success rate is 86.40. The failed transaction is quite less, which shows the rigidness of the system. To examine the proposed work we have done the simulation with a huge data set of credit and debit cards of different types of Credit cards like, Visa, Discover, RuPay, MasterCard, American Express.

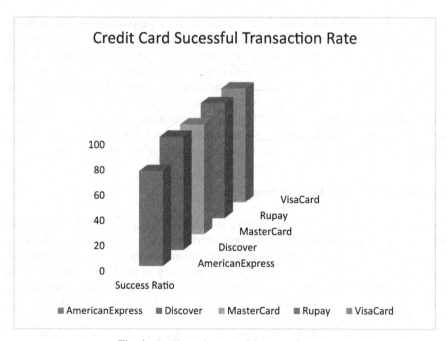

Fig. 4. Credit card successful transaction rate

As we can see in the below graph in Fig. 2 Credit Card successful Transaction ratio is the maximum of RuPay Card and the least success rate is of AmericanExpress (Fig. 4).

To simulate the proposed work have taken initially 100 credit card data and then increased it to 1000. Here are the results. Results show that in the context of the total transaction success ratio is the maximum of RuPay and the minimum of American Express (Fig. 5).

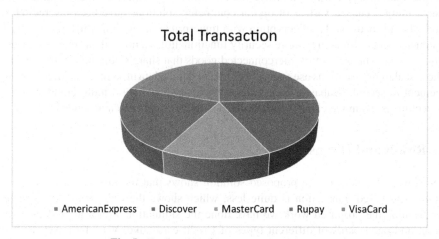

Fig. 5. Total transaction success rate summary

Results shows that Tokenization adds security, increases approval rates, and improves transaction administration, all of which improve the customer experience. To make online commerce more secure, a variety of digital commerce solutions have been offered. Next work should focus on data Encryption with fingerprint recognition, which has not been conducted so far, for adding more security functionalities, a novel data encryption technique, is made up of a set of interconnected goods that share a common infrastructure. These scalability solutions use encryption, tokenization, data masking, and identity management to secure databases, files, and containers across hybrid multi-cloud systems, protecting assets in the cloud, virtual, big data, and on-premise environments.

5 Conclusion and Future Scope

Tokenization is a security strategy that has a substantial impact on the adoption of HCE-based NFC services. The proposed EMV approach in this paper can be used for reliability, access control, identification, and security applications during the transaction process. Long with the magnetic stripe, this chip is another way to store the cardholder's the information on the back of the card. It's a reliable and secure and up-to-date way of data storage that helps to prevent fraud. The term "EMV" stands for "Europay, Mastercard, Visa." The two types of chips are Chip and Signature then Chip and PIN, variations of the worldwide chip technology standard to complete the transaction on a chip and signature card, you must sign it. Chip and PIN cards, on the other hand, work in a similar way to debit cards and use a Password that you create. These credit cards are available in one or both versions. Chip-and-Signature cards are the most popular in the United States, but this is changing, and more cards will have chip technology.

References

1. Solat, S.: Security of Electronic Payment Systems: A Comprehensive Survey. http://arxiv.org/abs/1701.04556 (2017)
2. Vishwakarma, P., Tripathy, A.K., Vemuru, S.: A hybrid security framework for Near Field Communication driven mobile payment model. Int. J. Comput. Sci. Inform. Secur. **14**(12), 337–348 (2016)
3. Ozdenizci, B., Ok, K., Coskun, V.: A tokenization-based communication architecture for HCE-enabled NFC services. Mob. Inf. Syst. **2016**, 1–20 (2016). https://doi.org/10.1155/2016/5046284
4. De Vivo, D., Gamess, E.: Application to quickly and safely store and recover credit card's information, using tokenization and following the PCI standards. Int. Res. J. Eng. Technol. **4**(8), 1446–1452 (2020)
5. Babatunde Iwasokun, G.: Encryption and tokenization-based system for credit card information security. Int. J. Cyber-Secur. Digt. Forensics **7**(3), 283–293 (2018). https://doi.org/10.17781/P002462
6. Garg, R.K., Garg, N.K.: Developing secured biometric payments model using Tokenization. In: 2015 International Conference on Soft Computing Techniques and Implementations (ICSCTI) (2015). https://doi.org/10.1109/icscti.2015.7489549
7. Zhang, X., Zeng, H., Zhang, X.: Mobile payment protocol based on dynamic mobile phone token. In: 2017 IEEE 9th International Conference on Communication Software and Networks (ICCSN) (2017). https://doi.org/10.1109/iccsn.2017.8230198
8. Nagaraju, S., Parthiban, L.: Trusted framework for online banking in public cloud using multi-factor authentication and privacy protection gateway. J. Cloud Comput. **4**(1), 1–23 (2015). https://doi.org/10.1186/s13677-015-0046-4
9. Scanio, S., Glasgow, J.W.: Payment card fraud, data breaches, and emerging payment technologies. Fidel. Law J. **XXI**, 59–94 (2015)
10. Andersson, D.: A Survey on Contactless Payment Methods for Smartphones. http://www.diva-portal.org/smash/get/diva2:947093/FULLTEXT02 (2016)
11. Technologies for Payment Fraud Prevention: EMV, Encryption and Tokenization – EMV Connection. https://www.emv-connection.com/technologies-for-payment-fraud-prevention-emv-encryption-and-tokenization/. Accessed 1 2022
12. Liu, W., Wang, X., Peng, W.: State of the art: secure mobile payment. IEEE Access **8**, 13898–13914 (2020). https://doi.org/10.1109/access.2019.2963480
13. Kakish, K., Shah, R.D.: Analysis of the risks of NFC mobile payment systems. In: Proceedings of the Conference on Information Systems Applied Research ISSN, vol. 2167, p. 1508. ISCAP, North Carolina, USA. Retrieved from https://scholar.google.ca/scholar?cluster=839353291 1470227721&hl=en&as_sdt=0,5 (2016)
14. Rajapashe, M., Adnan, M., Dissanayaka, A., Guneratne, D., Abeywardena, K.: Multi-format document verification system. Am. Acad. Sci. Res. J. Eng. Technol. Sci. **74**(2), 48–60 (2020). https://asrjetsjournal.org/index.php/American_Scientific_Journal/article/view/6454
15. Angelika, K.L.: Tokenization of assets: security tokens in Liechtenstein and Switzerland. TokenizationTokenization Assets MLR **2**(1) (2021)

16. Ozdenizci, B., Coskun, V., Ok, K., Karlidere, T.: A secure communication model for HCE based NFC Services. In: International Conference on Creative Technology, Thailand, pp. 19–22 (2015)
17. Urien, P., Aghina, X.: Secure mobile payments based on cloud services: concepts and experiments. In: 2016 IEEE 2nd International Conference on Big Data Security on Cloud (BigDataSecurity), IEEE International Conference on High Performance and Smart Computing (HPSC), and IEEE International Conference on Intelligent Data and Security (IDS) (2016). https://doi.org/10.1109/bigdatasecurity-hpsc-ids.2016.48

A Novel Approach to Secure Files Using Color Code Authentication

Keshav Kaushik[(✉)] [iD]

School of Computer Science, University of Petroleum and Energy Studies, Dehradun, India
officialkeshavkaushik@gmail.com

Abstract. In this modern era, where technologies are being evolved day by day and data is shared on various communication platforms in a huge volume and variety. There is a need of implementing security and privacy in every technology. The files that are being shared need to be protected with strong encryption. So that the confidential data will remain, secure and protected from unauthorized access. Data is a raw form of information that can be stored or transferred digitally over the network. Cybersecurity is applied to protect data from unauthorized access in order to maintain its integrity and availability. Information security refers to the use of defensive computerized protection measures to prevent unauthorized access to computers, databases, and websites. It protects customers by making the encrypting of communications and the validation of distinct clients helpful. This allows us to communicate critical data in a surprising manner. Nevertheless, there are several approaches available; the current state of the data security framework includes categorization, trustworthiness, and righteousness while accessing or modifying confidential internal records. This paper proposes an approach for securing the data from unauthorized access using color-coding authentication. It secures confidential data from being mishandled and information from being passed into the wrong hands by encrypting it and securing it using a process of automated passwords. Security is about the assurance of benefits. The validation model depends on some shading mixes. Thus, this paper aims for making sure about classified documents for conveying data utilizing encryption, unscrambling, and shading code validation.

Keywords: Authentication · Cybersecurity · Confidentiality · Cryptography · Encryption · Security · Privacy

1 Introduction

Information security is a growing concern for IT organizations, all things being equal. To address this growing worry, a rising number of IT companies are using strategies to safeguard their critical data. Apart from the foregoing concerns regarding data security, IT organizations are also grappling with the ever-increasing costs of capacity needed to secure that the organization's present and future demands are met. Data encryption is well known for keeping data safe from prying eyes. It uses an encryption key to convert data from one format, known as plaintext, to another one, known as cypher text. Currently,

© The Author(s), under exclusive license to Springer Nature Switzerland AG 2022
V. Sugumaran et al. (Eds.): AIR 2022, CCIS 1738, pp. 39–46, 2022.
https://doi.org/10.1007/978-3-031-23724-9_4

pressure and encryption techniques are implemented separately. Cryptography nowadays is firmly based on scientific hypotheses and software engineering practice; cryptographic computations are designed around computational hardness assumptions, making them almost impossible to crack by any adversary. It is theoretically sufficient to split such a foundation; nevertheless, no known viable methods can be used to accomplish so. In the digital era, the rise of such technology has produced a slew of legal difficulties. Because of its potential for use as a tool [1] of surveillance and dissidence, several laws have designated it as a weapon, restricting or outright prohibiting its use and use.

Any type of sophisticated data that has been stored is referred to as information. The certainty of advantages is what security is all about. Information security refers to the use of defensive computerised protection measures to prevent unauthorised access to computers, databases, and websites. It protects customers by making the encryption of content and the validation of distinct clients helpful. This allows us to communicate critical data in a surprising manner. Nevertheless, there are several approaches available; the current state of the data security framework includes categorization, believability, and righteousness while accessing or modifying confidential internal records. The validation model requires some shading mixtures. As a result, this article is designed to ensure the security of classified papers used to transmit data via encryption, decrypting, and coloring code checking. As the most crucial purpose, this technique aims to guarantee anonymity, ensuring that only the person with the decode key can interpret the received message. It also ensures that authentication is preserved, which we describe as a method of verifying one's identity in order to ensure that the communicating entity is who it claims to be. This means that users or the computer can verify their own credentials to those who are not personally acquainted with them. Data Integrity must also be maintained since it assures that the thoroughly checked has not been tampered with in any manner. An unauthorised party may alter the data, either purposefully or unintentionally. The integrity service verifies if data has been generated, sent, or saved by an authorised user since it last produced, communicated, or stored. This is accomplished by employing hashing on both the transmitter and the recipient's sides in order to generate a unique hashing algorithm and compare it to the one received. Then there is non-repudiation, which is a means for proving that the sender actually delivered this message and that the designated party got it, so the receiver cannot claim that it wasn't sent. If the non-repudiation feature was activated in this transaction, for example, a purchaser cannot refuse a purchase order after it has been submitted electronically. Finally, yet importantly, Access Control is the method of preventing unauthorized resource usage. This aim determines who has access to the information, whether they can access them, under what limits and circumstances they can access them, and what authorization level they have.

In this paper, the author has discussed the related work in Sect. 2, followed by working methodology in Sect. 3. The author also discussed the results obtained in Sect. 4 and conclusion is added in the Sect. 5.

2 Related Work

The volume of data in the cloud is growing because of the increased use of cloud-based technologies, necessitating the need for secrecy. Textual passwords are the most prevalent way of authentication. However, shoulder surfing, dictionary attacks, and eavesdropping are all-possible with these passwords. In general, passwords state that are simpler to guess for attackers. According to a review of the literature, text-based passwords have this security flaw. Text-based passwords can be replaced by pictographic passwords. Shoulder surfing may be facilitated with pictographic passwords. Accessibility may be an issue with pictographic password. This paper [2] employs color code identification, which provides the user with two-factor authentication. Each time a user signed in; a one-time passcode was generated. This system has been put to the test against a variety of security threats. The suggested method [3] enables for more reliable authorization control and highly secure authentication while accessing building facility equipment. The outcome of the unauthorized individual receiving a color grid code sequence and his face identification enables for strong security and access to the building's facility infrastructure architecture. The suggested scheme uses encrypted user access user credentials through a control box screen and a smart device application that detects and decodes color grid coded information combinations and then sends the user through the intelligent buildings network to the smart building for authentication confirmation, which provides a high level of security. In [4], it has been determined that people can only remember a few numbers of passwords as a result of users writing down, sharing, or using the same password for several locations. Text-based credentials are the most popular and easiest to memorize, although they are tough to learn. They are vulnerable to shoulder surfing and brute-force assaults. Graphic credentials, on the other side, are simple to remember and recall. One of the most cutting-edge studies to allow access to lawful uses is access control. Fingerprint, image-based, and graphical-based techniques have all been employed. In this paper [5], a three-level password verification is presented, with experimental results provided. In compared to existing systems, the three-level authentication delivers a trustworthy security level, according to the analysis of the results. The authors [6] of this study present a unique way of hiding harmful payload in picture information. As a result, metadata is information about the picture rights and how they are managed. Hackers commonly exploit this metadata to carry out a variety of harmful attacks, such as injecting malicious script within the picture metadata, and so on.

However, because to concerns such as higher user login time and limited password storage, they are not widely utilized. In today's world, when security breaches are becoming more common, more security authentication techniques are required to guarantee a user's identity. To render authentication mechanisms stronger and more resistant to assaults, the authors [7] suggested a unique hybrid strong authentication strategy that combines both text-based and visual password approaches. The purpose of each encryption algorithm [8] is to make decryption of the generated cipher text as difficult as possible without using the key. If a good encryption algorithm is used, then there is no strategy that is considerably better than trying every possible key methodically. In this study [9], a unique approach was used to establish colour document authentication using QR codes and digital watermarking. The suggested structure has high invisibility and optimal capacity, according to experimental results. The altered regions can also be precisely identified.

A new graphical password system is proposed in this article [10]. A challenge-response classification is what it is called. As a result, under our approach, a password is time-variant. A person who understands the passwords can successfully complete the assignment and reply properly. As a result, our password-based system is immune to shoulder surfing. When an adversary has videotaped a user's login procedure, he or she will still be unable to determine the passwords. Our password-based method has shown to be effective in first tests. The authors [11] divided existing graphical password schemes into recognition-based, pure-recall-based, cued-recall-based, and multifactor techniques in this research work. We also looked at the advantages and disadvantages of graphical password systems. In [12], Encryption: Strengths and Weaknesses of Public-key Cryptography - Public-key cryptography developed from earlier models like Küchlin to more advanced frameworks that have provided the data protection and privacy we need in contemporary world. The cryptography of the secret key lags behind asymmetric encryption. In [13], A Survey of Authentication of RFID Devices Using Elliptic Curve Cryptography- RFID is a wireless platform for automatic detection and data collection, and its main application for Internet of Things implementation. RFID's protection problem is becoming more relevant because of that. In the past, the basic logical and mathematical form. RFID is a wireless technique for automated data acquisition and recognition that is at the heart of the web of things. As a result, the RFID security problem is becoming increasingly significant. RFID identification was previously introduced using simple arithmetic and scientific methods, hash-based templates, and rudimentary PKI schemas. In this work, the researchers discuss various RFID security attacks as well as three distinct RFID authentication algorithms based on ECC, as well as why ECC is the best technique among all. In [14], Connections take in confidential data of all sorts, and security plays a critical role in every wireless network. Safety approve data integrity and data confidentiality standards as wired network maintenance, without significant security protocols being enforced, and wireless adapter is within the network adapter class. Text-based passwords are helpless to a word reference assault, shoulder surfing, listening in. To conquer a portion of these issues pictographic passwords are presented. The word reference assault is unimaginable with such a secret phrase. Yet, it experiences shoulder surfing.

3   Working Methodology

We should scramble secret knowledge and documents to prevent it from being abused or transmitted into the wrong hands by encrypting it and verifying it with a computerized secret phrase technique. Above all, the client will obfuscate the information included in a file, which will then be given to another client, who will have the opportunity to access the record simply by decoding the one-time constructed secret phrase. As a result, the technique may be divided into two main modules: encrypting and decryption of content in documents using shading code verification.

The primary module includes the section where the material that must be transmitted is hidden behind a separator so that the person for whom the information is intended may contact it. The following module, on the other hand, focuses on the part in which the client on the other end disentangles the partition in order to access the information using the key established by the shade plan confirmation procedure. The customer who is the intended recipient of the material in the documentation must complete the final module.

In this paper, the author has followed a specific methodology highlighted in Fig. 1. In step 1, the colors are assigned from a range of the colors and the values are assigned to them. Thereafter, the files are encrypted using the color code authentication by generating the password shown in Fig. 3. In step 3, the files are transmitted from the source to the destination where it is decrypted using the same color code authentication in the final step. The methodology used by the author is simple yet very efficient to secure the files using the color code authentication method.

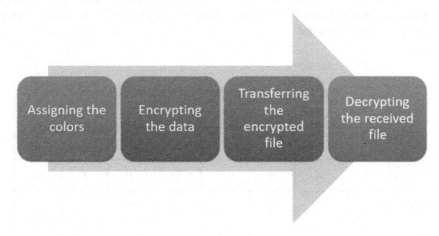

Fig. 1. Methodology

4   Results and Discussion

In the recent decade, a slew of password authentication methods have been presented. Nonetheless, the majority of them are affected by shoulder surfing, which is becoming a major issue. There have been proposals for graphical password systems that are impervious to shoulder surfing, but they come with their own set of downsides, such as usability concerns, longer login times, and tolerance levels. Users to store personal and secret information such as passwords and PIN numbers use Personal Digital Assistants. The use of these devices should be protected by identification. The implementation comprises of two main modules: Password Generation module and Color Recommendation Module (Fig. 2). At first, the Password Generation Module enters the image, allowing users to input values ranging from 1 to 8 for each of the eight colors. Customers can even give two distinct hues the same value.

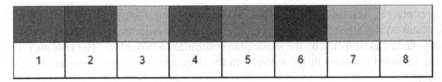

Fig. 2. Color generation

As a result, the authentication approach is immune to shoulder attacks, dictionary attacks, and eves dropping, among other threats. The Color Suggestion Module then appears, with a login interface that includes a color grid and an 8×8 number grid with digits 1 to 8 randomized inserted in the grid. The session passwords are generated based on the color ratings. The first color of each pair in the color grid indicates the number grid's row, while the second color represents the number grid's column (Fig. 3). Both the numerical grid and the color grid are randomly generated for each login, resulting in a unique session password.

	1	2	3	4	5	6	7	8
1	3	4	5	3	7	4	4	1
2	3	5	3	7	8	3	2	2
3	6	4	3	2	6	8	5	3
4	4	6	7	3	2	7	8	3
5	6	3	6	7	1	2	8	2
6	2	4	7	3	8	1	2	5
7	5	6	8	3	5	4	3	4
8	4	7	3	8	4	5	6	2

Fig. 3. Password generation

5   Conclusion

The approach used here to secure file is color code authentication scheme and is based on encryption and decryption of files. The password was generated by using the color scheme from a pool of available colors. The application was developed in java programming language and was successful in showing the desired results. In future, the application can be used for adding some more functionalities like single-sign on and use of salt for adding an additional layer of security. The most important things about any of the application are that how flexible the application is to accept any change or modification for its improvement. Wireless network security is important in any business, and it is also important to execute all network security plans for the organisation now and in the future to protect network resources from tampering, damage, and unauthorised usage. To safeguard the communications network and preserve IT assets, private data, and information, encryption and web security solutions are also highly useful.

References

1. Kaushik, K., Tanwar, R., Awasthi, A.K.: Security Tools. Information Security and Optimization 181–188 (2020). https://doi.org/10.1201/9781003045854-13.
2. Potey, M.M., Dhote, C.A., Sharma, D.H.: Secure authentication for data protection in cloud computing using color schemes. In: 2016 International Conference on Computation System and Information Technology for Sustainable Solutions (CSITSS). (2016). https://doi.org/10.1109/csitss.2016.7779398.
3. Hoon, Y.S. et al.: Building control box attached monitor based color grid recognition methods for user access authentication. Int. J. Internet Broadcasting and Commu. **12**(2), 1–7 (2020). https://doi.org/10.7236/IJIBC.2020.12.2.1
4. Dhamija, R., Perrig, A.: Deja Vu-A User Study: Using Images for Authentication. USENIX Security Symposium (2000)
5. Mishra, G.S., Mishra, P.K., Nand, P., Astya, R.: Amrita: user authentication: a three level password authentication mechanism. Journal of Physics: Conference Series **1712**, 012005 (2020). https://doi.org/10.1088/1742-6596/1712/1/012005
6. Kaushik, K., Surana, S.: An offensive approach for hiding malicious payloads in an image. Lecture Notes on Data Engineering and Communications Technologies 265–272 (2021). https://doi.org/10.1007/978-981-16-3961-6_23
7. Dabeer, S., Ahmad, M., Sarosh Umar, M., Hasan Khan, M.: A novel hybrid user authentication scheme using cognitive ambiguous illusion images. Advances in Intelligent Systems and Computing 107–118 (2019). https://doi.org/10.1007/978-981-15-0132-6_8
8. Mahalle, V.S., Shahade, A.K.: Enhancing the data security in Cloud by implementing hybrid (Rsa & Aes) encryption algorithm. In: 2014 International Conference on Power, Automation and Communication (INPAC). (2014). https://doi.org/10.1109/inpac.2014.6981152
9. Mohsin Arkah, Z., Alzubaidi, L., Ali, A.A., Abdulameer, A.T.: Digital color documents authentication using QR code based on digital watermarking. Advances in Intelligent Systems and Computing. 1093–1101 (2019). https://doi.org/10.1007/978-3-030-16657-1_102
10. Kameswara Rao, M., Vidya Pravallika, C., Priyanka, G., Kumar, M.: A shoulder-surfing resistant graphical password authentication scheme. Advances in Intelligent Systems and Computing **413**, 105–112 (2016). https://doi.org/10.1007/978-981-10-0419-3_13/COVER
11. Patel, S.S., Jaiswal, A., Arora, Y., Sharma, B.: Survey on graphical password authentication system. Data Intelligence and Cognitive Informatics. 699–708 (2021). https://doi.org/10.1007/978-981-15-8530-2_55
12. Alaa Zaidan, A., Othman, F., Zaidan, B.B, Raji, R.Z., Naji, A.W.: Securing cover-file without limitation of hidden data size using computation between cryptography and steganography. In: Proceedings of the World Congress on Engineering 2009 Vol I WCE 2009, July 1–3, London, U.K. (2009)

13. Monali, S., Patel, A.J.: A Survey of Authentication of RFID Devices Using Elliptic Curve Cryptography 2(4), 53–56 (2018). https://doi.org/10.13140/RG.2.2.36819.50725
14. Abdullah, A.M.: Advanced Encryption Standard (AES) Algorithm to encrypt and decrypt Data I Ako Muhammad Abdullah I Research Project (June 2017). https://www.researchgate.net/project/Advanced-Encryption-Standard-AES-Algorithm-to-Encrypt-and-Decrypt-Data. Accessed 13 Sep. 2021

Analysis of Ransomware Security on Cloud Storage Systems

Advait Deochakke[1] and Amit Kumar Tyagi[2](✉) ⓘ

[1] School of Computer Science and Engineering, Vellore Institute of Technology,
Chennai, Tamil Nādu 600127, India
advaitdeochakke@gmail.com
[2] Department of Fashion Technology, National Institute of Fashion Technology, New Delhi,
Delhi 110016, India
amitkrtyagi025@gmail.com

Abstract. Over the years cloud computing and cloud storage solutions have grown into over a 50-billion-dollar industry, and that signifies over 50 % of all corporate data being stored in the cloud as of 2021. In accordance, attacks over these files have grown exponentially, with average damages exceeding multiple millions of dollars per attack. Cloud storages are more susceptible to these attacks, due to the physical factor of accessing local storage being removed, and a simple connection to the internet. Despite the great convenience and arguably fulfilling core necessities during the pandemic, the Cloud storage model is vulnerable and an incredibly juicy target. These ransomware attacks are proving to be huge security risks around the world as such. Combine these with various other problems such as area of jurisdiction of law enforcement agencies and blockchain-based payments making tracing these payments a nigh-impossible task, and the threat is apparent at even the first glance. In this paper, (i) we analyse the insidious nature of ransomware and their power and threat levels, (ii) various papers and industry data to give a comprehensive analysis of the level of security that currently exists, (iii) discuss large security breaches in recent history, and (iv) consider up and coming solutions for cloud storage security. After going through these, we shall draw a final (v) conclusion, on the state of cybersecurity and cloud storage based on presented data.

Keywords: Cloud storage · Ransomware · Network security · Decentralized cloud storage · Dynamic data

1 Introduction

Ransomware is a type of malware attack on a computer system, which aims to coerce or threaten the victim to pay money in return for giving them access back to their encrypted and locked system. Ransomware encrypts the software and poses a real threat toward files which are not backed up, in the form of deletion of these files, making the victim lose access to the data, and voiding a vast amount of work and effort [1]. Another threat that ransomware poses is stealing of data. Once the attacker has discovered the various

© The Author(s), under exclusive license to Springer Nature Switzerland AG 2022
V. Sugumaran et al. (Eds.): AIR 2022, CCIS 1738, pp. 47–59, 2022.
https://doi.org/10.1007/978-3-031-23724-9_5

valuable files on the system and encrypts them, it will often lead to the attacker also making a copy of these valuable and sensitive files, which could in turn lead to the victim being blackmailed, the files being publicly released, or worse [1, 2].

In recent years, the threat of ransomware has risen as technologies like cryptocurrency come into the focus of development. The difficulty of tracing transactions and tracking down perpetrators of the attack to real world persons has been increased by Bitcoin wallets, and compounded with the real-world problem of prosecuting someone who is not in the same country as the victim, makes it much easier to get away after committing such crimes [3, 4].

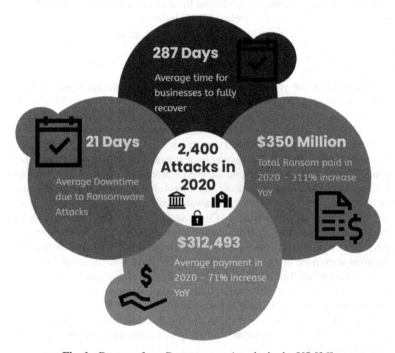

Fig. 1. Damage from Ransomware Attacks in the US [36]

Figure 1 shows some statistics with respect to damages via Ransomware Attacks in previous decade. The first documented ransomware was recorded in 1989, and called the AIDS trojan. Since then, use of such attacks has grown exponentially, hitting over 304 million attacks in 2020, rising to over 62% over 2019. Some high-profile examples are Locky, CryptoLocker, FBI MoneyPak, and WannaCry, which caused damages totaling over $4 Billion according to some estimates [2, 5]. Note that Ransomware doesn't just affect individuals, but can even grind the operations of large corporations to halt, prominent example being an attack on Ultimate Kronos Group's cloud storage, one of the largest human resources companies in the world, which caused damage to millions of workers and companies' dependent on their Private Cloud service [6]. Another example is DDS Safe, where hackers caused irreversible damage to over 400 doctor's offices and their patient data. LinuxEncoder1 is another large-scale ransomware which was the first to target Linux based servers across the globe [5]. Documentation of ransomware is often difficult, due to the largely non-representative nature of the data collected. Reporting various attacks, analyzing ransomware, finding solutions are all relatively relevant for users with high awareness of cybersecurity and a desire to contribute. As such, most data are collected from customers who have the knowledge and wherewithal to report such attacks to authorities and analysis labs such as BitDefender Labs. Similarly, corporate and government data is typically understated due to fear of backlash from backers, citizens, and users [2].

As resources and possessions stored in the cloud gain value, they become more lucrative targets to attack. As a result, attackers will utilize greater force and effort to take hold of these assets. In an era where organizations are quickly transitioning to cloud-based services, ransomware protection is of the utmost importance. Critical infrastructure such as pipelines, hospitals, government databases are constantly under threat. Many researchers have given solutions to combat such cloud-based cybercrime, and we shall discuss those along with newer and more novel solutions.

2 Nature of Cybercrime and Ransomware

Cybersecurity is an important factor in our times. As such, all analysis and data regarding cybersecurity, whether it be from experience, studies, or derived data, is shared on a wide scale, covering various large international organizations and through governments. As such, every day we get a clearer view into aspects of cybersecurity threats such as ransomware, from various sources such as Symantec, Deloitte, BitDefender Labs, etc., [5, 7]. Cloud computing is an emerging technology, and all models of its service, (a) Software as a Service (SaaS), (b) Platform as a Service (PaaS), and (c) Infrastructure as a Service (IaaS), are vulnerable to attacks. Such cloud service vulnerabilities typically include threats to the user's data, exploits in the API for accessing the cloud, threats from insiders which could bypass a great deal of protection, faults in the cryptography algorithms used, and misconfiguration of service deployment models by organizations [7]. Once a target is selected, the attackers use various methods to install the ransomware onto the system, and valuable data and system functionality is locked.

Research by Microsoft's Digital Crime Unit [9] shows that such attacks focus their target primarily on the healthcare sector, followed closely by the media & entertainment, and energy sectors. Findings from the Institute for Security and Technology's Ransomware Taskforce [4, 10] support these findings, as do reports from the Becker Hospital Review. The reason for the lopsided targeting statistics is due to the nature of these systems. Patient data is incredibly valuable to hospitals, and Internet of Things (IoTs) technologies are widespread in modern hospitals which mean hackers can critically affect patient health by locking the systems connected. Similarly, for energy sectors, where power grids are on threat. For attacks on the media and entertainment industry, they tend to focus on live streams of large broadcasters and encrypting source code for various applications such as video games [9, 11]. Figure 2 discusses industry the need of engagement on Ransomware in the previous decade.

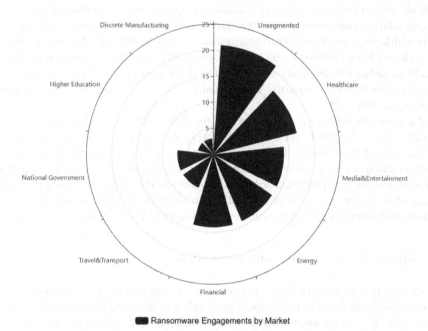

Fig. 2. Ransomware engagements by industry [10]

2.1 Technical Vectors of Attack

Vectors for ransomware attacks include e-mail spam and phishing attacks, a popular method including JavaScript trojan downloader, Nemucod. Exploit Kits are another aspect involved in these attacks. Exploit Kits are a sort of repository for managing various exploits for any given system, which vastly broadens the attack surface by attacking multiple possible vulnerabilities instead of just one. Another vulnerability commonly exploited is Microsoft's Remote Desktop Protocol, which allows anyone with credentials to log onto another machine with RDP enabled and use it as their own, as long as it is connected to the internet, often used in scam phishing-based attacks [3, 4]. Unpatched vulnerabilities can also lead to such ransomware deployments, some of which are part of zero-day exploits. Zero-day exploits involve utilizing bugs in the code which remained unknown, generally involving hacking into the developer's files to get hold of software before release. More advanced tactics utilize man-in-the-middle attacks to exploit the synchronization token system of cloud services, so that the attacker can intercept the token and replace it with a new one which provides access to the attacker. The compromised user may never know about it, as the attacker can also place the synchronization token right back in [7].

2.2 Socially Engineered Vectors

Phishing is a type of attack which uses social-engineering concepts and sends a target authoritative-looking emails or messages, typically including company logos and email ids similar to official ones, which can be easily mistaken if one does not look closely. Such phishing attempts may frequently involve Whaling or CEO fraud. Spear phishing involves specifically targeting the organization to gain access by compromising one of the many organization member accounts [12]. Stolen passwords are also a real threat, as many unaware users will use the same password or its iterations across multiple or all of their accounts. This could lead to the compromise of one system leading to another completely unrelated organization and their systems falling under threat, due to an employee of one organization using the same password for their account in another system and application [13].

2.3 Ransomware-as-a-Service

Sometimes the creator of the ransomware may not be the party who actually uses it, but will act as a seller for the ransomware, leading to the coining of the term Ransomware-as-a-Service (RaaS) [14]. Similar to SaaS solutions, the developers of the ExpoiltKits and other malware tools will lease their products to interested parties, letting any inexperienced, run-off-the-mill crook deploy and initiate ransomware attacks. Reports by Group-IB state that over two-thirds of all ransomware attacks in 2020 used RaaS solutions [15]. Two of the key players in this business are REvil and DarkSide, who were responsible for the JBS attacks and Colonial Pipeline attacks respectively, which we have previously mentioned [11]. In ransomware attacks on cloud systems, the responsibility is shared between the customer and the service provider, even though it might appear as if the user has less responsibility due to the assumed and contract-bound trust being handed to the service provider. Both must remain vigilant against such threats. In today's web of interconnected web services, a single breach can sometimes bring down entire networks [7].

3 Current Countermeasures

While ransomware is threatening, there are various countermeasures to mitigate its effects and ensure some degree of safety. We discuss various such widely used countermeasures below.

3.1 Repositories and Data Sharing

One of the best methods of making sure that countermeasures we use are solid and up to date, is using and sharing information repositories for this task. Maintaining such repositories and being aware of them helps organizations cover their bases, as the repositories will store countermeasures and solutions for multitudes of software vulnerabilities. Notable repositories include the MITRE Common Vulnerabilities and Exposures initiative from 1990, the National Institute of Standards and Technology's National Vulnerability Database. Typically, it may not be ideal for many users to actively keep track of such and such many vulnerability and threat management systems have been devised, such as Microsoft's Defender for Endpoint [7, 16].

3.2 Behavior Based Detection

System-based detection entails regular integrity checks for various files, detecting whether there have been suspicious API calls, or detecting keylogging and window captures, and finally monitoring resource usage of OS and I/O systems. Traffic analysis can unveil whether there exist significant fluctuations from the normal and expected rates [16]. File-based detection generally involves checking for signs of malicious activity in specific formats for files, typically involving disguised executables and other known ransomware file extensions and signatures. File activity monitoring such as files being accessed over the network beyond a certain expected threshold are commonly used, but can often result in false negatives [17].

Honeypot strategies involve setting up a VM or sacrificial storage to temporarily store new files in, and checking their immediate behavior. If files start getting encrypted, it serves as an early warning system. Throttling the throughput of these honeypots can further increase the time that is available to system administrators to cut off the honeypot and prevent cloud-wide infection [18].

3.3 Reverse Engineering

Reverse engineering involves discovering the key to the ransomware encryption and using it to recover infected files. The most important use case for this method is when prevention techniques used by antivirus software fail, resulting in system damage. Reverse engineering may be able to recover lost data without causing complete destruction or having to pay the ransom. The key disadvantage here being that the necessary prerequisite for this method, the existence of a decryption key of the targeted system, might not always be fulfilled [5, 19].

3.4 Risk Disclosure and Awareness

Getting affected by ransomware, for corporations, often means that there is a threat of bringing harm to shareholder and customer interests. With this statement in mind, it makes sense when a non-negligible number of incidents are either reported to be much less severe than in actuality, or go unreported and privately resolved. Awareness of cybersecurity entails reducing risks of employees leaking valuable and sensitive company data, whether they have malicious intentions in mind, or unintentionally let it happen. Underestimating dangers posed by cybersecurity threats and simply ignoring risk control instructions are some reasons due to which such breaches might occur. Peer behavior, previous experience, and regularly prompting employees to take action to ensure security are all key components to this [20, 21].

3.5 Decentralization and All-Or-Nothing Transforms

Decentralization inherently limits the ceiling of risk and threats that ransomware poses. The utilization of multiple independent and comparatively reduced risk of compromise, as there is no longer a single point of failure. All files are added only when the majority clears the file for addition to the main server, and verifying data integrity is easy due to multiple copies of data existing across the users. AONT facilitates both availability and security of data against malicious actors [22, 23]. Despite so many powerful countermeasures, ransomware still remains an extremely huge threat. We shall now look at various large breaches and ransomware related incidents in recent history.

4 Impact of Ransomware in Recent History

As long as data holds value, hackers will desire to utilize it as a means for profit or even furthering their agenda in niche cases.

4.1 Healthcare Incidents

A study by Comparitech shows over \$20 billion in losses due to ransomware attacks on clinics, hospitals, and healthcare organizations. J&J's chief information security officer, Marene Allison, further states that Johnson & Johnson Group receives over 15.5 billion cybersecurity incidents on a daily basis [24]. The WannaCry ransomware in 2017 also had a tremendous impact on hospitals, crippling tens of thousands of computers from the National Health Service hospitals in Great Britain [25].

4.2 Colonial Pipeline

Having to pay over \$4.4 million in bitcoin as ransom, the need to mitigate disruption of nationwide critical infrastructure is very visible. Amidst the 2021 April oil shortages, this feeling felt much more impactful than it would usually, in times of prosperity and abundance [26]. Even though the FBI were able to recover over \$2.3 million of the Bitcoin, catching the perpetrators from the DarkSide gang remained difficult, due to the very nature of such attacks [9, 27].

4.3 CD Projekt Red

Polish hit game developer, CD Projket Red, were hit in February of 2021, where the HelloKitty group got hold over the source code for their recently released billion-dollar game, Cyberpunk 2077, amongst others, and demanded high ransom, with CD Projekt Red denying to pay the fees, as they had backups in place [28]. This demonstrates good corporate practices, as not paying ransom discourages hackers from performing more malicious activities.

4.4 Ultimate Kronos Group

One of the most recent cases we will analyse in this paper, when hackers gained control of their Kronos Private Cloud service, leading to payroll systems of over dozens of private and government entities. Over 8,000 workers have experienced problems with their paychecks, upt o as recent as mid-January 2022 [6]. This is closely timed to the reporting of the Log4J vulnerability in Java running machines, on which Kronos' servers were based. However, there is no confirmation of this from Kronos Group [29].

4.5 REvil Group

Most likely one of the highest profiles RaaS groups, the Russian based operation has recently been declared as dismantled by the Russian Federal Service. Multiple ransomware attacks have been attributed to them, including the attack on JBS, the world's largest meat packer, the attack on Kaseya Group, a large software infrastructure management company based in America, and also the stealing various plans for Apple's up and coming products from one of their suppliers, Quanta Computer [26]. Its impact remains immeasurable, as a group member claimed to earn over $100 million in ransoms per month, and due to the similarities of its code and ransom structure with another highly prominent group, DarkSide. The similarities could imply that REvil is an offshoot of DarkSide, or a partner. Another important aspect is the peculiar code to check that the victim of the cyberattack is not situated in Russia, or more accurately the Commonwealth of Independent States which formed after the fall of the Soviet Union, perhaps leading to concerns about state-run hacker organizations.

5   Emerging Solutions

Few of existing solutions for tracing the cyber-attacks can be included here as:

5.1 Secure Network Protocols for Dynamic Data

B. Sengupta's work leverages Secure Network coding techniques in the construction of a protocol, DSCS I, enabling a guarantee for dynamic provable data possession. DSCS, we work well on a standard data model, while a second protocol introduced in the same paper, DSCS II, finds a use in being very efficient for real-world append-only data, but is not efficient for arbitrary modifications for generic data [30]. The protocol facilitates authenticity of data, as the storage server must keep the proof of data possession tags untampered, lest the challenge of testing integrity by customer fails. The protocol further necessitates the freshness of data, as the provider must keep the storage up to date if the authentication challenge is to be passed [30].

5.2 Analysis of Network Traffic on Multiple Classifiers

A paper by Ahmad O. has illustrated clearly how ransomware will affect all kinds of network traffic data, with the Locky ransomware as the test case [31]. The paper found over five times increase in TCP resets when a malicious software was introduced to the testbed, an increase of over 80 times in HTTP-POSTs. A sudden and incredibly high increase in the error frequencies for DNS names was also found, due to the large amount of pseudo-random domain names generated by the DGA algorithm in Locky. By analysis of network-based ransomware, the model was able to achieve over 97% accuracy in detecting the software, and signifies a leap in preventing network-based ransomware once samples are analyzed [31].

5.3 Dynamic Distributed Storage

Dynamic distribution provides a high degree of confidentiality, security, and resilience of data in the cloud. It utilizes fast and local encryption prior to the data leaving the local network, along with a permanently stored key with a filtered interface to prevent as much of the attack surface as possible. Storing the data over multiple cloud servers provides a high degree of redundancy, and can be scaled as high as desired. This helps in the event that the cloud provider faces a compromise in their servers, so that in the event where even some of the servers on which data is stored are affected, the data stored in the rest is still salvageable and as such can be restored and redistributed [8, 32].

5.4 Machine Learning and Artificial Intelligence

Symantec, a leading player in cybersecurity, has introduced its machine learning heuristic technology, Sapient. It applies natural language processing to help train computers in finding the hidden patterns in all the tens of thousands of cybersecurity incidents which could be happening on a daily basis for large organizations. Machine learning takes a step past recognizing threats and fixing them, to predicting such threats and acting on the data to minimize losses [10]. Symantec's Sapient blocked a full 100% of ransomware samples seen with cloud support. The WannaCry outbreak was also prevented at zero-day on systems with Symantec's Endpoint Protection enabled, showcasing the power of such techniques.

5.5 Decentralization

Albeit mainstream, it is still an emerging technology. Decentralization involves shifting the control over infrastructure from a single entity, and a single point of failure, to a trustless, distributed environment, with very few points of weakness. It further helps facilitate optimization of resources, and opens up a shared ledger to guarantee the validity of data movements. As no one "owns" the data, it becomes a collectively owned and maintained system, however it comes with the drawback of performance decreasing for all members as more and more members join the decentralized system, but that is the cost of security which must be paid [20, 33].

5.6 Key Backup

Key encryption uses a public-private key pair to encrypt the data, and the private key is stored locally. The "public" key can either be in the form of (1) Using a public key for encryption, making it easy to manage target data, or (2) Using group or individual keys for targets [34, 35]. Using a hook, we can latch onto the key backup which gets stored on the target's systems, and extract the key to prevent extensive harm to the victim [7]. As opposed to other solutions showcased in this paper, K. Lee's paper on key backup highlights a general case which does not require prior knowledge of the ransomware or its habits, utilizing the locally stored key in addition with a public key, which can be obtained after paying one set of ransom at a reasonable price [16]. Further, researchers are suggested to refer several possibilities with cyber security including issues, challenges and recommended countermeasures with modern techniques/ technologies in [37–45].

6 Conclusion

The number of criminals and cybersecurity threats in the world is far lesser in number than the number of experts constantly working towards improving security and reliability. However, due to exploits being much too easy to find than they are to fix, these few continue to be a large global threat, which the entire world is slowly coming to realize and act against.

The constant improvements in all fields related to security all over the world are slowly but surely leading to a privacy-guaranteed, and security-guaranteed environment, but the journey remains ever so dangerous. Without realizing and acknowledging the threats we face, we will not be able to act appropriately against them, and I hope that this paper facilitates to not only highlight the problem, but also help drive the development of improvements in all fields continuously.

References

1. Ransomware: What It Is & What To Do About It, Internet Crime Complain Center. https://www.ic3.gov/Content/PDF/Ransomware_Fact_Sheet.pdf. Last accessed 03 2022
2. Beaman, C., Barkworth, A., Akande, T.D., Hakak, S., Khan, M.K.: Ransomware: Recent advances, analysis, challenges and future research directions. Comput. Secur. **111**, 102490 (2021). https://doi.org/10.1016/j.cose.2021.102490
3. Deloitte Threat Intelligence and Analysis Report: Ransomware (August 2016). https://www2.deloitte.com/content/dam/Deloitte/us/Documents/risk/us-aers-ransomware.pdf. Last accessed 02 2022
4. Symantec ISTR: Ransomware Special Edition (2017). https://docs.broadcom.com/doc/istr-ransomware-2017-en. Last accessed 03 2022
5. "WannaCry" ransomware attack losses could reach $4 billion (May 2017). https://www.cbsnews.com/news/wannacryransomware-attacks-wannacry-virus-losses/. Last accessed 03 2022
6. Kronos Community report on the cyberattack (December 2021). https://community.kronos.com/s/feed/0D54M00004wJKHiSAO?language=en_US. Last accessed 02 2022
7. Does a Ransomware Attack Constitute a Data Breach? Increasingly, It May (Jan 2021). https://www.kroll.com/en/insights/publications/cyber/ransomware-attack-constitute-data-breach. Last accessed 04 2022
8. Ramesh, D., Mishra, R., Edla, D.R.: Secure data storage in cloud: an e-stream cipher-based secure and dynamic updation policy. Arab. J. Sci. Eng. **42**(2), 873–883 (2016). https://doi.org/10.1007/s13369-016-2357-2

9. Walden, K.: Assistant General Counsel, Microsoft Digital Crime Unit, at HEARING ON. STOPPING DIGITAL THIEVES: THE GROWING THREAT OF RANSOMWARE": US House of Energy and Commerce. https://energycommerce.house.gov/committee-activity/hea rings/hearing-on-stopping-digital-thieves-the-growing-threat-of-ransomware. Last accessed 12 2021
10. IBM X-Force Threat Report: Executive Summary (2021). https://www.ibm.com/downloads/cas/AWJ3PE1M. Last accessed 12 2021
11. The 2021 Evil Internet Minute, RiskIQ, https://www.riskiq.com/resources/infographic/evil-internet-minute-2021/. Last accessed 01 2022
12. Junger, M., Wang, V., Schlömer, M.: Fraud against businesses both online and offline: crime scripts, business characteristics, efforts, and benefits. Crime Sci. 9(1), 1–15 (2020). https://doi.org/10.1186/s40163-020-00119-4
13. Li, L., He, W., Xu, L., Ash, I., Anwar, M., Yuan, X.: Investigating the impact of cybersecurity policy awareness on employees' cybersecurity behavior. Int. J. Inf. Manage. 45, 13–24 (2019). https://doi.org/10.1016/j.ijinfomgt.2018.10.017
14. Manky, D.: Cybercrime as a service: a very modern business. Computer Fraud & Security. 2013, 9–13 (2013). https://doi.org/10.1016/s1361-3723(13)70053-8
15. Ransomware Uncovered 2020/2021, https://explore.group-ib.com/ransomware-reports/ran somware_uncovered_2020. Last accessed 01 2022
16. Lee, K., Yim, K., Seo, J.T.: Ransomware prevention technique using key backup. Concurrency and Computation: Practice and Experience. 30, e4337 (2017). https://doi.org/10.1002/cpe.4337
17. Securing your AWS Cloud environment from ransomware (April 2021). https://d1.awsstatic.com/WWPS/pdf/AWSPS_ransomware_ebook_Apr-2020.pdf. Last accessed 01 2022
18. Takahashi, T., Panta, B., Kadobayashi, Y., Nakao, K.: Web of cybersecurity: Linking, locating, and discovering structured cybersecurity information. Int. J. Commun Syst 31, e3470 (2017). https://doi.org/10.1002/dac.3470
19. Linux Ransomware Debut Fails on Predictable Encryption Key, Bitdefender Labs (Nov. 2015). http://labs.bitdefender.com/2015/11/linux-ransomware-debut-fails-onpredictable-enc ryption-key/. Last accessed 01 2022
20. Bacis, E., De Capitani di Vimercati, S., Foresti, S., Paraboschi, S., Rosa, M., Samarati, P.: Securing Resources in Decentralized Cloud Storage. IEEE Transactions on Information Forensics and Security 15, 286–298 (2020). https://doi.org/10.1109/tifs.2019.2916673
21. Li, H., No, W.G., Wang, T.: SEC's cybersecurity disclosure guidance and disclosed cybersecurity risk factors. Int. J. Account. Inf. Syst. 30, 40–55 (2018). https://doi.org/10.1016/j.accinf.2018.06.003
22. Castiglione, J., Pavlovic, D.: Dynamic distributed secure storage against ransomware. IEEE Transactions on Computational Social Systems. 7, 1469–1475 (2020). https://doi.org/10.1109/tcss.2019.2924650
23. Ateniese, G., Dagdelen, Ö., Damgård, I., Venturi, D.: Entangled cloud storage. Futur. Gener. Comput. Syst. 62, 104–118 (2016). https://doi.org/10.1016/j.future.2016.01.008
24. Ransomware attacks on US healthcare organizations cost $20.8bn in 2020. https://www.com paritech.com/blog/information-security/ransomwareattacks-hospitals-data/. Last accessed 01 2022
25. Cloud presents biggest vulnerability to ransomware (September 2021). https://www.sec uritymagazine.com/articles/96148-cloud-presentsbiggest-vulnerability-to-ransomware. Last accessed 01 2022
26. Report on Ransomware Trends, HC3 (May 2021). https://www.hhs.gov/sites/default/files/ran somware-trends2021.pdf. Last accessed 01 2022

27. US recovers millions in cryptocurrency paid to Colonial Pipeline ransomware hackers (June 2021). https://edition.cnn.com/2021/06/07/politics/colonial-pipeline-ransomware-rec overed/index.html. Last accessed 01 2022
28. Tweet title: Important Update, CDPROJEKTRED, https://twitter.com/CDPROJEKTRED/sta tus/1359048125403590660. Last accessed 01 2022
29. Apache Log4j Vulnerability Guidance: CISA, https://www.cisa.gov/uscert/apache-log4j-vul nerability-guidance. Last accessed 01 2022
30. Sengupta, B., Dixit, A., Ruj, S.: Secure cloud storage with data dynamics using secure network coding techniques. IEEE Transactions on Cloud Computing. **10**, 2090–2101 (2022). https://doi.org/10.1109/tcc.2020.3000342
31. Almashhadani, A.O., Kaiiali, M., Sezer, S., O'Kane, P.: A multi-classifier network-based crypto ransomware detection system: a case study of locky ransomware. IEEE Access. **7**, 47053–47067 (2019). https://doi.org/10.1109/access.2019.2907485
32. Lu, F., Li, W., Jin, H., Gan, L., Zomaya, A.Y.: Shadow-chain: a decentralized storage system for log data. IEEE Network **34**, 68–74 (2020). https://doi.org/10.1109/mnet.011.1900385
33. What is Decentralization in Blockchain?, https://aws.amazon.com/blockchain/decentraliza tion-in-blockchain/. Last accessed 01 2022
34. Share of corporate data stored in the cloud in organizations worldwide from 2015 to 2021, https://www.statista.com/statistics/1062879/worldwide-cloud-storageof-corporate-data/. Last accessed 01 2022
35. Annual number of ransomware attacks worldwide from 2016 to 2020, https://www.statista.com/statistics/494947/ransomware-attacks-peryear-worldwide/. Last accessed 01 2022
36. Institute for Security and Technology, Ransomware Task Force Report: April 2021. https://securityandtechnology.org/wp-content/uploads/2021/04/IST-Ransomware-Task-Force-Rep ort.pdf. Last accessed 01 2022
37. Vishnuram, G., Tripathi, K., Kumar Tyagi, A.: Ethical Hacking: Importance, Controversies and Scope in the Future. 2022 International Conference on Computer Communication and Informatics (ICCCI). (2022). https://doi.org/10.1109/iccci54379.2022.9740860
38. Deshmukh, A., Sreenath, N., Tyagi, A.K., Eswara Abhichandan, U.V.: Blockchain Enabled Cyber Security: A Comprehensive Survey. In: 2022 International Conference on Computer Communication and Informatics (ICCCI) (2022). https://doi.org/10.1109/iccci54379.2022.9740843
39. Nair, M.M., Tyagi, A.K., Goyal, R.: Medical cyber physical systems and its issues. Procedia Computer Science. **165**, 647–655 (2019). https://doi.org/10.1016/j.procs.2020.01.059
40. Tyagi, A.K., Aghila, G.: A wide scale survey on botnet. Int. J. Comp. Appl. **34**(9), 10–23 (2011)
41. Kumar, A.: Cyber Physical Systems (CPSs) – Opportunities and Challenges for Improving Cyber Security. Int. J. Comp. Appl. **137**, 19–27 (2016). https://doi.org/10.5120/ijca20169 08877
42. Rekha, G., Malik, S., Tyagi, A.K., Nair, M.M.: Intrusion detection in cyber security: role of machine learning and data mining in cyber security. Advances in Science, Technology and Engineering Systems Journal **5**, 72–81 (2020). https://doi.org/10.25046/aj050310
43. Mishra, S., Tyagi, A.K.: Intrusion Detection in Internet of Things (IoTs) Based Applications using Blockchain Technolgy. 2019 Third International conference on I-SMAC (IoT in Social, Mobile, Analytics and Cloud) (I-SMAC) (2019). https://doi.org/10.1109/i-smac47947.2019.9032557

44. Tyagi, A.K., Sreenath, N.: Cyber Physical Systems: Analyses, challenges and possible solutions. Internet of Things and Cyber-Physical Systems. **1**, 22–33 (2021). https://doi.org/10.1016/j.iotcps.2021.12.002
45. Kumari, S., Tyagi, A.K., Aswathy S.U.: The Future of Edge Computing with Blockchain Technology: Possibility of Threats, Opportunities and Challenges. Recent Trends in Blockchain for Information Systems Security and Privacy, CRC Press (2021)

A Novel Approach for an Automated Advanced MITM Attack on IoT Networks

Keshav Kaushik(✉) ⓘ, Vanshika Singh, and V. Prabhu Manikandan

School of Computer Science, University of Petroleum and Energy Studies, Dehradun, India
officialkeshavkaushik@gmail.com

Abstract. Man-in-the-middle (MITM) attacks target any insufficiently protected contact between two entities, whether it's a data transfer between two parties or an interaction between two users through an online messaging system. Commercial site credentials and verification, interconnections protected by public or private credentials, and any other circumstance where an existing transaction might provide adversary access to the personal information are all vulnerable. An attack's purpose is to acquire personal data such as login passwords, banking information, and credit card information. In this paper, the authors have implemented an automated advanced MITM attack on IoT/Wireless networks. The authors have used Xerosploit and Fluxion tools to exploit the IoT/Wireless network. Wireless networks having weak encryption algorithms and keys are exploited. Moreover, the results of these two used tools are then compared. At last, the preventive measures against the advanced MITM attacks are highlighted.

Keywords: Cyber-attacks · Man-in-the-middle · MITM · Wireless networks · IoT networks

1 Introduction

1.1 A Subsection Sample

A man-in-the-middle attack (MITM) is a typical kind of networking attack that permits attackers to listen in on the correspondence between two targets. The assault happens in the middle of two authentically imparting attacks, permitting the attacker to "tune in" to a discussion they ought to typically not have the option to stand by listening to, subsequently the name "man-in-the-middle." For example [1], the integrity of information on the way among inverters and a cloud server can be undermined by authenticated third-party, gadgets, and inside network inside security parameters i.e., MITM assault.

An attack's goal is to steal personal information, such as login credentials, payment information, and credit/debit payment information [2]. Customers of accounting systems, SaaS firms, online business portals, and other sites that need registration are common targets. MITM encircles an expansive scope of methods and expected results, contingent upon the target and the goal. For instance, in SSL stripping, attackers layout an HTTPS association among themselves and the server, yet with an unstable HTTP

V. Sugumaran et al. (Eds.): AIR 2022, CCIS 1738, pp. 60–71, 2022.
https://doi.org/10.1007/978-3-031-23724-9_6

connection with the client/user, and that implies data is sent in a simple message without encryption. These kinds of assaults can be for surveillance or monetary benefit, or to simply be problematic," says Turedi. "The harm caused can go from little to immense, contingent upon the aggressor's objectives and capacity to cause misdemeanor.

Data gathered because of the MITM attack might be used for a variety of purposes, involving wholesale deception, unauthorized financial transfers, or an unauthorized secret key change. Overall, a MITM attack is like a postal carrier reading your bank statement, capturing your account information, and then resealing the package and sending it to your doorway. There are numerous endeavors [3] made in recreating the Man-in-the-middle attack. In this paper [4], the authors exhibited a Bluetooth MITM given secure simple pairing (SSP) utilizing of band (OOB) affiliation model. They have executed every one of the three matching models specifically Numeric correlation, Just works, and Passkey section. The sharing of keys throughout the matching is finished utilizing the Diffie Hellman key trade method.

Internet of Things (IoT) gadgets [5], encompassing tablets and smart mobiles, are generally sent in different areas of application going from smart homes to modern conditions. A significant number of these gadgets depend on Bluetooth Low Energy (BLE) as a correspondence convention for their control or the exchange of information [6]. Trivial assaults can without much of a stretch objective these gadgets to compromise about because of their low-security highlights and intrinsic vulnerabilities in their product and correspondence parts.

The powerful advancement of the Smart Medical Devices in the Healthcare framework has taken on a creative change in working on the clinical frameworks and controlling infections and working on the QoS (Quality of Service) for the Patients. Be that as it may, Smart Medical Devices [7] are not resistant to security weaknesses, protection breaks, and actual dangers. The MITM assaults (DDoS, Jamming, Node-Injection, and Node-Hijacking) can make genuine dangers to the Smart Medical Devices because of the uncertain correspondence interaction and absence of secrecy in gadget availability through Heterogeneous Wireless Medical Sensor Networks (WMSNs). The principle point of the exploration is to distinguish significant security weaknesses in Smart Medical Devices in Heterogeneous WMSNs.

Right now, Bluetooth Low Energy (BLE) has become generally famous in different wellbeing and wellness applications, home systems administration, digital watches, and other smart apparatuses. BLE fills in as a driver innovation for IoT. It is anticipated [8] that by 2023 a greater number than 1.6 billion BLE gadgets will be delivered every year and 90% of Bluetooth gadgets will incorporate BLE innovation. A MITM [9] assault is one of the most notable assaults on computer networking. Address Resolution Protocol (ARP) Poisoning is one of the few MITM versions that is often used in data retrieval and on-the-fly management [10]. Traditional MITM attacks using ARP Poisoning reveal the attacker's identity and, as a result, their location.

Tools that the authors have used to perform MITM attacks for testing purposes include:

- XEROSPLOIT: Xerosploit [11] is a python-based structure that joins the force of Bettercap and NMAP to make influential Man-in-the-Middle attacks. It has several modules that enable it to recognize and respond to assaults, as well as perform DOS and packet inspection. Bettercap and NMAP are in charge of this. NMAP, hping3, construct ruby-dev, libpcap-dev, libgmp3-dev, tabulate, and terminal tables are among the requirements.

- FLUXION: Fluxion [12] is a research tool for security audits and social engineering. It's a rewrite of vk496's linset, with (hopefully) fewer issues and more features. The script uses a social engineering attack to try to acquire the WPA/WPA2 key from a targeted access point. It works with Kali's most recent version (rolling). The setting of Fluxion's assaults is primarily manual, however, an experimental auto-mode takes care of some of the parameters. Scan for a target IoT/wireless network using Fluxion. Attack with the Handshake Snooper. Take a picture of a handshake using the Captive Portal. Then it creates a rogue (fake) Access Point (AP) that imitates the original. Creates a DNS server that directs all queries to the attacker's captive portal host. The captive portal, which requests users for their WPA/WPA2 key, is served via a web server. Creates a jammer, which de-authenticates all clients connected to the original AP and redirects them to the rogue AP. All captive portal authentication attempts are compared to the handshake file that was obtained before. Once a proper key is supplied, the attack will instantly end. Clients will be able to re-join the destination access point when the key has been recorded.

2   Related Work

Cyber-attacks are quickly becoming a serious criminal offense as well as a fiercely debated issue. A MITM attack is a kind of hack in which an unauthorized third party joins and stays unnoticed in an online debate between two or more users. The virus that is now attacking is often monitoring and changing occupation that was previously detected by the two users. A man-in-the-middle attack enables an outsider to be, read, and edit sensitive information without establishing any indications of tampering. This work [13] also examines the most referenced MITM research and survey papers on 'Google Scholar.' The purpose of this article is to assist readers in comprehending and familiarizing themselves with the issue of a 'man-in-the-middle assault.'

The attackers are interested in the data that transfers between the endpoints, as well as the privacy and reliability of that data. An attacker may break confidentiality and integrity by intercepting and changing communications through communication acquisition. In addition, the adversary may intercept, modify, or delete messages to prohibit one of the parties from interacting with the other, culminating in a violation of the availability issue. In this research, we go into MITM attacks in great detail [14].

In this study [15], a viable MITM attack is demonstrated and documented. A hacker uses MITM to divert traffic between a client and a telecommunication route. The most frequent approach to hijack a Wi-Fi network is to use a combination of methods known as ARP spoofing and SSL ripping to signal out the connection. For security, the SSL certificate and HTTP packet created at a computer's application-level are linked to the information being sent. MITM is one of the most used computer-based hacking techniques. In this article [16], the authors have looked at how an attacker uses the free source Ettercap tool in a Kali Linux environment to carry out a MITM attack. The sniffer program Ettercap is included in the Kali Linux environment. It is used for sniffing, MITM attacks, and other types of assaults including DDOS, traffic shaping, DNS spoofing, and so on. This study aims to demonstrate how to employ this assault in an academic setting to teach a core cybersecurity course.

Connected cars provide important data that must be shared in a secure setting with neighbours. Nevertheless, VANET may add untrusted nodes, such as MITM attackers, who want to spread and exchange harmful material with the cars, contaminating the network with hacked data. Relationship building among connected cars might improve security in this aspect since each engaged vehicle will create and spread genuine, accurate, and trustworthy material across the network. In this paper [17], we present a new trust model for connected automobiles called the MITM at-tack-resistant trust model, which efficiently detects dishonest nodes committing MITM attacks and revokes their privileges.

The authors [18] presented a new plug-and-play MITM detection for local networks in this research. Vesper employs an approach based on impulse response analysis, which is often used in the field of acoustic signal treatment. A brief and powerful pulse of ICMP echoes queries may represent the connection between two network sites, similar to how reflections in a cave record the form and architecture of the surroundings. The goal of this article is to perform a MITM attack in an HTTP/2 scenario by leveraging a known TLS flaw. To the authors' knowledge [19], no study has been undertaken on how MITM attacks against HTTP/2 services may be initiated.

In this paper [20], the authors presented a MITM-Intrusion Heuristic Detection paradigm for detecting, isolating, and reconfiguring attacked nodes in this article. The IDS approach aids in the preparation of nodes for potential assaults. The MITM attack targeting cyber-physical systems is investigated in this work underneath the random access protocol (RAP) paradigm; in that, an adversary intercepts and modifies sent data before processing it to reduce the performance of the system. This study [21] used cross-site scripts and telnet pivoting to replicate typical assaults on cyber-physical controller systems. The authors [22] compiled a list of known and undisclosed vulnerabilities and used a tree-based attack method to exploit them. When attempting to infiltrate CPS devices and systems, the authors assessed the average amount of time for cyber attackers of various skill levels.

In this paper [23], the authors present a strategy for preventing a MITM from interrupting operations and preventing the remote health monitoring system from raising warnings. To optimize the efficiency for regular data transmission while ensuring the stability of healthcare information, the framework delivers a size reduction signature extracted from data gathered with authentication and encryption, where the key is taken from obtained strength signal. The method [24] described in this research will assist organizations in detecting insider threats early and functioning more successfully in cyberspace.

Our research [25] intends to solve the difficulties of gathering such data in a continuous delivery setting, as well as to determine the effect of MITM attacks on traffic behavior. A test case is also presented to give some quantitative analysis of the data acquired. A quicker and more efficient preventive technique for MITM attacks on VANET is still required, according to this review research. This review [26] research could have been used as proof of concept and a roadmap for building new VANET security approaches.

3 Working Methodology

The first phase starts with scanning the IoT/Wi-Fi network with the Xerosploit and Flux-ion tools. After that, the target is identified to perform the attack. The target is exploited using Xerosploit and Fluxion individually, and thereafter results are observed. This paper also highlights the preventive measures against MITM. The entire methodology followed by the authors during the implementation is shown in Fig. 1.

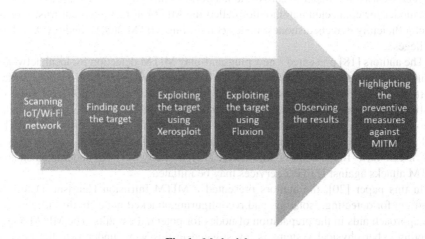

Fig. 1. Methodology

Xerosploit is a penetration testing toolkit powered by NMAP and bettercap. This tool can be installed and used in any Linux system. Here we are using Kali Linux 2021.4 for attacking and Ubuntu 21.10 as victims in the virtual box. We start by starting the tool, selecting the target, and then choosing the attack. The first module is "move".

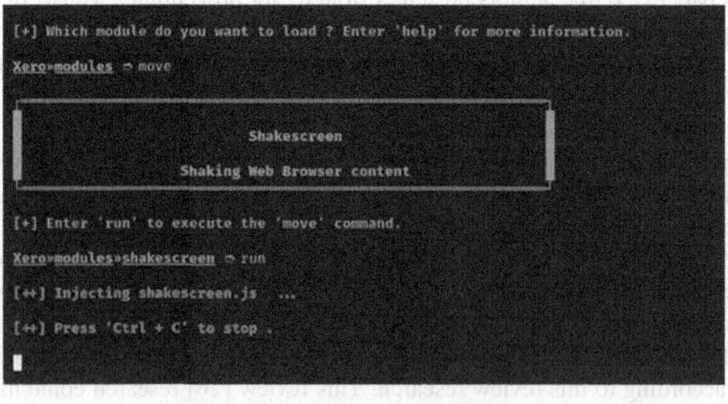

Fig. 2. Shaking the screen with a move

This module uses the security flaws in HTTP and shakes the browser page visited by the victim. From Fig. 2 we can see the browser is being shaken in the victim, system. The second module is "sniff" (Fig. 3).

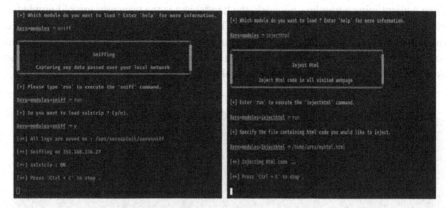

Fig. 3. Using the Sniffing and inject module of Xerosploit

As the name implies, with the help of this module we can see the network traffic of the victim machine. This module uses elements of NMAP to sniff the traffic. If the site visited by the victim is HTTP then we will be able to see the full site address. The third module is "injecthtml" (Fig. 4). Which if successful has so much potential to do anything with the victim browser. Here we just injected a sample alert HTML code, which can be seen above the content of the original website.

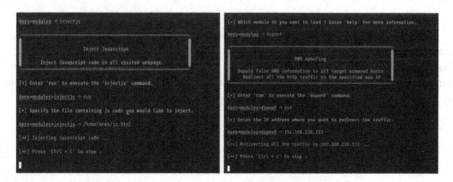

Fig. 4. Injecting JavaScript and performing DNS spoofing

Since JavaScript programs can be inserted almost anywhere into an HTML document using the <script> tag. We can write custom JS code to virtually do anything. The fourth module is similar to the third module, which is "injects", which injects JavaScript code. As we can see from Fig. 4, some content is the JS code and not from the URL we visited. Fifth and the final module is "depoof". When we use this attack on the victim, the victim is redirected to any Website of our choice. As we can see from Fig. 4, the victim has tried to access google.com but the content in the browser is the content from the website that is chosen. This attack has so much malicious potential with it.

Thereafter, the authors used Fluxion, which is a MITM WPA tool available on Github. This tool has multiple attacks, in which we are going to use "Handshake Snooper". When a client joins a wireless network, the handshake is the transmission of knowledge between the access point and the client. This data comprises several different keys, which are exchanged in phases. To do the attack we have to first select the channel to monitor, the tool will choose a Wi-Fi adapter, monitor the channels, and show us the results (Fig. 5), from which we can choose the Wi-Fi to attack.

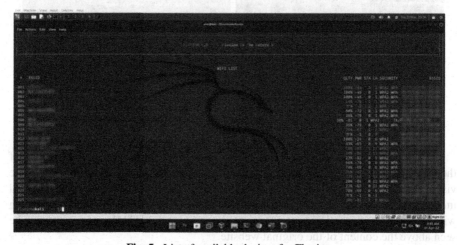

Fig. 5. List of available devices for Fluxion

After choosing the WIFI and the network interface for attacking, we can select the method. For this, we choose the aireplay-ng de-authentication method. Then after that, the tool tries to do a de-auth attack and tries to capture the handshake. When the handshake capture is successful (Fig. 6), the tool will close all the previous tabs opened by it for the user to monitor the attack and prompts that the attack is completed.

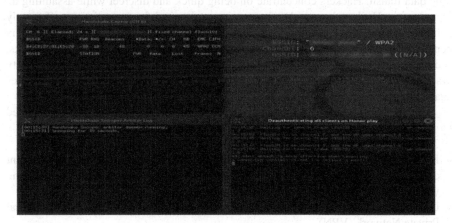

Fig. 6. The output of handshake snooper

4 Results and Discussion

The handshake is a. cap file stored in /attacks/Handshake Snooper/handshakes/ directory. Then we can use aircrack-ng and rockyou wordlist to crack the password. As you can see from Fig. 7 the key is found successfully for the Wi-Fi which we at-tacked. This has happened because the key was insecure and common that the key cracking took hardly any time and we found the key.

Fig. 7. Attack on the target

The Fluxion Monitors the Wi-Fi and shows us live updates about that Wi-Fi, as shown in Fig. 7, additionally, we can also see updates of the de-authentication attack performed on the Wi-Fi every 30s until a handshake is captured. A handshake is an information shared between the client and the access point, the de-auth attack will but this info transfer between the client and the access point, and when the client tries to communicate back to the access point Fluxion captures it in a.cap file, from which we can get many details about the client request and the access point data (Fig. 8).

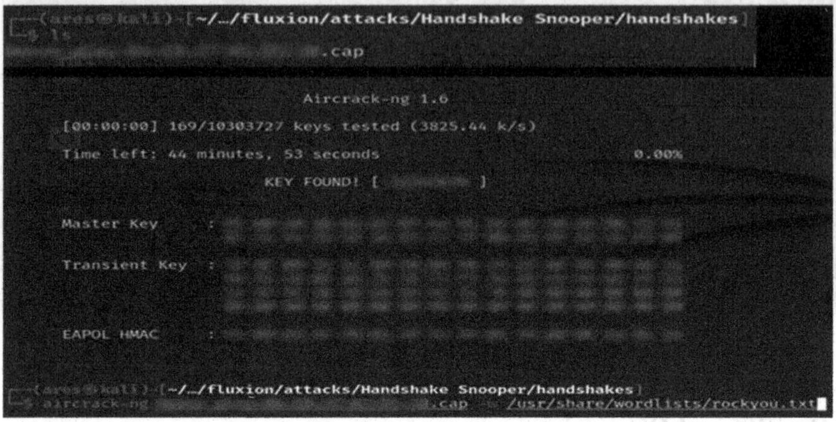

Fig. 8. Advanced MITM attack successful

4.1 Preventive Measures Against MITM

MITM attacks are gaining traction among hackers as a way to take advantage of real-time data transit. Hackers concentrate on being quick and discreet while assaulting an organization. Hackers have to be clever to go undetected for some time to effectively penetrate, steal critical information, or harm an organization in other ways. Hackers benefit from MITM attacks because they provide a degree of stealth. MITM attacks, if done correctly, may go unnoticed, leaving the targeted organization's cyber security systems and/or team unable to control and resolve the problem. The preventive measures against MITM are highlighted in Fig. 9.

MITM is a dangerous attack and can lead to the data leakage but it can be prevented by following the measures given below:

- By conducting awareness campaigns to educate the staff about the most prevalent cyber assaults and dangers, as well as what they should do to prevent jeopardizing your company's security.
- Using guaranteed encrypted communications from your enterprise, use a Virtual Private Network (VPN).
- Using SSL/TLS to encrypt your e-mails. Additionally, PGP/GPG encryption is a viable option.
- Two-factor authentication should be implemented.
- Make sure your browsers are up to date. Make sure your company is constantly using the most recent edition of secure browsers.
- Make sure that employees are not using public Wi-Fi.

Fig. 9. Preventive measures against MITM

5 Conclusion

MITM attacks are a kind of eavesdropping attack in which the attackers try to stop a conversation or data transfer in the middle of it. After positioning themselves in the "middle" of the transfer, the attackers pretend to be both legitimate parties. This allows the attacker to capture data and information from both parties while concurrently sending malicious sites or other material to both transacting parties in a way that may not be detected until it is too late. In this paper, the authors have implemented a novel approach to perform automated advanced MITM on IoT/Wi-Fi networks. Xerosploit and Fluxion tools are used in the implementation. Xerosploit is a penetration testing toolbox fully intent on executing man-in-the-center attacks to test. It incorporates various modules that take into account several attacks, as well as DOS attacks and scanning of ports.

References

1. Choi, J., Ahn, B., Bere, G., Ahmad, S., Mantooth, H.A., Kim, T.: Blockchain-Based Man-in-the-Middle (MITM) Attack Detection for Photovoltaic Systems. 2021 IEEE Design Methodologies Conference (DMC). (2021). https://doi.org/10.1109/dmc51747.2021.9529949
2. Verma, S., Sharma, J., Kaushik, K., Vyas, V.: Mounting Cases of Cyber-Attacks and Digital Payment. Cybersecurity Issues, Challenges, and Solutions in the Business World, 59–80 (2022). https://doi.org/10.4018/978-1-6684-5827-3.ch005
3. Khatod, V., Manolova, A.: Effects of Man in the Middle (MITM) Attack on Bit Error Rate of Bluetooth System. 2020 Joint International Conference on Digital Arts, Media and Technology with ECTI Northern Section Conference on Electrical, Electronics, Computer and Telecommunications Engineering (ECTI DAMT & NCON) (2020). https://doi.org/10.1109/ectidamtncon48261.2020.9090721

4. Saravanan, K., Vijayanand, L., Negesh, R.K., Cse, L., Eee, L.: A Novel Bluetooth Man-In-The-Middle Attack Based On SSP using OOB Association model (Mar. 2012). https://doi.org/10.48550/arxiv.1203.4649

5. Bhardwaj, A., Kaushik, K., Kumar, M.: Taxonomy of Security Attacks on Internet of Things. Blockchain Technologies. 1–24 (2022). https://doi.org/10.1007/978-981-19-1960-2_1

6. Lahmadi, A., Duque, A., Heraief, N., Francq, J.: MitM Attack Detection in BLE Networks Using Reconstruction and Classification Machine Learning Techniques. In: Koprinska, I., et al. (eds.) ECML PKDD 2020. CCIS, vol. 1323, pp. 149–164. Springer, Cham (2020). https://doi.org/10.1007/978-3-030-65965-3_10

7. Kaushik, K., Tayal, S., Bhardwaj, A., Kumar, M.: Advanced Smart Computing Technologies in Cybersecurity and Forensics. (2021). https://doi.org/10.1201/9781003140023

8. Zeadally, S., Siddiqui, F., Baig, Z.: 25 Years of Bluetooth Technology. Future Internet. **11**, 194 (2019). https://doi.org/10.3390/fi11090194

9. Samineni, N.R., Barbhuiya, F.A., Nandi, S.: Stealth and semi-stealth MITM attacks, detection and defense in IPv4 networks. In: 2012 2nd IEEE International Conference on Parallel, Distributed and Grid Computing (2012). https://doi.org/10.1109/pdgc.2012.6449847

10. Bhardwaj, A., Kaushik, K., Maashi, M.S., Aljebreen, M., Bharany, S.: Alternate data stream attack framework to perform stealth attacks on active directory hosts. Sustainability. **14**, 12288 (2022). https://doi.org/10.3390/su141912288

11. How to Perform Advanced Man-in-the-Middle Attacks with Xerosploit « Null Byte :: WonderHowTo. https://null-byte.wonderhowto.com/how-to/perform-advanced-man-middle-attacks-with-xerosploit-0384705/. Accessed 11 April 2022

12. Fluxion - Penetration Testing Tools. https://en.kali.tools/?p=235. Accessed 11 April 2022

13. Mallik, A.: MAN-IN-THE-MIDDLE-ATTACK: UNDERSTANDING IN SIMPLE WORDS. Cyberspace: Jurnal Pendidikan Teknologi Informasi **2**, 109 (2019). https://doi.org/10.22373/cj.v2i2.3453

14. Bhushan, B., Sahoo, G., Rai, A.K.: Man-in-the-middle attack in wireless and computer networking—A review. 2017 3rd International Conference on Advances in Computing, Communication & Automation (ICACCA) (Fall) (2017). https://doi.org/10.1109/icaccaf.2017.8344724

15. Chordiya, A.R., Majumder, S., Javaid, A.Y.: Man-in-the-Middle (MITM) Attack Based Hijacking of HTTP Traffic Using Open Source Tools. In: 2018 IEEE International Conference on Electro/Information Technology (EIT) (2018). https://doi.org/10.1109/eit.2018.8500144

16. Pingle, B., Mairaj, A., Javaid, A.Y.: Real-World Man-in-the-Middle (MITM) Attack Implementation Using Open Source Tools for Instructional Use. In: 2018 IEEE International Conference on Electro/Information Technology (EIT) (2018). https://doi.org/10.1109/eit.2018.8500082

17. Ahmad, F., Kurugollu, F., Adnane, A., Hussain, R., Hussain, F.: MARINE: man-in-the-middle attack resistant trust model in connected vehicles. IEEE Internet Things J. **7**, 3310–3322 (2020). https://doi.org/10.1109/jiot.2020.2967568

18. Mirsky, Y., Kalbo, N., Elovici, Y., Shabtai, A.: Vesper: using echo analysis to detect man-in-the-middle attacks in LANs. IEEE Trans. Inf. Forensics Secur. **14**, 1638–1653 (2019). https://doi.org/10.1109/tifs.2018.2883177

19. Patni, P., Iyer, K., Sarode, R., Mali, A., Nimkar, A.: Man-in-the-middle attack in HTTP/2. In: 2017 International Conference on Intelligent Computing and Control (I2C2) (2017). https://doi.org/10.1109/i2c2.2017.8321787

20. Mohapatra, H.: Handling of man-in-the-middle attack in WSN through intrusion detection system. International Journal of Emerging Trends in Engineering Research **8**, 1503–1510 (2020). https://doi.org/10.30534/ijeter/2020/05852020

21. Zhang, X.-G., Yang, G.-H., Wasly, S.: Man-in-the-middle attack against cyber-physical systems under random access protocol. Inf. Sci. **576**, 708–724 (2021). https://doi.org/10.1016/j.ins.2021.07.083
22. Bhardwaj, A., Alshehri, M.D., Kaushik, K., Alyamani, H.J., Kumar, M.: Secure framework against cyber attacks on cyber-physical robotic systems. Journal of Electronic Imaging **31** (2022). https://doi.org/10.1117/1.jei.31.6.061802
23. Salem, O., Alsubhi, K., Shaafi, A., Gheryani, M., Mehaoua, A., Boutaba, R.: Man-in-the-middle attack mitigation in internet of medical things. IEEE Trans. Industr. Inf. **18**, 2053–2062 (2022). https://doi.org/10.1109/tii.2021.3089462
24. Kaushik, K.: A systematic approach to develop an advanced insider attacks detection module. J. Eng. Appl. Sci. **8**, 33 (2021). https://doi.org/10.5455/jeas.2021050104
25. Calvert, C., Khoshgoftaar, T.M., Najafabadi, M.M., Kemp, C.: A procedure for collecting and labeling man-in-the-middle attack traffic. International Journal of Reliability, Quality and Safety Engineering **24**, 1750002 (2017). https://doi.org/10.1142/s0218539317500024
26. Al-shareeda, M.A., Anbar, M., Hasbullah, I.H., Manickam, S., Abdullah, N., Hamdi, M.M.: Review of Prevention schemes for Replay Attack in Vehicular Ad hoc Networks (VANETs). In: 2020 IEEE 3rd International Conference on Information Communication and Signal Processing (ICICSP) (2020). https://doi.org/10.1109/icicsp50920.2020.9232047

Fog Computing Paradigm with Internet of Things to Solve Challenges of Cloud with IoT

Aarti Rani$^{(\boxtimes)}$, Vijay Prakash , and Manuj Darbari

Babu Banarsi Das University, Lucknow, Uttar Pradesh, India
aarti.singh18oct@bbdu.ac.in

Abstract. The Internet of Things is a ground-breaking and innovative concept. It aims to bring all objects online, reduce human intervention, and make work simple and quick. In IoT heterogeneous physical and virtual things are connected in a network incorporated into electronic devices, software, sensors, and connections, and substance become more useful by exchanging data with other connected objects over the Internet. The variety of Internet- Connected devices and sensors has risen in recent years. Despite the widespread use of cloud computing, certain applications and services are still unable to benefit from this modern computing standard due to cloud computing's intrinsic drawbacks, such as unbearable delay, a lack of mobility, and context awareness. For the solution to this problem a new computing paradigm that supports the computational needs of real-time applications for mostly geographically scattered IoT devices and sensors is known as Fog computing. Fog is not a cloud computing replacement. It is a cloud technology alternative. It extends the cloud services. We have explored the current scenario of Fog computing and related concepts in this study. Fog increases the superiority of service while simultaneously reducing bandwidth latency. Fog allows for faster connection and additional computing capability closer to the end-use and diminishes the processing workload on the cloud computing framework.

Keywords: Internet of things · Applications of IoT · Technology · Challenges of cloud with IoT · Fog computing · Fog computing in IoT

1 Introduction

IoT concept promises to integrate appliances and "things" into the Internet environment, including medical equipment, refrigerators, cameras, and sensors. This paradigm is a new type of interaction between objects and people that allows smart cities, infrastructure, and services to be built to improve quality of life and resource use. Improve by opening the door [1]. M-to-M communication, which allows "anything" to connect to the Internet, is not only realism, but actually, it is necessary for our daily life and interaction. We can move disruptive applications like air quality, transportation, smart parking, elder care, living ecosystems, smart grids, smart farming, and medical systems with the help of IoT, and rely on the consistent quality of service (QoS) [2]. We need enough networks and better computing methods to provide low latency and rapid response times for applications if we want to get the most out of IoT.

© The Author(s), under exclusive license to Springer Nature Switzerland AG 2022
V. Sugumaran et al. (Eds.): AIR 2022, CCIS 1738, pp. 72–84, 2022.
https://doi.org/10.1007/978-3-031-23724-9_7

Cloud-based IoT systems, on the other hand, are far from end-users and face several issues, including faster reaction times, heavy cloud server loads, and a lack of universal mobility. The high bandwidth cost of connection and the high redundancy of data make sending a very large quantity of data sensed by IoT devices to the cloud inefficient in the period of big data. As a substitute for transferring data to the cloud, it might be more cost-effective to put apps and hand them out faster to IoT data. Fog computing is a notion that is well suited to dealing with these kinds of issues [3]. Fog is a new thought that purpose to get the cloud closer to the end-user while also enhancing service quality [4]. Fog is a smart layer that sits in the middle of the cloud and the IoT, allowing for reduced latency, location alertness, and a geographic spread of IoT devices. While at the network's boundary, Fog computing inherits cloud main features and provides end-users with processing, storage, and network services [5].

The paper is planned as follows: A formal discussion of the Internet of Things, applications, and technology is discussed in Sect. 2. Discuss Cloud computing, their challenges with IoT, and comparisons in Sect. 3. Discuss Fog computing and its architecture and its role in IoT in Sect. 4. Last Sect. 5 discusses the conclusion.

2   Internet of Things

The Internet of Things (IoT) is a term that describes the number of hardware objects which are constantly connected to the Web and acquiring and transmission of data all over the world. The IoT is a collection of computers and other network devices, mechanical and digital machinery, products, creatures, and humans, all of which have a unique identifier (UID) and are not interconnected to one another. It is able of sending data through a network. Human or human-computer interaction is required. The Internet of Things is becoming an increasing area of life and might be seen all around us. Ultimately, the IoT is a game-changer that links together a diverse set of expert machines, frameworks, smart devices, and sensors [6]. The IoT has an interdisciplinary vision to extend its utility to a variety of fields, including the environment, industry, public/private sector, medicine, and transportation as presented in Fig. 1. As a result, the Internet of Things' primary purpose is to enable objects to connect to other objects and individuals via networks, pathways, or services at any time and from any location. Smart homes, phones, transportation, industrial systems, cameras, smart toys, buildings, smart home appliances, industrial systems, and a plethora of other objects may now communicate through the Internet [7]. An easy explanation of IoT is "IoT or Internet of Things is a network of associated devices that interrelate and exchange information with each other. The technology allows the link of two or more devices that connect and transfer and get information through the internet".

2.1   IoT Applications

IoT applications appear to be promising in the next years as shown in Fig. 2. To create integrated smart solutions, this technology will most likely be combined with additional technical trends such as AI and programmed things. Technology integration will cause upheaval in several industries, resulting in new opportunities. IoT-based solutions offer efficient monitoring and management of linked devices as well as the automation of daily operations. As a result, task performance is more efficient and convenient.

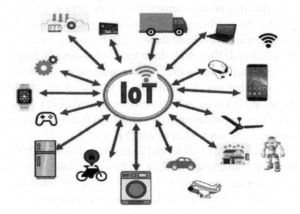

Fig. 1. IoT devices

Fig. 2. IoT applications

The Internet of Things' potential applications is not only many, but also diversified, as they touch practically every element of people's, institutions', and society's daily lives. Manufacturing and industry, healthcare, agriculture, smart cities, security, and emergencies are all examples of IoT areas. The number of devices and features that the IoT can do is predicted to continue to grow. The ambiguity of the representation of "thing" indicates this. The IoT aids in the development of smart nations and smart cities. The Internet of Things (IoT) aids cities in terms of management by combining it with vital infrastructural facilities, such as mobility and medical. It also helps in different areas such as water management, trash, and emergency management. In comparison to the conventional approach, which was impeded by information delay, which can be critical in real emergencies, its real-time and exact data allows for faster responses. Traditional technologies and resources are used in current court systems. Outside of basic legal responsibilities, they rarely use current analytics or automation. Superior analytics, better evidence, and improved processes are brought to judicial systems by the Internet of Things, which speeds up processes, eliminates unnecessary procedures, manages corruption, lowers costs, and improves satisfaction. The optimization and data analysis of IoT assist consumers both personally and professionally. The Internet of Things functions as a team of personal assistants, counselors, and security. It improves our quality of life, work, and pleasure. Current manufacturing technology makes use of standard technologies as well as modern distribution and analytics.

2.2 Technology

The creation of a computing system in which electronic artifacts can be distinctively acknowledged and can think and act in concert with other objects to accumulate data on which programmed events are based necessitates and use of clustering of better and more effective innovations, which can only be accomplished through the combination of various techniques that enable artifacts to be distinctively recognized and converse with one another [8].

The main goal of the IoT is to connect things and substances all over the world through the internet, wireless sensor networks (WSNs), and smartphones so that they can share information automatically, much as people do. Numerous strategies can be employed to accomplish this purpose. Radio Frequency Identification (RFID) identifies mobile phones, sensors, actuators, and embedded devices, and nanotechnology allows them to communicate with one another [9]. Sensors, scanning and monitoring systems, supply chain management; smart grids, smart air quality monitoring, smart farming, and data analytics are all instances of IoT in action. The IoT's basic concept is to agree to the independent exchange of valuable information among imperceptibly embedded different exclusively certain real-world devices in our vicinity, fueled by advanced technologies like RFID and Wireless Technologies, which are detected by sensing devices and then processed for the result, based on which an automatic achievement is carried out [10].

3   Internet of Things

The cloud-to-IoT integration, known as CoT, has numerous advantages. It can, for example, assist in the management of IoT resources and the provision of cost- effective andwell-organized IoT services. It enables fast, minimal deployment and adaptability for complicated data processing and implementation, in addition to improving IoT data and processing flow. The CoT concept is complex; it brings the latest challenges to the IoT system that a conventional centralized cloud computing system cannot address, like latency, capability limitations, limited resource devices, network breakdown heavily congested, and greater security [11]. Furthermore, for IoT applications with time-sensitive operations or insufficient Internet connection, the centralized solution is ineffective. Milliseconds can be critical in a variety of situations, including telemedicine and medical care. A similar situation occurs in vehicle-to-vehicle communications, in which it is impossible to prevent mishaps or accidents. Delays are caused by the centralized cloud strategy [12]. To overcome these difficulties, a more capable cloud computing model with lower latency constraints is required [13]. To improve these issues, Cisco recommended a novel technique known as Fog computing [14].

Challenges of Cloud with IoT: Unluckily, nothing is perfect, and cloud technology, especially for IoT applications, has several flaws which are presented through Fig. 3. Due to the distance between clients and data processing centers, the cloud cannot provide very low latency for many IoT programs. In any Web system, system problems and network outages can occur for any reason, enabling consumers to access an interruption; to avoid difficulties, many businesses use several connection routes with automated redundancy. Many organizations deploy numerous connected channels with managed failover to avoid issues. Confidential data is communicated across interconnected global channels

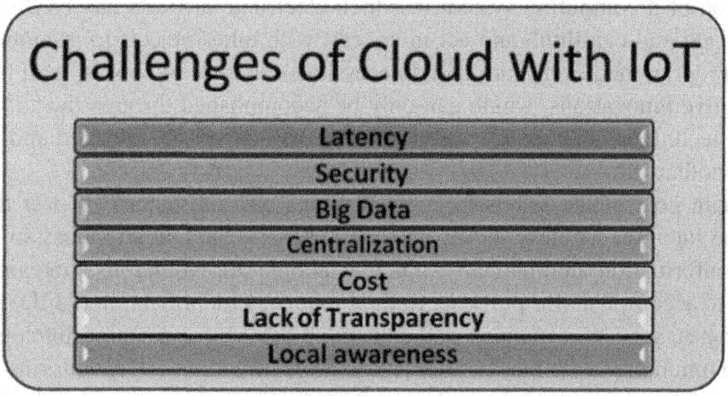

Fig. 3. Challenges of cloud with IoT

Table 1. Assessment between cloud computing and fog computing [15].

Parameters	Cloud Computing	Fog Computing
Distance	Multiple hops	One hope
server nodes	Few	Very large
Location of Service	Within the Internet	At the edge of the local network
Latency	High	Low
Delay Jitter	High	Very Low
Security	Undefined	Can be defined
Location awareness	No	Yes
Geo-distribution	Centralized	Distributed
Resource Management	Centralized	Centralized/ Distributed
Response Time	High	Low
Transmission	Device to Cloud	Device to Device
Capacity	Cloud Computing does not provide any reduction in data while sending or transforming data	Fog Computing reduces the amount of data sent to cloud computing.

with thousands or millions of gigabytes of data from some of the other users; it's no surprise that the network is vulnerable to cyber-attacks or data theft (Table 1).

4 FoG Computing

The fog environment, which can be positioned nearer to IoT devices/sensors, is made up of conventional network elements including gateways, switches, set-top boxes, proxy servers, Ground Stations, and others. These elements can execute applications and provide a broad range of computing, storage, networking, and other functionalities. As a result, Fog computing can build massive geographical dispersion of Cloud-based services thanks to the networking components. The National Institute of Standards and Technology defines fog computing as "Between smart end-devices and conventional cloud or data centers, there exists a horizontal, physical or virtual resources paradigm. "This approach enables geographically segregated, delayed applications to leverage from pervasive, scalable, layered, pooled, and distributed computing, storage, and network access. [16]. Fog computing is a decentralized computing approach that brings the typical cloud computing technology to the edge of the network. At the network's edge, fog computing provides processing, storage, monitoring, and service capabilities. Fog in the IoT is a great supplement to prior cloud computing offerings. There is currently a significant effort focusing on various scenarios in IoT applications across several businesses in which the IoT can be applied [17]. Data, Volume, Latency, and Bandwidth are three criteria of today's networks that Fog addresses. Fog is a new technology that is mostly utilized in conjunction with the Internet of Things. Data and Fog computing is used to distribute services from the network core to the network edge. This technology provides data, computation, storage, and application services to end-users in the same way that Cloud does. Fog is a decentralized computing approach that pulls data from a centralized location, processes it, and sends it to a network edge device (set-top box, access point). Fog computing is a technology in which the service is hosted locally and used by the user.To put it another way, fog computing is a methodology that allows IoT data to be processed nearby in smart devices not sent to the cloud. The computation, storage, and networking resources are all available in the cloud and fog structures. Data acquired by sensors is not transferred to a cloud server in fog computing; instead, it is sent to devices such as network edges or set-top boxes [15]. Fog computing is related to cloud computing in certain ways. Both computer technologies offer their registered clients application, storage, data, and computational services. Fog computing, on the other hand, provides services closer to end-users than cloud computing, which provides services distantly.

End- users can get data, compute, storage, and application services from both Cloud and Fog. Fog, on either side, differs from Cloud in terms of proximity to end-users, geographical distribution, and mobility assistance. Fog computing is characterized as "an extremely virtualized environment that offers networking, storage, and compute resources across obsolete CC information centers, typically but not always located at the network edge"[4]. A fog structure has several edge nodes with limited processing capabilities, which are commonly referred to as fog nodes. These fog nodes have fewer processing and storage facilities. Cloudlets are edge and numerous server nodes in a fog

Table 2. IoT challenges

Iot challenges	Challenges solved by fog computing
Latency issue	All computing processes, such as data processing and analysis, and other time-sensitive operations, are conducted close to end-users in the fog, making it an ideal solution for latency problems in a variety of IoT applications
Bandwidth issue	Fog enables IoT devices to do hierarchical data processing from the cloud. This allows data processing to be customized to the application's requirements as well as the presence of networking and computing resources. As a consequence, the amount of data transferred to the cloud is decreased, resulting in lower network traffic
Resource-constrained devices	When operations that require a huge amount of resources can't be moved to the cloud, so to handle this situation Fog computing used its capabilities. Device intricacy, lifetime costs, and power consumption can all be declined as a result
Uninterrupted services	Fog computing can operate separately even if the communication network to the cloud is sporadic, ensuring continuous services
Security Issues	Because resource-constrained devices lack adequate security features, Fog acts as a proxy, allowing these devices to upgrade their software and security information. The fog could also be used to evaluate the security status of nearby devices
Real-time communications	In contrast to the batch analysis used in the cloud, fog computing solicitations allow simultaneous communications among fog nodes
Physical distribution	Unlike the integrated cloud, fog allows for distributed applications and services to be hosted everywhere
Accessibility and consistency	Data can be recovered at every moment without fail, and computation and transmission can continue without interruption

network [18], which play a part in the shared computing environment rather than outside the network edge Clients, may be able to get a real-time response for critical latency applications by using fog devices. Even though Cisco coined the term, numerous researchers and industries characterized fog computing in a variety of ways. Yi et al. cover a wide range of fog computing topics [20]. It is defined as a "geographically shared computing framework with a pool of requirements that contains different universally linked heterogeneous computing devices at the network edge that is not entirely flawlessly supported by cloud services to collectively offer transmission, storage, and elastic computation in remote surroundings to an enormous scale of users nearby," according to the specification. "System-level flat architecture that splits storage, resources, computing services, and networking from every place together with the range from Cloud to Things," The Open Fog Consortium claims [19].

Fog computing is best suited to IoT-based systems with globally distributed end devices, where cloud communication is spotty but minimal delay is needed. Fog is fit for IoT applications that create terabytes of data regularly and can't transport it to and from the cloud. From an IDC analysis, edge devices are expected to contribute 10% of global data by 2020. As a result, there will be greater demand for fog computing systems that provide low latency while still offering comprehensive intelligence. Envision, a New York-based renewable energy company has experienced a 15% rise in production from its massive network of wind turbines thanks to the fog. The company is currently analyzing up to 20 terabytes of data each second from 3 million sensors on the 20,000 turbines it oversees. By relocating processing to the edge, Envision was able to decrease data management time between 10 min to seconds, giving them actionable intelligence and significant economic gains. Fog computing is being used by Plat One, some other IoT company, to improve data handling for its over 1 million sensors. The ParStream platform is used by hundreds and thousands of devices, including lighting systems and parking, port and mobility management, and a network of 50,000 coffee makers, to transmit real-time sensor data [20]. According to Joe Skorupa, Distinguished Vice President Analyst for Gartner's General Managers team, "With real-time business processes on the line, the massive number of devices, combined with the sheer volume, velocity, and structure of IoT data, causes issues, particularly in the areas of security, data, storage management, servers, and the data center network. To achieve the business requirements connected with IoT, data center managers will need to employ more forward-looking capacity management in these areas. "Over the projection period, the fog computing market is expected to grow at a CAGR of 55.6 percent, from $ 22.28 million in 2017 to $ 203.48 million in 2022. With the rise of interconnected devices and cloud technology, fog computing's prominence is expected to increase. The growth of fog computing is being fueled by a rising growth of real applications, increased awareness of data security, and the need to analyze at the network's edge.

The predicted term of the market is between 2017 and 2022. Cisco Systems, Inc. (United States), Microsoft Corp. (United States), ARM Holding Plc. (United king-dom), Dell Inc. (United States), Intel (United States), Fujitsu (Japan), GE Digital (United states), Nebbiolo Technologies (United States), Schneider Electric Software, LLC (Japan), Toshiba Corporation (Japan), and PrismTech Corporation (United States) are the major players in fog computing development [20]. Thus according to Zion Industry Report, the global fog business has the potential to approach $768 million U.S. dollars by 2025 [20].

4.1 The FoG Computing Architecture

The Fog is associated with the physical and conceptual components that resemble hardware and software needed to create an IoT network. The system consists of IoT devices, nodes, aggregation nodes, data services, remote cloud storage, and a localized data storage server/cloud. Fog is a middle layer. The Fog layer is a group of Fog nodes, which act as a virtual representation of IoT. While transferring data to the cloud layer, the Middle layer conducts preliminary processing of data, enabling speedier decision-making and execution.

- **IoT devices** are devices that use various wired and wireless technologies to connect to an IoT network. These gadgets generate massive amounts of data regularly. Zwave, HART, NFC, Bluetooth, BLE, Zigbee, NFC, ISA- 100.11A, 6LoWPAN, and other wireless technologies are all employed in IoT. IPv4, IPv6, MQTT, CoAP, XMPP, AMQP, and other IoT protocols are used.
- **A fog node** is a device that can compute, store data, and connect to the internet. To assist end devices, additional fog nodes are scattered across such a broader area. Different topologies are used to connect fog nodes. Depending on the requirements, fog nodes can be located in a factory, on top of the buildings, close to a railway track, on transportation, and so on. Examples include switches, embedded servers, controllers, routers, cameras, and other fog nodes. These fog nodes process highly sensitive data.

  - Responsibilities of a Fog node are:
  - Real-time data were taken by IoT devices
  - For real-time analytics, run IoT-enabled applications.
  - capable of handling temporary data storage
  - Sends cloud summaries of data collected from devices regularly.

- **Cloud:** All of the fog nodes connect and transmit information to the cloud layer. Data that is less sensitive is processed, analyzed, and stored at the cloud layer [21] (Fig. 4).

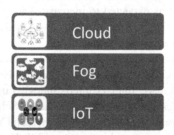

Fig. 4. The structural design of fog computing

Significance of Fog Computing

- Fog, in comparison to cloud technology, offers better security.
- Data is analyzed at the Fog layer before being transferred to the cloud layer, reducing bandwidth usage and operating costs.
- Fog computing minimizes latency, resulting in faster response times.
- Fog computing allows for improved data handling with not as much latency and bandwidth use.

- Fog is important for concurrent data analysis, and it has a wide geographical dispersion.
- There are a lot of nodes.
- Wireless access has a major impact.
- Streaming and real-time applications are prevalent.
- Heterogeneity

4.2 FoG Computing in IoT

Data storage gets extremely expensive and complicated whenever the sensor or program generates a big amount of data. When dealing with massive amounts of data, network bandwidth becomes expensive, necessitating the use of large data centers to tackle the problem. Fog has emerged as a viable alternative to traditional data management techniques. Fog has great potential for the collection of data; data distribution process, storage, and network connectivity resources. It saves a lot of energy, reduces the density of space and instance, and improves the data's effectiveness and performance. The fog paradigm is valuable for applications that require huge amounts of data, fast network activities, and immediate processing. Real-time, hybrid, and independent data centers benefit from Fog, which improves operational reliability and effectiveness. Fog can also help keep systems up and running while saving funds on electricity, data center security, and dependability. By concentrating computer resources across a huge number of nodes, fog computing saves money. The availability, efficiency, and utility of fog nodes define their position. It also relieves the strain on corporate data centers. An additional major benefit of fog is the reduction in data congestion. Fog computing advantages include actual working on time, and heterogeneous and autonomous data centers, which facilitate better effectiveness and safety. Fog computing can also save you cost on energy, data center security, and dependability while keeping your things running smoothly. By sharing system resources across a vast network, fog computing cuts costs. The availability, efficiency, and utility of fog nodes define their position. It also relieves the strain on corporate data centers. Nevertheless, this technique offers great ability can save governments, organizations, and even individual customers a large amount of money [19]. Fog brings the cloud's capabilities closer to where data is generated and processed. As a result, more people will be able to access the Internet simultaneously. It offers a network and services similar to cloud technology, but it also has more quality and reliability. According to IDC, network edge devices will produce 45 percent of all data by 2025, with 10 percent of that data coming from mobile phones, wearable technology, smart home devices, transportation, as well as other edge devices. In the next five years, Fog is considered to be the only technology that will outlast AI, Internet of Things app development, and 5G [20].

Fog computing can be used to resolve challenges that occur during cloud integration with IoT [30]. Many of the shortcomings of present computer systems based primarily on cloud technology and end-user device connected to IoT systems could be overcome with fog computing. Fog computing, can resolve numerous IoT difficulties as described in Table 2 (Fig. 5).

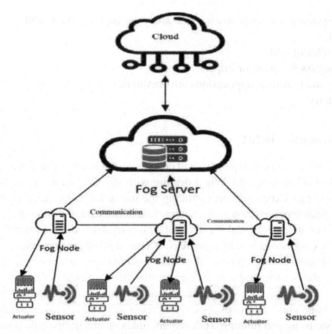

Fig. 5. Communication between cloud servers, Fog devices, and sensors

4.3 Areas Where FoG Works with IoT

- Real medical assessment using fog technology, in which patients with electronic scans can be supervised in actual for medical emergencies and the adequate doctors are alerted as soon as possible.
- One key field is real-time rail monitoring, which involves deploying fog nodes to railway tracks to analyze track conditions for high-speed trains. High-speed data analysis is provided by fog nodes, which improves the railway system's safety and reliability.
- Another area is real-time air quality monitoring using fog computing because poor air quality ultimately gets impacts the ambient conditions in our environment.
- Optimization of the pipeline for Pipelines is used to carry gas and oil. As a result, with such a gas pipeline system, real-time pressure monitoring and a flow compressor are required.
- The IoT and cloud paradigms are increasingly driving increased agricultural production at cheaper costs. The Fog Nodes technology minimizes overall latency caused by data transport to the cloud for processing.

The Fog paradigm comes since the cloud is not suitable for numerous IoT applications. Fog has distributed architecture that satisfies IoT requirements and manages huge amounts of data generated by sensors, which would be prohibitively exclusive and time-taking to send to the cloud for processing and analysis. Fog reduces the amount of bandwidth and provides an ease of communication among sensors and the cloud, allowing IoT to have a greater impact.

5 Conclusion

The fog paradigm can be regarded as a technique to provide improved services more quickly and cost-effectively, as well as a way to avoid the more extensive internet, whose speeds are often constrained by the carrier. IoT has a very bright and scalable future.The majority of affluent countries are investing billions of dollars in Smart Infrastructure to replace present infrastructure. The IoT promises to improve human lives and business productivity. Through globally dispersed and locally intelligent networks of smart devices and a rich ecosystem of application development, it has the potential to enable the extension and advancement of core services in health care, transportation, air quality monitoring, logistics, security, and education. However, significant efforts will be necessary to mobilize the industry to advance beyond the early stages of market development and into market maturity by utilizing the IoT's hidden possibility. The market may place varying demands on mobile networks in terms of service distribution, customer billing models, and ability to supply IoT services, among other things, posing a challenge to mobile service providers. In summary, this paper present a detailed study about Fog computing and its contributions to the IoT, and how this technology explores guidelines and open issues related to the cloud with the Internet of Things.

References

1. Gupta, H., Dastjerdi, A.V., Ghosh, S.K., Buyya, R.: iFogSim: a toolkit for modeling and simulation of resource management techniques in the internet of things, edge and fog computing environments: iFogSim: a toolkit for modeling and simulation of internet of things. Softw.: Pract. Exp. **47**(9), 1275–1296 (2017). https://doi.org/10.1002/spe.2509
2. Okafor, K.C., Achumba, I.E., Chukwudebe, G.A., Ononiwu, G.C.: Leveraging fog computing for scalable IoT datacenter using spine-leaf network topology. J. Electr. Comput. Eng. **2017**, 1–11 (2017). https://doi.org/10.1155/2017/2363240
3. Yousefpour, A., Ishigaki, G., Jue, J.P.: Fog computing: towards minimizing delay in the internet of things. In: 2017 IEEE International Conference on Edge Computing (EDGE) (2017). https://doi.org/10.1109/ieee.edge.2017.12
4. Saad, M.: Fog computing and its role in the internet of things: concept, security and privacy issues. Int. J. Comput. Appl. **180**, 7–9 (2018). https://doi.org/10.5120/ijca2018916829
5. Garcia Lopez, P., et al.: Edge-centric computing. ACM SIGCOMM Comput. Commun. Rev. **45**, 37–42 (2015). https://doi.org/10.1145/2831347.2831354
6. Kumar, S., Tiwari, P., Zymbler, M.: Internet of Things is a revolutionary approach for future technology enhancement: a review. Journal of Big Data **6**(1), 1–21 (2019). https://doi.org/10.1186/s40537-019-0268-2
7. Hussein, A.H.: Internet of things (IOT): research challenges and future applications. Int. J. Adv. Comput. Sci. Appl. **10** (2019). https://doi.org/10.14569/ijacsa.2019.0100611
8. Khoo, B.: RFID as an enabler of the internet of things: issues of security and privacy. In: 2011 International Conference on Internet of Things and 4th International Conference on Cyber, Physical and Social Computing (2011). https://doi.org/10.1109/ithings/cpscom.2011.83

9. Jain, D., Krishna, P.V. Saritha, V.: A study on internet of things based applications', arXiv preprint arXiv:1206.3891 (2012)
10. Farooq, M.U., Waseem, M., Mazhar, S., Khairi, A., Kamal, T.: A review on internet of things (IoT). Int. J. Comput. Appl. **113**(1), 1–7 (2015). https://doi.org/10.5120/19787-1571
11. Atlam, H.F., Alenezi, A., Walters, R.J., Wills, G.B., Daniel, J.: Developing an adaptive risk-based access control model for the internet of things. In: 2017 IEEE International Conference on Internet of Things (iThings) and IEEE Green Computing and Communications (Green-Com) and IEEE Cyber, Physical and Social Computing (CPSCom) and IEEE Smart Data (SmartData) (2017). https://doi.org/10.1109/ithings-greencom-cpscom-smartdata.2017.103
12. Wen, Z., Yang, R., Garraghan, P., Lin, T., Xu, J., Rovatsos, M.: Fog orchestration for internet of things services. IEEE Internet Comput. **21**, 16–24 (2017). https://doi.org/10.1109/mic.2017.36
13. Aburukba, R.O., AliKarrar, M., Landolsi, T., El-Fakih, K.: Scheduling Internet of Things requests to minimize latency in hybrid Fog–Cloud computing. Futur. Gener. Comput. Syst. **111**, 539–551 (2020). https://doi.org/10.1016/j.future.2019.09.039
14. Proceedings of the first edition of the MCC workshop on Mobile cloud computing - MCC'12 (2012). https://doi.org/10.1145/2342509
15. Bonomi, F., Milito, R., Zhu, J., Addepalli, S.: Fog computing and its role in the internet of things. Proceedings of the first edition of the MCC workshop on Mobile cloud computing - MCC'12. (2012). https://doi.org/10.1145/2342509.2342513
16. Luan, T.H., Gao, L., Li, Z., Xiang, Y., Wei, G., Sun, L.: Fog computing: focusing on mobile users at the edge. arXiv (2015). https://arxiv.org/abs/1502.01815
17. Iorga, M., Feldman, L., Barton, R., Martin, M.J., Goren, N.S., Mahmoudi, C.: Fog computing conceptual model. https://www.nist.gov/publications/fog-computing-conceptual-model. Last Accessed 02 Feb 2022
18. Peter, N.: Fog computing and its real time applications. Int. J. Emerg. Technol. Adv. Eng. **5**(6), 266–269 (2015)
19. Whaiduzzaman, M., Naveed, A., Gani, A.: MobiCoRE: mobile device based cloudlet resource enhancement for optimal task response. IEEE Trans. Serv. Comput. **11**, 144–154 (2018). https://doi.org/10.1109/tsc.2016.2564407
20. Yi, S., Hao, Z., Qin, Z., Li, Q.: Fog computing: platform and applications. In: 2015 Third IEEE Workshop on Hot Topics in Web Systems and Technologies (HotWeb) (2015). https://doi.org/10.1109/hotweb.2015.22
21. Saurabh, Dhanaraj, R.K.: A review paper on fog computing paradigm to solve problems and challenges during integration of cloud with IoT. J. Phys. Conf. Ser. **2007**, 012017 (2021). https://doi.org/10.1088/1742-6596/2007/1/012017

Dynamic Resource Allocation in Fog Computing Environment

Gaurav Goel[1]([✉]) [iD] and Rajeev Tiwari[2] [iD]

[1] Department of Computer Science and Engineering, Chandigarh Engineering College,
Landran, Mohali, India
gaurav.goel9@gmail.com
[2] School of Computer Science, University of Petroleum and Energy Studies, Bidholi Dehradun
Uttarakhand, Dehradun, India
errajeev.tiwari@gmail.com

Abstract. Transforming IoT-devices applications in a cloud environment for processing may not be a good solution, especially for applications/approaches that are time-sensitive. A possible solution for the same is to use the Fog environment because the Fog devices are established near the IoT-devices. Nowadays, Data computation of applications is processed near the IoT devices instead of the cloud. Consideration regarding resource management for the IoT devices-Fog-Cloud structure is required and can be accomplished by task offloading, task scheduling, and application management. In this work, an evaluation was done in the Fog structure, and a talk was done on how dynamically allocated resources affect the execution time in comparison to the static resource allocation. After the result evaluation, dynamic resource allocation showed better execution time in comparison to static resource allocation. In this work, a comparison was the contrast between FCFS and Round Robin on parameter cost and makespan. After the result evaluation, the Round Robin algorithm showed better performance on FCFS.

Keywords: Resource scheduling · Fog · Cloud · Optimization

1 Introduction

IoT devices are playing a crucial role in every human's life. Today's every human task is somehow involved with the IoT (internet-of-things). Nowadays, IoT devices are involved in every area like healthcare, smart industries, shopping malls, smart Grid, many business applications, etc. [1–3] For controlling a large amount of data produced by sensors, smart devices, smartwatches, mobiles, and smart meters are processed with the cloud environment. A high level of intelligent work is being done with the integration of IoT devices and cloud services. Services of the cloud system are impacted due to the increasing of IoT (internet-of-things) devices. The issue of latency and response time is going to be faced by time-sensitive applications. CISCO introduced the extension of Cloud named Fog to overcome the problem of latency and response time [4, 5].

V. Sugumaran et al. (Eds.): AIR 2022, CCIS 1738, pp. 85–93, 2022.
https://doi.org/10.1007/978-3-031-23724-9_8

Fog is situated at a central layer between the IoT (internet-of-things) devices and the cloud which reduces the distance between the IoT (internet-of-things) devices and computation devices. Micro Computing clusters are used as a combination of devices and the Fog nodes for effective communication and computation as shown in Fig. 1. Fog node can be any device with computation power like it can be a router, switch, smartphone, and base station. Fog reduces the issue of latency and response time because computation is performed near to the IoT devices [6–8]. Due to the introduction of Fog nodes, computation power, security, and reliability is improved in the IoT-Fog-Cloud system. Fog Computing is used in tremendous applications like agriculture, healthcare, weather forecasting, smart traffic management, e-waste handling, and smart industries due to their benefits [9, 10].

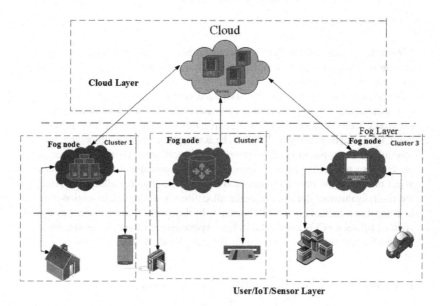

Fig. 1. Architecture of fog system

In the architecture of the Cloud environment, the Cloud system is situated a long aside from the IoT (internet-of-things) devices. That's why the issue of, memory,latency, and network bandwidth appear in the earlier system. With the introduction of the Fog system, a problem of latency, memory, and network consumption is overcome to some extent in the IoT-Fog-Cloud system. Because devices are located at the edge of the network [14, 15]. Various types of techniques/optimization algorithms are provided by many researchers for dealing with resource management. Still, there is the requirement of raising the concern about the issue of resource-management in the Fog environment [16].

2 Motivation

In IoT-Fog-Cloud environments, many heterogeneous devices shared their data in the system for computation. It is difficult to process synchronization and resource management in the system due to the large level of heterogeneity. Many researchers have provided different optimization techniques for resource-management in the IoT-Fog-Cloud system. Poor resource management leads to high costs and adverse effects on the performance of the system. QoS in the Fog network can be achieved through task scheduling, resource allocation, application management, and task offloading. So, to achieve efficient resource scheduling in IoT-Fog-Cloud environments, task scheduling, resource allocation, application management, and task offloading could play a vital role.

2.1 The Goal of This Work

In this work, Simulation setup has been evaluated for resource allocation in the Fog environment, and how cost & makespan is varied with efficient optimization algorithms. The principal contribution of this work is as follows:

1. How Dynamic allocation of tasks affects the execution time in comparison to static.
2. Evaluation of FCFS and Round Robin algorithms on parameter cost and makespan.

2.2 Organization of Work

This work is further classified into various segments. Segment 3 is Related work about resource provisioning, resource management, and scheduling techniques. Section 4 is about the methodology of work. The Result and simulation setup segment are discussed in Sect. 5. Section 6 is a discussion of the conclusion.

3 Related Work

This section enlightens the existing works on resource-management strategies in the Fog-Cloud structure.

Bushra Jamil et al. [11] describe the case study on the healthcare system. Researchers describe how efficient resource scheduling algorithms lessen the reaction time and consumption of energy in the Fog devices structure. Researchers proposed a scheduler for minimizing network usage and delay in the Fog environment. Through the algorithms SJF and FCFS, researchers represented the energy consumption in the Fog environment.

Samson Busuyi et al. [12] discuss the problem of placement of VM and task allocation in a Cloud/Fog system. The authors also provide a solution for both problems by providing an efficient technique. A provided technique is successfully improving Quality-of-Services in a Cloud/Fog system through allocation of cost.

Seema A. Alsaidy et al. [13] describe the concept regarding the problems of task scheduling in cloud systems. Researchers compared the proposed LJFP-PSO and MCT-PSO with earlier PSO techniques on parameters of total energy consumption, makespan, total execution time, and degree of imbalance. Proposed algorithms are providing good performance over basic PSO.

Ali Shakarami et al. [17] provide a review on resource provisioning in Fog/Edge Computing. Researchers discussed the review based on five categories- meta heuristic-based, framework-based, machine learning-based, model-based, and game-theoretic-based.

Mohamed Abu Sharkh et al. [18] proposed a dynamic algorithm for the solution of resource allocation. The authors used the SIMist simulator in the proposed work and efficiently utilized the performance of the network on parameters cost, cloud capacity, and network capacity.

Jianwen Xu et al. [19] discusses the concept of disaster response in emergency services. Researchers provided a concept, of how it's difficult to manage a network in the situation of an earthquake. Because all network services suffered during these disasters. Under this situation, the deployment of Fog nodes can work for networks and help humans to provide networks during disasters.

Mohammad S. Aslanpour et al. [20] describe a taxonomy of metrics for the real society for evaluating the performance of the Fog, edge, and cloud. Researchers also provided various types of applications for the computing environment. The authors also described some open issues for the computing environment.

Huaqing Zhang et al. [23] used the concept of the Stackelberg sub-game, student project matching game, and moral hazard (contact theory) for the resource-management in the Fog structure. The above techniques, fortunately, reduce the communication gaps between the ADSSs (Authorized data service subscribers), DSO (data service operators), and FNs (Fog nodes). An optimal utilization is seen in the result by using these above-mentioned techniques.

Siqi Luo et al. [24] proposed a novel technique MCC (Micro Computing cluster) of resource sharing for communication and computation among mobile nodes in the Fog environment. By using coalitional game theory, efficient resource cooperation is noticed among mobile devices during the execution of the task. MCC mechanism successfully reduces service delay and saves energy in the fog system.

Yan sun et al. [25] used a crowdfunding algorithm for the management of assets in the Fog environment. With the help of this technique, authors have successfully encouraged resources owner to participate in the resource pool for finishing tasks. An incentive mechanism is helpful in task completion and reducing SLA violations as shown through simulation results.

4 Methodology

Resource allocation in the Fog environment is working towards methodology as shown in Fig. 2. The methodology is working on the three-tier architecture of the IoT system, Fog system, and cloud System. IoT devices sense miscellaneous type of data from equipped sensors [21, 22] so a number of tasks need to computed systematically in the IoT devices-Fog-cloud system. Dynamically allocation of tasks required to be done to Fog nodes and Cloud servers [26, 27].

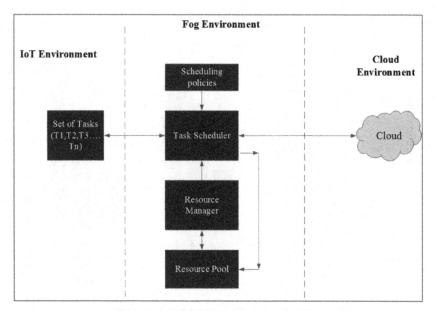

Fig. 2. Methodology of working scenario

In this approach, FCFS and Round-Robin algorithm will work as scheduling policies as shown in Fig. 2 towards the middle layer Fog environment. The task scheduler and resource manager will play a vital role in efficiently managing resources available in the resource pool [13, 28]. Computation of tasks can be done through the Fog environment and cloud environment. Results of computed tasks are to be reverted to IoT devices for further necessary action [29, 30].

5   Results and Discussion

This segment outlines the outcomes for the dynamic allocation of Fog devices to the applications and a Comparison of FCFS and RR (Round-Robin) algorithms on parameter makespan, and cost.

The YAFS toolkit [31] was run on a processor Core i3 (Frequency 2.40 Ghz) with a 64-bit Windows-7 system and a RAM capacity of 8 GB. For YAFS (yet another Fog Simulator) tool whole simulation was done for instructions 500,1000 and 2000 of each 10 bytes in size. For dynamic allocation simulation, the simulated time was set to 2000,5000, and 10000 in the YAFS tool.

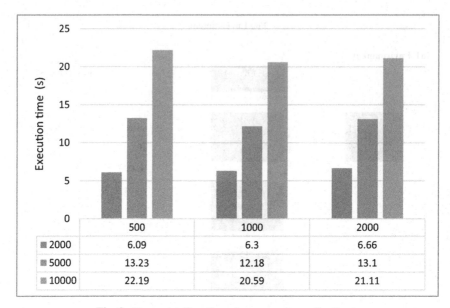

Fig. 3. Dynamic allocation of resources to applications.

Resources are allocated dynamically to applications/tasks [31] in the YAFS tool. The simulation was done for 401 nodes and 2242 edges. As shown in Fig. 3, Execution time is shown for instructions 500,1000 and 2000. Plotting represents a linear type of execution time during the dynamic allocation of resources to applications, and a very stable type of variation has been noticed. In [33], the authors contrast comparisons in SJF, FCFS, MPSO, and the proposed technique TRAM. A large type of variation has been noticed during resource allocation. In this contrast, the dynamic allocation of resources seems better as experienced in the YAFS tool.

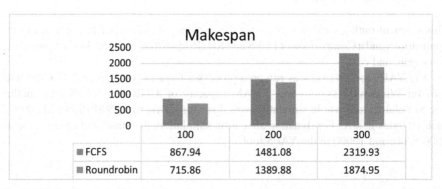

Fig. 4. FCFS and round robin algorithm for the various number of tasks on parameter makespan.

The Fog workflow Sim toolkit [32] was run on a processor Core i3 (Frequency 2.40Ghz) with a 64-bit Windows-7 system and a RAM capacity of 8 GB. For the Fog

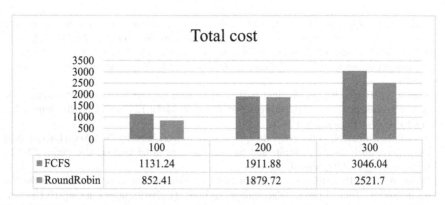

Fig. 5. FCFS and round robin algorithm for the various number of tasks on parameter total cost.

workflow Sim tool whole simulation was done by considering MIPS 1600 for 2 cloud servers, MIPS 1300 for 5 Fog devices, and MIPS 1000 for 10 IoT devices. A comparison was done on FCFS and Round Robin for parameters Total cost and makespan in the toolkit for 100,200, and 300 tasks as shown in Fig. 4 and Fig. 5.

Makespan represents the total time of execution for the completion of tasks in a system. Minimization of makespan represents an efficient utilization of resources for an application. Figure 4 represents the comparison between FCFS and Round Robin optimization algorithm. As per the simulation results shown, the Round Robin algorithm has shown an efficient performance over FCFS.

Total cost describes the cost of using bandwidth, memory, and CPU utilization for the execution of tasks. If the number of resources utilized is high per fog node then it will raise the cost of the system. Figure 5 represents the comparison between FCFS and Round Robin optimization algorithm. As per the simulation results, the Round Robin algorithm has shown an efficient performance over FCFS because the value of cost for a different number of tasks is low for Round Robin.

6 Conclusion

Task scheduling, resource allocation, and application management are considered a component of resource scheduling. By efficiently managing the resource, QoS parameters like cost, makespan, and latency can be enhanced. This work aimed to highlight the dynamic allocation of resources that helps to improve or strengthen the execution time of the system in comparison to static allocation. It also aimed to provide the Round Robin scenario is execute finer in Fog structure than FCFS on QoS framework makespan, and cost.

References

1. Peralta, G., Garrido, P., Bilbao, J., Agüero, R., Crespo, P.M.: Fog to cloud and network coded based architecture: minimizing data download time for smart mobility. Simul. Model. Pract. Theory. 101, 102034 (2020). https://doi.org/10.1016/j.simpat.2019.102034

2. Mahmud, R., Ramamohanarao, K., Buyya, R.: Application management in fog computing environments. ACM Comput. Surv. **53**, 1–43 (2021). https://doi.org/10.1145/3403955
3. Vambe, W.T., Chang, C., Sibanda, K.: A Review of quality of service in fog computing for the internet of things. Int. J. Fog Comput. **3**, 22–40 (2020). https://doi.org/10.4018/ijfc.202 0010102
4. Kumar, S., Tiwari, R.: An efficient content placement scheme based on normalized node degree in content centric networking. Clust. Comput. **24**(2), 1277–1291 (2020). https://doi. org/10.1007/s10586-020-03185-0
5. Tiwari, R., Kumar, N.: A novel hybrid approach for web caching. In: 2012 Sixth International Conference on Innovative Mobile and Internet Services in Ubiquitous Computing (2012). https://doi.org/10.1109/imis.2012.39
6. Wang, A., Yan, P., Batiha, K.: A comprehensive study on managing strategies in the fog environments. Trans. Emerg. Telecommun. Technol. **31** (2019). https://doi.org/10.1002/ett. 3833
7. Hussein, M.K., Mousa, M.H.: Efficient task offloading for iot-based applications in fog computing using ant colony optimization. IEEE Access **8**, 37191–37201 (2020). https://doi.org/ 10.1109/access.2020.2975741
8. Kaur, K., Garg, S., Kaddoum, G., Gagnon, F., Jayakody, D.N.K.: EnLoB: energy and load balancing-driven container placement strategy for data centers. In: 2019 IEEE Globecom Workshops (GC Wkshps) (2019). https://doi.org/10.1109/gcwkshps45667.2019.9024592
9. Haghi Kashani, M., Rahmani, A.M., Jafari Navimipour, N.: Quality of service-aware approaches in fog computing. Int. J. Commun Syst **33**, e4340 (2020). https://doi.org/10. 1002/dac.4340
10. Rehman, S., Javaid, N., Rasheed, S., Hassan, K., Zafar, F., Naeem, M.: Min-min scheduling algorithm for efficient resource distribution using cloud and fog in smart buildings. In: Barolli, L., Leu, F.-Y., Enokido, T., Chen, H.-C. (eds.) BWCCA 2018. LNDECT, vol. 25, pp. 15–27. Springer, Cham (2019). https://doi.org/10.1007/978-3-030-02613-4_2
11. Jamil, B., Shojafar, M., Ahmed, I., Ullah, A., Munir, K., Ijaz, H.: A job scheduling algorithm for delay and performance optimization in fog computing. Concurr. Comput. Pract. Exp. **32** (2019). https://doi.org/10.1002/cpe.5581
12. Akintoye, S., Bagula, A.: Improving quality-of-service in cloud/fog computing through efficient resource allocation. Sensors. **19**, 1267 (2019). https://doi.org/10.3390/s19061267
13. Alsaidy, S.A., Abbood, A.D., Sahib, M.A.: Heuristic initialization of PSO task scheduling algorithm in cloud computing. J. King Saud Univ. – Comput. Inf. Sci. **34**, 2370–2382 (2022). https://doi.org/10.1016/j.jksuci.2020.11.002
14. Tiwari, R., et al.: Automated parking system-cloud and IoT based technique. Int. J. Eng. Adv. Technol. (IJEAT) **8**(4C), 116–123 (2019)
15. Khan, E., Garg, D., Tiwari, R., Upadhyay, S.: Automated toll tax collection system using cloud database. In: 2018 3rd International Conference On Internet of Things: Smart Innovation and Usages (IoT-SIU) (2018). https://doi.org/10.1109/iot-siu.2018.8519929
16. Tiwari, R., Kumar, N.: Dynamic web caching: for robustness, low latency and disconnection handling. In: 2012 2nd IEEE International Conference on Parallel, Distributed and Grid Computing (2012). https://doi.org/10.1109/pdgc.2012.6449945
17. Shakarami, A., Shakarami, H., Ghobaei-Arani, M., Nikougoftar, E., Faraji-Mehmandar, M.: Resource provisioning in edge/fog computing: a comprehensive and systematic review. J. Syst. Architect. **122**, 102362 (2022). https://doi.org/10.1016/j.sysarc.2021.102362
18. Sharkh, M.A., Kalil, M.: A dynamic algorithm for fog computing data processing decision optimization. In: 2020 IEEE International Conference on Communications Workshops (ICC Workshops) (2020). https://doi.org/10.1109/iccworkshops49005.2020.9145296
19. Xu, J., Ota, K., Dong, M.: Fast deployment of emergency fog service for disaster response. IEEE Network **34**, 100–105 (2020). https://doi.org/10.1109/mnet.001.1900671

20. Aslanpour, M.S., Gill, S.S., Toosi, A.N.: Performance evaluation metrics for cloud, fog and edge computing: a review, taxonomy, benchmarks and standards for future research. Internet of Things. **12**, 100273 (2020). https://doi.org/10.1016/j.iot.2020.100273

21. Tiwari, R., Kumar, K., Khan, G., Patel, R.B., Singh, B.P.: Load balancing in distributed web caching: a novel clustering approach. AIP Conf. Proc. (2010). https://doi.org/10.1063/1.352 6228

22. Rajeev, T., Gulista, K.: Load balancing in distributed web caching. In: Meghanathan, N., Boumerdassi, S., Chaki, N., Nagamalai, D. (eds.) CNSA 2010. CCIS, vol. 89, pp. 47–54. Springer, Heidelberg (2010). https://doi.org/10.1007/978-3-642-14478-3_5

23. Zhang, H., Zhang, Y., Gu, Y., Niyato, D., Han, Z.: A hierarchical game framework for resource management in fog computing. IEEE Commun. Mag. **55**, 52–57 (2017). https://doi.org/10.1109/mcom.2017.1600896

24. Luo, S., Chen, X., Zhou, Z., Chen, X., Wu, W.: Incentive-aware micro computing cluster formation for cooperative fog computing. IEEE Trans. Wireless Commun. **19**, 2643–2657 (2020). https://doi.org/10.1109/twc.2020.2967371

25. Sun, Y., Zhang, N.: A resource-sharing model based on a repeated game in fog computing. Saudi J. Biol. Sci. **24**, 687–694 (2017). https://doi.org/10.1016/j.sjbs.2017.01.043

26. Kumar, S., Tiwari, R.: Dynamic popularity window and distance-based efficient caching for fast content delivery applications in CCN. Eng. Sci. Technol. an Int. J. **24**, 829–837 (2021). https://doi.org/10.1016/j.jestch.2020.12.018

27. Chithaluru, P., Tiwari, R., Kumar, K.: Performance analysis of energy efficient opportunistic routing protocols in wireless sensor network. Int. J. Sens. Wirel. Commun. Control **11**, 24–41 (2021). https://doi.org/10.2174/2210327909666191026092311

28. Chithaluru, P., Tiwari, R., Kumar, K.: ARIOR: adaptive ranking based improved opportunistic routing in wireless sensor networks. Wireless Pers. Commun. **116**(1), 153–176 (2020). https://doi.org/10.1007/s11277-020-07709-0

29. Tiwari, R., Sille, R., Salankar, N., Singh, P.: Utilization and energy consumption optimization for cloud computing environment. In: Khanna, K., Estrela, V.V., Rodrigues, J.J.P.C. (eds.) Cyber Security and Digital Forensics. LNDECT, vol. 73, pp. 609–619. Springer, Singapore (2022). https://doi.org/10.1007/978-981-16-3961-6_50

30. Tiwari, R., Mittal, M., Garg, S., Kumar, S.: Energy-aware resource scheduling in FoG environment for iot-based applications. In: Tiwari, R., Mittal, M., Goyal, L.M. (eds.) Energy Conservation Solutions for Fog-Edge Computing Paradigms. LNDECT, vol. 74, pp. 1–19. Springer, Singapore (2022). https://doi.org/10.1007/978-981-16-3448-2_1

31. Lera, I., Guerrero, C., Juiz, C.: YAFS: A Simulator for IoT scenarios in fog computing. IEEE Access **7**, 91745–91758 (2019). https://doi.org/10.1109/access.2019.2927895

32. Liu, X., et al.: FogWorkflowSim: an automated simulation toolkit for workflow performance evaluation in fog computing. In: 2019 34th IEEE/ACM International Conference on Automated Software Engineering (ASE) (2019). https://doi.org/10.1109/ase.2019.00115

33. Wadhwa, H., Aron, R.: TRAM: technique for resource allocation and management in fog computing environment. J. Supercomput. **78**(1), 667–690 (2021). https://doi.org/10.1007/s11227-021-03885-3

Vehicle as Fog Server in Intelligent Transportation System

Deep Chandra Binwal[1]([✉]) [iD], Rajeev Tiwari[1] [iD], and Monit Kapoor[2] [iD]

[1] University of Petroleum and Energy Studies, Dehradun 248001, India
deepchandra_mits@yahoo.co.in
[2] CUIET, Chitkara University, Punjab 140401, India
monit.kapoor@chitkara.edu.in

Abstract. The world is moving towards an autonomous vehicle system very fast. The computing power required for vehicular applications is increasing day by day. Vehicular fog computing is a way forward for meeting the ever-increasing demand for computing resources. In this work, we are proposing a machine learning (ML) supported approach for solving the issue of scheduling latency-sensitive, real-time, safety-related applications to optimal resources in vehicular fog computing (VFC). The goal is to satisfy the quality of service (QoS) and minimize resource consumption. We set up a simulation with real-world data, using SUMO and iFogSim2 to prove that there is a possibility of a trade-off between the multiple objectives of QoS (i.e., latency), energy consumption, and network utilization in VFC. Analysis of results depicts the usefulness of the ML-based approach in optimizing the resources with a much wider input parameter set for refined results.

Keywords: Latency-sensitive · Dynamic workload · Real-time · Vehicular fog computing

1 Introduction

The important role of vehicular fog computing (VFC) in intelligent transportation system (ITS) is becoming evident in the past few years with researchers and academia bringing forth many new applications of VFC. Some of the prominent applications are smart parking reservation system [1, 2] crowd-sourcing of road and traffic conditions [3] smart real-time traffic management system [4] emergency message delivery system [5, 6]. Conventional cloud computing provides massive computing capability and is used in abundance for most compute-intensive tasks, but has an inherent limitation of providing higher latency because of large (to and from) transmission delays [7]. Many tasks in modern connected vehicles are latency-sensitive [8] e.g. autonomous driving, collision prevention system, turn speed computation, and smart/adaptive traffic light system. The concept of fog computing was proposed [9] to reduce the latency in computation as compared to the cloud by bringing the computational resources much closer to the end-user as compared to the cloud.

V. Sugumaran et al. (Eds.): AIR 2022, CCIS 1738, pp. 94–101, 2022.
https://doi.org/10.1007/978-3-031-23724-9_9

In ITS the static fog micro servers are installed at roadside units (RSU), base stations, routers, and switches. The static fog system is infrastructure-based (i.e., akin to cloud-based infrastructure), thus, has fixed capacity and involves installation and maintenance of micro fog servers by fog service providers. The idea of utilizing vehicles as infrastructure (i.e. computational and communication resources) was first proposed in [4]. One of the most important characteristics of a vehicular network is its dynamic nature because of vehicle mobility. Mobility results in dynamic workload generation in the vehicular fleet at any given place and time. Hence, the need for dynamic computational resources to meet dynamic workload requirements.

The limitation of the static fog nodes is that the dynamic computational resource requirement of the vehicular network may not be fulfilled at times, because of a sudden spurt in demand. On the other hand, if we deploy additional micro fog servers at static fog locations (considering maximum possible demand), it may result in the under-utilization of costly infrastructure because of less demand [4, 10]. Hence, installing and maintaining static fog infrastructure is costly. In VFC the requirement of installing computational infrastructure is escaped by utilizing surplus resources on the vehicle's onboard units (OBU), collaboratively, on-demand basis [11]. Hence there is no additional cost involved in utilizing vehicular fog nodes (VFN). The two most important characteristics of vehicular networks are dynamic workload (i.e. processing request) generation and dynamic resource availability [4, 12]. The problem of latency and energy optimization in dynamic VFC is being actively researched for the last couple of years [13–17].

The autonomous vehicle concept is coming to reality with the advancement of VFC research. Authors in [18] have highlighted the open research challenges associated with static and dynamic vehicular object detection in autonomous vehicles. With the number of smart, connected vehicles on the roads increasing every day, there are many related challenges to solve regarding the security of the predominantly radio networks in vehicular networks [19, 20]. As the cyber security threats on autonomous vehicle infrastructure are on the increase, the authors in [19] have explored an approach to detect the cyber-attacks in the autonomous fleet of heavy vehicles using big data analysis techniques.

The research in VFC is still at a nascent stage. Many real-time applications are being proposed by researchers in vehicular networks. An architecture for a smart parking system to increase the efficiency of parking lots in smart cities has been proposed in [21]. In the past couple of years, few researchers have proposed solutions related to VFC application offloading to cloud and(or) edge to reduce latency and energy consumption. Despite that, a lot needs to be achieved in terms of quality of service (QoS) enforcement and optimization of resource utilization in VFC. In this preliminary work, we are proposing the use of machine learning (ML) in application scheduling/offloading and optimizing the resources in VFC to achieve QoS compliance and optimize resource utilization.

2 System Model

A generic representation of vehicular fog computing architecture is presented in Fig. 1. It is a three-tier architecture consisting of a cloud computing (CC) layer at the top, that is responsible for mass computation but has its limitation in providing real-time services, particularly for latency-sensitive e.g. safety applications in ITS [22]. The CC layer is most suitable for mass storage, archive, and centralized decision-making activities. The middle layer is the static fog computing node (FCN) layer, typically installed at RSU, routers, base stations, and much closer to end-users. The fog layer is made of fixed, infrastructure-based micro-servers that can provide limited computational services but with low latency. This layer is suitable for latency-sensitive applications but has the limitation of computational capacity and, it is not cost-effective to install for huge computational capacity. The third layer is the VFC layer and is most promising for providing a massive chunk of computational resources to latency-sensitive ITS applications [20]. This layer is made up of collaborative vehicular nodes sharing their excess computational resources on-demand. Thus, this layer can adapt to the dynamic demand changes in vehicular networks. Most importantly, this layer does not involve any installation or maintenance cost in contrast to the other two layers in this architecture.

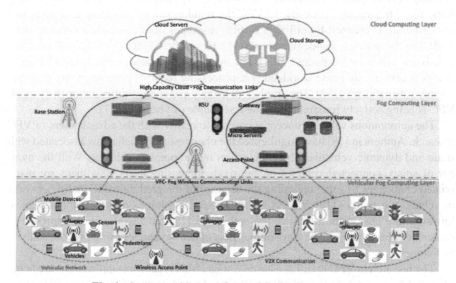

Fig. 1. System architecture for a vehicular fog computing

The network-level connectivity in VFC is by vehicle to vehicle (V2V) and vehicle to everything (V2X) modes using cellular, DSRC, or, any other mode of wireless communication. For this discussion, we assume seamless connectivity among all nodes in VFC. Firstly, the latency in VFC applications is one of the important characteristics that must be minimized for the future generation of ITS applications. Secondly, as the connectivity between various nodes in VFC is by radio medium, the energy consumption of nodes in transmit/reception and also during processing need optimization. This is particularly relevant with the current trend towards all-electric vehicles on road, where saving battery power will be a key consideration. Thirdly, the network bandwidth consumption also becomes a cause of concern, specifically during peak traffic hours, where network resources will be under stress to meet QoS demand for applications. Hence, network bandwidth utilization needs to be minimized.

3 Application Characteristics in VFC

With the advancements in ITS and autonomous driving dream coming to a reality, real-time applications are becoming more important in VFC. Here, for the sake of keeping the discussion simple but without loss of generality, we will discuss the safety applications e.g., collision avoidance system, road turn radius indicator, and accident information dissemination system. Applications are divided into latency-tolerant and latency-sensitive. Latency-tolerant applications can be processed at cloud servers, without loss of utility. Whereas, every latency-sensitive application has a well-defined maximum latency associated with it. This means, that if the task is not completed within the defined maximum latency limits, then it loses its utility e.g., if the collision avoidance warning message is received after the maximum permissible latency for avoiding a collision is elapsed, it is bound to result in a collision. Hence, strict latency limits must be achieved for processing all latency-sensitive applications in VFC. The typical value of maximum latency limit is up to 100 ms for latency-sensitive applications in VFC. Table 1 represents a snapshot of a typical application feature in VFC.

Table 1. Features of application data from source

Source_Loc (Lat, Long)	Source_speed (km)	App_Id	App_type	Max_lat (ms)	Data_size (Byte)	Time_arrival
39.654,76.092	42	a-1	LS	40	300	221001
39.642,76.097	62	a-2	LS	40	300	221011
39.541,76.103	27	a-3	LT	–	–	231002
–	–	–	–	–	–	–
38.638,77.112	56	a-100	LS	40	300	631941

Legend: LS-Latency-sensitive, LT Latency-tolerant

4 Research Directions

A literature survey on the subject and the above discussion brings forth the problem of optimum utilization of vehicular fog layer resources so that the cost of installing and maintaining is minimum, latency requirements are satisfied and the energy consumption is optimized. As part of the research in this domain of latency-sensitive applications in VFC, it is proposed to develop techniques to efficiently segment the vehicular network into zones or areas. The goal of such techniques would be as follows. Firstly, to achieve minimum network bandwidth utilization as discussed in Sect. 2. Secondly, this will enable the global problem of vehicular fog optimization to be broken down into multiple smaller local problems. The local optimum solution for vehicular fog optimization problems will ultimately converge into an optimal solution globally. The final global solution will encompass (static) fog layer optimization as well. Thirdly, the application processing will be limited to the zone or area, thus achieving twin goals of minimum latency and energy consumption optimization, because of a smaller number of transmission/re-transmissions over the radio links.

5 Proposed Solution Strategy

As part of the proposed solution for the optimization process, we are proposing the use of machine learning (ML) techniques to continuously enhance the performance in a closed loop. The block diagram level explanation of the proposed system is depicted in Fig. 2. Here the input parameters are taken from Table 1 and the output parameters are the results of the optimization process (Table 2). The feedback process is based on ML-based algorithms to continuously refine the performance of the system. Optimal clustering and scheduling of applications are proposed to be implemented using suitable ML-based algorithms for optimum performance. This system should be able to monitor the performance in the form of Table 2 and take corrective action, whenever needed in terms of compliance to QoS parameters (i.e., latency), minimization of overall energy consumption, and network bandwidth consumption.

Table 2. Results of application after processing

App_id	Dest_type	N/W_BW used(kB)	Energy_consumed (pW)	Time_completion	Latency (ms)	QoS compliance
a-1	VFN1	234	2011	221037	36	yes
a-2	VFN2	304	1907	221062	51	no
a-3	CC	5023	7270	261165	–	–
–	–	–	–	–	–	–
a-100	SF	371	3213	631979	38	yes

Legend: CC-cloud computing, SF-static fog node, VFN-vehicular fog node

Fig. 2. Block diagram of the proposed solution

6 Simulation Setup

For proving the concept presented, we set up a simulation (without the inclusion of ML element) using random, real-world vehicular data (location: a section of street Madhya

Marg in Chandigarh, India) about smart vehicle applications. The input data was captured using the 'open street map' [23] by loading a 1.5 km length section of the map from the open street map and running SUMO. The FCD (floating car data) file generated by sumo is used for generating real-world vehicular data for simulation. The FCD file from SUMO was used as input for the simulation running on 'iFogSim2'. The simulation was run on the hardware using a laptop (Intel(R) Core-i5 10th Gen processor, 8GB RAM, Windows-10, 64 Bit). Because of the unavailability of the real-world data for the workload size, and maximum permissible latency parameters in Table 1 these values are chosen empirically. The simulation was run for 100 s in the iFogSim2 simulator. The input data and output results are depicted in Table 1 and Table 2 respectively. The processing nodes (i.e., VFN, SF) have different locations, speeds/directions, and hardware configurations. Figure 3 depicts the section of the map used for the experiments.

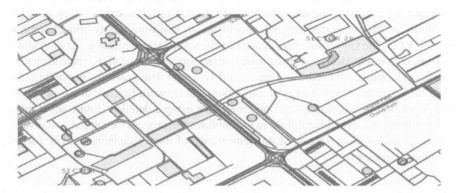

Fig. 3. Section of the road (Madhya Marg, Chandigarh, India) taken from OSM

7 Results and Discussion

Results of simulation on real-world data show that for the same type of application (i.e., max permissible latency of 40 ms) and same data size of 300 bytes, the end-to-end latency achieved for applications a-1, a-2, are different. This difference is because the application requests originated from a source that is at a different location, has a different speed and direction, and is also processed at nodes having different parameters and at different times. Network bandwidth and the energy consumption is highest for processing in the cloud followed by static fog and least for processing at vehicular fog nodes. This is of course related to a greater number of transmissions and receptions and higher idle & busy power consumption rates for SF and CC servers as compared to VFN. Based on the analysis of results for latency-sensitive applications, there is a possibility of a trade-off between end-to-end latency, energy consumption, and network bandwidth consumption. The trade-off can be achieved by dynamically scheduling/offloading applications to the most suitable VFN or SF for the application, based on the application and source characteristics. For many safety-critical applications in VFC, the latency value must be strictly satisfied. Whereas, energy consumption and, network utilization may not have an immediate bearing on the safety of vehicle/road users. Therefore, the strict latency limits must be satisfied. Whereas, overall energy consumption and network bandwidth consumption minimization are desirable characteristics.

8 Conclusion

Latency-sensitive request processing mandates strict QoS satisfaction, particularly for safety-critical applications in connected vehicles. The QoS for vehicular applications encompasses latency, reliability (i.e., packet delivery ratio), energy consumption, and network bandwidth consumption. The maximum permissible latency for the safety-critical applications must be satisfied, or else the application loses its utility. Whereas, for optimal network performance, the energy consumption and network bandwidth consumption are desired to be the least possible. In this research work, we propose the suitability of ML supported scheduling scheme for real-time, safety-critical applications in VFC. The QoS parameters depend on the source (i.e., request generating node) and destination (i.e., data processing node) parameters and application type and characteristics. The simulation results on real-world vehicular data prove the possibility of a trade-off between latency, energy consumption, and network bandwidth consumption. The simulation results suggest an opportunity for using a detailed feature set at input along with the ML-based algorithms in the optimization process for refined, and diverse parameter trade-offs at the output. Implementation of these techniques will be part of our future research work.

References

1. Zhang, Y., Wang, C.-Y., Wei, H.-Y.: Parking reservation auction for parked vehicle assistance in vehicular fog computing. IEEE Trans. Veh. Technol. **68**, 3126–3139 (2019). https://doi.org/10.1109/tvt.2019.2899887
2. Qasem, M.H., Abu-Srhan, A., Natoureah, H., Alzaghoul, E.: Fog computing framework for smart city design. Int. J. Interact. Mob. Technol. (iJIM) **14**(01), 109 (2020). https://doi.org/10.3991/ijim.v14i01.9762
3. Zhu, C., Pastor, G., Xiao, Y., Ylajaaski, A.: Vehicular fog computing for video crowdsourcing: applications, feasibility, and challenges. IEEE Commun. Mag. **56**, 58–63 (2018). https://doi.org/10.1109/mcom.2018.1800116
4. Wang, X., et al.: A city-wide real-time traffic management system: enabling crowdsensing in social internet of vehicles. IEEE Commun. Mag. **56**, 19–25 (2018). https://doi.org/10.1109/mcom.2018.1701065
5. Hou, X., Li, Y., Chen, M., Wu, D., Jin, D., Chen, S.: Vehicular fog computing: a viewpoint of vehicles as the infrastructures. IEEE Trans. Veh. Technol. **65**, 3860–3873 (2016). https://doi.org/10.1109/tvt.2016.2532863
6. Liu, B., et al.: A novel framework for message dissemination with consideration of destination prediction in VFC. Neural Comput. Appl. (2021). https://doi.org/10.1007/s00521-021-05754-9
7. Shrestha, R., Bajracharya, R., Nam, S.Y.: Challenges of future VANET and cloud-based approaches. Wirel. Commun. Mob. Comput. **2018**, 1–15 (2018). https://doi.org/10.1155/2018/5603518

8. Tang, C., Wei, X., Zhu, C., Wang, Y., Jia, W.: Mobile vehicles as fog nodes for latency optimization in smart cities. IEEE Trans. Veh. Technol. **69**, 9364–9375 (2020). https://doi.org/10.1109/tvt.2020.2970763

9. Bonomi, F., Milito, R., Zhu, J., Addepalli, S.: Fog computing and its role in the internet of things. In: Proceedings of the First Edition of the MCC Workshop on Mobile Cloud Computing - MCC '12 (2012). https://doi.org/10.1145/2342509.2342513

10. Hussain, M., Alam, M.S., Beg, M.M.S.: Vehicular fog computing-planning and design. Procedia Comput. Sci. **167**, 2570–2580 (2020). https://doi.org/10.1016/j.procs.2020.03.313

11. Xiao, X., Hou, X., Chen, X., Liu, C., Li, Y.: Quantitative analysis for capabilities of vehicular fog computing. Inf. Sci. **501**, 742–760 (2019). https://doi.org/10.1016/j.ins.2019.03.065

12. Zhou, Z., Liao, H., Wang, X., Mumtaz, S., Rodriguez, J.: When vehicular fog computing meets autonomous driving: computational resource management and task offloading. IEEE Network **34**, 70–76 (2020). https://doi.org/10.1109/mnet.001.1900527

13. Zadobrischi, E., Dimian, M.: Vehicular communications utility in road safety applications: a step toward self-aware intelligent traffic systems. Symmetry. **13**, 438 (2021). https://doi.org/10.3390/sym13030438

14. Alharbi, H.A., Elgorashi, T.E.H., Elmirghani, J.M.H.: Energy efficient virtual machines placement over cloud-fog network architecture. IEEE Access **8**, 94697–94718 (2020). https://doi.org/10.1109/access.2020.2995393

15. Mekki, T., Jmal, R., Chaari, L., Jabri, I., Rachedi, A.: Vehicular fog resource allocation scheme: a multi-objective optimization based approach. In: 2020 IEEE 17th Annual Consumer Communications & Networking Conference (CCNC) (2020). https://doi.org/10.1109/ccnc46108.2020.9045361

16. Mahmud, R., Ramamohanarao, K., Buyya, R.: Application management in fog computing environments. ACM Comput. Surv. **53**, 1–43 (2021). https://doi.org/10.1145/3403955

17. Zhang, K., Peng, M., Sun, Y.: Delay-Optimized resource allocation in fog-based vehicular networks. IEEE Internet Things J. **8**, 1347–1357 (2021). https://doi.org/10.1109/jiot.2020.3010861

18. Jain, S., Kumar, A., Kaushik, K., Krishnamurthi, R.: Autonomous driving systems and experiences: a comprehensive survey. In: Autonomous and Connected Heavy Vehicle Technology, pp. 65–80. Elsevier (2022). https://doi.org/10.1016/B978-0-323-90592-3.00003-3

19. Kaushik, K., Bathla, G., Naeem, U., Kumar, A.: Cybercriminal approaches in big data models for automated heavy vehicles. In: Autonomous and Connected Heavy Vehicle Technology, pp. 303–333. Elsevier (2022). https://doi.org/10.1016/B978-0-323-90592-3.00018-5

20. Binwal, D.C., Kapoor, M.: A survey on architecture, applications, and challenges in vehicular fog computing. Int. J. Sens. Wirel. Commun. Control **12**, 194–211 (2022). https://doi.org/10.2174/2210327912666220127130014

21. Tiwari, R., et al.: Automated parking system-cloud and IoT based technique. Int. J. Eng. Adv. Technol. **8**, 116–123 (2019)

22. Tiwari, R., Mittal, M., Garg, S., Kumar, S.: Energy-aware resource scheduling in FoG environment for iot-based applications. In: Tiwari, R., Mittal, M., Goyal, L.M. (eds.) Energy Conservation Solutions for Fog-Edge Computing Paradigms. LNDECT, vol. 74, pp. 1–19. Springer, Singapore (2022). https://doi.org/10.1007/978-981-16-3448-2_1

23. OpenStreetMap. https://www.openstreetmap.org/. Last Accessed 02 Jan 2022

Measuring the Impact of Blockchain-Based Supply Chain Traceability Systems on Consumer Trust

Tejaswi Khanna[1](✉) ⓘ, Parma Nand[1] ⓘ, and Vikram Bali[2] ⓘ

[1] School of Engineering and Technology, Sharda University, Greater Noida 201306, India
{tejaswi.khanna,parma.nand}@sharda.ac.in
[2] IMS Engineering College, Ghaziabad, India

Abstract. Traceability systems are characterised as systems which provide functionality for collecting real time data of a product when it travels in the supply chain. As its characteristic, traceability systems share data transparently between multiple participants of the supply chain. Blockchain has been a driver technology for such systems. This work presents analysis of primary data collected from consumers of food products in India. The purpose of the work is to ascertain the level of trust that consumers have in packaged food brands in India like Britannia, Bambino (but not limited to) which sell packaged food items like (but not limited to) Britannia breads, Nestle Maggi, MTR Rajma Chawal Ready to Eat. The analysis infers that traceability systems are essential for enhancing trust and brand credibility in the consumer perspective. Also, the onus of providing such a system falls upon the government and the manufacturer.

Keywords: Blockchain analysis · Traceability systems · Primary data collection · Correlation

1 Introduction

Supply Chain Traceability Systems (SCTS) assure integrity of the products which are moving through the supply chain and its participants [1]. For many businesses, in order to improve sustainability performance and curbing illegal activities, there is a requirement of implementing SCTS [2]. Traceability systems require involved parties of the supply chain to share data about shipping and other aspects about the product being processed by the vendor. Hence, there is a requirement of designing efficient and effective SCTS. Such is a challenge as observed by [3]. A case of vegetable SCTS has been presented by [4] modeled using UML. The products, processes and quality information have been modeled in the research.

Food traceability systems are complex, in the way they require an all-round view of processes, material and information flow, infrastructure and people involved in the supply chain [5]. In a 2019 interview of vegetable farmers of a Chinese province garnered attention towards the complexity of such supply chains. Furthermore, social influence and usefulness of SCTS impacted positively on the farmers' intention to participate in

V. Sugumaran et al. (Eds.): AIR 2022, CCIS 1738, pp. 102–112, 2022.
https://doi.org/10.1007/978-3-031-23724-9_10

the traceability efforts. A lack of databases and lagging technological research have been observed in Western Australia Halal food supply chain by [6]. Discussing about implementation of SCTS, data can be captured through RFID and collected using Wireless Sensor networks [7]. Such system has been observed to have comparable data accuracy in the case of Traceability systems for Recirculation Aquaculture [8].

A comprehensive review of agri-supply chain research and techniques of the past decade have been presented in [9]. Small data granularity, slowing digital transformation, managing traditional strategies to manage inventory, and lack of workable data and insight can be looked at as key challenges for the agri-supply chain. An implementation of SCTS based on blockchain for apple supply chain has been presented in [10]. In addition to food supply chain, implementation frameworks of SCTS in pharmaceutical have also been researched [11–13]. In regards to illegal drug trade, [14] have observed that blockchain based drug traceability is a viable solution for the problem which has claimed multiple lives on a global level. [15] have implemented drug traceability using Hyperledger Fabric and showcased that blockchain based SCTS provide higher levels of efficiency and data safety. Combining the power the IoT with blockchains, [16] proposed a solution for smart tracking and tracing of drugs over BIoT. A case study presented has shown the feasibility and efficiency of their platform.

The organization of the paper is in five sections. Section 1 introduces the problem and need for SCTS. Section 2 throws light on the literature review from the perspective of impact analysis. This section is further divided into sub categories of impact analysis identified by the authors. Section 3 presents with the methodology of conducting the analysis. Hypothesis of this work is also laid out in this section. Section 4 shares the findings of the work with Sect. 5 ending the work with concluding remarks and future directions.

2 Literature Survey: Impact Analysis

Impact analysis (IA) is a way to identify the probable implications of a change. The analysis looks at the tentative modification to understand what components would need to be updated, or deleted, as well as it determines the amount of effort that will be required to make the change happen [17]. Multiple participants have different needs and expectations out of system [18]. For a change to be manifested in the existing system or working scheme of things, an evaluation is required. Evaluation on many different assessment and estimation levels. These levels can be complexity assessments (how difficult the change will be for the programmer to implement), a level of effort estimate (how long the change should take), and maybe a risk assessment (how dangerous the change will be to implement). Now, the requirement of a well-functioning SCTS is a change that many businesses and industries need to inculcate in their daily workings and dealings. In data centric terms, the major change that SCTS are going to drive is all round data visibility. Whereas, speaking in perspective of operational efficiency, it can provide better knowledge and an improved source of the truth. This research proposes impact analysis of SCTS as:

- Impact on brand trust and credibility.
- Impact on environment sustainability.
- Impact on economic circularity.

2.1 Impact on Brand Trust and Credibility

Recently, spread of Covid-19 disease in the food supply chain have blown the consumer's trust and this has increased the need of traceability systems in the food supply chain. Frameworks have been defined that identify consumer's confidence in food and food supply chains which is established by assurances regarding individual food products and supply chain actors [19]. Traceability in supply chains impact the trust and brand credibility. Food safety concerns have been a point of convergence for many policy makers. In this direction, [20] have investigated the effect of traceability on consumers' trust in the retailers. Subsequently, this also influences the choice of the retailer in order to buy food products. The researchers have also emphasized on the upward impacts of blockchain based traceability systems on consumers.

In addition to food safety, consumer satisfaction is another driver for businesses to implement SCTS. Data identification, data recording, data integration and accessibility have been identified as the important principles for implementing effective supply chain traceability [21]. The consequences spotlight blockchain's position as a technological functionality for enhancing control in the waste product movement and product return control activities. After analysing 300 face-to-face questionnaire surveys from the Chinese consumers, [22] have concluded that outlook and perceived behavioural control qualities significantly and positively affect the usage intention in adopting blockchain based traceability system. They have utilized Partial Least Square for the analysis paradigm.

2.2 Impact on Environment Sustainability

Supply chains directly impact energy efficiency and environmental sustainability [23]. The production in today's industrious society is largely dependent on the businesses creating distributing products. In an assessment of how the Indian mango food supply chain impacts the environment, [24] suggested that reduction of supply uncertainty can be considered to be improvement in the operational inefficiency. In addition, optimization of transportation routes and resource consumption further enhance the system efficiency. The supply chain appears to be a mechanism that can be used to encourage sustainable agriculture production while also providing economic, environmental, and social benefits [25]. In order to reach sustainable goals in the hospitality industry, blockchain based traceability systems can be utilized to decrease food waste and reduction of rework or recall [26]. With blockchain technology, tracing of carbon footprint of green products of a company becomes easier [27].

2.3 Impact on Economic Circularity

Circular economy (CE) is another indirect consequence of sustainable businesses. It can also be viewed as a major driver of sustainability [28]. From an environmental viewpoint, convergence of CE principles within sustainable supply chain management provides distinct advantages. [29].

It has been observed that product traceability is a challenge in the domain of supply chain management. This can further be used by businesses to move in the direction of implementing circular economy. [30] UNCTAD's work on the circular economy at the national and global levels, in collaboration with other international organizations, puts this vital issue at the service of the international community. UNCTAD promotes the circular economy by supporting actions aimed at extracting value from waste streams, as well as debates centered on collaborative economy sectors, the investigation of innovative business models, and consumer awareness and behavioral adjustments [31].

The enterprise's performance depends on the trustworthiness of its product data quality. Because verifiable traceability in product data is unavailable or is weak, such confidence does not extend to the sharing and reuse of product data across the product life cycle [32]. Only 1.07% of the food goods in two Brazilian supermarkets had traceability information, according to an analysis of 4577 food products [33].

The importance of having a well-functioning STCS can become a positive aspect for providing circular economy. Circular economy, since it thrives on the all-round view of the product life cycle, ultimately depends on the efficiency of the traceability of the products in a supply chain.

3   Methodology

A survey of 107 consumers was conducted about the importance of supply chain data being shared transparently. All the respondents have been confirmed with knowing about blockchain technology and its implication on providing real time data traceability for supply chains. All questions of the questionnaire are in the form of Likert scale where the respondents can indicate strengths about the traceability systems and express how much they agree or disagree with a particular statement.

Following Variables have been identified:

Q1: Quality Rating.
Q2: Packaging Rating.
Q3: Pricing Rating.
Q4: transparent data sharing.
Q5: ingredient data access.
Q6: Brand Trust.

The work hypothesizes that there is a correlation between the pairs (Q6,Q1), (Q6,Q2), (Q6,Q3), (Q6,Q4) and (Q6,Q5). Hence, the null becomes that there is no correlation among these variable pairs. Spearman's correlation has been applied and the results have been recorded. The survey was first shared with a group of scientists and engineers and other peers in the academic field. Based on their feedbacks, a refinement process was applied to the questionnaire. This updated questionnaire was shared with 750 participants, from whom 107 participants responded and the responses were analysed based on statistical tools. Figure 1 represents the flowchart depicting the methodology and the procedure.

The purpose of the work is to ascertain the level of trust that consumers have in packaged food brands in India like Britannia, Bambino (but not limited to) which sell packaged food items like (but not limited to) Britannia breads, Nestle Maggi, MTR Rajma Chawal Ready to Eat.

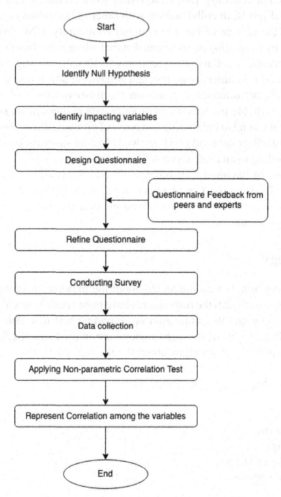

Fig. 1. Flowchart of methodology

4   Results and Discussions

Survey was conducted with consumers from Tier 1 and Tier 2 cities in India. The consumers have been able to provide a consensus that the responsibility of managing SCTS of food products falls majorly on the Packaging food brands, manufacturers and government. The variable Q6 are positively correlated with all the other variables since the p-value are all less than 0.05. The significance factor are all shared in their respective tables.

4.1   Correlation Between Q1 and Q6: Correlated Positively

Brand trust is positively correlated with Quality and significance factor is 0.207 as shown in Table 1.

Table 1. Spearman's correlation between brand trust and quality rating

Variable	Q1: Quality Rating		Q6: Brand trust in terms of genuineness
1. Q1: Quality Rating	Spearman's rho	—	
	p-value	—	
2. Q6: Brand trust in terms of genuineness	Spearman's rho	0.207	—
	p-value	0.016	—

Note. All tests one-tailed, for positive correlation.
$*p < .05, **p < .01, ***p < .001$, one-tailed

4.2   Correlation Between Q2 and Q6: Correlated Positively

Brand trust and Packaging rating have a positive correlation with significance factor of 0.152 as shown in Table 2.

Table 2. Spearman's correlation between brand trust and packaging

Variable	Q2: Packaging rating		Q6: Brand trust in terms of genuineness
1. Q2: Packaging rating	Spearman's rho	—	
	p-value	—	
	VS-MPR†		
2. Q6: Brand trust in terms of genuineness	Spearman's rho	0.152	—
	p-value	0.059	—
	VS-MPR†	2.192	—

4.3 Correlation Between Q3 and Q6

Brand Trust and Pricing do share significance correlation with significance factor as 0.209, as shown in Table 3.

Table 3. Spearman's correlation between brand trust and pricing

Variable	Q3: Pricing rating		Q6: Brand trust in terms of genuineness
1. Q3: Pricing rating	Spearman's rho	—	
	p-value	—	
	VS-MPR†		
2. Q6: Brand trust in terms of genuineness	Spearman's rho	0.209*	—
	p-value	0.031	—
	VS-MPR†	3.423	—

4.4 Correlation Between Q4 and Q6: Positive Correlation

Brand Trust is positively correlated to transparent data sharing with significance factor of 0.178 as shown in Table 4.

Table 4. Spearman's correlation between brand trust and importance of transparent data

Variable	Q4: Importance of transparent data sharing		Q6: Brand trust in terms of genuineness
1. Q4: Importance of transparent data sharing	Spearman's rho	—	
	p-value	—	
	VS-MPR†	—	
2. Q6: Brand trust in terms of genuineness	Spearman's rho	0.178*	—
	p-value	0.033	—
	VS-MPR†	3.256	—

4.5   Correlation Between Q5 and Q6: Positive Correlation

Brand trust is positively correlated to ingredient data sharing with significance factor of 0.176 as shown in Table 5.

Table 5. Spearman's correlation between brand trust and importance of ingredient data

Variable	Q5: Importance of ingredient data access		Q6: Brand trust in terms of genuineness
1. Q5: Importance of ingredient data access	Spearman's rho	—	
	p-value	—	
	VS-MPR†	—	
2. Q6: Brand trust in terms of genuineness	Spearman's rho	0.176*	—
	p-value	0.035	—
	VS-MPR†	3.133	—

Note. All tests one-tailed, for positive correlation
$*p < .05, **p < .01, ***p < .001$, one-tailed
†Vovk-Sellke Maximum p -Ratio: Based on the p -value, the maximum possible odds in favor of H_1 over H_0 equals $1/(-e \, p \log(p))$ for $p \leq 37$ [34]

One striking observation from the responses is the responsibility of providing an efficient SCTS. The bar chart in Fig. 2 represents the responses. The participants could select multiple options.

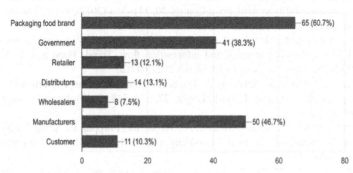

Fig. 2. Respondents opinion on responsible parties for managing transparent data sharing

5   Conclusion

The hypothesis that brand trust is correlated with pricing, packaging and quality of the product being sold stands true. In fact, it is positively correlated with all the variables. Almost 37.4% of respondents have moderate trust and similar percentage have high trust in the branded products. Almost 40% of respondents have faced some issues with their purchased food product. Since, 67.3% of respondents buy their food products from their retailers, there is high importance given to the transparent data sharing of the products as well as their ingredients.

In addition to Packaging food brand and manufacturers, government is also considered to be highly responsible for promoting and managing transparent data sharing of packaged food products. The work presents an interesting fact that the government's role in providing such a system is quite high. Hence, government needs to create regulations and apply certain mandates to provide better data sharing which is transparent and viewable by all the parties.

To achieve such a role blockchain's technological framework should be viewed as a solution. Stakeholders of the supply chains and the product brand must consider implementing SCTS via blockchains. Furthermore, SCTS efficacy can be evaluated by either running transactions using test data or via simulations. Real time implications can be evaluated if the SCTS is implemented using blockchain for a significant time duration.

References

1. Khan, S., Haleem, A., Khan, M., Abidi, M., Al-Ahmari, A.: Implementing traceability systems in specific supply chain management (SCM) through critical success factors (CSFs). Sustainability **10**, 204 (2018). https://doi.org/10.3390/su10010204
2. Hastig, G.M., Sodhi, M.S.: Blockchain for supply chain traceability: business requirements and critical success factors. Prod. Oper. Manag. **29**, 935–954 (2020). https://doi.org/10.1111/poms.13147
3. Dai, H., Ge, L., Zhou, W.: A design method for supply chain traceability systems with aligned interests. Int. J. Prod. Econ. **170**, 14–24 (2015). https://doi.org/10.1016/j.ijpe.2015.08.010
4. Hu, J., Zhang, X., Moga, L.M., Neculita, M.: Modeling and implementation of the vegetable supply chain traceability system. Food Control **30**, 341–353 (2013). https://doi.org/10.1016/j.foodcont.2012.06.037
5. Islam, S., Cullen, J.M., Manning, L.: Visualising food traceability systems: a novel system architecture for mapping material and information flow. Trends Food Sci. Technol. **112**, 708–719 (2021). https://doi.org/10.1016/j.tifs.2021.04.020
6. Poniman, D., Purchase, S., Sneddon, J.: Traceability systems in the Western Australia halal food supply chain. Asia Pac. J. Mark. Logist. **27**, 324–348 (2015). https://doi.org/10.1108/apjml-05-2014-0082
7. Parreño-Marchante, A., Alvarez-Melcon, A., Trebar, M., Filippin, P.: Advanced traceability system in aquaculture supply chain. J. Food Eng. **122**, 99–109 (2014). https://doi.org/10.1016/j.jfoodeng.2013.09.007
8. Qi, L., Zhang, J., Xu, M., Fu, Z., Chen, W., Zhang, X.: Developing WSN-based traceability system for recirculation aquaculture. Math. Comput. Model. **53**, 2162–2172 (2011). https://doi.org/10.1016/j.mcm.2010.08.023

9. Khandelwal, C., Singhal, M., Gaurav, G., Dangayach, G.S., Meena, M.L.: Agriculture supply chain management: a review (2010–2020). Mater. Today Proc. **47**, 3144–3153 (2021). https://doi.org/10.1016/j.matpr.2021.06.193

10. Nand, P., Khanna, T., Bali, V.: FruitBlock: a layered approach to implement blockchain based traceability system for agri supply chain. Int. J. Bus. Inf. Syst. **1**, 1 (2020). https://doi.org/10.1504/ijbis.2020.10035479

11. Bali, V., Khanna, T., Soni, P., Gupta, S., Chauhan, S., Gupta, S.: Combating drug counterfeiting by tracing ownership transfer using blockchain technology. Int. J. E-Health Med. Commun. **13**, 1–21 (2022). https://doi.org/10.4018/ijehmc.309429

12. Kumar, R., Tripathi, R.: Traceability of counterfeit medicine supply chain through Blockchain. In: 11th International Conference on Communication Systems & Networks (COMSNETS) (2019). https://doi.org/10.1109/comsnets.2019.8711418

13. Bali, V., Soni, P., Khanna, T., Gupta, S., Chauhan, S., Gupta, S.: Blockchain application design and algorithms for traceability in pharmaceutical supply chain. Int. J. Healthcare Inf. Syst. Informatics **16**, 1–18 (2021). https://doi.org/10.4018/ijhisi.289460

14. Molina, J.C., Delgado, D.T., Tarazona, G.: Using blockchain for traceability in the drug supply chain. In: Uden, L., Ting, I.-H., Corchado, J.M. (eds.) KMO 2019. CCIS, vol. 1027, pp. 536–548. Springer, Cham (2019). https://doi.org/10.1007/978-3-030-21451-7_46

15. Uddin, M.: Blockchain Medledger: hyperledger fabric enabled drug traceability system for counterfeit drugs in pharmaceutical industry. Int. J. Pharm. **597**, 120235 (2021). https://doi.org/10.1016/j.ijpharm.2021.120235

16. Liu, X., Barenji, A.V., Li, Z., Montreuil, B., Huang, G.Q.: Blockchain-based smart tracking and tracing platform for drug supply chain. Comput. Ind. Eng. **161**, 107669 (2021). https://doi.org/10.1016/j.cie.2021.107669

17. Arnold, R.S., Bohner, S.A.: Impact analysis-towards a framework for comparison. In: Conference on Software Maintenance (1993). https://doi.org/10.1109/icsm.1993.366933

18. Olander, S.: Stakeholder impact analysis in construction project management. Constr. Manag. Econ. **25**, 277–287 (2007). https://doi.org/10.1080/01446190600879125

19. Patidar, A., Sharma, M., Agrawal, R.: Prioritizing drivers to creating traceability in the food supply chain. Proc. CIRP **98**, 690–695 (2021). https://doi.org/10.1016/j.procir.2021.01.176

20. Garaus, M., Treiblmaier, H.: The influence of blockchain-based food traceability on retailer choice: The mediating role of trust. Food Control **129**, 108082 (2021). https://doi.org/10.1016/j.foodcont.2021.108082

21. Islam, S., Cullen, J.M.: Food traceability: a generic theoretical framework. Food Control **123**, 107848 (2021). https://doi.org/10.1016/j.foodcont.2020.107848

22. Lin, X., Chang, S.-C., Chou, T.-H., Chen, S.-C., Ruangkanjanases, A.: Consumers' intention to adopt blockchain food traceability technology towards organic food products. Int. J. Environ. Res. Public Health **18**, 912 (2021). https://doi.org/10.3390/ijerph18030912

23. Centobelli, P., Cerchione, R., Esposito, E.: Environmental sustainability and energy-efficient supply chain management: a review of research trends and proposed guidelines. Energies **11**, 275 (2018). https://doi.org/10.3390/en11020275

24. Krishnan, R., Agarwal, R., Bajada, C., Arshinder, K.: Redesigning a food supply chain for environmental sustainability – an analysis of resource use and recovery. J. Clean. Prod. **242**, 118374 (2020). https://doi.org/10.1016/j.jclepro.2019.118374

25. De Fazio, M.: Agriculture and sustainability of the welfare: the role of the short supply chain. Agric. Agric. Sci. Procedia **8**, 461–466 (2016). https://doi.org/10.1016/j.aaspro.2016.02.044

26. Kopanaki, E., Stroumpoulis, A., Oikonomou, M.: The impact of blockchain technology on food waste management in the hospitality industry. Ent. Res. Innov. **7**, 428–437 (2021). https://doi.org/10.54820/cqrj6465

27. Saberi, S., Kouhizadeh, M., Sarkis, J., Shen, L.: Blockchain technology and its relationships to sustainable supply chain management. Int. J. Prod. Res. **57**, 2117–2135 (2018). https://doi.org/10.1080/00207543.2018.1533261

28. Schöggl, J.-P., Stumpf, L., Baumgartner, R.J.: The narrative of sustainability and circular economy – a longitudinal review of two decades of research. Resour. Conserv. Recyc. **163**, 105073 (2020). https://doi.org/10.1016/j.resconrec.2020.105073

29. Genovese, A., Acquaye, A.A., Figueroa, A., Koh, S.C.L.: Sustainable supply chain management and the transition towards a circular economy: evidence and some applications. Omega **66**, 344–357 (2017). https://doi.org/10.1016/j.omega.2015.05.015

30. Bressanelli, G., Perona, M., Saccani, N.: Challenges in supply chain redesign for the circular economy: a literature review and a multiple case study. Int. J. Prod. Res. **57**, 7395–7422 (2018). https://doi.org/10.1080/00207543.2018.1542176

31. Pacini, H.: Circular economy: a new normal? In: United Nations Conference on Trade and Development, May 2018, vol. 61. Available: https://unctad.org/system/files/official-document/presspb2017d10_en.pdf

32. Hedberg, T.D., Krima, S., Camelio, J.A.: Method for enabling a root of trust in support of product data certification and traceability. J. Comput. Inf. Sci. Eng. **19**, (2019). https://doi.org/10.1115/1.4042839

33. Matzembacher, D.E., Stangherlin, I.d.C., Slongo, L.A., Cataldi, R.: An integration of traceability elements and their impact in consumer's trust. Food Control **92**, 420–429 (2018). https://doi.org/10.1016/j.foodcont.2018.05.014

34. Sellke, T., Bayarri, M.J., Berger, J.O.: Calibration of p values for testing precise null hypotheses. Am. Stat. **55**, 62–71 (2001). https://doi.org/10.1198/000313001300339950

Comparison of Routing Protocols with Performance Parameters in MANET Using NS3

Jaykumar Bhosale[1]($^{(\boxtimes)}$) (iD), Sheetal Zalte[1], and Bharat Jadhav[2]

[1] Shivaji University, Kolhapur, India
bhosalejaykumar45@gmail.com
[2] Yashavantrao Chavan Institute of Science, Satara, Maharashtra, India

Abstract. A provisional network known as (MANET) Mobile Ad-hoc Network (MANET) that can be set up voluntarily in the event of a disaster to communicate between participants. MANETs are used in various potential applications like communication, search and rescue operations in battlefield, in home and industrial networks, in entertainment, and in sensor networks. Numerous routing protocols of different types are advised for use with mobile ad-hoc networks to get optimal routing performance. Dark side of this technology is that it poses a variety of challenges, including variable topology, resource constraints, and unreliable connectivity. In this paper, significant evaluation analysis has been carried out with four different routing protocols like Ad hoc On Demand Distance Vector Routing protocol (AODV) Dynamic Source Routing protocol (DSR.), Destination Sequenced Distance Vector (DSDV), and Link State Routing Protocol (OLSR). In this study, performance parameter throughput is included and NS3 simulator is used to simulate these routing protocols.

Keywords: MANET · Data transmission · Routing · Throughput · NS3 simulator

1 Introduction

In this particular type of ad-hoc network, the nodes are portable, like mobile phones, laptops, digital devices are used as participants to form infrastructure spontaneously as shown in Fig. 1 [1]. Co-operation of participants is the key of successful communication. So, MANET offers the advantage of rapid infrastructure-free deployment and no centralized management. Main applications of MANETs are in disaster areas, military, war areas, instant business meetings and so on. [2] People and automobiles will appreciate the convenience of the controller. These can be used to work on the internet in regions where there isn't already one. When it comes to communication infrastructure, or when it comes to the use of such, Wireless expansion is required for infrastructure. By enlarging Multi-hop is supported by a wide range of mobile nodes in ad hoc networks.

They can enhance the range of Wi-Fi by using routing networks. The range is determined by the concentration of wireless signals. All MANET nodes act as senders as well as receivers.

The different features of MANET are

V. Sugumaran et al. (Eds.): AIR 2022, CCIS 1738, pp. 113–119, 2022.
https://doi.org/10.1007/978-3-031-23724-9_11

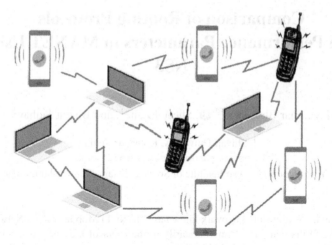

Fig. 1. Infrastructure of MANET

- Infrastructure-less-as there is no centralized authority
- wireless link-frequent breakage occurs
- Frequently disconnected network topologies
- Resource constrained-due to small size, it has limited energy and storage power

The focal goal of the paper is to estimate the performance of proactive and reactive protocols by measuring performance parameter throughput.

There are five sections in this paper; first section presented the introduction followed by a description of MANET and various routing protocols in Literature Review Section. The section three elaborates routing process in MANET. Fourth section describes the simulation followed by a conclusion in the preceding section.

2 Literature Review

In normal conditions, AODV outperforms DSR significantly, while in a limited context, DSR outperforms AODV [8]. The author examined three routing protocols: DSDV, DSR, and AODV, taking into account factors like Path disclosure, network Overhead, Regular Broadcast, Node Overhead, and so on. Author concluded that DSR/AODV performs better than proactive protocol like DSDV [9].

The study [10] compares several routing protocol types, such as proactive, reactive, and hybrid routing protocol. Author concludes that hybrid protocols are better in scalability than other types of protocol. It also reduced bottlenecks and single point of failure problems. In paper [11] the author concluded that for moderate sized network, AODV performs low than DSR protocol.

Reactive routing protocols are employed to reduce control traffic overhead and increase scalability [8].

In [3], using performance measures such as control overhead, Packet Delivery Ratio, latency, and throughput, the effectiveness of reactive and proactive routing systems is examined by the author. Author concluded that in case of average PDR, DSR protocol is best and OLSR also performs well in case of mobility conditions.

2.1 Routing Protocols in MANET

The core categories of the protocol for the MANET are On-demand and Table driven.

Routes are identified only when they are truly needed with reactive or on-demand routing. So, if node wants to interact with the another node, the response protocols will look up the route on demand and provide a path for packet transmission and reception. A sequence of network-wide request messages is often used for route finding. In table driven routing, every node maintains the path between two nodes indefinitely. As a result, constructing and sustaining routes is accomplished by a combo of periodic routing updates initiated by a distance vector or link status method event [3].

2.2 AODV (Ad Hoc on Demand Distance Vector Routing)

The DSR and DSDV protocols are combined in this routing protocol. Whenever, a node wishes to transmit packets towards its intended recipient, to keep it under control. RREQs are broadcast over the network, and the source node using the ring search approach is being expanded. The forward path establishes itself in intermediary nodes with a lifetime association in its route table RREP is a protocol for recording and replaying events. When a source node moves, a route error (RERR) is communicated to the impacted nodes. A source node could resume the routing procedure after receiving a (RERR). Information about the area is retrieved from a Hello packet broadcast over the network [4].

2.3 DSR (Dynamic Source Routing Protocol)

DSR is supposed to enable on-demand routing, but it does not keep account of frequent topology changes. The process of discovering and maintaining routes results in a rise in bandwidth consumption. These events take place when observed routes become inactive or when the network topology changes. By using effective caching techniques at each node, this cost may be reduced in DSR at the expense of memory and CPU resources. The source route header, which is present in every package, is the last place where bandwidth costs are incurred. DSR requires a lot more routing information because it depends on source routing. Before actual packet transmission, one route must be discovered in the DSR. In interactive applications, this initial search time might degrade performance. Furthermore, the path's quality is unknown until the call is made. Only during path construction can it be identified. All intermediary nodes in a session must keep an eye on the performance of this route.

This increased costs due to latency and additional expenses. DSR has significant scalability issues due to source routing. To reply to routing queries, nodes employ routing caching. As a result, the hosting server experiences uncontrolled feedback and repeated updates. Furthermore, the first requests are unstoppable and spread all the required messages everywhere in the network. Therefore, as the network grows, performance may degrade after a certain period of time [5].

2.4 DSDV (Destination Sequenced Distance Vector)

A well-known proactive or table-driven routing technique for MANET is DSDV [5]. The DSDV routing method's basis is the amount of hops required to reach the target node. The DSDV protocol makes use of routing updates, which is stored in each node, to transmit data packets between entire networks. The DSDV protocol has three primary characteristics: it eliminates high routing cost, solves the "count to infinite" problem, and prevents loops. Each mobile node stores a routing table that holds all the routes to the targets as well as some additional information [5].

2.5 OLSR (Link State Routing Protocol)

OLSR is proactive routing technique that communicates by using multipoint relaying [6]. Optimization techniques in O.L.S.R. can be made in two ways: first, by reducing the volume of control packets and second, by reducing the total of associations used to promote link state messages. As you may know, each node keeps the network's topology knowledge up to date by replacing link state communication with the other nodes on a regular basis. Neighbor sensing, capable flooding, and computing an ideal route using a variety of shortest-path algorithms are the three main strategies that make up the OLSR routing class. Neighbor sensing is the assessment of changes in the node's immediate vicinity. Using this topological knowledge, each node determines the optimum route to every known target and records it in a routing table. The most constructive path is then calculated using the shortest path algorithm. When data broadcasting begins, routes to all destinations are immediately available and remain so for a set length of time until the information is finished [7].

3 Routing in MANET

In a computer network, routing is the process of determining data transmission paths. This method is used to switch topology and connectivity information. Routing method actually computes the pathways and the distance between nodes. Mobile Ad-hoc Networks are multi-hop wireless networks that self-organize and configure themselves. The network's state changes on a regular basis. This is primarily due to the fact that the nodes' mobility. All nodes in these networks leverage multi-hop forwarding by working together over a shared random access wireless channel. The nodes of the network perform both hosting and server responsibilities.

Routers transport data to and from other network nodes. Due to lack of foundation in MANET, a routing mechanism is usually required in wireless networks since a destination node may be out of range of a source node releasing packets, making it difficult to transport the packets between the source and the destination in an efficient manner. In a typical wireless network, a ground station may communicate with every mobile node inside a cell without requiring broadcast routing.

Each node in an ad-hoc network has to be able to interact with the others [9]. In addition to the limitations of dynamic topology, this introduces other issues including unexpected connection changes. Routing is challenging because mobility necessitates frequent changes to the network design and requires a strong and adaptable route-finding and maintenance technique [12, 13].

4   Simulation

In this section, four different routing protocols are simulated specifically AODV, DSR, DSDV, and OLSR in a particular network including mobile nodes. Random waypoint model is used for mobility in the 300 m × 1500 m topology boundary. Node mobility scenarios are created for 25, 50, 75, 100 and 125 Nodes for simulation time of 200 s. Each node begins at the top and traveling from a random starting point to a random destination at a random pace.

As indicated in Table 1, several simulation parameters were employed using the NS3 simulator.

Table 1. Simulation parameters

NS3 parameters	Values
Connection type	UDP
No. of nodes	25/50/75/100/125
The transmit power	7.5 d Bm
Traffic flow	CBR
Node speed	20 m/s
Routing protocols	AODV, DSR, DSDV,OLSR
Pause time	0 s
Mobility model	Random waypoint

The performance metric aids in the identification of networks that are severely impacted by routing algorithms in order to reach the desired level of service (QoS). The following performance metric is taken into account in this study.

The percentage of all data packets arriving at the recipient from the source over the course of a certain period is known as throughput. Throughput is measured in bytes or bits per second (byte/sec or bit/sec).

Table 2. Throughput in percentage for different number of nodes

No of Nodes	OLSR	AODV	DSDV	DSR
25	4.096	6.656	4.096	6.144
50	1.536	7.68	2.048	4.096
75	6.144	13.312	4.096	6.144
100	4.096	7.168	2.048	6.144
125	5.12	3.072	4.096	2.048

Table 2 shows study shows that in a network with a reasonable number of nodes, AODV and DSR perform well.

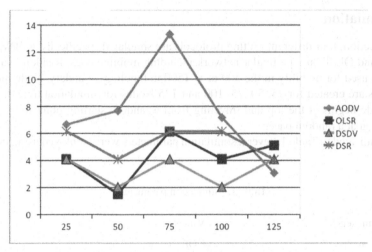

Fig. 2. Throughput vs. number of nodes

Figure 2 indicates that AODV and DSR significantly improved than DSDV and OLSR in simulation for moderate range of nodes. OLSR works well in dense network.

5   Conclusion

In this paper, the proposed work illustrates the performance of reactive routing protocols. The paper demonstrated the simulation of reactive and proactive protocols using NS3 simulation. In this work, we have created scenarios by varying the number of nodes with 0 s pause time. The study shows that throughput varies with different numbers of nodes. When it came to the evaluation metrics throughput, AODV and DSR outperformed other routing protocols such as DSDV and OLSR Even when the network had a moderate number of nodes, AODV and DSR outperformed DSDV. Overall, the study found that in a network with a moderate number of nodes, AODV and DSR perform better as compared to others. In the future, research will extend with different performance parameters.

References

1. Zalte, S., Ghorpade, V.R.: A survey on secure routing protocols for mobile ad-hoc network. Int. J. Comput. Appl. **8**, 13–19 (2018). https://doi.org/10.26808/rs.ca.i8v1.02
2. Kaur, G., Thakur, P.: Routing protocols in MANET: an overview. In: 2019 2nd International Conference on Intelligent Computing, Instrumentation and Control Technologies (ICICICT). (2019). https://doi.org/10.1109/icicict46008.2019.8993294
3. Mohapatra, S., Kanungo, P.: Performance analysis of AODV, DSR, OLSR and DSDV Routing Protocols using NS2 Simulator. Procedia Eng. **30**, 69–76 (2012). https://doi.org/10.1016/j.proeng.2012.01.835
4. Perkins, C.E., Royer, E.M.: Ad-hoc on-demand distance vector routing. In: Proceedings WMCSA'99. Second IEEE Workshop on Mobile Computing Systems and Applications (1999). https://doi.org/10.1109/mcsa.1999.749281

5. Jonson, D.: The dynamic source routing protocol for mobile ad hoc networks (DSR), Internet Draft, draft-ietf-manet-dsr-08. txt (2003)
6. Abusalah, L., Khokhar, A., Guizani, M.: A survey of secure mobile Ad Hoc routing protocols. IEEE Commun. Surv. Tutorials **10**, 78–93 (2008). https://doi.org/10.1109/surv.2008.080407
7. Kulla, E., Ikeda, M., Hiyama, M., Barolli, L.: Evaluation of a MANET Testbed in Indoor Stairs Environment Considering OLSR Protocol. In: 2011 International Conference on Complex, Intelligent, and Software Intensive Systems (2011). https://doi.org/10.1109/cisis.2011.32
8. Misra, R., Mandal, C.R.: Performance comparison of AODV/DSR on-demand routing protocols for ad hoc networks in constrained situation. In: 2005 IEEE International Conference on Personal Wireless Communications. ICPWC 2005 (2005). https://doi.org/10.1109/icpwc.2005.1431307
9. Shrivastava, P.K., Vishwamitra, L.K.: Comparative analysis of proactive and reactive routing protocols in VANET environment. Measur.: Sens. **16**, 100051 (2021). https://doi.org/10.1016/j.measen.2021.100051
10. Mishra, A., Singh, S., Tripathi, A.K.: Comparison of MANET routing protocols. Int. J. Comput. Sci. Mob. Comput **8**, 67–74 (2019)
11. Gupta, A.K., Sadawarti, H., Verma, A.K.: Review of various routing protocols for MANETs. Int. J. Inform. Electron. Eng. **1**(3), 251 (2011)
12. Jadhav, S.S., Kulkarni, A.V., Menon, R.: Mobile Ad-Hoc Network (MANET) for disaster management. In: 2014 Eleventh International Conference on Wireless and Optical Communications Networks (WOCN) (2014). https://doi.org/10.1109/wocn.2014.6923074
13. Prasad, R., Shivashankar, P.: Enhanced energy efficient secure routing protocol for mobile ad-hoc network. Global Transitions Proc. **3**(2), 412–423 (2022). https://doi.org/10.1016/j.gltp.2021.10.001

Developments Towards Sustainable Healthcare Sector

Light Weighted Model Based on Convolutional Neural Network for Detection of COVID-19 Using Chest X-Ray Images

Jitendra Mehta$^{(\boxtimes)}$ [ID], Ramesh Pandey [ID], and Ravi Prakash Tewari [ID]

Department of Applied Mechanics, Motilal Nehru National Institute of Technology Allahabad, Prayagraj, UP, India
`jitendramehta4@gmail.com, {ramesh,rptewari}@mnnit.ac.in`

Abstract. Since the discovery of COVID-19, new variants have been emerging. The latest in this series is BA.2, which is the subvariant of omicron and is more transmissible than the previous ones. People infected with this virus must be diagnosed at the earliest to provide the needed clinical attention. Radiological images of the chest are crucial in diagnosing the severity of BA.2 infection RT-PCR (Reverse Transcription-Polymerase Chain Reaction) is one of the approved diagnostics for COVID-19. Moreover, it takes time to give the result as compared to imaging techniques like X-ray and CT scans. Deep learning methods offer a clearer understanding and assist in extracting important data from X-ray images. In the absence of clinical assistance, this research emphasises the benefits of employing deep learning to ascertain the infection's existence. We present a light-weighted convolutional neural network-based deep learning binary classification model in this paper. Dataset consists of 16808 publically available images. The accuracy of our model is 98.76% which is effective to diagnose such patients.

Keywords: COVID-19 · Deep learning · X-ray · CNN

1 Introduction

A novel coronavirus (COVID-19), developed from SARS-CoV-2, has caused a global epidemic in the previous two years [1]. COVID-19 is expected to affect 474,731,929 people, and cause 6,123,493 deaths by March 20, 2022 [2]. However, 410,621,633 patients have been recovered. The novel coronavirus causes fever, dry cough, myalgia, dyspnoea, and headache [3]. In order to identify COVID-19, the RT-PCR test is considered to be the state of the art method [4]. RT-PCR inspection also has a high rate of false negatives [5]. Regrettably, the only effective methods of combating this communicable disease are clinical immunizations and precision drug/therapy techniques. COVID-19 has been classified as one of the most dangerous diseases threatening human civilization.

Imaging procedures including CT scans and X-rays are utilized to identify COVID-19 [6–8]. Its versatility and three-dimensional lung imaging make it preferred over X-rays. [9, 10], however, X-ray is preferred as it is economical. Professionals like radiologists and physicians generally interpret medical images. Because, depending on the ailment,

© The Author(s), under exclusive license to Springer Nature Switzerland AG 2022
V. Sugumaran et al. (Eds.): AIR 2022, CCIS 1738, pp. 123–132, 2022.
https://doi.org/10.1007/978-3-031-23724-9_12

medical data varies greatly from one patient to the next and, diagnoses become a time-consuming job. Inexperienced clinicians also significantly rely on interpretation. The healthcare system's pandemic readiness has been tested. A neural network, for example, can be used to construct an automated, precise, and cost-effective medical image processing framework. A neural network can imitate the accuracies of a trained human brain while also interpreting large amounts of data. In this study, a lightweight CNN model is suggested that outperforms previously published CNN models in binary classification.

The paper is structured in sequence as: First section deals with the introduction of the paper, Background of the research done by different researchers in this area is discussed in Sect. 2. In next section, methodology of the research was explained. Section 4, includes results and discussion. Section 5 concluded our research study.

2 Background

Deep learning has steadily been employed in health-related industries as artificial intelligence has advanced, and its widespread application in different areas has demonstrated that Deep learning may help humans solve simple problems. This section summarizes the research on utilizing AI to detect chest illnesses. COVIDX-Net classifier having seven convolutional layers was suggested by Hemdan [11] as a deep learning method for diagnosing COVID-19 in X-ray images. Wang and Wong [12] deep model (COVID-Net) for COVID19 detection was 92.4% accurate. Narin identified COVID-19 with 98% accuracy using X-rays and ResNet50 [13].

In applications that leverage image-based data, artificial intelligence systems have consistently produced accurate and dependable results. Deep learning techniques have recently been used by researchers to examine and interpret chest X-ray scans in order to detect COVID-19. Summary of the studies employing deep learning to identify COVID-19, and their accuracy is shown in the Table 1.

3 Methodology

This investigation is conducted using a database of chest X-rays, [43, 44]. This study includes 16808 radiographs of COVID-19 affirmative and healthy patients, sample of which is shown in Fig. 1. This database is currently one of the most popular publically available X-ray databases. The resolution of each image is kept at 432×288.

This study's main purpose is to achieve adequate categorization results from publicly available data and to achieve that goal we develop a CNN-based deep learning model that can detect COVID-19 positivity. The proposed model framework is shown in Fig. 2.

The summary of the model is shown in Fig. 3. The following layers make up the proposed CNN architecture:

– **Convolution layer:** A Convolutional Neural Network's most essential component is the convolution layer, which uses convolution instead of matrix multiplication. Its parameters are made up of kernels, which are learnable filters. The convolutional layer converts the appearance of features identified in local regions of the input image into a feature map. Non-linear layers are introduced in deep learning by means of an

Table 1. Studies employing deep learning to identify COVID-19, and their accuracy.

Author (Year) [reference no.]	Classification	Technique employed	Pre-trained/self-made model used	Dataset (Chest X-Ray images)	Accuracy (%)
Hussain (2021) [14]	Binary and Multiclass	–	CoroDet	2100	Binary – 99.10 Multiclass – 94.20
Haritha (2020) [15]	Binary	Transfer learning	VGG	1824	99.49
Ouchicha (2020) [16]	Ternary	RNN	CVDNet	2905	97.20
Ucar & Korkmaz (2020) [17]	Binary	Data augmentation	SqueezeNet	5949	98.30
Jain (2020) [18]	Multiclass	DNN	–	1832	97.77
Mahmud (2020) [19]	Multiclass	Transfer learning	CovXNet	5856	90.20
Panwar (2020) [20]	Multiclass	–	VGG-16	337	88.10
R. Mohammadi (2020) [21]	Binary	Transfer learning	VGG-16, VGG-19, MobileNet, and InceptionResNetV2	348	MobileNet – 99.10 InceptionResNetV2 – 96.80 VGG-16 – 93.60 VGG-19 – 90.80
Channa (2020) [22]	Binary	–	–	3606	91.67
Irmak (2020) [23]	Binary	–	–	–	99.20
Shibly (2020) [24]	Binary	–	RCNN	283	97.36
Rodrigues (2020) [25]	Binary	–	AlexNet, VGG-11, SqueezeNet, and DenseNet-121	407	
Narin (2020) [13]	Binary	Transfer learning	ResNet50	100	98
Karlita(2020) [26]	Binary	–	MobileNetV2	656	81
Sharma (2020) [27]	Multiclass	Transfer learning	–	352	93.80
Zhang (2020) [28]	Binary	–	COVID19XrayNet	1078	91.08
Khan (2020) [29]	Multiclass	–	DCNN	284	89.60

(continued)

Table 1. (*continued*)

Author (Year) [reference no.]	Classification	Technique employed	Pre-trained/self-made model used	Dataset (Chest X-Ray images)	Accuracy (%)
Apostolopoulos (2020) [30]	Multiclass	Deep transfer learning	MobileNetV2	3905	99.18
Sethy (2020) [31]	Binary	–	ResNet50 and SVM	–	95.40
Albahali & Albattah (2020) [32]	Multiclass	–	ResNet152	–	87
Toraman (2020) [33]	Multiclass	–	CapsNet	2331	89.48
Wang (2020) [12]	–	–	COVID-Net	13962	93.33
Mukherjee (2021) [34]	Binary	–	CNN	260	96.92
Rafi (2020) [35]	Binary	–	Base-CNN, ResNet-50, DenseNet-121 and EfficientNet-B4	5907	Base-CNN – 84.50 ResNet-50 – 97.31 DenseNet-121 – 96.50 EfficientNet-B4 – 98.86
Jin (2021) [36]	Binary	–	AlexNet	1743	98.64
Santoso & Purnomo (2020) [37]	Multiclass	–	Xception	618	90.09
Varela Santos & Melin (2021) [38]	Binary	–	–	848	97.69
Chattopadhyay (2021) [39]	Binary	FFNN	–	22	60
Rangarajan & Ramachandran (2021) [40]	Binary	Data augmentation and Generative Adversarial Network (GAN)	VGG16, MobileNetV2, Xception, NASNetMobile and InceptionResNetV2	–	VGG16 – 98.60 MobileNetV2 – 97.90 Xception – 98.10 NASNetMobile – 92.70 InceptionResNetV2 – 97.10
Hemdan (2020) [11]	Binary	–	COVIDX-Net	50	90

(*continued*)

Table 1. (*continued*)

Author (Year) [reference no.]	Classification	Technique employed	Pre-trained/self-made model used	Dataset (Chest X-Ray images)	Accuracy (%)
Farooq & Hafeez (2020) [41]	Multiclass	–	COVID-ResNet	2862	96.23
Cheng (2021) [42]	Multiclass	Data Augmentation	DPN-SE	1412	84

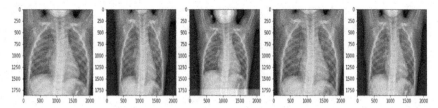

Fig. 1. Chest X-ray dataset images.

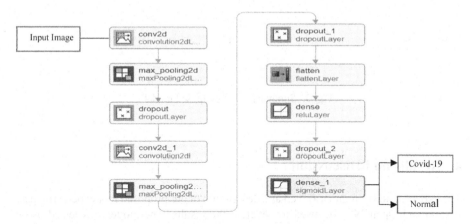

Fig. 2. Proposed model architecture.

activation function. The Rectified Linear Unit is the most prevalent instance of this function type.

- **Pooling layer:** A pooling or down sampling layer follows the convolution layer to lower the input's spatial extent and the network's parameter count. A pooling layer highlights a convolution layer by down sampling feature map output.
- **Dropout layer:** This layer is used to alleviate the issue of overfitting.

- **Flatten layer:** This layer is applied to flatten the entire network in our model. The flatten layer reduces the matrix of pooled feature maps to a single column. After that, it's sent to the neural network to be processed further.
- **Dense layer:** A dense layer, often known as a fully connected layer. Two dense layers are used after the flatten layer.

```
Layer (type)                 Output Shape            Param #
=================================================================
conv2d (Conv2D)              (None, 150, 150, 32)    2432

max_pooling2d (MaxPooling2D  (None, 75, 75, 32)      0
)

dropout (Dropout)            (None, 75, 75, 32)      0

conv2d_1 (Conv2D)            (None, 75, 75, 64)      51264

max_pooling2d_1 (MaxPooling  (None, 37, 37, 64)      0
2D)

dropout_1 (Dropout)          (None, 37, 37, 64)      0

flatten (Flatten)            (None, 87616)           0

dense (Dense)                (None, 256)             22429952

dropout_2 (Dropout)          (None, 256)             0

dense_1 (Dense)              (None, 1)               257

=================================================================
Total params: 22,483,905
Trainable params: 22,483,905
Non-trainable params: 0
```

Fig. 3. Summary of the proposed model

4   Results and Discussion

The experimental outcomes as well as a description of our proposed model performance. Python and OpenCV were used to generate the results. The model was tested using Scikit-learn and NumPy. The training vs validation accuracy is 98.76% and the training vs validation losses is around 0.0314 as shown in Fig. 4(a) and 4(b) respectively. Hussain [14] model has 99.10% accuracy but the details of the dataset is missing. Haritha [15] model has 99.49% accuracy but the dataset is small as only 1824 images are used. R. Mohammadi [23] model achieved an accuracy of 99.10% but only 348 images are used. Irmak [25] model achieved an accuracy of 99.20 but the details about the dataset is missing. Apostolopoulos [32] model has an accuracy of 99.18% but only 3905 images are used. Rafi [37] model has an accuracy of 98.86% but only 5907 images are used. On the other hand, the proposed model used 16808 images and achieved an accuracy of 98.76%.

Fig. 4. (a) Training vs validation accuracy, (b) training vs validation losses

5   Conclusion

A deep learning algorithm for detecting COVID-19 has been developed. This is crucial in a doctor's decision-making process. In addition, when time, and the patient's ailment are limited, the doctor may have to choose one modality above the others. Our proposed model may be helpful to radiologists and clinicians to choose most favorable approach so that they can save the life of the patients.

References

1. Wu, F., et al.: A new coronavirus associated with human respiratory disease in China. Nature **579**, 265–269 (2020). https://doi.org/10.1038/s41586-020-2008-3
2. COVID Live – Coronavirus Statistics – Worldometer. https://www.worldometers.info/corona virus/. Accessed 24 Mar 2022

3. Huang, C., et al.: Clinical features of patients infected with 2019 novel coronavirus in Wuhan, China. The Lancet **395**, 497–506 (2020). https://doi.org/10.1016/S0140-6736(20)30183-5

4. Ai, T., et al.: Correlation of chest CT and RT-PCR testing for coronavirus disease 2019 (COVID-19) in China: a report of 1014 cases. Radiology **296**, E32–E40 (2020). https://doi.org/10.1148/radiol.2020200642

5. Xie, X., Zhong, Z., Zhao, W., Zheng, C., Wang, F., Liu, J.: Chest CT for typical coronavirus disease 2019 (COVID-19) pneumonia: relationship to negative RT-PCR testing. Radiology **296**, E41–E45 (2020). https://doi.org/10.1148/radiol.2020200343

6. Kanne, J.P.: Chest CT findings in 2019 Novel Coronavirus (2019-nCoV) infections from Wuhan, China: key points for the radiologist. Radiology **295**, 16–17 (2020). https://doi.org/10.1148/radiol.2020200241

7. Rubin, G.D., et al.: The role of chest imaging in patient management during the COVID-19 pandemic: a multinational consensus statement from the Fleischner society. Radiology **296**(1), 172–180 (2020). https://doi.org/10.1148/radiol.2020201365

8. Dong, D., et al.: The role of imaging in the detection and management of COVID-19: a review. IEEE Rev. Biomed. Eng. **14**, 16–29 (2021). https://doi.org/10.1109/RBME.2020.2990959

9. Kim, H., Hong, H., Yoon, S.H.: Diagnostic performance of CT and reverse transcriptase polymerase chain reaction for coronavirus disease 2019: a meta-analysis. Radiology **296**, E145–E155 (2020). https://doi.org/10.1148/radiol.2020201343

10. Ye, Z., Zhang, Y., Wang, Y., Huang, Z., Song, B.: Chest CT manifestations of new coronavirus disease 2019 (COVID-19): a pictorial review. Eur. Radiol. **30**(8), 4381–4389 (2020). https://doi.org/10.1007/s00330-020-06801-0

11. Hemdan, E.E.-D., Shouman, M.A., Karar, M.E.: COVIDX-Net: A Framework of Deep Learning Classifiers to Diagnose COVID-19 in X-Ray Images. arXiv:2003.11055 [cs, eess] (2020)

12. Wang, L., Lin, Z.Q., Wong, A.: COVID-Net: a tailored deep convolutional neural network design for detection of COVID-19 cases from chest X-ray images. Sci Rep. **10**, 19549 (2020). https://doi.org/10.1038/s41598-020-76550-z

13. Narin, A.: Detection of Covid-19 patients with convolutional neural network based features on multi-class X-ray chest images. In: 2020 Medical Technologies Congress (TIPTEKNO), pp. 1–4 (2020). https://doi.org/10.1109/TIPTEKNO50054.2020.9299289

14. Hussain, E., Hasan, M., Rahman, M.A., Lee, I., Tamanna, T., Parvez, M.Z.: CoroDet: a deep learning based classification for COVID-19 detection using chest X-ray images. Chaos, Solitons Fractals **142**, 110495 (2021). https://doi.org/10.1016/j.chaos.2020.110495

15. Haritha, D., Swaroop, N., Mounika, M.: Prediction of COVID-19 cases using CNN with X-rays. In: 2020 5th International Conference on Computing, Communication and Security (ICCCS), pp. 1–6 (2020). https://doi.org/10.1109/ICCCS49678.2020.9276753

16. Ouchicha, C., Ammor, O., Meknassi, M.: CVDNet: a novel deep learning architecture for detection of coronavirus (Covid-19) from chest x-ray images. Chaos, Solitons Fractals **140**, 110245 (2020). https://doi.org/10.1016/j.chaos.2020.110245

17. Ucar, F., Korkmaz, D.: COVIDiagnosis-Net: deep Bayes-SqueezeNet based diagnosis of the coronavirus disease 2019 (COVID-19) from X-ray images. Med. Hypotheses **140**, 109761 (2020). https://doi.org/10.1016/j.mehy.2020.109761

18. Jain, G., Mittal, D., Thakur, D., Mittal, M.K.: A deep learning approach to detect Covid-19 coronavirus with X-Ray images. Biocybernetics Biomed. Eng. **40**, 1391–1405 (2020). https://doi.org/10.1016/j.bbe.2020.08.008

19. Mahmud, T., Rahman, M.A., Fattah, S.A.: CovXNet: a multi-dilation convolutional neural network for automatic COVID-19 and other pneumonia detection from chest X-ray images with transferable multi-receptive feature optimization. Comput. Biol. Med. **122**, 103869 (2020). https://doi.org/10.1016/j.compbiomed.2020.103869

20. Panwar, H., Gupta, P.K., Siddiqui, M.K., Morales-Menendez, R., Singh, V.: Application of deep learning for fast detection of COVID-19 in X-Rays using nCOVnet. Chaos, Solitons Fractals **138**, 109944 (2020). https://doi.org/10.1016/j.chaos.2020.109944

21. Mohammadi, R., Salehi, M., Ghaffari, H., Rohani, A.A., Reiazi, R.: Transfer learning-based automatic detection of Coronavirus disease 2019 (COVID-19) from chest X-ray images. J. Biomed. Phys. Eng. **10**, 559–568 (2020). https://doi.org/10.31661/jbpe.v0i0.2008-1153

22. Channa, A., Popescu, N., Malik, N. ur R.: Robust technique to detect COVID-19 using Chest X-ray Images. In: 2020 International Conference on e-Health and Bioengineering (EHB), pp. 1–6 (2020). https://doi.org/10.1109/EHB50910.2020.9280216

23. Irmak, E.: A novel deep convolutional neural network model for COVID-19 disease detection. In: 2020 Medical Technologies Congress (TIPTEKNO), pp. 1–4 (2020). https://doi.org/10.1109/TIPTEKNO50054.2020.9299286

24. Shibly, K.H., Dey, S.K., Islam, M.T.-U., Rahman, M.M.: COVID faster R-CNN: a novel framework to Diagnose Novel Coronavirus Disease (COVID-19) in X-Ray images. Inform. Med. Unlocked. **20**, 100405 (2020). https://doi.org/10.1016/j.imu.2020.100405

25. Rodrigues, L., Rodrigues, L., da Silva, D., Mari, J.F.: Evaluating Convolutional Neural Networks for COVID-19 classification in chest X-ray images. In: Anais do Workshop de Visão Computacional (WVC), pp. 52–57. SBC (2020). https://doi.org/10.5753/wvc.2020.13480

26. Karlita, T., Yuniarno, E.M., Purnama, I.K.E., Purnomo, M.H.: Detection of COVID-19 on chest X-Ray images using inverted residuals structure-based convolutional neural networks. In: 2020 3rd International Conference on Information and Communications Technology (ICOIACT), pp. 371–376 (2020). https://doi.org/10.1109/ICOIACT50329.2020.9332153

27. Sharma, A., Rani, S., Gupta, D.: Artificial intelligence-based classification of chest X-Ray images into COVID-19 and other infectious diseases. Int. J. Biomed. Imaging **2020**, e8889023 (2020). https://doi.org/10.1155/2020/8889023

28. Zhang, R., et al.: COVID19XrayNet: a two-step transfer learning model for the COVID-19 detecting problem based on a limited number of chest X-Ray images. Interdiscip. Sci.: Comput. Life Sci. **12**(4), 555–565 (2020). https://doi.org/10.1007/s12539-020-00393-5

29. Khan, A.I., Shah, J.L., Bhat, M.M.: CoroNet: A deep neural network for detection and diagnosis of COVID-19 from chest x-ray images. Comput. Methods Programs Biomed. **196**, 105581 (2020). https://doi.org/10.1016/j.cmpb.2020.105581

30. Apostolopoulos, I.D., Aznaouridis, S.I., Tzani, M.A.: Extracting possibly representative COVID-19 biomarkers from X-ray images with deep learning approach and image data related to pulmonary diseases. J. Med. Biol. Eng. **40**(3), 462–469 (2020). https://doi.org/10.1007/s40846-020-00529-4

31. Sethy, P.K., Behera, S.K., Ratha, P.K., Biswas, P.: Detection of coronavirus disease (COVID-19) based on deep features and support vector machine. Int. J. Math. Eng. Manag. Sci. **5**, 643–651 (2020). https://doi.org/10.33889/IJMEMS.2020.5.4.052

32. Albahli, S., Albattah, W.: Detection of coronavirus disease from X-ray images using deep learning and transfer learning algorithms. J. Xray Sci. Technol. **28**, 841–850 (2020). https://doi.org/10.3233/XST-200720

33. Toraman, S., Alakus, T.B., Turkoglu, I.: Convolutional capsnet: a novel artificial neural network approach to detect COVID-19 disease from X-ray images using capsule networks. Chaos Solitons Fractals **140**, 110122 (2020). https://doi.org/10.1016/j.chaos.2020.110122

34. Mukherjee, H., Ghosh, S., Dhar, A., Obaidullah, S.M., Santosh, K.C., Roy, K.: Shallow convolutional neural network for COVID-19 outbreak screening using chest X-rays. Cogn. Comput. (2021). https://doi.org/10.1007/s12559-020-09775-9

35. Rafi, T.H.: A holistic comparison between deep learning techniques to determine Covid-19 patients utilizing chest X-Ray images. Eng. Appl. Sci. Lett. **3**(4), 85–93 (2020). https://doi.org/10.30538/psrp-easl2020.0054

36. Jin, W., Dong, S., Dong, C., Ye, X.: Hybrid ensemble model for differential diagnosis between COVID-19 and common viral pneumonia by chest X-ray radiograph. Comput. Biol. Med. **131**, 104252 (2021). https://doi.org/10.1016/j.compbiomed.2021.104252

37. Santoso, F.Y., Purnomo, H.D.: A Modified deep convolutional network for COVID-19 detection based on chest X-ray images. In: 2020 3rd International Seminar on Research of Information Technology and Intelligent Systems (ISRITI), pp. 700–704 (2020). https://doi.org/10.1109/ISRITI51436.2020.9315479

38. Varela-Santos, S., Melin, P.: A new approach for classifying coronavirus COVID-19 based on its manifestation on chest X-rays using texture features and neural networks. Inf. Sci. (NY) **545**, 403–414 (2021). https://doi.org/10.1016/j.ins.2020.09.041

39. Chattopadhyay, S.: A novel approach to detect abnormal chest X-rays of COVID-19 patients using image processing and deep learning. Artif. Intell. Evol. **11**, 23–41 (2021). https://doi.org/10.37256/aie.222021977

40. Rangarajan, A.K., Ramachandran, H.K.: A preliminary analysis of AI based smartphone application for diagnosis of COVID-19 using chest X-ray images. Expert Syst. Appl. **183**, 115401 (2021). https://doi.org/10.1016/j.eswa.2021.115401

41. Farooq, M., Hafeez, A.: COVID-ResNet: A Deep Learning Framework for Screening of COVID19 from Radiographs. arXiv:2003.14395 [cs, eess]. (2020)

42. Cheng, B., Xiang, W., Xue, R., Yang, H., Zhu, L.: A self-attention mechanism neural network for detection and diagnosis of COVID-19 from chest X-Ray images. In Review (2021). https://doi.org/10.21203/rs.3.rs-577494/v1

43. COVID-19 Radiography Database: https://www.kaggle.com/tawsifurrahman/covid19-radiography-database. Accessed 24 Mar 2022

44. Cohen, J.P.: ieee8023/covid-chestxray-dataset (2022)

Forecasting COVID-19 Cases Using n-SARS-CoV-2 Variants

Soham Parekh📧, Rishabh Agarwal$^{(\boxtimes)}$📧, Tanaya Jadhav📧, and Amit Joshi📧

Department of Computer Engineering and IT, College of Engineering, Pune, Maharashtra, India
{parekhsk18.comp,agarwalrs18.comp,jadhavtn18.comp,
adj.comp}@coep.ac.in

Abstract. This work proposes a novel Deep Learning-based model to forecast the total number of confirmed COVID-19 cases in four of the worst-hit states of India. Along with statewide restrictions and public holidays, a novel parameter is introduced for training the proposed model, which considers the Alpha, Beta, Delta, and Omicron variants and the degree of their prevalence in each of the four states. Recurrent Neural Network-based Long-Short Term Memory is applied to the custom dataset, with the lowest Mean Absolute Percentage Error being 0.77% for the state of Maharashtra. SHapley Additive exPlanations values are used to examine the significance of the various parameters. The proposed model can be applied to other countries and can include newer variants of the novel coronavirus discovered in the future.

Keywords: COVID-19 · Machine learning · LSTM · Variants · Forecasting

1 Introduction

A novel coronavirus called n-SARS-CoV-2 was discovered in China towards the end of 2019. The disease caused by this virus, termed COVID-19 swept across various countries in the world, causing a pandemic. Since then, the world has witnessed three major waves of the coronavirus. Globally, the virus has had a major impact; it has gravely affected people physically and mentally. In January 2020, COVID-19 emerged in India, and since then, the countrywide number has increased tremendously. There were 145,380 cases in India by 26th May 2020 with about 4167 deaths due to COVID-19 [1]. The second wave impacted India severely with a peak of about 414,000 cases per day. Due to the sudden hike in the daily cases, there was a scarcity of proper health facilities for the patients. There were no beds available for patients and there was an acute shortage of oxygen, ventilators, medicines, etc. in hospitals. Accurate prediction of future cases can help in efficient management and planning of these essential resources.

To check the spread of COVID-19, certain restrictions like lockdowns and social distancing were enforced in various regions around the world. As the virus spread, it also underwent several mutations which resulted in new variants of the virus named Alpha, Beta, Delta, and Omicron. These variants were different from the original strain in terms of transmissibility and fatality. Previous research has identified the effects of

V. Sugumaran et al. (Eds.): AIR 2022, CCIS 1738, pp. 133–144, 2022.
https://doi.org/10.1007/978-3-031-23724-9_13

different factors on the spread of the virus [1–3]. It is also seen that the contribution of non-invasive features like age and oxygen levels to the disease and mortality rates is significant and can help in their prediction [4].

Artificial intelligence (AI) can be crucial in the prediction of daily cases and deaths. There are several advantages of using AI models to reduce the spread of coronavirus and fight against the pandemic [5]. Machine learning models can be used for the forecasting of confirmed cases and can replace existing statistical models [6]. Various models have been implemented for the forecasting of COVID-19 confirmed cases, recovered cases, and deaths and compared based on their accuracy and error rates [7–10]. Prediction of future cases can help hospitals prepare for the varying caseloads. Moreover, state-wise predictions can help in supplying resources to the severely hit states by those with a surplus of resources. This will also help governments plan future steps and precautions like restrictions, lockdowns, etc. to reduce the spread of the pandemic. In this work, we propose a machine learning model for the prediction of cases that focuses on multiple variables. It accounts for different variants and their transmissibility. This will help policymakers look at various scenarios by adjusting the multiple variables used. The proposed model is also analyzed to find the contribution of different factors used in forecasting the number of cases. These accurate predictions can be used to prepare for future waves of COVID-19 by predicting the cases and preparing the necessary resources. This work provides a comprehensive literature review of the topic in Sect. 2, followed by the proposed methodology in Sect. 3, results and discussion in Sect. 4, and conclusion and future scope in Sect. 5.

2 Literature Review

There has been a lot of research into the prediction of COVID-19 cases and their severity using deep learning. Zivkovic et al. implemented a novel hybrid method of machine learning and achieved an accuracy of 97.63% while considering only weekly new cases as the parameter [11]. Painuli et al. used the Autoregressive Integrated Moving Average (ARIMA) approach for forecasting the number of positive cases in the future. They considered the confirmed cases as a parameter and achieved an accuracy of 93.62% [12]. Arora et al. applied the Bi-directional Long Short Term Memory (LSTM), Deep LSTM, and Convolutional LSTM to Indian datasets for predicting new cases daily and weekly. They achieved error rates in the range of 3%–8% [13]. Kırbas, et al. did a comparative study between ARIMA, Nonlinear Autoregression Neural Network (NARNN), and LSTM in various European countries. LSTM was found to give the best results [14]. Shahid et al. used the LSTM, BiLSTM, and Gated recurrent network (GRU) models for the prediction of new, recovered, and death cases and achieved an accuracy of 99% for recovered cases in China [15]. Alzahrani et al. used statistical methods like AR, MA, and ARIMA. ARIMA showed the highest coefficient of determination(R2) value of 0.99 [16]. Ahmad et al. used Shallow Single-Layer Perceptron Neural Network (SSLPNN) and Gaussian Process Regression (GPR) for classifying and predicting the positive cases of COVID-19 in different regions of Asia. They achieved a root mean square error (RMSE) score of 0.91 and 0.95 [17]. Ribeiro et al. employed six different models for the prediction of confirmed cases and achieved errors in the range 0.87%–6.90% [18]. Tomar et al. used LSTM for predicting positive, recovered, and deceased cases 30 days ahead. They were able to achieve a minimum error percentage of 1.64% on total cases and 3.7% on daily cases [19]. Car et al. used multilayer perceptron (MLP) for the prediction of new, recovered, and deceased cases. They achieved R2 scores of 0.986, 0.994, and 0.979 for confirmed, deceased, and recovered respectively [20]. Shastri et al. used stacked LSTM, BiLSTM, and Convolutional LSTM for predicting COVID-19 cases. They achieved mean absolute percentage error (MAPE) ranging from 2–3.3% [21]. Sokhansanj et al. applied a deep neural network sequence model to predict disease severity and applied the model to the Omicron variant. They achieved an accuracy of 70% [22]. Aljameel et al. used logistic regression (LR), RF, and extreme gradient boosting (XGB) for the prediction of COVID-19 tests. RF was observed to perform the best with an accuracy of 0.95 [23]. Zagrouba et al. used Support Vector Machines (SVM) for predicting the outbreak of the pandemic. They achieved an accuracy of 98.88% while training and 96.79% during validation [24]. Chandra et al. used LSTM, Encoder-Decoder LSTM, and Bi-LSTM for forecasting the spread of COVID-19. The LSTM model outperformed the other two with the lowest RMSE of 13102 [25]. Bedi et al. applied a modified SEIRD model to four of the most affected states of India and predicted total confirmed cases. They used the LSTM model for trend predictions and compared the results with SEIRD [26]. Zain et al. proposed a hybrid CNN-LSTM model using a time-series dataset and found that the hybrid worked better than individual Convolutional Neural Network (CNN) or LSTM with a MAPE of 0.43 [27]. Zoabi et al. proposed a model built using decision trees. They could predict the outcome of COVID-19 tests with a confidence interval of 95% [28]. Ghafouri-Fard et al. used ANFIS, Recurrent neural network (RNN), LSTM, ARIMA, and MLP for the prediction of COVID-19 cases. They found the MAPE value to be the lowest for ARIMA and LSTM [29]. Oshinubi et al. compared the RMSE and relative-RMSE (rRMSE) for different models like extreme machine learning (ELM), MLP, LSTM, GRU, CNN, and deep neural network (DNN) for the prediction of daily positive cases [30]. From this survey, it can be observed that LSTM models are relatively more accurate in forecasting COVID-19 cases.

3 Proposed Methodology

3.1 Dataset

Several factors contribute to the change in the number of cases and need to be considered while predicting the cases ahead of time. Therefore, a few important parameters were considered and manually collated for a novel dataset [31]. The total confirmed cases in four of the worst affected states in India were taken into consideration for this work. The dataset is sourced from official government websites and consists of total confirmed cases from 10 March 2020 to 20 January 2022 for the states - Maharashtra (MH), Tamil Nadu (TN), Karnataka (KA), and Kerala (KL) [32]. The dataset is represented graphically in Fig. 1.

Holidays. India is culturally and religiously diverse and celebrates a variety of festivals where people usually step out of their homes and meet in large groups. These can involve mass gatherings and violate social distancing norms, causing a rise in positive cases. Thus, the regional holidays for the different states as well as the national holidays were recognized and used as a parameter in the dataset. These were sourced from the official Government of India website for public holidays [33]. Since the weekends are holidays for the general population, they are categorized differently. National and regional holidays were given a higher numeric value of 3 in the dataset; weekends were represented by the value 2 and weekdays were assigned the number 1.

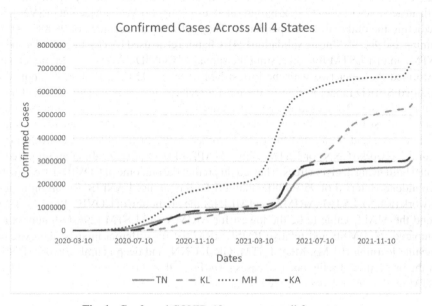

Fig. 1. Confirmed COVID-19 cases across all four states

Restrictions. Amid the rising COVID-19 cases, the State government and the Central government of India imposed several restrictions to combat the spread of the virus and prevent public gatherings. People were instructed to stay at home and only emergency and essential services were open. Various lockdown phases (increasing severity) and unlock phases (decreasing severity) were imposed in different states at different times which majorly influenced the COVID-19 curve.

Restrictions like night curfews and Section 144 (a section under the Indian Penal Code that bans gatherings of more than four people) helped control public gatherings and limit the movement of people. These restrictions were prioritized based on their severity and were categorized from 1 to 4. The restrictions under Level 4 include total lockdown whereas Level 3 includes strict orders like night curfew and Section 144. Level 2 includes restrictions with more relaxations like the reopening of public places, lenient travel guidelines, and upliftment of curfews. Level 1 was assigned to dates where there were no restrictions or lockdowns in place. The values were processed from publicly available government data from the respective State Government websites [34–38] and the Ministry of Home Affairs, Government of India website [39].

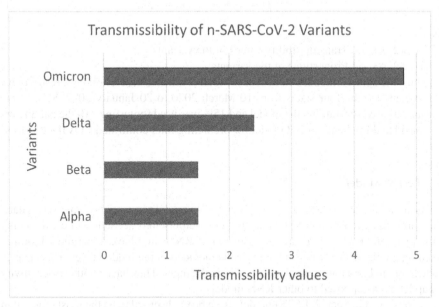

Fig. 2. Transmissibility values for all four variants

Variants. Viruses change or mutate over time which results in occurrences of different variants. In late 2020, the first variant of the n-SARS-CoV-2 coronavirus was identified. As the pandemic progressed, newer variants of the virus were identified. The variants often have different properties and may differ in terms of the speed with which they get transmitted and the severity of the associated disease. The variants may also react differently to vaccines, medicines, and public health measures taken by the people and are, therefore, an important aspect while considering the severity of the pandemic. In India, the Alpha and Beta variants were dominant during the first wave. Delta and Omicron were newer variants that were the dominant strains in the second and third waves respectively.

Genome sequencing provides an idea of the prevalence of each strain in a country. In India, this information is publicly available through the Indian SARS-CoV-2 Genomics Consortium (INSACOG) which is an amalgamation of several state-level laboratories recognized by the Indian Government [40]. For the four states chosen, this data is parsed into four different time series consisting of the daily ratios of these variants. These values represent the contribution of each variant to the spread of the virus. Every variant has a numeric value associated with its transmissibility [41]. Figure 2 shows these transmissibility values of the four n-SARS-CoV-2 variants taken into consideration.

The weighted sum used to calculate the final parameter is represented using the equation below:

$$\tau = \lambda_1\phi_1 + \lambda_2\phi_2 + \lambda_3\phi_3 + \lambda_4\phi_4 \tag{1}$$

where:

$\lambda_1, \lambda_2, \lambda_3, \lambda_4$ Transmissibility values of the variants

$\phi_1, \phi_2, \phi_3, \phi_4$ Proportions of the variants

Thus, the dataset includes values for the total confirmed cases, holidays, restrictions, and variants for the four states from 10 March 2020 to 20 January 2022. 85% of the dataset was used for training the model and 15% was used for testing. All the parameters are considered by the proposed model for predicting total confirmed COVID-19 cases.

3.2 LSTM Model

RNNs are a subclass of Deep Learning which help model sequential or time-series data. They are sequential in nature taking previous outputs into account while calculating subsequent outputs. LSTMs are an extension of RNNs and have a learning algorithm based on gradients. They have memory cells included in the hidden layer. This enables the network to learn long-term dependencies in the input. They have relative insensitivity to gap length as opposed to other RNN models.

As observed in Sect. 2, LSTM models have been observed to be the most efficient in processing and predicting time series data and therefore, have been chosen for predicting the total COVID-19 cases. In this work, the model was trained with two LSTM layers for 50 epochs with an early stopping limit of 10 epochs. Adam was used as the optimizer with an initial learning rate of 0.01.

3.3 SHapley Additive exPlanations (SHAP)

As the model developed in this work depends on several parameters to make predictions, it is essential to quantify the findings which unravel the hidden aspects of the model.

SHAP is a framework for interpreting predictions of a model and is considered the state-of-the-art tool for Machine Learning Explainability [42]. SHAP values help understand the results of complex models. They quantify the contributions of various features to the output of the model. In simpler terms, this helps understand the weightage of each parameter as concluded by the model. The proposed model was evaluated with the SHAP Python library to explain its decisions concerning the four factors taken into consideration.

4 Results and Discussion

There were four separate models trained using the proposed methodology. The predictions of these models are plotted against the actual values in Figs. 3, 4, 5 and 6. The Mean Absolute Percentage Error (MAPE) values of these models ranged from 0.0077 to 0.0424. The Root Mean Squared Error (RMSE) values ranged from 46889.44 to 91720.89. These values are represented in Table 1. The MAPE values show an improvement of 1.23 percentage points as opposed to the state-of-the-art LSTM models [21]. This improvement in the MAPE could be attributed to the additional consideration of the transmissibility values of n-SARS-Cov-2 variants.

This claim is further strengthened by the SHAP values displayed in Fig. 7. The variants factor played a major role in the model's predictions along with the previously confirmed cases. This indicates that the government can allocate more resources to genome testing as the prevalence of different variants can indicate the severity of the spread. The restrictions also majorly influenced the final forecast and continue to be a good measure to contain the transmission.

Small deviations can be observed in the performance of the model in the various states. For example, the model performed better in Maharashtra and Karnataka as opposed to Tamil Nadu and Kerala. This can be explained by the varying levels of COVID-19 testing in the chosen states. The differences in the test positivity rates strengthen this assertion. Due to the relatively recent onset of the pandemic, the dataset includes data for 681 days which reduces the accuracy compared to the model's potential as this dataset size is lesser than ideal.

However, it can be observed that all four models display a spike in January 2022, before the spike in the actual cases. This indicates the robustness of the models as this prediction can be crucial for policymakers and healthcare providers to plan as the pandemic progresses. The overestimation of the models for January 2022 can also be explained by the severe underreporting of cases due to reduced testing (indicated by the high test positivity rates) and the increased availability of at-home test kits.

Table 1. Error values for all four models

	MH	KL	TN	KA
MAPE	0.0077	0.0424	0.0183	0.0091
MAE	52661.83	222018.97	50833.49	28357.01
RMSE	91720.89	280839.06	56888.89	46889.44

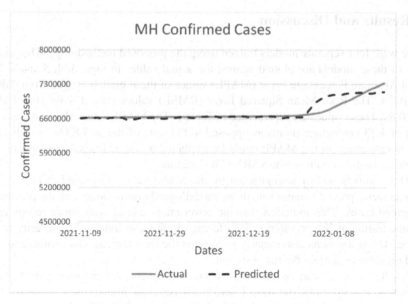

Fig. 3. Predictions for the state of Maharashtra

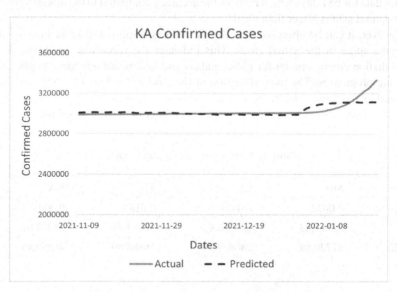

Fig. 4. Predictions for the state of Karnataka

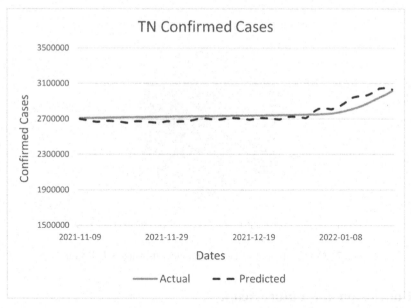

Fig. 5. Predictions for the state of Tamil Nadu

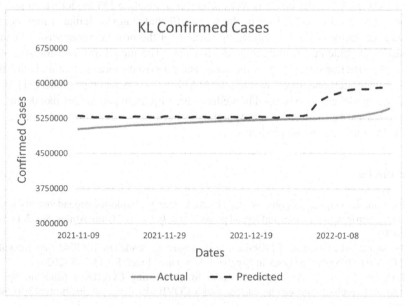

Fig. 6. Predictions for the state of Kerala

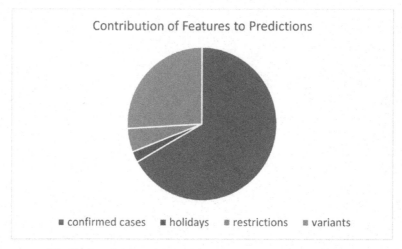

Fig. 7. Contribution of features to predictions using SHAP values

5 Conclusion and Future Scope

For better preparedness, as the pandemic progresses, it is essential to improve the accuracy of COVID-19 modeling. This work proposes a novel LSTM model which predicts the total confirmed cases of four of the worst affected states of India. It incorporates an important factor of the ever-changing variants of the novel coronavirus and can be extended to include newer mutations and lineages. The model also considers the holidays and restrictions prevalent in the area. The proposed model performs better than pre-existing models and improves upon the MAPE by 1.23 percentage points [21]. In the future, this model can also be used to predict other important parameters like deaths and recovered cases. The addition of more parameters like test positivity rate and vaccinations could help in more accurate predictions.

References

1. Bherwani, H., Gupta, A., Anjum, S., Anshul, A., Kumar, R.: Exploring dependence of COVID-19 on environmental factors and spread prediction in India. NPJ Clim. Atmos. Sci. 3(1), 1–13 (2020)
2. Ogundokun, R., Lukman, A., Kibria, G., Awotunde, J., Aladeitan, B.: Predictive modelling of COVID-19 confirmed cases in Nigeria. Infect. Dis. Model. 5, 543–548 (2020)
3. Hassanat, A., et al.: A simulation model for forecasting COVID-19 pandemic spread: analytical results based on the current Saudi COVID-19 data. Sustainability 13(9), 4888 (2021)
4. Mahdavi, M., et al.: A machine learning based exploration of COVID-19 mortality risk. PLoS ONE 16(7), e0252384 (2021)
5. Asada, K., et al.: Application of artificial intelligence in COVID-19 diagnosis and therapeutics. J. Pers. Med. 11(9), 886 (2021)
6. Ardabili, S., et al.: COVID-19 outbreak prediction with machine learning. Algorithms 13(10), 249 (2020)

7. Devaraj, J., et al.: Forecasting of COVID-19 cases using deep learning models: is it reliable and practically significant? Results Phys. **21**, 103817 (2021)
8. Zeroual, A., Harrou, F., Dairi, A., Sun, Y.: Deep learning methods for forecasting COVID-19 time-series data: a comparative study. Chaos Solitons Fractals **140**, 110121 (2020)
9. Ghany, K., Zawbaa, H., Sabri, H.: COVID-19 prediction using LSTM algorithm: GCC case study. Inform. Med. Unlocked **23**, 100566 (2021)
10. Papastefanopoulos, V., Linardatos, P., Kotsiantis, S.: COVID-19: a comparison of time series methods to forecast percentage of active cases per population. Appl. Sci. **10**(11), 3880 (2020)
11. Zivkovic, M., et al.: COVID-19 cases prediction by using hybrid machine learning and beetle antennae search approach. Sustain. Cities Soc. **66**, 102669 (2021)
12. Painuli, D., Mishra, D., Bhardwaj, S., Aggarwal, M.: Forecast and Prediction of COVID-19 using Machine Learning. Data Science for COVID-19, 1st edn. Academic Press, London (2021)
13. Arora, P., Kumar, H., Panigrahi, B.: Prediction and analysis of COVID-19 positive cases using deep learning models: a descriptive case study of India. Chaos Solitons Fractals **139**, 110017 (2021)
14. Kırbaş, İ, Sözen, A., Tuncer, A., Kazancıoğlu, F.: Comparative analysis and forecasting of COVID-19 cases in various European countries with ARIMA, NARNN and LSTM approaches. Chaos Solitons Fractals **138**, 110015 (2020)
15. Shahid, F., Zameer, A., Muneeb, M.: Predictions for COVID-19 with deep learning models of LSTM, GRU and Bi-LSTM. Chaos Solitons Fractals **140**, 110212 (2020)
16. Alzahrani, S., Aljamaan, I., Al-Fakih, E.: Forecasting the spread of the COVID-19 pandemic in Saudi Arabia using ARIMA prediction model under current public health interventions. J. Infect. Public Health **13**(7), 914–919 (2020)
17. Ahmad, F., Almuayqil, S.N., Humayun, M., Naseem, S., Ahmad Khan, W., Junaid, K.: Prediction of COVID-19 cases using machine learning for effective public health management. Comput. Mater. Continua **66**(3), 2265–2282 (2021)
18. Ribeiro, M., da Silva, R., Mariani, V., Coelho, L.: Short-term forecasting COVID-19 cumulative confirmed cases: perspectives for Brazil. Chaos Solitons Fractals **135**, 109853 (2020)
19. Tomar, A., Gupta, N.: Prediction for the spread of COVID-19 in India and effectiveness of preventive measures. Sci. Total Environ. **728**, 138762 (2020)
20. Car, Z., Baressi Šegota, S., Anđelić, N., Lorencin, I., Mrzljak, V.: Modeling the spread of COVID-19 infection using a multilayer perceptron. Comput. Math. Methods Med. **2020**, 1–10 (2020)
21. Shastri, S., Singh, K., Kumar, S., Kour, P., Mansotra, V.: Time series forecasting of Covid-19 using deep learning models: India-USA comparative case study. Chaos Solitons Fractals **140**, 110227 (2020)
22. Sokhansanj, B.A., Zhao, Z., Rosen, G.L.: Interpretable and Predictive Deep Modeling of the SARS-CoV-2 Spike Protein Sequence. medRxiv (2021)
23. Aljameel, S., Khan, I., Aslam, N., Aljabri, M., Alsulmi, E.: Machine learning-based model to predict the disease severity and outcome in COVID-19 patients. Sci. Program. **2021** (2021)
24. Zagrouba, R., et al.: Modelling and simulation of COVID-19 outbreak prediction using supervised machine learning. Comput. Mater. Continua **66**(3), 2397–2407 (2021)
25. Chandra, R., Jain, A., Singh Chauhan, D.: Deep learning via LSTM models for COVID-19 infection forecasting in India. PLoS ONE **17**(1), e0262708 (2022)
26. Bedi, P., Dhiman, S., Gole, P., Gupta, N., Jindal, V.: Prediction of COVID-19 trend in India and Its four worst-affected states using modified SEIRD and LSTM models. SN Comput. Sci. **2**(3), 1–24 (2021). https://doi.org/10.1007/s42979-021-00598-5
27. Zain, Z., Alturki, N.: COVID-19 pandemic forecasting using CNN-LSTM: a hybrid approach. J. Control Sci. Eng. **2021**, 1–23 (2021)

28. Zoabi, Y., Deri-Rozov, S., Shomron, N.: Machine learning-based prediction of COVID-19 diagnosis based on symptoms. NPJ Digit. Med. **4**(1), 1–5 (2021)

29. Ghafouri-Fard, S., Mohammad-Rahimi, H., Motie, P., Minabi, M.A., Taheri, M., Nateghinia, S.: Application of machine learning in the prediction of COVID-19 daily new cases: a scoping review. Heliyon **7**(10), e08143 (2021)

30. Oshinubi, K., Amakor, A., Peter, O.J., Rachdi, M., Demongeot, J.: Approach to COVID-19 time series data using deep learning and spectral analysis methods. Aims Bioeng. **9**(1), 1–21 (2022)

31. Novel COVID-19 Dataset. https://bit.ly/covid-19-dataset-variants. Accessed 31 July 2022

32. Home - COVID-19 India Data by DataMeet. https://projects.datameet.org/covid19/. Accessed 31 July 2022

33. State and UT Holiday Calendar|National Portal of India. https://www.india.gov.in/state-and-ut-holiday-calendar. Accessed 31 July 2022

34. COVID-19 Archives BombayChamber. http://bombaychamber.com/knowledgecenter?CovidArchives.html. Accessed 31 July 2022

35. Novel Coronavirus Government of Maharashtra. https://arogya.maharashtra.gov.in/1175/Novel--Corona-Virus. Accessed 31 July 2022

36. Government Circulars - COVID-19 INFORMATION PORTAL. https://covid19.karnataka.gov.in/new-page/Government%20Circulars/en. Accessed 31 July 2022

37. Government of Tamil Nadu: Government Orders|Tamil Nadu Government Portal. https://www.tn.gov.in/go_view/dept/26. Accessed 31 July 2022

38. Kerala State IT Mission C. GoK Dashboard|Official Kerala COVID-19 Statistics. https://dashboard.kerala.gov.in/covid/government-orders.php. Accessed 31 July 2022

39. Circulars for Covid-19|Ministry of Home Affairs|GoI. https://www.mha.gov.in/notifications/circulars-covid-19. Accessed 31 July 2022

40. COVID-19 Genomic Surveillance. https://clingen.igib.res.in/covid19genomes/. Accessed 31 July 2022

41. Duong, D.: Alpha, Beta, Delta, Gamma: what's important to know about SARS-CoV-2 variants of concern? Can. Med. Assoc. J. **193**(27), E1059–E1060 (2021)

42. Lundberg, S.M., Lee, S.I.: A unified approach to interpreting model predictions. In: Advances in Neural Information Processing Systems. 30, Curran Associates, Inc., CA, USA (2017)

COVID-19 Vaccines Analysis to Predict Its Impact Across the World

Ishita Sarkar[✉] [ID], Sridevi Vattikuti, and K. S. Jasmine [ID]

RV College of Engineering®, Bangalore, India
{ishitasarkar.mca20,srideviv.mca19,jasmineks}@rvce.edu.in

Abstract. In recent years, due to the widespread of COVID-19 pandemic, a large amount of data set is available about the various types of vaccines used by different countries for the protection of their citizens. So it is very important and useful if one is able to perform effective analysis of the same to make the awareness and the effectiveness of each vaccine known to mankind. It is found that COVID-19 vaccines increase the immune system, prepare the body to fight against the virus, and reduce the probability of contracting COVID-19.this can be done with the help of regression techniques such as The MAE, MSE, RMSE values to predict and evaluate the observations with more efficiency. The RMSE technique measures the standard deviation of results and provides more accuracy. This analysis helps to find out how COVID-19 vaccines are provided in various countries and the countries where 80% of the population is vaccinated.

Keywords: COVID-19 · Vaccination · The MAE · MSE · RMSE value

1 Introduction

Coronavirus disease (COVID-19) is an infectious disease caused by the SARS-CoV-2 virus. The virus spreads more easily indoors and in crowded places, hence spreading rapidly and causing a pandemic. COVID-19 vaccines provide an effective way to reduce the risk of getting affected by COVID-19. So various countries worked to provide enough vaccines to vaccinate the country's huge population. A wide range of vaccines is developed by different companies to achieve maximum effectiveness. The goal is to analyse how effective vaccines are and how many countries have achieved vaccination for more than 80% of their population and also the popular vaccines. Visualization of data is also done. Various graphs and heat maps can be plotted. Check specifically for a geographical area for how many are vaccinated and from which area has the highest number of vaccinated people. It also checks for the fastest country to vaccinate its people and also shows the impact of different vaccines. So a machine learning technique "An extra-trees regressor", This class implements a meta estimator that fits many randomized decision trees on different sub of the dataset and uses averaging and control over-fitting to improve predictive accuracy [9].

V. Sugumaran et al. (Eds.): AIR 2022, CCIS 1738, pp. 145–155, 2022.
https://doi.org/10.1007/978-3-031-23724-9_14

2 Proposed System

Unique Technical Features

- Using Python Libraries to evaluate and analyze the vaccination data
- Predicting the total and daily vaccination in India
- A thorough analysis of the dataset

Use of Python and Python Libraries- Python is a high-level general-purpose programming language used to create server applications. It is an Object-Oriented programming language that helps us to perform inheritance, overriding, and polymorphism. A Python library, on the other hand, means a collection of modules consisting of lines of code that you can use by importing the modules into any program. Modules such as Pandas, Scikit-Learn, and NumPy are also used for data analysis and Machine Learning. Even Matplotlib is an amazing library that is used for data visualization.

Machine Learning Algorithm-The Extra Tree Model class implements a meta estimator that fits multiple randomized decision trees (also known as extra-trees) on different dataset properties. Also, it uses averaging to boost forecasting accuracy and limit overfitting.

3 Implementation

In the proposed analysis the data requires to go through a pre-processing stage where missing data is being removed. After which some analysis is performed on the optimized dataset where it checks for the countries using a particular vaccine, countries to reach 80% vaccination mark, etc. Once the initial analysis is being performed the dataset is cleared further to make it optimized for training a Machine Learning algorithm. Firstly, as the predictions are made for India only we store the rows which have the country like India; Once the data is isolated, feature scaling is performed so that the data can be standardized to a fixed range. The next step is to split the dataset into training and test data. The size of the training data is 0.80 for the entire dataset and the test data consists of the remaining 0.20 for the entire data. After splitting the dataset, the Machine Learning algorithm is applied first to fit the data which builds "a forest of trees from the training set (x, y)", after which the score can be checked where the coefficient of determination of the prediction is returned and followed by that the predict method is used to predict regression target for X. Once that is done the MAE, MSE, and RMSE is checked [5, 11].

3.1 Analysis

From Fig. 1 which depicts a geographical graph, one can analyze and conclude that the rate of vaccination is different in different countries. Only a few counties were able to achieve over 60 k per million vaccination landmarks.

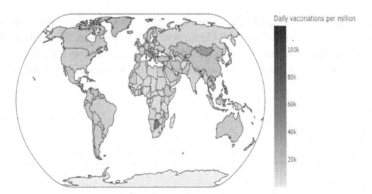

Fig. 1. Daily vaccinations

Total Vaccinations per country grouped by Vaccines

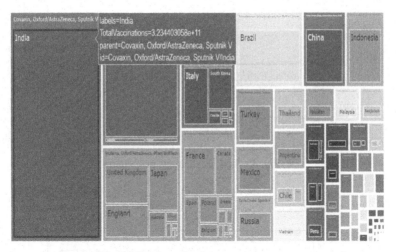

Fig. 2. Total vaccinations per country

Figure 2 shows the total vaccinations to date (as per dataset) for every country and the vaccines which they use, that is the reason why we have grouped the vaccines used by one particular country as we know it's not necessary to have only one type of COVID-19 vaccine in a country so to get the total estimation we clubbed all the vaccines available in one country to calculate the total vaccinations completed [15].

From the graph presented in Fig. 3, we can spot that China has over 3 billon of its population vaccinated and followed by India with over 1.8 billion. This data is different from the above graph as the above graph stated total vaccination for India as per the grouped vaccine but this graph states just the total estimated vaccination including both the doses (Fig. 4).

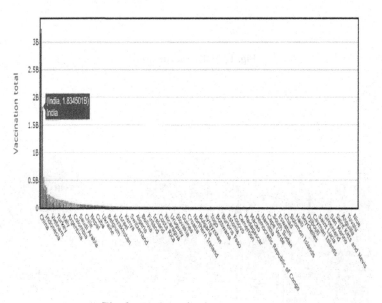

Fig. 3. Total vaccinations per country

Fig. 4. Vaccination percent v/s total

It shows the relation between the total vaccination done to what percentage of vaccination is being done based on the countries and vaccines.

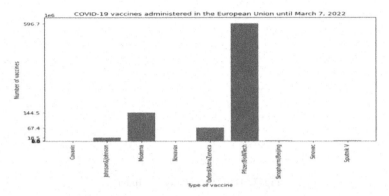

Fig. 5. Vaccinations administered in European Union

The above graph in Fig. 5 shows that Pfizer and Moderna are the 2 greatly administered vaccinations in the European Union (Fig. 6).

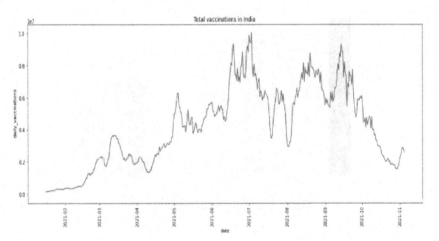

Fig. 6. Vaccinations in India

The graph explains the rate of vaccinations done in India. Initially (2021-02) the rate of vaccination was very low and increased gradually over time and (2021-07) reached the highest in daily vaccines and reduced over time (Fig. 7).

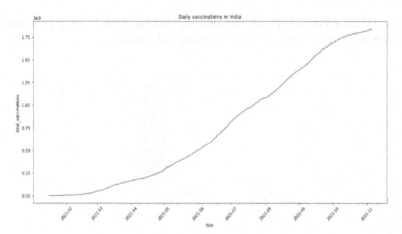

Fig. 7. Daily vaccinations in India

The graph explains the rate of vaccinations done in India. Initially, the rate of vaccination was very low but reached the highest in daily vaccines over a few months (Fig. 8).

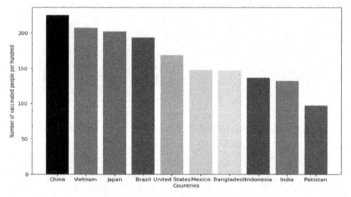

Fig. 8. Vaccinated people per hundred

From the above graph, we can see that China has the highest number of vaccinated people per hundred followed by Vietnam, Japan, and other countries (Fig. 9).

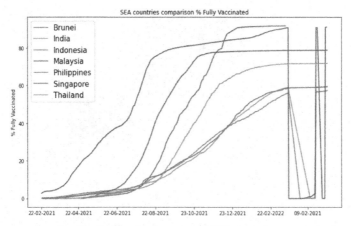

Fig. 9. Vaccination rates of SEA countries

Singapore has the highest vaccination rate among all the SEA countries. Most SEA countries have a vaccination rate close to 60% (Figs. 10 and 11).

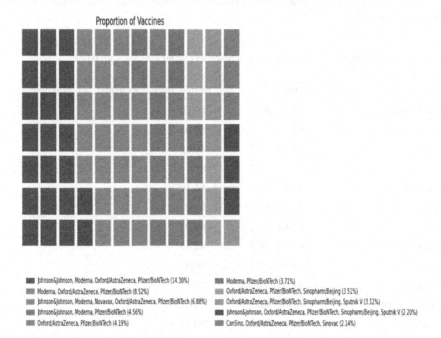

Fig. 10. The proportion of the Vaccines

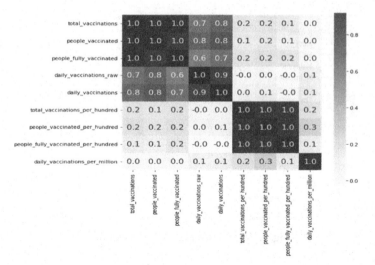

Fig. 11. Correlation between the features

The above heatmap represents the correlation between the different attributes of the dataset (Table 1).

Table 1. Fastest countries to reach vax = 80% along with dates

Country	Date	people_fully_vaccinated_per_hundred
South Korea	01-01-2022	80.20
Cambodia	01-01-2022	80.01
Singapore	01-01-2022	80.10
Chile	01-01-2022	80.16
Portugal	01-01-2022	81.10
Malta	01-01-2022	80.03
Cuba	01-01-2022	80.01
Gibraltar	01-02-2022	82.11
Spain	01-02-2022	80.05
Denmark	01-02-2022	80.12
Faeroe Islands	01-02-2022	82.41
Seychelles	01-03-2022	80.54
Argentina	01-03-2022	80.02

(*continued*)

Table 1. (*continued*)

Country	Date	people_fully_vaccinated_per_hundred
United Arab Emirates	01-03-2022	80.18
Canada	02-03-2022	80.05
Qatar	03-03-2022	87.90
Cayman Islands	03-12-2021	80.73
Ireland	05-03-2022	80.03
China	06-01-2022	80.49
Brunei	07-01-2022	80.99
Pitcairn	07-09-2021	100.00
Uruguay	09-03-2022	80.02
Guernsey	11-01-2022	81.01
Australia	11-03-2022	80.12
Niue	13-03-2022	87.79
Cook Islands	14-03-2022	81.04

3.2 Predicting the MAE, MSE and RMSE Value

Many regression models rely on distance metrics to determine convergence to the best results. Even the definition of the "best" result needs to be explained quantitatively by the metric. Typical metrics used are mean average error (MAE), root mean square error (MSE), or root mean square error (RMSE). MAE uses the average of all observations to evaluate the absolute distance from the observation (of the data set entry) to the prediction of the regression. Use the absolute value of the distance to properly consider negative errors. This is exactly the situation described in the image above. Another way is to square the distance so that the result is positive. This is done by MSE, and due to the nature of the power function, high errors (or distances) have higher metric weights than low errors. The MSE setback is the fact that the unit of the metric is also squared. Therefore, if the model tries to predict the price in US dollars, MSE will return a number in units (US dollars), which is meaningless. It then uses RMSE to reset the MSE error to its original 1 by taking the square root of the MSE error while maintaining the character of penalizing higher errors [4].

Making Predictions
Y_pred_I=EXTRAindia.predict(X_test_I)
Output:

```
In [97]:  M Y_pred_I

Out[97]:  array([1.09545646, 1.09213283, 1.08430854, 1.06446381, 1.06434142,
                 1.06585156, 1.06446381, 1.06544722, 1.06434142, 1.06544722,
                 1.0645862 , 1.06585156, 1.06495338, 1.065692  , 1.065692  ,
                 1.10824185, 1.07144865, 1.09213283, 1.06470859, 1.06524232,
                 1.065692  , 1.08018888, 1.06532482, 1.1000787 , 1.10868571,
                 1.10771899, 1.10700305, 1.10735182, 1.10939327, 1.10952654,
                 1.10964893, 1.11003696, 1.11040958, 1.10938784, 1.10824185,
                 1.10824185, 1.10747421, 1.10714693, 1.10824185, 1.10681692,
                 1.10824185, 1.10792272, 1.10824185, 1.10771899, 1.10824185,
                 1.10792388, 1.10812217, 1.10820195, 1.10824185, 1.10824185,
                 1.10820195, 1.10824185, 1.10824185, 1.10820195, 1.10820195,
                 1.10824185, 1.08880669, 1.08880669, 1.08880669, 1.08880669,
                 1.08880669, 1.08880669, 1.08880669, 1.08880669, 1.08880669,
                 1.08880669, 1.08880669, 1.08880669, 1.08880669, 1.08880669,
                 1.08880669, 1.08880669, 1.08880669, 1.08880669, 1.08880669,
                 1.08880669, 1.08880669, 1.08880669, 1.08880669, 1.08068702,
                 1.0887668 , 1.08880669, 1.10012217, 1.10824185, 1.08880669,
                 1.08880669])
```

The MAE, MSE, and RMSE Values

print('MAE:',metrics.mean_absolute_error(Y_test_I, Y_pred_I))
print('MSE:',metrics.mean_squared_error(Y_test_I, Y_pred_I))
print('RMSE:',np.sqrt(metrics.mean_squared_error(Y_test_I, Y_pred_I)))
Output:

```
In [96]:  M  print('MAE:',metrics.mean_absolute_error(Y_test_I, Y_pred_I))
             print('MSE:',metrics.mean_squared_error(Y_test_I, Y_pred_I))
             print('RMSE:',np.sqrt(metrics.mean_squared_error(Y_test_I, Y_pred_I)))

             MAE: 0.408461936457182
             MSE: 0.19229460289697306
             RMSE: 0.43851408517512075
```

4 Conclusion

This paper analyses the overall population which is being vaccinated during the pandemic and the types of vaccines which were being used across the globe. Our initial analysis is based on the growth of vaccination in various countries and we could infer from the graphical analysis that in the list of SEA countries most of the countries have crossed the 60% vaccination mark. We have taken India into consideration for most of the analysis. We could observe that India was among the top 10 countries which had a higher rate of vaccinated people per hundred. India was even successful in catering over 1 Billion vaccines and the other observations include the vaccines used in the European Union and found that Pfizer is the commonly used vaccine there. Using the heatmap, we could also observe the correlation between the different attributes of the dataset. Later a regressor model is used to report the lowest value of forecasted errors using the MAE, MSE, and RMSE. The MAE value was 0.408, MSE was 0.192 and RMSE was 0.438. The MAE tells us how an error can be significant that we can expect on average between the actual data and the predicted data. The variance of residuals is evaluated by the MSE, which would be the average of the squared difference between the original and projected values in the data set. The standard deviation of residuals is evaluated by the RMSE. Thus the lower value of MAE, MSE, and RMSE implies that the accuracy of our regression model is high.

References

1. Singh, S., Singh, N.: Big data analytics. In: 2012 International Conference on Communication, Information & Computing Technology (ICCICT) (2012). https://doi.org/10.1109/iccict.2012. 6398180
2. Mittal, S., Sangwan, O.P.: Big data analytics using machine learning techniques. In: 2019 9th International Conference on Cloud Computing, Data Science & Engineering (Confluence) (2019). https://doi.org/10.1109/confluence.2019.8776614
3. Komalavalli, C., Laroiya, C.: Challenges in big data analytics techniques: a survey. In: 2019 9th International Conference on Cloud Computing, Data Science & Engineering (Confluence) (2019). https://doi.org/10.1109/confluence.2019.8776932
4. Qi, J., Du, J., Siniscalchi, S.M., Ma, X., Lee, C.-H.: On mean absolute error for deep neural network based vector-to-vector regression. IEEE Sig. Process. Lett. **27**, 1485–1489 (2020). https://doi.org/10.1109/lsp.2020.3016837
5. Shaikh, S., Gala, J., Jain, A., Advani, S., Jaidhara, S., Roja Edinburgh, M.: Analysis and prediction of COVID-19 using regression models and time series forecasting. In: 2021 11th International Conference on Cloud Computing, Data Science & Engineering (Confluence) (2021). https://doi.org/10.1109/confluence51648.2021.9377137
6. Paul, N., Gokhale, S.S.: Analysis and classification of vaccine dialogue in the coronavirus era. In: 2020 IEEE International Conference on Big Data (Big Data) (2020). https://doi.org/ 10.1109/bigdata50022.2020.9377888
7. Imran, S.A., Islam, Md.T., Shahnaz, C., Islam, Md.T., Imam, O.T., Haque, M.: COVID-19 mRNA vaccine degradation prediction using regularized LSTM model. In: 2020 IEEE International Women in Engineering (WIE) Conference on Electrical and Computer Engineering (WIECON-ECE) (2020). https://doi.org/10.1109/wiecon-ece52138.2020.9398044
8. Darapaneni, N., Jain, P., Khattar, R., Chawla, M., Vaish, R., Paduri, A.R.: Analysis and prediction of COVID-19 pandemic in India. In: 2020 2nd International Conference on Advances in Computing, Communication Control and Networking (ICACCCN) (2020). https://doi.org/ 10.1109/icacccn51052.2020.9362817
9. Cotfas, L.-A., Delcea, C., Roxin, I., Ioanas, C., Gherai, D.S., Tajariol, F.: The longest month: analyzing COVID-19 vaccination opinions dynamics from tweets in the month following the first vaccine announcement. IEEE Access **9**, 33203–33223 (2021). https://doi.org/10.1109/ access.2021.3059821
10. Dumre, R., Sharma, K., Konar, K.: Statistical and sentimental analysis on vaccination against COVID-19 in India. In: 2021 International Conference on Communication information and Computing Technology (ICCICT) (2021). https://doi.org/10.1109/iccict50803.2021.9510179
11. Tamilselvan, S., Kumar, S., Priya, J., Ramesh, R.: COVID vaccination analysis and prediction using machine learning. In: 2021 Smart Technologies, Communication and Robotics (STCR) (2021). https://doi.org/10.1109/stcr51658.2021.9588837
12. Beatty, A.L., et al.: Analysis of COVID-19 vaccine type and adverse effects following vaccination. JAMA Netw. Open **4**, e2140364 (2021). https://doi.org/10.1001/jamanetworkopen. 2021.40364
13. Voysey, M., Clemens, S.A.C., Madhi, S.A., et al.: Safety and efficacy of the ChAdOx1 nCoV-19 vaccine (AZD1222) against SARS-CoV-2: an interim analysis of four randomised controlled trials in Brazil, South Africa, and the UK. The Lancet **397**, 99–111 (2021). https://doi. org/10.1016/s0140-6736(20)32661-1
14. Gee, J., et al.: First month of COVID-19 vaccine safety monitoring—United States, December 14, 2020–January 13, 2021. MMWR. Morb. Mortal. Wkly. Rep. **70**, 283–288 (2021). https:// doi.org/10.15585/mmwr.mm7008e3
15. Han, X., Xu, P., Ye, Q.: Analysis of COVID-19 vaccines: types, thoughts, and application. J. Clin. Lab. Anal. **35** (2021). https://doi.org/10.1002/jcla.23937

Lung Cancer Detection Using Ensemble Learning

Fayeza Sifat Fatima[1], Arunima Jaiswal[1]([⊠]) [iD], and Nitin Sachdeva[2]

[1] Indira Gandhi Delhi Technical University for Women, Delhi, India
{fayezasifat028mtcse20,arunimajaiswal}@igdtuw.ac.in
[2] Galgotia's College of Engineering and Technology, Greater Noida, India
nitin.sachdeva@galgotiacollege.edu

Abstract. From time to time, lung cancer has appeared in the category of nearly the most lethal maladies since humankind existed. It is even among the most incessant fatalities and major reasons of mortality among all cancers. Lung cancer cases are significantly growing. In India, there are around 70 thousand instances each year. Because the condition is usually asymptomatic in its early stages, it is practically extremely difficult to identify. As a result, early cancer identification is beneficial for preserving lives. Early discovery can improve a patient's chances of rehabilitation and recovery. Technology has a critical part in accurately identifying cancers. Based on these findings, several researchers have offered various ways. Several Computer-aided diagnostics (CAD) methodologies and systems have been suggested, developed and created in recent years to handle this problem using computer technology. Also, there are some factors like smoking, taking alcohol, anxiety etc. that also helps us to detect if patient is having cancer or not has also been taken into considerations by many researchers. Taking on an assortment of techniques such as machine learning, Ensemble learning and deep learning approaches and numerous ways based on image processing techniques and text information, those systems contribute to a great extent to ascertain the cancer malignancy degree. We had in view integrating or putting together the Ensemble learning algorithms like Stacking, blinding, Max voting, boosting and XGBoost through this so as to build an advanced method to assess and scrutinize the outturn. On comparing Blinding ensemble learning technique proves to be the most efficient technique based on the performance metrics like accuracy, F1 score, precision and recall.

Keywords: Lung cancer disease · Ensemble learning · Machine learning · Deep learning · Blending · Detection

1 Introduction

Lung cancer stands as the world's largest reason of cancer deaths. It is the leading cause of death for women and men both. It's also tough to detect in time to make an impact. Favourable prognoses depend on early identification. Lung cancer screening, also known as low-dose CT screening, can aid in the detection of lung cancer at an

V. Sugumaran et al. (Eds.): AIR 2022, CCIS 1738, pp. 156–167, 2022.
https://doi.org/10.1007/978-3-031-23724-9_15

early stage, when it is most curable [1]. Lung cancer possesses poor prognoses that vary widely on the basis of the tumour stage at the time of diagnosis. Lung cancer has two divisional forms of clinical practise: "Small cell lung cancer" (SCLC) and the "non-small cell lung cancer" (NSCLC). In point of fact, it is a terminal tumour defined through uncontrolled cell-tissue production. It is almost caused by long-term cigarette or tobacco usage. "International Agency for Research on Cancer" (IARC) created the Global Cancer Observatory database in the year 2018 and according to it, the incidence and rate of mortality in 185 nations and 36 kinds of malignancies, has lung cancer ranking first for men and third for women. In 2018, there were about 9.6 million cancer fatalities reported, with 1.8 million deaths attributed to lung cancer accounting for 18.4% of all deaths [3]. Lung cancer has two divisions: "Small cell lung cancer" and "Non-small cell lung cancer". Thirdly, Carcinoid lung cancer is a lesser widespread type of lung cancer. SCLC is divided into two types: "small cell carcinoma" & "mixed small cell/large cell malignancy", sometimes known as combination small cell lung cancer [4]. The numerous types of SCLC are called by the various kinds of cells viewed in tumour and the way they appear under a microscope. Cigarette smoking is virtually always linked to small cell lung cancer. Chemotherapy is generally used to treat SCLC. There are three subtypes of NSCLC that is "squamous cell carcinomas", "large cell carcinomas" & "adenocarcinomas". As a result, large scale cancer or mixed small cell cancer is a condition in which a patient exhibits signs of the two cancer types [5]. Adenocarcinoma (NSCLC) has frequency more than small cell lung cancer (SCLC) & advances more slowly. SCLC has a connection with smoking. Also, it grows more quickly, eventually transforming into a big tumour that spreads throughout the body [6]. Lung cancer is caused by a tumour termed as nodule that develops from cells in the respiratory system's airways. These cells are constantly in direct contrast in chest X-rays, they form themselves as spherical objects. However, by routinely discovering the lung nodules, considerable enhancement of survival of patient can be made. But since lung nodule cannot be discovered rapidly using chest X- ray imaging, analyzing these diagnostic photos has become a time consuming & difficult process [7]. A computer-aided diagnostic (CAD) system would have to recognise the existence of tiny nodule found on a big 3D lung CT image [8]. Figure 1 is a 2D slice of a CT scan showing an early-stage lung cancer nodule. The CT scan, being filled around with air, bone as well as noise created by the tissues, this noise, would have to be processed prior to the CAD system searching efficiently. Our classification pipeline includes "image pre-processing", "malignancy classification detection" & "nodule candidate" [9].

Many lung cancer detection systems are created. Certain systems, however, have a deficit of acceptable accuracy in detection, and it is a must that certain systems would be created so as to achieve the highest, that is, 100% accuracy in detection. The diagnosis as well as categorization of lung cancer laid their basis upon learning by machine and approaches through processing of the image.

Techniques of learning by machine aid in the before time recognition and examining the lung nodules through evaluation of Computed tomography (CT) scan images generated by systems of artificial intelligence [8]. These systems are known as DSS: Decision Support Systems because they assess pictures through the processes of "pre-processing", "Segmentation", "feature extraction", and "Classification" [10].

Aside from image datasets, we can also detect whether a patient has lung cancer or not by a variety of other factors that cause these nodules to form in the lungs, such as excessive smoking, coughing, anxiety, chest pain, alcoholic person, shortness of breath, and so on. These are the attributes that help researchers or doctors to determine whether a patient has cancer or not. So, in this study, we will employ datasets containing features that are the primary cause of lung cancer and can assist us in determining the various causes of lung cancer. Next section consists of extensive study on work that has been done in this field up till now.

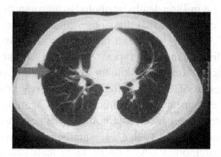

Fig. 1. 2D CT scan slice containing a small early-stage Lung Cancer nodule of 5 mm [9]

2 Related Work

We examined current breakthroughs and research in this sector in light of the growing need for awareness and early detection/prediction of Lung Cancer. We primarily focused on studies published in the last five years and to assure the relevance and validity of the results, we screened papers from high-quality and well-known journals that were relevant to our study. Table 1 summarizes our observations.

Table 1. Analysis of existing works

Author	Year	Classifier/algorithms	Dataset	Outcome/efficiency
P. Aonpong et al. [11]	2021	Genotype-guided radiomics method (GGR) (DEEP Learning)	NSCLC Dataset	83.28% Accuracy
Pang, Shanchen et al. [12]	2020	Deep learning + DenseNet + Adaboost	Shandon Provincial Hospital	89.85% Accuracy

(continued)

Table 1. (*continued*)

Author	Year	Classifier/algorithms	Dataset	Outcome/efficiency
Bhandary et al. [13]	2020	Deep learning	Dataset of Chest X-Ray and Lung cancer (LIDC-IDRI)	Accuracy for X-Ray pictures is 96%, & accuracy for Ct image 97.27%
Shakeel et al. [14]	2020	Neural network & Ensemble Classifier	Database of "Cancer imaging archive" (CIA) dataset	The suggested technique identified the tumour with the greatest degree of accuracy
Boban et al. [15]	2020	"MLP, SVM, KNN"	CT images	Highest accuracy achieved by KNN
Sree kumar et al. [16]	2020	CNN	LIDC IDRI	Sensitivity 86%
Banerjee et al. [17]	2020	"Random forest, SVM & ANN"	LIDC IDRI	Highest accuracy by ANN 96%"
Elnakib et al. [18]	2020	SVM	LDCT images	96.25%
Bhatia et al. [19]	2019	XGBoost and Random Forest	LIDC-IDRI	84%
K. Roy et al. [20]	2019	Random forest algorithm and SVM classification	CT scan images	94.5%
Günaydin et al. [21]	2019	SVM, KNN, Decision Tree, Naïve Bayes, & ANN	JSRT Dataset	ANN 82.43% & Decision Tree 93.24%
G. Jakimovski et al. [22]	2019	Convolutional Deep Neural Network (CDNN) & Regular CDNN	Dataset from the South Carolina University & Neuro Imaging	0.909% and 0.872%
Gian Son Tran et al. [23]	2019	2-D Deep CNN	LIDC-IDRI	Accuracy of 97.2%
Faisal et al. [24]	2018	SVM	UCI dataset	90.9% Accuracy
Alam et al. [25]	2018	Multi-class SVM classifier	UCI dataset	Cancer detection precision of 97% & cancer prognosis precision of 87%

(*continued*)

Table 1. (*continued*)

Author	Year	Classifier/algorithms	Dataset	Outcome/efficiency
Singh and Gupta [26]	2018	"Knn classifier, decision tree classifier, random forest classifier,	Database of Lung image	Accuracy 88.55%
Alakwaa et al. [9]	2017	3D Convolutional Neural Networks (CNNs)	CT scan dataset	Accuracy 86.6%
Makajua [27]	2017	SVM	Lung Image Database (LICD)	92% Accuracy
QingZeng Song et al. [28]	2017	CNN, DNN, SAE	LIDC-IDRI	84.15% Accuracy
Q. Dou et al. [29]	2017	A 3D CNNs	The luna16 challenge data	94.4% Accuracy

This study provides a brief overview of the various strategies used for lung cancer diagnosis utilizing CT images. Area and eccentricity are determined and sent into classifier which determines if the lung nodule in the image is malignant or not. Also, we observed that many researchers have used X-ray and CT scan images for the detection also some researchers opt for factor-based datasets. In some work only few features have been extracted for the cancer nodules. The primary restrictions restricting research in this sector are a smaller sample size of studies and non-validated models. Because the sample size is limited in some of the research, statistically meaningful findings are not obtained. Also, Ensemble learning is not much used by the researchers in this field.

So, in our implementation we will be trying to overcome these limitations that we observed from our literature review using ensemble techniques as on analysing the above review it gives the better results. Some of the predominantly used datasets that have been used through the years by a large number of researchers are as follows: Radiogenomics dataset of NSCLC: dataset has 211 285,411 images of 211 subjects. It includes CT (Computed Tomography), PET (Positron Emission Tomography) images and quantitative values are acquired [30]. LIDC IDRI Dataset: Dataset consist of 244,527 images of diagnostics & screening of CT images of annotated lesions. It has 7371 labelled lesions as "nodule" by one radiologist [31]. Lung Cancer Dataset Kaggle: The data set includes several aspects such as smoking, anxiety, alcohol, chest discomfort, coughing, and so on. A total of 16 attributes were gathered from 284 individuals, whether they were diagnosed with cancer or not [32].

3   Implementation Details

In this research paper, out of one of the discussed datasets above dataset we opted for the Lung cancer dataset available on Kaggle where we have 16 attributes and 309 instances of patients recorded from the lung prediction system also available on "data.world" [32]. The dataset is used to evaluate Ensemble learning approaches like XGBoost, Stacking, MaxVoting, Blending, and Boosting to see which one produces the best results. Table 2 gives the details about the dataset.

Table 2. Dataset details

S. no.	Attributes	Value type
1	Age	Numerical
2	Gender	Male or female
3	Smoking	Numerical
4	Yellow fatigue	Numerical
5	Anxiety	Numerical
6	Peer pressure	Numerical
7	Chronic disease	Numerical
8	Fatigue	Numerical
9	Allergy	Numerical
10	Wheezing	Numerical
11	Alcohol	Numerical
12	Coughing	Numerical
13	Shortness of breath	Numerical
14	Swallowing difficulty	Numerical
15	Chest pain	Numerical
16	Result	Yes or No

For the implementation, we chose Python as the programming language and Jupyter Notebook as the platform. And we have incorporated ensemble learning techniques. Tthey are used to integrate several approaches in order to get better results than a single algorithm, and its outcomes are comparably better than ml techniques. For the data pre-processing we load and check the dataset surprisingly there were no null values so, there was no need to fill null values with mean or 0. After that we checked the values and types of the data, to ensure the values are in float or integer. After that, we altered the values of Male and Female to 0 and 1, respectively. Next, we checked whether our dataset is overcrowded or not. To checked that we used the T-SNE scatter plot on our dataset and from the result we get to know that our dataset was not overcrowded as shown in Fig. 2.

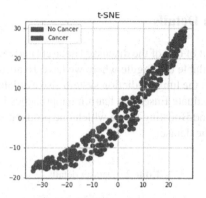

Fig. 2. T-SNE scatter plot

After that for the feature extraction we consider every feature and didn't eliminate. Following that, we utilised SMOTE (Synthetic minority oversampling technique) to eliminate the imbalance data, hence resolving the overfitting problem in the data. Following that, we used heat maps to assess the correlation of our datasets, and then we determined the confusion matrix for each ensemble classifiers that we would be utilising. After that split the dataset into training and testing taking standard size as 80:20 ratio where testing size was 20% and random state was 50.

After preparing the model, we used 5 different supervised ensemble classifiers to see which one produced the greatest accuracy with our model in terms of accuracy, F1score, precision and recall. The confusion matrix and AUC & ROC curve for each classifier were analysed. Figure 3 displays the workflow, in which we described how the dataset is imported, processed, extracted, and then separated into training and testing data. Following that, we incorporate it into ensemble learning techniques, and it determines whether or not a person is suffering from cancer.

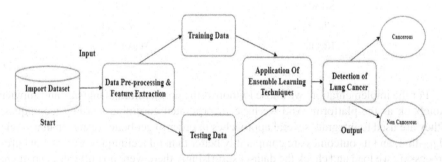

Fig. 3. Workflow of application of ensemble learning techniques

4 Results

In this section, we discuss the outcomes of implementing our techniques and compare the accuracy of several techniques to see which one works best. The outcomes are listed below (Table 3 and Figs. 4, 5, 6 and 7).

According to the aforementioned implementation and findings, blending proved to be the best technique on all performance criteria and provided the highest accuracy score of 96.77% and AUC results of 98.11%, followed by stacking and boosting. As a result, we may conclude that ensemble approaches are effective in the detection of lung cancer.

Table 3. Analysis of existing works

Algorithm	Accuracy	Precision	Recall	F1 score
XGBoost	0.8870	0.9259	0.9433	0.9345
Max Voting	0.9193	0.9444	0.9622	0.9532
Stacking	0.9516	1.0	0.9433	0.9708
Blending	**0.9677**	**1.0**	**0.9622**	**0.9807**
Boosting	0.9354	0.9803	0.9433	0.9615

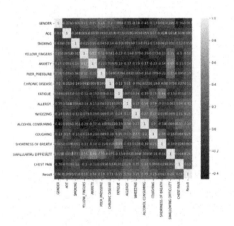

Fig. 4. Heatmaps correlation

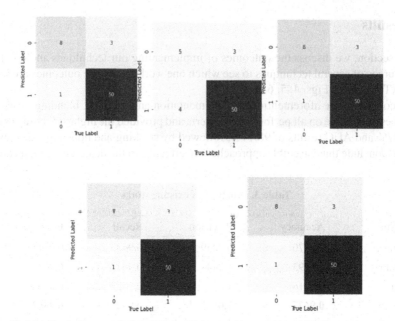

Fig. 5. Confusion matrix for XGBoost, max voting, stacking, blending & boosting

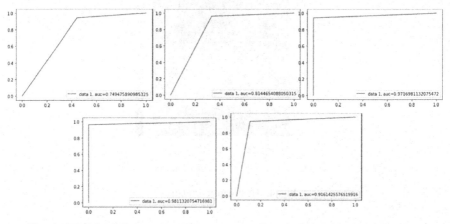

Fig. 6. AUC & ROC curve for XGBoost, max voting, stacking, blending & boosting

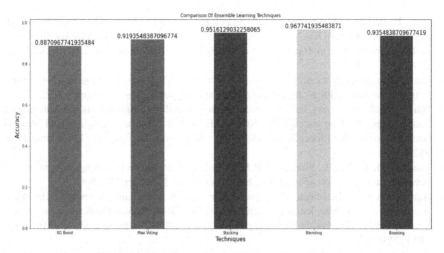

Fig. 7. Comparison of ensemble learning techniques

5 Conclusion and Future Scope

Lung cancer, one of the most common cancer types, was investigated in this paper. We used 5 different ensemble learning approaches, including Blending, Boosting, Stacking, Max Voting, and XGBoost, and compared them. Blending proved to be the best learning technique with 96.77% accuracy, also, on the basis of AUC & ROC curve it provided the best accuracy followed by Boosting and Stacking. On the ground of our analysis of the past research, it can be concluded that the models based on single techniques/algorithms are not the best affirmation and ensemble learning techniques performs better as compare to ml approaches. Even for predictions, a unified approach is always preferable. Ensemble approaches should be given more attention since they can support the discovery of the best- fitting solution. The next rational step in the predictive healthcare systems should be the real-time medical settings. Deep learning is still an early bid, and more significance should be placed on identifying and implementing the best approach that is possible using feature extraction and segmentations techniques. Further research and investigations are required, as well as validation of the suggested models of convolutional neural networks. Validation of the presented models is paramount before they can be used in the screening technique for lung cancer, enhancing detection in earlier stages. Furthermore, research and trials will be undertaken using technology breakthroughs, and clinicians will be challenged to improvise them and furthermore adopt them.

References

1. Thakur, S.K., Singh, D.P., Choudhary, J.: Lung cancer identification: a review on detection and classification. Cancer Metastasis Rev. **39**(3), 989–998 (2020). https://doi.org/10.1007/s10555-020-09901-x
2. Ibrahim, I., Abdulazeez, A.: The role of machine learning algorithms for diagnosing diseases. J. Appl. Sci. Technol. Trends **2**, 10–19 (2021). https://doi.org/10.38094/jastt20179

3. Bray, F., Ferlay, J., Soerjomataram, I., Siegel, R.L., Torre, L.A., Jemal, A.: Global cancer statistics 2018: GLOBOCAN estimates of incidence and mortality worldwide for 36 cancers in 185 countries. CA: A Cancer J. Clin. **68**, 394–424 (2018). https://doi.org/10.3322/caac. 21492

4. Lung Cancer Basics|American Lung Association. https://www.lung.org/lung-health-diseases/ lung-disease-lookup/lung-cancer/basics/lung-cancer-types. Accessed February 2022

5. Nai, Y., et al.: Improving lung lesion detection in low dose positron emission tomography images using machine learning. In: 2018 IEEE Nuclear Science Symposium and Medical Imaging Conference Proceedings (NSS/MIC) (2018). https://doi.org/10.1109/nssmic.2018. 8824292

6. Pandiangan, T., Bali, I., Silalahi, A.R.J.: Early lung cancer detection using artificial neural network. Atom Indones. **45**, 9 (2019). https://doi.org/10.17146/aij.2019.860

7. Rahane, W., Dalvi, H., Magar, Y., Kalane, A., Jondhale, S.: Lung cancer detection using image processing and machine learning healthcare. In: 2018 International Conference on Current Trends towards Converging Technologies (ICCTCT) (2018). https://doi.org/10.1109/icctct. 2018.8551008

8. Qader Zeebaree, D., Mohsin Abdulazeez, A., Asaad Zebari, D., Haron, H., Nuzly Abdull Hamed, H.: Multi-level fusion in ultrasound for cancer detection based on uniform LBP features. Comput. Mater. Continua **66**, 3363–3382 (2021). https://doi.org/10.32604/cmc.2021. 013314

9. Alakwaa, W., Nassef, M., Badr, A.: Lung cancer detection and classification with 3D convolutional neural network (3D-CNN). Int. J. Adv. Comput. Sci. Appl. **8** (2017). https://doi.org/ 10.14569/ijacsa.2017.080853

10. Saba, T.: Recent advancement in cancer detection using machine learning: systematic survey of decades, comparisons and challenges. J. Infect. Public Health **13**, 1274–1289 (2020). https://doi.org/10.1016/j.jiph.2020.06.033

11. Aonpong, P., Iwamoto, Y., Han, X.-H., Lin, L., Chen, Y.-W.: Genotype-guided radiomics signatures for recurrence prediction of non-small cell lung cancer. IEEE Access **9**, 90244– 90254 (2021). https://doi.org/10.1109/access.2021.3088234

12. Pang, S., Zhang, Y., Ding, M., Wang, X., Xie, X.: A Deep model for lung cancer type identification by densely connected convolutional networks and adaptive boosting. IEEE Access **8**, 4799–4805 (2020). https://doi.org/10.1109/access.2019.2962862

13. Bhandary, A., et al.: Deep-learning framework to detect lung abnormality – a study with chest X-Ray and lung CT scan images. Pattern Recogn. Lett. **129**, 271–278 (2020). https://doi.org/ 10.1016/j.patrec.2019.11.013

14. Shakeel, P.M., Burhanuddin, M.A., Desa, M.I.: Automatic lung cancer detection from CT image using improved deep neural network and ensemble classifier. Neural Comput. Appl. **34**, 9579–9592 (2020). https://doi.org/10.1007/s00521-020-04842-6

15. Boban, B.M., Megalingam, R.K.: Lung diseases classification based on machine learning algorithms and performance evaluation. In: 2020 International Conference on Communication and Signal Processing (ICCSP) (2020). https://doi.org/10.1109/iccsp48568.2020.9182324

16. Sreekumar, A., Nair, K.R., Sudheer, S., Ganesh Nayar, H., Nair, J.J.: Malignant lung nodule detection using deep learning. In: 2020 International Conference on Communication and Signal Processing (ICCSP) (2020). https://doi.org/10.1109/iccsp48568.2020.9182258

17. Banerjee, N., Das, S.: Prediction lung cancer – in machine learning perspective. In: 2020 International Conference on Computer Science, Engineering and Applications (ICCSEA) (2020). https://doi.org/10.1109/iccsea49143.2020.9132913

18. Elnakib, A., Amer, H.M., Abou-Chadi, F.E.Z.: Early lung cancer detection using deep learning optimization. Int. J. Online Biomed. Eng. (iJOE) **16**, 82 (2020). https://doi.org/10.3991/ijoe. v16i06.13657

19. Bhatia, S., Sinha, Y., Goel, L.: Lung cancer detection: a deep learning approach. In: Bansal, J.C., Das, K.N., Nagar, A., Deep, K., Ojha, A.K. (eds.) Soft Computing for Problem Solving. AISC, vol. 817, pp. 699–705. Springer, Singapore (2019). https://doi.org/10.1007/978-981-13-1595-4_55

20. Roy, K., et al.: A comparative study of lung cancer detection using supervised neural network. In: 2019 International Conference on Opto-Electronics and Applied Optics (Optronix) (2019). https://doi.org/10.1109/optronix.2019.8862326

21. Gunaydin, O., Gunay, M., Sengel, O.: Comparison of lung cancer detection algorithms. In: 2019 Scientific Meeting on Electrical-Electronics & Biomedical Engineering and Computer Science (EBBT) (2019). https://doi.org/10.1109/ebbt.2019.8741826

22. Jakimovski, G., Davcev, D.: Using double convolution neural network for lung cancer stage detection. Appl. Sci. **9**, 427 (2019). https://doi.org/10.3390/app9030427

23. Tran, G.S., Nghiem, T.P., Nguyen, V.T., Luong, C.M., Burie, J.-C.: Improving accuracy of lung nodule classification using deep learning with focal loss. J. Healthc. Eng. **2019**, 1–9 (2019). https://doi.org/10.1155/2019/5156416

24. Faisal, M.I., Bashir, S., Khan, Z.S., Hassan Khan, F.: An evaluation of machine learning classifiers and ensembles for early stage prediction of lung cancer. In: 2018 3rd International Conference on Emerging Trends in Engineering, Sciences and Technology (ICEEST) (2018). https://doi.org/10.1109/iceest.2018.8643311

25. Alam, J., Alam, S., Hossan, A.: Multi-stage lung cancer detection and prediction using multi-class SVM classifie. In: 2018 International Conference on Computer, Communication, Chemical, Material and Electronic Engineering (IC4ME2) (2018). https://doi.org/10.1109/ic4me2.2018.8465593

26. Singh, G.A.P., Gupta, P.K.: Performance analysis of various machine learning-based approaches for detection and classification of lung cancer in humans. Neural Comput. Appl. **31**(10), 6863–6877 (2018). https://doi.org/10.1007/s00521-018-3518-x

27. Makaju, S., Prasad, P.W.C., Alsadoon, A., Singh, A.K., Elchouemi, A.: Lung cancer detection using CT scan images. Proc. Comput. Sci. **125**, 107–114 (2018). https://doi.org/10.1016/j.procs.2017.12.016

28. Song, Q., Zhao, L., Luo, X., Dou, X.: Using deep learning for classification of lung nodules on computed tomography images. J. Healthc. Eng. **2017**, 1–7 (2017). https://doi.org/10.1155/2017/8314740

29. Dou, Q., Chen, H., Yu, L., Qin, J., Heng, P.-A.: Multilevel contextual 3-D CNNs for false positive reduction in pulmonary nodule detection. IEEE Trans. Biomed. Eng. **64**, 1558–1567 (2017). https://doi.org/10.1109/tbme.2016.2613502

30. Bakr, S., et al.: A radiogenomic dataset of non-small cell lung cancer. Sci. Data **5** (2018). https://doi.org/10.1038/sdata.2018.202

31. Hancock, M.C., Magnan, J.F.: Lung nodule malignancy classification using only radiologist-quantified image features as inputs to statistical learning algorithms: probing the Lung Image Database Consortium dataset with two statistical learning methods. J. Med. Imaging **3**, 044504 (2016). https://doi.org/10.1117/1.jmi.3.4.044504

32. Lung Cancer. https://www.kaggle.com/datasets/mysarahmadbhat/lung-cancer. Accessed February 2022

Detection of Pneumothorax from Chest X-Ray Data Using Machine Learning: A Comprehensive Survey

Arpan Garg and Bobbinpreet Kaur[✉] [iD]

Chandigarh University, Mohali, India
bobbinece@gmail.com

Abstract. Chest radiography is one of the most common and well-known medical imaging procedures. In humans, chest radiography is a very effective and reliable method of detecting thoracic and pneumothorax disorders. Due to recent improvements in computer technology, computer vision, and publically available large-scale datasets, machine learning-based techniques to automated pneumothorax diagnosis in chest radiography have risen in favour among academics. Our study examines existing machine learning approaches, datasets, and strategies for identifying pneumothorax in chest X-rays. The study includes widely available and publicly available labelled Chest X-Ray datasets with their requirements, as well as a detailed description of the labellers and labelling procedures used by them. Then, for Chest X-Ray images, popular and successful Image Processing approaches are provided. The paper then goes on to discuss the existing machine learning architectures in use, as well as the efficacy of Deep Convolutional Neural Networks in this regard. Finally, they look at gaps in the current literature for pneumothorax diagnosis, as well as uncharted territory and possible future collaborations in Machine Learning-based automated pneumothorax detection on Chest X-Rays.

Keywords: Diagnostic imaging · Medical photography · Convolutional Neural Networks · Pneumothorax identification · Medical imaging

1 Introduction

Medical imaging is the science of processing images of specified internal tissues of the human body obtained through non-intrusive means for medical research purposes. It's an inverted reasoning metric of some sort. Medical pictures as a discipline include diagnostic imaging, radiology, endoscopy, medical thermography, medical photography, and microscopes. In the medical field, digital image processing is widely used. Even said, manual processing is still required for many of the strategies. Automatic picture segmentation and feature evaluation can help doctors diagnose and treat diseases with greater precision. This will help to improve performance and speed up the diagnosis procedure. Because of the varied image quality produced by equipment and dose, automatic medical image segmentation is problematic.

V. Sugumaran et al. (Eds.): AIR 2022, CCIS 1738, pp. 168–178, 2022.
https://doi.org/10.1007/978-3-031-23724-9_16

Medical imaging is a valuable source of information on anatomy and organ function in addition to diagnosing disorders. Image processing techniques have been combined with machine learning approaches to produce computer-aided diagnostic and decision-making skills in medical imaging. X-rays have the benefits of low cost and quick reproducibility [1, 2].

In the diagnosis of chest X-rays, pneumothorax is a common and straightforward recurring ailment. As a potentially life-threatening condition, pneumothorax necessitates prompt diagnosis and, in some cases, prompt treatment. This disorder develops when air escapes through the space between the lungs and the chest wall. A blunt trauma chest injury, some surgical procedures, or lung illness can all lead to pneumothorax. Shortness of breath or chest pain are common symptoms. When the pneumothorax is severe, a needle or tube is utilized to evacuate the excess air [3].

Pneumothorax disease can be categorized as shown Fig. 1.

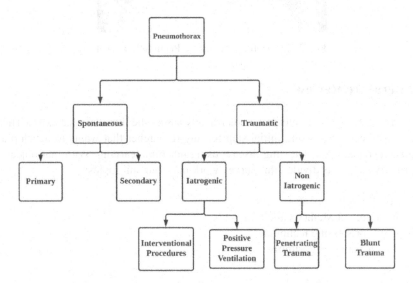

Fig. 1. Classification of Pneumothorax disease [2]

- Primary Pneumothorax- Primary spontaneous pneumothorax is most common in young, tall, and thin guys who have had no previous thoracic trauma or lung disease.
- Secondary Pneumothorax- Secondary pneumothorax is a type of spontaneous pneumothorax that happens whenever lung disease occurs. COPD, asthma, as well as tuberculosis are the root factors of secondary pneumothorax.
- Iatrogenic Pneumothorax- Iatrogenic pneumothorax is also referred to as traumatic pneumothorax, resulting in pleural injury, with air inserted into the pleural space secondary to medical diagnostic or therapeutic intervention, as shown in Fig. 2.

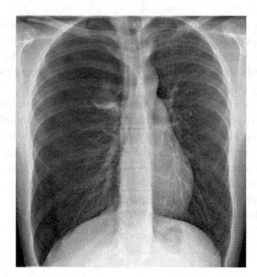

Fig. 2. Iatrogenic or traumatic Pneumothorax [3]

2   Literature Review

In this article, we outline, interpret, and critically assess the literature that exists. There-fore, it will become a strong initial step for any researcher that wants to develop and establish a standard for detecting disease using machine learning. With that objective, our primary subject is divided this survey work into four sub-topics:

- Datasets Survey;
- Survey based on Methods and findings;
- Image pre-processing technique;
- Machine learning Algorithms;

2.1   Datasets Survey

Datasets By their very nature, neural networks are data hungry. Data is considerably more important when it comes to Convolutional Neural Networks. It's not only about the quantity or number of training photographs; it's about the visual quality, subject relevance, and labelling quality as well. These parameters have a direct impact on the quality, accuracy, and performance of the models one tries to develop (depending on the application). Those factors become even more significant and important when the applied domain is Bioinformatics. Creating a high-quality medical picture collection takes a lot of time and effort, and many of them are not available to researchers publically.

2.2 Survey Based on Methods and Findings

The correctness of the ground truth labels is a highly critical and crucial feature of these datasets. It may be argued that it is the most crucial feature of a dataset. Even if a competent neural network can handle a few erroneous or irrelevant input data/images, it is common knowledge that training a model using inaccurate data will never yield accurate predictions.

2.3 Image Pre-processing Technique

Data does not always appear in the exact form that we desire. As a result, data pre-processing is a critical step in developing a high-quality machine learning model. These pre-processing approaches became more crucial with the rise of Convolutional Neural Networks than they were for prior machine learning techniques that incorporated processes like "feature extraction." Because CNNs execute their own feature extraction, the data we supply as input must be clean, and having the anticipated Region of Interest (ROI) on the image in contrast to the rest of the image is advantageous. This will have an impact on CNN's ability to learn "what we need it to learn." An innovative method for removing off-distribution samples from a dataset is proposed in Reference.

Image Enhancement. Experiments have demonstrated the importance of Image Enhancement methods in CNN Models. It evaluates and contrasts the ability of five different Image Enhancement approaches to improve model quality: SMQT (Successive Means Quantization Transform), CLAHE (Contrast Limited Adaptive Histogram Equalization), Adaptive Gamma Correction, Laplace Operator, and Wavelet Transform are all examples of transforms. The CLAHE and Laplace Operator approaches are shown to significantly improve the model's accuracies and recall rates.

Image Segmentation. There are three types of image segmentation methods: model-based, rule-based, and machine learning-based. A Model-based technique, such as Reference, is an example. Pixels and their features are the basis for ML algorithms. To segment images, shallow learning techniques such as Support Vector Machine (SVM) and Deep Neural Network (DNN) were commonly utilized. Shallow learning-based approaches rely on handcrafted features. Machine Learning-based approaches learn them automatically, obviating the need for human feature extraction stages, but this necessitates a large dataset. Rule-based approaches segment images according to a set of criteria based on shape, patterns/texture, colour intensities, pixel location, and pixel influence on other pixels in the image, whereas Machine Learning-based approaches learn them automatically, obviating the need for human feature extraction stages.

2.4 Machine Learning Algorithms

ML algorithms can learn a variety of patterns and relationships from supplied training data, both visible and invisible. There are two types of identification: supervised and unsupervised. Semi-supervised learning is a combination of these two approaches used by some algorithms. Humans affect ML models through supervised learning approaches, which involve training with expected outputs to associated inputs.

Unsupervised learning methods look for qualities in the input data on their own. Pathology Detection in Chest X-Rays is mostly accomplished by supervised training, in addition to the picture pre-processing techniques outlined in the previous section.

Survey related with Publicly available dataset, existing methods, and their results in Table 1.

Table 1. Summary sheet of publicly available dataset

Ref no	Type of disease	Method	Source	Image samples and modalities
[4]	Tuberculosis	Manual		10,848 DICOM Images
[5]	Cardiomegaly, Atelectasis, Tortuous, Aorta, Hypo-inflated Lung, Lung	Mixed	From Two Indian hospitals	Frontal and lateral view of 8,121 DICOM image
[6]	Lung Nodule	Manual	Collected from Japan (13 Centers) and US (1 Institute)	247 DICOM image Samples
[7]	Tuberculosis	Manual		138 PNG/DICOM Images
[8]	Enlarged Cardio	Automated	Beth Israel Deaconess	377,110 JPEG/DICOM Images

The images obtained using this algorithm and the results obtained by manual segmentation were compared and there were minor variations with visual observations. Thus, it can be concluded from the literature that no gold standard method exists, that can be used for lung segmentation from CT slices shown in Table 2.

Table 2. Survey based on findings of various researchers

Ref no	Method analysis	Findings
[9]	Ultrasound Sonography as an e-FAST method,	A hand-held device to conduct ultrasound for e-fast examination was used. The results shows the higher levels of sensitivity for ultrasound as compared to x-ray. Ultrasound was more sensitive in identifying occult traumatic pneumathoraces in comparison to xray
[10]	Ultrasonography, Pathophysiology	Worked out on a case study of an 83-year-old male with persistent underlying Pulmonary obstructive disorder. Initially, ultrasonography reported a "lung point sign" signalling a suspected pneumothorax. Further examination revealed the absence of pneumothorax, with a large bulla in the patient. Initially, ultrasonography reported a "lung point sign" signalling a suspected pneumothorax. Further examination revealed the absence of pneumothorax, with a large bulla in the patient. Author found that the "lung point sign" is not always indicative of a pneumothorax. At the end also discussed the significance of both clinical correlation and under-standing of the underlying pathophysiology
[11]	Phase Stretch Transform (PST),	Build a diagnostic assistance tool, demonstrated the use of PST for extracting and enhancing features of chest X-ray pictures. Edge detection in chest X-ray allows to detect a patient with pneumothorax with a higher precision to the limit of collapsed lung, which is otherwise difficult for a radiologist to find with a naked eye

(*continued*)

Table 2. (*continued*)

Ref no	Method analysis	Findings
[12]	Chest radiography	The study chose newborns to see if treating chest radiography (CR) diagnosed pneumothoraxes in infants receiving respiratory support with Needle aspiration findings resulted in fewer infants receiving CDs within 6 h of diagnosis. Researcher reported that Needle aspiration minimized the rate of Chest Drain intrusion in indicative CR pneumothorax new-borns. It can be used in diagnosable infants as the initial method of draining radiologically verified pneumothorax
[13]	Chest tomography	Study included the finding of Chest tomography method applied on patients who suffered from chest trauma but at that time patients was in stable condition. The results of this study indicated Pneumothorax with hemothoraces (13%) in 25 of the patients
[14]	Chest Radiography	To assist a physician in diagnosing a pneumothorax, a machine learning-based pneumothorax diagnosis technique from a chest radiography image is required. To efficiently classify relatively large chest radiography images, an ensemble model of identical 50-layer ResNet models with three-sized chest radiography images was created
[15]	ML Classifier	With the help of Web-based training, anesthesiologists can learn LUS for the aim of pneumothorax exclusion. When the need for training grows, this efficient and cost-effective option should be considered

A 3D histogram thresholding approach was paired with an edge-highlighting wavelet preprocessing step in the first stage. For cases of under segmentation, a supervised texture classification refinement stage utilizing an SVM classifier was applied in the second stage.

The construction of a machine learning system for the identification and categorization of pneumothorax, pleural effusion, normal, and CT slices impacted by other diseases is the third scientific contribution. Basic arithmetic and morphological procedures are used in the segmentation and ROI extraction techniques created. Along with the segmented lung, the pneumothorax region is present when the lung regions are segmented. This paper also includes algorithms for calculating the extent to which the lung has been impacted by the condition, which will show the severity of the disorder.

3 Discussions

Regardless of the radiologist's involvement, the merger of Chest X-Ray and ML has the benefit of attaining of frequent outcome, essentially following image restoration and when the patient is still confined on the inspection bed. This condition might conceivably play a role in tiny peripheral hospitals or places with radiological personnel shortages due to numerous causes, including a heavy load of pneumothorax patients, and could also act as aid during nighttime activities for new radiologists. In the situation of staff shortages and overburdening patient loads, a first reading from an AI-based instrument might drastically reduce wait times and enable quicker risk categorization. For a more thorough diagnosis later, a doctor will check up on the reading of the AI system. A basic preliminary diagnosis can be easily obtained as our ML algorithm is released as open source and only open-source photos have been used to construct it.

This has multiple consequences for acutely pressing patient numbers or worker shortages from low-income countries. In terms of diagnostic precision, our findings are only modestly inferior to those of a previously published study based on a much larger dataset, but the results cannot be meaningfully compared due to the distinct datasets. Nevertheless, according to seasoned radiologists, the diagnostic precision was comparable and even marginally superior, and our method did not require complicated pre-processing of lung segmentation compared to the aforementioned research, reducing the time needed to a minimum and substantially increasing the overall viability.

Since all the data used in this analysis is access-free and the ML model itself is also sponsored without access constraints, our ML classifier can be directly connected to more developments. Our findings suggest that, while also retaining high sensitivity and precision, the dynamic pre-processing stage of lung segmentation can be skipped. The drawbacks of the Chest X-Ray and machine learning system must be well understood, despite displaying good precision.

In identifying pneumothorax lesions, Chest X-Ray has shown high sensitivity [6]. In the other hand, pneumothorax demonstrates a wide variety of possible features of Chest X-Ray and indicates a heterogeneous presence of Chest X-Ray at different locations, as the distinguishing trait of variable density and fibrosis areas in extreme advanced and di advanced areas, Dispersed patchy or conglomerate field glass from single or multiple conglomerate ground glass, in the early stages of diffusing lung consolidation. We've also discovered that the majority of false-negative cases are newfangled-stage pneumothorax, while the majority of false-positive cases are pneumothorax pathologies, such as ground-glass opacities, that have some similarities to pneumothorax. Inui and colleagues reviewed Chest X-Ray photographs of 112 cases of RT-PCR-confirmed pneumothorax from the Diamond Princess Cruise ship. In less than 2/3rd (61 percent) of cases, chest lung opacities were present; 20 percent of emblematic patient shave negative chests, indicating that the Chest X-Ray results investigated (e.g., consolidations, ground-glass opacity) are not unique to pneumothorax. In general, the Chest X-Ray limitations are the limit for such ML models since the dataset is created by Chest X-Ray. Therefore, it is important to treat with care the general accuracy of ML models since it reflects the average output within the whole dataset and does not indicate difficulty in those subsets. Diagnostic precision is likely to be good if only early pictures of patients with pneumothorax (with ground glass as an identifying feature) are taken in one group and only pathologies with non-similar characteristics, such as lobar pneumonia, tumors and fibrosis, are given in the control group. The more cases of advanced stage pneumothorax (with consolidation and fibrosis) and associated non-pneumothorax pathologies are applied to the process, the lower the accuracy, precisely because some illnesses, such as some common cases of pneumonia, pulmonary toxicity, pneumonia organization, acute eosinophilic pneumonia, can have the same characteristics as pneumothorax. We included some pneumothorax-like pathologies in the planning, validation, and test data collection.

It is not omitted, however, that neural networks will extract characteristics of pneumothorax and pneumothorax-like pathologies that are invisible to the human eye on Chest X-Ray images and that will make a somewhat clearer differentiation between the two groups. A significantly broader sample would be suitable to test this theory, and more ML strategies such as multi-view fusion could be applied. On the one hand, our research is limited by the heterogeneous nature of the dataset, which is a result of many sources and a small number of images. The Machine learning technique, on the other hand, currently avoids analysing complete 3D datasets of DICOM pictures during publication. The reasoning for this was that much of the open access material was only usable as non-DICOM photographs containing slices of lung pathological changes. However, it is very feasible to expand the model to operate with volumes of expected comparable outcomes in terms of pneumothorax detection, as harbour pneumothorax is extremely unlikely to be an entirely negative Chest X-Ray slice (no densities/opacities). Though, in the clinical practice, 2D Machine learning models are critical for the approach of the assessment of pathological modifications in a lone slice regarding the risk of pneumothorax.

Although our findings suggest that the dynamic pre-processing step of lung segmentation can be skipped, the absence of lung segmentation can result in a perceived bias due to extra thoracic artefacts, such as ICU patient incubation tubes. And it's something you can't ignore.

4   Conclusion

The discussion in this paper was organized into four key sections. We looked examined practically all the current publicly available datasets of Chest X-Rays in the first segment.

A thorough examination of the datasets was also presented. We found how large-scale datasets may help the research community build high-quality DL models that produce consistent findings. Even if it is possible to collect millions of Chest X-Rays in a single day, labelling the data remains a challenge. Automated labelling is vital in developing complete annotated and useable datasets because manual labelling, while not ideal, is expensive and wasteful. Despite their higher potential, rule-based labellers presently beat ML-based labellers due to ML-based models' lack of training data. Then, we observed how various image processing techniques may help with the utilization of small-scale datasets in machine learning model training. However, as more large-scale datasets become available, DL algorithms, particularly well-performing CNN-based algorithms, are rapidly replacing manual processes like feature extraction. Attempts to construct unique CNN architectures, rather than attempting to build various new manual processing procedures, have been shown to be more effective in recent literature, allowing the algorithm to learn the "features" and how to ignore any noisy representations in the input data. As a result, in the DL research community, enthusiasm for developing new manual processing methodologies like feature extraction has gradually and increasingly been displaced by optimization and development of new DL-based algorithms.

The ribs around the lungs are not continuous in some CT slices, which was discovered during work on the extraction and classification of pleural effusion and pneumothorax. The pleural effusion region could not be retrieved in these cases, resulting in incorrect slice classification. As a result, the segmentation strategy can be refined further to improve classification results. Pleural illnesses include hemothorax, in which the pleural space is filled with blood, pyopneumothorax, in which the pleural cavity is filled with pus and air, and hydropneumothorax, in which the pleural cavity is filled with fluid and gas. This research can be used to classify disorders like hemothorax, pyopneumothorax, and hydropneumothorax.

References

1. Noppen, M., De Keukeleire, T.: Pneumothorax. Respiration **76**, 121–127 (2008). https://doi.org/10.1159/000135932
2. MacDuff, A., Arnold, A., Harvey, J.: Management of spontaneous pneumothorax: British Thoracic Society pleural disease guideline 2010. Thorax **65**, ii18–ii31 (2010). https://doi.org/10.1136/thx.2010.136986
3. Yarmus, L., Feller-Kopman, D.: Pneumothorax in the critically Ill patient. Chest **141**, 1098–1105 (2012). https://doi.org/10.1378/chest.11-1691
4. Ryoo, S., Kim, H.J.: Activities of the Korean institute of tuberculosis. Osong Public Health Res. Perspect. **5**, S43–S49 (2014). https://doi.org/10.1016/j.phrp.2014.10.007
5. Demner-Fushman, D., et al.: Preparing a collection of radiology examinations for distribution and retrieval. J. Am. Med. Inform. Assoc. **23**, 304–310 (2015). https://doi.org/10.1093/jamia/ocv080
6. Shiraishi, J., et al.: Development of a digital image database for chest radiographs with and without a lung nodule. Am. J. Roentgenol. **174**, 71–74 (2000). https://doi.org/10.2214/ajr.174.1.1740071
7. Jaeger, S., Candemir, S., Antani, S., Wáng, Y.X., Lu, P.X., Thoma, G.: Two public chest X-ray datasets for computer-aided screening of pulmonary diseases. Quant. Imaging Med. Surg. **4**(6), 475–477 (2014). https://doi.org/10.3978/j.issn.2223-4292.2014.11.20

8. Johnson, A.E.W., et al.: MIMIC-CXR, a de-identified publicly available database of chest radiographs with free-text reports. Sci. Data **6** (2019). https://doi.org/10.1038/s41597-019-0322-0

9. Kirkpatrick, A.W., et al.: Hand-held thoracic sonography for detecting post-traumatic pneumothoraces: the Extended Focused Assessment with Sonography for Trauma (EFAST). J. Trauma Acute Care Surg. **57**(2), 288–295 (2004)

10. Aziz, S.G., Patel, B.B., Ie, S.R., Rubio, E.R.: The lung point sign, not pathognomonic of a pneumothorax. Ultrasound Q. **32**, 277–279 (2016). https://doi.org/10.1097/ruq.000000000 0000199

11. Suthar, M., Mahjoubfar, A., Seals, K., Lee, E.W., Jalaii, B.: Diagnostic tool for pneumothorax. In: 2016 IEEE Photonics Society Summer Topical Meeting Series (SUM) (2016). https://doi.org/10.1109/phosst.2016.7548806

12. Murphy, M.C., et al.: Effect of needle aspiration of pneumothorax on subsequent chest drain insertion in newborns. JAMA Pediatr. **172**, 664 (2018). https://doi.org/10.1001/jamapediatrics.2018.0623

13. Abbasi, S., Farsi, D., Hafezimoghadam, P., Fathi, M., Zare, M.A.: Accuracy of emergency physician-performed ultrasound in detecting traumatic pneumothorax after a 2-h training course. Eur. J. Emerg. Med. **20**, 173–177 (2013). https://doi.org/10.1097/mej.0b013e328356 f754

14. Jun, T.J., Kim, D., Kim, D.: Automated diagnosis of pneumothorax using an ensemble of convolutional neural networks with multi-sized chest radiography images. arXiv preprint arXiv:1804.06821 (2018)

15. Edrich, T., et al.: A comparison of web-based with traditional classroom-based training of lung ultrasound for the exclusion of pneumothorax. Anesth. Analg. **123**(1), 123–128 (2016)

Analyzing Patient Reviews for Recommending Treatment Using NLP and Deep Learning-Based Approaches

Tauheed Shahid, Suraj Singh, Shatmanyu Gupta, and Shanu Sharma[✉] [ID]

Department of Computer Science and Engineering, ABES Engineering College, Ghaziabad,
India
{tauheed.18bcs1108,suraj.18bcs1028,
shatmanyu.18bcs1030}@abes.ac.in, shanu.sharma16@gmail.com

Abstract. Nowadays technological advancement can be seen in the medical field starting from medical devices, data collection, analysis to diagnosis and treatment recommendations for diseases. Drug and treatment recommendation is one of the most popular applications, which is now observed and used by everyone in this digital era. These types of recommendation systems usually require a huge set of data from the patients and an efficient Machine learning-based model to conclude significant insights that can help in the prediction of the best possible medications for a particular disease. The health-related recommendation systems can be proved as a significant tool in the healthcare sector for speeding up various decision-making processes such as health insurance, clinical pathway-based treatment methods, and assisting doctors by recommending drugs using a patient's health profile. People frequently utilize social media to explore their health issues, therefore there is now a wealth of information on social networks that may be leveraged to create various health-related recommendation systems. In this research, a deep learning-based based drug recommendation system using N-Gram is provided, which uses patient review data as input and sentiment analysis to choose the appropriate treatment for the ailment. The accuracy achieved, shows the efficacy of the proposed approach for the real time applicability of the model.

Keywords: Recommender system · Drugs recommendation · Deep learning · N-grams · Reviews

1 Introduction

In the past few years, health was the most discussed topic on the internet due to the Global Covid outbreak. Due to the lockdown and availability and popularity of the virtual space, almost all people were looking for health-related solutions on the internet [1]. Thus, the majority of people log on for health-associated troubles to educate themselves. On the other side, the young, as well as the old generation, is also searching out fitness-related facts on the web. At some point, part of the population is also involved in searching for similar stories to resolve or to assist their mental health-related issues [2]. Thus, it can

© The Author(s), under exclusive license to Springer Nature Switzerland AG 2022
V. Sugumaran et al. (Eds.): AIR 2022, CCIS 1738, pp. 179–190, 2022.
https://doi.org/10.1007/978-3-031-23724-9_17

be seen that nowadays, people are actively participating in sharing and discussing their health-related issues on the internet through various platforms, and thus a wide range of related data is available on the internet. This type of patient-related data available on social media can be proved as a significant tool in the healthcare sector such as suggesting health insurance, clinical pathway-based treatment methods, and drug recommendations based on the patient's health profile or assisting doctors [3].

A drug recommendation system is a framework for the healthcare sector that recommends the best drugs for a particular disease by analyzing data related to patients such as their background, reviews, other diseases, etc. [4, 5]. Any healthcare system requires studying huge data of the patients to conclude significant insights and help in the prediction of the best possible medications for the disease. With the advancements in machine learning (ML) and deep learning (DL) technologies, this huge amount of patient data can be used to extract meaningful insights for the betterment of the healthcare sector [6, 7]. Over the past decade, researchers have been analyzing the emotional impact of user experience and the severity of adverse drug reactions by extracting sentiment and semantic information from patient data [8, 9].

In this paper, a drug recommendation framework is proposed, and its operation is illustrated. The framework makes use of modern technologies, such as machine learning, natural language processing, sentiment analysis, etc., to uncover the interesting records that are hidden in the data and minimize medical errors made by doctors when prescribing medications. A database module, data preparation, data visualization, recommendation, and a section for model evaluation make up the proposed framework's many modules. The publicly accessible dataset on Kaggle [10] is used to create the suggested recommender architecture using machine learning N-Gram and Lightgbm algorithms. The main objective of the proposed work is to provide an optimized model for the medication suggestion framework to achieve the measurements like great exactness, adaptability, and proficiency.

With the goal of offering a better platform for the automation of Drug Recommendation, the work on the proposed system is presented as Sect. 2 represents the background and related work present on the Drug Recommendation System. Section 3 represents the adopted methodologies for the proposed system. Section 4 represents the outcome of our proposed system and the last section i.e.; Sect. 5 represents the conclusion and future scope of the presented work.

2 Background and Related Work

In today's era, the most significant and researched topic on the internet is health care or health-related information. In this digital space, everyone is looking for quick solutions, so the majority of people go online for health-related issues to educate themselves [1]. Nearly 60% of adults, according to a study [2], look online for adequate health information, with 35% of respondents focusing solely on online illness diagnosis. Previous studies have also shown that users are often looking for stories from "patients like them" on the Internet, which is hard to find among their friends and family [3, 4]. This kind of affected person-related facts available on social media may be proved as a substantial tool in the healthcare area from a specific point of perspective including health insurance, clinical pathway-based remedy strategies, and other drugs primarily based on the affected person's fitness profile or assisting doctors.

To draw important conclusions and aid in the prediction of the best treatments for a condition, a healthcare system needs to analyze vast amounts of patient data. With the development of machine learning (ML) and deep learning (DL) technologies, it is now possible to use this enormous amount of patient data to derive insightful information that will improve the healthcare industry [6, 7]. By collecting sentiment and semantic data from patient data, researchers have spent the last ten years examining the emotional influence of user experience and the severity of adverse drug reactions [8, 9].

For as long as decade, analysts have been examining the enthusiastic effect of client experience and the seriousness of antagonistic medication responses by extricating feeling and semantic data [11]. Past examinations have shown that wellbeing-related client-produced content is helpful according to various perspectives. One of the benchmark papers in this space was composed by Jane Sarasohn-Kahn [2]. It expresses that clients are regularly searching for stories from "patients like them" on the Internet, which is elusive among their loved ones. For as long as decade, analysts have been examining the enthusiastic effect of client experience and the seriousness of antagonistic medication responses by extricating feeling and semantic data [12, 15]. Leilei Sun [1] inspected enormous scope treatment records to find the best treatment solution for patients. The thought was to utilize a productive semantic bunching calculation assessing the similitudes between treatment records. In like manner, the creator made a system to evaluate the sufficiency of the proposed treatment. This construction can endorse the best treatment regimens to new patients according to their segment areas what's more, unexpected problems. An Electronic Medical Record (EMR) of patients assembled from various centers for testing. The outcome shows that this system further develops the fix rate. Xiaohong Jiang et al. [1] analyzed three unmistakable calculations, choice tree calculation, support vector machine (SVM), and backpropagation brain network on treatment information. SVM was picked for the drug proposition module as it performed really well in every one of the three novel limits - model precision, model capability, model adaptability. Furthermore, proposed the slip-up actually take a look at framework to guarantee investigation, accuracy and organization quality.

Because of an absence of trust and nature of client communicated clinical language, broad examination in the clinical and wellbeing area has not been finished [13, 14]. Along these lines, we expect to construct a stage where patients and clinicians can look by side effects and get drug proposals, symptoms of medications and acquire bits of knowledge into patients' portfolio.

3   Proposed Framework

The pipeline used to develop the proposed drug recommendation framework is presented in Fig. 1.

Fig. 1. Process for the development of proposed framework

3.1 Dataset Description

The dataset used in the experiments is a patient medication survey dataset containing ascribes like unique Id, drug name, condition (disease of the patient), date, helpful count, audits, and appraisals given by the patient as shown in Table 1.

Table 1. Data heads and their attributes

Attributes	Description of attribute	Type of attributes
DrugName	It is a categorical attribute which specifies the name of the drug prescribed by the practitioner	Categorical
Condition	It is a categorical attribute which states that in which condition or disease the drug is prescribed by the practitioner	Categorical
Review	It is the text review given by patient about the drug	Text
Rating	It is the overall patient satisfaction score	Numerical
Date	It is a date attribute which tells the date of entry of review	Date
Useful count	It is the number of patients that find the review useful	Numerical

3.2 Data Understanding and Pre-processing

It comprises of dataset collection, reviewing, cleaning and dataset preprocessing. The real-world information is raw information which can be splitted and unorganized and is unable to be used for training of the model. So, information cleaning is used to

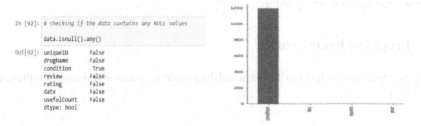

Fig. 2. Checking and counting null values

clean information. It consists of null/missing values processing, correlation analysis and removing duplicate data. The result is presented in Fig. 2.

Data Exploration: Following steps are followed during Data Exploration

(i) Analyzing patient ids to check if a patient has written more than one review
(ii) Find count of drugs for each condition by analyzing condition and quantity of drugs.

Data Cleaning; Following steps are followed during Data Cleaning

(i)   Find the count of missing or empty fields for all the dimensions.
(ii) These none values can be removed, ignored or filled so the rows with missing values can be deleted.
(iii) Remove the redundancy in the dataset to normalize the data
(iv) Delete the rows with only drug as only one drug is unable to recommend the best one.
(v)   Words like don't need, never, etc. should be removed from stop words as they don't possess any specific results about the attitude of review. At last removal of stop words is done to clean the reviews.

3.3 Data Visualization

Data Visualization is the process to visualize the data and relationships among different attributes and how one attribute depends on the other Some snapshots of relationships of attributes are shown below:

(i) Standard Data Cleaning techniques are applied to look at invalid qualities, copy columns, eliminating anomalies, and text from lines in this examination. Hence, eliminated each of the 1200 invalid qualities lines in the conditions segment.
(ii) Figure 3 shows top conditions with maximum number of drug available. After removing conditions that have no meaning, the dataset reduces to 212141 rows.

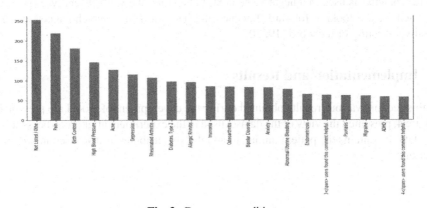

Fig. 3. Drugs per conditions

3.4 Approaches

Sentiment Analysis-Sentiment analysis is a technique for NLP that determines the emotional undertone of a body of text. This is a common method used by companies to gather and classify opinions. To mine text for sentiment and subjective information, it uses data mining, machine learning, and artificial intelligence. In Sentiment Analysis, predefined labels positive or negative is given to text document [16].

N-gram model-N-grams are a chunk of subsequent words, by studying these sequences we can efficiently understand the context in which a particular word is used. Example – the word 'book' can be used in different contexts like – to 'book' tickets, read the 'book'. Here the word book is used as the verb in the first phrase while as a noun in the latter. So, in order to efficiently understand the context of the word, N-grams look at the after the word and before the word and then determine if the word is used as a noun or verb in the sentence or in other context. N in N-grams denotes the number of words machine will look at before and after the target word. Ex- This 'book', A 'book', Your 'book' are all examples of bi-grams where before word 'book' is a noun. Bi-grams are the two pairs of words to look at before and after the target word while sliding over the words. The context can be extended by going to tri-grams which means looking at three pairs of words before and after the target word [17, 18].

Feeling investigation helps assessing the exhibition of items or administrations from client created substance. Vocabulary based opinion investigation approaches are liked 28 over learning-based ones when preparing information isn't satisfactory. Existing vocabularies contain just unigrams alongside their feeling scores. It is seen that opinion n-grams shaped by joining unigrams with intensifiers or invalidations show further developed outcomes. Such opinion n-gram vocabularies are not openly accessible. This paper presents a procedure to make such a vocabulary called Senti-N-Gram. Proposed rule-based methodology removes the n-grams opinion scores from an irregular corpus containing item surveys and relating numeric rating in 10-point scale. The scores from this computerized system are contrasted and that of the human annotators utilizing ttest and viewed as genuinely same N-grams can also be used to capture words in positive or negative context or viceversa. Example – 'the staff were not friendly, terrible really'. In this sentence 'Not friendly' and 'friendly terrible' is enough context to elucidate that the word 'friendly' is used in a negative context. In isolation the word 'friendly' is positive in when we are looking forward 'terrible' and backward 'not' which cancels out the positive meaning of the word [19, 20].

4 Implementation and Results

In this section, various results obtained during the development of model are presented. Figure 4, presented the view of the dataset used in the experiment after pre-processing of the data. It contains the patient unique Id and the six attributes as discussed in previous section.

```
# checing the sample of new dataset
data.sample(5)
```

	uniqueID	drugName	condition	review	rating	date	usefulCount
112607	170298	Quetiapine	Generalized Anxiety Disorde	"\n\n\n please tell the ones who is sufferin...	10	25-Jul-16	45
141096	136119	Acamprosate	Alcohol Dependence	"I was a two bottle plus red wine drinker ever...	9	28-Jan-14	97
35338	170518	Quetiapine	Bipolar Disorde	"I have been taking seroquel for a little over...	10	8-Oct-15	16
26858	209685	Lupron Depot	Endometriosis	"I started this about 6 -7 weeks ago after lap...	8	11-Oct-16	10
121226	122848	Linaclotide	Constipation, Chronic	"I've had chronic constipation for as lon...	9	23-Mar-14	113

Fig. 4. Dataset description

Some of the results obtained during visualization of the dataset are presented in Fig. 5 and 6, which shows the popular drugs, and most common conditions among patients respectively.

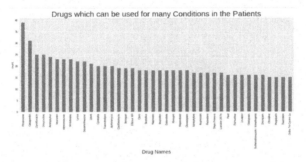

Fig. 5. Popular drugs

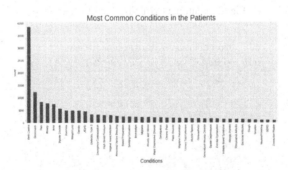

Fig. 6. Most common conditions in patients

Furthermore, during sentiment analysis of reviews, the world cloud of all reviews is presented in Fig. 7, followed by the world cloud of positive and negative reviews in Fig. 9 and 10 respectively. The weightage of positive and negative reviews is presented in Fig. 8.

After the classification of positive and negative sentiments, the analysis through 1–4 g is performed to check that which corpus best classifies the emotions. After analysis of

Fig. 7. World cloud of reviews

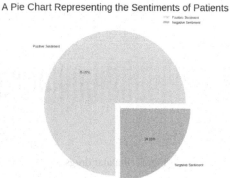

Fig. 8. Sentiment visualization of patients

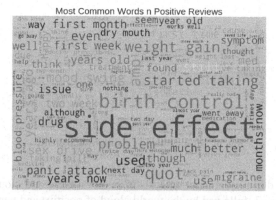

Fig. 9. World cloud of positive reviews

1–4 g, it has been observed that 4-g classifies emotions much better than other grams, thus 4 g is used for further processing.

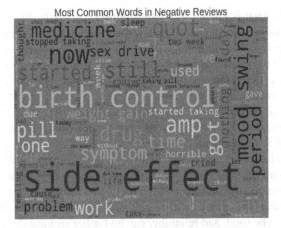

Fig. 10. World cloud of negative reviews

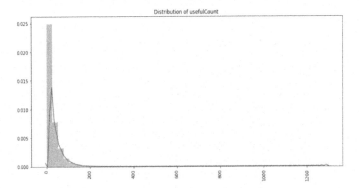

Fig. 11. Distribution of useful counts

From the distribution of useful Count shown in Fig. 11, it can be observed that the contrast between least and greatest is 1291, which is high. Likewise, the deviation is gigantic, which is 36. The justification behind this is that the more medications individuals search for, the more individuals read the survey regardless of whether their items are fortunate or unfortunate, which makes the most of the help exceptionally high. Thus, when designing the model, standardization is done on conditions.

Furthermore, for the prediction of reviews through sentiment analysis, various ML models have been used and tested such as Random Forest, Naïve Bayes, and Linear Regression. For this purpose, the raw text of the review is converted into a numeric data representation through a vectorization approach so that it can be used by a numerical classifier. Vectorization is done via the TF-IDF method which involves creating tokens (i.e. individual words or groups of words extracted from the text). Once the list of tokens is created, they are assigned an index integer identifier which allows them to be listed. It can help in providing the count of number of words in the document and normalize them in such a way that de-emphasizes words that appear frequently (like "a", "the", etc.). This creates what is known as a bag (multiset) of words. Such a representation associates a real-valued vector to each review representing the importance of the tokens (words) in the review. This represents the entire corpus of reviews as a large matrix where each row of the matrix represents one of the reviews and each column represents a token occurrence. Term-Frequency Inverse Document-Frequency (TF-IDF) is a way of handling the excessive noise due to words such as "a", "the", "he", "she", etc. Clearly such common words will appear in many reviews, but do not provide much insight into the sentiment of the text and their high frequency tends to obfuscate words that provide significant insight into sentiment.

For emotion analysis using a word dictionary, deep learning with an n-gram app-roach is used, where Harvard emotional dictionary is adopted. For feature analysis idea of attempting to derive importance out of the vectorized features by k-clustering by sim-ilarity. To compensate the limitation of natural language processing, Lightgbm machine learning model can be used, and reliability can be further secured through useful count The accuracy of the various tested models is presented in Table 2, and the output of the prediction task for a particular condition is presented in Fig. 12.

condition	drugName	total_pred mean
ADHD	Adderall	0.070960
	Adderall XR	0.042328
	Adzenys XR-ODT	0.010250
	Amantadine	0.011098
	Amphetamine	0.013925
	Amphetamine / dextroamphetamine	0.046908
	Aptensio XR	0.005885
	Armodafinil	0.028856
	Atomoxetine	0.047597
	Bupropion	0.083736
	Catapres	0.044449
	Clonidine	0.059211
	Concerta	0.059579
	Cylert	0.014713
	Daytrana	0.031764
	Desoxyn	0.133611
	Desvenlafaxine	0.006131
	Dexedrine	0.064658
	Dexmethylphenidate	0.041450
	Dextroamphetamine	0.052630
	Dextrostat	0.045610
	Dyanavel XR	0.016457
	Evekeo	0.008692
	Focalin	0.046282
	Focalin XR	0.044685
	Guanfacine	0.070408
	Intuniv	0.078066
	Kapvay	0.127024
	Lisdexamfetamine	0.045679
	Metadate CD	0.037710

Fig. 12. Prediction results

Table 2. Accuracy of tested models

Vectorizer	Model	Accuracy
TF-IDF	Linear regression	78.2%
	Naive Bayes	75.2%
	Random forest	83.1%
	N-Gram based model	89.4

5   Conclusion and Future Work

Reviews have now become part of our daily life, such as E-commerce reviews, Restaurant Reviews, fashion reviews, etc. Inspired by this, Sentiment Analysis on drug reviews is presented in this paper, where various ML-based approaches have been used to analyze the sentiments behind patient reviews to recommend drugs for a particular condition using Sentiment Analysis on Reviews. The result shows the Deep Learning frame work using N gram achieved an accuracy of 89.4%. As future work productivity of proposal framework can be expanded by including age of the individual, segment data during the preparation stage. Additionally, the brand and the substance contents accessible in the medication can work on the suggested prescriptions.

References

1. Sun, L., Liu, C., Guo, C., Xiong, H., Xie, Y.: Data-driven automatic treatment regimen development and recommendation. In: Proceedings of the 22nd ACM SIGKDD International Conference on Knowledge Discovery and Data Mining (2016). https://doi.org/10.1145/2939672.2939866
2. Sarasohn-Kahn, J.: The Wisdom of Patients: Health Care Meets Online Social Media (2008)
3. Guidelines for Telemedicine. https://www.mohfw.gov.in/pdf/Telemedicine.pdf Accessed 20 Dec 2021
4. Shani, G., Gunawardana, A.: Evaluating recommendation systems. In: Ricci, F., Rokach, L., Shapira, B., Kantor, P. (eds.) Recommender Systems Handbook, pp. 257–297. Springer, Boston (2011). https://doi.org/10.1007/978-0-387-85820-3_8
5. Bao, Y., Jiang, X.: An intelligent medicine recommender system framework. In: IEEE 11th Conference on Industrial Electronics and Applications (ICIEA), June 2016. https://doi.org/10.1109/iciea.2016.7603801
6. Park, D.H., Kim, H.K., Choi, I.Y., Kim, J.K.: A literature review and classification of recommender systems research. Expert Syst. Appl. **39**(11), 10059–10072 (2012). https://doi.org/10.1016/j.eswa.2012.02.038
7. Mu, R.: A survey of recommender systems based on deep learning. IEEE Access **6**, 69009–69022 (2018). https://doi.org/10.1109/ACCESS.2018.2880197
8. Calero Valdez, A., Ziefle, M., Verbert, K., Felfernig, A., Holzinger, A.: Recommender systems for health informatics: state-of-the-art and future perspectives. In: Holzinger, A. (ed.) Machine Learning for Health Informatics. LNCS (LNAI), vol. 9605, pp. 391–414. Springer, Cham (2016). https://doi.org/10.1007/978-3-319-50478-0_20

9. Fernandez-luque, L., Karlsen, R., Vognild, L.K.: Challenges and opportunities of using recommender systems for personalized health education. Stud. Health Technol. Inform. **150**(903), 903–907 (2009)

10. Drug Review Data Set. https://www.kaggle.com/datasets/jessicali9530/kuc-hackathon-winter-2018. Accessed 12 Jan 2022

11. Goel, V., Gupta, A.K., Kumar, N.: Sentiment analysis of multilingual Twitter data using natural language processing. In: 8th International Conference on Communication Systems and Network Technologies (CSNT), Bhopal, India, pp. 208–212 (2018). https://doi.org/10.1109/CSNT.2018.8820254

12. Shimada, K., et al.: Drug-recommendation system for patients with infectious diseases. In: AMIA Annual Symposium Proceedings, p. 1112 (2005). PMID: 16779399; PMCID: PMC1560833

13. Pandey, S.C.: Data mining techniques for medical data: a review. In: 2016 International Conference on Signal Processing, Communication, Power and Embedded System (SCOPES), pp. 972–982 (2016). https://doi.org/10.1109/SCOPES.2016.7955586

14. Tekade, T.N., Emmanuel, M.: Probabilistic aspect mining approach for interpretation and evaluation of drug reviews. In: International Conference on Signal Processing, Communication, Power and Embedded System (SCOPES), Paralakhemundi, pp. 1471–1476 (2016). https://doi.org/10.1109/SCOPES.2016.7955684

15. Doulaverakis, C., Nikolaidis, G., Kleontas, A., Kompatsiaris, I.: GalenOWL: ontology-based drug recommendations discovery. J. Biomed. Semant. **3**(1), 14 (2012). https://doi.org/10.1186/2041-1480-3-14

16. Popescu, A.-M., Etzioni, O.: Extracting product features and opinions from reviews. In: Kao, A., Poteet, S.R. (eds.) Natural Language Processing and Text Mining, pp. 9–28. Springer, London (2007). https://doi.org/10.1007/978-1-84628-754-1_2

17. Gopalakrishnan, V., Ramaswamy, C.: Patient opinion mining to analyze drugs satisfaction using supervised learning. J. Appl. Res. Technol. **15**(4), 311–319 (2017). https://doi.org/10.1016/j.jart.2017.02.005

18. Gräßer, F., Kallumadi, S., Malberg, H., Zaunseder, S.: Aspect-based sentiment analysis of drug reviews applying cross-domain and cross-data learning. In: Proceedings of the 2018 International Conference on Digital Health, April 2018. https://doi.org/10.1145/3194658.3194677

19. Ozsoy, M.G., Özyer, T., Polat, F., Alhajj, R.: Realizing drug repositioning by adapting a recommendation system to handle the process. BMC Bioinform. **19**(1) (2018). https://doi.org/10.1186/s12859-018-2142-1

20. Leveraging N-grams to Extract Context From Text. https://towardsdatascience.com/leveraging-n-grams-to-extract-context-from-text-bdc576b47049. Accessed 10 Mar 2022

IoT Based Low-Cost Pulse Oximeter for Remote Health Monitoring

Sajal Kumar Babu Degala$^{(\boxtimes)}$ ⓘ, Ramesh Pandey ⓘ, Ashutosh Mishra ⓘ,
Abhishek Kumar Tiwari ⓘ, and Ravi Prakash Tewari ⓘ

Department of Applied Mechanics, Motilal Nehru National Institute of Technology Allahabad,
Prayagraj, UP, India
sajal.kumar3@gmail.com, {ramesh,amishra,aktiwari,
rptewari}@mnnit.ac.in

Abstract. In the Remote Health monitoring system measurement of heart rate and oxygen saturation (SpO2) are the most important parameters needed to be monitored. Effective measurement of these parameters may reduce the risk of sudden death or heart stroke and other diseases. In this paper, we developed a low-cost pulse oximeter which can measure SpO2 level and Heart rate with the best accuracy and transmit these data to a secure server where the data is stored and can be accessed by a medical practitioner. Both Heartrate and SpO2 are measured using a single customized Pulse oxygen sensor module. The sensor module is developed by using components such as BP34 Photodiode, and CA3140AEZ Operational Amplifier for detecting and measuring SpO2 and Heart rate values. By using above said components cost of the developed oximeter gets reduced and accuracy has been improved. The data transmission from the sensor to the Cloud server is done by using hypertext transfer protocols (HTTPS) protocol to defend data from security loopholes.

Keywords: Health monitoring · Low cost · IoT · HTTPS · Cloud server · Pulse oximeter · Telemedicine

1 Introduction

India is the world's second-biggest country by population and the world's largest democracy. However, it lags many other countries in terms of delivering health care to both urban and rural populations. For better infrastructure, 75% of qualified doctors practice in urban regions, whereas 70% of India's population suffers from weak rural healthcare facilities [1]. The use of emerging technologies to improve healthcare infrastructure is critical. In the coming years, emerging technologies such as blockchain-based electronic medical records and mobile apps will revolutionize the way healthcare is delivered. The utilization of IoT in healthcare is anticipated to reach $409.9 billion by 2022. In 2020, the global IoT market in the healthcare industry is had grown at a rate of over 37% [2].

Blood oxygen saturation indicates the fraction of arterial haemoglobin that is saturated with oxygen. Pulse oximetry can be performed using two non-invasive techniques:

V. Sugumaran et al. (Eds.): AIR 2022, CCIS 1738, pp. 191–198, 2022.
https://doi.org/10.1007/978-3-031-23724-9_18

transmission and reflectance (SpO2). The Pulse Oximetry (SpO2) method is commonly used as a standard for determining a person's health status by measuring the amount of oxygen dissolved in their blood. Abnormal dissolved O2 levels are detected in patients with health problems like pneumonia, cardiovascular illnesses, and asthma, and they're also used to check for potential abnormalities in new born babies [3]. Other methods for measuring SpO2 and pulse rate are either prohibitively expensive, inconvenient, or time-consuming. Arterial Blood Gas analysis produces less desirable SpO2 (arterial oxygen saturation) measurements that are not the same as the more desirable SpO2 (peripheral oxygen saturation) findings (ABG test). This ABG test provides an accurate assessment of arterial gases such as carbon dioxide and oxygen, but it's an invasive test which requires blood needed to be extracted from the artery of a patient and is an expensive procedure that is normally performed in intensive-care facilities. The secure, non-invasive, adaptive, and low-cost pulse oximeter technique is effective since the SpO2 measures correspond well enough with actual SpO2 values, as proved in this case.

2 Related Work

Many research works have been carried out that focus on developing IoT-based Pulse Oximeter using different sensors and Communication Protocols. Patient monitoring was designed using wireless technology by Sagar R Patil et al. [4] Sensors were used to keep track of patients' vital parameters. The downside was that the obtained values were inaccurate, and the output was skewed. Anil, Maradugu et al. [5] propose a system in which by using an android application, various biological characteristics of the patient's body, such as SpO2, temperature and heart rate were transferred to a web server, where the medical practitioner can access information from a remote location without having to be present at the centre. With the wireless monitor, Nubenthan et al. [6] designed a system for surveillance of dengue patients. The mobile-based application was cited as a drawback in this system since data from sensors was not sent via GSM modules. Using wireless technologies, Kathikamani R et al. created a [7] patient health monitoring system. The information collected is kept in a cloud server and analyzed. The disadvantage was that it was on localhost rather than using the web service application peripheral interface. Dong et al. [8] created a portable device for atrial blood pressure monitoring, however, it didn't preserve medical data for further study. Aadil et al. [9] proposed a wireless body area network (WBAN) for remote health monitoring that made use of the Internet of Things. To assess blood oxygen levels in athletes, Fu et al. [10] used a sensor network and a Wireless data transmission protocol, although this article only looks at one health indicator, making comprehensive health monitoring impossible.

3 Materials and Method

Figure 1 shows the schematic diagram of the designed Pulse Oxygen Sensor module. This module consists of Red and Infrared LED, CA3140AEZ Op Amp, BPW34 PIN Photodiode, OLED Display, ESP8266 Wi-Fi Module and ATMega328P 5V Microcontroller. The explanation and Purpose of each block are explained separately which gives a clear idea about the designed Pulse Oxygen Sensor. All the components used here are low in cost which makes the overall pulse oximeter economical. The selection of components is done in such a way that the overall gives better accuracy when compared to existing systems.

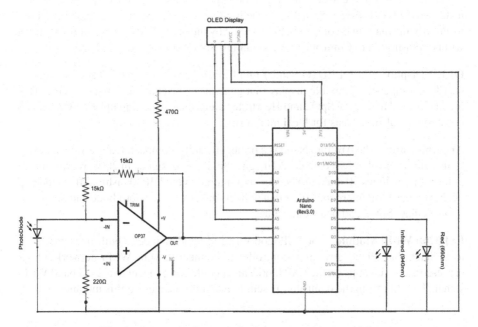

Fig. 1. Schematic diagram of pulse oxygen sensor module.

3.1 Hardware

This section explains briefly about different components used in the development of the Pulse oxygen sensor module.

Infrared and Red LED. To measure pulse oxygen level and Heart rate we need two lights of 660 nm and 940 nm wavelength. At 660 nm Red light will be emitted and at 940 nm infrared light will be emitted so these two different lights were used in our module. The reason for employing two different wavelengths is that oxygenated hemoglobin absorbs more infrared light whereas deoxygenated hemoglobin absorbs more red light. Depending up on the absorbance of these lights SpO2 and heart rate values can be estimated.

Light transmitted is measured using a detector (or) Photodiode.

BPW34 Photodiode. The BPW34 is a PIN photodiode in a tiny, flat, top-view, clear plastic container with high speed and high radiant sensitivity. It is sensitive to near-infrared and visible light. Photodiode detects both red and infrared light transmitted through the finger or ear lobe. This detected signal has useful data that will help in the calculation of SpO2 and heart rate values.

CA3140AEZ Operational Amplifier. The CA3140AEZ is a BiMOS Operational Amplifier with MOSFET input/bipolar output. On a single monolithic chip, it combines the benefits of high voltage PMOS and high voltage bipolar transistors. High input impedance, low input current, and high speed performance are provided by gate protected MOSFET (PMOS) transistors in the input circuit. Op-Amp in our module is used to amplify the magnitude of the signal detected by the photodiode. This amplified signal will be transmitted to Controller for calculating SpO2 and Heartrate values.

OLED Display. The OLED (Organic Light Emitting Diode) is an LCD alternative. The OLED is a super-thin, flexible display that generates a brighter and crisper image. This module is used to display SpO2 and Heartrate values that are getting uploaded to a cloud server on a real-time basis for local monitoring.

Arduino Nano. The Arduino Nano is a project friendly, compact, feature-rich, and versatile Microcontroller based on the ATmega328p. It was designed in 2008 by Arduino.cc in Italy and includes 30 male I/O headers configured in the DIP30 fashion. It is made up of an Atmega 328P microcontroller that collects data from the photodiode and processes it to calculate SpO2 and heart rate values.

ESP8266 Wi-Fi Module. The ESP8266 Wi-Fi Module includes a built-in TCP/IP protocol stack that allows any microcontroller to connect to your Wi-Fi network. Other processors can run apps on the ESP8266. This module can connect to a 2.5G band Wi-Fi signal. The data from the controller is sent to a cloud server using this module.

3.2 Flow Chart and Working

Figure 2 shows a flow chart that explains the working of the IoT-based Pulse Oximeter which will measure SpO2 and heart rate and transmit data from the controller to a cloud server.

Initially when the Pulse oximeter is started, and the finger is placed on the sensor module detects the finger and initiates the controller. Red and Infrared light passes through the finger and depending on oxygenated and deoxygenated hemoglobin some part of the light will get observed and the remaining light reaches the photodiode. The value of the amount of light detected by the photodiode will be transmitted to the controller and depending on light intensity values controller will calculate SpO_2 and heart rate. After calculating the values, the controller connects to a Wi-Fi network using the ESP8266 Wi-Fi module and starts sending data to a cloud server while also displaying the SpO_2 and heart rate on an OLED display.

Data encryption is done by controller before sending data to cloud server. Encryption is done by adding a private key to the data. The same private key is stored on the serverside which helps in the decryption of data once the data is received from controller. The need for encryption of data is to protect it from security loopholes like unnecessary open ports of devices which will help the attacker to access data. The encrypted data is transmitted to the server using a post request. The server used in our model is HostGator's paid VPS Server which is one of the best servers in terms of security and uptime. Once data is successfully transmitted to the server this data is decrypted by matching the private

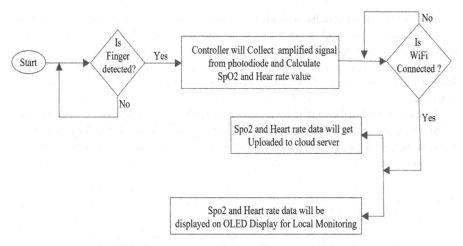

Fig. 2. Flow chart of IoT-based pulse oximeter.

key in the sent data with the private key stored on the server-side. After decryption, the data is stored, and this stored data can be accessed at any time by the medical practitioner by logging in to the server using credentials provided to them. The medical practitioner can also view data on a real-time basis in the form of graphs and values along with timestamp. Medical practitioner can also generate of data in the server.

4   Results and Discussion

A developed pulse oximeter provides very accurate readings when compared to existing pulse oximeters. Figure 3 shows the output of the Pulse oximeter.

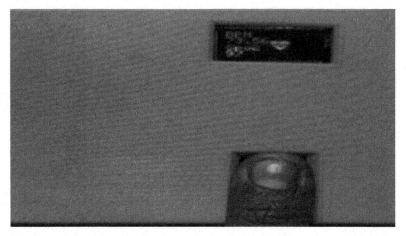

Fig. 3. Developed IoT-based pulse oximeter showing SpO$_2$ and heart rate values.

To test the designed pulse oximeter 10 different healthy subjects were selected and for each subject, SpO$_2$ and Heart rate were measured using the Designed Pulse oximeter and portable Oximeter available on the market. The comparison of measured values was plotted as shown in Fig. 4 and Fig. 5 both SpO$_2$ and Heart rate values were very close. Results clearly show that by using a customized sensor module best accuracy has been obtained.

It is also found that by using own customized pulse oxygen sensor the speed of data transmission from IoT device to cloud server has also increased. As the data transmitted to the server is encrypted changes in data leaking because of security loopholes are also eliminated.

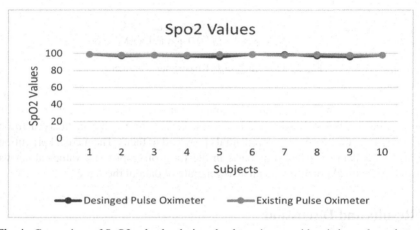

Fig. 4. Comparison of SpO2 value by designed pulse oximeter with existing pulse oximeter

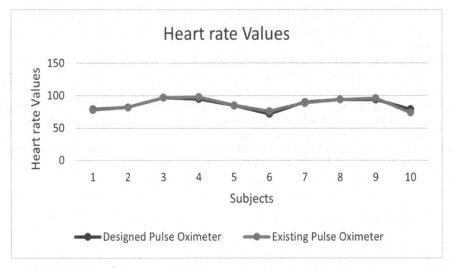

Fig. 5. Comparison of heartrate by designed pulse oximeter with existing pulse oximeter.

5 Conclusion

In the real world, our proposed pulse oximeter could be used in IoT and embedded systems. Using Internet of Things technologies, this system might be used to monitor heartbeat and SpO2. The results were compared to those obtained using a portable oxygen meter available in the market. Our developed oximeter provided the best accuracy as we see in Figs. 4 and 5. After obtaining the data, the portal displays the SpO2 level and the heartbeat with the date and time of measurement. The cost developed model is also very less as components used in development are economical. This system uses local Wi-Fi communication, and cloud-based remote monitoring to monitor the heartbeat and SpO2.

References

1. Semwal, N., Mukherjee, M., Raj, C., Arif, W.: An IoT based smart e-health care system. J. Inf. Optim. Sci. **40**, 1787–1800 (2019). https://doi.org/10.1080/02522667.2019.1703269
2. Akkaş, M.A., Sokullu, R., Ertürk Çetin, H.: Healthcare and patient monitoring using IoT. Internet Things **11**, 100173 (2020). https://doi.org/10.1016/j.iot.2020.100173
3. Ewer, A., et al.: Pulse oximetry as a screening test for congenital heart defects in newborn infants: a test accuracy study with evaluation of acceptability and cost-effectiveness. Health Technol. Assess. **16**, 1–184 (2012). https://doi.org/10.3310/hta16020
4. Priya, B., Rajendran, S., Bala, R., Gobbi, R.: Remote wireless health monitoring systems. In: 2009 Innovative Technologies in Intelligent Systems and Industrial Applications (2009). https://doi.org/10.1109/citisia.2009.5224177
5. Kumar, M.A., Sekhar, Y.R.: Android based health care monitoring system. In: 2015 International Conference on Innovations in Information, Embedded and Communication Systems (ICIIECS) (2015). https://doi.org/10.1109/iciiecs.2015.7192877
6. Nubenthan, S., Ravichelvan, K.: A wireless continuous patient monitoring system for dengue; Wi-Mon. In: 2017 International Conference on Wireless Communications, Signal Processing and Networking (WiSPNET) (2017). https://doi.org/10.1109/wispnet.2017.8300150

7. Bell, A., Rogers, P., Farnell, C., Sparkman, B., Smith, S.C.: Wireless patient monitoring system. In: 2014 IEEE Healthcare Innovation Conference (HIC) (2014). https://doi.org/10.1109/hic.2014.7038896

8. Ferretto, L.R., et al.: A physical activity recommender system for patients with arterial hypertension. IEEE Access **8**, 61656–61664 (2020). https://doi.org/10.1109/access.2020.2983564

9. Aadil, F., Mehmood, B., Ul Hasan, N., Lim, S., Ejaz, S., Zaman, N.: Remote health monitoring using IoT-based smart wireless body area network. Comput. Mater. Continua **68**, 2499–2513 (2021). https://doi.org/10.32604/cmc.2021.014647

10. Fu, Y., Liu, J.: System design for wearable blood oxygen saturation and pulse measurement device. Proc. Manuf. **3**, 1187–1194 (2015). https://doi.org/10.1016/j.promfg.2015.07.197

Machine Learning and Deep Learning Enabled Applications in Different Sectors

Development of Homogenous Cross-Project Defect Prediction Model Using Artificial Neural Network

Abhishek Gautam[(⊠)] [iD], Anant Gupta, Bharti Singh, Ashwajit Singh,
and Shweta Meena

Delhi Technological University, Delhi, India
abhigautamls29@gmail.com, {bhartisingh,shwetameena}@dtu.ac.in

Abstract. Defect prediction is an extremely new software quality assurance study field. A project team's goal is to provide a high-quality product with no or few flaws. The quantity of flaws in a product is connected to its quality, which is also restricted by time and money. As a result, defect prediction is critical in the field of software quality. This study provides an in-depth look of the software defect/fault prediction. It covers important aspects of software defect prediction. It emphasizes several significant outstanding concerns for the future and explains the key areas of software defect prediction practice. This paper discusses methods for homogenous defect prediction (HDP), which compares metrics within projects. Our aim is to improve the quality of the software by removing the defects so that the working could be more efficient and the results would be more optimum. Our model will help in identifying the problematic modules, which would save a lot of resources that are required for the assurance of the software quality. All the algorithms and techniques of an HDP model will be Universal, but depending on the type of dataset used, the model can be used in multiple industries, for instance food, healthcare, business, and many more. We have built a HDP model using multiple activation functions. HDP models will only be applicable to balanced datasets but we have taken an unbalanced dataset for the model in order to show how to balance a dataset using multiple balancing techniques before moving to the actual development of the HDP model.

Keywords: Homogeneous metrics · Cross-project · Machine learning · Neural network · Defect prediction

1 Introduction

Before deploying software systems, most organizations wish to anticipate the number of problems or identify defect-prone modules. So, there are two most common techniques that we can apply to ensure that the final draft of the software is completely working without any issues or bugs. The first one being Software Testing (which is pretty expensive and generally only be used by huge corporations having huge expenditure for the task) and the second one being developing a defect prediction model. A key goal in

V. Sugumaran et al. (Eds.): AIR 2022, CCIS 1738, pp. 201–212, 2022.
https://doi.org/10.1007/978-3-031-23724-9_19

software engineering is to be able to predict defect-prone software modules. This would allow for more efficient testing resource allocation and better-informed decisions about release quality. As a result, numerous defect prediction studies have been conducted.

We can clearly observe that a lot of corporations like NASA, Microsoft, etc. are actually prioritizing defect prediction models over software testing, even after having the desired expenditure for doing the software testing, and this shift can also become steep in the upcoming years. With each and every new and more efficient development of the models there, this shift will become exponentially higher.

Two things must be clear before everything, when it comes to defect prediction. First, no single prediction technique dominates, and second, the employment of various datasets, data pre-processing, validation systems, and performance statistics makes it difficult to make sense of the multiple prediction outcomes. The lack of agreed-upon reporting methods, as well as the necessity to share code and algorithms, exacerbates these discrepancies. This makes it difficult for academics and, more crucially, practitioners to know which defect prediction approaches to use and how well they are likely to perform.

Many corporations desire to estimate the amount of defects (faults) in software systems before they are deployed in order to estimate the quality and maintenance work that will be required. To aid with this, a plethora of software measures and statistical models have been developed, as well as a sizable literature. To forecast faults, the vast majority of prediction models employ size and complexity criteria. Others rely on data from tests, the "quality" of the development process, or a multivariate approach.

2   Related Work

The use of Deep learning is visible in a variety of fields including software engineering. The application of Deep learning can be first seen in software defect prediction in 2015, and it has been applied more frequently since then. Many academics have looked at the use of deep learning in software fault prediction till date. Deep learning-based software defect prediction is further separated into two types based on the feature type:

2.1   Prediction of Defects Based on Hand-Crafted Characteristics

How to integrate existing features to develop more effective features when utilizing various types of traditional hand-crafted features remains a problem when using various types of traditional hand-crafted features. Deep learning models provide the capacity to combine features effectively. Consequently, deep learning models might be utilized to improve model performance in such instances.

2.2   Prediction of Defects Based on Deep Characteristics

Hand-crafted features are not used in deep feature-based software fault prediction. Instead, deep features are generated from source codes or ASTs using this technique. In 2016, Wang et al. used DBN to forecast software defects. They employed machine learning models to classify chosen AST sequences taken from source codes as input to the DBN model, which generates new expressive features. Their model beat state-of-the-art machine learning methods in WPDP and cross-version defect prediction studies. Then, in 2017, Li et al. introduced a CNN-based defect prediction model that combined word embedding with a CNN model to predict defects. Despite the fact that they classified using logistic regression rather than multiple machine learning algorithms, their outcomes were positive.

2.3 Dependent and Independent Variable

A dependent variable is any variable whose value changes when the value of the parameters on which the dependent variable is linked to, changes, whereas an independent variable's value changes as a result of a process, programme, event, or other computing-specific interaction. It is assigned to a variable value, item, or process in computer programming.

Independent variables can be used in practically any software programme or application. Based on the context in which it is utilized, any independent variable can have any arbitrary value. It can influence the value of a dependent variable directly or indirectly.

3   Research Methodology

We have tested our homogeneous defect prediction model on various datasets (listed below), in all the models we have used CV (Cross Validation) technique in order to test and train the model. In CV what happens is 50% data is used for testing purposes and 50% data is used for training purposes and this keeps going on and on. Figure 1 represents the paths/links involved in the process of development.

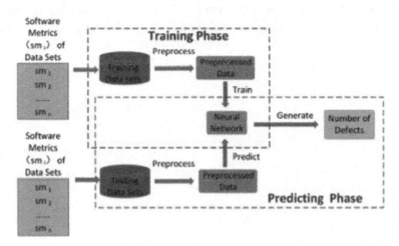

Fig. 1. Flowchart of the process [7]

Steps involved in the development of the model are mentioned below:

3.1 Select the Right Dataset

Problems faced during selecting the right datasets:-

- Studies on the accuracy of defect prediction models have focused on either project or product metrics, rather than the combined impact of both.
- Although it is widely assumed that software size is related to software quality, there is a plethora of data indicating size measurements are a good predictor of faults.
- Neither change metrics nor code metrics were shown to be superior for defect elimination in the defect prediction model.
- Developers rely on complexity measurements to properly allocate QA resources, however these indicators fail to identify important binaries in complex systems.

3.2 Balancing the Datasets (if Required)

If we have a number of positive values in our data collection that are almost identical to negative ones. Then we'll be able to declare that our dataset is balanced (Table 2).

Table 1. Datasets used in the proposed research

Name	Total instances	Repository	Programming languages	Author
PC3	1100	PROMISE	NICKLE	Mike Chapman, NASA
CM1	345	PROMISE	C	Robert Chapman, NASA
KC3	201	Tere-PROMISE	PERL	Mike Chapman, NASA
JM1	9592	PROMISE	NICKLE	Mike Chapman, NASA

Table 2. Description of datasets

Name	Description
PC3	Defect data from the NASA Metrics Data Program. Flight software data for an earth-orbiting satellite. McCabe's data is used, and Halstead has source code extractors. These characteristics were developed in the 1970s in order to scientifically characterize code properties linked to software quality
CM1	This is a PROMISE Software Engineering Repository data collection that has been made publicly available to encourage repeatable, verifiable, refutable, and/or improved software engineering predictive models
KC3	A faulty data set from NASA's Metrics Data Program. It is unknown what kind of programme it is. McCabe provided the data, and Halstead had source code extractors. These characteristics were developed in the 1970s as a way to objectively characterize code characteristics linked to software quality
JM1	This is also a PROMISE data collection that has been made publicly available in order to facilitate repeatable, verifiable, refutable, and/or improved software engineering predictive models

3.3 Problems with Unbalanced Datasets

Unbalanced datasets are quite common when you work with raw data or datasets, for instance, consider a dataset containing classes A and B, in which 90% of the data belongs to class A and 10% to class B. This dataset appears to be unbalanced. A typical and undesirable outcome of such a dataset is that a naïve classifier may achieve 90% accuracy by constantly predicting class A.

So clearly we need to do something to balance the datasets. Moreover, it is always advised to verify the dataset before actually starting developing the HDP model.

3.4 SMOTE for Balancing the Unbalanced Datasets

While working with huge datasets there will be thousands of instances (sometimes even more) and all these instances will have a minority and majority number of classes. Sometimes when majority classes dominate over the minority classes, then a huge deviation from the results is seen. So to avoid this we used a technique called SMOTE, which will try to fill up this gap in between the two classes. SMOTE will not only increase the overall data instead it will try to make the dataset a lot more efficient to move forward with. The Synthetic Minority Oversampling Technique, or SMOTE, is a technique used for increasing some instances or cases for the minority or lesser classes. This finally results in more synthetic cases or instances in the overall datasets. So, after the addition of those synthetic cases, our dataset may be called a pseudo dataset.

This may cause some issues with our final result but without using SMOTE, we can't move forward with the imbalanced datasets.

- Developing the model using Artificial Neural Networks.
- Sigmoid Activation Function has been used to develop the model.
- We used the results given by these activation functions in order to analyze the datasets.

3.5 Choosing the Right Neural Network

There are a lot of neural networks that are already deployed. Based on the requirement we have to choose the perfect fit for the task. For the development of this model ANN is the best fit and the reasons for choosing ANN [8] are as follows:-

- ANN can implement tasks that a linear program cannot.
- If there's some declination in the specific function of ANN, it can continue without some issues by its parallel features.
- ANN determines and does not require to be reprogrammed.
- ANN can be executed in any application.

4   Results and Analysis

Our Defect Prediction model has given us appreciable results with high precision values and an accuracy of about 80 percent. All the major Accuracy Curves and Loss Curves have been shown below along with their precision, accuracy and recall. F-measure and G-measure are also shown respectively.

4.1 Performance Measures - Accuracy, Precision, F Measure, Recall and Sigmoid Function

Before everything, let's make a universal set of all the possible outputs. The actual output can be 1 (true) or 0 (false). But during verification of these outputs there can be an extraordinary reversal/error too, eventually we have more cases added in our universal set.

These cases are:

- True Positive (Tp) - Prediction is Positive and we verified it correctly.
- True Negative (Tn) - Prediction is Negative and we verified it correctly.
- False Positive (Fp) - Prediction is Positive but we verified it incorrectly.
- False Negative (Fn) - Prediction is Negative but we verified it incorrectly.

Based on all of these cases of our universal set, the following formulas can be derived

- *Accuracy* - The fraction of predictions which are correctly observed. In mathematical terms, the ratio of all correctly verified cases to all of the cases. i.e.

$$\text{Accuracy} = (Tp + Tn)/(Tp + Fp + Tn + Fn) \tag{1}$$

- *Precision* - In predictive analytics, precision refers to how close are our model predictions to the observed values or benchmark values. Precision is the ratio of all the correctly verified positives to all the positives observed.

$$Precision = Tp/(Tp + Fp) \tag{2}$$

- *Recall* - Recall is the ratio of all the correctly verified positives to all of the positives in real. It is also considered as Sensitivity.

$$Recall = Tp/(Tp + Fn) \tag{3}$$

- *F-Measure* - It is measured by calculating the average (generally harmonic mean) of precision and recall.
- *Sigmoid Function* - A mathematical function with a distinctive "S"-shaped curve, also known as a sigmoid curve, is known as a sigmoid function.

The relation between the input and output points i.e. (p, y) can be defined as:-

$$F(p) = 1/(1 + e^{\wedge}(-p)) \tag{4}$$

The sigmoid function is utilized as it exists between two points (0 to 1). Due to this, it is specifically useful in models where the probability must be predicted as an output.

We have used sigmoid function to program neural networks as the activation function. Since we only want the output between 0 (zero) and 1 (one) along with non-linear nature, thanks to the sigmoid function which will give us the assurity that the output function will be non-linear.

Such outputs are sometimes called sigmoid units. Different-Different activation functions have different-different brackets or limits on both of the sides. For instance Hyperbolic Tangent Activation Function (sometimes called as tan h) have the output limit of +1 to −1 (Fig. 2).

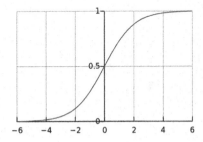

Fig. 2. Graph representing the sigmoid function

Moreover sigmoid function is one of the most convenient commonly used activation functions for these kinds of projects. The reason for this being is basically the monotonic nature of sigmoid function. Along with that, the sigmoid function is continuous and differentiable at all possible points on the x axis of the number line. So we need not take care of a lot of points of collisions in between different points, this makes it one of the easiest activation functions to use.

4.2   Results of JM1 Dataset

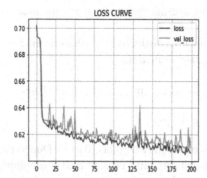

Fig. 3. Loss curve of the dataset JM1

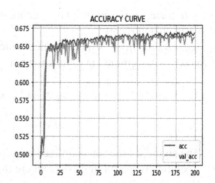

Fig. 4. Accuracy curve of the dataset JM1

4.3   Results of KC3 Dataset

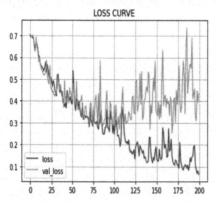

Fig. 5. Loss curve of the dataset KC3

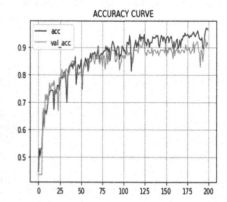

Fig. 6. Accuracy curve of the dataset KC3

4.4   Results of PC3 Dataset

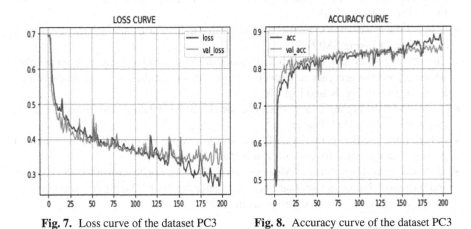

Fig. 7. Loss curve of the dataset PC3   **Fig. 8.** Accuracy curve of the dataset PC3

4.5   Results of CM1 Dataset

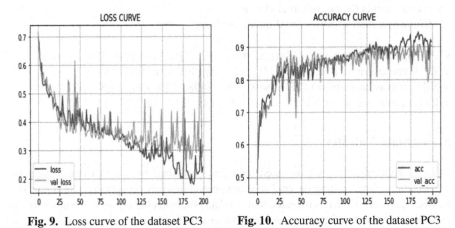

Fig. 9. Loss curve of the dataset PC3   **Fig. 10.** Accuracy curve of the dataset PC3

Table 3. Datasets used in the proposed research

Dataset	Recall	Precision	Accuracy	F measure	G measure
JM1	0.7017	0.6582	0.6692	0.6792	0.6677
KC3	0.9999	0.9236	0.9563	0.9603	0.9514
PC3	0.9151	0.8436	0.8728	0.8779	0.8708
CM1	0.9953	0.8560	0.9123	0.9204	0.9028

4.6 Observations from the Results Obtained

- Losses or measures of the model errors made are comparatively low as seen in the Fig. 3, Fig. 5, Fig. 7, and Fig. 9.
- In Fig. 5 the losses may seem high but that is due to the noises made during balancing of the datasets using SMOTE.
- The actual values and the predicted values are comparatively close to each other which depicts the accuracy and precision of the defect prediction model as presented in Fig. 4, Fig. 6, Fig. 8, and Fig. 10.
- In our model the highest precision can be seen in the KC3 dataset and lowest precision can be seen in the JM1 dataset.
- In Fig. 4, the prediction model performs poorly because the precision, f-measure and g-measure are comparatively lower than that of other datasets.
- The maximum values of the G-Measure and F-Measure can be seen in the KC3 dataset and the reason being, the total number of instances in the KC3 dataset is minimum as compared to the rest of the datasets taken (Table 1).

4.7 Performance of the Model

For evaluating the model, we have to compare the values given by our model with the actual target values, and this work is done by forming a confusion matrix. It's an n * n matrix where n is the no. of target classes.

Confusion matrix values of all the datasets are:-

- PC3: confusion matrix: {'TP': 615, 'TN': 559, 'FP': 114, 'FN': 57}
- KC3: confusion matrix: {'TP': 121, 'TN': 98, 'FP': 10, 'FN': 0}
- JM1: confusion matrix: {'TP': 3840, 'TN': 3498, 'FP': 1994, 'FN': 1632}
- CM1: confusion matrix: {'TP': 214, 'TN': 171, 'FP': 36, 'FN': 1}.

5 Threats Validity

A lot of HDP algorithms have been built and published by a lot of researchers and organizations. The existing defect gathering procedures rely on optional bug repair keywords. Recent research has revealed that the data obtained contains noise. Automatically gathered defect data might contain noise but gradually on making some changes in our final algorithms, we can actually decrease the noise upto a specific point. This study showcases methods for dealing with faulty data noise. First, the influence of noise on defect prediction models is assessed and noise levels that are acceptable are established. We test the noise resistance of two greatly-known defect prediction methods and show that addition of false positive and false negative noises alone does not result in significant results variations for big defect datasets. However, the prediction performance suffers a lot when the dataset has 20%–35% of FP and FN noises. Second, we apply a noise detection and removal approach to solve the issue. Our system can correctly detect noisy occurrences with a respectable degree of accuracy as concluded by the research. Furthermore, after employing our approach to remove disturbances, defect prediction accuracy improves significantly.

6   Conclusion

While training new models, transfer learning proved to be very beneficial as it helps in the saving of cost and time. It also improves the performance of neural networks. Our proposed HDP model yielded promising results, it gives a deep understanding of how to perform defect prediction across projects with heterogeneous metric datasets. We also successfully proved that even in the unbalanced datasets we can actually apply homogeneous defect prediction models by just balancing the dataset using one of the many balancing techniques (we discussed two of the most common and highly efficient dataset balancing techniques). Getting the highest efficiency is totally a hit and trial at the end of the process. In our case we are actually getting some good efficiency (Table 3) but maybe in the future it becomes quite normal and a lot more efficient techniques have been developed. This same model can be used in multiple industries, for instance food, healthcare, business, and many more, we just need to change the dataset to the respective industry's dataset. All the algorithms and techniques of this HDP model will be exactly the same or Universal throughout. We will try to develop a HDP model using other deep learning techniques like CNN and RNN too in future. We are also interested to learn about developing heterogeneous defect prediction models. Moreover, we are also looking forward to building more software defect prediction models with improved efficiency and results. Defect Prediction is one of the most widely used methods to successfully test the model nowadays. With the immense development in this field the best is yet to come.

References

1. Balogun, A.O., et al.: SMOTE-based homogeneous ensemble methods for software defect prediction. In: Gervasi, O., et al. (eds.) ICCSA 2020. LNCS, vol. 12254, pp. 615–631. Springer, Cham (2020). https://doi.org/10.1007/978-3-030-58817-5_45
2. Wang, A., Zhang, Y., Yan, Y.: Heterogeneous defect prediction based on federated transfer learning via knowledge distillation. IEEE Access 9, 29530–29540 (2021). https://doi.org/10.1109/access.2021.3058886
3. Amasaki, S., Aman, H., Yokogawa, T.: An extended study on applicability and performance of homogeneous cross-project defect prediction approaches under homogeneous cross-company effort estimation situation. Empir. Softw. Eng. 27(2), 1–29 (2022). https://doi.org/10.1007/s10664-021-10103-4
4. Pan, S.J., Yang, Q.: A survey on transfer learning. IEEE Trans. Knowl. Data Eng. 22, 1345–1359 (2010). https://doi.org/10.1109/tkde.2009.191
5. Minku, L.L.: A novel online supervised hyperparameter tuning procedure applied to cross-company software effort estimation. Empir. Softw. Eng. 24(5), 3153–3204 (2019). https://doi.org/10.1007/s10664-019-09686-w
6. Shihab, E.: Practical software quality prediction. In: 2014 IEEE International Conference on Software Maintenance and Evolution (2014). https://doi.org/10.1109/icsme.2014.114
7. Qiao, L., Li, X., Umer, Q., Guo, P.: Deep learning based software defect prediction. Neurocomputing 385, 100–110 (2020). https://doi.org/10.1016/j.neucom.2019.11.067
8. Advantages and Disadvantages of ANN. https://www.tutorialspoint.com/what-are-the-advantages-and-disadvantages-of-artificial-neural-networks

9. Bal, P.R., Kumar, S.: Extreme learning machine based linear homogeneous ensemble for software fault prediction. In: Proceedings of the 13th International Conference on Software Technologies (2018). https://doi.org/10.5220/0006839501030112
10. Zhang, F., Mockus, A., Keivanloo, I., Zou, Y.: Towards building a universal defect prediction model with rank transformed predictors. Empir. Softw. Eng. **21**, 2107–2145 (2015). https://doi.org/10.1007/s10664-015-9396-2

Detection of Offensive Comments for Textual Data Using Machine Learning

Rhea Hooda[1], Arunima Jaiswal[1]([✉]) [ID], Isha Bansal[1], Mehak Jain[1], Pranjli Singh[1], and Nitin Sachdeva[2]

[1] Indira Gandhi Delhi Technical University for Women, Delhi, India
{rhea065btcse18,arunimajaiswal,isha049btcse18,mehak055btcse18,
pranjli054btcse18}@igdtuw.ac.in
[2] Galgotia's College of Engineering and Technology, Greater Noida, India
nitin.sachdeva@galgotiacollege.edu

Abstract. Social Media is an essential part of our lives today that provides us to connect with others all around the world. Social Media facilitates the sharing and spreading of information, thoughts, and ideas. However, just like any other innovation, it influences people in a harsh or another way. They have become a platform for spreading hatred, negative comments, and cyberbullying. Cyberbullying is bullying that occurs via digital technologies for example social media, messaging platforms, gaming platforms, and mobile phones. Cyberbullying includes posting, sending or sharing negative, mean, and harmful content. A lot of efforts are being made by researchers for the detection of cyberbullying on social networking sites. The research in this paper focuses on detecting offensive comments for textual data. The data set has been taken from Kaggle, containing 35,000 comments. A rigorous testing has been performed using various Machine learning techniques, among them SVM outperforms with an accuracy of 92.2%.

Keywords: Cyberbullying · Machine learning · Social media · Comments · Offensive

1 Introduction

Over the past decade, social media networking has become an essential medium of communication. Social Media helps users to connect and share their ideas, thoughts, and opinions with people around the world. However, because of social media, there has been a rise in cyberbullying. Cyberbullying can be interpreted as harassment or a crime that occurs on social media platforms. It includes passing negative, mean, false content about an individual that could lead to defamation and harassment. Both short-term and long-term implications can arise from cyberbullying. Victims of cyberbullying can experience a variety of physical, psychological, and emotional consequences. Furthermore, it can lead to anxiety issues, depression, or even drastic measures such as suicide [1]. A sudden increase in cyberbullying cases has been experienced in recent days. India appears as a place where the existence of cyberbullying is seen most often, with more than 37%

V. Sugumaran et al. (Eds.): AIR 2022, CCIS 1738, pp. 213–223, 2022.
https://doi.org/10.1007/978-3-031-23724-9_20

of the families affected by it. A rise of 36% is experienced for cyber related crimes such as cyberstalking, especially among women and children was reported from 542 in 2017 to 739 in 2018 [2]. Child Rights and You (CRY) estimates that 1 in 3 adults are bullied every day [3]. Covid Pandemic period has brought every human being in a virtual digital environment. Due to COVID-19's lockdown, most people's internet usage increased, which led to a spike in cyberbullying [4]. Based on the statistics, Instagram is the most common platform for cyberbullying, followed closely by Facebook and Snapchat. Therefore, in this research, we have presented an overview of the various approaches to analyze and classify cyberbullying related cases with the help of social media platforms.

2 Related Work

Till date, Several deep learning models for hostility and bullying detection on social media in the Hindi language has been developed [9]. The problem with bullying detection in Hindi is that it has fewer resources. The models used were CNN, multi-CNN, Bi-LSTM, IndicBert, and mBert. The accuracy achieved was 96%. The model that outperformed all other models in terms of accuracy is IndicBert presented in [25]. The described CNN model comprises word embedding, max-pooling, and dense layers. Naive Bayes algorithm and Random Forest Classifier (RF) are also used. RF gives better accuracy with an increase in the number of trees. CNN outperforms giving better accuracy (97.08%). It also eliminates feature extraction and feature selection steps. Another model for the classification of cyberbullying comments using the BERT model was proposed in [26]. This model was based on transformers. It analyzed and compared different models such as SVM, Naive Bayes, and BERT and concluded that BERT performed best with an accuracy of 91.90%. The dataset was taken from Twitter. This model has a lot more scope. The BERT model can be combined with other models for better accuracy. In [27], authors proposed two types of variations in previous models. The first method suggests using the Bi-LSTM model instead of Bi-GRU. The second method suggests using CNN instead of CapsNet. Therefore, it has the advantages of both the models, the Bi-LSTM model, and the CNN model with F1 Score of 94.03 and 93.89. The comments were collected from Twitter, YouTube, and MySpace. Future work is to apply BERT models to the classification of cyber-bullying comments. Authors in [28], proposed a method using BERT models. They used compact BERT models and compared the results of some selected compact BERT models. They chose 5 compact BERT models for comparison. BERT Base performed best with an accuracy of 91.56%. The problem with BERT is that it does not perform well on smaller datasets. Future work is to explore other models out of the 24 compact BERT models and try out their combinations. In [29], authors proposed a method for the detection of cyberbullying using LSTM-CNN. The methodology includes prepossessing, word embedding, spatial dropout layer, and a combination of Bi-LSTM with CNN layer. Accuracy and precision were considered prominent metrics for analyzing the model. LSTM-CNN outperforms all traditional machine learning algorithms with an accuracy of 95.2%. [30] presents a Comparative Study of Various State-of-the-Art Hate Speech Detection Techniques for Hindi-English Code-Mixed Data. They used algorithms to compare Support Vector Machines, Naive Bayes, Decision Tree, and Character based CNN. The character-based CNN model performed best. They analyzed the datasets taken from Twitter, and Facebook. They used Roman, Devanagari Scripts. But the drawback was that some comments were not able to classify correctly which were sarcastic. CNN performed best with an accuracy of 82%. The future scope is to experiment with code-mixed data of minority languages. Additionally, authors used deep learning models to detect hate speech from code-mixed Hindi-English tweets in [31]. They compared 3 Deep Learning models. CNN-1d, LSTM, Bi-LSTM. CNN-1d performed best. They used a benchmark dataset of some other paper. They used domain-specific word embeddings and trained the embeddings. But they are not able to classify code-switched codes in Hindi. CNN-1d performed best with an accuracy of 82.6%. The future work is to classify sarcasm and misinformation correctly. Authors in [32] focused on cyberbullying detection using neural network architecture to classify tweets taken from Twitter as cyber-aggressive and non-cyber-aggressive. They proposed a simple framework having N-gram parameters with TF-IDF for feature extraction and feeding it to the dense layers of MultiLayered Perceptron (MLP). The results of the proposed approach were compared with the other old hybrid models of CNN-LSTM and CNN-BiLSTM. The proposed model outdid other models with an accuracy of 91% which too in less training time and lesser layers. In [33], authors proposed a cyberbullying detection model on bilingual comments, namely English and Hindi, taken from Facebook and Twitter. They proposed an LSTM autoencoder model followed by a supervised machine learning classifier. The model outperformed the previous best results with an F1-score of 81% and 72% for the English and Hindi corpus respectively. In [34], authors developed a model for detecting Arabic hate speech on Twitter Platform and then classifying the hate tweets into different classes based on the type of hate in the tweet. Deep neural networks, specifically LSTM, CNN + LSTM, GRU, and CNN + GRU, were used in the experiments, and the outcomes were compared to the SVM baseline model. The results proved that an ensemble model of CNN + LSTM performed best. [5] used deep learning and machine learning algorithms to solve the issue of detecting online bullying. The methodology includes data collection and preprocessing with GloVe, SSWE, and word2vec word embeddings followed by the application of classification models. The machine learning techniques used are SVM, LR, NB, and RF, while CNN, LSTM, and BLSTM are deep learning models. F-measure, precision, recall were chosen as result metrics. CNN with SSWE outperformed other models with 80% precision. In [6], authors have discussed that deep learning models can be used to determine whether a comment is abusive. They further classified it as a threat, insult, toxic, severe toxic, identity hate, or obscene. The classification algorithms used are ANN, CNN, and LSTM with GloVe and without GloVe embeddings. The results obtained had a high accuracy of 97.27% with CNN and GloVe. The model proposed by [7] was based on deep learning with word embeddings. The proposed system involved Glove as the word embedding method. The system uses Convolution Neural Network (CNN) as the deep neural network model that operates through many layers. A comparison of the proposed system with traditional algorithms of machine learning and neural networks found that it performed better with a testing accuracy of 94%. Deep learning and word embeddings were used by the authors of [8] to detect cyberbullying. Experiments were done with three deep learning algorithms, namely LSTM, BLTM, and GRU. The methodology involved data preprocessing steps followed by feature extraction using four-word embedding models, namely word2vec,

ELMO, Reddit, and GloVe. The results were analyzed on the basis of Recall and the average time taken to train the model and it was found that BLSTM performs best with ELMO in cyberbullying detection. Also, GRU outperforms other models in terms of time efficiency.

Using Multi Interactive Attention and Language-Environment Cognitive Models, authors in [10] proposed a method. They compared different models such as LSTM, Bi-LSTM, Bi-LSTM + CNN, MIALC. They classified the Chinese comments. The model was unique and hence gave very good results. The model MIALC performed best with an accuracy of 97.01%. Future work is to find out the varying categories of cyberbullying comments that the comments can be classified [11]. In this case, the authors suggested a BERT base model with one neural network layer serving as the classifier. The approach was tested on two datasets: Formspring and Wikipedia talk pages. The data was first oversampled as the number of bullying comments were lesser than nonbullying comments and were fed to the BERT model. The experimental results were compared with some other existing models namely CNN, RNN, LR, MLP, and it was found that the proposed approach performed better with an accuracy of 98% on the Formspring dataset and 96% on Wikipedia dataset. A machine learning-based model to identify and stop bullying on Twitter was put forth by authors in [12]. The data collection and preprocessing are followed by feature extraction with TF-DIF and then classification with SVM and NB. The result was analyzed based on accuracy, precision, recall, and F-measure. In [13], authors presented a technique for preprocessing tweets using Sentimental Analysis. The supervised machine learning methods used were Vector Machine and Naive Bayes. SVM outperforms NB with an average accuracy value of 92.02%. The average accuracy of 81.1% was achieved by NB classifiers on the 4-gram language model. By combining natural language processing and machine learning, authors developed a method for detecting online abusive and bullying messages [14], where BoW and TF-IDF feature vectors were used.

3   Implementation Details

This section provides a summary of the dataset information, the methods employed, and the work-flow that was used. In Fig. 1, the workflow is shown. The first stage is gathering data. The information came from Kaggle [15]. The dataset has 35,000 comments. There are 65.75% offensive comments and 34.24% non-offensive remarks, respectively. 70% of the dataset was used for training purposes, and the remaining 30% was used for testing purposes.

The dataset contains 2 fields:

- Comment
- Id of the comment
- And Label, which was categorized into two categories, Offensive and Non-Offensive.

The dataset contained 35,000 comments which were collected from various social media sites.

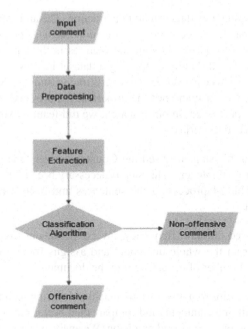

Fig. 1. Proposed workflow

Next step is Data Preprocessing [16] which is a technique used to clean the raw data and make it suitable for classification models. This will make the data to be easily parsed by the machine and additionally improve the accuracy of the results. Real-world datasets are highly prone to inconsistent, noisy, or missing data. If the data mining algorithms are applied on such a dataset, they will not give quality results as they will not be able to identify patterns effectively. Hence, data preprocessing is a crucial step to improve the data quality before applying any classification algorithm to it. We handled the noisy data by using a large dataset since the more the data, the better the estimation. To handle the missing values, we assumed the comments to be Offensive as it is better to classify the comment as Offensive rather than Non-Offensive.

The following steps are involved in the data preprocessing stage:

- Importing libraries
- Importing datasets
- Handling missing values
- Removing the stop words
- Removing punctuation marks
- Expanding abbreviations
- Removing unnecessary text or characters
- Converting all the upper-case letters to lower
- Data splitting into training and testing datasets.

Next step is feature extraction [17]. The feature extraction techniques help in examining the similarities between the pieces of text. One of the key steps that ought to be followed when processing raw data is feature extraction. The aim is to better understand the text that we are analyzing. A component of natural language processing is this stage. Reducing the number of related or redundant features in the dataset is the main goal of feature extraction. The difficulty of training a dataset increases with the number of features in the dataset. This can even lead to overfitting within the Classification model. Feature extraction selects or combines the important features and thereby reduces the amount of data to be processed. In our research, we did feature extraction using count vectorizer [18] and TF-IDF [19].

Countvectorizer: In this step, we used the Countvectorizer function. It converts the comments into an array of integers. This step is necessary because the machine learning models are not capable of processing the sentences and instead require an array of integers as their input.

TF-IDF: We also used the term frequency–inverse document frequency. It basically collects the words from the whole document and assigns some probabilities to each word based upon the number of occurrences in the document.

Following this, we aim to apply various machine learning techniques on a dataset that contains cyberbullying comments and compare their performance on various metrics such as accuracy, F1-score, recall, and precision. We analyzed several machine learning algorithms, such as Decision Trees, Random Forests, Naive Bayes, Support Logistic Regression, and Vector Machines along with feature extraction models, such as TF-IDFs and Count Vectorizations, for performance analysis.

The details about the classifiers used areas follows.

Naive Bayes: It is a classifier which works on the principle of Bayes Theorem [20]. It comprises a set of algorithms (having different ways to calculate the probability) working under the same assumption that every pair of features is independent of each other.

Support Vector Machines: By using SVM, the algorithm seeks an N-dimensional hyperplane [21], where N is the number of features that classify the data. It maximizes the distance of support vectors (points on the boundary) from the hyperplane and in this way, the most optimal hyperplane is found.

Logistic Regression: A classification algorithm that predicts the probability of a query point belonging to each of the classes in question [22]. The value of Y_predicted can be outside the probability range of 0, 1 so a sigmoid function is used to bring it back in this range. Sigmoid(z) = (1/(1 + exp(−z))).

Decision Tree: Based on its name, this model [23] consists of nodes representing the features of dataset, edges representing the decision rules, and leaves representing the outcomes. The algorithm is designed to find a splitting node such that the partition of the data about this node results in maximum reduction of node impurity. A particular node is stopped from splitting if the number of data points on that node is less than a limit and we assign that node as a leaf node having a label as the majority class of the set of all points at that node.

Random Forest Classifier: A random forest [24] utilizes decision trees. Decision trees are created by randomly choosing a portion of the training data, and the outcome is based on each tree's output.

We also observed that the dataset contained the following:

- Percentage of offensive comments in the dataset are: 65.75
- Percentage of non-offensive comments in the dataset are: 34.24.

Thereafter, we applied various supervised machine learning techniques. These include:

- Multinomial Naïve Bayes (MNB)
- Decision Tree (DT)
- Support Vector Machine (SVM)
- Random Forest (RF)
- Logistic Regression (LR).

We employed trained models to identify the labels on testing data after these models had been trained on training datasets. For every machine learning model, we also evaluated precision, recall, accuracy, F1-score, AUC, and assessed the confusion matrix for each model. For each model, we have also presented the ROC curves (receiver operating characteristic curve).

4 Discussions

This section briefs about the results obtained by applying aforesaid techniques for bullying detection. We evaluated machine learning models on various performance metrics, including accuracy (A), precision (P), recall (R), F1-score (F), and AUC.

In the graph shown in Fig. 2, we have plotted various algorithms on the x-axis and their respective accuracy scores on the y-axis. The algorithms are arranged in descending order of their accuracy scores.

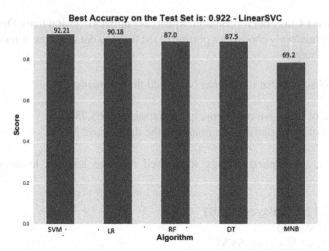

Fig. 2. Results obtained for machine learning techniques

In Fig. 2, we have plotted various algorithms on the x-axis and their respective accuracy scores on the y-axis. The algorithms are arranged in descending order of their accuracy scores.

Comparison Between Different Models Based on Various Performance Metrics
Table 1 shows the performance of different machine learning models on various performance metrics such as Accuracy, Precision, Recall, F1-score and AUC. We used the criterion as 'Entropy' in the Random Forest classifier and Decision tree classifier. For Multinomial Naive Bayes, SVM and Logistic Regression, the parameters used were by default.

Table 1. Comparison table

Model	A	P	R	F	AUC
DT	88.65	91.60	91.11	91.36	87.5
LR	90.18	92.06	93.10	92.58	88.8
MNB	78.54	75.88	98.79	85.83	69.2
RF	88.85	90.41	92.91	91.64	87.0
SVM	92.21	94.21	93.34	94.07	91.4

We can see that SVM outperformed all the other models with an accuracy of 92.21%. SVM also performed the best in other performance metrics as well such as precision, recall, F1-score, AUC score.

ROC Curve

We have also plotted the ROC curves (receiver operating characteristic curve) for all the models.

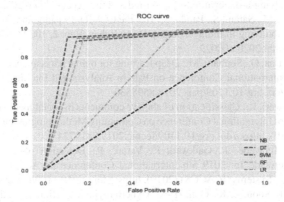

Fig. 3. ROC curve

Figure 3 denotes the ROC curve. In the ROC curve, we can notice that the curve of SVM is the most closer to the top-left corner which indicates that SVM performed best in comparison to the other models.

The area under the curve of each model is the most important here, as the area under the curve indicates the AUC score.

5 Conclusion

In this paper, we examined a dataset with 35,000 comments containing 65.75% offensive comments. A series of machine learning techniques were applied including SVM, Naive Bayes, Random Forest, Logistic Regression, Decision Tree, and SVM was found to be the most accurate model at 92.2%. Furthermore, SVM performed the best in other performance metric scores as well, including precision, recall, and AUC. Future work will revolve around enhancing the implementation of existing machine learning techniques, thus improving accuracy and results. Additionally, deep learning models may be used to improve results.

References

1. What Is Cyberbullying? https://www.verywellfamily.com/types-of-cyberbullying-460549. Accessed 05 Apr 2022
2. IndiaSpend.com, R.M.: In one year alone, cyberbullying of Indian women and teenagers rose by 36%. https://scroll.in/article/956085/in-one-year-alone-cyberbullying-of-indian-women-and-teenagers-rose-by-36. Accessed Apr 2022
3. Cyber Bullying: A Disregarded Issue in India. https://legalserviceindia.com/legal/article-2358-cyber-bullying-a-disregarded-issue-in-india.html. Accessed Feb 2022
4. Jain, O., Gupta, M., Satam, S., Panda, S.: Has the COVID-19 pandemic affected the susceptibility to cyberbullying in India? Comput. Hum. Behav. Rep. 2, 100029 (2020). https://doi.org/10.1016/j.chbr.2020.100029
5. Marwa, T., Salima, O., Souham, M.: Deep learning for online harassment detection in tweets. In: 2018 3rd International Conference on Pattern Analysis and Intelligent Systems (PAIS) (2018). https://doi.org/10.1109/pais.2018.8598530
6. Anand, M., Eswari, R.: Classification of abusive comments in social media using deep learning. In: 2019 3rd International Conference on Computing Methodologies and Communication (ICCMC) (2019). https://doi.org/10.1109/iccmc.2019.8819734
7. Banerjee, V., Telavane, J., Gaikwad, P., Vartak, P.: Detection of cyberbullying using deep neural network. In: 2019 5th International Conference on Advanced Computing & Communication Systems (ICACCS) (2019). https://doi.org/10.1109/icaccs.2019.8728378
8. Al-Hashedi, M., Soon, L.-K., Goh, H.-N.: Cyberbullying detection using deep learning and word embeddings. In: Proceedings of the 2019 2nd International Conference on Computational Intelligence and Intelligent Systems (2019). https://doi.org/10.1145/3372422.3373592
9. Akhter, A., Uzzal, K.A., Polash, M.M.A.: Cyber bullying detection and classification using multinomial Naïve Bayes and fuzzy logic. Int. J. Math. Sci. Comput. 5, 1–12 (2019). https://doi.org/10.5815/ijmsc.2019.04.01
10. Niu, M., Yu, L., Tian, S., Wang, X., Zhang, Q.: Personal-bullying detection based on multi-attention and cognitive feature. Autom. Control Comput. Sci. 54, 52–61 (2020). https://doi.org/10.3103/s0146411620010083
11. Yadav, J., Kumar, D., Chauhan, D.: Cyberbullying detection using pre-trained BERT model. In: 2020 International Conference on Electronics and Sustainable Communication Systems (ICESC) (2020). https://doi.org/10.1109/icesc48915.2020.9155700
12. Dalvi, R.R., Baliram Chavan, S., Halbe, A.: Detecting a Twitter cyberbullying using machine learning. In: 2020 4th International Conference on Intelligent Computing and Control Systems (ICICCS) (2020). https://doi.org/10.1109/iciccs48265.2020.9120893
13. Atoum, J.O.: Cyberbullying detection through sentiment analysis. In: 2020 International Conference on Computational Science and Computational Intelligence (CSCI) (2020). https://doi.org/10.1109/csci51800.2020.00056
14. Islam, M.M., Uddin, M.A., Islam, L., Akter, A., Sharmin, S., Acharjee, U.K.: Cyberbullying detection on social networks using machine learning approaches. In: 2020 IEEE Asia-Pacific Conference on Computer Science and Data Engineering (CSDE) (2020). https://doi.org/10.1109/csde50874.2020.9411601
15. mehak2610: GitHub - mehak2610/CyberBullying-Detection-Dataset. https://github.com/mehak2610/CyberBullying-Detection-Dataset. Accessed Dec 2021
16. Kotsiantis, S., Kanellopoulos, D., Pintelas, P.: Data preprocessing for supervised leaning. world academy of science, engineering and technology, open science index 12. Int. J. Comput. Inf. Eng. 1(12), 4104–4109 (2007)

17. Khalid, S., Khalil, T., Nasreen, S.: A survey of feature selection and feature extraction techniques in machine learning. In: 2014 Science and Information Conference (2014). https://doi.org/10.1109/sai.2014.6918213

18. Sayeedunnisa, S.F., Hegde, N.P., Khan, K.U.R.: Wilcoxon signed rank based feature selection for sentiment classification. In: Bhateja, V., Tavares, J.M.R.S., Rani, B.P., Prasad, V.K., Raju, K.S. (eds.) Proceedings of the Second International Conference on Computational Intelligence and Informatics. AISC, vol. 712, pp. 293–310. Springer, Singapore (2018). https://doi.org/10.1007/978-981-10-8228-3_27

19. Zhang, Y., Gong, L., Wang, Y.: An improved TF-IDF approach for text classification. J. Zhejiang Univ. Sci. **6**, 49–55 (2005). https://doi.org/10.1631/jzus.2005.a0049

20. Eells, E.: Review: Bayes's theorem. Mind **113**, 591–596 (2004). https://doi.org/10.1093/mind/113.451.591

21. Veinott, A.F.: The supporting hyperplane method for unimodal programming. Oper. Res. **15**, 147–152 (1967). https://doi.org/10.1287/opre.15.1.147

22. Wright, R.E.: Logistic regression. In: Grimm, L.G., Yarnold, P.R. (eds.) Reading and Understanding Multivariate Statistics, pp. 217–244. American Psychological Association (1995)

23. Dam, H.K., et al.: Lessons learned from using a deep tree-based model for software defect prediction in practice. In: 2019 IEEE/ACM 16th International Conference on Mining Software Repositories (MSR) (2019). https://doi.org/10.1109/msr.2019.00017

24. Biau, G., Scornet, E.: A random forest guided tour. TEST **25**, 197–227 (2016). https://doi.org/10.1007/s11749-016-0481-7

25. Singh, N., Sinhasane, A., Patil, S., Balasubramanian, S.: Cyberbullying detection in social networks: a survey. SSRN Electron. J. (2020). https://doi.org/10.2139/ssrn.3648738

26. Desai, A., Kalaskar, S., Kumbhar, O., Dhumal, R.: Cyber bullying detection on social media using machine learning. In: ITM Web of Conferences, vol. 40, p. 03038 (2021). https://doi.org/10.1051/itmconf/20214003038

27. Kumar, A., Sachdeva, N.: A Bi-GRU with attention and CapsNet hybrid model for cyberbullying detection on social media. World Wide Web **25**, 1537–1550 (2021). https://doi.org/10.1007/s11280-021-00920-4

28. Behzadi, M., Harris, I.G., Derakhshan, A.: Rapid cyber-bullying detection method using compact BERT models. In: 2021 IEEE 15th International Conference on Semantic Computing (ICSC) (2021). https://doi.org/10.1109/icsc50631.2021.00042

29. Gada, M., Damania, K., Sankhe, S.: Cyberbullying detection using LSTM-CNN architecture and its applications. In: 2021 International Conference on Computer Communication and Informatics (ICCCI) (2021). https://doi.org/10.1109/iccci50826.2021.9402412

30. Rani, P., Suryawanshi, S., Goswami, K., Chakravarthi, B.R, Fransen, T., McCrae, J.P.: A comparative study of different state-of-the-art hate speech detection methods in Hindi-English code-mixed data. In: Proceedings of the Second Workshop on Trolling, Aggression and Cyberbullying, Marseille, France, pp. 42–48. European Language Resources Association (ELRA) (2020)

31. Kamble, S., Joshi, A.: Hate speech detection from code-mixed Hindi-English tweets using deep learning models. arXiv. (2018). https://doi.org/10.48550/arXiv.1811.05145

32. Sadiq, S., Mehmood, A., Ullah, S., Ahmad, M., Choi, G.S., On, B.-W.: Aggression detection through deep neural model on Twitter. Future Gener. Comput. Syst. **114**, 120–129 (2021). https://doi.org/10.1016/j.future.2020.07.050

33. Kumari, K., Singh, J.P., Dwivedi, Y.K., Rana, N.P.: Bilingual Cyber-aggression detection on social media using LSTM autoencoder. Soft. Comput. **25**, 8999–9012 (2021). https://doi.org/10.1007/s00500-021-05817-y

34. Al-Hassan, A., Al-Dossari, H.: Detection of hate speech in Arabic tweets using deep learning. Multimedia Syst. **28**, 1963–1974 (2021). https://doi.org/10.1007/s00530-020-00742-w

Analyzing Various Handwriting Recognition Phenomenon for Predicting Gender, Age and Handedness

Ayushi Agarwal[1] and Mala Saraswat[2]([✉]) [ID]

[1] ABES Engineering College, Ghaziabad, India
[2] Bennett University, Greater Noida, U.P., India
malasaraswat@gmail.com

Abstract. Handwriting recognition, in the current scenario is becoming an important task to recognize ones general identity by investing minimum time for it. As handwriting recognition plays a very significant role for authentication of documents, genuineness of historical manuscripts and many more. It is now becoming an exploiting field of research as one can copy others handwriting but can never write the same in an identical manner. From here comes rise of a new field of research for researchers. Now this handwriting recognition concept is being used for classifying gender, age, handedness, ethnicity and many more aspects just by analyzing written data of the writers. The focus for this exploration is to study and summarize various techniques used so far for analyzing the handwriting and recognizing the possible features of a person. This concept has built up its importance by raising its usage in various fields such as; for forensic scrutiny, identification of writers, word perceiving, verification of signature etc. The advancement of this research for this concept has increased by observing the attractive positive results for its outcomes and the eagerness of building a computerized system for processing handwriting so that it could replace the manual analysis. From prediction till recognition of correct identity of the writers', this complete process takes place majorly in three basic steps: segmentation, features extractions and classification. SVM, KNN and RFC supervised machine learning algorithms are being used for classification purpose. Few of plenty of researches done by researchers for the same purpose had also purposed approaches by using the unsupervised machine learning techniques as well. Thus, both the phenomenon may be utilized for fulfilling the defined query with most appropriate possible computational approach.

Keywords: Supervised machine learning · Unsupervised learning algorithms · Handedness · Ethnicity · Word spotting · Segmentation · Features extractions · Classification · Computational approaches

1 Introduction

Every person is different from one other in contrast to each and every aspect that could differentiate them. Like for initially every persons' cells are different. Each have different blood group. Likewise everyone have different genes, body shape, nature, habits.

V. Sugumaran et al. (Eds.): AIR 2022, CCIS 1738, pp. 224–234, 2022.
https://doi.org/10.1007/978-3-031-23724-9_21

Moreover everyone have different figure prints, face features, choices etc. Similarly, everyone have different handwriting design. Male and female both have different writing styles, writing pattern, writing texture. Through handwriting we can understand five main human traits like; gender, age, ethnicity, handedness and nationality [1]. Handwriting features [2, 3] that are used for extracting the information about the writers are such as; slant, curvature, line separation, chain code, characters shape, texture, legibility, direction, gradient direction, allograph features, shape, structure, wavelet domain local binary pattern etc. [2–4, 6, 8].

Thus, through vast set of features, a specific set of features is used for handwriting recognition. Due to large variety of features for analyzing writers' handwriting, researchers got more interest for doing more impressive researches using supervised and unsupervised machine learning algorithms in the field of machine learning and explaining numerous proposals.

The three basic steps that are included in the process of handwriting recognition are as follows; segmentation, features extraction and classification. The most suitable algorithms used for segmentation process are edge detection and k-means clustering. Further moving on with the steps; the most prominently algorithms that are used for feature extraction are: m-RMR, PCA. The features that are being extracted by using these algorithms are as follow; tortuosity, direction, curvatures, chain codes and dimension reduction [4, 6, 7].

Moving to the third step which is the final step for the process that is classification, algorithms used frequently by the researchers are SVM, KNN, CNN [8, 9, 11] and RFC. Among these classification algorithms researchers have given more choice for classification process to SVM and RFC. Since RFC is leading supervised learning algorithm and SVM makes use of kernel function which results in more prominent and accurate result. Thus, following the combination of these processes and algorithms the outcomes by the handwriting is more accurate and possesses efficiency.

All cognate aspects can be pulled out from scanned handwriting images. For fulfilling this aspect there is requirement of image processing as well. This conveys that the handwriting recognition is not an isolated process. Rather it's a combined concept generated by merging the understandings from Digital Image Processing and Machine Learning supervised learning methods.

Here, through this research work it is observed that recognition problems can be classified as lazy learners as well as eager learner. In case of lazy learner classification problem many researches followed KNN algorithm as it takes more time for learning and takes less time for prediction comparatively. While many researches that had followed eager learner classification approach had exploited the knowledge of ANN and CNN which has enhanced this field of research.

Taking a look on the research outcomes, it can help us in many fields. As everyone have different pattern of writing this approach can be used for verification of the signature digitally as well as physically. This would help in preventing any sort of frauds that are increasing day by day. It was found that the handwriting recognition methodology is not only fruitful digitally but it can give good results physically as well. Soon in this digitized world this approach would find its space with nearly 100% accuracy to bypass all manual recognition approaches.

This would then save time in Forensics, as they have to hire experts for handwriting experts for extracting general features of culprits' characters and for selecting the correct group of suspects for interrogation. This will not only save time for forensics investigation but would provide reliable approach for recognition through handwriting to various other sectors as well. Through this application there raise a new complex problem of automatic classification of individuals in the fields such as; in Forensic Biometrics investigation, for understanding Psychology attributes, for human computer interaction and in Biometric security.

This research approach can also provide benefits to neurologists, psychologists for having basic knowledge about their patients so that they can treat them with more efficiency to improve their health. This approach can also be applied for authentication of documents, for understanding historical manuscripts. These learning have also manifested existence for connection between handwriting pattern and from handwriting the person's personality traits. In this field of human computer interaction, if the system can automatically predict the gender of the individual may provide more interactive and impressive communication.

The data studied from recognition of various things through handwriting had also concluded that the male handwriting is more barbed; hasten, disordered, shabby and inclined. While from female handwriting data study it was concluded that their writing is more adorning, embellishing, analogous, graceful, fragile, accordant, tidy and wide ranging.

From this the objective of doing this survey is:

- To identify the differences in the handwriting designs from person to person.
- By using the above stated objectives next is to understand the more appropriate learning technique suitable for predicting the gender, age, handedness.
- To identify ethnicity, nationality and many other traits of the individual writers'.

Above objectives can be used in various applications in different sectors such as healthcare, automotive industries, business field services, pedagogy, demography based writers' recognition, designation verification, impression verification, postal address interpretation, background investigation processing etc. Upcoming, in Sects. 2 and 3; there will be summarized literature review from various research works, it will also give the highlight of the various Machine Learning algorithms used for different approaches. Section 4 will cover various data sets used, Sect. 5 analyzes and compares the discussed work and finally Sect. 6 provides a conclusion for the discussed concept in this complete survey followed by references content.

2   Related Works

This section consists of two phases namely; the first is the literature review and the second is for understanding the algorithms that are being used in different research papers so far. The literature review helped to understand acutely that there are many traits of human behavior that can be predicted by the help of artificial intelligence concepts. The artificial intelligence further consists of the combination of practical approach from machine learning and deep learning. Thus, one can effortlessly understand that machine learning is the subgroup of artificial intelligence. Then deep learning is subgroup of machine learning.

In deep learning, algorithms aim to mimic human brain for incorporating intelligence into the machine. From here after, the machine learning, automatically learns from the data and results in incorporation of intelligence into machines with precision. Thus, it can be stated that an artificial intelligence algorithm imitates the ability of human intelligence.

So chronology here is, first the chief concept is the deep learning then with the improvements in the algorithms there comes the machine learning and finally with more enhancements the artificial intelligence concepts came into the picture. But today, all these three conceptual and computational studies are used in combination with each other.

The study and research with these technologies is now increasing day by day which has showcased that the gender and age of a person are not the only traits that can be predicted through it but their age, nationality, ethnicity, handedness, emotions, nature, gestures, thinking, thought process and many more traits can be understood and predicted with their complete inner study.

This section of the survey is going to cover all the various classifiers used by the researchers in their research works for the purpose of handwriting recognition and utilizing the outcomes for predicting various features. Ning Bi et al. in this research work they showed the contribution of the KMI application for features selection and carried out classification by exploring two datasets with SVM motion for recognizing the gender of the writers' [1].

Ahmed et al. exploited the features like; Local Binary Pattern (LBP), Histogram of Oriented Gradient (HOG) and extracted them by division motion based upon fractal texture analysis and at last employed the computation of SVM, DT, RFC and KNN for classification [2].

Abdeljalil Gattal et al., captured the characters' details in handwriting are collected by compiling distinctive layouts from oriented basic image features. Advancing on, the oriented basic image features histograms and its columns histograms had been extracted from a numerous writing illustration of male and feminine handwriting so accustomed train a support vector machine classifier [3].

Somaya et al. considered several geometric, angular, congruent features for distinguishing handwritings were put forward. The assumed target using these features and classification of handwritings was performed for locating age, gender and nationality with precision. Then the features were combined and correlated using random forests and kernel discriminant analysis algorithms [4]. Marzinotto et al. proposed a brand new approach consisting of two-level classification for handwriting characterization [5]. Morera et al. suggested a technique on entreaty of deep neural networks for resolving several automatic demographic classification problems based upon handwriting. They'd identifies three problems that were required to induce resolved here were; predicting gender, handedness and combined combination for gender-and-handedness categorization that they had used Convolutional Neural Network (CNN) for his or her classification to supply the ultimate prediction [6]. Maken et al. the complete prediction for gender identification system which solely depends on the scenario of features extraction. Here, the varied and distinct characteristics' had made the classing accurate and efficient. This paper relates the problem minutely along with understructure to create more detailed systems [7]. Gattal et al. proposed a fresh method by using cloud of line distribution and hinge feature to determine gender from handwriting. Then, SVM classifier combines the allocated classes based on maximal of the two predefined values emanated from COLD and hinge features for classification [8]. Gil Levi et al. worked by studying the representations through use of Deep-Convolutional Neural Networks (CNN), a relevant rise in execution can be achieved from these tasks [9]. Maken et al. identifies gender from handwriting using the critical points of variance between the two genders. Here, classification had been carried out using support vector machine, KNN and at last, to enhance the classification rates they had used majority voting [10]. Rahmanian et al. explored the potentiality and range of deep CNNs in automated classification for two handwritings rooted upon enumeration problems, that is handedness and gender been classified [11]. Further, Siddiqui et al. carried out classification using artificial neural networks and support vector machine [12].

3 Phases in Handwriting Recognition

Here, through the literature work for the purposed task, the complete Handwriting Recognition can be performed in a set of different phases. The Handwriting Recognition is executed in set of five phases. These can be named as: Image Acquisition, Image Preprocessing, Segmentation, Feature Extraction and lastly Classification. But when this concept is exploited by many other authors, they mainly focus and present only last three steps. First two steps are considered as per the data used by them.

In Image Acquisition phase, which is the initiation of the whole process, here the task is to gather the data for exploration. Here, the proposed concept is to identify various traits of human in online mode. So to do so, one requirement is to capture the data. For this, many people make use of good quality cameras. Some don't prefer to invest in expensive cameras rather they use normal and simple cameras to capture and then perform the preprocessing phase to enhance the quality of the captured data so as to have good results. That's why the first two steps are designed in such a way that many researchers or authors sometimes use only one of these or both as per their requirement. So the preprocessing phase involves the morphological operations, noise removal, size normalization and many more sub operations to enhance the picture quality.

When discussing about the segmentation, it is basically a division process which works in such a way that it isolated the individual character from the handwritten character image. This is carried out using the threshold based, edge based, region based and clustering techniques. The different steps in segmentation are line, word and character segmentation.

Then comes the fourth phase, this is one of the most important phases of the recognition process. The complete feature extraction process can be grouped into three major sub phases, namely; Statistical Features, Global transformation and series expansion and lastly the Structural Features. There are many alternative features that are getting used for the predictions through writers' handwriting data. Feature extraction strategy is being used for both manual and computerized identification. Features that are mostly being extracted for study are like; *Chain code feature, Curvature feature, Character shape, Direction feature, dimension reduction, histogram of oriented gradient, plane, Local binary pattern, Tortuosity feature, slope, Space Gradient, size, Slanting characters* and plenty of more.

- Slant - the slant in the western writing is the predominant angle for the downward stokes of the letters.
- Slope - the slope concept is used to determine upward and downward slope for the line of writing. As through many studies it is noted that, in about 67% of the cases the slope of line of writing is upwards towards the right direction.
- Direction feature determines the flow of writing that is whether it is smooth writing pattern or there are breaks in between.
- The curvature feature determines the curve nature of the alphabets and writing which is then calculated by gradient descent approach.
- Tortuosity - this is a property for extracting the twisted character for the curves of the letters. So this basically identifies the twisted curves.
- Chain code - the chain code is considered to be a lossless compression algorithm which is harnessed for understanding monochromic images.
- Boundary noise - this is basically that characteristic which determines the noise in the writing flow, which helps in predicting the nature of writing person.
- Dimension reduction - for announcing or designing the final model which is a probabilistic process, dimension reduction came into existence for feature selection and then feature extraction.
- Other local and global features that are used for feature reading and its extraction are like;
- Speed - which indicates that how fast the writer had written the text.
- Writing Direction - this indicated the direction of writing along the x and y direction which is further used for calculating the slant or slope.
- Local Curvature radius
- Vicinity Curliness
- Vicinity Aspect
- Vicinity Slope
- Vicinity Linearity
- Ascender/Descenders
- Context Map.

Lastly here comes the classification phase, this is the final phase for recognition process which provides the results. Researchers throughout the world are working to find and evolve a robust and volatile method to solve the problem and make the recognition of different approaches easy, approachable and executable, but the progress id still ongoing in this direction and not converged yet.

The whole human population can be classified on the basis of different human traits into various different classes such as; gender, age, nationality, handedness, ethnicity, races and plenty of more. Here this review paper covers the various undifferentiated works of grate researchers where the main focus is on identifying the gender, age and handedness.

4 Datasets Used

As the Machine Learning algorithms can be categorized as supervised and unsupervised learning algorithms. The selection preference from any of two algorithms for learning and exploring depends on the factors connected to structure, volume and quality of the content of dataset that is being utilized for task and for defining use cases of the defined problems. Taking a look for the dataset; many of researchers in their researches had operated for their proposed approaches with the following datasets; *QUWI databases, KHATT dataset, IAM dataset containing English texts, ICDAR2013, ICDAR2015, ICFHR2016.*

Each proposed notion has a varying level of accuracy, precision, and efficiency depending on the strategy and algorithm used. Very few researchers had employed their own developed dataset, however because they had used unsupervised algorithms for the evaluation, we believe their suggested methods and approaches to be ineffective. This gave us the idea to create our own dataset and propose a novel method for predicting human qualities using supervised learning. This will assist us in exploring new ideas as well as in suggesting a new, clearly defined dataset for fresh methodologies.

- QUWI DATABASE-QUWI dataset is a collection for various datasets which belongs to Qatar University Writer Identification organization. The QUWI dataset is generated by the volunteering of 1017 volunteers, which consists of handwriting samples for each volunteer. This dataset had stored samples of handwritten scripts written in bi-languages namely Arabic and English. The volunteers participated for the collection of handwriting data were of various ages, nationality and gender and education levels. All of them were asked to repeat an identical content to assemble their writing sample. This complete dataset is employed in two ways; one for the text that is dependent and another is independent to writers' identifications chore.
- KHATT DATABASE-This is kwon for KFUPM Handwritten Arabic Tex T. This dataset gathers the content for only written in Arabic language. There were all around 1000 writers' handwriting samples compiled and stored in it. All were from different countries so this consists of enormous types of writing sample for process and having effective results through various computational predictions.
- IAM DATASET-This dataset was first time published in the year 1999, in ICDAR 1999. This dataset consists of the varieties of English handwriting for 657 writers'. In this dataset there were around 1539 pages for scanned texts and it consists of 13353 images of handwritten scripts for 657 writers.
- ICDAR DATASET: ICDAR is defined as the International Conference on Document Analysis and Recognition in this context. The organization holds competitions every two years, and each hosting year, many datasets are produced as a result of these competitions. As a result, many datasets are available and being utilized to forecast and understand human qualities as well as for other views or hypotheses.

5 Comparison of Various Works

Table 1 compares and analyzes different research works based on features such as approach used, dataset, accuracy, advantage and disadvantage of the given approach and identifying character.

Table 1. Analysis of various approaches

Ref	Methodology	Dataset	Advantage/Disadvantage	Performance	Identifying character
[1]	KMI, SVM	ICDAR2013, RDF database in Chinese	Flexible, approachable, improved accuracy	Combined 72% (approx.) success to predict gender	Gender prediction
[2]	ANN, SVM, RFC, KNN	ICDAR2015, QUWI databases	Results with more accuracy Complex concept	KNN - 69% SVM - 70% (Approx.) is able to discriminate between gender	Discrimination between male and female
[3]	BIFs histograms, SVM	ICDAR2013, ICDAR2015, QUWI databases, ICFHR2016	Effective, efficient, robust	72% success in predicting gender	Gender prediction
[4]	RFC, Kernel discriminant analysis	QUWI databases	Not too flexible nut a good approach for prediction	70% approx. able to predict age, gender and nationality	Age, gender and nationality
[5]	Unsupervised learning algorithms; PCA, SNE	IRONOFF database	Good result giving approach Time consuming, less accuracy, can be uncertain with other dataset	Very complex approach with approx. 60%–66% accuracy in predicting age traits	Age

(continued)

Table 1. (*continued*)

Ref	Methodology	Dataset	Advantage/Disadvantage	Performance	Identifying character
[6]	SVM, GMM	IAM dataset - English, KHATT dataset - Arabic	Good approach to work with for prediction	SVM - 65% GMM - 67% approx. success for finding gender and handedness	Gender and handedness
[7]	OCR, SVM, RFC, KNN	QUWI databases, KHATT dataset	Flexible, accurate	Approx. 70% success for finding gender	Gender prediction
[13]	SVM, GMM	IAM DATA BASE	Better results than humans. Feature extraction process is complex	SVM - 62.19% GMM - 67.06% Success for gender and handedness prediction	Gender, Handedness
[14]	GMM	IAM DATA BASE	Classification results were comparatively accurate	Gender classification rate for test set: Online – 64.25%, Offline – 55.39%, Combination – 67.57%	Gender
[15]	KNN (k-Nearest Neighbor) Regularized logistic regression Decision tree and random forest	QUWI DATA BASE	Random forest method has shown the best results combining the classification methods Not all features separately (single feature) were used in LASSO technique	KNN – 71.54%, tree – 62.53%, random forest – 72.57% for finding gender	Gender

6 Conclusion

After the whole study of around fifty research papers, it can be concluded that for the prediction of human features both the Supervised Machine Learning algorithms and the Unsupervised Machine Learning algorithms can be experimented and utilized.

In case of supervised learning the algorithms that are utilized in few of the research papers are; Regression, Classification, Naive Bayes Model, Decision Tress, Random Forest Model, Neural Networks models, Convolutional Neural Networks models, Artificial Neural Networks models, Support Vector Machine, many more. Algorithms that are being used from Unsupervised Learning for different prediction approaches and ideas so far are; k-means clustering, K-nearest neighbor, Principal Component Analysis and plenty of more.

The concept proposals where only the supervised algorithms are being employed for the task are easy to grasp and are less complex concepts whereas the proposals within which for the completion of the research tasks the unsupervised algorithms are used are bit more complex concepts and provided less accuracy as compared to the supervised ones. But when either the algorithms are utilized in combination or certain unique traits they need provided more efficient results.

Unsupervised learning proposals had taken longer for the completion of the task and as compared to the present supervised learning algorithms is less time consuming. Alone unsupervised learning cannot provide the specified output because it finds the hidden patterns first and then proceed for training through unlabeled data. In contrary to the current supervised learning models predicts the output model fast as here training is completed through labeled data. For the prediction and identification purpose the classification and regression algorithms works more efficiently as compared to the clustering and association algorithms.

References

1. Bi, N., Suen, C.Y., Nobile, N., Tan, J.: A multi-feature selection approach for gender identification of handwriting based on kernel mutual information. Pattern Recogn. Lett. **121**, 123–132 (2019). https://doi.org/10.1016/j.patrec.2018.05.005
2. Ahmed, M., Rasool, A.G., Afzal, H., Siddiqi, I.: Improving handwriting based gender classification using ensemble classifiers. Expert Syst. Appl. **85**, 158–168 (2017). https://doi.org/10.1016/j.eswa.2017.05.033
3. Gattal, A., Djeddi, C., Siddiqi, I., Chibani, Y.: Gender classification from offline multi-script handwriting images using oriented Basic Image Features (oBIFs). Expert Syst. Appl. **99**, 155–167 (2018). https://doi.org/10.1016/j.eswa.2018.01.038
4. Al Maadeed, S., Hassaine, A.: Automatic prediction of age, gender, and nationality in offline handwriting. EURASIP J. Image Video Process. **2014**(1), 1–10 (2014). https://doi.org/10.1186/1687-5281-2014-10
5. Marzinotto, G., et al.: Age-related evolution patterns in online handwriting. Comput. Math. Methods Med. **2016**, 1–15 (2016). https://doi.org/10.1155/2016/3246595
6. Morera, Á., Sánchez, Á., Vélez, J.F., Moreno, A.B.: Gender and handedness prediction from offline handwriting using convolutional neural networks. Complexity **2018**, 1–14 (2018). https://doi.org/10.1155/2018/3891624

7. Maken, P., Gupta, A., Gupta, M.K.: A study on various techniques involved in gender prediction system: a comprehensive review. Cybern. Inf. Technol. **19**, 51–73 (2019). https://doi.org/10.2478/cait-2019-0015

8. Gattal, A., Djeddi, C., Bensefia, A., Ennaji, A.: Handwriting based gender classification using COLD and hinge features. In: El Moataz, A., Mammass, D., Mansouri, A., Nouboud, F. (eds.) ICISP 2020. LNCS, vol. 12119, pp. 233–242. Springer, Cham (2020). https://doi.org/10.1007/978-3-030-51935-3_25

9. Levi, G., Hassncer, T.: Age and gender classification using convolutional neural networks. In: 2015 IEEE Conference on Computer Vision and Pattern Recognition Workshops (CVPRW) (2015). https://doi.org/10.1109/cvprw.2015.7301352

10. Maken, P., Gupta, A.: A method for automatic classification of gender based on text-independent handwriting. Multimed. Tools Appl. **80**, 24573–24602 (2021). https://doi.org/10.1007/s11042-021-10837-9

11. Rahmanian, M., Shayegan, M.A.: Handwriting-based gender and handedness classification using convolutional neural networks. Multimed. Tools Appl. **80**, 35341–35364 (2021). https://doi.org/10.1007/s11042-020-10170-7

12. Siddiqi, I., Djeddi, C., Raza, A., Souici-meslati, L.: Automatic analysis of handwriting for gender classification. Pattern Anal. Appl. **18**, 887–899 (2014). https://doi.org/10.1007/s10044-014-0371-0

13. Liwicki, M., Schlapbach, A., Loretan, P., Bunke, H.: Automatic detection of gender and handedness from on-line handwriting. J. Soc. Psychol. **2007**(March), 179–183 (2007)

14. Liwicki, M., Schlapbach, A., Bunke, H.: Automatic gender detection using on-line and off-line information. Pattern Anal. Appl. **14**, 87–92 (2010). https://doi.org/10.1007/s10044-010-0178-6

15. Xie, Q., Xu, Q.: Gender prediction from handwriting. Data Min. Course Proj. **2013**, 10–13 (2013)

Indoor Human Fall Detection Using Deep Learning

Viraj Patel$^{(\boxtimes)}$ ⓘ, Suraj Kaple ⓘ, and Vishal R. Satpute

Department of Electronics and Communication Engineering, Visvesvaraya National Institute of
Technology, Nagpur, India
virajpatel0505@gmail.com, suraj.kaple@students.vnit.ac.in,
vrsatpute@ece.vnit.ac.in

Abstract. Falls are a paramount concern for aged people and can prove fatal if the
person remains unattended for a long time. Fall detection systems can prove useful
to avoid such situations and also help in eliminating fear among older people. In
this work, a system uses a hybrid version of a Long Short-Term Memory (LSTM)
network and Convolutional Neural Network (CNN) called the Long-term Recurrent Convolutional Network (LRCN) to detect falls in the real-time indoor environment. Our results suggest that using spatial and temporal information provides
the best solution for indoor fall detection.

Keywords: Fall detection · Long short-term memory network · Convolutional
neural network

1 Introduction

A fall is an event that results in a person coming to rest on the ground, floor, or other
lower-level surfaces by mistake [1]. Globally, more than 28% of people aged above 65
and more than 32% of people aged above 70 experience a fall each year causing injuries
like hip fracture, traumatic brain injuries, limb injuries, etc. Research has shown that the
fatal fall rate increases exponentially with increasing age. Apart from the trauma of the
event, fall incurred costs also impact the families. These costs depend upon the level of
injury and time the person was lying unattended. Hence, apart from the measures taken
to avoid a fall event, it is equally necessary to have an alarm system to detect a fall and
report it to the guardian as soon as possible.

There have been some wearable sensor-based approaches made toward detecting
fall. Qiang Li et al. [2] have proposed a fall detection method using posture information
derived from accelerometers and gyroscopes. Two accelerometers are placed at different
body locations which determine the static posture of human. Unintentional motion is
classified as a fall by analysing angular velocity and linear acceleration using the gyroscope. The combination of accelerometer and gyroscope helps increase the precision
and recall. This method has a fast response rate and is computationally less intense. In
recent years, developments in deep learning have enabled solving fall detection problem
effectively. Xiaogang Li et al. [12] have presented a fall detection system using CNN.

V. Sugumaran et al. (Eds.): AIR 2022, CCIS 1738, pp. 235–242, 2022.
https://doi.org/10.1007/978-3-031-23724-9_22

They have used the AlexNet convolutional neural network architecture with slight modifications to predict ADL (Activities of Daily Life) and Fall. They have directly fed colour image frames of the video to CNN to identify the deformation and posture of human and to predict if a fall occurs. They have applied a 10-fold cross-validation technique to estimate the execution of the approach. Na Lu et al. [13] have put forward a 3D CNN combined with LSTM based method for fall detection. They have used 3D CNN as it extracts both the spatial as well as temporal motion features present in the video. Furthermore, the features obtained from the 3D CNN are used to identify the region of interest (ROI) in every frame by incorporating a soft attention mechanism using LSTM. The training of 3D CNN is done on a different dataset containing no fall activities which is then merged with LSTM for training on the fall dataset. Wen-Nung Lie et al. [5] have put forward a DL algorithm comprising of estimation of a 2D human skeleton using CNN for every RGB frame for a single person. Additionally, the LSTM network is used to efficiently predict short-term actions into 5 classes. A Residual Network known as DeeperCut is used as the CNN architecture to extract 14 human skeleton joints. Using the hip and chin coordinates, the centroid of the human skeleton is computed. Then the 14 coordinates are converted to skeleton-centred coordinates w.r.t. the computed centroid to have translational invariance ultimately making the LSTM more robust. Kripesh Adhikari et al. [14] proposed a CNN model preceded by background subtraction to extract human silhouette and classify activities into six classes and predict fall activity based on transition speed of movement. Priyanka et al. [7] proposed a heuristic design comprising background subtraction for finding the region of interest (ROI) but this method fails in the case of a person lying on the floor as the person then is completely below the threshold height below which fall is declared. Martinez-Villaseñor et al. [15] have put forward a multimodal fall detection system based on wearable and ambient sensors along with vision devices by using LSTM and CNN for their analysis. Dina Chahyati et al. [16] used LSTM and CNN and combined both the results using the majority voting strategy. Anahita Shojaei-Hashemi et al. [10] proposed a method to extract 3D locations of major body joints and then use transfer learning to classify fall and non-fall activities.

This work presents a Long-term Recurrent Convolutional Network (LRCN) method which uses Convolutional Neural Network (CNN) followed by a Long Short-Term Memory (LSTM) network to extract the spatial information and to find a temporal relation between frames respectively. Real-time predictions are made to detect fall events or non-fall events.

2   Methodology

Feature design and extraction of discriminative features from training data is handled by the LRCN model allowing it to cover more real-life scenarios. To develop a human fall detection system, two different features are needed. They are (1) Spatial features and (2) Temporal features. Temporal features analyze the changes in those spatial features in the time domain. These models are end to end trainable. While the earlier models assumed a constant visual representation or carried out simple temporal averaging for sequential processing, recurrent convolutional models develop and learn compositional representation in time and space. The work flow block diagram of the proposed methodology is as shown in Fig. 1.

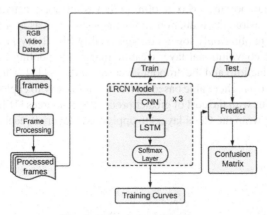

Fig. 1. Proposed methodology

2.1 Dataset Preprocessing

"NTU RGB + D Human Action Recognition Dataset" [17] is a wide-ranging database of RGB and depth videos. It involves 60 action classes majorly classified as daily actions, medical actions and mutual actions. The main objective of this project is human fall detection. Hence, by narrowing down the dataset, four actions "Falling Down", "Jump Up", "Sit Down", and "Standing Up" that closely resemble falling were chosen. Actions were performed by 40 different subjects under 17 different scenarios and were captured by three kinect V2 cameras concurrently with different horizontal imaging viewpoints namely −45°, 0°, +45°. The resolution of RGB video is 1920 × 1080. The videos contain 60 frames on an average out of which only 25 equally distributed frames were extracted. These 25 frames were processed as follows:

- Conversion from RGB to Grayscale
- Resizing frame dimensions to 64 × 64
- Frame normalization i.e. mapping pixel values from [0, 255] to [0, 1].

2.2 Convolutional Neural Network

A Convolutional Neural Network (CNN) has the ability to capture the spatial dependencies in the frame by making use of relevant filters [3]. The purpose of the CNN is to convert the frames into a format that is more efficient and easy in processing while retaining critical features for accurate prediction [4]. Following a convolutional layer, the pooling layer is used for the reduction of convolved features' spatial size [24]. The processing power needed to operate the data is lowered because of dimensionality reduction [6]. The extraction of positional and rotational invariant dominating features helps in keeping the operation of the model's training process smooth and is better done using a pooling layer [8]. There are two major types of pooling layers [23]. They are max pooling and average pooling. Max pooling removes all noisy activations (denoising) and performs dimensionality reduction simultaneously whereas as a noise-suppressing measure, average pooling only lowers dimensionality [9]. Every layer of the CNN is a formation of the convolutional layer (feature maps), the pooling layer (denoising & dimensionality reduction) and the dropout layer (overfitting) [11]. The number of layers may be improved to a higher value based on frame complexity to explore more low-level features. This comes with the cost of greater processing resources [18]. Time-distributed wrapper is used to wrap the CNN layers to apply CNN layers to each of the time slices of an input.

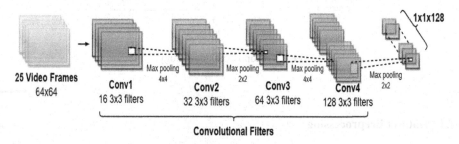

Fig. 2. CNN architecture

The input to the convolutional neural network as shown in Fig. 2 is a tensor having a shape (BATCH SIZE, SEQ LENGTH, rows, cols, 1) where SEQ LENGTH is the sequence length which is equal to 25, rows and cols are the frame height and width respectively and are equal to 64 [22]. This model included 4 convolutional layered architecture having 16, 32, 64 and 128 filters respectively. The size of each filter matrix is 3 × 3. Each one of the convolutional layers uses a rectified linear unit (ReLU) as an activation function. Following this is a max-pooling layer and a dropout layer with a probability equal to 0.4 to avoid over-fitting. The layer's output, a 3D feature vector, is flattened to obtain a tensor of shape (BATCH SIZE, SEQ LENGTH, 128).

2.3 Long Short Term Memory

In many circumstances, the output at each step, whether in time or space, is dependent not just on the current input but also on previous inputs. This type of data is known as sequential data and video is an example of time-sequenced sequential data [19]. A recurrent neural network (RNN) is the popular choice in the case of video classification in the field of deep learning [8]. The feedback loop in RNN simulates the correlation existing between video frames. RNNs might be deep in terms of layers, time, or both. However, because of the "vanishing gradient" phenomena, a normal RNN does not train successfully when it is deep in time [20]. A modified version of RNN i.e. LSTM neural network was introduced to address this issue and allow the neural network to handle extended sequences. Figure 3 is the LSTM unit having three types of gates input, output and forget [21]. Such 128 LSTM units formed the first LSTM layer followed by the second LSTM layer which has 32 units. The output of the LSTM network was fed to a dense layer which in turn passed on to the softmax activation function.

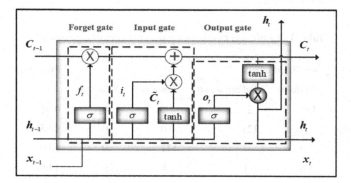

Fig. 3. LSTM unit

This function classified output into four classes: "Falling Down", "Jump Up", "Sit Down" and "Stand up". Finally, activities apart from "Falling down" were grouped under the "Non-Fall" category. On this final set of predictions, the rolling average is computed for a predetermined time period and the activity is classified as a "Falling Down" class or a "Non-Fall" class.

3 Results and Discussions

The dataset has 2121 videos, approximately 530 of each category i.e. falling down, jump up, sit down and stand up. Out of which 75% i.e. 1590 videos were used for training and 25% i.e. 531 videos were used for testing. Figure 4 shows the accuracy and loss function curves obtained during the training phase.

From Table 1, it can be observed that "falling down" metric parameters like the recall is 0.95 and the precision is 0.85. It means out of 128 total falling down actions, 121 were predicted correctly and 7 were predicted incorrectly as sit down actions. Also out of

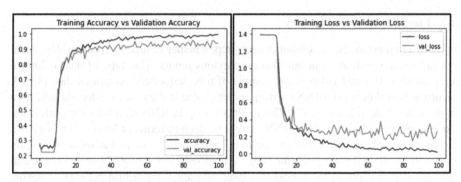

Fig. 4. Training curves

143 predicted as falls, 121 were actual falls, and others were non-falls. It was observed that sitting down majorly contributes to a false positive rate of falling down. The overall accuracy obtained is 94.54%.

Table 1. Confusion matrix along with performance parameters

Actual labels	Predicted labels				Precision	Recall
	Sit down	*Falling down*	*Jump up*	*Stand up*		
Sit down	**134**	21	0	0	**0.95**	**0.86**
Falling down	7	**121**	0	0	**0.85**	**0.95**
Jump up	0	1	**121**	0	**1.00**	**0.99**
Stand up	0	0	0	**126**	**1.00**	**1.00**

4 Conclusion

This project work proposed to use a deep learning Long-term Recurrent Convolutional model-based fall detection system. We trained the model on raw video as input. A CNN model is constructed which extracts spatial information from videos. The output of the CNN model is fed as input to the LSTM network which finds temporal relationships in the sequential data. Finally, the model classifies the input into four different human activity classes. The human activity classification accuracy obtained is 94.54%. The model was then tested on a sample video to identify "Falling Down" and "Non-fall" activities.

Acknowledgment. The funding for this work is received from the SERB funded research project entitled, "Development of a simple and low cost unified smart video surveillance system for suspicious human activity recognition in wide area surveillance" having sanction number [EEQ/2018/001103].

References

1. WHO global report on falls prevention in older age. https://www.who.int/publications/i/item/9789241563536. Accessed 07 Feb 2021
2. Li, Q., Stankovic, J.A., Hanson, M.A., Barth, A.T., Lach, J., Zhou, G.: Accurate, fast fall detection using gyroscopes and accelerometer-derived posture information. In: 2009 Sixth International Workshop on Wearable and Implantable Body Sensor Networks (2009). https://doi.org/10.1109/bsn.2009.46
3. Gajbhiye, P., Naveen, Ch., Satpute, V.R.: VIRTUe: video surveillance for rail-road traffic safety at unmanned level crossings; (Incorporating Indian scenario). In: 2017 IEEE Region 10 Symposium (TENSYMP) (2017). https://doi.org/10.1109/tenconspring.2017.8070015
4. Jirafe, A., Jibhe, M., Satpute, V.R.: Camera handoff for multi-camera surveillance. In: Kumar, R., Dohare, R.K., Dubey, H., Singh, V.P. (eds.) Applications of Advanced Computing in Systems. AIS, pp. 267–274. Springer, Singapore (2021). https://doi.org/10.1007/978-981-33-4862-2_29
5. Lie, W.-N., Le, A.T., Lin, G.-H.: Human fall-down event detection based on 2D skeletons and deep learning approach. In: 2018 International Workshop on Advanced Image Technology (IWAIT) (2018). https://doi.org/10.1109/iwait.2018.8369778
6. Pawade, A., Anjaria, R., Satpute, V.R.: Suspicious activity detection for security cameras. In: Kumar, R., Dohare, R.K., Dubey, H., Singh, V.P. (eds.) Applications of Advanced Computing in Systems. AIS, pp. 211–217. Springer, Singapore (2021). https://doi.org/10.1007/978-981-33-4862-2_22
7. Sase, P.S., Bhandari, S.H.: Human fall detection using depth videos. In: 2018 5th International Conference on Signal Processing and Integrated Networks (SPIN) (2018). https://doi.org/10.1109/spin.2018.8474181
8. Gangal, P.P., Satpute, V.R., Kulat, K.D., Keskar, A.G.: A novel approach based on 2D - DWT and variance method for human detection and tracking in video surveillance applications. In: 2014 International Conference on Contemporary Computing and Informatics (IC3I) (2014). https://doi.org/10.1109/ic3i.2014.7019593
9. Gangal, P.P., Satpute, V.R., Kulat, K.D., Keskar, A.G.: Object detection and tracking using 2D—DWT and variance method. In: 2014 Students Conference on Engineering and Systems (2014). https://doi.org/10.1109/sces.2014.6880123
10. Shojaei-Hashemi, A., Nasiopoulos, P., Little, J.J., Pourazad, M.T.: Video-based human fall detection in smart homes using deep learning. In: 2018 IEEE International Symposium on Circuits and Systems (ISCAS) (2018). https://doi.org/10.1109/iscas.2018.8351648
11. Gupta, A., Stapute, V.R., Kulat, K.D., Bokde, N.: Real-time abandoned object detection using video surveillance. In: Afzalpulkar, N., Srivastava, V., Singh, G., Bhatnagar, D. (eds.) Proceedings of the International Conference on Recent Cognizance in Wireless Communication & Image Processing, pp. 837–843. Springer, New Delhi (2016). https://doi.org/10.1007/978-81-322-2638-3_94
12. Li, X., Pang, T., Liu, W., Wang, T.: Fall detection for elderly person care using convolutional neural networks. In: 2017 10th International Congress on Image and Signal Processing, BioMedical Engineering and Informatics (CISP-BMEI) (2017). https://doi.org/10.1109/cisp-bmei.2017.8302004
13. Lu, N., Wu, Y., Feng, L., Song, J.: Deep learning for fall detection: three-dimensional CNN combined with LSTM on video kinematic data. IEEE J. Biomed. Health Inform. **23**, 314–323 (2019). https://doi.org/10.1109/jbhi.2018.2808281
14. Adhikari, K., Bouchachia, H., Nait-Charif, H.: Activity recognition for indoor fall detection using convolutional neural network. In: 2017 Fifteenth IAPR International Conference on Machine Vision Applications (MVA) (2017). https://doi.org/10.23919/mva.2017.7986795

15. Martinez-Villasenor, L., Ponce, H., Perez-Daniel, K.: Deep learning for multimodal fall detection. In: 2019 IEEE International Conference on Systems, Man and Cybernetics (SMC) (2019). https://doi.org/10.1109/smc.2019.8914429

16. Chahyati, D., Hawari, R.: Fall detection on multimodal dataset using convolutional neural network and long short term memory. In: 2020 International Conference on Advanced Computer Science and Information Systems (ICACSIS) (2020). https://doi.org/10.1109/icacsis51025.2020.9263201

17. Shahroudy, A., Liu, J., Ng, T.-T., Wang, G.: NTU RGB+D: a large scale dataset for 3D human activity analysis. In: 2016 IEEE Conference on Computer Vision and Pattern Recognition (CVPR) (2016). https://doi.org/10.1109/cvpr.2016.115

18. Parate, M.R., Satpute, V.R., Bhurchandi, K.M.: Global-patch-hybrid template-based arbitrary object tracking with integral channel features. Appl. Intell. **48**, 300–314 (2017). https://doi.org/10.1007/s10489-017-0974-4

19. Abdo, H., Amin, K.M., Hamad, A.M.: Fall detection based on RetinaNet and MobileNet convolutional neural networks. In: 2020 15th International Conference on Computer Engineering and Systems (ICCES) (2020). https://doi.org/10.1109/icces51560.2020.9334570

20. Sharma, S., Dhama, V.: Abnormal human behavior detection in video using suspicious object detection. In: Kumar, A., Paprzycki, M., Gunjan, V.K. (eds.) ICDSMLA 2019. LNEE, vol. 601, pp. 379–388. Springer, Singapore (2020). https://doi.org/10.1007/978-981-15-1420-3_39

21. Nale, R., Sawarbandhe, M., Chegogoju, N., Satpute, V.: Suspicious human activity detection using pose estimation and LSTM. In: 2021 International Symposium of Asian Control Association on Intelligent Robotics and Industrial Automation (IRIA) (2021). https://doi.org/10.1109/iria53009.2021.9588719

22. Ramirez, H., Velastin, S.A., Meza, I., Fabregas, E., Makris, D., Farias, G.: Fall detection and activity recognition using human skeleton features. IEEE Access **9**, 33532–33542 (2021). https://doi.org/10.1109/access.2021.3061626

23. Thombare, P., Gond, V., Satpute, V.R.: Artificial intelligence for low level suspicious activity detection. In: Kumar, R., Dohare, R.K., Dubey, H., Singh, V.P. (eds.) Applications of Advanced Computing in Systems. AIS, pp. 219–226. Springer, Singapore (2021). https://doi.org/10.1007/978-981-33-4862-2_23

24. Chen, Y., Du, R., Luo, K., Xiao, Y.: Fall detection system based on real-time pose estimation and SVM. In: 2021 IEEE 2nd International Conference on Big Data, Artificial Intelligence and Internet of Things Engineering (ICBAIE) (2021). https://doi.org/10.1109/icbaie52039.2021.9390068

Colour Detection for Interior Designs Using Machine Learning

Tarcisius Forjong Dewingong[1]([✉]) [iD], Mary Echabuo Afor[1], Pradeep Kumar Mishra[1], Sasmita Mishra[2], Gouri Sankar Mishra[1], and Bello Ibrahim Aliyu[1]

[1] Department of Computer Science and Engineering, School of Engineering and Technology, Sharda University, Greater Noida, India
dewingongt@gmail.com, {pradeepkumar.mishra, gourisankar.mishra}@sharda.ac.in
[2] Department of Business Management, C. V. Raman Global University, Bhubaneswar, Odisha, India
sasmitamishra@cgu-odisha.ac.in

Abstract. Colours have a significant impact on human psychology and emotions. An essential part of interior design is choosing appropriate colours for a facility's areas. Simply gazing at the colours does nothing but satisfy the eyes. However, understanding its origins and selecting the best colour becomes difficult. This paper presents a solution for colour detection systems in interior design. Using machine learning to teach the system how to recognise colour in RGB space and predict its name and values. Open-Source computer vision (OpenCV) is used in this system for computer vision and to process the image which has to be detected while Pandas a python library collects the data from the dataset and analysis them to give the appropriate prediction of the colour name and values. The Colour Detection method is implemented using the Colour Detection and Segmentation approach in image processing and the result is displayed by double-clicking on any part of the image to detect the colour at that point of the image.

Keywords: Colour detection · Interior design · Image processing · OpenCV · Machine learning · RGB colour model

1 Introduction

The boom and the evolution of technology, lead to diverse levels of innovation in areas such as real estate and construction for example. Among other fields that are affected by the evolution of technology stands interior design. Interior design is one of the fast-growing fields among others, be it at the level of commercial or residential or any hospitality space, everyone is looking for a unique concept that reflects their taste for interior designs [1]. This has objects, lighting and other tools involved as putting these together brings out the aesthetics of interior design. Interior design is architectural, that is, getting the layout to be right as per the client's needs. In this project, we look at the interior design with the overall flow and the texture, colour schemes, merging, and

V. Sugumaran et al. (Eds.): AIR 2022, CCIS 1738, pp. 243–254, 2022.
https://doi.org/10.1007/978-3-031-23724-9_23

blending of colours (decor schemes). This further defines Interior design as a profound artiste that conveys a clear understanding of the message a colour carries.

Before going into the project's hypothesis, it's essential to first grasp the concept of colour detection. Colour detection refers to the process of determining the name of any colour in a given image. People do this behaviour naturally and without putting any effort as emotions might be the main booster at the said time for the said colour detected by humans over machines. However, in the situation of computers, it is not the case as computers do not portray any result based on emotions but facts and specifics, unlike humans who are either moved by emotions and likewise colourized settings might and could ignite an emotion (coloured). The signal is being forwarded to the cortex via light receptors in the eyes, which identify the colour. Humans have associated specific lights with their colour designations from birth, hence this is not an exaggeration. In this project, the same method works well for detecting colour names.

Machine Learning has been at the heart of most detection approaches. As per Arthur Samuel, machine learning (ML) is defined as "A field of research that offers machines the capability to acquire knowledge without even being explicatively programmed". Machine Learning (ML) is the ability to execute and enhance a computer's learning process based on its experiences without any need for human interaction [2]. The procedure begins with the provision of quality data, which will then be utilised to educate our machines (computers) through the creation of machine learning techniques based on the information and other approaches. The type of information we have now and the task we're aiming to automate influence the algorithms we apply. This approach uses a dataset of 865 colour names and RGB values to teach the computer how to predict a colour name and its RGB value automatically. The RGB colour space is a colour system whereby the red, green, and blue lights are mixed in various ways to produce a wide range of colours [3]. In the RGB model, each red, green, and blue colour component of an image is represented by an $M \times N \times 3$ pixel matrix with M rows and N columns of pixels.

Computer vision is an interdisciplinary branch of science that uses digital images or videos to perform operations that human vision is capable of. From an engineering standpoint, it aims to comprehend and automate operations that the visual system is capable of performing. Gathering, processing, and interpreting data from digital images are all part of computer vision activities. Open-Source computer vision (OpenCV) is used for the processing of images and colour detection. This project's concept is to create an application that allows users to obtain the name of a colour by simply clicking on it. The distance between each colour is calculated to determine the shortest one using a data file containing the colour name and values.

2 Literature Survey

There are a good number of proposed techniques for colour detection as per some existing facts that depict and brings concrete understanding and comprehension to the preference of this said project of colour detection.

Duth, Sudharshan and Deepa, M. [4] provides a way for identifying two-dimensional pictures in MATLAB via colour thresholds and RGB Colour model to determine the user's preferred colour in the image. In their methodology, the system reads an inputted image, it then creates RGB Colour bands of the Image and calculates and plot the colour band histogram in red, green, and blue. After plotting the colour band histogram, it subtracts the two pictures to create a 2-dimensional black and white image after converting the 3-D RGB image to a grayscale image, with the use of the bounding box and its attributes, it recognises the linked element mark in the connected area of the image and filters the noisy picture parts with a median filter., and compute the metric for each marking area. It is a good approach but the algorithm has some flaws. It just evaluates the picture element's intensity values but ignores any link among them, extra pixels that don't appear to be part of the required region are detected, and these inaccuracies grow as the noise level rises.

N. Otsu (1979) [5] from the standpoint of discriminant analysis, suggested a way for mechanically picking out a criterion from a grey level bar graph in his article. This immediately addresses the issue of determining the usefulness of benchmarks. By maximising the discriminating measure character from the alphabeting addition, the discriminant criteria find the corresponding best threshold or set of thresholds.

Wyszecki G and Stiles WS (1982) [6] proposes a project still on colour detection which makes credible elaboration and that explains colour science concepts and methodologies. To recognize the shade in the image or of an object the RGB display is employed. The RGB literally expatiates as the Red Green Blue. The RGB display is a colouring model which uses red, green and blue lights to generate various effects to produce a diverse or specific range of colours. This proposed research work labels the regarded colour science ideas and policies.

M. Sezgin et al. [7] he categorised image threshold approaches, published their formulas in a standardised notation, and compared effectiveness in his research. The threshold approach is classified as a histogram, spatial clusters, volatility, attributes of objects, high connection, or a surface in its natural grayscale. It also recognises approaches that have advanced thresholds more than the Non-Destructive Testing (NDT) and documentary image applications.

Nikhil Pandey, Aayushi Saxena and Amanya Verma [8]. Their paper proposed a colour detection system that is developed in python using the OpenCV library and pandas. The system detects colour in an image when clicked on a particular area of the image. The image processing and colour detection techniques were successfully implemented.

Neal N. Xiong, et al. [9] proposed a unique real-time colour picture segmentation algorithm based on RGB colour space colour similarity is proposed in their paper. The dominant colour is identified first using colour and brightness information in RGB colour space, and then colour similarity may be estimated using the suggested colour component calculation technique, which generates a colour-class map. The pixels are then classified using the information from the associated colour-class map. For the reason of probable measurement imperfection, they also propose a colour correction and light source adjustment approach. They develop a unique approach for detecting a fire in a live video that is built with these features by integrating a suggested segmentation algorithm with a colour sensor in real-time colour image division for Cyber-physical systems (CPS). Experiments indicated that the suggested technique for fire identification based on vision and detection in movies was successful, with accurate findings that could be employed in a real-time assessment or analysis.

Masato Takahashi, et al. [10] developed colour charts containing the colours of the human skin and tongue as a guide to aid doctors in more precisely identifying the colour of patients during a telemedicine check-up. The suggested procedure was unanimously judged to be feasible in terms of a colour inspection after a subjective assessment by eight medical specialists. The colour chart that has been created can also be utilized for automated colour correction.

Resti, Yulia and Burlian, et al. (2020) [11] used the k-means technique and three unique metric distances: Manhattan, Euclidean, and Minkowski to construct and analyse a can waste sorting system that is based on the CYMK (Cyan, Magenta, Yellow, and Black) digital image colour model. The use of experimental results to enact three distinct metric ranges on the k-means cluster analysis system for classifying cans wastages into three different types reveals that the average precision of k-means cluster analysis for two distances, Euclidean and Minkowski, seems to be similar, with an accuracy level difference of 1% or less, whereas the Manhattan distance seems to have a much lower level of accuracy. Because it has an average accuracy of less than 70% for both simulation and experiment data, which each implements three distances, this technique is not appropriate for constructing a can classification system.

P. Raguraman et al. (2021) [12]. The purpose of this work is to extract the needed colour field from an RGB picture. The OpenCV platform is used to implement numerous processes. The key advantage of this approach is that it can differentiate monochrome colours. The process of recognising colour shades with an exact forecast of their names is the major goal of this programme.

Deborah T. Joy, et al. (2021) [13]. This study suggests that a computer be taught to recognise and describe colours accurately enough to be helpful. The suggested detection approach takes advantage of a camera and the data it receives to identify colour based on RGB values. Calls to a function that performs loops on realigning the distance depending on the closest match were used in the algorithm.

Raghav puri, Archit Gupta, Manas Sikri (2018) [14]. The study created a technique for distinguishing contours, shapes, and colours of various geometrical objects in binary photographs using Python, Open-Source Computer Vision Library, and Numpy. For processing the images, the most basic operations are employed, which include loading them and identifying distinct forms and colours within the provided sample images. The publication of Alasdair McAndrew (2004) [15] gives a thorough introduction to MATLAB-based digital image processing.

3   Methodology

There are several methods for detecting colours, ranging from physical approaches to the most recent machine learning techniques and even web scraping techniques. The RGB model, CYMK colour model, HSL colour model, and other popular colour detection systems are only a few examples. For colour detection, the proposed system employs the RGB colour model. The process is as follows.

- Read Image: The first stage of the method is to input a high-quality image, read the input image using the cv2.imread (img_name) method of the OpenCV library. The image may be uploaded from any folder.
- Import dataset: The second step is to import the dataset containing the colour names and RGB values. For this, a CSV file was used, read the CSV file using pandas' library.
- RGB colour Extraction: The RGB colours are extracted from the input image in this step. Each primary colour is assigned an intensity value ranging from 0 to 255. A variety of colours may be created by blending three primary colours at varying intensities.
- Calculate the distance coordinates: The minimum distance from all colours is calculated to find the shortest one and to get the most matching colour to calculate.
- Display the image in a window: The image with shades of colour is displayed in the rectangular window. The RGB values and colour name are updated once the double-click is triggered. The Cv2.imshow() method is used to display an image. The colour name and intensity level may be acquired using the cv2.rectangle and cv2.putText() methods (Fig. 1).

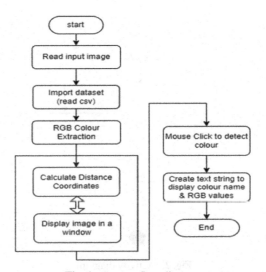

Fig. 1. System flow diagram

The flow of the detecting system, as depicted in the preceding phases, is shown in the diagram above. Based on concepts and qualities connected, the aforementioned system flow makes the process more efficient. When employing RGB colour combinations, as opposed to CMYK and HSL approaches, colour detection is a very straightforward operation. In comparison, RGB has a higher level of precision. As a result, the accurateness is determined by mapping the initial RGB values to the actual colour values and calculating the error. Now, to make the system more user-friendly and pleasant to use, a web application was constructed utilising the Django framework and Python as the based programming language, which allows a user to upload an image, double-click it, and retrieve its RGB value as well as the colour match that is closest to it. Python libraries like OpenCV and pandas were used in this system for the detection process (Fig. 2).

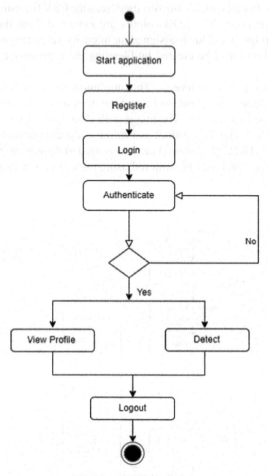

Fig. 2. Activity diagram

The activity diagram shown above depicts the flow of the system from the beginning to the end, and also many decision paths that occur whilst the activity is being carried out. An activity diagram is a diagram that portrays the behaviour of the system. The activity diagram has been used to show both sequential and parallel processing of activities.

The RGB Color Space
The colour space is the most extensively used colour space, in which a colour point in the space is defined by the three colour components of the associated pixel: (R) red, (G) green, and (B) blue. However, because there are so many colour spaces, it's easier to

group them into fewer groups based on their definitions and qualities. The colour spaces were classified into the following groups by Nicolas et al. [17].

The primary colour spaces are the real RGB, subtractive CMY, and imaginary XYZ primary spaces, which are founded on the premise that it is possible to match any colour by combining an adequate proportion of the three fundamental colours. The RGB to CMY conversion is shown below [18].

$$C' = 1 - R \quad C = \min\left(1, \max\left(0, C' - K'\right)\right)$$

$$M' = 1 - G \quad M = \min\left(1, \max\left(0, M' - K'\right)\right)$$

$$Y' = 1 - B \quad Y = \min\left(1, \max\left(0, Y' - K'\right)\right)$$

$$K' = \min\left(C', M', Y'\right)$$

and the conversion from RGB to XYZ is

$$\begin{bmatrix} X \\ Y \\ Z \end{bmatrix} = \begin{bmatrix} 0.412453 & 0.357580 & 0.180423 \\ 0.212671 & 0.715160 & 0.072169 \\ 0.019334 & 0.119193 & 0.950227 \end{bmatrix} \begin{bmatrix} R \\ G \\ B \end{bmatrix}.$$

4   Results and Discussions

The initial step in detecting colour in the image processing job is to have an image. You have the option of uploading photographs from your hard drive or capturing images from your camera. A 3-D matrix of size M × N × 3, with each RGB component that represents a colour image in the most prevalent form, is the RGB format of an image with a resolution of M × N. The red, green, blue parts of the picture are represented by the input image matrix.

Fig. 3. Input image

An original image of a room from which the colour must be extracted is shown in Fig. 3. The primary colours are extracted from this image using the cv2.imread() method in OpenCV to gain correct information on the subject of the amount of these colours contained in the image. The minimal distance between all colours in our dataset is determined using the function getColorName(R, G, B) to get the most matching colour.

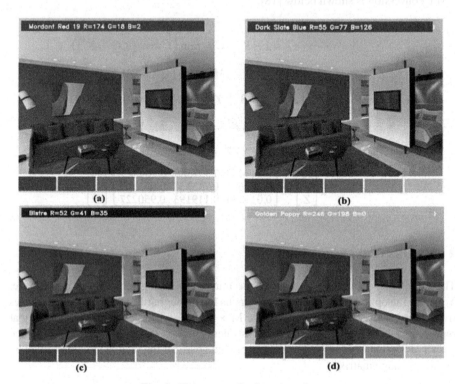

Fig. 4. The output of colour detection

When you double-click on a particular portion of the image, Fig. 4 displays the colour name as well as the RGB colour values. (a) display image with RGB colour intensity values (r-174, g-18, b-2) for Mordant Red 19, (b) display image with RGB colour intensity values (r-55, g-77, b-126) for Dark State Blue, (c) display image with RGB colour intensity values (r-52, g-41, b-33) for Bistre, and (d) display image with RGB colour intensity values (r-246, g-198, b-0) for Golden Poppy. Other test results from different images are displayed in Fig. 5 below.

Fig. 5. Test cases on different images

A dataset of 865 colours and their RGB values is used to test the result. The end product appears to be a success, as it can anticipate or recognise a colour with 97% accuracy. When it comes to accuracy, adjusting the updated distances can help increase the accuracy of the RGB distance calculation process. When compared to parallel colour models, the RGB model has the extra benefit of categorization on all-colour neutral grounds, which makes it easier to compute distances frequently with more precision (Table 1).

Table 1. Dataset

Colour name	Code	R	G	B
Air Force Blue (Raf)	#5d8aa8	93	138	168
Air Force Blue (Usaf)	#00308f	0	48	143
Air Superiority Blue	#72a0c1	114	160	193
Alabama Crimson	#a32638	163	38	56
Alice Blue	#f0f8ff	240	248	255
Alizarin Crimson	#e32636	227	38	54
Alloy Orange	#c46210	196	98	16
Almond	#efdecd	239	222	205
Amaranth	#e52b50	229	43	80
Amber	#ffbf00	255	191	0
Amber (Sae/Ece)	#ff7e00	255	126	0
American Rose	#ff033e	255	3	62
Amethyst	#96c	153	102	204
Android Green	#a4c639	164	198	57
Anti-Flash White	#f2f3f4	242	243	244
Antique Brass	#cd9575	205	149	117
Antique Fuchsia	#915c83	145	92	131
Antique Ruby	#841b2d	132	27	45
Antique White	#faebd7	250	235	215
Ao (English)	#008000	0	128	0
Apple Green	#8db600	141	182	0
Apricot	#fbceb1	251	206	177
Aqua	#0ff	0	255	255

The following table depicts a portion of our dataset; the dataset utilised for this study is a CSV file including 865 colour names, colour codes, and RGB values.

5 Future Work

Although this study focuses on colour recognition in interior designs, several features might be added to the programme to improve usability in any context. Features include the ability to recognise colour in a live video and the ability to capture a photo using the camera. This idea might be used in a multitude of fields, including exterior design. Exterior design is also a crucial component that should not be overlooked. The external design may sometimes easily grab a lot of attention, to the point where people are curious about the name of a certain colour. Colour detection systems might also be used to sort mining (diamond, gold) materials. Most mining companies use manual means for sorting gold, diamond and other minerals and without good eyesight, it is very difficult to tell the difference between these minerals, thus this project will also facilitate the sorting of minerals for mining industries as well. Finally, a colour detection system could also be used for pollution detection. Air pollution is one of the sectors that is least monitored or found at the most inconvenient times. The ability to detect the colour of the atmosphere could be extremely useful in preventing incidents or accidents (such as fires) from wreaking havoc on a given environment, thus limiting the danger and facilitating data. Finally, colour detection systems can be used for both information and communication systems.

6 Conclusion

In this research paper, using Machine learning we present a solution for colour detection systems in interior design to teach the system how to recognise colour in RGB space and predict its name and values. The various steps are implemented using OpenCV for computer vision and image processing, while the Pandas library is used to gather and analyse the data from the dataset. The Colour Detection method is implemented using the Colour Detection and Segmentation approach in image processing. A dataset of 865 colours and their RGB values is used to test the result. The end product appears to be a success, as it can anticipate or recognise a colour with 97% accuracy. The outcomes are efficient and close.

References

1. Guanggen, L., Matthews, A.: Color recognition of design object of manual decoration element based on convolution neural network under the impact of COVID-19. J. Intell. Fuzzy Syst. **39**, 8739–8746 (2020). https://doi.org/10.3233/jifs-189270
2. Praba, R., Darshan, G., Roshanraj, T.K., Prakash, B.S.: Study on machine learning algorithms. Int. J. Sci. Res. Comput. Sci. Eng. Inf. Technol. **7**, 67–72 (2021). https://doi.org/10.32628/cseit2173105
3. Goel, V., Singhal, S., Jain, T., Kole, S.: Specific color detection in images using RGB modelling in MATLAB. Int. J. Comput. Appl. **161**, 38–42 (2017). https://doi.org/10.5120/ijca201791 3254
4. Sudharshan Duth, P., Mary Deepa, M.: Color detection in RGB-modeled images using MAT LAB. Int. J. Eng. Technol. **7**, 29 (2018). https://doi.org/10.14419/ijet.v7i2.31.13391
5. Otsu, N.: A threshold selection method from gray-level histograms. IEEE Trans. Syst. Man Cybern. **9**, 62–66 (1979). https://doi.org/10.1109/tsmc.1979.4310076
6. Billmeyer, F.W.: Color Science: Concepts and Methods, Quantitative Data and Formulae, 2nd edn., by Gunter Wyszecki and W. S. Stiles, John Wiley and Sons, New York, 1982, 950 pp. Price: $75.00. Color Research Application 8, 262–263 (1983). https://doi.org/10.1002/col.5080080421
7. Sankur, B.: Survey over image thresholding techniques and quantitative performance evaluation. J. Electron. Imaging **13**, 146 (2004). https://doi.org/10.1117/1.1631315
8. Pour Yousefian Barfeh, D., Ramos, E.: Color detection in autonomous robot-camera. J. Phys.: Conf. Ser. **1169**, 012048 (2019). https://doi.org/10.1088/1742-6596/1169/1/012048
9. Xiong, N.N., Shen, Y., Yang, K., Lee, C., Wu, C.: Color sensors and their applications based on real-time color image segmentation for cyber physical systems. EURASIP J. Image Video Process. **2018**(1), 1–16 (2018). https://doi.org/10.1186/s13640-018-0258-x
10. Takahashi, M., Takahashi, R., Morihara, Y., Kin, I., Ogawa-Ochiai, K., Tsumura, N.: Development of a camera-based remote diagnostic system focused on color reproduction using color charts. Artif. Life Robot. **25**(3), 370–376 (2020). https://doi.org/10.1007/s10015-020-00627-1

11. Resti, Y., Burlian, F., Yani, I., Rosiliani, D.: Analysis of a cans waste classification system based on the CMYK color model using different metric distances on the k-means method. J. Phys: Conf. Ser. **1500**, 012010 (2020). https://doi.org/10.1088/1742-6596/1500/1/012010

12. Raguraman, P., Meghana, A., Navya, Y., Karishma, S., Iswarya, S.: Color detection of RGB images using Python and OpenCv. Int. J. Sci. Res. Comput. Sci. Eng. Inf. Technol. **7**, 109–112 (2021). https://doi.org/10.32628/cseit217119

13. Joy, D.T., Kaur, G., Chugh, A., Bajaj, S.B.: Computer vision for color detection. Int. J. Innov. Res. Comput. Sci. Technol. **9**, 53–59 (2021). https://doi.org/10.21276/ijircst.2021.9.3.9

14. Puri, R., Gupta, A., Sikri, M.: Contour, shape, and colour detection using OpenCV – Python. Int. J. Adv. Electron. Comput. Sci. **5**(3), 4–6 (2018)

15. McAndrew, A.: Introduction to Digital Image Processing with MATLAB. Course Technology, Boston (2004)

16. Zhang, J., Pan, R., Gao, W., Zhu, D.: Automatic recognition of the color effect of yarn-dyed fabric by the smallest repeat unit recognition algorithm. Text. Res. J. **85**, 432–446 (2014). https://doi.org/10.1177/0040517514548811

17. Vandenbroucke, N., Macaire, L., Postaire, J.-G.: Color image segmentation by pixel classification in an adapted hybrid color space. Application to soccer image analysis. Comput. Vis. Image Underst. **90**, 190–216 (2003). https://doi.org/10.1016/s1077-3142(03)00025-0

18. Khattab, D., Ebied, H.M., Hussein, A.S., Tolba, M.F.: Color image segmentation based on different color space models using automatic GrabCut. Sci. World J. **2014**, 1–10 (2014). https://doi.org/10.1155/2014/126025

A Review on Estimation of Workload from Electroencephalogram (EEG) Using Machine Learning

Mansi Sharma$^{(\boxtimes)}$ ⓘ and Ela Kumar ⓘ

Indira Gandhi Delhi Technical University for Women (IGDTUW), Delhi, India
mmansi069@gmail.com, ela_kumar@igdtuw.ac.in

Abstract. Human workload plays a very important role in daily productivity while performing tasks. The mental workload in participants utilizing an electroencephalogram (EEG) can be described as the ratio of mental effort to brain capacity. It is a complex signal that requires high-level processing and long-term training to extract useful patterns and results. Recently, machine learning approaches have shown tremendous promise in this area. Many researchers have utilized the availability of large EEG datasets and growing capabilities of deep learning to estimate cognitive workload with satisfactory outcomes. To identify mental tasks, they used machine learning methods like K Nearest Neighbor (KNN) and Support Vector Machine (SVM). The findings of Artificial Neural Network (ANN) and Logistic Regression (LR) classifiers were also satisfactory. Furthermore, when the optimal network design was identified, the Noise Reduction Autoencoder (SDAE) beat several existing mental load estimators. In this paper, we review several research papers on the Deep learning applications to electroencephalogram (EEG) that have been published in recent years, and they span a wide range of topics including epilepsy, cognitive and emotional monitoring. In order to guide future research, we collected trends from this substantial literature and highlighted noteworthy approaches. The ability to reliably and automatically classify these signals is a critical step toward formation of the electroencephalogram (EEG) more useful in a variety of applications and reducing the need for skilled specialists. A systematic review of the literature on the application of deep learning for electroencephalogram (EEG) categorization was conducted to attain this goal.

Keywords: Mental workload · Electroencephalogram (EEG) · Deep learning · Brain computer interface (BCI)

1 Introduction

The voltage signal produced by synchronized brain activity is known as an electroencephalogram (EEG). The EEG is created by the brain which has millions of neurons that communicate with one another. The EEG can be measured in two different methods: The electrodes can either be placed on or near the scalp, or they can be implanted into the skull. EEG signals alter as synchronized brain activity changes with developmental, mental state, and cognitive activities.

© The Author(s), under exclusive license to Springer Nature Switzerland AG 2022
V. Sugumaran et al. (Eds.): AIR 2022, CCIS 1738, pp. 255–264, 2022.
https://doi.org/10.1007/978-3-031-23724-9_24

1.1 Classification of Workload and Relationship to Brain-Computer Interface (BCI)

The amount of mental resources an individual utilizes for a given task and at a given moment influences their capacity to absorb information and make decisions in reaction to their surroundings, which is referred to as cognitive workload. A scale with two opposed ends can be characterized as it.

- When too much information is being processed - Overload
- When the processing information is below the threshold level - Underload.

Workload level monitoring provides information on the state of agent workloads and helps you manage them using a variety of methods [1].

In [1], most experiments use one of two common workload-inducing approaches. The first is a task battery, in which individuals are required to complete multiple tasks in two or more independent task windows. NASA's Multi-Attribute Task Battery (MATB) popularized this format, which tries to boost mental workload through multitasking, with studies including mental workload employing the Multi-Attribute Task Battery or similarly inspired task. The another style involves inducing workload using mental arithmetic, with highly complex arithmetic problems resulting in a high workload level.

Traditionally, mental load levels are assessed through a person's oral or written feedback. However, the reliability of these self-reported measures depends on the individual's metacognition abilities [5]. The goal of a brain-computer interface (BCI) is to develop a different kind of communication that gives the human brain a way to operate an object without using muscles. Using machine learning techniques, it converts electroencephalography (EEG) information derived from brain activity into control commands [3].

1.2 Challenges in EEG Processing

An important method for measuring mental workload has been demonstrated to be the electroencephalogram (EEG) including Neuromarketing, Psychology, Neuroscience, and analysing the mental capability of humans in different situations, However, it still has a number of flaws that make it difficult to do meaningful analysis or processing. For starters, the Electroencephalogram possesses a poor signal-to-noise ratio (SNR) because amplified brain activities is frequently buried in many ambient sources due to physiological and active impacts of specific noise or higher amplitude, referred to as 'artefacts.' As a result, they required to reduce the impacts of the noise circles and recover the genuine brain activity from the signal recording. It's also a signal that isn't fixed. In other words, the statistics are always different. As a result, the classifier trained in temporary user data can summarize data from the same person that was recorded at several periods. This is a significant issue in real electroencephalogram applications that often have to work with limited data volumes [7].

Brain-computer interface research and development are rife with signal processing issues, especially for those relying on motor imagery electroencephalography (MI-EEG). Choosing the most efficient techniques for feature extraction and selection is difficult since EEG data is highly non-stationary, non-linear, and artifact-prone. Data fusion is one of the issues, namely how to combine data from many EEG channels to decrease the dimensionality of the data and perhaps improve classification outcomes. To choose the best categorization methods for the given features, more study is needed. Research into features and classifiers should concentrate on figuring out the best practices to use for patients with central nervous system (CNS) impairment or illness, in addition to establishing the best strategies to employ for those individuals [22].

1.3 Improvement Through Deep Learning

To solve the aforementioned challenges, a new strategy is necessary to boost generality and flexible application possibilities. In this context, deep learning (DL) can significantly simplify the processing of the pipeline, so you can automatically teach pre-processing, extraction modules, classifications, and competitive performance in target operations. In practice, DL architectures are very successful in handling complex data, such as images, audio, and text signals, such as a large-scale visualization problem, such as leading to a variety of social steps, such as large visualization problems in Industrial applications. Deep Learning, Sealing Machine Learning, Computing Model to Study Hierarchical Expression of Input Data through Continuous Nonlinear Conversion. The Deep Neural Network (DNN) that inspired previous models such as Perceptron is a model [7]. A folded layer of artificial "neurons" is attached to the linear transformation with each data. The linear level of each layer conversion is supplied through the nonlinear activation function. It's worth noting that the parameters of these transformations are investigated by reducing the cost function directly. The term "deep" refers to a network with various layers, however there is no agreement on how to quantify depth in neural networks, and hence no agreement on what constitutes a true deep network.

1.4 Understanding EEG In-depth

The hypothesis that consciousness levels and ranges are correlated with the nonlinear complexity of brain activity is gaining acceptance. This idea is based on what is considered to be an essential feature of conscious experience, namely that every conscious event which is made up of many different parts and is distinct. This idea is that transient complexity is often thought of as concurrent differentiation (subsets of the system are interactively diverse) (subsets of the system are interactively distinct) and integration (the system as a whole exhibits coherence) (differentiation) [23] (Fig. 1).

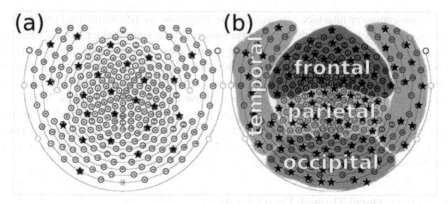

Fig. 1. Channel selection from the high density (256 electrodes) EEG [23]

Electroencephalogram (EEG) data is captured in real-time from a human subject through n, values ranging from a few to 512 different EEG channels. These EEG channels are divided into various groups i.e., Frontal, Parietal, Occipital and Temporal.

Types of EEG Channels

- Frontal: These EEG channels are mainly concentrated in the central front part of the brain.
- Parietal: These EEG channels are mostly found on the brain's top mid-section.
- Occipital: These EEG channels are located in the brain's rear region.
- Temporal: These EEG channels are situated on both sides of the brain.

EEG Channel Naming Convention

- The initial symbol, F stands for frontal, P for parietal, T for temporal, and O for occipital. The second character, a digit, serves as the electrode's entry point into the primary gyrus or lobule. (F1 indicates a point of entry into the superior frontal gyrus, for instance).
- The third character is a lowercase letter that indicates the distance between electrodes that enter the same gyrus or lobule in the anterior-posterior (A-P) plane. In the superior frontal gyrus, for example, the electrode F1a is the most anterior, followed by F1b, F1c, and so on.

Hardware in EEG

Electrode caps are generally used to help in the placement of electrode and make affixing electrodes to the scalp easier. Caps make sure of electrodes are correctly placed and that sufficient contact with the scalp is maintained.

2 Methods

2.1 Data Acquisition and Pre-processing

Measuring EEG data while the individual is performing various degrees of a mental task is referred to as a mental workload task. Many methods have been used to classify mental workload levels, involving driving simulation studies [19], live pilot studies [20], and responsible tasks [14]. The workload was classified in driver and pilot studies based on subject behavioural statistics such as response time and path deviation. The workload was classified in an accountability research based on a rise in the number of actions that the subject is liable for. This type of task is commonly used in two areas: BMI performance monitoring or cognitive stress monitoring [18]. An Emotive EPOC (excess post-exercise oxygen consumption) EEG headset with a 128 Hz sampling rate and 16-bit A/D resolution was used to collect EEG data. AF4, F7, FC5, F3, T7, P7, O2, O1, P8, T8, FC6, F8, F4, AF3 are among the fourteen electrodes on the gadget. The preparation of this data is carried out in the four steps below [1, 2, 10]:

- High-pass filter the raw data at 1 Hz
- Elimination of line noise
- Perform Artifact Subspace Reconstruction (ASR)
- Re-reference data to baseline.

In [4, 12], a flight simulator task to generate scalp EEG data, it was used to categorise the workload state of an operator as high or low while performing. This assignment was created to simulate aircraft operations, especially those involving remote piloting. The information was gathered for the 2011 Cognitive State Assessment Competition [13, 14] and the competition organizers make this information publicly available. Two electrooculogram (EOG) channels (vertical and horizontal) and 19 EEG channels at normal 10–20 locations were used (Fp2, Fp1, Fz, F3, F7, F8, F4, T5, T3, Cz, C3, C4, T4, T6, P4, Pz, P3, O1, O2).

Eight subjects (13 tests in two subjects, 15 tests in six subjects) participated in a total of one hundred eighteen recordings over the course of a month. Each recording day consisted of three 15-min EEG sessions, allowing the workload monitor's temporal performance to be assessed on a variety of measures [3]. For validation of the Mental Workload classifiers constructed in their prior work [15], the author used an EEG database. Participants were required to complete a simulated Human Machine task based on the Automatic Augmented Cabin Air Management System (ACAMS) [13, 16], with physiological data being simultaneously collected under varied workloads. To vary the difficulty levels of each session, a cyclic-loading schedule with eight subsequent stages was adopted. The baseline conditions of 5 min each were used in the first and last phases. In ACAMS, the six successive task-load circumstances were programmed with 1, 3, 4, 3, and 1 failure (denoted by Non-negative Tensor Factorization (NTF), or number of failed subsystems). Each workload condition was 15 min long. The control conditions NTF = 1 and NTF = 4 were chosen for examination in this study and classified as low and high Workload levels, respectively [5]. Eight subjects completed scenarios in the Multi-Attribute Activity Battery (MATB) [10] environment over five testing days spaced out over a month in another task intended to improve cognitive workload prediction. Tasks involving monitoring, resource management, communication, and tracking were given and adjusted to create three levels of difficulty: low, medium, and high [17, 18]. The number of resource allocation errors, communication response time and monitoring task reaction times were all recorded and utilized to confirm which subject had low and high difficulty levels [6, 18].

Another author discussed the four jobs of the multi-attribute task battery before focusing on Open MATB three primary contributions: task customization, software extensibility, and experiment replicability. Those four tasks are [12]:

The system monitoring task.

- The tracking task
- The communication task
- The resource management task.

The data was also recorded as part of a Cognitive State Assessment task utilizing a 14 channel EEG in the standard 10–20 position in one experiment (AF3, F3, F7, AF4, T7, P7, O2, O1, P8, T8, F4, FC6, F8, and FC5). Eight subjects (10 tests each) participated in a total of 80 EEG recordings in a noise-free environment. Prior to processing the signal and extracting features, they removed artifacts using Independent Component Analysis (ICA) and then data was filtered using the Butterworth filter to have signal from 0.5 to 45 Hz. Nonlinear properties of Hurst exponent and Higuchi fractal dimension were retrieved after filtering the data and removing artifacts [9].

Brain Waves in Normal EEG
Brain waves are formed when a group of neurons fires in a specific sequence to relay signals to other groups of neurons. Different forms of brain activity and states of consciousness are linked to these electrical patterns.

- **Alpha waves**: Alpha brain waves are a type of electrical activity that the brain produces. You're likely to experience alpha waves when you're dreaming, meditating, or engaging in mindfulness - based. According to study, this kind of brain wave may help to lessen the signs of depression and to improve creativity.
- **Beta Waves**: Beta waves, which appear as separate peaks on spectrograms, can be observed in various parts of the cortex in healthy people. When compared to posterior regions of the cortex, beta waves are more commonly observed in frontal or central locations. They happen in the majority of conscious, waking states. It's a quick activity that indicates alertness and attentiveness.
- **Theta Waves**: Theta waves are produced by the theta rhythm, a neuronal oscillation in the brain that supports a number of cognitive and behavioural functions in many animals, including learning, memory, and spatial navigation.
- **Delta Waves**: The low, deep, sluggish delta waves lie at the very bottom of the brain wave spectrum. They happen when you're in a deep, dreamless sleep (Table 1).

Table 1. Brain waves and their frequency ranges

EEG waves name	Frequency
Alpha waves	8 to 13 Hz
Beta waves	13 Hz (14 to 30 Hz)
Theta waves	4 to 7.5 Hz
Delta waves	1 to 3.5 Hz

2.2 Approach and Algorithm

Various algorithms used by different authors to obtain desired outcomes were:

- Neighborhood Component Analysis (NCA),
- Artificial Neural Network (ANN),
- Stacked Denoising Autoencoder (SDAE),
- K-Means,
- Grey Wolf Optimizer (GWO),
- K-Nearest Neighbor,
- Deep recurrent neural network (RNN),
- Convolution Neural Network,
- Random Forest Classifier,
- Support Vector Regression (SVR) model,
- Logistic Regression.

The STEW dataset's effectiveness is evaluated using a 9-point workload scale and a Support Vector Regression classifier training is selected features from local component analysis. In order to train a Support Vector Regression (SVR) classifier, Neighborhood Component Analysis (NCA) algorithm is used [1]. The author also used the Grey Wolf Optimizer (GWO) optimizer to extract various sorts of characteristics (frequency, statistical, nonlinear, and linear) from the EEG signal. The most common algorithms discussed were K-Means, K-Nearest Neighbor, Support Vector Machine (SVM). The retrieved features were loaded into the defined classifiers, such as SVM, K-Means, and KNN, and the performance accuracy of each classifier was compared [9–12].

Another author discussed the temporary use of Artificial Neural Networks in classifying user activity. Networks are trained using 150 min of EEG data in the process of confirming the drop-off [3, 6, 11]. The EL-SDAE integrated learning model is also proposed to be divided into two MW categories by extracting high-EEG features. Stacked denoising autoencoder (SDAE) that stores local information. Autoencoder stacked denoising (SDAE) [5].

It is discussed that the examination of a long-term visual protocol that attracts the workload of the brain is performed and Identification of common features using the Neighborhood Component Feature Selection (NCFS) in two visual tasks. It used dual split function uses a deep structure using Long short-term memory (LSTM) and Bidirectional short-term memory (BLSTM) [8].

In Fig. 2, Electroencephalogram (EEG) data is captured from the human subjects using an EEG cap. Further, captured data is processed for noise removal. The preprocessed data is used in training of efficient machine learning models. The trained model is used in real time to evaluate the workload of human subjects.

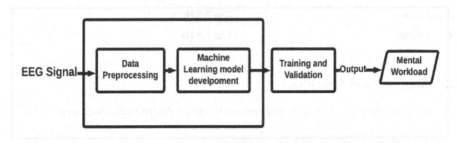

Fig. 2. Widely followed workflow of EEG processing for mental workload analysis.

2.3 Outcomes

This section discusses the respective results obtained by the authors of the reviewed papers following the application of several approaches on data that has already been processed. Various algorithms including Long Short-Term Memory and Bidirectional Long Short-Term Memory (LSTM-BLSTM) (86.33% and 82.57%) [2], SDAE (92%) [5], deep LSTM formats (93%) [6]. Many algorithms used while comparison failed to achieve higher accuracy like Random Forest classifier KNN classifier (57.3%), CNN + LSTM network separator (58.68%), (57.19%), MLP network separator (58.2%) [10]. It is observed that the Support vector machine (SVM) outperformed other classifiers because it is a supervised classifier [12]. The results obtained from Deep recurrent neural networks (RNN) were also highly accurate (92.8%) of cross-sectional activity compared to conventional phase dividers [8].

3 Limitations

EEG establishes thresholds for specific expertise and experience, time constraints, and consistency of measurement throughout time at various frequency band filter settings, which are often subjectively defined, and potential changes. It relies heavily on unclear criteria for doing so with low amplitude associated with background EEG [21]. The utility of EEG applications is also limited by individual variability. This phenomenon is driven by physiological differences between people of different sizes, yet it can greatly restrict the effectiveness of strategies that aim to extrapolate the findings to all participants. Many practical uses of EEG rely on the capability to extrapolate from one group of people to another invisible group, which is why so much effort has gone into inventing strategies to cope with inter-individual variability, which is also lacking [7].

4 Conclusion

Recognition of sentiments, mental workload, sleeping phase score, seizure detection, motor imagery, and event-related potential are just a few of the EEG tasks that have been successfully implemented using deep learning classification. The input formulization and network design of these deep network research differed greatly. Various research evaluated several public datasets, allowing for us to immediately contrast categorization performance depending on their structure. Out of all algorithms like Neighborhood Component Analysis (NCA), Support Vector Regression (SVR) model, Artificial Neural Network (ANN), Grey Wolf Optimizer (GWO)and deep neural network, Stacked denoising autoencoder (SDAE), Deep recurrent neural network (RNN), K-Means, K-Nearest Neighbor, Convolution Neural Network, Random Forest Classifier, Logistic Regression, and others, it's been observed that Support Vector Machine (SVM) and Artificial Neural Network (ANN's) outperformed other types of deep networks [18].

Despite the fact that much study has been done in this sector, there is currently little evidence of its use in daily life. This is mostly due to the fact that collecting EEG data necessitates specialized apparatus, expert personnel, and expensive resources. It will not be surprising to find a big section of the population wearing high-tech bands or caps (like smartwatches) capable of simply acquiring data (brain waves) and utilizing in real-time in the future.

References

1. Lim, W.L., Sourina, O., Wang, L.: STEW: simultaneous task EEG workload dataset. IEEE Dataport **26**, 2106–2114 (2018). https://dx.doi.org/10.21227/44r8-ya50
2. Das Chakladar, D., Dey, S., Roy, P.P., Dogra, D.P.: EEG-based mental workload estimation using deep BLSTM-LSTM network and evolutionary algorithm. Biomed. Signal Process. Control **60**, 101989 (2020). https://doi.org/10.1016/j.bspc.2020.101989
3. Casson, A.J.: Artificial neural network classification of operator workload with an assessment of time variation and noise-enhancement to increase performance. Front. Neurosci. **8**, 372 (2014). https://doi.org/10.3389/fnins.2014.00372
4. Cegarra, J., Valéry, B., Avril, E., Calmettes, C., Navarro, J.: OpenMATB: a multi-attribute task battery promoting task customization, software extensibility and experiment replicability. Behav. Res. Methods **52**(5), 1980–1990 (2020). https://doi.org/10.3758/s13428-020-01364-w
5. Yang, S., Yin, Z., Wang, Y., Zhang, W., Wang, Y., Zhang, J.: Assessing cognitive mental workload via EEG signals and an ensemble deep learning classifier based on denoising autoencoders. Comput. Biol. Med. **109**, 159–170 (2019). https://doi.org/10.1016/j.compbiomed.2019.04.034
6. Hefron, R.G., Borghetti, B.J., Christensen, J.C., Kabban, C.M.S.: Deep long short-term memory structures model temporal dependencies improving cognitive workload estimation. Pattern Recogn. Lett. **94**, 96–104 (2017). https://doi.org/10.1016/j.patrec.2017.05.020
7. Roy, Y., Banville, H., Albuquerque, I., Gramfort, A., Falk, T.H., Faubert, J.: Deep learning-based electroencephalography analysis: a systematic review. J. Neural Eng. **16**, 051001 (2019). https://doi.org/10.1088/1741-2552/ab260c
8. Gupta, S.S., Taori, T.J., Ladekar, M.Y., Manthalkar, R.R., Gajre, S.S., Joshi, Y.V.: Classification of cross task cognitive workload using deep recurrent network with modelling of temporal dynamics. Biomed. Signal Process. Control **70**, 103070 (2021). https://doi.org/10.1016/j.bspc.2021.103070

9. Chandra, S., Sharma, G., Gomes, A.: Estimation of workload using EEG data and classification using linear classifiers. Int. J. Sci. Eng. Res. **6**(10), 198–203 (2015)

10. Pandey, V., Choudhary, D.K., Verma, V., Sharma, G., Singh, R., Chandra, S.: Mental workload estimation using EEG. In: 2020 Fifth International Conference on Research in Computational Intelligence and Communication Networks (ICRCICN) (2020). https://doi.org/10.1109/icrcicn50933.2020.9296150

11. Miller, D.: The U.S. Air Force-Developed Adaptation of the Multi-Attribute Task Battery for the Assessment of Human Operator Workload and Strategic Behavior, vol. 152 (2010)

12. Estepp, J.R., Klosterman, S.L., Christensen, J.C.: An assessment of non-stationarity in physiological cognitive state assessment using artificial neural networks. In: 2011 Annual International Conference of the IEEE Engineering in Medicine and Biology Society (2011). https://doi.org/10.1109/iembs.2011.6091616

13. Christensen, J.C., Estepp, J.R., Wilson, G.F., Russell, C.A.: The effects of day-to-day variability of physiological data on operator functional state classification. Neuroimage **59**, 57–63 (2012). https://doi.org/10.1016/j.neuroimage.2011.07.091

14. Yin, Z., Zhang, J.: Cross-session classification of mental workload levels using EEG and an adaptive deep learning model. Biomed. Signal Process. Control **33**, 30–47 (2017). https://doi.org/10.1016/j.bspc.2016.11.013

15. Lorenz, B., Nocera, F., Rottger, S., Parasuraman, R.: Automated fault-management in a simulated space fight micro-world. Aviat. Space Environ. Med. **73**, 886–897 (2002)

16. Sauer, J., Wastell, D.G., Hockey, G.R.J.: A conceptual framework for designing micro-worlds for complex work domains: a case study of the cabin air management system. Comput. Hum. Behav. **16**, 45–58 (2000). https://doi.org/10.1016/s0747-5632(99)00051-5

17. Wilson, G.F., Russell, C.A., Monnin, J.W., Estepp, J.R., Christensen, J.C.: How does day-to-day variability in psychophysiological data affect classifier accuracy? Proc. Hum. Factors Ergon. Soc. Annu. Meet. **54**, 264–268 (2010). https://doi.org/10.1177/154193121005400317

18. Craik, A., He, Y., Contreras-Vidal, J.L.: Deep learning for electroencephalogram (EEG) classification tasks: a review. J. Neural Eng. **16**, 031001 (2019). https://doi.org/10.1088/1741-2552/ab0ab5

19. Hajinoroozi, M., Mao, Z., Jung, T.-P., Lin, C.-T., Huang, Y.: EEG-based prediction of driver's cognitive performance by deep convolutional neural network. Signal Process.: Image Commun. **47**, 549–555 (2016). https://doi.org/10.1016/j.image.2016.05.018

20. Li, F., et al.: Deep models for engagement assessment with scarce label information. IEEE Trans. Hum.-Mach. Syst. **47**, 598–605 (2017). https://doi.org/10.1109/thms.2016.2608933

21. Gemein, L.A.W., et al.: Machine-learning-based diagnostics of EEG pathology. Neuroimage **220**, 117021 (2020). https://doi.org/10.1016/j.neuroimage.2020.117021

22. Padfield, N., Zabalza, J., Zhao, H., Masero, V., Ren, J.: EEG-based brain-computer interfaces using motor-imagery: techniques and challenges. Sensors **19**, 1423 (2019). https://doi.org/10.3390/s19061423

23. Schartner, M., et al.: Complexity of multi-dimensional spontaneous EEG decreases during propofol induced general anaesthesia. PLoS ONE **10**, e0133532 (2015). https://doi.org/10.1371/journal.pone.0133532

A Comprehensive Review on Image Captioning Using Deep Learning

Rupendra Kumar Kaushik$^{(\boxtimes)}$ (iD), Sushil Kumar Sharma, and Lokesh Kumar

Institute of Technology and Management, Aligarh, India
rupendrakumarkaushik@gmail.com

Abstract. Our brain is capable of annotating or classifying any image that emerges in front of us. What about computers, though? How can a computer process an image and identify it with a caption that is both relevant and accurate? It appeared unachievable a few years ago, but with the advancement of Computer Vision and Deep Learning algorithms, as well as the availability of appropriate datasets and AI models, building a relevant caption generator for an image is becoming easier. Caption generation is also becoming a booming business around the world, with numerous data annotation companies making billions. Furthermore, this image caption generation process is used to transform images into a series of words from a series of pixels. Image captioning can be thought of as an end-to-end Sequence to Sequence challenge from beginning to end. It is necessary to process both the words or comments as well as the visuals in order to achieve this goal. In this paper, we also reviewed the feature vectors that are obtained by using recurrent neural networks for the language component and convolutional neural networks for the image component, respectively.

Keywords: Image captioning · Convolution neural network · Deep learning

1 Introduction

Developing image description systems in the future may make it possible for those who are visually impaired to "see" the environment more clearly. It has lately received a great deal of attention and has come to the top of the list of the most critical issues in the field of computer vision. Moreover, the salient features of early image information gathering methods relied on static object class libraries in the picture to capture information, which was then described using statistical language models in early image description generating methods. Using a dependency model, Aker and Gaizauskas [1] summarised multiple web papers containing image location details and proposed a systematic method for self-labelling geotagged photographs. Using a network-scale approach, Li et al. [2] proposed an n-gram strategy in which candidate phrases are gathered and combined to construct sentences describing pictures beginning from zero. To assess visual motion as well as the likelihood of collocated nouns, sceneries, and prepositions, Yang et al. [3] presented a language model learned on the comprehensive archive of newswire text data, and then used these estimates as hidden Markov model parameters. Visual explanation

© The Author(s), under exclusive license to Springer Nature Switzerland AG 2022
V. Sugumaran et al. (Eds.): AIR 2022, CCIS 1738, pp. 265–275, 2022.
https://doi.org/10.1007/978-3-031-23724-9_25

is created by speculating the nearest POS (nouns, prepositions and verbs) which will be used to construct the phrase. Moreover, Kulkarni et al. [4] suggested using a identifier to indicate subjects in a photograph, categorizing every potential area and operating it with a association function, and then using a conditional random field (CRF) prediction picture tag to provide a natural linguistic explanation of the object. Object detection is also used in this process. In their study, Lin et al. [5] used a three-dimensional optical inspection arrangement to extract target, features, and connections from the picture and arrange them into a sequence of semantic trees. After that, they learned how to write text descriptions for the contextual trees they had discovered previously using the grammar they had learned. A number of indirect approaches have been developed to deal with picture explanation issues, like as the process of reformulating a given query technique given by Yagcioglu et al. [6], which consists of obtaining comparable pictures from a vast data sets and applying the spread indicated in connection with the obtained pictures. It is necessary to use the expression to generate an expanded query, after which the candidate descriptions are rearranged using the cosine similarity among the dispersed presentation and the expanded query vector, and the most closely-matched explanation is chosen to serve as the input picture description. In summary, the approaches mentioned are innovative and each has its own set of characters, but they all have the drawback of not making instinctual feature inspection on entity or operations on the picture, and also they do not provide a full mature generalized model to address the problem. Until the entrance of the era of big data and the emergence of DL/NLP learning methods, the efficacy and popularisation of artificial neural networks have achieved advancements in the field of picture description and seen new prospects. The following is a breakdown of the paper's structure. Initially, we evaluate the recent development of image interpretation methods in this paper and summarise the underlying structure as well as some improved methods. The second section delved into the fundamental models and approaches and cantered on the implementation of an attention mechanism (A.M.) to improve the model and compensate for the flaws of the encoder-decoder mechanism. The third section introduces the utilization of the A.M. along with the algorithm used for prediction and also evaluation metrics. The fourth section recaps previous work and suggests future work direction and expectations.

2   Image Captioning Techniques

- Retrieval based captioning
- Template-based captioning
- Neural network based captioning methods

  - Encoder-Decoder mechanism based
  - Attention mechanism based

    - Soft attention
    - Hard attention.

2.1   Retrieval Based Captioning

Visual and multimodal space can be used to retrieve captions. Captions are fetched from a group of already existing captions in these approaches. Visually related photos with captions from the training dataset are initially found via retrieval-based algorithms as like Fig. 1. Candidate captions are what they're called. This captions pool is used to choose captions for the query image [7–9]. These methods give captions that are both inclusive and syntactically correct. They can't, however, provide image-specific and semantically correct captions.

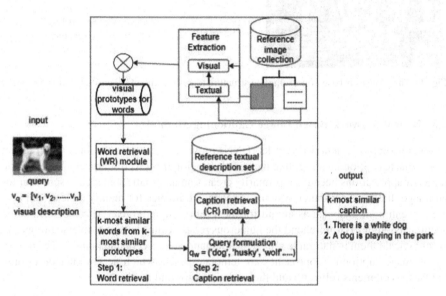

Fig. 1. Retrieval method for image captioning

2.2   Template Based Captioning

Captions are generated in template-based systems by using fixed templates with a predetermined number of unfilled spots. In these techniques, different objects, traits, and behaviors are first recognized, and then the blank areas in the templates are filled in by the participants as like in Fig. 2. For example, Farhadi et al. [11] load the template slots for making picture captions with a triplet of scene components, which is then used to generate the captions. Li et al. [10] achieve this goal by extracting sentences that are related to the objects, attributes, and connections that have been recognized. Objects, traits, and prepositions are inferred using a conditional random field (CRF), and then the gaps are filled in using a conditional random field (CRF). Captioning methods that use templates can provide captions that are grammatically correct. On the other hand, templates have already been specified and are unable to create captions of variable length. Later on, parsing-based language models for picture captioning were developed, which are more powerful than the fixed template-based solutions that were previously available. Consequently, we will not examine these template-based methods in this study.

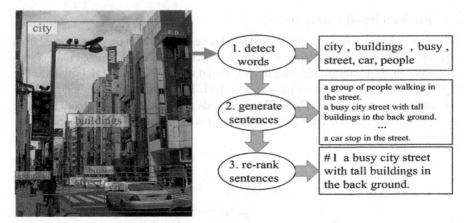

Fig. 2. The process is based on a template structure to demonstrate CNN used by Microsoft [12]

2.3 Neural Network-Based Image Captioning Method

Deep convolutional neural networks (CNN) provide a highly useful benefit. In recent years, image captioning has gotten increased attention from AI researchers. It has a wide range of applications because it primarily creates an automatic sentence description for an image. It allows computer systems to recognize images for mainly educational purposes, sentiment analysis, as an aid for the visibly impaired, etc. The model must be accurate enough to comprehend the numerous relationships between diverse things and communicate them in natural language in a semantically acceptable manner. The majority of image captioning approaches are template-based, which necessitates describing the various elements (objects) and their relationships and attributes.

Encoder-Decoder Mechanism Based
Figure 3 shows the encoder-decoder (CNN-RNN)-based models that can be used to generate the image-to-caption component. The encoder sections include multiple convolutions, max pooling, and fully linked layers for convolution of the input picture. We've eliminated them from the end because we're not dealing with image classification. The feature vector will be generated as the encoder part's final output.

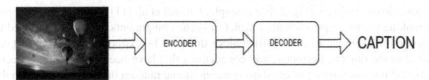

Fig. 3. Overview of encoder-decoder mechanism

We'll concentrate on the decoder after we've generated the feature vector. An RNN-based model is used for the decoder. The most significant distinction between CNN and RNN is feedback memory. A specific RNN layer is a function of both the current and prior inputs. As a result, the RNN layers will have two inputs: one for the feature vector and the other for the previous layer's output.

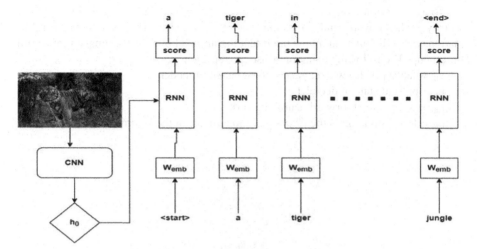

Fig. 4. Detailed view of working of the encoder-decoder mechanism

Figure 4 shows the step by step procedure of the encoder-decoder mechanism in which, the image will first be processed through the encoder, and the feature vector will be created, as seen in the tiger example. The feature vector and the <start> tag will then be fed into the first RNN layer, which will generate the first word in the sequence. This anticipated word and the feature vector will be fed into the next layer, which will predict the second word. This sequence of events will continue until the output is the <end> tag. Finding the odds of the word's existence in the dictionary is used to predict the words.

Drawbacks of Encoder-Decoder Mechanism
One of the most significant drawbacks of old approaches is the image input. The image is being supplied as the input to every RNN layer at each timestamp, which can introduce extra information into the model and slow down the overall computational pace. As a result of this constraint, the model has difficulty correctly predicting the word sequence. Instead of passing the entire image at each timestamp, you can simply pass the sections of the image that you believe will aid in the image prediction at each timestamp. This will speed up the model and improve the correctness of the predictions. With the use of an attention mechanism, this limitation can be overcome.

Attention Mechanism Based
A 'traditional' image captioning system would encode the image using a feature vector generated by a pre-trained CNN. While utilising RNN to decode the caption, this feature vector would remain the same. The Attention model, on the other hand, provides a variable feature vector based on the previously created word. These aid captioning by allowing you to look at different portions of the image.

While the Recurrent Neural Network is producing a new word, the attention mechanism concentrates on the appropriate part of the image; so, the decoder only uses those certain parts of the image.

To an Attention model, which is a type of a neural network, you pass in yt–1 (previously predicted word) and hj (present state of the decoder). Therefore, with this information, you will understand how important the jth pixel of the input image is at the tth timestamp. The following equation is used to represent it:

$e_{jt} = f_{att}(y_{t-1}, h_j)$ where, $y_{t-1} = $ what has the encoder

$h_j = $ present state of decoder

$f_{att} = $ simple feed forward neural network

$e_{jt} = $ how important is the jth pixel of input image at the tth time stamp

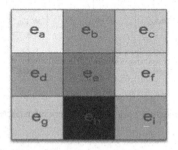

Fig. 5. Representation of pixel values by ej that changes wrt time

Figure 5 shows which pixel value is important at that particular instant of time. Darker the shade more important the pixel value at that timestamp in this figure.

The neural network in the attention model does a linear transformation of the input h_j and y_{t-1} i.e.,

$U_{att} * y_{t-1} + W_{att} * h_j$

where, $U_{att} = $ weight given to y_{t-1} (what has the encoder produced so far) $W_{att} = $ weight given to h_j (present state of decoder)

Once the linear layers are structured, we will add a non-linear mapping on top of it using the tanh activation function:

$$f_{att} = V^T_{att} * tanh (U_{att} * y_{t-1} + W_a * h_i)$$

where, $V^T_{att} = $ Dense layer which is introduced to make e_{jt} a scalar value
tanh = activation function

The output needs to be in the range of (0,1), i.e., it should have a probability distribution.

$$\alpha_{jt} = Softmax(e_{jt})$$

The α_{jt} depicts our Attention weights (the probability distribution) of all the pixel values in the feature vector.

Once we have this value, we only need to compute a weighted sum of the Attention weights on our feature map ($\mathbf{h_j}$).

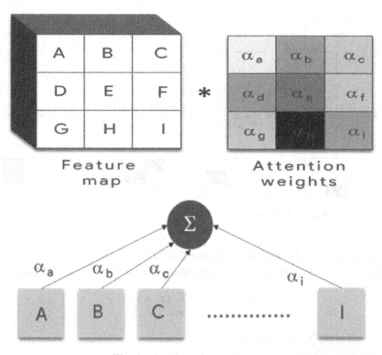

Fig. 6. Creation of context vector

Figure 6 shows how feature maps is multiplied by the attention weights to produce the context vector which provides the chance of each word in the input sentence S occurring in the output sentence.

This weighted sum produces the Context vector,

$$C_t = \sum_{j-1}^{T} (a_{j_t} h_j)$$

Figure 7 shows, how after insertion of attention mechanism, the model focuses on a relevant area of the image and transfers it to the RNN layer from where it calculates the score of the word in the form of probability and that word which has got highest probability is obtained as output and so on.

Soft Attention

In the beginning, Dzmitry et al. [13] thought of and applied the soft attention model to the field of machine translation. The word "soft" really relates to the probability distribution of attention rather than the actual attention itself. The context vector Zt [11, 14] provides

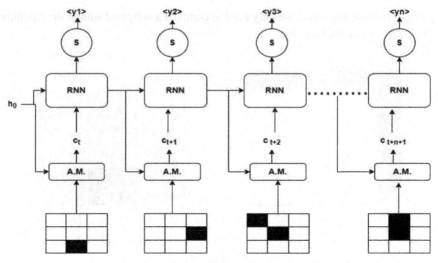

Fig. 7. Detailed view of working of attention mechanism

the chance of each word in the input sentence S occurring in the output sentence. Finally, the probability distribution is calculated by taking the weighted total of all areas.

$$\underset{p(s\,t\,|\,a)}{E} \quad |z| = \sum_{i=1}^{L} (a_{t,i} \, a_i)$$

where, E = probability distribution

Z_t = context vector

S_t = attention location at time

ta_i = annotation vector

$a_{t,i}$ = weight of each annotation vector at time t.

A deterministic attention model is composed by computing a soft weighted attention vector [13].

$$\Phi(\{a_i\}, \{\alpha_i\}) = \sum_{i=1} (a_i \alpha_i)$$

where, φ = function that returns a single vector given the set of annotation vectors and their corresponding weights.

αi = weight of each annotation vector.

The objective function can be written as:

$$L = -\log(P(y\,|\,x)) + \lambda \sum_{i}^{L} (1 - \sum_{i=1}^{L} (a_i \alpha_i))^2$$

where, L = penalized negative log-loss likelihood

P (y|x) = probability of y given x

λ = hyperparameter set by cross-validation.

Soft attention can be incorporated and modelled for direct training because it is parameterized. Gradients can be communicated back to other portions of the model via the attention mechanism module.

Hard Attention

When compared to previous A.M., which concentrates over finding the weighted aggregation for all areas, this A.M. concentrates on single point and is the way of arbitrarily picking a distinct site. It takes and does sampling of the unrevealed state of the input in comparison than sampling the unseen state of the whole encoder, and it does so by using probability. Calculating the context vector Zt [11] is accomplished by the use of the following formula:

$$z_t = \sum_{i=1}^{L} (s_{t,i} a_i)$$

where $s_{t,i}$ refers to whether to select the ith position in the L feature maps, if selected, set to 1, otherwise the opposite.

For the purpose of performing gradient backpropagation, it is necessary to find the slope of the module by Monte Carlo sampling. One disadvantage of intense attention is that data is selected using maximum sampling or random sampling techniques, which are both inefficient. There is thus no link among the final objective function and the attention distribution, and the backpropagation approach cannot be used for training as a consequence of these findings.

3 Applications of Attention Mechanism

Question Answering Model: With the help of the attention models, you can find the answers to questions asked from the model by passing it to the text from which you want the model to find the answers. The model will use the attention mechanism to answer the questions [15].

Visual Q&A Model: Attention models can also answer questions related to images passed to them. As seen in the video, when the model was passed with an image of a pizza and asked how many slices of pizza are present in the image, it correctly gave the output. [16].

Seq2Seq Model: Language translation is another application of the attention model. If you pass a sequence of words of a particular language into the model, the encoder will encode the words and pass them to the decoder. The decoder will then decode the words and will give the output as a sequence of words translated into another language [17].

3.1 How Are Predictions Made?

- **Greedy search:** This approach determines the likelihood of the terms occurring in the English language based on their frequency of occurrence in the English lexicon.

It examines the words in a sample, calculates the probability of each word, and then produces the word with the greatest likelihood of being correct. However, although this enhances the computing speed of the model, the accuracy of the model may not be up to par.

- **Beam search:** Beam search may be used as an alternative to greedy search. If you use beam search, the model identifies the k most probable words instead of just one, and these k words are transmitted to the next timestamp instead of being kept in the model. It operates on the basis of the breadth-first search algorithm.

3.2   How Are Predictions Evaluated?

The BLEU score is used as the evaluation metric for the predicted word. It determines the difference between the predicted word from the human-created word.

- The BLEU metric is utilized to assess the outcome of the captions created by the test set. It just takes the proportion of n-grams in the anticipated phrase that is there in the ground truth and uses it as the input [18].
- BLEU is a well-known evaluation measure for comparing the likeness of a hypothesis sentence to a set of base sentences that may be used to test the hypothesis phrase. It provides a number between 0 and 1 based on a single hypothesis phrase and several reference sentences provided by the user [18].

4   Conclusion

This paper discusses numerous deep neural network-based picture captioning approaches, including template, retrieval, and neural network-based methods. This article examines the advantages and disadvantages of the most regularly utilized approaches. A comparison of different techniques reveals the benefits and drawbacks of semantic image comprehension with an end-to-end learning strategy. The fact that image captioning may be used for image retrieval, video captioning, and video movement and that a wide variety of image captioning processes are currently available, experimental data imply that this work still needs the development of higher-performance systems and improvements. First and foremost, it must figure out how to generate human equivalent natural language; second, it must determine whether the sentence generated is correct grammatically; and third, it must figure out how to make the caption meaning as explicit and consistent as feasible in relation with the specified picture content.

References

1. Aker, A., Gaizauskas, R.: Generating image descriptions using dependency relational patterns. In: Proceedings of the 48th Annual Meeting of the Association for Computational Linguistics, vol. 49, no. 9, pp. 1250–1258 (2010)
2. Li, S., Kulkarni, G., Berg, T.L., Choi, Y.: Composing simple image descriptions using web-scale N-grams. In: Proceeding of Fifteenth Conference on Computational Natural Language Learning, pp. 220–228. Association for Computational Linguistics, Portland (2011)

3. Yang, Y., Teo, C.L., Daume, H., Aloimonos, Y.: Corpus-guided sentence generation of natural images. In: Proceeding of the Conference on Empirical Methods in Natural Language Processing, Edinburgh, UK, pp. 444–454 (2011)
4. Kulkarni, G., et al.: Baby talk: understanding and generating simple image descriptions. In: CVPR 2011 (2011). https://doi.org/10.1109/cvpr.2011.5995466
5. Lin, D., Fidler, S., Kong, C., Urtasun, R.: Generating multi-sentence natural language descriptions of indoor scenes. In: Proceedings of the British Machine Vision Conference 2015 (2015). https://doi.org/10.5244/c.29.93
6. Yagcioglu, S., Erdem, E., Erdem, A., Cakici, R.: A distributed representation based query expansion approach for image captioning. In: Proceedings of the 53rd Annual Meeting of the Association for Computational Linguistics and the 7th International Joint Conference on Natural Language Processing (Volume 2: Short Papers) (2015). https://doi.org/10.3115/v1/p15-2018
7. Gong, Y., Wang, L., Hodosh, M., Hockenmaier, J., Lazebnik, S.: Improving image-sentence embeddings using large weakly annotated photo collections. In: Fleet, D., Pajdla, T., Schiele, B., Tuytelaars, T. (eds.) ECCV 2014. LNCS, vol. 8692, pp. 529–545. Springer, Cham (2014). https://doi.org/10.1007/978-3-319-10593-2_35
8. Hodosh, M., Young, P., Hockenmaier, J.: Framing image description as a ranking task: data, models and evaluation metrics. J. Artif. Intell. Res. 47, 853–899 (2013). https://doi.org/10.1613/jair.3994
9. Ordonez, V., Kulkarni, G., Berg, T.L.: Im2text: describing images using 1 million captioned photographs. In: Advances in Neural Information Processing Systems, pp. 1143–1151 (2011)
10. Farhadi, A., et al.: Every picture tells a story: generating sentences from images. In: Daniilidis, K., Maragos, P., Paragios, N. (eds.) ECCV 2010. LNCS, vol. 6314, pp. 15–29. Springer, Heidelberg (2010). https://doi.org/10.1007/978-3-642-15561-1_2
11. Liu, X., Xu, Q., Wang, N.: A survey on deep neural network-based image captioning. Vis. Comput. 35(3), 445–470 (2018). https://doi.org/10.1007/s00371-018-1566-y
12. Dzmitry, B., Cho, K., Bengio, Y.: Neural machine translation by jointly learning to align and translate (2014). http://arxiv.org/abs/1409.0473
13. Karimpour, Z., Sarfi, A., Asadi, N., Ghasemian, F.: Show, attend to everything, and tell: image captioning with more thorough image understanding. In: 2020 10th International Conference on Computer and Knowledge Engineering (ICCKE) (2020). https://doi.org/10.1109/iccke50421.2020.9303609
14. Bachrach, Y., et al.: An attention mechanism for neural answer selection using a combined global and local view. In: 2017 IEEE 29th International Conference on Tools with Artificial Intelligence (ICTAI) (2017). https://doi.org/10.1109/ictai.2017.00072
15. Nguyen, V.-Q., Suganuma, M., Okatani, T.: Efficient attention mechanism for visual dialog that can handle all the interactions between multiple inputs. In: Vedaldi, A., Bischof, H., Brox, T., Frahm, J.-M. (eds.) ECCV 2020. LNCS, vol. 12369, pp. 223–240. Springer, Cham (2020). https://doi.org/10.1007/978-3-030-58586-0_14
16. Hao, S., Lee, D.-H., Zhao, D.: Sequence to sequence learning with attention mechanism for short-term passenger flow prediction in large-scale metro system. Transp. Res. Part C: Emerg. Technol. 107, 287–300 (2019). https://doi.org/10.1016/j.trc.2019.08.005
17. Liu, S., Zhu, Z., Ye, N., Guadarrama, S., Murphy, K.: Improved image captioning via policy gradient optimization of SPIDEr. In: 2017 IEEE International Conference on Computer Vision (ICCV) (2017). https://doi.org/10.1109/iccv.2017.100
18. Vinyals, O., Toshev, A., Bengio, S., Erhan, D.: Show and tell: a neural image caption generator. In: 2015 IEEE Conference on Computer Vision and Pattern Recognition (CVPR) (2015). https://doi.org/10.1109/cvpr.2015.7298935

Classical Models vs Deep Leaning: Time Series Analysis

Mahima Choudhary(✉) ⓘ, Saumya Jain ⓘ, and Greeshma Arya ⓘ

Indira Gandhi Delhi Technical University for Women, Delhi, India
mahimachoudhary971@gmail.com, greeshmaarya@igdtuw.ac.in

Abstract. There has been a lot of ongoing discussion on the performance of the classical methods used for time series prediction like ARIMA versus various deep learning models such as LSTM, CNN etc. While traditional forecasting methods like ARIMA, SARIMAX and so on may perform well on a particular time series after tuning the model parameters properly, they may not perform as well for a different dataset since the future values are predicted based on the past observations only and the model parameters are chosen independently for each dataset. Moreover, manual selection of model parameters and some pre-processing of data is required based on your dataset. Deep learning models on the other hand, are more versatile and data-driven. Models like LSTM which are known to work well for sequential data are able to extract the relationship between different time step values from the raw data itself and a particular model architecture can work equally for several datasets of similar type. In this paper performance comparison of classical time series forecasting methods with most commonly used neural network models is done. After studying the work already done on the subject, three traditional methods were chosen: ARIMA, SARIMA and Holt-Winters Method along with the commonly used neural network models: MLP, CNN and LSTM. For comparing a dataset containing currency values of various countries from 1999 to 2021 is used for forecasting values for two countries: US and Australia. The error metric values including root mean square error (RMSE) and mean absolute percentage error (MAPE) obtained from the experiments suggested the values predicted by the three classical methods, especially ARIMA and Holt-Winters Method, were more accurate than the neural network models.

Keywords: Time series · Deep learning · Machine learning · Stationarity · Currency value prediction

1 Introduction

Time series forecasting has applications in a lot of important practical domains including FOREX prediction, sales forecasting, weather forecasting and many more. A lot of research work has been done for improving upon the efficiency and accuracy of time series prediction and many new machine learning algorithms have been proposed for the same. Application of neural networks has been proposed as a better alternative to the existing widely used classical methods like ARIMA, SARIMA, etc. [2]. However, scant evidence is available about their relative performance in terms of accuracy and computational requirements.

For the same reason, we compare the performance of traditional methods used for time series forecasting with neural networks, by taking a dataset containing currency prices of various countries from 1999 to 2021. To experiment with different algorithms, we chose two countries: Australia and the US.

A time series is in general affected by 4 components that are as follows:

- **Trend** that can be described as the tendency of the time series to increase, decrease or stagnate over long periods of time.
- **Seasonality** that is the seasonal variance or fluctuations in the time series within a year. A number of factors can cause seasonal fluctuations of the data such as climate, weather conditions and so on. For example, an increase in ice-cream sales in the summer results in fluctuation.
- **Cyclicity** is when a particular behavior in the time series repeats itself over long periods of time, the time period usually being two or more years.
- **Irregularity** or noise is the presence of spikes or troughs which occur at irregular intervals and do not follow a particular pattern. They are caused by unpredictable influences [3].

In order to reduce the complexity, some traditional algorithms like Auto Regressive Moving Average (ARMA) assume that the time series on which the model is fitted is stationary. Stationarity of a time series can be described as a statistical equilibrium in which mean, variance and auto-covariance of the series are independent of time and there is no presence of trend and seasonal components in the data [3].

We use the most widely used traditional methods: ARIMA, SARIMA and Holt-Winters method because of their capability to handle non-stationary data with trend and seasonal components. In case of neural networks, we use a Multilayer Perceptron (MLP) as a base model to make a comparison with two other more complicated neural networks: CNN which we believe will be able to extract features from the time series dataset because of its widespread application with feature extraction in image classification and LSTM which is known to work really well with sequential datasets such as time series datasets.

In order to compare the accuracy of different models, two error metrics are chosen: Mean Absolute Percentage Error (MAPE) and Root Mean Square Error (RMSE). MAPE is independent of the scale of data but overlooks the impact of extreme deviations while forecasting. RMSE, on the other hand, compliments the effect since it penalize extreme deviations [3].

The performance of different algorithms is dependent on certain parameters which need to be chosen carefully so as to produce the lowest possible values of RMSE and MAPE.

A grid search framework is used for searching the model parameters which give the most accurate results, for the traditional methods as well as the neural network models.

2 Methodology

2.1 Data-Extraction, Summary and Exploration

In order to study the performance of various algorithms we chose two countries from our dataset: The United States and Australia. There are 5724 values present in both the time series out of which 62 values are missing at random time steps. From the distance plots (Fig. 1) obtained for both The US and Australia it is observed that the distribution of data is almost normal in case of The US and rightly skewed in case of Australia. From both these observations, we decide to apply median imputation to the time series to take care of the missing values.

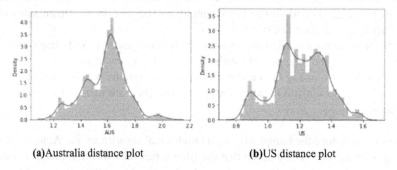

(a)Australia distance plot   (b)US distance plot

Fig. 1. Australia and US dollar distance plots

In order to interpret the values of RMSE and MAPE obtained after fitting the model better, we transform the data using the rank function in pandas. Figure 2 contains the plot of both the time series after the pre-processing is done.

Before fitting the model on the dataset, we split it into train and test sets. Ninety percent of the data is used as a train set for fitting the model and the rest 10% is used for testing the fitted model.

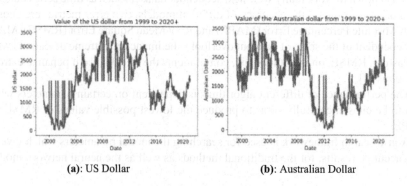

(a): US Dollar   (b): Australian Dollar

Fig. 2. Values of the US and Australian dollar

2.2 Model Building

Applying Classical Machine Learning Algorithms. In order to search for the most optimal parameters for each algorithm, a grid search framework is used in which forecasting is done for the test set over different parameter ranges. Each model configuration produces values of RMSE and MAPE which are stored for comparison. After the search operation is completed, the model configuration with the lowest values of RMSE and MAPE is selected. A one step forecast is done for each time step in the test dataset for each model configuration.

The Machine Learning Algorithms used are:

- ARIMA
- SARIMA
- Holt Winters

ARIMA- ARIMA (Auto Regressive Integrated Moving Average) is an extension of ARMA (Auto Regressive Moving Average) and representation of stationary as well as non-stationary time series by applying finite differencing to the data points [3, 5]. ARIMA model has three important parameters: p which decides the order of the autoregressive term (AR) or the number of lags, d which decides the order of differencing and q which decides the order of the moving average term (MA) or the number of lagged errors introduced inside the time series.

The order of p and q are decided on the basis of PACF and ACF plots of the time series. The number of lags to be used for making the predictions can be determined by PACF plot. PACF plot refers to partial autocorrelation function. PACF helps us in determining the correlation between the series and its own lags overlooking any contributions from the intermediate lags. Plotting the PACF will help us in determining which lags are significant for the given series.

The ACF plot helps us to find out the number of lagged error terms(q) that are required to remove the autocorrelation from the series (Figs. 3 and 4).

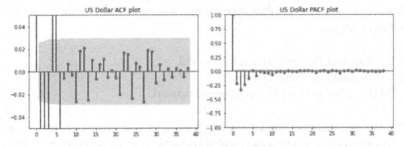

Fig. 3. US DOLLAR: ACF and PACF plots

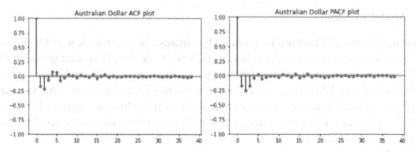

Fig. 4. AUSTRALIAN DOLLAR: ACF and PACF plots

From the ACF and PACF plots obtained for both the countries, we decide to perform the grid search operation from one to five for p, zero to three for d and one to five for q for both the countries respectively.

SARIMA- SARIMAX is short for seasonal auto regressive integrated moving average with exogenous factors. Seasonal ARIMA or SARIMA finds its application in time series where the series exhibits a variation which is seasonal in nature. The multiplicative process of SARIMA are formed by P i.e., a seasonal autoregressive notation and Q i.e., a seasonal moving average notation in the form of (p, d, q) (P, D, Q)$_s$. The letter 's' which is subscripted gives the length of the seasonal period. For example, in a quarterly data the value of s = 4, in an hourly data time series the value of s = 7, and in a monthly data the value of s = 12 [8].

On the basis of the ACF and PACF plot we performed grid search for various model parameters over different ranges.

Holt-Winters - Holt winters method which is also known as triple exponential smoothing is applied for prediction using data that has both trend as well as seasonality. The model is fitted on the training set with multiplicative seasonality as well as multiplicative trend. The fitted model is tested using the test set and walk forward validation which forecasts the value of a single time step at a time.

Applying Deep Learning Algorithms. To test if deep learning models work better on our time series data, we apply three types of neural network models. The Deep Learning Algorithms used are:

- MLP (Multilayer Perceptron) as a base model
- CNN (Convolutional Neural Network)
- LSTM (Long Short-Term Memory) neural network.

The data is scaled from 0 to 1 using MinMaxScaler from scikit learn before splitting it into test and train sets. The data is scaled back after making the predictions using the inverse scaler transform.

For applying the deep learning models to both the time series, we present the test and train sets of univariate time series in the form of a supervised learning problem to the neural network by feeding Input vectors with p features (y_t, y_{t-1}, y_{t-2}......y_{t-p+1}) into the input layer. The next time step in the series is provided as an output so that our model can provide an estimate value of this output during a one-step forecast using walk forward validation [4]. We repeat evaluation on the test set 10 times for each model parameter configuration and take average of RMSE and MAPE of all these evaluations. We consider model parameters with the lowest RMSE and MAPE after performing the grid search [4].

In order to make the modeling of the time series easier, we also provide the option for differencing the time series prior to fitting our model. It takes care of removing any trends or seasonality from the time series. The differencing is reversed before returning the predictions.

MLP (Multilayer Perceptron)- Multilayer perceptron comprises at least three layers: Input layer, one or more hidden layers and an output layer which are fully connected with multiple neurons inside each layer of the network. It is an example of a feedforward artificial neural network.

The inputs are pushed through neurons in each layer which adds weights to the inputs and bias and then passes it through an activation function before passing it to the next layer. For example, a neuron with three inputs would require four weights, one for each input and one for the bias. The activation function in each neuron decides how strong the output signal will be and provides the threshold at which the neuron is activated.

We test the model on relu (rectified linear unit) and leaky relu activation functions. We feed the outputs generated by the output layer back to the neural network through backpropagation algorithm to update the weights during each epoch and use an adam optimizer to minimize the MSE loss function. TensorFlow, an open-source library is used to build the model.

The grid search operation was performed for a number of model parameters: number of inputs fed to the neural network (100–300), number of epochs (50–200), number of nodes in each layer (25–100), batch size (1–500) and differencing parameter which decides if the time series is to be differenced before fitting the model (0, 1, 12).

CNN (Convolutional Neural Network)- A CNN comprises of a convolutional layer and a pooling layer in between the input and fully connected layer which eventually produces the final output. The convolutional layers perform a convolution on the input sequences fed to the neural network and helps in detecting the similarity between two sequences, similar to a cross correlation. The neurons act as filters whose values are basically weights which are updated during each epoch to minimize the loss or cost function. Feature maps are generated by these filters which summarize the presence of all the features inside the time series such as trend or seasonality. The results from the convolutional layer are passed through the pooling layer which reduces the dimensions of the feature maps. The extracted features are then passed through the fully connected layer as inputs and applies an activation function and derives a function that attempts at tying the features it receives from the previous layers together [6].

The model is tested for various activation functions (sigmoid, relu (rectified linear unit), leaky relu, selu, elu) and optimizers (adam, adagrad, stochastic gradient descent) to minimize the value of loss or cost function while keeping the model parameters constant.

Grid search framework is used to search for the most optimal model parameters with minimum loss function. The parameters used are: number of inputs fed to the neural network (100–300), number of epochs (50–200), batch size (1–500), number of filters inside the convolutional layer (32, 64, 128), kernel size used in the convolutional layer (3, 5, 7, 9), differencing parameter (0, 1, 12).

LSTM (Long Short-Term Memory)- LSTM is a type of recurrent neural network that was invented to solve the problem of vanishing gradient encountered in RNN and to learn long term dependencies in between inputs that are separated by longer time lags as compared to RNNs. They are useful for maintaining the state of the input internally. LSTM consists of three gates: input gate which decides whether to pass through the new input or not, a forget gate performs the task of deciding which information is unimportant and deleting it and an output gate which decides the output. The three gates operate in an analog fashion using sigmoid function which generates outputs in the range 0 to 1 [7].

We perform experiments on the time series data using various architectures of LSTM, with a single LSTM layer as well as stacked LSTM (multiple LSTM layers). The model was tested for one to five hidden layers and dropout layers with dropout rate from 0.2 to 0.5 are also added to prevent over-fitting. We test these architectures while keeping the other model parameters constant. Various combination of activation functions (relu, leaky relu, selu, elu) and optimizers (adam, adagrad, stochastic gradient descent) are also tested.

Keeping the architecture of the neural network constant, grid search operation for various model parameters is performed to find the optimal configuration with minimum value of RMSE. The parameters tested were: number of inputs fed to the neural network (100–300), number of epochs (50–200), batch size (1–500), number of neurons inside each layer (25–100), differencing parameter (0, 1, 12).

For deep learning models, out of all the combinations of activation functions and optimizers tested, it is observed that the combination of (rectified linear unit) activation function as well as adam optimizer produce the most favorable results with lowest RMSE and MAPE values for both Australian and US dollar in case of all the three models.

3   Results

RMSE and MAPE values obtained from all the classical time series forecasting algorithms as well as deep learning model are listed. These values are obtained after performing grid search over various model parameter ranges and only the lowest values are mentioned along with the model configuration (Tables 1, 2 and Figs. 5, 6).

Table 1. RMSE and MAPE values of classical methods and deep learning models for the US Dollar

Error metric	ARIMA	Holt-Winters method	SARIMA	MLP	CNN	LSTM
RMSE	159.5554	164.2568	183.7251	252.3343	238.7199	237.3826
MAPE	21.2361	23.2616	37.5343	100.326	70.3791	68.5324

Table 2. RMSE and MAPE values of classical methods and deep learning models for Australian Dollar

Error metric	ARIMA	Holt-Winters method	SARIMA	MLP	CNN	LSTM
RMSE	113.1385	115.8311	116.8753	301.6424	286.3153	286.4686
MAPE	4.3157	4.3925	4.8760	12.3394	11.8416	11.8372

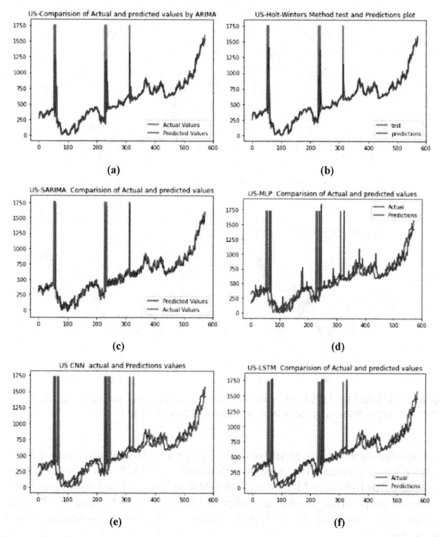

Fig. 5. US DOLLAR: plots of classical methods and deep learning models (a) ARIMA, (b) Holt-Winters, (c) SARIMA, (d) MLP (e) CNN (f) LSTM

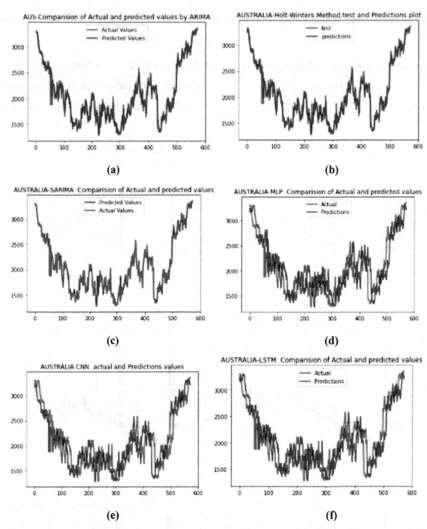

Fig. 6. AUSTRALIAN DOLLAR: plots of classical methods and deep learning models (a) ARIMA, (b) Holt-Winters, (c) SARIMA, (d) MLP (e) CNN (f) LSTM

The values of RMSE and MAPE obtained for the three classical methods are less than the deep learning model. The value of both RMSE and MAPE is lowest for ARIMA followed by Holt-Winters Method and SARIMA for both US and Australian Dollar. Among the deep learning models, the difference between the RMSE and MAPE values does not seem to be significant for both the currencies. MLP has the highest error metric values (Table 3).

Table 3. Standard deviation of RMSE and MAPE values of classical methods and deep learning models for the US and Australian Dollar

Error metric	LSTM (US)	LSTM (AUS)	CNN (US)	CNN (AUS)	MLP (US)	MLP (AUS)
RMSE	0.0343	0.0532	0.2386	0.5763	0.9376	1.9876
MAPE	0.0035	0.0321	0.5478	0.8754	0.8565	0.4532

Ten evaluations were done for each model configuration in deep learning and the RMSE and MAPE values were recorded. A mean of all the ten evaluations was considered as the final value for both the error metrics. Standard deviation of RMSE and MAPE values were also recorded. From table three, it can be observed that the values of standard deviation for both RMSE and MAPE are lowest in case of LSTM for both the currencies.

4 Conclusion

Root Mean Square Error (RMSE) and Mean Absolute Percentage Error (MAPE) were obtained for the data of the US Dollar and Australian Dollar for three classical machine learning models (ARIMA, Holt-Winters Method, SARIMA) and three deep learning models (MLP, CNN, LSTM).

The values of RMSE and MAPE obtained on testing the classical time series forecasting techniques were lower than that of the deep learning neural networks. Amongst the three classical methods, the values for ARIMA for both US and Australian Dollar were lower than SARIMA and Holt-Winters Method. Hence, from the experiment results we conclude that ARIMA is the most favorable model for time series forecasting amongst all the models tested.

For the deep learning models the differences in the values obtained for RMSE and MAPE in LSTM and CNN models were not very significant for both the countries, but the values of standard deviation of RMSE and MAPE obtained from the ten evaluations of both the models suggests that the LSTM model is most stable out of the three models applied since it gave the lowest value of standard deviation.

References

1. Zhang, G.P., Berardi, V.L.: Time series forecasting with neural network ensembles: an application for exchange rate prediction. J. Oper. Res. Soc. **52**, 652–664 (2001). https://doi.org/10.1057/palgrave.jors.2601133
2. Makridakis, S., Spiliotis, E., Assimakopoulos, V.: Statistical and machine learning forecasting methods: concerns and ways forward. PLoS ONE **13**, e0194889 (2018). https://doi.org/10.1371/journal.pone.0194889
3. Adhikari, R., Agarwal, R.K.: An Introductory Study on Time Series Modeling and Forecasting (2013). arXiv.cs.LG:1302.6613
4. Brownlee, J.: How to Grid Search Deep Learning Models for Time Series Forecasting. https://machinelearningmastery.com/how-to-grid-search-deep-learning-models-for-time-series-forecasting/. Accessed 08 Feb 2022

5. Kumar, M., Anand, M.: An application of time series arima forecasting model for predicting sugarcane production in India. Stud. Bus. Econ. **9**, 81–94 (2014)
6. Time Series Forecasting. https://towardsdatascience.com/temporal-coils-intro-to-temporal-convolutional-networks-for-time-series-forecasting-in-python-5907c04febc6. Accessed 07 Jan 2022
7. Yadav, A., Jha, C.K., Sharan, A.: Optimizing LSTM for time series prediction in Indian stock market. Procedia Comput. Sci. **167**, 2091–2100 (2020). https://doi.org/10.1016/j.procs.2020.03.257
8. Permanasari, A.E., Hidayah, I., Bustoni, I.A.: SARIMA (Seasonal ARIMA) implementation on time series to forecast the number of Malaria incidence. In: 2013 International Conference on Information Technology and Electrical Engineering (ICITEE) (2013). https://doi.org/10.1109/iciteed.2013.6676239

Probabilistic Evaluation of Distinct Machine Learning Algorithms

Shyla[1](✉) [iD] and Vishal Bhatnagar[2] [iD]

[1] NSUT East Campus (Formerly Ambedkar Institute of Advanced Communication Technologies and Research), Guru Gobind Singh Indraprastha University, New Delhi 110031, India
shylasinghit@gmail.com
[2] NSUT East Campus (Formerly Ambedkar Institute of Advanced Communication Technologies and Research), New Delhi 110031, India

Abstract. Education is the basic requirement for living a good life with valuable prestige and self-assurance. Several approaches for educational learning are being adapted by various institutions to enhance the learning quality. The schools, training institutes and colleges follow similar criteria to evaluate students' knowledge by conducting exams and tests after completion of course work. To estimate the quality of learning and teaching, educational evaluation is vital. In this paper authors considered a dataset on knowledge status of several students which includes educational objectives and educational features as the duration and time interval devoted to study, the total repetitive number of study sessions conducted, the difficulty level, and the type of questions being asked. The dataset is used for analysis of its features to understand the relationship between different instances to compute the knowledge status of different students and to use machine learning algorithms for analysis and classification of dataset.

Keywords: Pandas · Python · Support vector machine · Linear regression · NumPy

1 Introduction

Prospective Educational data analytics for learning is used by many educational institutions and initiatives [1]. Found that industries, business intelligence, and educational institutions use information analytics for analyzing the performance of different students based on various aspects such as time spent achieving objectives, methods applied to achieve goals, and usage of platforms to enhance learning.

Data analytics and modeling is used to enhance the learning of students, which is the emerging area of research where different tools and models are used precisely to compute the facts from fiction [2]. Found that the data analytics procedure is followed to extract the necessary information for learning assessment. The analytical models represent more comprehensive information about students learning through manual methods and online methods.

The schools, training institutes, and colleges follow similar criteria to evaluate students' knowledge by conducting exams and tests after the completion of coursework. To

V. Sugumaran et al. (Eds.): AIR 2022, CCIS 1738, pp. 287–299, 2022.
https://doi.org/10.1007/978-3-031-23724-9_27

estimate the quality of learning and teaching, educational evaluation is vital. The dataset was gathered from [3] "UCI Machine Learning Repository". The dataset is gathered using a user knowledge model which collects user responses from a web-based environment. Data such as learning activities, feedback, replies concerning learning objects, and domain-specific objects such as text reading, problem-solving, and test navigation are used to evaluate the student's existing knowledge, which is then transformed into five features. The objective of the paper is to calculate the accuracy and precision of several machine learning classification methods to determine the optimal model for the dataset's classification. The data analysis model is used as a modeling framework to analyse the students' knowledge status. [4] found that the model is used to create and build a strong analysis for different datasets related to educational institutions. Data relevant to research is produced commercially on large scale. The inclination of institutions towards enhanced learning scenarios gives opportunities to design the best models.

Fig. 1. Generic research model [4, 5]

Figure 1 depicts a general data analysis model. The model mainly consists of Problem Definition, Research Objectives, Research Strategy, and Results Implications. The problem definition defines the problem found during the study, Research objectives define the goals that are to be achieved, Research Strategy involves the procedure to be followed for obtaining the objectives, and Result Implications show the overall outcomes.

1.1 Problem Statement

The schools, training institutes, and colleges follow similar criteria to evaluate students' knowledge by conducting exams and tests after the completion of coursework. The dataset is obtained from [4, 5] where the author used an object model to form a domain-dependent dataset in an adaptive learning environment. The dataset includes the previous knowledge and efforts made by students to obtain knowledge. The procedure of considering prior knowledge to evaluate current knowledge is used to create an adaptive learning environment.

1.2   Objectives

The preliminary objective of the paper is to apply the methodology for analyzing students' datasets, and their features, understanding the relationships between distinct instances, computing the knowledge status of different students, and using machine learning algorithms for dataset analysis and classification.

- To compute the accuracy and precision made by several machine learning classification algorithms using a research framework.
- To compare the performance of the algorithm to find an appropriate model for the dataset classification.

This paper is categorized into the following sections: Sect. 1 is an introduction, which gives a brief description of the paper; Sect. 2 is research methodology; Sect. 3 defines the literature review, which defines the work of various researchers in the same field; Sect. 4 is dataset description which thoroughly explains the characteristics of the dataset, Sect. 5 is an improvised analysis that explains the classification algorithms used by authors, Sect. 6 shows overall accuracy analysis and Sect. 7 concludes the overall paper and future scope in the opted area.

2   Research Methodology

Research methodology is the procedure to be followed by authors to conduct the research systematically. It involves methods such as identifying the research problem, selecting the research procedure, and analyzing the research findings. The problem definition defines the problem statement, Data analysis sector involves methods for preparing data and data visualization, Machine Learning Classifiers involve testing and predictions and Performance Evaluation involves the evaluation of machine learning algorithms.

- Problem Definition. The associated problem is to define How different factors are responsible for evaluating the knowledge status of different students.
- Data Analysis. The data analysis involves the pre-processing of raw data and generating results as geometrical graphs to represent the relationship between different attributes.
- Machine Learning Classifiers. In this paper authors used machine learning classifiers for testing and prediction. In this paper, authors used SVM, Logistic Regression, and KNN classification algorithms.
- Performance Evaluation. This includes determining the performance matrices and the best-suited classification algorithm using various machine learning algorithms.

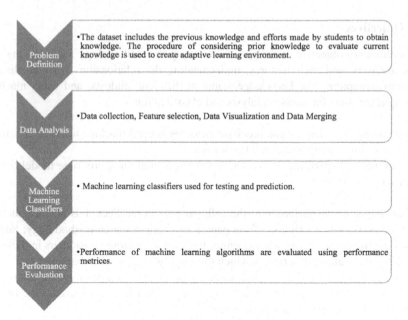

Fig. 2. Research methodology [4, 5]

Figure 2 depicts that the model consists of four sectors as Problem Definition, Data Analysis, Machine Learning Classifiers, and Performance Evaluation.

3 Literature Survey

The [5] authors used Neural Networks for predicting students' academic potential and performed data analysis for finding the different factors responsible for affecting the performance of students. The authors used 11 attributes and two hidden layers of neurons for the input and output of variables. The authors computed performance matrices that shows regression, error value, and performance and found that the neural network shows an accuracy of 84.8%. The [6] used three different datasets for performance assessment of various algorithms used for the prediction of brain-computer interface. The authors found that the evaluation of a new algorithm needs to get responses and feedback from the complete system to break the loop. [6, 7] provides a comparative evaluation of different machine learning algorithms involving pattern recognition for valid and accurate detection of any disease. The authors found that the SVM has a 94.60% accuracy for heart disease diagnosis, the Naive Bayes has a 95% accuracy, and functional trees have a 97% accuracy. [7] founded an algorithm to forecast breast cancer illness, the authors conducted a comparative analysis of several algorithms such as SVM, Decision Tree (C4.5), Naive Bayes (NB), and k-NN and found that SVM has a 97.13% accuracy rate and even a low error rate. [8] authors classified and compared various supervised machine learning algorithms to produce general hypotheses and determine the efficient classification algorithm for making predictions. Authors used several algorithms such as Random Forest (RF), NB, SVM, and Neural Network to optimize the input weights and minimization of norm least-square scheme, [9] proposed a novel strategy employing a hybrid algorithm that combines swarm optimization algorithm with extreme machine learning classification algorithm. The author [9, 10] used an enhanced PSO to evaluate the output weights. The lookup behavior of the particles is improved by PSO to determine the better response with 91.33% accuracy, the sensitivity of 95.46, and specificity of 97.33. [10] used an SVM algorithm for the analysis of sentiments using social media data. The method merges a hybrid optimization technique for feature selection. The recall, accuracy, precision, and f-measure percentages for the experiment are 94.83%, 91.91%, 98.34%, and 96.55%, respectively, and the results are comparatively better than other existing methods based on deep convolutional neural networks. It is found that the technique of feature selection by using the hybrid optimization method has better performance in sentiment analysis.

[11] authors considered the various factors used by researchers to predict the graduation time of different students and indicated that the assessment of academics is an important factor to predict graduation time. For the prediction, machine learning techniques such as SVM, Naive Bayes, Decision Trees, and Neural Networks were used, with SVM and Naive Bayes showing the best classification results. The results showed that the accuracy for academic assessment is 83.65% for Naïve Bayes, 79.5% for Decision Tree, 95% for Neural Network, and SVM 87.5%.

The different approaches are being used by different authors to evaluate the performance of students' knowledge. The researchers analyzed a single dataset as well as multiple data sets to determine the performance of machine learning algorithms using various methodologies utilized by different researchers. The performance evaluation of students involves different datasets for classification and analysis. The researchers used overall accuracy, precision, and recall value to conclude the best algorithm for prediction and learning. In this paper, the authors used a single dataset of students' knowledge status and used machine learning algorithms to compute the algorithm with the best precision and recall value. The knowledge status of a student is predicted by using earlier knowledge and current domain-dependent data.

4   Dataset Description

The dataset is an actual dataset that contains the knowledge status of several students about electrical DC machines. [3, 12] found that this dataset is constituted of 403 rows and 6 columns. The dataset is divided into a training sample and a testing sample where training has 258 instances and testing has 145 instances. The dataset is obtained from [3, 12] where the author designed an object model from domain-dependent data for an adaptive learning environment. The dataset includes earlier knowledge of students and the current efforts made by students for learning to specify current knowledge status based on previous knowledge and overall efforts. The data is domain-dependent student knowledge data, followed by dynamic data from the user knowledge model. Students interacted with the user modeling system via a web environment, which collected data from students as learning activities, feedback, learning objects, and domain-specific objects such as text reading, problem-solving, and test navigation, which was then converted into five features as follows: (STG, SCG, PEG, STR, LPR). The dataset includes features such as the time interval and duration devoted to studies, the total number of study sessions conducted, and the questions or subject difficulty level.

The box and whisker plots are used for graphically representing the class distribution of different attributes using quartiles. [1, 12] found that the whiskers are lines attached with boxes to represent the variability outward the range of the upper and lower quartiles. The concentric circles outside the range denote outliers.

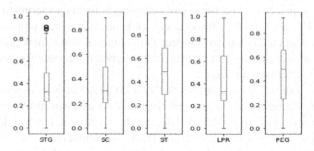

Fig. 3. Box and whisker plot

Figure 3 shows the whisker plot for each attribute's class distribution. The graph shows the discrete view of all the attributes. The statistical analysis includes the plotting of data for every attribute as univariate, bivariate, and multivariate plots.

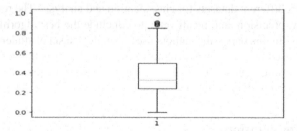

Fig. 4. Outlier for STG attribute

Figure 4 shows the outlier detected for the STG attribute. The dots above the maximum value in the boxplot represent the outliers. The STG features hold the maximum number of different values between all the numeric independent features. The STG features are concentrated around 0.50 and the rest of the features are evenly distributed. The line between the box represents the median value, and the endpoints of the box shows the first and third quartile within the minimum and maximum value. The dots represent the outliers that are to be eliminated while the rest of the features reside away from the center of the boxplot. The outliers lie near the beginning and end of the distribution. The values of data are presented as colors in the plots. The plots are made by using the python seaborn package.

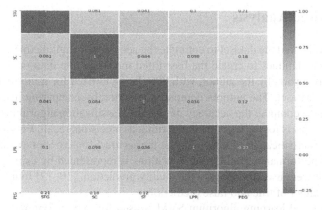

Fig. 5. Heatmap plot

In Fig. 5 authors create a heatmap matrix of 5 rows and 5 columns to display the values for the class distribution of each attribute affecting the knowledge status of students.

The multivariate plots are used to find the relation between different variables used in the dataset. It consists of multiple dependent variables. The path, factor, and multivariate analysis can be made using these plots. [12] found that the purpose is to predict the structural relationship among multiple attributes.

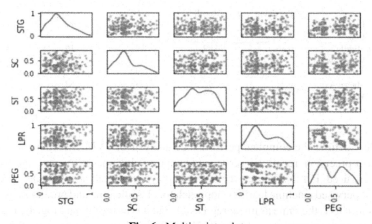

Fig. 6. Multivariate plot

Figure 6 shows the scatterplot which represents all the pairs of attributes. This scatterplot represents the structured relationship between pairs of attributes. The diagonal histogram indicates the Predictable relationship and high degree of correlation.

5 Improvised Analysis

The authors validated the dataset to compute the accuracy of multiple machine-learning classification techniques to create the best-fitted model for the dataset. The dataset is divided into two parts by the author, with 80% being utilized for training and 20% for validating the dataset. The authors compute prediction by comparing it with the validation dataset to compute the accuracy of various classification algorithms to generate classification reports for the individual algorithm as precision, recall, F1-score, and support value, the classification report computes the accuracy, macro average, and weighted average. The performance analysis of algorithms is represented by using performance metrics which were used to compute the quality prediction. [10, 12] found that quality defines the number of true and false predictions.

The supervised learning algorithm SVM is used for maximizing the margin value during classification and regression. [13] found that the primary objective is to find the dimensions using hyperplane for the representation of separation among different classes. [14] found that optimization routines are used for solving quadratic optimization in SVM training. The classification operation is made by generating hyperplanes by using coordinates of individual attribute observation. The primary objective is to accumulate classes for finding hyperplanes given by authors.

Table 1. Performance analysis of SVM

	Precision	Recall	F1-Score	Support
High	1.00	1.00	1.00	11
Low	1.00	1.00	0.96	17
Middle	0.86	0.89	0.92	19
Very_low				5
Accuracy			0.97	52
Macro Avg	0.95	0.97	0.96	52
Weighted Avg	0.97	0.97	0.97	52

Table 1 defines the complete performance analysis of SVM classifiers as accuracy, In terms of precision, recall, F1-score, and support value, macro average and weighted average are used. For the dataset, the SVM displays an overall accuracy of 0.97.

The supervised machine learning approach for classification and prediction is logistic regression. This is the same as linear regression, but it is termed binary logistic regression because there exist only two classes. [15] found that logistic regression is defined as binomial and multinomial regression. In the binomial regression, the dependent attribute holds two possibilities as success rate and failure rate while multinomial regression holds three or more attribute values as class a, class b, and class c.

$$q = \frac{e^{(a0+a1p)}}{(1+e^{(a0+a1p)}} \quad q = \frac{e^{(a0+a1p)}}{(1+e^{(a0+a1p)})} \tag{1}$$

The [15] authors used the equation of logistic regression where (p) denotes input values which are segregated with coefficients and weights of input values. The (q) denotes the output values. The rule for logistic regression is that the classification is made possible by using binary values instead of any other values.

Table 2. Performance analysis of logistic regression

	Precision	Recall	F1-Score	Support
High	1.00	0.73	0.84	11
Low	0.65	1.00	0.87	17
Middle	0.83	0.79	0.87	19
Very_low				5
Accuracy			0.87	52
Macro Avg	0.62	0.63	0.71	52
Weighted Avg	0.73	0.77	0.83	52

Table 2 defines the performance of the Logistic Regression classifier as accuracy, in terms of precision, recall, F1-score, and support value, macro, and weighted averages were used. The dataset's overall accuracy for the Logistic Regression is 0.87.

KNN is a supervised learning technique that is used for finding the classification and regression [15] found that the KNN method evaluates the similarity between existing and new data points using the distance function, and then assigns data to the nearest neighbor. The output is stated as class members and if the $k = 1$ then the class to which the data point is nearest is allocated. [16] found that the KNN can be performed in the presence of test data and is called an instance-based learning algorithm [17] found that there exist several ways to measure distance: "Euclidean distance", "hamming distance", "Manhattan distance" and "Minkowski distance". Authors used Euclidean distance for calculating the distance between data points p and q in space by (Ooi et al. 2013).

$$\text{Distance } (P, Q) = \sqrt{\frac{\sum_{i=1}^{n}(xi-yi)^2}{n}}\sqrt{\frac{\sum_{i=1}^{n}(xi-yi)^2}{n}} \tag{2}$$

Here P and Q are feature vectors where P is (a1, a2, a3,....., an) and Q is (b1, b2, b3.....bn) and n represent the feature space dimensionality.

$$\text{Sim } (P,Q) = \frac{P.\,Q}{|P||Q|}\frac{P.\,Q}{|P||Q|} \tag{3}$$

Table 3. Performance analysis of K-nearest neighbors

	Precision	Recall	F1-Score	Support
High	1	0.97	0.98	11
Low	1	0.95	0.96	17
Middle	0.84	0.89	0.90	19
Very_Low				5
Accuracy			0.94	52
Macro Avg	0.9	0.95	0.92	52
Weighted Avg	0.9	0.95	0.94	52

Table 3 defines the complete performance analysis of k-NN classifiers as accuracy, Macro average and weighted average with respect to precision, recall, F1-score and support value. The k-NN shows overall accuracy of 0.89 for the dataset.

6 Discussion

Authors validated the dataset to compute the accuracy of multiple machine-learning classification techniques to create the best-fitted model for the dataset. The dataset is divided into two parts by the author, with 80% being utilized for training and 20% for validating the dataset. The authors compute prediction by comparing it with the validation dataset to estimate the accuracy of classification algorithms to generate classification reports for individual algorithms. In terms of precision, recall, F1-score, and support value, the classification report computes the accuracy, macro average, and weighted average. The SVM makes use of kernels to work in both linear and non-linear modes. The SVM can detect hyperplanes by defining linear separation with dataset dimensions. SVM performance is not affected by outliers as SVM uses the relevant data point to find the support vectors. [17] found that the SVM requires a lesser number of training samples which makes it away from the overfitting problem. The inputs are mapped to higher dimensions using fewer training samples.

The SVM is better comparatively as it outperforms KNN and Logistic Regression in the presence of outliers, presence of large features using lesser training samples. SVM can work in both linear and non-linear ways while logistic regression works only in a linear way.

The Fig. 7 illustrates the overall accuracy of different classification machine learning algorithms like SVM, Linear Regression, and KNN. The outcomes show that SVM holds the maximum accuracy among the rest of the algorithms.

The Fig. 8 illustrates the overall results of various classification algorithms as SVM, Linear Regression, and KNN. The results show the algorithm's macro average values for precision, recall, and F1-score. Because there are some features that do not contribute and decrease total accuracy, SVM is more accurate than KNN and Logistic Regression.

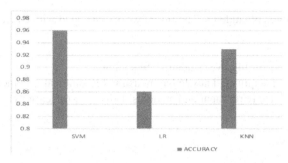

Fig. 7. Overall accuracy

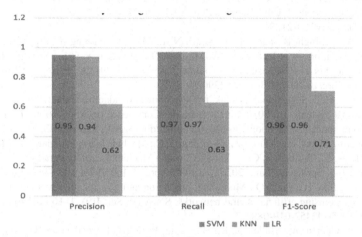

Fig. 8. Overall outcomes

7 Conclusion and Future Scope

The efficiency of educational learning is being studied using data analytics and various modeling techniques which is an emerging research area. The knowledge status of students is necessary to evaluate their learning performance. In this paper the authors analyzed the dataset, and its features, to understand the relationship between different instances, to compute the knowledge status of different students, and to use machine learning algorithms for analysis and classification. The authors' research is important in the field of educational learning because the dataset features are derived from student data such as learning activities, feedback, answers to learning objectives, and prerequisite objectives such as reading books, study time, problem-solving, exercises, and tests. The students' responses are then converted into five features. According to the research, a dataset on student knowledge status can be categorized or predicted by algorithms such as SVM, KNN, and Logistic Regression. The KNN achieves an overall accuracy of 89%, Logistic regression overall accuracy is 87% and SVM accuracy is 97%. The accuracy or precision results computed by authors are obtained by using a dataset on the knowledge status of students. The future work associated with educational learning includes in [17].

- The impact of e-learning over students' education.
- The efficiency of acquiring knowledge by using different learning methods.
- The impact of the environment and students' behaviour on learning.

References

1. Altabrawee, H., Ali, O.A.J., Ajmi, S.Q.: Predicting students' performance using machine learning techniques. J. Univ. Babylon Pure Appl. Sci. **27**, 194–205 (2019). https://doi.org/10. 29196/jubpas.v27i1.2108
2. Naidu, V.R., Singh, B., Farei, K.A., Suqri, N.A.: Machine learning for flipped teaching in higher education—a reflection. In: Al-Masri, A.N., Al-Assaf, Y. (eds.) Sustainable Development and Social Responsibility—Volume 2. ASTI, pp. 129–132. Springer, Cham (2020). https://doi.org/10.1007/978-3-030-32902-0_16
3. Kahraman, H.T., Sagiroglu, S., Colak, I.: Development of adaptive and intelligent web-based educational systems. In: 2010 4th International Conference on Application of Information and Communication Technologies (2010). https://doi.org/10.1109/icaict.2010.5612054
4. Virvou, M., Alepis, E., Tsihrintzis, G.A., Jain, L.C.: Machine learning paradigms. In: Virvou, M., Alepis, E., Tsihrintzis, G.A., Jain, L.C. (eds.) Machine Learning Paradigms. ISRL, vol. 158, pp. 1–5. Springer, Cham (2020). https://doi.org/10.1007/978-3-030-13743-4_1
5. Lau, E.T., Sun, L., Yang, Q.: Modelling, prediction and classification of student academic performance using artificial neural networks. SN Appl. Sci. **1**(9), 1–10 (2019). https://doi. org/10.1007/s42452-019-0884-7
6. Sajda, P., Gerson, A., Muller, K.-R., Blankertz, B., Parra, L.: A data analysis competition to evaluate machine learning algorithms for use in brain-computer interfaces. IEEE Trans. Neural Syst. Rehabil. Eng. **11**, 184–185 (2003). https://doi.org/10.1109/tnsre.2003.814453
7. Fatima, M., Pasha, M.: Survey of machine learning algorithms for disease diagnostic. J. Intell. Learn. Syst. Appl. **09**, 1–16 (2017). https://doi.org/10.4236/jilsa.2017.91001
8. Asri, H., Mousannif, H., Moatassime, H.A., Noel, T.: Using machine learning algorithms for breast cancer risk prediction and diagnosis. Procedia Comput. Sci. **83**, 1064–1069 (2016). https://doi.org/10.1016/j.procs.2016.04.224
9. Zhang, M.-L.: A k-nearest neighbor based multi-instance multi-label learning algorithm. In: 2010 22nd IEEE International Conference on Tools with Artificial Intelligence (2010). https://doi.org/10.1109/ictai.2010.102
10. Patra, A., Singh, D.: A survey report on text classification with different term weighing methods and comparison between classification algorithms. Int. J. Comput. Appl. **75**(7), 14–18 (2013)
11. Mohammad Suhaimi, N., Abdul-Rahman, S., Mutalib, S., Abdul Hamid, N.H., Hamid, A.: Review on predicting students' graduation time using machine learning algorithms. Int. J. Mod. Educ. Comput. Sci. **11**, 1–13 (2019). https://doi.org/10.5815/ijmecs.2019.07.01
12. Sulmont, E., Patitsas, E., Cooperstock, J.R.: Can you teach me to machine learn?. In: Proceedings of the 50th ACM Technical Symposium on Computer Science Education (2019). https://doi.org/10.1145/3287324.3287392
13. Suykens, J., Vandewalle, J.: Least squares support vector machine classifiers. Neural Process. Lett. **9**, 293–300 (1999). https://doi.org/10.1023/A:1018628609742

14. Vishwanathan, S.V.M., Narasimha Murty, M.: SSVM: a simple SVM algorithm. In: Proceedings of the 2002 International Joint Conference on Neural Networks, IJCNN 2002 (Cat. No. 02CH37290) (2020). https://doi.org/10.1109/ijcnn.2002.1007516

15. Bijalwan, V., Kumar, V., Kumari, P., Pascual, J.: KNN based machine learning approach for text and document mining. Int. J. Database Theory Appl. **7**, 61–70 (2014). https://doi.org/10.14257/ijdta.2014.7.1.06

16. Ooi, H.-L., Ng, S.-C., Lim, E.: ANO detection with k-nearest neighbor using Minkowski distance. Int. J. Signal Process. Syst. **1**, 208–211 (2013). https://doi.org/10.12720/ijsps.1.2.208-211

17. Nugrahaeni, R.A., Mutijarsa, K.: Comparative analysis of machine learning KNN, SVM, and random forests algorithm for facial expression classification. In: 2016 International Seminar on Application for Technology of Information and Communication (ISemantic) (2016). https://doi.org/10.1109/isemantic.2016.7873831

Empirical Analysis of Humor Detection Using Deep Learning and Machine Learning on Kaggle Corpus

Pariksha Prajapati[1], Arunima Jaiswal[1](✉) (iD), Aastha[1], Shilpi[1], Neha[1], and Nitin Sachdeva[2]

[1] Department of Computer Science and Engineering, Indira Gandhi Delhi Technical University for Women, New Delhi, India
{pariksha109btcse18,arunimajaiswal,aastha131btcse18,
shilpikumari129btcse18,neha142btcse18}@igdtuw.ac.in
[2] IT Department, Galgotia College of Engineering and Technology, Greater Noida, India
nitin.sachdeva@galgotiacollege.edu

Abstract. Humor is a multifaceted personality trait that makes us stand out as individuals and social groups. Humor is an important part of interpersonal communication. Due to its subjective nature, it remains difficult to find the underlying structure of comedy, recognize humor, and even develop techniques or techniques for extracting humor. Humor can also provide important information about linguistic, psychological, neurological and social issues. Humor, on the other hand, remains an undefined phenomenon due to its complexity. It's difficult to generalize or define reactions that make others laugh. For example, cognitive and cultural knowledge are two multifactorial factors that must be explored in order to understand the characteristics of humor. It's hard to understand the universal characteristics of humor, but it does give you an idea of the hidden structure that underlies comedy. In this paper we implemented comparative analysis of various machine learning (logistic regression, decision tree, random forests, passive aggressive classifier) and deep learning (CNN, LSTM) techniques for classifying tweets as humorous and nonhumorous. We considered a data-set from kaggle which contains humorous and non-humorous tweets in two different sets such as train and test in csv format. The results of this research demonstrate enhanced accuracy was obtained for humor prediction using deep learning as compared to machine learning.

Keywords: Humor · Deep learning · Machine learning · Classification

1 Introduction

Humor is the propensity of encounters to incite chuckling and give entertainment. The term comes from the humoral medication of the old Greeks, which instructed that the equilibrium of liquids in the human body, known as humors, controlled human wellbeing and feeling. Individuals of any age and societies answer humor. The vast majority can

V. Sugumaran et al. (Eds.): AIR 2022, CCIS 1738, pp. 300–312, 2022.
https://doi.org/10.1007/978-3-031-23724-9_28

encounter humor, be entertained, grin etc. More complex types of humor, for example, parody require a comprehension of its social importance and setting, and in this manner will quite often interest a more developed crowd. For the past years, social media has developed into an information and entertainment platform for the people in the world. We know how much usage of social media increased during the pandemic. With benefits like work from home, online chat it also increased stress, anxiety and unhappiness among people. It was highly needed to understand the importance of happiness, some fun in life and spreading them with the people we love and know. Hence, usage of social media and knowing whether it can bring laughter and happiness to people became very important. So, we tried to detect humor in textual social media platform like Twitter. It is widely done on sentences, paragraphs, plain text, code mixed etc. The problem many researchers and we also faced was distinguishing humourous and non humorous text. As one person might find a text humorous while others may not.

One country might find one joke humorous while other might think of it as offensive. We began our work by choosing our dataset from kaggle. For which we investigate many related papers distributed on the comparable theme. Then we found a dataset on printed media which is twitter as many people tweet on this site which are generally text. Classification of text has been done using deep learning and machine learning techniques. Deep Learning techniques [1], Glove [2] along with CNN and LSTM [3] were used. Machine Learning techniques [4], Logistic Regression, Decision Tree, Random Forest and Passive Aggressive were used with TF-IDF vectorizer.

2 Related Work

Classifying any text as humorous or not is not an easy job for any computational model [5]. Understanding humor requires a quantitatively huge amount of knowledge on linguistics and common sense world-wide to know that an interpretation of the premise that is initially given is in conflict with a hidden interpretation that fits the entire joke rather than just the part of it [6]. Various humor detection techniques use word based features to separate jokes from non-jokes [7–10]. This method is only effective when words used in the non-joke dataset are totally different from the joke dataset. For word-based humor detectors to accurately capture the differences between jokes and non-jokes, contextual-aware language models must be used [11]. According to humor theory, the order of words is important, since stating the punchline before the setup would only cause the joke to lose its humor [12]. The use of large pre-trained models, such as the recent BERT-like models, is thus a suitable approach for the task of detecting comedy. These models do not lend themselves well to understanding wordplay, since their tokens are unable to grasp morphological similarities because the models don't know the letters assigned to the tokens. In spite of this, BERT-like models have shown promising results on English humor recognition dataset [1, 13, 14]. There are other sets of techniques that are mainly used for classifying text into humorous or not using only a fixed number of features, they are known as neural networks. These techniques include some general deep learning methods such as RNN, LSTM, CNN and many more. In recurrent neural networks (RNN), the network can be enhanced by recurrent connections to prior states in the case of sequences of varying lengths. An LSTM (Long Short Term Memory) is an extension of an RNN that provides access to and forgetting of previously seen information through a series of gates. An LSTM cell that utilizes the last hidden states of multiple LSTM cells may be used to represent a sequence using a fixed-length feature vector [15, 16]. Additionally, if the length of a sequence is known, an artificial neural network could have its input size set to this length, allowing for CNN (convolutional neural networks) to be used.

3 Implementation Details

Dataset Description, techniques used and workflow applied has been discussed in detail under this section.

3.1 Dataset Description

Data for this research has been taken from Kaggle corpus [17]. It contains about 8000 tweets classified into humorous and nonhumorous tweets. Figure 1 shows the glimpse of the dataset used. The dataset contains 8000 rows and 4 columns. For every text\tweet the column provides whether the text is humorous or not. Dataset contains four columns:

- **id**- unique identifier for each text
- **text**- statement given\tweet
- **is_humor-** shows the given text is humorous or not
- **Is_humour controversy**- either take 0 or 1 value

	id	text	is_humor	humor_controversy
0	1	TENNESSEE: We're the best state. Nobody even c...	1	1.0
1	2	A man inserted an advertisement in the classif...	1	1.0
2	3	How many men does it take to open a can of bee...	1	0.0
3	4	Told my mom I hit 1200 Twitter followers. She ...	1	1.0
4	5	Roses are dead. Love is fake. Weddings are bas...	1	0.0

Fig. 1. Dataset

Total number of tweets are 8000 among which number of humorous and non humorous tweets are distributed as described below:

- Humorous tweets: 4932(61.65%)
- Non Humorous: 3068(38.35%) (Fig. 2)

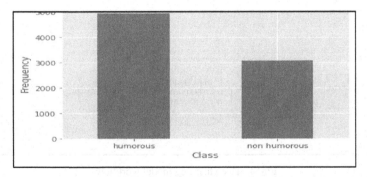

Fig. 2. Humor class distribution

Figure 3 and 4 shows the workflow of Machine Learning and Deep Learning Techniques.

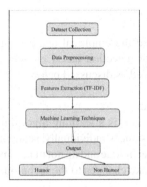

Fig. 3. Machine learning model workflow

Figure 3 shows the workflow of machine learning techniques starting with data collection as no research can move forward without prior data available or data collection of own. Followed by data pre-processing which includes cleaning of data before it could be actually used. So that it does not give errors while process. The process then followed is feature extraction using Term Frequency Inverse Document Frequency which is an algorithm based on word statistics. Then applying the machine learning techniques to give the output.

Figure 4 shows the workflow of the deep learning techniques applied. It starts with feeding the input. Followed by applying the Embedding layer which is used to represent discrete values variables as continuous vectors. Then applying the deep learning techniques (CNN &LSTM). The result is the output if the tweet is humorous or not.

In the Embedding layer GloVe ("GloVe: Global Vectors for Word Representation", n.d.) [2] was implemented which stands for global vectors for word representation. It is a pre-trained learning calculation that can be utilized to urge vector representations for words. The method is prepared on amassed worldwide word-word co-occurrence measurements from a corpus, which comes about in straight substructures of the word

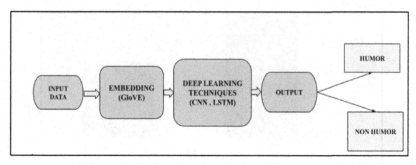

Fig. 4. Deep learning model workflow

vector space. This unsupervised calculation was created by Stanford for producing word Embeddings.

4 Techniques Applied

In this research, we performed the empirical analysis of machine learning and deep learning techniques for humor detection based on accuracy. The following machine learning techniques were applied as discussed below:

- Passive Aggressive Classifier
  A passive Aggressive classifier, is a learning algorithm where we train any system gradually by supplying it instances individually, sequentially, mini-batches i.e., small groups. Passively, keep the technique and do not make any changes when the prediction is correct. In aggressive, make changes to the technique to correct it when the guess is incorrect [18].
- Decision Tree Classifier
  When the dataset is small and can be transformed into a simple technique then Decision Trees [4, 19] classifiers are employed in classification tasks. In various situations and areas, we use the predictive technique. To create decision trees, we can use an algorithm approach that can break the dataset in numerous ways based on different conditions.
- Random Forest Classifier
  A portion that is selected randomly from training data, the random classifier (forest classifier) produces a class or group of decision trees. To get the final prediction it gathers votes from various Decision Trees. It is a meta estimator.
- Logistic Regression
  It is used for assigning observations to different sets of classes. Logistic Regression creates a probability value which might be converted to various different classes applying the logistic sigmoid function, whereas linear regression gives continuous numerical output or values. The following deep learning techniques were applied:
- CNN
  It is possible for a Convolutional Neural Network (ConvNet/CNN) [20] to deal with input images, assign weight and bias (learnable) to aspects and objects in the images and recognize them as distinct.

- LSTM
  This is a recurrent neural network (RNN) with memory cells. Better than Vanilla RNN for long sequence data. RNNs with large short-term memory are a subset of RNNs. It can learn to rely on something for a long time. Avoid long-term addiction. All recurrent neural networks (RNNs) can be thought of as a chain of iterative modulation. The is a chain-like structure, but it's repeating.

5 Results Discussion

Word clouds for humorous and nonhumorous data are shown in Fig. 5 and 6. The results for various machine learning and deep learning techniques are discussed in the below sections.

Fig. 5. Word cloud of humorous tweets

Fig. 6. Word cloud of non humorous tweets

5.1 Machine Learning Techniques

In this section results of various machine learning techniques implemented are discussed with their Precision value [21], Recall, F1 score and Accuracy [22, 23]. Machine Learning Techniques that are applied here are Passive Aggressive, Logistic Regression, Decision Tree and Random Forest respectively.

Table 1. Machine learning techniques

Technique	Precision	Recall	F1 score	Accuracy
Passive aggressive	0.81	0.81	0.81	0.814
Logistic regression	**0.84**	**0.83**	**0.84**	**0.83**
Decision tree	0.76	0.71	0.70	0.71
Random forest	0.82	0.82	0.82	0.82

As shown in the Table 1 Logistic Regression have the highest precision value (0.84), recall (0.84), F1 score (0.84) and accuracy (0.83) among all four machine learning techniques. Whereas, Decision Tree shows the Lowest precision value (0.76), recall (0.71), F1 score (0.70), and accuracy (0.71). The other two machine learning techniques almost show similar results with Random Forest having slightly better accuracy (0.82) than Passive Aggressive having accuracy (0.814).

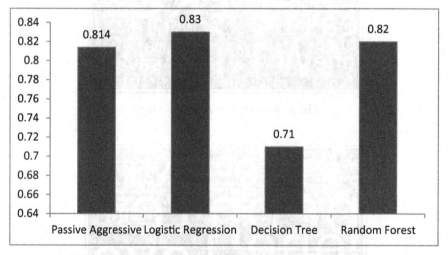

Fig. 7. Accuracy vs. machine learning techniques

Figure 7 depicts the graph of accuracy Vs. implemented machine learning techniques. It is clear from the graph that Logistic Regression have the highest accuracy of 0.83, after that Passive Aggressive and Random Forest Techniques have similar accuracy of 0.81 and the lowest accuracy is shown by the Decision Tree which is 0.71. Therefore, Logistic Regression is the yields the highest accuracy among all four Machine Learning Techniques techniques applied on the Kaggle corpus whereas Decision Tree yields the lowest accuracy on the same dataset.

Confusion Matrix [23] for the highest accurate technique(Logistic Regression) and lowest accurate technique(decision Tree) is given in Fig. 8 and 9. The confusion matrix was designed on total 1600 tweets from Kaggle corpus. The True Positive percentage is

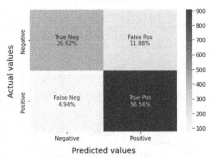

Fig. 8. Logistic regression confusion matrix

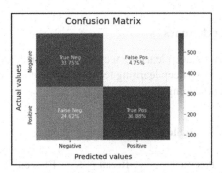

Fig. 9. Decision tree confusion matrix

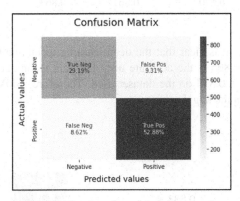

Fig. 10. Random forest confusion matrix

higher in case of Fig. 7 which is 56.56% (905 data values) and lower in case of Fig. 10 which is 36.88%(590 data values). And True Positive percentage for Fig. 11 which is 52.88% (846 data values) is slightly greater than Fig. 10 which is 52.50%(840 data values).

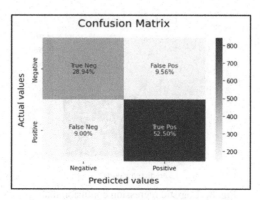

Fig. 11. Passive aggressive confusion matrix

5.2 Deep Learning Techniques

Here in this section various deep learning techniques are discussed and compared with their Accuracy. For these two deep learning techniques are considered namely CNN and LSTM with GloVe as embedding layer.

Table 2. Deep learning techniques

Technique	Precision	Recall	F1-score	Accuracy
GloVe + CNN	0.834	0.832	0.833	0.833
GloVe + LSTM	0.870	0.861	0.863	0.865

From the Table 2, it is clear that the deep learning technique GloVe+LSTM with highest accuracy of 0.865 is the accurate deep learning technique than GloVe+CNN which has accuracy of 0.833 on the dataset used. Therefore, GloVe+CNNis the most effective technique on the kaggle corpus.

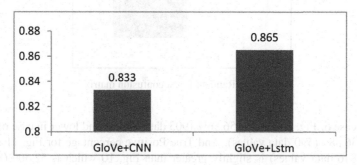

Fig. 12. Accuracy vs. deep learning techniques

Among the two implemented deep learning techniques with same embedding LSTM proves to be better than CNN technique with higher performance on kaggle corpus as shown in Fig. 12.

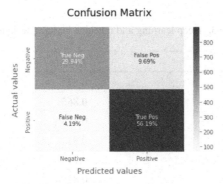

Fig. 13. GloVe+LSTM confusion matrix

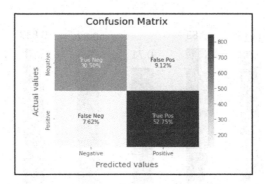

Fig. 14. GloVe+CNN confusion matrix

In The Confusion Matrix True Positive percentage is higher in case of Fig. 13 which is 56.19% (899 data values) and lower in case of Fig. 14 which is 52.75% (844 data values).

5.3 Comparative Analysis of ML and DL

Under this section, empirical analysis of humor detection using Deep Learning & Machine Learning techniques on Kaggle Corpus has been done. From the above two sections A and B accuracies of Machine Learning and Deep Learning techniques applied are plotted in the graph as shown in Fig. 15 and Table 3.

From the Fig. 15 and Table 3, it can be seen that the highest accuracy of 0.865 is shown by GloVe+LSTM then GloVe+CNN with accuracy of 0.833, these are deep learning techniques. Following that machine learning techniques Logistic Regression gives the accuracy of 0.83 and Passive Aggressive and Random Forest gives the accuracy of 0.814

and 0.82 respectively. The lowest accuracy of 0.71 is shown by Decision Tree which is also a machine learning technique. Hence, it is clear that deep learning techniques are more accurate techniques and shows higher performance than machine learning techniques on kaggle corpus.

Table 3. Deep learning and machine learning techniques

Technique	Accuracy
GloVe+CNN	0.833
GloVe+LSTM	**0.865**
Passive aggressive	0.814
Logistic regression	0.83
Decision tree	0.71
Random forest	0.82

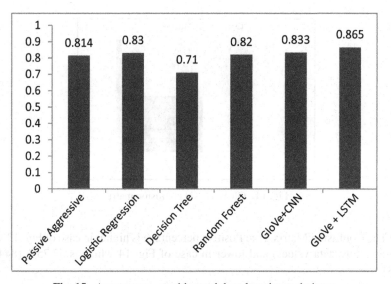

Fig. 15. Accuracy vs. machine and deep learning techniques

6 Conclusions

In this research work, the techniques for humor detection on social media data were stretched to comparison between machine learning and deep learning techniques. Various machine learning techniques with TF-IDF vectorizer and deep learning techniques CNN and LSTM with GloVe which is used for representing words as vectors, were considered. The architecture can learn to differentiate between humorous and non humorous texts on a given scale of positive and negative dataset. Deep Learning techniques (GloVe+CNN and GloVe+LSTM) prove to be more effective than machine learning techniques. Altogether, the novel deep learning techniques can easily distinguish and recognize if the text posted on social media is humorous or not. It is important to understand the power of social media. It creates an impact that can be very important and dangerous also. Hence, every research should create a positive impact. Our research will help in analysis of text or tweets as humorous or non humorous. The research distinguishes and finds a tweet as humorous or nonhumorous. There are various techniques applied but the one used here is applied on kaggle corpus. The above result will show it's accuracy.

7 Future Scope

The future improvement of this research can be applied to code mixed data, audio, images, videos etc. using other computational algorithms. It could be useful for various social media platforms which use hash tags other than twitter like YouTube. Face book, Instagram etc. Extracting text from images or videos could use this model to find humorous or not. Various complaint centres could see that social media post could be nonhumorous and just named as humour, so that society lives peacefully and such posts in the name of fun, comedy, humor are deleted or reported easily.

References

1. Sane, S.R., Tripathi, S., Sane, K.R., Mamidi, R.: Deep learning techniques for humor detection. In: Proceedings of the Tenth Workshop on Computational Approaches to Subjectivity, Sentiment and Social Media Analysis (2019). https://doi.org/10.18653/v1/w19-1307
2. Pennington, J., Socher, R., Manning, C.: Glove: global vectors for word representation. In: Proceedings of the 2014 Conference on Empirical Methods in Natural Language Processing (EMNLP) (2014). https://doi.org/10.3115/v1/d14-1162
3. Zia, T., Zahid, U.: Long short-term memory recurrent neural network architectures for Urdu acoustic modeling. Int. J. Speech Technol. 22(1), 21–30 (2018). https://doi.org/10.1007/s10 772-018-09573-7
4. Patel, H.H., Prajapati, P.: Study and analysis of decision tree based classification algorithms. Int. J. Comput. Sci. Eng. 6, 74–78 (2018). https://doi.org/10.26438/ijcse/v6i10.7478
5. Fan, X., et al.: Humor detection via an internal and external neural network. Neurocomputing 394, 105–111 (2020). https://doi.org/10.1016/j.neucom.2020.02.030
6. Winters, T., Delobelle, P.: Dutch Humor Detection by Generating Negative Examples (2020). http://arxiv.org/abs/2010.13652
7. Mihalcea, R., Strapparava, C.: Making computers laugh: investigations in automatic humor recognition. In: Proceedings of Human Language Technology Conference and Conference on Empirical Methods in Natural Language Processing, pp. 531–538 (2005)
8. Taylor, J.M., Mazlack, L.J.: UC Merced Proceedings of the Annual Meeting of the Cognitive Science Society Title Computationally Recognizing Wordplay in Jokes Publication Date Computationally Recognizing Wordplay in Jokes (2004). https://escholarship.org/content/ qt0v54b9jk/qt0v54b9jk.pdf
9. Kiddon, C., Brun, Y.: That's what she said: double entendre identification. In: Proceedings of the 49th Annual Meeting of the Association for Computational Linguistics: Shortpapers, Portland, Oregon, 19–24 June, pp. 89–94 (2011)

10. Cuba Gyllensten, A., Sahlgren, M.: Measuring issue ownership using word embeddings. In: Proceedings of the 9th Workshop on Computational Approaches to Subjectivity, Sentiment and Social Media Analysis (2018). https://doi.org/10.18653/v1/w18-6221

11. Choube, A., Soleymani, M.: Punchline detection using context-aware hierarchical multi-modal fusion. In: Proceedings of the 2020 International Conference on Multimodal Interaction (2020). https://doi.org/10.1145/3382507.3418891

12. Ritchie, G.: Developing the Incongruity-Resolution Theory. https://homepages.abdn.ac.uk/g.ritchie/pages/papers/aisb99.pdf

13. Annamoradnejad, I., Zoghi, G.: ColBERT: using BERT sentence embedding for humor detection, April 2020. http://arxiv.org/abs/2004.12765

14. Weller, O., Seppi, K.: Humor detection: a transformer gets the last laugh. In: Proceedings of the 2019 Conference on Empirical Methods in Natural Language Processing and the 9th International Joint Conference on Natural Language Processing (EMNLP-IJCNLP) (2019). https://doi.org/10.18653/v1/d19-1372

15. Ziser, Y., Kravi, E., Carmel, D.: Humor detection in product question answering systems. In: Proceedings of the 43rd International ACM SIGIR Conference on Research and Development in Information Retrieval (2020). https://doi.org/10.1145/3397271.3401077

16. Cuza, C.M., Medina Pagola, J.E., Ortega-Bueno, R., Muñiz-Cuza, C.E., Rosso, P.: UO-UPV: deep linguistic humor detection in Spanish social media. In: Proceedings of the Third Workshop on Evaluation of Human Language Technologies for Iberian Languages (IberEval 2018) (2018). https://ceur-ws.org/Vol-2150/HAHA_paper2.pdf

17. Train dataset visualization. https://www.kaggle.com/code/vfdev5/train-dataset-visualization. Accessed 13 Nov 2021

18. Crammer, K., Dekel, O., Keshet, J., Shalev-Shwartz, S., Singer, Y.: Online passive-aggressive algorithms. J. Mach. Learn. Res. 7, 551–585 (2006)

19. Ali, J., Khan, R., Ahmad, N., Maqsood, I.: Random forests and decision trees. Int. J. Comput. Sci. Issues. 9(5), 272 (2012)

20. Nanda, A., et al.: TECHSSN at HAHA @ IberLEF 2021: humor detection and funniness score prediction using deep learning techniques. In: IberLEF 2021, Málaga, Spain, September 2021 (2021). https://ceur-ws.org/Vol-2943/haha_paper1.pdf

21. Sokolova, M., Japkowicz, N., Szpakowicz, S.: Beyond accuracy, f-score and ROC: a family of discriminant measures for performance evaluation. In: Sattar, A., Kang, B.-h (eds.) AI 2006. LNCS (LNAI), vol. 4304, pp. 1015–1021. Springer, Heidelberg (2006). https://doi.org/10.1007/11941439_114

22. Goutte, C., Gaussier, E.: A probabilistic interpretation of precision, recall and f-score, with implication for evaluation. In: Losada, D.E., Fernández-Luna, J.M. (eds.) ECIR 2005. LNCS, vol. 3408, pp. 345–359. Springer, Heidelberg (2005). https://doi.org/10.1007/978-3-540-31865-1_25

23. Visa, S., Ramsay, B., Ralescu, A., VanDerKnaap, E.: Confusion matrix-based feature selection. In: Proceedings of the 22nd Midwest Artificial Intelligence and Cognitive Science Conference 2011, pp. 120–127 (2011). https://openworks.wooster.edu/facpub/88

Rumour Stance Classification on Textual Social Media Content Using Machine Learning

Anahita Singla[1], Arunima Jaiswal[1]([email]) (iD), Shruti Aggarwal[1], Parvati Sohni[1], Pragya Arora[1], and Nitin Sachdeva[2]

[1] Department of Computer Science and Engineering, Indira Gandhi Delhi Technical University for Women, New Delhi, India
{anahita012btcse18,arunimajaiswal,shruti020btcse18,
parvati040btcse18,pragya077btcse18}@igdtuw.ac.in
[2] IT Department, Galgotia College of Engineering and Technology, Greater Noida, India
nitin.sachdeva@galgotiacollege.edu

Abstract. Rumour stance classification involves the analysis of how the users react to the rumours linked with the news on social media platforms. It involves the identification of the attitude of the users towards the veracity of the rumour they are conversing about. Spreading of misinformation is a dangerous tendency and it has been widely recognized that it is important to prevent its spreading. Stance classification is a key step toward the verification of rumours. People on social media display various stances, perspectives and judgement towards rumours being spread on a social media platform. These various reactions may be unambiguous, i.e., they either deny the rumour in consideration or support the rumour. While there may be others who just comment on the rumour or ask for its veracity or claim its proof. This paper is focused on predicting user stance, ie, Accepting (S), Rejecting (D), Info-requesting (Q), or Opinion-giving (C). The paper focuses on a user stance classification analysis of rumour and non-rumour events using support vector machines, Gaussian process, multi-layer perceptron, decision tree, adaptive boosting, random forests and naive Bayes.

Keywords: Machine learning · Stance classification · Rumour analysis

1 Introduction

Modern times have made social media platforms very notable, important and eminent for news. People use these platforms to propagate events and news. They also express their opinions and views on the same. These social media platforms like Twitter, Facebook, Reddit, etc. keep generating massive amounts of data unceasingly. Any kind of breaking news makes its appearance first and foremost on these platforms nowadays. They have become the first thing people go to if they wish to gather information or consume any news. This is often owing to the simplicity to collect, share and discuss the news and therefore the ability to remain alert to the most recent news and be updated quicker than the standard media.

V. Sugumaran et al. (Eds.): AIR 2022, CCIS 1738, pp. 313–322, 2022.
https://doi.org/10.1007/978-3-031-23724-9_29

Stance classification can be described as the work of associating the attitude of a user to a rumour and the stance taken by them towards that given rumour. It is calculated in a certain short paragraph text. This text is written under a post that could be a rumour as a response. The most common stances are of showing support/acceptance and of rejecting a rumour. However, when the authenticity of a rumour is undetermined, people hardly express stances that are definite. Dataset imparted by SemEval that specifies users' reactions as well as stances in the form of these four main categories – accept (S), reject (D), request for more information (Q) and finally an opinion (C). In this paper, tweets in the English language are taken from Twitter threads of conversations surrounding an event that is notable and could be a rumour and are provided as information in conjunction with the rumours around it [1]. For scenarios like the one above, it's important to analyze people's attitudes towards rumours on different platforms and reveal their truthfulness as soon as possible. Several ways and methods have been proposed to verify the authenticity of rumours on social media.

This paper focuses on an analysis of event-related rumours. This will be based on user stances. The objective is to ascertain if a tweet in the thread is accepting (S), rejecting (D), info-requesting (Q), or opinion giving (C) on the initial rumour that initialised the thread of conversational tweets. It is a task, wherein the stance of the user towards a particular rumour that originated because of a tweet needs to be predicted, in the backdrop of a particular conversation thread. This problem can be viewed as an open stance classification task. This is regarded as an important part of resolving rumours by taking into account the reactions of people to new rumours [2, 3].

- Accept (S): when the person who responds to the tweet is in clear support or favour of the truthfulness of the rumour.
- Reject (D): when the person who responds to the tweet is in clear denial about the rumour's truthfulness.
- Request for information (Q): when the person who responds to the tweet can neither confirm nor deny the veracity of the rumour and hence the author seeks additional further information.
- Opinion (C): when the person who responds to the tweet makes their own comment and shares their own opinion and doesn't analyse the truthfulness of the rumour.

Therefore, in this work, we have presented an overview of the various approaches to classify user stances on the social media platforms, features used, the performance of techniques employed along with their analysis and comparison.

2   Related Work

With the current situation, it is very important to study the behaviour and stance of people towards rumours emerging on social media as well as to determine the veracity of these rumours as soon as possible. Different methods have been proposed to check the veracity of the rumours on social media platforms [4]. 'Rumour Detection and Classification for Twitter Data' is a comprehensive study where the J48 decision tree Classifier with SRDC and TRDC is used to get an F-Measure was more on a mixed and Obama rumour data sets which is one of the rumour topics they selected, respectively [5]. Another research is "Towards Automated RealTime Detection of Misinformation on Twitter" where sentiment and semantic analysis used some examples of rumours and, according to a verified news channel and general public tweets and detect rumours from that data using sentiment and semantic analysis [6]. Derczynski and Procter [7] used a sequential technique based on LSTM and was developed through modelling the conversational type structure of the tweets. Lukasik et al. [8] and Zubiaga et al. [9] considered in their research work the sequential nature of the Twitter threads. Hawkes processes were used by Lukasik et al. [8] for the classification of the temporal tweet sequences. In the work by Zubiaga et al. [9], the conversational type structure of the source tweets and their replies were modelled as a tree and a linear chain. [10] used a logistic regression classifier along with selected features based on text content and propagation state. Through a thorough literature review, we have concluded that a lot of work has been devoted to enhancing the validity and effectiveness of machine learning models. We aim to extract and utilize the most effective part of a tremendous number and types of features.

3 Implementation Details

This section briefs about the dataset details, techniques used and the applied workflow.

3.1 Dataset Description

The data for this paper consists of Twitter conversations focussed on news-related rumours collected by [3]. This data was classified using four labels (SDQC): "support(accept), deny(reject), query(info-request) and comment(opinion)". The data is distributed into two sets: "training and test sets. Our training data consist of four thousand two hundred and thirty-eight tweets on two hundred and ninety-seven Twitter conversations. These Twitter threads were associated with 7 dissimilar breaking news. Test data includes one thousand and forty-nine tweets focussing on two new rumorous topics" (Table 1).

Table 1. Dataset description - development, training and testing set

	Number of threads	Number of branches	Number of tweets
Development set	25	215	281
Testing set	28	772	1049
Training set	272	3030	4238
Total	325	4017	5568

We have utilised several Twitter data characteristics. These characteristics were taken into account and then the most relevant attributes were used to improve classification performance. The attributes that are used include:

Attribute set A based on the structure of data include

- Number of Retweets: Number of people tweeting or sharing the same tweet again.
- Question Mark Presence: the presence of question mark "?" with (0 for the absence of a question mark and 1 for the presence of a question mark) as binary values
- Number of Question Marks: number of question marks existing in the tweet
- Existence of Hashtags: If there is no hashtag in the tweet, we give the value as 0 and if there is at least one hashtag in the tweet, we give the value as 1
- Text Length: The text length is the length of text being used including the number of characters post removal of various selected Twitter objects such as hashtags, mentions, and URLs, etc. present on Twitter
- URL Count: the numerical value of URL links present as a hyperlink in the selected tweets of the dataset are also considered.

Attribute Set B based on individualistic properties, having a tree data structure with nodes and leaves and branches reflecting the conversation thread includes.

- Similarity of text in a tweet to source tweet: We consider the similarity of each tweet with the first original tweet.
- Similarity of text in a tweet with a replied tweet: The tweet which is a reply to another tweet and the extent of similarity of this tweet with the earlier tweet in the same thread.
- Depth of tweet: This is calculated by counting the tweet node from the root node tweet to each tweet in the ranking, this gives a depth value.

Attributes Set C based on emotional responses [11]. We used the following different emotion techniques for recognizing emotions associated with each tweet -

- Emolex: It is an array list of English words and their interrelation to positive and negative sentiments and the eight basic emotions - "sadness, joy, disgust, anger, fear, anticipation, trust, Surprise [12, 13]
- EmoSenticNet: SenticNet concepts are assigned using six WordNet Affect emotions [14, 15]
- Dictionary of Affect in Language (DAL): eight thousand seven hundred forty-two English words specified by 3 scores representing activation, imagery and pleasantness [16]
- Affective Norms for English Words (ANEW): a set of one thousand and thirty-four words commonly used. It is characterized on the basis of the affective dimensions of dominance, arousal, and valence [17]
- Linguistic Inquiry and Word Count: It calculates the fraction of text words in a specified text which belongs to a psychological and topical group that indicates various affective, cognitive, social, etc. processes [18].

3.2 Workflow

Data Collection: The data consists of Twitter conversations focussed on news-related rumors collected by [3]. They were tagged as (SDQC): support, deny, query and comment. The data is distributed into training and test sets. Training data consist of 4,238 tweets on 297 Twitter conversations in total including related direct and nested replies. These conversations were associated with seven different breaking news stories. Test data consist of 1049 tweets focussing on two new rumorous topics.

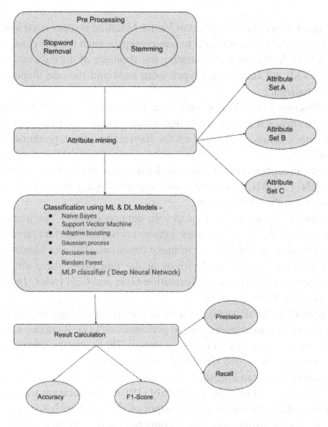

Fig. 1. Workflow diagram

Data Preprocessing: This step involves data cleaning, data transformation, and data reduction [22]. In Data Cleaning we remove stopwords, apply stemmization and remove punctuation marks from the given tweets to be able to extract the features for emotion techniques and other attribute sets.

Feature Extraction: The cleaned and transformed tweets (data) is passed further to extract the desired information and features [22]. This helps classify the data using different attribute sets. In our work, we have used TF-IDF for feature extraction. It basically collects the words from the whole document and assigns some probabilities to each word based on the number of occurrences in the document.

Classification Using Machine Learning Techniques: As seen in Fig. 1, the extracted features are used to create a feature matrix and label matrix which are passed as arguments to the classification techniques. The classification techniques utilize the feature matrix to classify the tweets into 4 classes: support (accept), deny (reject), query (info-request), and comment (opinion). The details about the classifiers used are as follows:

- **Support Vector Machine:** The Support Vector Machine is supervised learning, where we create a boundary i.e. hyperplane to separate space such that the classes are divided into subsets [19]. In this work considering the structure of the data set, we have used Non-linear SVM. All four kernel types were used and the one displaying the best results was finalized.
- **Gaussian Process:** The Gaussian process is a flexible framework for regression and various extensions of it are available that make it more versatile compared to other algorithms. Since Gaussian is based on the Bayesian method, predictions made by it are uncertain.
- **Multi-Layer Perceptron:** MLP comes under the class of feedforward artificial neural network (ANN) [21]. MLP falls under the category of a supervised learning technique called backpropagation for training.
- **Decision Tree:** A parameter is used to split data repeatedly. The tree contains two components- internal nodes and leaves. Leaves correspond to class labels and internal nodes correspond to attributes used to make decisions [19]. For identification of the attribute to be used in making decisions at the first node, there are two attribute selection measures usually used: Information Gain and Gini Index. In this work, we have used the Gini Index.
- **Adaptive Boosting:** AdaBoost is a statistical classification algorithm that can be used with other algorithms to improve overall performance [21]. It creates a tree with only two leaves. Such a structure is called a stump. These stumps correspond to weak learners that can use only one variable to make a decision.
- **Random Forest:** Random Forest drops in the category of supervised learning and it is based on the decision tree algorithm only [19]. In the decision tree algorithm, the prediction is made on the basis of the output of a single tree but in a random forest algorithm, we take multiple trees into account to give us better results. The more trees in the forest the higher the accuracy.
- **Naive Bayes:** The Naive Bayes algorithm comes under the category of supervised learning that is based on the Bayes theorem [20]. It is used to classify a set into smaller subsets. In this work, we have used Gaussian Naive Bayes since the value of attributes is not discrete and attributes have continuous values.

Results: Results of the performed experiment are calculated and analyzed as follows: The results are displayed in the form of performance metrics like Accuracy, Precision, Recall, and F1-Score along with the classification report of the 4 classes: support (accept), deny (reject), query (info-request) and comment (opinion). These results can be compared by creating bar graphs and comparison tables to analyze the stance of users over rumors. The highest F1-Score given by a technique would specify which technique is most efficient in analyzing the stance of users over various kinds of rumors.

4   Results and Discussion

This section depicts the results obtained by applying machine learning techniques to the aforesaid dataset. We have experimented with using each attribute set individually and in combination with other sets and represented the findings by comparing the performance of all classifiers with all these combinations of attribute sets. Based on these results we found the classifier with the combination of attribute sets that gives the best performance.

It was found that some attributes did not improve the classification performance. Therefore, emotion techniques described in attribute set C were used. It was decided on having only 16 attributes that produce the best results. These attributes are covered under attribute set A, B & C.

Table 2. Comparison between results from different algorithms

Technique	Accuracy	Precision	Recall	F1-score
Support vector machine	0.524	0.45	0.56	**0.451**
Gaussian process	0.775	0.491	0.437	0.447
Multi-layer perceptron	0.758	0.462	0.436	0.445
Decision tree	0.521	0.313	0.373	0.321
Adaptive boosting	0.742	0.441	0.411	0.419
Random forest	0.747	0.443	0.386	0.402
Naive Bayes	0.703	0.432	0.378	0.371

The kernel types for SVM were explored and we tried to test these 4 kernels: linear, RBF, polynomial and sigmoid. We also wanted to deal with class imbalance so we utilized their distribution in the training data and weighed these classes. The best results as observed in Table 2 were obtained for the support vector machine classifier with the RBF kernel.

Table 3. Comparison between results obtained after using various feature sets

Features	Accuracy	Precision	Recall	F1-score
Set A	0.729	0.4	0.36	0.37
Set B	0.765	0.41	0.3	0.32
Set C	0.74	0.18	0.24	0.2
Set A + B	0.781	0.53	0.42	0.44
Set A + C	0.739	0.41	0.35	0.37
Set A + B + C	0.793	0.56	0.42	0.46

Overall

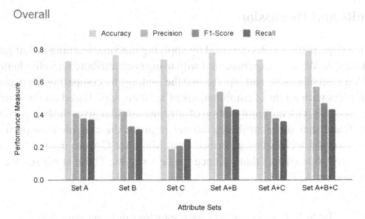

Fig. 2. Overall analysis of performance based on all attribute sets

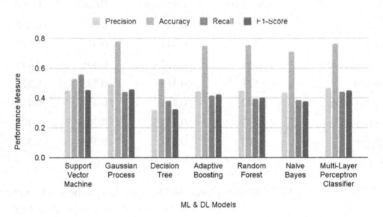

Fig. 3. Comparing the performance of different algorithms

It is observed that the best results are obtained by using all the attribute sets together as seen in Table 3 and Fig. 2.

It is observed from Fig. 3 that out of all the algorithms used, the best performance was achieved using the support vector machine classifier with the RBF kernel.

5 Conclusion and Future Work

In this paper, the classification of user stances towards rumours is done therefore, a selected set of attributes was designed which include Retweet count, Question marks (?), Number of question marks, Hashtag (#), Length of text, text similarity to source tweet and replied tweets, Tweet depth, emotion techniques like LIWC Assent, LIWC Cause, LIWC Certain, LIWC Sad attributes, DAL Activation, ANEW Dominance, Emolex Negative, Emolex Fear, Through the techniques used we were able to successfully detect rumours with F1 score of 0.45, through the help of the finite set of reliable attributes.

According to our work, SVM (using RBF Kernel) shows the best results as compared to other Machine Learning and basic deep learning algorithms, i.e. Naive Bayes, Adaboost, MLP Classifier, Random Forest, Gaussian Process and Decision Tree.

Some enhancements that can be made in the future are as follows. Addition of figurative language like sarcasm. The detection of sarcasm is important in rumour stance classification as it is "the use of words or expressions to mean the opposite of what they actually say". In sentiment analysis, it has an important effect but it gets ignored in social media analysis because it is considered too tricky to handle. Speech figures like Simile and metaphors can be added. Use of more emotions to improve classification performance. Few emotions which can be considered are embarrassment, confusion, and shock. Rumour detection can be extended to audio, video & images. Future work may also include observations with other algorithms which may produce higher accuracy for rumour detection. Use of other more sophisticated deep learning techniques like convolution, recurrent neural networks and hybrids.

References

1. Derczynski, L., Bontcheva, K., Liakata, M., Procter, R., Wong Sak Hoi, G., Zubiaga, A.: SemEval-2017 task 8: rumoureval: determining rumour veracity and support for rumours. In: Proceedings of the 11th International Workshop on Semantic Evaluation (SemEval-2017) (2017). https://doi.org/10.18653/v1/s17-2006
2. Procter, R., Vis, F., Voss, A.: Reading the riots on Twitter: methodological innovation for the analysis of big data. Int. J. Soc. Res. Methodol. **16**, 197–214 (2013). https://doi.org/10.1080/13645579.2013.774172
3. Zubiaga, A., Liakata, M., Procter, R., Wong Sak Hoi, G., Tolmie, P.: Analysing how people orient to and spread rumours in social media by looking at conversational threads. PLoS ONE **11**, e0150989 (2016). https://doi.org/10.1371/journal.pone.0150989
4. Shu, K., Sliva, A., Wang, S., Tang, J., Liu, H.: Fake news detection on social media. ACM SIGKDD Explor. Newsl. **19**, 22–36 (2017). https://doi.org/10.1145/3137597.3137600
5. Hamidian, S., Diab, M.T.: Rumour detection and classification for Twitter data. ArXiv, abs/1912.08926 https://arxiv.org/abs/1912.08926 (2019)
6. Jain, S., Sharma, V., Kaushal, R. : Towards automated real time detection of misinformation on Twitter. In: 2016 International Conference on Advances in Computing, Communications and Informatics (ICACCI) (2016). https://doi.org/10.1109/icacci.2016.7732347
7. Kochkina, E., Liakata, M., Augenstein, I.: Turing at SemEval-2017 task 8: sequential approach to rumour stance classification with branch-LSTM. In: Proceedings of the 11th International Workshop on Semantic Evaluation (SemEval-2017) (2017). https://doi.org/10.18653/v1/s17-2083
8. Lukasik, M., Srijith, P.K., Vu, D., Bontcheva, K., Zubiaga, A., Cohn, T.: Hawkes processes for continuous time sequence classification: an application to rumour stance classification in Twitter. In: Proceedings of the 54th Annual Meeting of the Association for Computational Linguistics, vol. 2: Short Papers (2016). https://doi.org/10.18653/v1/p16-2064
9. Zubiaga, A., Kochkina, E., Liakata, M., Procter, R., Lukasik, M.: Stance classification in rumours as a sequential task exploiting the tree structure of social media conversations. In: Proceedings of COLING 2016, the 26th International Conference on Computational Linguistics: Technical Papers, pp. 2438–2448. The COLING 2016 Organizing Committee, Osaka (2016)
10. Xuan, K., Xia, R.: Rumor stance classification via machine learning with text, user and propagation features. In: 2019 International Conference on Data Mining Workshops (ICDMW) (2019). https://doi.org/10.1109/icdmw.2019.00085

11. Vosoughi, S., Roy, D., Aral, S.: The spread of true and false news online. Science **359**, 1146–1151 (2018). https://doi.org/10.1126/science.aap9559

12. Mohammad, S., Kiritchenko, S., Sobhani, P., Zhu, X., Cherry, C.: SemEval-2016 task 6: detecting stance in tweets. In: Proceedings of the 10th International Workshop on Semantic Evaluation (SemEval-2016) (2016). https://doi.org/10.18653/v1/s16-1003

13. Plutchik, R.: The nature of emotions: human emotions have deep evolutionary roots, a fact that may explain their complexity and provide tools for clinical practice. Am. Sci. **89**(4), 344–350 (2001). http://www.jstor.org/stable/27857503

14. Ekman, P.: An argument for basic emotions. Cogn. Emot. **6**, 169–200 (1992). https://doi.org/10.1080/02699939208411068

15. Poria, S., Gelbukh, A., Hussain, A., Howard, N., Das, D., Bandyopadhyay, S.: Enhanced SenticNet with affective labels for concept-based opinion mining. IEEE Intell. Syst. **28**, 31–38 (2013). https://doi.org/10.1109/mis.2013.4

16. Whissell, C.: Using the revised dictionary of affect in language to quantify the emotional undertones of samples of natural language. Psychol. Rep. **105**, 509–521 (2009). https://doi.org/10.2466/pr0.105.2.509-521

17. Kittross, J.M.: The measurement of meaning. Audiov. Commun. Rev. **7**, 154–156 (1959). https://doi.org/10.1007/bf02767021

18. Chung, C.K., Pennebaker, J.W.: Linguistic inquiry and word count (LIWC). In: Applied Natural Language Processing, pp. 206–229 (2012). https://doi.org/10.4018/978-1-60960-741-8.ch012

19. Kwon, S., Cha, M., Jung, K., Chen, W., Wang, Y.: Prominent features of rumor propagation in online social media. In: 2013 IEEE 13th International Conference on Data Mining (2013). https://doi.org/10.1109/icdm.2013.61

20. Granik, M., Mesyura, V.: Fake news detection using naive Bayes classifier. In: 2017 IEEE First Ukraine Conference on Electrical and Computer Engineering (UKRCON) (2017). https://doi.org/10.1109/ukrcon.2017.8100379

21. Ahmad, I., Yousaf, M., Yousaf, S., Ahmad, M.O.: Fake news detection using machine learning ensemble methods. Complexity **2020**, 1–11 (2020). https://doi.org/10.1155/2020/8885861

22. Agarwal, V., Sultana, H.P., Malhotra, S., Sarkar, A.: Analysis of classifiers for fake news detection. Procedia Comput. Sci. **165**, 377–383 (2019). https://doi.org/10.1016/j.procs.2020.01.035

Robotics and Computer Vision
for Intelligent Automation in Industries

Theft Detection: An Optimized Approach Using cGAN and YOLO

Manas Nighrunkar$^{(\boxtimes)}$ ⓘ, Shaunak Mahajan ⓘ, Akshay Kulkarni ⓘ,
and Amit Joshi ⓘ

Department of Computer Engineering, College of Engineering Pune,
Pune 411005, Maharashtra, India
`nighrunkarmanas@gmail.com`

Abstract. Theft detection is one of the ways to reduce crime in today's chaotic society. Lot of the researchers have worked on this topic. Most of the thefts happen in low-lighting conditions. Hence, the main challenge is to increase the accuracy of the theft detection systems using an optimization technique. In the past, such systems were based on IoT resulting in false alarms in most of the cases. This work suggests a theft detection system build on You Only Looks Once (YOLO) for detection of weapons and a technique based on conditional generative adversarial network (cGAN) which is used for optimization of the results. Proposed work compares the YOLOv3 and YOLOv5 model for the detection of the weapons on a custom dataset. The accuracy for cGAN, YOLOv3 and YOLOv5 are 97.8%, 89.9% and 87.5% respectively. Also, this work presents a comparative study between the results before and after using the proposed optimization. Proposed work can be deployed at high risk areas which are highly prone to theft.

Keywords: Theft detection · cGAN · YOLO

1 Introduction

Detection of object is a key aspect of the artificial intelligence domain. This computer vision technique can be applied in countless fields starting from object tracking, traffic monitoring, security of autonomous driving, medical and many other industrial applications. Automated surveillance systems are one of the primary applications of object detection technique in the security area which has crucial importance because of their high accuracy, efficiency and reliability. The purpose of using this technique in surveillance systems can be varied according to the specific need or role the system must serve. Majority of the surveillance systems currently present in the society use weapon detection and face recognition to reduce the criminalities in public as well as private places. Rapid advancement in deep learning algorithms in the past few years is leveraged by computer vision to perform object detection.

V. Sugumaran et al. (Eds.): AIR 2022, CCIS 1738, pp. 325–332, 2022.
https://doi.org/10.1007/978-3-031-23724-9_30

Recently some researchers have proposed automatic weapon detection for surveillance systems using single shot detector (SSD) & Faster- Recurrent Convolutional Neural Network (R-CNN) algorithms. Faster R-CNN is the most efficient algorithm in R-CNN series [1].

The first deep learning algorithm which was applied to object detection was region based CNN. The approach used in this algorithm is dividing the image in various regions and classifying them into different classes and then combining them to get the original image with the required object detected. Selective search method is used in region based CNNs for generating the region proposals. Improved versions of R-CNN namely faster R-CNN & fast R-CNN were proposed in 2015. Some researchers have worked on the problem of negative samples in case of fast R-CNN and have proposed two methods as a solution for it namely hard negative sample mining and alternative training [2]. You only look once (YOLO) is one of the best performing algorithms for object detection that works by splitting the input image in a number of equal dimension grids. YOLO uses non-maximal suppression technique to suppress the boxes with low probability scores and to obtain the final bounding boxes with highest probability [3]. Next version of YOLO named as YOLOv2 came in 2016. The first version of YOLO had localization error issues and relatively low recall which were resolved in YOLOv2 while maintaining the accuracy level. The third version of YOLO known as YOLOv3 came in 2018 which was improved version of YOLOv2 in terms of accuracy and speed. YOLOv3 uses Darknet-53 for feature extraction purpose [4]. In the research work published recently, comparison between SSD vs YOLOv2 vs YOLOv3 for accuracy and speed is done. According to this work, the SSD is fastest in comparison of speed whereas the YOLOv3 is the most accurate model amongst all [5].

2   Literature Review

In 2020 Ying-jie liang et al. summarized various weapon detection models and algorithms such as YOLOv2, SSD513, Retina Net, R-CNN, Scale Normalization for Image Pyramids (SNIP). The models were trained on datasets such as Pascal Voc, Moc COCO, KITTI, Open images v5, Flickr 30k [6]. In 2021 Haogang Feng et al. analyzed the workflow of yolo models on various GPU and Non-GPU based single board computer (SBC) such as NVIDIA Jetson Nano & Raspberry Pi 4B with Intel Neural Compute [7]. Jeong-ah Kim et al. Studied Faster R-CNN, YOLO, SSD methods to recognize vehicle types in real time. Limitation in datasets is a major problem in accuracy rate of model. Some features of car and van cannot be distinguished by models, so unbiased training must be implemented in future scope [8]. Madhusri maity et al. performed a elaborate review of existing deep learning methods YOLO and R-CNN for vehicle detection. R-CNN has limitation of greater time complexity, so Fast R-CNN is better method than traditional, though it has problem of inaccurate region making which was solved in later proposed R-CNN model [9].

Zhang Menghan et al. suggested a algorithm on top of YOLOv3 to reduce the size of model and increase its performance compared to traditional convolutional structure. In result the Mobile Net v3 network has highest efficiency among all backbone networks [10]. Chien-Yao Wang et al. presented a scaling approach that changes the depth, resolution, width and structure of the network. Presented method gives accuracy of 56% Average Precision (AP) on COCO dataset for YOLOv4 large model [11]. BIN LIU et al. did a comparative study in 2017 on faster R-CNN involving regional proposal network (RPN), VGG16, ResNet101 and PvaNet. A "caffe" framework is used to train the network. The mAP for VGG16, Resnet101, PVANET are 69.4%, 72.5%, 84.9% respectively [12]. Harsh Jain et al. proposed a object detection model using R-CNN & SSD algorithm. Researchers have used custom dataset created using Fatkun Batch image downloader which is labelled manually. SSD model took more time than R-CNN and gave less accuracy for same training conditions. R-CNN has 10.8% greater accuracy than the SSD model [1]. In the research work proposed by Pandiya et al. a comparative study of three deep learning approaches has been performed. The approaches include AlexNet, VGG16 and InceptionNet [13].

3 Proposed Methodology/Solution

The implemented theft detection system contains connected network of Motion detection, Image enhancement and weapon detection model. Figure 1 displays the flow of data and actions in the system.

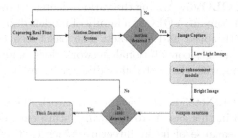

Fig. 1. Block diagram of proposed theft detection system.

3.1 Experimental Setup for Weapon Detection Module

Dataset. The setup uses custom made dataset for training. The images in dataset are collected from various sources like Google Images, Open image dataset, unsplash images, etc. A software named "Vott" is used to annotate every image manually by having 3 classes handguns, rifles, knives (Fig. 2).

Fig. 2. Sample image from custom dataset with class "Gun" and "Knife"

All annotated images were augmented with help of "Roboflow" software. Augmentations executed on dataset:-

1. Outputs per training example: 3
2. Flip: Horizontal
3. Blur: Up to 2.75px
4. Noise: Up to 5% of pixels.

After Augmentation the final dataset contained 3000 training image set around 300 validation image and 100 testing image. The dataset was then converted to comma separated value (CSV) format needed by YOLOv3.

Architecture of YOLOv3. Among the various deep learning models present in the computer vision domain, YOLO is a family of models designed for performing object detection with speed and accuracy. The basic idea behind the working of YOLO is that a single convolutional network does a job of predicting the bounding boxes along with the probability directly from input images in a single evaluation round.

YOLOv3 uses DarkNet53 as the backbone network, the use of backbone network or DarkNet53 in this case is to perform feature extractor on inputs. The name DarkNet is beacause of its architecture which contains 53 convolutional layers. For every convolutional layer or operation in DarkNet there is a convolution layer followed by batch normalization and leaky relu. So, total of 106 convolutional layers are present in YOLOv3 network.

The number of layers in YOLOv3 i.e. 106 is responsible for slow speed of v3 model but it increases the accuracy significantly. One of the salient feature of YOLOv3 is that it predicts or detects in three different scales. The scales are purely decided on downsampling of input image size by 32, 16, 8.

The feature map size has its own importance in YOLOv3, the smaller size of feature map i.e. 13×13 is responsible for detecting larger objects whereas feature map of 52×52 detects smaller objects more efficiently [14]. YOLOv3 uses 9 anchor boxes in its network. These anchors are generated by K-Means clustering which then are assigned in descending order to 3 different scales. Anchors and Grids are collectively used to generate bounding boxes on resulting images. 3 bounding boxes are predicted using 3 anchors at each scale. YOLOv3 predicts around 11,000 bounding boxes per image of size 416×416 which is ten times the number from YOLOv2 or any other CNN network, and for the same reason the time taken by YOLOv3 is greater.

Architecture of YOLOv5. All YOLO models are made up of three main architectural networks: Backbone, Neck and Head. Backbone network is the core of a deep learning model, it is used to extract key features from a given input image. YOLOv5 uses Cross Stage Partial Networks (CSPNet) or popularly known as CSPDarkNet. The CSPNet uses the method of split merge strategy which allows for greater flow in the network. Neck network is specifically used to generate feature pyramids by using the extracted feature from backbone network. Pyramids help generalise object scaling in the input. In simple words, it is a series of layers to combine extracted image features and provide them to the prediction network. As input could have the same object with different size, shape and orientation, model neck plays a crucial role in identifying such objects. Feature pyramids are useful to detect objects in completely unseen input images. Feature pyramids are generated using model neck PANet in YOLOv5. Model head is the layer that generates predictions using anchor boxes. Its main work is to perform final detection of objects on input images. It generates prediction along with probabilities, objectness score, and bounding boxes. The difference between YOLOv4 and YOLOv5 is on the basis of backbone and neck network whereas, the head network is the same for both the YOLO versions. Among the layers, the YOLOv5 uses leaky ReLU and sigmoid activation function whereas, adaptive moment estimation (ADAM) & Stochastic gradient descent (SGD) as optimizer function options in networks. For loss calculation of class probability and object score YOLOv5 uses Binary cross-entropy with logits loss functions given by PyTorch. The model has an additional option to use focal loss as its loss function while training.

Training of YOLOv3

1. Input image size - 416×416
2. Validation split - 0.1
3. Batch size for freeze - 4
4. Batch size for unfreeze - 32
5. Epochs - 51.

Training of YOLOv5

1. Model used - YOLOv5s
2. Batch size - 32
3. Input image train resize - 640×640px
4. Epochs - 500.

The model is trained on NVIDIA V100 Tensor Core GPU with architecture of NVIDIA-Volta, 640 cores of Tensor, 32 GB memory (RAM) and a bandwidth of 900 GB per second.

4   Result and Discussion

The weapon detection module is based on YOLOv3 and YOLOv5. The YOLOv3 model is trained for 51 epochs resulting in validation loss of approximately **10.09** and YOLOv5 model is trained on 200 epochs resulting in mAP of **0.875**. The module localizes whether, input image is having gun, rifle or knife in the form of label. Also, it generates the confidence score of detected weapon. This module is tested on the actual images as well as enhanced images. Model is tested on 40 actual low light images and 40 corresponding enhanced images. The main finding are as follows:

1. In most of the cases, the confidence score of detected weapon is increased as shown in the Fig. 3, YOLOv3 and YOLOv5 gives similar results.

Fig. 3. Confidence score is increased from **0.72** to **0.81**

2. In some of the cases, weapon was not detected before enhancement of the image. But, weapon is detected after the enhancement as shown in the Fig. 4.

Fig. 4. Detection of knife with confidence score of **0.43** in YOLOv3 and rifle with confidence score of **0.67** in YOLOv5

3. In some of the cases, enhanced image is detected with multiple weapons as shown in the Fig. 5.

Fig. 5. Detection of Multiple weapons in same images

4. In some of the cases of YOLOv5, dark image has detected wrong weapon with wrong localization whereas, with enhanced image it detects correct weapons in right area as seen in the Fig. 6.

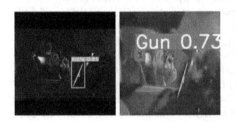 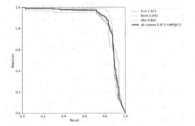

Fig. 6. Detection of right weapons in same images

Fig. 7. Precision-Recall curve for YOLOv5

The Precision-Recall (PR) curve for YOLOv5 is as shown in the Fig. 7.

5 Conclusion

Theft detection in low light conditions is highly inaccurate as, extraction of the features for any CNN model becomes difficult resulting in false negative output. Hence, the need for optimization arises. The proposed system is tested on YOLOv3 and YOLOv5 models and trained on a custom dataset consisting of approximately 3000 images. Comparative study between actual images and enhanced images shows that both models give better results in the form of either confidence score or detection of the correct weapon/multiple weapons.

Acknowledgements. We are thankful to the Dept of Computer Engineering and IT for providing the high computing GPU server facility procured under TEQIP-III (A world bank project) for our project/research work.

References

1. Jain, H., Vikram, A., Kashyap, A., Jain, A., et al.: Weapon detection using artificial intelligence and deep learning for security applications. In: 2020 International Conference on Electronics and Sustainable Communication Systems (ICESC), pp. 193–198. IEEE (2020)
2. Liu, Y.: An improved faster R-CNN for object detection. In: 2018 11th International Symposium on Computational Intelligence and Design (ISCID), vol. 2, pp. 119–123. IEEE (2018)
3. Redmon, J., Divvala, S., Girshick, R., Farhadi, A.: You only look once: unified, real-time object detection. In: Proceedings of the IEEE Conference on Computer Vision and Pattern Recognition, pp. 779–788 (2016)
4. Redmon, J., Farhadi, A.: YOLOv3: an incremental improvement. arXiv preprint arXiv:1804.02767 (2018)
5. Peng, G.: Performance and accuracy analysis in object detection (2019)
6. Liang, Y.J., Cui, X., Xu, X., Jiang, F.: A review on deep learning techniques applied to object detection. In: 2020 7th International Conference on Information Science and Control Engineering (ICISCE), pp. 120–124. IEEE (2020)
7. Feng, H., Mu, G., Zhong, S., Zhang, P., Yuan, T.: Benchmark analysis of yolo performance on edge intelligence devices. In: 2021 Cross Strait Radio Science and Wireless Technology Conference (CSRSWTC), pp. 319–321. IEEE (2021)
8. Kim, J.A., Sung, J.-Y., Park, S.: Comparison of faster-RCNN, YOLO, and SSD for real-time vehicle type recognition. In: 2020 IEEE International Conference on Consumer Electronics-Asia (ICCE-Asia), pp. 1–4. IEEE (2020)
9. Maity, M., Banerjee, S., Chaudhuri, S.S.: Faster R-CNN and yolo based vehicle detection: a survey. In: 2021 5th International Conference on Computing Methodologies and Communication (ICCMC), pp. 1442–1447. IEEE (2021)
10. Menghan, Z., Zitian, L., Yuncheng, S.: Optimization and comparative analysis of YOLOv3 target detection method based on lightweight network structure. In: 2020 IEEE International Conference on Artificial Intelligence and Computer Applications (ICAICA), pp. 20–24. IEEE (2020)
11. Wang, C.-Y., Bochkovskiy, A., Liao, H.-Y.M.: Scaled-YOLOv4: scaling cross stage partial network. In: Proceedings of the IEEE/CVF Conference on Computer Vision and Pattern Recognition, pp. 13029–13038 (2021)
12. Liu, B., Zhao, W., Sun, Q.: Study of object detection based on faster R-CNN. In: 2017 Chinese Automation Congress (CAC), pp. 6233–6236. IEEE (2017)
13. Pandiya, M., Dassani, S., Mangalraj, P.: Analysis of deep learning architectures for object detection-a critical review. In: 2020 IEEE-HYDCON, pp. 1–6. IEEE (2020)
14. Muehlemann, A.: TrainYourOwnYOLO: building a custom object detector from scratch (2019)

A Parser Based Apparel Transformation to Aid in Cloth Virtual Try-On

Deepak Kumar Jha, Badrivishal A. Paurana$^{(\boxtimes)}$ ⓘ, Seshu Tarapatla,
Praveen Thamatam, Banothu Jayanth Nath Nayak, and Anamika Singh

Electronics And Communication Engineering, Visvesvaraya National Institute
of Technology (VNIT), Nagpur, India
{deepak.jha,badrivishal.paurana}@students.vnit.ac.in,
anamikasingh@ece.vnit.ac.in

Abstract. Presenting a tailored state-of-art Deep Learning model pipeline for providing the seamless experience of different fashion designing and editing tasks. Some of the end-user features offered to the world of virtual fashion are: Pose Transfer, various features for top garments, trying out coats/jackets over upper-body garments i.e., layering of outfits at different levels, content removal, introducing stickers to garments on the body, opacity control for layered cloth. These are some of the features which we believe are going to bring a revolutionary step toward the world of virtual fashion try-on. The model separately segments and encodes different garments to provide us the flexibility to try clothes in different orders which provides us different visual experience.

Keywords: Cloth virtual try-on · Key points · Body mask ·
Generative model

1 Introduction

Our overall goal of achieving a 2D virtual try-on depends upon pipelining two of the state of art models that are present in the open world of Pose estimation and Parser generation with a deep learning model for artificial image generation of Virtual Try-On. Entire model is divided into three sub-parts in which one will generate the key points of the body structure and the other will parse the 2D image into different categories of clothes and body parts and finally, the third model will take care of the image generation. The networks we choose to implement in this model are "Open Pose: Realtime Multi-Person 2D Pose Estimation using Part Affinity Fields" for the key point generation, "Self-Correction for Human Parsing" for segmentation and the CycleGAN, MUNIT state-of-the-art models for image generation and modification as per the given mask and key points collectively as a generative model.

V. Sugumaran et al. (Eds.): AIR 2022, CCIS 1738, pp. 333–340, 2022.
https://doi.org/10.1007/978-3-031-23724-9_31

2   Related Works

Our strategy is the successor of Global Flow Field Local Attention and is using its global flow components and much of its loss components. Using the proposed model pipeline it can be observed that we have achieved quite similar results even without using Global Flow Field Local Attention. The Dressing in Order model is capable of many more features compared to GFLA which can only be used to handle pose transfer.

Inspired by Attribute-decomposed Generative Adversarial Network (ADGAN) like in case of ADGAN the garments, we also condition the generation on 2D pose and train on pose transfer. For achieving this we have followed some of the features of ADGAN in our model. We prepared our model as a modification of ADGAN. We encode garments in shape and texture separately while ADGAN encodes the garments into a single 1D vector.

Separate encoding allowed us to edit the share and texture of each individual separately. Results obtained by our 2D encoding are much superior than ADGAN's 1D encoding for capturing complex geometrical properties. Although ADGAN encodes garments separately, finally it fuses all the encodings into a single vector so the order and type of garments are fixed and can't be modified as per user's choice while in our pipeline of RNN garment can be superimposed on target one at a time.

3   Model Pipeline

3.1   OpenPose

The first stage as discussed in the model involves the network to analyze and produce key points of the subject, the points on the body that are sufficient enough to represent the pose of a person present in the image. This helps us to understand the person's posture and to perform affine transformations on the clothes to fit the person more naturally. Hence we use the Open Pose Model (Fig. 1).

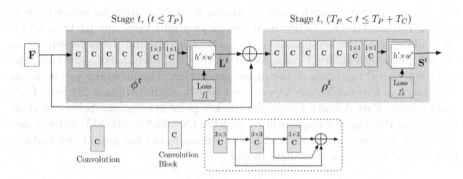

Fig. 1. Open pose model architecture

This method adopts a non-parametric representation of the subject's body parts. These representations are called 'Part Affinity Fields' (PAFs) which 2D are vector fields used to encode the positions of all the body parts including their location and orientation as well. Since this model has an ability to perform in real time understanding the persons posture with the best accuracy. This model is adopted to generate Key points for our Virtual Try on model.

Single person pose estimation: The primary reason for the model to be implemented is that traditionally the pose estimation of a person involves observing the entire image for the body parts and analyzing the spatial dependencies between them. In order make the network more refined in terms of speed, PAFs were introduced in this model. These PAFs contains the sets of flow fields that generates a non-structural pairwise relationships of body parts and connecting them as shown in the figure.

This network actually takes an RGB image of size w × h as input producing the pose. First the model predicts 2D confidence maps of body parts and a set of vector fields of Part Affinity Fields L

The set $S = (S_1, S_2 \ldots S_j)$ has J confidence maps where $S_j \in R(wxh)$,

And the set L has c vectors one for each body part $L = (L_1, L_2, \ldots L_c)$

Then the network iteratively tries to predict the affinity fields to find the part association. This will follow a Convolution Network of 7 × 7 layers with 3 kernels of size 3 × 3. The 3 outputs are concatenated, this helps in keeping both the lower and higher-level features.

The image is sent through a CNN (primary 10 stages of VGG-19 and fine-tuned). This generates feature maps F at first stage of input.

$$L^1 = \psi^1(F), \psi^1 \text{ refers to 1st stage of CNN}$$

$$L^t = \psi^t(F, L^{t-1}), \text{ where, } 2 \leq t \leq T_P, \text{ for the rest of stages}$$

where T_p is equal to total number of PAF stages involved. The confidence maps will be refined on every stage of CNN making the segmentation of limbs more accurate and cost effective for the next stage, and using those confidence map output at the last stage the dots are connected on the body parts making the pose of the body.

3.2 Self Correction for Human Parsing

Human Parsing aims to classify regions of the image to fixed semantic categories like body parts/clothes. For this, we use semantic segmentation. Semantic segmentation is a method by which each pixel is assigned to a different fixed class.

For the training, we are using the LIP dataset (Look into Person) to train the model, which comprises of 50,000 images with elaborate pixel-wise annotation. For this task, we use 19 semantic human body parts as labels, like a hat, coat, right leg, left leg, etc.

The model chosen was Self Correction for Human Parsing. SCHP uses model aggregation, wherein it uses the information learned by the previous models to

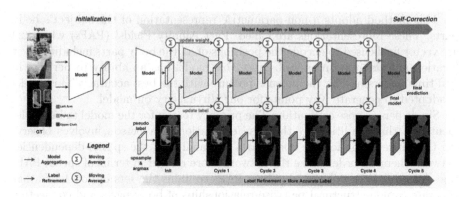

Fig. 2. Self correction for human parsing architecture

improve on itself. It performs multiple training cycles to progressively aggregate the learned model to generate the best model. These are called self-correction cycles (Fig. 2).

It uses Label Refinement which uses the context that soft, multiclass labels have more hidden information in comparison to the one-hot encoded labels, which in turn helps reduce label noises. After every self correction cycle, the information from the updated annotations will reduce some of the errors in the original ground truth.

Furthermore, SCHP can be integrated with other future human parsing models to improve them. With this SCHP was able to achieve an mIoU score of 59.36% in the LIP dataset showing that it improves and performs better than all the other human parsing models and is the best model (Fig. 3).

Fig. 3. Semantic segmentation results

4   Experiments

4.1   Implementation

The model is trained on Deepfashion Dataset with a similar proportion of training and testing data in PATN for pose transfer on 256 × 176 resolution images. Openpose, a state-of-art library for real time key point generation was used and

Self-Correction-Human-Parser which is another state-of-art model for human parser generation, pipelining these two models whose outputs are given to the DiOr model which decodes different body parts as all different parts are encoded as different colors as an output of parser model which helps in segmentation.

Compared method	Task	Others	Ours
GFLA	Pose transfer	47.728%	**52.1%**
ADGAN	Pose transfer	42.52%	**57.3%**
GFLA	Virtual try - on	19.358%	**80.43%**

4.2   Applications

We are here to demonstrate various functionality or features that can be achieved using our model pipeline. In order to make the demonstration clearer we are adding the graphical representation of features achieved by our model.

Texture Transfer shown in Fig. 4a, texture transfer allows us to change the cloth from source to target. In order to achieve this, we have simply replaced the garment texture map with the required feature map encoded from source.

Pose Transfer as shown in Fig. 4b, our work allows the user to change the pose as desired. The only requirement is the target image whose pose is to be changed and the source image whose pose is to be transferred.

(a) Texture Transfer   (b) Pose Transfer

Fig. 4. Demonstration of (a) Texture Transfer and (b) Pose Transfer.

Tucking in/out is a unique feature that can be achieved by our model because of independent injection of garment segment on target gives us a way to control the order of garments which results in tucked-in or tucked-out image. This can be observed from Fig. 5.

Layering of outfits is also possible only because of independent garment segmentation and encoding. Garments from the same category, i.e. a jacket over a shirt which belongs to the same category, are superimposed to give different visual effects can also be handled as shown in Fig. 6a.

Removal of designs as shown in Fig. 6b, allows us to choose the dimension of rectangular window from where we want to remove the content engraved on garment which could be used by fashion designers to experiment with different patterns on garments for different visual effects.

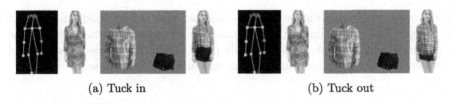

(a) Tuck in   (b) Tuck out

Fig. 5. Demonstration of (a) Tuck in and (b) Tuck out features.

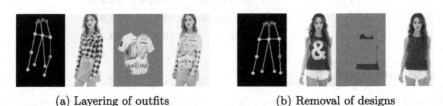

(a) Layering of outfits   (b) Removal of designs

Fig. 6. Demonstration of visual effects (a) Layering of outfits and (b) Removal of designs feature achieved by the model.

Transparency Control of Outfit shown in Fig. 7a, the transparency of an outfit can be used by a fashion outfit designer mostly in the case of layering the garments to observe and design the outfits by deciding and observing the visual patterns.

Design Testing/Insertion as shown in Fig. 7b, our model allows the inserting of designs. Which allows us to experiment with different designs and choose one that suits us best to us which allows us to check the garments on our body before ordering any customized garment for us.

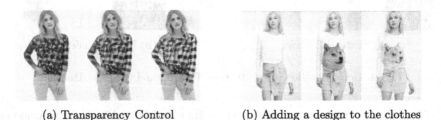

(a) Transparency Control   (b) Adding a design to the clothes

Fig. 7. Graphical Representation of features (a) Transparency Control (b) Adding a design to the clothes achieved by the model.

Garment Reshaping as shown in Fig. 8, can be achieved by replacing the shape mask of one garment with another garment of source. Another advantage of our model is that it can work with handling the removal of sleeves with ease, but in the particular case where the model needs to generate the sleeves, we are bound to use a comparatively large impanting ratio nearly equal to 0.501. The proposed model after deploying is capable of imprinting short sleeves, but when it needs to generate full length sleeves, the model performs with less confidence.

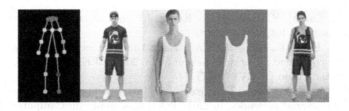

Fig. 8. Garment has been reshaped as per target image

4.3 Limitations and Work to be Done

The limitation comes with working resolution of the model. It has been trained and tested over the datasets of images with resolution of 256×176 which is on the lower resolution side compared to modern internet usage. This can be improved with training the model with much higher resolution images and more image varieties for much better eye pleasing results. The generative model is trained and tested on deep fashion dataset which contains only few dozens of different faces, so in order to make the model robust for custom image finetuning of generative model with the variety dataset is required.

5 Conclusion

The model pipeline consisting of openpose for key-points generation, Self-Correction-Human-Parser for mask generation along with the generative model has provided us with different fashion editing and fashion designing tasks which we hope is going to be a revolutionary step contributing towards digital transformation. The major achievement of this work is, providing the unmatched fashion editing features taking 2D images as an input which is economically more friendly as compared to the other existing 3D models as rendering 3D templates which are less economical.

References

1. Cui, A., McKee, D., Lazebnik, S.: Dressing in order: recurrent person image generation for pose transfer, virtual try-on and outfit editing. In: Proceedings of the IEEE/CVF International Conference on Computer Vision (ICCV) (2021)
2. Ren, Y., Yu, X., Chen, J., Li, T.H., Li, G.: Deep image spatial transformation for person image generation. arXiv preprint arXiv:2003.00696 (2020)
3. Ren, Y., Li, G., Liu, S., Li, T.H.: Deep spatial transformation for pose-guided person image generation and animation. IEEE Trans. Image Process. **29**, 8622–8635 (2020)
4. Cao, Z., Hidalgo, G., Simon, T., Wei, S.-E., Sheikh, Y.: Openpose: realtime multi-person 2d pose estimation using part affinity fields. IEEE Trans. Pattern Anal. Mach. Intell. **43**(1), 172–186 (2019)
5. Zhu, Z., Huang, T., Shi, B., Yu, M., Wang, B., Bai, X.: Proceedings of the IEEE Conference on Computer Vision and Pattern Recognition, pp. 2347–2356 (2019)

6. Huang, X., Liu, M.-Y., Belongie, S., Kautz, J.: Multimodal unsupervised image-to-image translation. In: ECCV (2018)
7. Zhu, J.-Y., Park, T., Isola, P., Efros, A.A.: Unpaired image-to-image translation using cycle-consistent adversarial networks. In: 2017 IEEE International Conference on Computer Vision (ICCV) (2017)
8. Isola, P., Zhu, J.-Y., Zhou, T., Efros, A.A.: Image-to-image translation with conditional adversarial networks. In: 2017 IEEE Conference on Computer Vision and Pattern Recognition (CVPR) (2017)

Real-Time Sign Language Detection Leveraging Real-Time Translation

Neha Challa, Kriti Baishya, Vinayak Rohatgi, and Keshav Gupta(✉) ⓘ

Department of Computer Science and Engineering, School of Engineering and Technology, Sharda University, Greater Noida, India
{2019003269.neha,2018015118.kriti,
2018007478.vinayak}@ug.sharda.ac.in, keshav.gupta@sharda.ac.in

Abstract. The outlook for the disabled people has been instantiated through the phenomena of analysing the gestures through signs which is converted in real-time into text. The aid to the people possessing an anomaly of being unable to hear or to speak through automation has been excruciatingly scrutinized over the past years. Diverse modus operandi has been induced for collation of Sign Language Detection with Text-to-Speech, escalating its utilization among common people having any disability. With the actuation of this prospect, these people can convey any message to the ones unknown to sign language. In the proposed articulation, we've tried to consummate the prowess of Convolutional Neural Networks for Sign Language Detection and thereby contemplating the efficiency through increasing the depth of the network. The output we got was phenomenal giving us a potent outlook for amalgamating it into the real-time.

Keywords: Convolutional Neural Network (CNN) · American Sign Language (ASL) · Computer Vision (CV) · Gesture recognition

1 Introduction

Due to the inefficiency of an individual to hear or speak in an appropriate manner because of bodily limitations, led to the instigation of Sign Language so that they can communicate effectively [1]. As per the claim of World Health Organization (WHO), approximately 700 million people or we can say one in every ten of the global population will be possessing disabling hearing deprivation [2]. The sign language involves varied gestures and motions formulated through a person's hands, fingers, etc. [3]. Through these gestures it becomes extremely easy for the disabled ones to communicate among themselves. The incorporation of Sign Language permits a disabled person to comprehend himself into the worldly situations and it allows them to feel that they are the part of the society as well [4]. But this Sign Language would be known by people who're unable to hear or speak and not necessarily known by the normal beings. Thus, it becomes prominent to pivot over this prospect for aiding the differently abled ones. As a result, the inculcation of plethora of technological prospects became eminent. Varied advancements were carried out to automate the process of detecting the sign language and thus

© The Author(s), under exclusive license to Springer Nature Switzerland AG 2022
V. Sugumaran et al. (Eds.): AIR 2022, CCIS 1738, pp. 341–351, 2022.
https://doi.org/10.1007/978-3-031-23724-9_32

Machine Learning and Deep Learning aspect came into picture as well [5]. Even though various techniques were scrutinized and analogized for potent solutions but turned out to be difficult to use and expensive in nature. Initially, the main focus was on creating a classification model [6] to detect varied hand gestures and thereby their meanings. But this system wasn't feasible for real-time applicability.

Thus, the induction of text-to-speech [7] stood a great outlook for aiding the disability and varied researchers got their hands on for creating such system. Different types of approaches were juxtaposed for elucidating the detection and conversion process and yet many of them were capable of achieving an optimal accuracy but got rolled out in terms of computational complexity [8]. Thus, we decided to assuage a system for Sign Language Detection using frameworks like HTML, CSS, JSON and JavaScript [9] and Computer Vision for real-time analysis. The induction of CNNs with addition of layers got us into an ideation of impact of depth over a problem domain along with the effect of it on computational complexity. Through the creation of our own dataset in real-time referencing American Sign Language (ASL) [10] dataset and contemplating it over our proposed system gave us great results. Thus, the conversion of a sign language gesture into text-to-speech along with the applicability of compound words was achieved with high potency. The paper initiates with the brief Introduction about the problem statement and our approach in Sect. 1. Moreover, the related work prospect is displayed in Sect. 2 with methodological prospect elucidated in Sect. 3. Furthermore, we discussed about the Implementation outlook in Sect. 4 and Experimental Results in Sect. 5. Also, Sect. 6 comprises of Conclusion and Future Scope of the proposed modus operand.

2   Related Work

With the perspicacity of our structured workflow, we scrutinized over recent researches in this domain. The inculcation of transliteration for Sign Language inducing ASL Dataset was carried out for Alphabetical Gestures which gave higher efficacy but stood out as a conventional prospect as it dealt with Static Images and required frames for processing [11]. Moving on to dynamic outlook a higher accuracy rate of above 90% was proposed utilizing the ASL dataset but had a condition of video being in the visible range for successful recognition [12].

Furthermore, Sign Language Linguistics was contemplated for gesture recognition using ASL dataset with eminent accuracy of above 95% but had a void in terms of inculcation of compound words [13]. Regional Pattern Accommodation utilizing ASL dataset for sign language variations actuation was proposed gaining an efficacy of 93.88% but had training discrepancy over certain epochs [14]. Integration of compound words was amalgamated over interdisciplinary principle of American Sign Language with 86.50 accuracy rate which turned out to be low for real-time modus operand [15]. The infusion of Principal Component Analysis (PCA) was also done consummating the efficacy of around 96% but the accuracy suffered when the test specimen had a consistently diversified hand position or orientation within the bounding box than the training specimen [16]. Convolutional Neural Network (CNN) was imposed on New Zealand Sign Language dataset for elucidating the applicability of it through a simple camera gaining an accuracy of 82.50% but had certain shortcomings in terms of lighting and skin color which deteriorated its accuracy to a greater extent [17]. Microsoft Kinect was also used with ASL dataset where utilizing depth data through the Kinect Sensor, per-pixel classification technique was induced to dissect human hand into sections for detecting the sign language with an efficiency of 90% but needed 3D hand models for increasing the overall efficacy [18].

Snapshot based Learning on the basis of Fingerspelling method on ASL dataset has also been incorporated gaining an accuracy of 93.30% where the processing of frames for static images turns out to be low [19]. Moreover, weakly supervised training based on Instance Learning has been applied over ASL dataset expelling the output of 86% but it's low when compared to other approaches [20]. Furthermore, Arabic Sign Language Detection model has also been developed with an efficacy of 90% with the need of increasing its scope [1]. Spanish Sign Language Detection utilizing Statistical Translation System was carried out gaining an efficacy of 92% with the limitation redundancy in statistical modus operand [19]. Thus, hovering around varied approaches we collated some prominent minutes of each approach and tried to consummate into our system for creating the most optimal solution for the people in need.

3   Methodology

After the imploration upon the related work, we summarized our structural outlook and initiated with the implementation. We explicitly examined varied dataset and selected the most famous American Sign Language Dataset as a reference for creating our own dataset. Furthermore, we incorporated the HTML, CSS, JSON and JavaScript framework. We also used Tensorflow module as it works best with the images. Also, we used that library for real-time data creation aiding the real- time gesture recognition. For our implementation we initiated with creating a self-made dataset from scratch thereby analyzing the impact of incrementing layers. We first started with using the CNN methodology, but the 01-layer model [21] gave us extremely poor layers as it wasn't able to fetch appropriate features for gesture recognition.

The 02-Layer model gave somewhat better outlook but wasn't enough for real-time induction. Thus, we increased the number of layers and made it a 03-Layered CNN structure where we got an insight of the strength of depth over a problem statement and the efficacy of CNNs for extracting minute features. Here we got great results and it became one of the models to be considered for our real-time analysis. Furthermore, we went on increasing the number of layers i.e., 04-Layered CNN, 05- Layered CNN, etc. But this time we encountered the problem of overfitting and the disadvantage of adding more layers into a network. Thus, after 05-Layered CNN structure our results weren't promising and we stopped ourselves for increasing the complexity of the model. As a result, the explication of the layered network got us to the best possible modus operand for achieving our end goal. Hence, we went on to make the application totally based on Tensorflow module and HTML, CSS and JavaScript framework as the best choice. Let's see each CNN models graphical representation Fig. 1, Fig. 2 and Fig. 3.

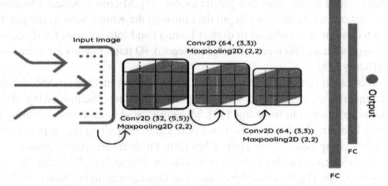

Fig. 1. Pictorial representation of 03-layered CNN system [28].

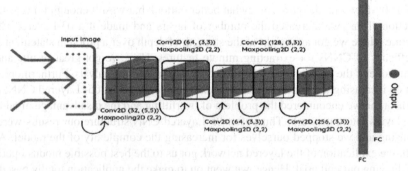

Fig. 2. Pictorial representation of 04-layered CNN system [28].

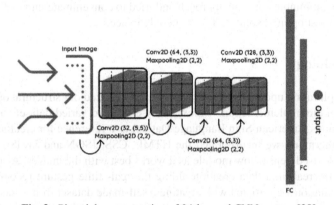

Fig. 3. Pictorial representation of 05-layered CNN system [28].

- *03-Layered CNN Architecture:* A Deep Neural Network with 03-Layers possessing different filter sizes i.e., (32, (5,5)), (64, 3,3)), (64, (3,3)) amalgamated with Max-Pooling Layer for prominent feature extraction ending with Fully-Connected (FC) Layers, formulating and generating the output.
- *04-Layered CNN Architecture:* A Deep Neural Network with 04-Layers possessing different filter sizes i.e., (32, (5,5)), (64, 3,3)), (64, (3,3)), (128, (3,3)) amalgamated with Max-Pooling Layer for prominent feature extraction ending with Fully-Connected (FC) Layers, formulating and generating the output.
- *05-Layered CNN Architecture:* A Deep Neural Network with 04-Layers possessing different filter sizes i.e., (32, (5,5)), (64, 3,3)), (64, (3,3)), (128, (3,3)), (256, (3,3)) amalgamated with Max-Pooling Layer for prominent feature extraction ending with Fully-Connected (FC) Layers, formulating and generating the output.

After the contemplation of our methodology, we were able to recognize the sign language in real-time using tensorflow library and translate it into text for the Alphabetical as well as Compound Words with higher effectivity. We also converted it into text-to-speech for certain emergency words providing an initiation for the normalization of sign language among the common beings as well and thereby aiding the needful ones.

4 Implementation and Tools

The methodological outlook gave us a strong prowess of visualizing our outcome, diminishing every constraint implicitly seen in related work for sign language recognition. Let's see each the implementation in detail to get a more precise view of our modus operandi. *The Dataset:* We incorporated the American Sign Language (ASL) dataset as a reference for creating our own real-time image database for Alphabets and Compound Words through varied open sources. ASL dataset is the world's most widely used sign language dataset comprising of static and dynamic symbols that can be used for depiction of a gesture in real-time [22]. Figure 4 represents the ASL dataset.

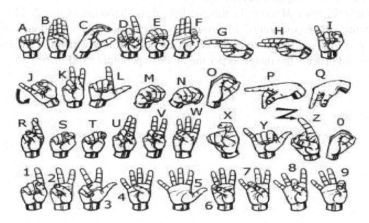

Fig. 4. Pictorial representation of American sign language dataset [13].

We then collated all the gestures along with the emergency gestures for creating our database using our team member as a host for annotating those gestures. The novelty in our dataset is the inclusion of not only static or dynamic letter gestures but also the compound as well as hazard word gestures for aiding the disabled people with more ease.

We used Tensorflow JavaScript (Tensorflow.js) as an important library to incorporate the application with all the necessary libraries and audio and video module.

- *The Tools Utilized:* We induced HTML and CSS framework for the training purpose along-with the OpenCV python library for Data Collection and real-time gesture recognition. The models have been trained over several epochs using CPU processing itself generating potent results.
- *Procedure used:* The JavaScript and CSS modules in the project use Tensorflow to train the model. The translated words can also be copied as well as predicted in any light condition. The Json module also plays an important role for the development of user level interface. The project can also be run on a local host as per our convenience.
- *Accuracy Parameters:* The dataset was differentiated into Train, Validation and Test for gauging the efficacy of model. Thus, the training, validation and test accuracy was considered for depiction of strength of our modular phenomenon. The parametric approach wasn't taken into consideration as major focus was on real-time applicability rather than demonstrating the numbers itself.

The Generalised and Proposed Architecture: Our basic flow for Sign Language Recognition consists of three modules majorly,

- *The Data Collection Module:* It fetches data from the dataset offered by the user in real-time. As we're creating our own dataset to train our model it would use that dataset for training and testing over the articulated model [23].
- *The Image Processing Module:* It fetches input provided by the user and verifies its presence by checking into the database. If the module is unable to analyse the hand gesture it alerts to adjust it accordingly [24].
- *The Image Capture Module:* In this module, the calculation of threshold value for determining the separation of foreground and background which is done using Tensorflow to find and return contours is carried out, through which our model would capture and process the image as per the modus operandi [25] (Fig. 5).

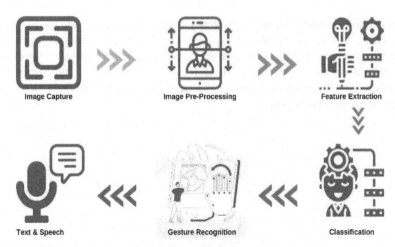

Fig. 5. Pictorial representation of the general system architecture

5   Experimental Results and Analysis

After the implementation process it was time to test our result in real-time to benchmark the prowess of our modus operand. Figure 6 and Fig. 7 represents the applicability of compound words demonstrating the words like "Help".

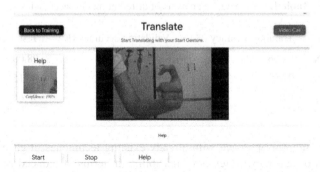

Fig. 6. Real-time result demonstration for compound word "Help".

Fig. 7. Real-time result demonstration for compound words "start, stop, help".

Furthermore, demonstration of Emergency words in form of text and sound was done for enhancing the use-case of our approach. We were fascinated by the real-time scrutiny we did after the creation of this outlook over the disabled ones and were overwhelmed by the response we got from them. The text- to-speech conversion turned out to be a game-changer in this domain. Figure 7 illustrates the Emergency words detection in real-time through training (Fig. 8).

Fig. 8. Real-time result demonstration of training

Moreover, Table 1 demonstrates the accuracies for our 03, 04, and 05 Layered CNN Architecture for Training, Validation and Test.

Table 1. Comparative analysis of different models accuracies.

Model	Training accuracy (%)	Validation accuracy (%)	Test accuracy (%)
03-Layer CNN	98.06	98.30	98.00
04-Layer CNN	97.50	96.89	97.15
05-Layer CNN	97.22	96.00	96.65

On comparing our approach with already existing techniques, it gave us an extra edge in terms of accuracy, in terms of feasibility, in terms of reduced computational complexity, and in terms of real-time applicability. Table 2 demonstrates this comparison in more detail.

When we train our model, it should be ensured that the model avoids over fit and fit the data well. Therefore, scientists divided the data into two parts namely training set and validation set.

The training accuracy, validation accuracy and test accuracy are very important parameters to determine the performance of any model; the training accuracy is determined by using the training set. In order to avoid overfitting of the model, validation set is used and to determine its accuracy validation accuracy is used. Test accuracy, on the other hand is found during the testing procedure.

Table 2. Comparative analysis of different approaches for sign language recognition

S. No	Approach	Result (Accuracy)
1	Sign language variations and regional pattern accommodation [14]	93.88%
2	Induction of PCA with neural network [16]	96.10%
3	Result snapshot-based learning based on fingerspelling [19]	93.30%
4	Proposed approach	97.00%

6 Conclusion and Future Work

The experimental results depicted above demonstrates the effectivity of our approach and the possibility of applicability of the proposed modus operandi in real-time to greater extent. We infused this model in real-time and it proved out to be one of the best outlooks for sign language recognition. Moreover, more dataset can be aggregated with the collation of static, dynamic and compound phenomenon's consummating the proficiency of any proposed articulation. Text-to-Speech should be integrated with a web app providing ease of access to the effected ones and also for the normal beings. We tried creating an application which not only detects words but also alphabets for the ease of use. Apart from automating or bringing technological plethora into this domain it's necessary to create awareness about the problem among the common beings and not only the deaf and dumb, because than only the empathetic bond would be created and thus the technology would aid the transformed behavioral stance.

References

1. Suharjito, Anderson, R., Wiryana, F., Ariesta, M.C., Kusuma, G.P.: Sign language recognition application systems for deaf-mute people: a review based on input-process-output. Procedia Comput. Sci. **116**, 441–448 (2017). https://doi.org/10.1016/j.procs.2017.10.028
2. Zhuang, F., et al.: A comprehensive survey on transfer learning. Proc. IEEE **109**, 43–76 (2021). https://doi.org/10.1109/jproc.2020.3004555
3. Szegedy, C., et al.: Going deeper with convolutions. In: 2015 IEEE Conference on Computer Vision and Pattern Recognition (CVPR) (2015). https://doi.org/10.1109/cvpr.2015.7298594
4. Cortes, C., Vapnik, V.: Support-vector networks. Mach. Learn. **20**, 273–297 (1995). https://doi.org/10.1007/bf00994018
5. Kau, L.-J., Su, W.-L., Yu, P.-J., Wei, S.-J.: A real-time portable sign language translation system. In: 2015 IEEE 58th International Midwest Symposium on Circuits and Systems (MWSCAS) (2015). https://doi.org/10.1109/mwscas.2015.7282137
6. Shahriar, S., et al.: Real-time american sign language recognition using skin segmentation and image category classification with convolutional neural network and deep learning. In: TENCON 2018 - 2018 IEEE Region 10 Conference. (2018). https://doi.org/10.1109/tencon.2018.8650524

7. Nair, M.S., Nimitha, A.P., Idicula, S.M.: Conversion of Malayalam text to Indian sign language using synthetic animation. In: 2016 International Conference on Next Generation Intelligent Systems (ICNGIS) (2016). https://doi.org/10.1109/icngis.2016.7854002

8. Mahesh, M., Jayaprakash, A., Geetha, M.: Sign language translator for mobile platforms. In: 2017 International Conference on Advances in Computing, Communications and Informatics (ICACCI) (2017). https://doi.org/10.1109/icacci.2017.8126001

9. Kumar, S., Wangyal, T., Saboo, V., Srinath, R.: Time series neural networks for real time sign language translation. In: 2018 17th IEEE International Conference on Machine Learning and Applications (ICMLA) (2018). https://doi.org/10.1109/icmla.2018.00043

10. Shivashankara, S., Srinath, S.: American sign language recognition system: an optimal approach. Int. J. Image Graph. Signal Process. **10**, 18–30 (2018). https://doi.org/10.5815/ijigsp. 2018.08.03

11. Peressotti, F., Scaltritti, M., Miozzo, M.: Can sign language make you better at hand processing? PLoS ONE **13**, e0194771 (2018). https://doi.org/10.1371/journal.pone.0194771

12. Jérôme, F., Benoît, F., Anthony, C.: Deep learning applied to sign language. In: CEUR Workshop Proceedings, vol. 2491 (2019)

13. Schembri, A., Stamp, R., Fenlon, J., Cormier, K.: Variation and change in varieties of British sign language in England. In: Braber, N., Jansen, S. (eds.) Sociolinguistics in England, pp. 165–188. Palgrave Macmillan, London (2018). https://doi.org/10.1057/978-1-137-562 88-3_7

14. Koller, O.: Quantitative Survey of the State of the Art in Sign Language Recognition arXiv (2020). https://doi.org/10.48550/arXiv.2008.09918

15. Abiyev, R.H., Arslan, M., Idoko, J.B.: Sign language translation using deep convolutional neural networks. KSII Trans. Internet Inf. Syst. **14** (2020). https://doi.org/10.3837/tiis.2020. 02.009

16. Pivac, L.: Learner autonomy in New Zealand sign language interpreting students. In: McKee, D., Rosen, R.S., McKee, R. (eds.) Teaching and Learning Signed Languages, pp. 197–221. Palgrave Macmillan, London (2014). https://doi.org/10.1057/9781137312495_10

17. Dong, C., Leu, M.C., Yin, Z.: American sign language alphabet recognition using Microsoft Kinect. In: 2015 IEEE Conference on Computer Vision and Pattern Recognition Workshops (CVPRW) (2015). https://doi.org/10.1109/cvprw.2015.7301347

18. Kania, K., Markowska-Kaczmar, U.: American sign language fingerspelling recognition using wide residual networks. In: Rutkowski, L., Scherer, R., Korytkowski, M., Pedrycz, W., Tadeusiewicz, R., Zurada, J.M. (eds.) ICAISC 2018. LNCS (LNAI), vol. 10841, pp. 97–107. Springer, Cham (2018). https://doi.org/10.1007/978-3-319-91253-0_10

19. Kelly, D., Mc Donald, J., Markham, C.: Weakly supervised training of a sign language recognition system using multiple instance learning density matrices. IEEE Trans. Syst. Man Cybern. Part B (Cybern.) **41**, 526–541 (2011). https://doi.org/10.1109/tsmcb.2010.2065802

20. Ibrahim, N.B., Selim, M.M., Zayed, H.H.: An automatic Arabic sign language recognition system (ArSLRS). J. King Saud Univ. – Comput. Inf. Sci. **30**, 470–477 (2018). https://doi. org/10.1016/j.jksuci.2017.09.007

21. Jimenez, J., Martin, A., Uc, V., Espinosa, A.: Mexican sign language alphanumerical gestures recognition using 3D Haar-like features. IEEE Lat. Am. Trans. **15**, 2000–2005 (2017). https:// doi.org/10.1109/tla.2017.8071247

22. Mohandes, M., Deriche, M., Liu, J.: Image-based and sensor-based approaches to Arabic sign language recognition. IEEE Trans. Hum.-Mach. Syst. **44**, 551–557 (2014). https://doi.org/10. 1109/thms.2014.2318280

23. Gallo, B., San-Segundo, R., Lucas, J.M., Barra, R., D'Haro, L.F., Fernandez, F.: Speech into sign language statistical translation system for deaf people. IEEE Lat. Am. Trans. **7**, 400–404 (2009). https://doi.org/10.1109/tla.2009.5336641

24. Lopez-Ludena, V., San-Segundo, R., Martin, R., Sanchez, D., Garcia, A.: Evaluating a speech communication system for deaf people. IEEE Lat. Am. Trans. **9**, 565–570 (2011). https://doi.org/10.1109/tla.2011.5993744

25. Dwivedi, S.A., Attry, A.: Juxtaposing deep learning models efficacy for ocular disorder detection of diabetic retinopathy for ophthalmoscopy. In: 2021 6th International Conference on Signal Processing, Computing and Control (ISPCC) (2021). https://doi.org/10.1109/ispcc53510.2021.9609368

Intelligent Pesticide Recommendation System Based on Plant Leaf Disease and Pests

Mayank Sharma[1], Mukund Rastogi[1], Prajwal Srivastava[1], and Mala Saraswat[2]([envelope]) [iD]

[1] ABES Engineering College, Ghaziabad, India
{mayank.18bcs1153,mukund.18bcs1021,prajwal.18bcs1005}@abes.ac.in
[2] Bennett University, Greater Noida, U.P., India
malasaraswat@gmail.com

Abstract. Agriculture plays a major role in the population's good health and country's GDP, but both of these will have an effect if we do not look in this field constantly. The major issues in the agriculture farm is plant's leaf disease and pests which cause major damages to the crops. To tackle this, farmers use fertilizers and pesticides but because of lack of knowledge they can use any kind of fertilizer and pesticides for any leaf's disease and pests. Thus we planned to give a suitable approach by recommending fertilizers and pesticides for particular leaf's disease and pests with the help of today's technology like deep learning. In our paper, we have proposed a detection system using deep learning to detect leaf's disease and pests and then recommend fertilizers and pesticides. For this, we have trained our dataset in various pre-learned Convolutional Neural Network (CNN) models and rectified the best pre-learned model which has high accuracy. To detect leaf's disease, we trained our leaf dataset in pre-learned CNN model like Inception V3, MobileNet V2, and EfficientNet_lite1 and found out that EfficientNet_lite1 gives high accuracy for leaf dataset and to detect pests we trained our pest dataset in pre-learned CNN model like MobileNet V2, EfficientNet_lite1, and ResNet50 and found out that ResNet50 gives high accuracy for pest dataset.

Keywords: CNN · Agriculture · Pesticides · Deep learning · Recommender system

1 Introduction

Agriculture is the backbone of the Indian economy. Almost half of the country's national income is attained from the agriculture sector which plays a significant role in the economic sector of our Indian economy. The advancement in the agriculture sector is nowadays bulk of raw material for industries coming from agriculture and rural sectors. Around 70% of the Indian population get employment through agriculture. The population is increasing very rapidly so there is a demand for food and raw materials from the agriculture sector. So for this purpose the advancement of the agriculture sector must be done, the goal of this research is to improve the quality of crops and help the farmer to avoid the damages in the field by the pest. Fertilizer for the crop will increase the output from the agriculture sector and can help a farmer to be financially good. Our goal is to

© The Author(s), under exclusive license to Springer Nature Switzerland AG 2022
V. Sugumaran et al. (Eds.): AIR 2022, CCIS 1738, pp. 352–361, 2022.
https://doi.org/10.1007/978-3-031-23724-9_33

inform farmers about the crop quality and what exactly should be used in the particular crop and also tell them about the insect damaging the field. To accomplish this research, both Software and Hardware requirements have to be fulfilled. The information about the field is provided in real-time. To achieve this approach, we have used a deep learning approach. The trend of machine learning and artificial intelligence has rapidly increased in various sectors and it has to be also increased in the agriculture sector too for solving several kinds of problems prevailing in the field.

In this research paper, we have focused on to choose the best model for the leaf images dataset and pest image dataset so that the model can detect the image class and we recommend the pesticides to the farmer. We have chosen CNN models like MobileNet V2, Inception V3, and EfficientNet_lite1 to train the leaf images dataset and found out that EfficientNet_lite1 gives best accuracy among the three used. EfficientNet_lite1 is a convolutional neural network engineering and scaling strategy that consistently scales all elements of width, goal utilizing a compound coefficient. EfficientNet_lite1 utilizes a compound coefficient to consistently scale network width and goal in a principled way. For the pest images dataset we chose CNN models like MobileNet V2, EfficientNet_lite1 and ResNet50 V2 and found out that ResNet50 V2 gives best accuracy among the three used. ResNet50 is a convolutional neural network which has 50 layers in total. These layers are used to solve complex tasks and increase the accuracy.

Our main focus is to recommend Pesticides to the Farmers based on Plant's leaf diseases and the presence of pests in the fields. Efficiently managing soil and crop with technologies such as AI, ML, and Deep Learning. We can examine the health of the crop for the diagnosis of pests, disease deficiencies etc. Prior information about the disease of the crop helps the farmers or users to control the disease accordingly before it causes major defects in the field. It has also resolved the issue of over spraying of herbicides and fertilizer as a result it will cause the poison or excess of the harmful chemicals in the vegetables and fruits this method will prevent the overuse of the chemicals.

2   Related Work

Pant et al. proposed a paper in 2021 where they identify disease in capsicum plants leaves. They use image dataset of 597 images which is divided into 2 classes (healthy and infected with disease) and trained it with VGG model based on CNN and get 95.5% of accuracy.[1] Liu and Wang proposed a paper in 2020 where they mainly focus on identifying types of leaves disease and less on pest disease. They have image dataset of 15000 images that divided into 12 classes (11 classes of leaves disease and only 1 class of pest), trained it with CNN model, yolo V3, and improved YoloV3 and found that improved yolo V3 gives best accuracy of 92% [2]. Burhan et al. proposed a paper in 2020 where they identify the disease and pest in the rice crop. They used image dataset of 3355 images divided into 4 classes (3 classes of diseases and 1 class of pest), trained it with CNN model like VGG16, VGG19, ResNet50, ResNet50V2 and ResNet101V2 and found out that ResNet101V2 gives best accuracy of 86.79% [3]. Liu et al. proposed a paper in 2019 to detect pests. They uses 8800 images dataset, trained it with CNN model like PestNet, VGG16, ResNet50 and ResNet101 and found out that PestNet gives best accuracy of 75.46% [4]. Jiang et al. proposed a paper in 2019 to identify Apple leaf disease detection. They used 21377 images of image dataset, trained it with ZFNet, VGGNet, combination of VGGNet and Inception and ResNet101 and found out that combination of VGGNet and Inception gives best accuracy of 78.80% [5]. Muammer and HaNBAY proposed a paper in 2019 where they identify whether the leaves have disease or pest. They used a dataset of 1965 images divided into 8 classes and trained it with different CNN models like ALexNet, VGG16 and VGG19. They found out that VGG16 get best accuracy of 92% [6]. Arsenouic et al. proposed a paper in 2019 to detect plant leaf disease where they use the image dataset of 5432 image that divided into 38 classes, trained it with PlantdiseaseNet model and get 93.67% of accuracy [7]. Liu et al. proposed a paper in 2018 where they identify disease in apple leaves. They have made their own architecture model of CNN. They have used dataset of total 13689 images, trained it with AlexNet, ResNet20, GoogLeNet, VGGNet-16, and with their own CNN model and found out that they get 95.62% of accuracy with their own CNN model [8]. Krishnaswamy et al. proposed a paper in 2018 where they detect tomato leaves disease. They trained a dataset of 13262 images with VGG16 and AlexNet and found out that AlexNet provide better accuracy of 95% [9]. Amara et al. proposed a paper in 2017 where they identify disease in banana leaves using LeNet model based on CNN where they get 92.88% of accuracy. They use image dataset having only 3 classes (healthy, black sigatoka and black speckle) of total 3700 images only [10]. Wang et al. proposed a paper in 2017 where they identify the disease of plant leaves. They use image dataset of total 1644 image that are divided into 12 clusters, trained it with CNN model like VGG16, VGG19, InceptionV3, and ResNet50 and found out that they get best accuracy of 90.4% with VGG16 model [11]. DeChant et al. proposed a paper in 2017 where they have found out if a maize plant have leaf-blight infection or not. They have a dataset of 1796 images having only two classes, trained it with simple CNN model and get 95% of accuracy [12]. Brahimi et al. proposed a paper in 2017 to identify tomato leaf disease detect. They uses 14828 images dataset, trained it with AlexNet and GoogleNet and found out that GoogleNet gives best accuracy of 95% of accuracy [13]. Ramcharan et al. proposed a paper in 2017 to identify leaf disease of image dataset of 14000 images, trained it with InceptionV3 CNN model and found only 93% of accuracy [14]. Besides plant disease identification, Saraswat et al. used RNN for book recommendation [15]. A related work [9] mentioned above proposed a method which achieves the accuracy of 95% and used 13262 images of only tomato leaves, another related work [4] proposed a method to detect only pests which achieves accuracy of 75.46% and used 8800 of images. On the comparison of these work, our work is far better than these as we used two dataset in our research. One dataset is the plant's leaves having 22000 images of all kinds of leaves which were divided into 10 different leaf diseases classes and achieve 97% of accuracy. Another dataset is of pests having 21226 images which was divided into 93 classes of pests and achieves 93% of accuracy. We have used large datasets and divided them into more classes to make our CNN model stable so that it gives us more accurate results.

3 Proposed Method

Image Acquisition: We have used the images dataset for plant leaf disease detection which is a secondary dataset having 10 classes and a total 22000 images in which 18000 images are used for training and 4000 images for testing. We have also used another image based secondary dataset for pest detection which has 93 classes and total 21226 images in 17020 images used for training and 4206 images used for testing. In the insect classification dataset, insects are classified based on GBIF (Global Biodiversity Information Facility) Id. So we found corresponding insects from the GBIF database. Both the datasets are already divided into different classes. The proposed approach is presented in Fig. 1 and explained below.

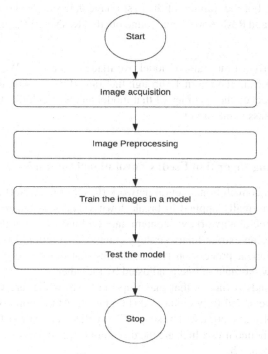

Fig. 1. Proposed method

Image Preprocessing: First step of image pre-processing involves image resizing which is performed on both datasets. Images in the training dataset had varying sizes, along these lines images must be resized prior to being utilized as a contribution to the model. Square images were resized to the shape 256 × 256 pixels. Rectangular images were resized to 256 pixels on their most brief side, then, at that point, the centre 256 × 256 square was edited from the picture.

After resizing, Augmentation is implemented on the dataset for more accurate outcomes. In particular, augmentations were acted in memory and the outcomes were not saved, the supposed in the nick of time augmentation that is presently the standard way for utilizing the methodology. The primary sort of augmentation performed was level flips of a more modestly edited square picture that was extended to the expected side utilizing flat reflections inside the picture. Test-time augmentation was acted to allow a fit model for each opportunity of making a hearty expectation. This included making five trimmed forms of the info picture and five edited adaptations of the evenly flipped rendition of the picture, then, at that point, averaging the forecasts.

Train Images in a Model: After pre-processing, we had to choose some CNN model like MobileNet V2, Inception V3, ResNet50 V2 and EfficientNet_lite1 for training the images dataset. For the training of leaf image dataset, we chose MobileNet V2, Inception V3 and EfficientNet_lite1 and found out that EfficientNet_lite1 gives best accuracy for leaf image dataset. For the training of the pest image dataset, we chose MobileNet V2, EfficientNet_lite1 and ResNet50 V2 and found out that ResNet50 V2 gives best accuracy for pest detection.

Test the Model: To test the trained model, we made a small UI. We passed an image that we have taken from the internet, through the trained model with the help of the UI application and checked the accuracy of that model and to check that the trained model gives the correct class name or not.

3.1 Deep Learning Algorithm Used: Convolutional Neural Network (CNN)

In deep learning, a convolutional neural network (CNN or ConvNet) is a class of deep neural networks, normally applied to break down visual symbolism. Presently when we think about a neural network, we contemplate grid increases yet that isn't true with ConvNet. It utilizes an extraordinary strategy called Convolution. Now in science convolution is a numerical process on two capacities that delivers a third capacity that communicates how the state of one is adjusted by the other.

There are 3 kinds of layers that make up the CNN which are the convolutional layers, pooling layers, and fully-connected (FC) layers. At the point when these layers are stacked, a CNN architecture will be shaped. Notwithstanding these three layers, there are two additional boundaries which are the dropout layer and the activation work which are characterized beneath.

3.2 CNN Models Used to Compare

Inception V3: The Inception V3 is a deep learning model dependent on Convolutional Neural Networks, which is utilized for picture arrangement. The inception V3 is a predominant rendition of the essential model Inception V1 which was presented as GoogleNet in 2014. As the name recommends it was created by a group at Google.

The inception V3 is only the high-level and improved form of the inception V1 model. The Inception V3 model involved a few procedures for enhancing the organization for better model transformation.

MobileNet V2: MobileNets are little, low-idleness, low-power models defined to meet the asset requirements of an assortment of utilization cases. As per the examination paper, MobileNetV2 works on the cutting edge execution of portable models on numerous benchmarks and errands just as across a range of various model sizes. It is an exceptionally powerful component extractor for object identification and division. For example, for recognition, when combined with Single Shot Detector Lite, MobileNetV2 is around 35% quicker with similar precision as MobileNetV1.

EfficientNet_lite1: The analysts previously planned a pattern network by playing out the neural engineering search, a strategy for robotizing the plan of neural networks. It upgrades both the precision and productivity as estimated on the drifting point tasks each second (FLOPS) premise. This created design utilizes the portable reversed bottleneck convolution (MBConv). The analysts then, at that point, increased this standard organization to acquire a group of deep learning models, called EfficientNet_lite1.

ResNet50 V2: ResNet has numerous variations that suddenly spike in demand for a similar idea yet have various quantities of layers. Resnet50V2 is utilized to signify the variation that can work with 50 neural organization layers. This model was tremendously fruitful, as can be determined from the way that its group won the top situation at the ILSVRC 2015 order rivalry with a blunder of just 3.57%. Moreover, it likewise started things out in the ImageNet recognition, ImageNet restriction, COCO location, and COCO division in the ILSVRC and COCO rivalries of 2015.

4 Implementation

4.1 Models Used to Compare for Plant Leaf Disease Detection

For the plant leaf disease classification, we have compared InceptionV3, MobileNetV2 and EfficientNet_lite1 to find the best one as presented in Table 1.

Table 1. Models used and experimental result for plant leaf disease detection

S. no	Model	Performance metrics	Accuracy	Precision	Recall	F1-score
1	InceptionV3	Accuracy	85%	84.9%	84.6%	84.7%
2	MobileNetV2	Accuracy	89%	86.3%	85.9%	85.9%
3	EfficientNet_lite1	Accuracy	97%	90%	89.7%	89.9%

4.2 Models Used to Compare for Pest Detection

For the pest classification, we have compared MobileNetV2, EfficientNet_lite1 and ResNet50V2 to find the best one as presented in Table 2.

Table 2. Models used and experimental result for pest detection

S. no	Model	Performance metrics	Accuracy	Precision	Recall	F1-score
1	MobileNetV2	Accuracy	65%	47.7%	47.6%	47.8%
2	EfficientNet_lite1	Accuracy	75%	75.3%	75.5%	75.5%
3	ResNet50V2	Accuracy	93%	86.6%	86.9%	86.7%

5   Results

5.1   Plant Leaf Disease Detection

In Fig. 2, we had described the observation of Accuracy and Validation accuracy of Different models which we had applied to Plant Leaf Disease Classification. Blue color represents the Accuracy of different models and orange color denotes validation accuracy on testing data. InceptionV3 gives the least accuracy on our dataset while Efficient-Net_lite1 gives the best accuracy and validation accuracy on the Plant Leaf Dataset. The difference between accuracy and val_accuracy is small in EfficientNet_lite1 as compared to other models.

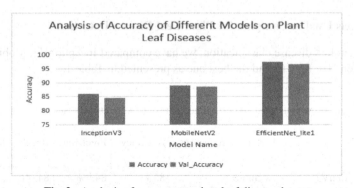

Fig. 2. Analysis of accuracy on plant leaf disease dataset

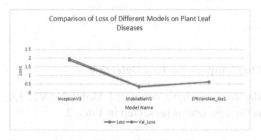

Fig. 3. Analysis of loss on plant leaf disease dataset

In Fig. 3, we had demonstrated the loss and validation loss of various models which we had used in this research. We came to the conclusion that if the loss will be high, accuracy must be below. In the InceptionV3 model, losses will be much higher as compared to EfficientNet_lite1. Hence, we can use EfficientNet_lite1 to detect leaf disease because its losses are less and accuracy will be high. Blue color denotes Loss and orange color denotes validation loss in the Plant leaf disease dataset.

5.2 Pest Detection

In Fig. 4, we had explained the observation of accuracy and validation accuracy in the insect identification dataset. The X-axis denotes accuracy in two different colors and Y-axis shows the model's name used. ResNet50V2 gives the best accuracy which is 93% while MobileNetV2 gives the least accuracy that is 65%. But Validation accuracy is less in Resnet50V2 as compared to accuracy. Blue colors show accuracy and orange color represents validation accuracy.

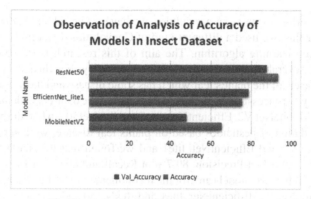

Fig. 4. Analysis of accuracy on insect dataset

In Fig. 5, we had demonstrated the loss and validation loss presented in the given model which we had applied to the insect identification dataset. The X-axis represents Loss and val_loss while Y-axis denotes model names in the insect identification model. MobileNetV2 gives higher loss and val_loss as compared to other models. ResNet50V2 gives the least loss and validation loss. Blue color indicates loss and orange color denotes val_loss in the insect dataset.

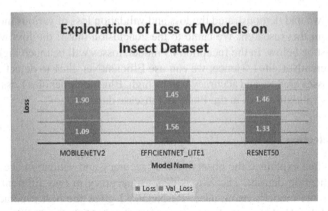

Fig. 5. Analysis of loss on insect dataset

6 Conclusion and Future Scope

To reduce the effect of pests on agriculture, we have proposed an idea to recommend pesticides. For this, we used a different kind of Convolutional Neural Network (CNN) which is a deep learning algorithm. The aim of this research is to identify the best model among several models which gives best accuracy. For this, we had taken the secondary datasets of the plant's leaf which has some disease and the secondary dataset of pests. After pre-processing the dataset, we compared the datasets with the models like Inceptive V3, MobileNet V2, EfficientNet_lite1 and ResNet50. To find the best model for the recommendation of pesticides based on plants leaf disease, we compare Inceptive V3, MobileNet V2 and EfficientNet_lite1 and we found that EfficientNet_lite1 gives 97% of Accuracy, 90% of Precision, 89.7% of Recall and 89.9% of F1-Score which is the best among other two models and for the recommendation of pesticides for pests, we compare MobileNet V2, EfficientNet_lite1 and ResNet50 and we found that ResNet50 gives 93% of Accuracy 86.6% of Precision, 86.9% of Recall and 86.7% of F1-Score which is the best among other two models. For the future perspective, we have decided to train our datasets with other models as well in a hope to find more accuracy. For the convenience of farmers, we have decided to build a mobile application so that we can put our trained model in the application and farmers can use the application and find out the pesticides conveniently. We also decided to use a bot so that it can roam around the field and click an image whenever it finds any pests on leaves or disease on leaves.

References

1. Pant, H., Lohani, M.C., Pant, J., Petshali, P.: Capsicum plant leaves disease detection using convolution neural networks. Int. J. Curr. Res. Rev. **13**, 185–190 (2021). https://doi.org/10.31782/ijcrr.2021.13704
2. Liu, J., Wang, X.: Tomato diseases and pests detection based on improved Yolo V3 convolutional neural network. Front. Plant Sci. **11** (2020). https://doi.org/10.3389/fpls.2020.00898

3. Burhan, S.A., Minhas, S., Tariq, A., Nabeel Hassan, M.: Comparative study of deep learning algorithms for disease and pest detection in rice crops. In: 2020 12th International Conference on Electronics, Computers and Artificial Intelligence (ECAI) (2020). https://doi.org/10.1109/ecai50035.2020.9223239

4. Liu, L., et al.: PestNet: an end-to-end deep learning approach for large-scale multi-class pest detection and classification. IEEE Access. **7**, 45301–45312 (2019). https://doi.org/10.1109/access.2019.2909522

5. Jiang, P., Chen, Y., Liu, B., He, D., Liang, C.: Real-time detection of apple leaf diseases using deep learning approach based on improved convolutional neural networks. IEEE Access. **7**, 59069–59080 (2019). https://doi.org/10.1109/access.2019.2914929

6. Liu, J., Wang, X.: Plant diseases and pests detection based on deep learning: a review. Plant Methods **17**, 22 (2021). https://doi.org/10.1186/s13007-021-00722-9

7. Arsenovic, M., Karanovic, M., Sladojevic, S., Anderla, A., Stefanovic, D.: Solving current limitations of deep learning based approaches for plant disease detection. Symmetry **11**, 939 (2019). https://doi.org/10.3390/sym11070939

8. Fang, T., Chen, P., Zhang, J., Wang, B.: Identification of apple leaf diseases based on convolutional neural network. In: Huang, D.-S., Bevilacqua, V., Premaratne, P. (eds.) ICIC 2019. LNCS, vol. 11643, pp. 553–564. Springer, Cham (2019). https://doi.org/10.1007/978-3-030-26763-6_53

9. Rangarajan, A.K., Purushothaman, R., Ramesh, A.: Tomato crop disease classification using pre-trained deep learning algorithm. Procedia Comput. Sci. **133**, 1040–1047 (2018). https://doi.org/10.1016/j.procs.2018.07.070

10. Amara, J., Bouaziz, B. and Algergawy, A.: A deep learning-based approach for banana leaf diseases classification. In: Mitschang, B., et al. (eds.) Datenbanksysteme für Business, Technologie und Web (BTW 2017) - Workshopband. Bonn: Gesellschaft für Informatik e.V., S. 79–88 (2017)

11. Wang, G., Sun, Y., Wang, J.: Automatic image-based plant disease severity estimation using deep learning. Comput. Intell. Neurosci. **2017**, 1–8 (2017). https://doi.org/10.1155/2017/2917536

12. DeChant, C., et al.: Automated identification of northern leaf blight-infected maize plants from field imagery using deep learning. Phytopathology®. **107**, 1426–1432 (2017). https://doi.org/10.1094/phyto-11-16-0417-r

13. Brahimi, M., Boukhalfa, K., Moussaoui, A.: Deep learning for tomato diseases: classification and symptoms visualization. Appl. Artif. Intell. **31**, 299–315 (2017). https://doi.org/10.1080/08839514.2017.1315516

14. Ramcharan, A., Baranowski, K., McCloskey, P., Ahmed, B., Legg, J., Hughes, D.P.: Deep learning for image-based cassava disease detection. Front. Plant Sci. **8** (2017). https://doi.org/10.3389/fpls.2017.01852

15. Saraswat, M., Srishti: Leveraging genre classification with RNN for book recommendation. Int. J. Inf. Technol. **14**, 3751–3756 (2022). https://doi.org/10.1007/s41870-022-00937-6

Flood Damage Detection Using Satellite Images

Amey Dhongade[✉][iD], Akanksha Thorat[iD], Divya Alone[iD], Suraj Sawant[iD], and Amit Joshi[iD]

Department of Computer Engineering, College of Engineering Pune,
Pune 411005, Maharashtra, India
ameymakarand@gmail.com,
{thoratak18.comp,alonedv18.comp,sts.comp,adj.comp}@coep.ac.in

Abstract. After a hazardous event such as a hurricane, timely and reliable situational awareness for all intents and purposes is critical to emergency managers and first responders. One of the most fairly effective ways to achieve this goal is damage assessment, generally contrary to popular belief. Recently, disaster researchers basically have used satellite images or drone images to detect the damage done by a flood to urban areas, which is quite significant. In this paper, with the help of Convolutional Neural Networks detecting damage caused by hurricanes is highlighted. The dataset posted by NOAA (National Oceanic and Atmospheric Administration) during Hurricane Harvey is used to train the models. This work focuses on identification of damages done precisely to buildings and roads. To achieve this, twelve convolutional neural network models namely VGG-16, Resnet50, Inceptionv3, Densenet, Alexnet, Squeezenet, Shufflenet, Resnext, Wideresnet, Googlenet, Mobilenetv3 and a customised convolutional model is used. Hurricane Harvey Dataset is used for damage detection, that is available on Kaggle. To improve the robustness, a customised dataset is used. In this work, an attempt is made to find damages for buildings and roads. For the hurricane Harvey, the best accuracy was shown by Resnet50 (93.56%) and for the customised Dataset, GoogleNet showed the higher accuracy (90.65%). The customised approach is proven to be acceptable in comparison with the existing models.

Keywords: Flood damage detection · Satellite imagery · CNN

1 Introduction

When a hurricane hits the coast, emergency managers must assess the situation and damage caused by the flood to effectively respond to the disaster and allocate resources for future rescue and recovery work. The traditional practice of assessing disaster and damage conditions relies heavily on several emergency response teams and volunteers that tour the affected area and conduct assessments. However, this process is labor-intensive and time- consuming. Thanks to

V. Sugumaran et al. (Eds.): AIR 2022, CCIS 1738, pp. 362–374, 2022.
https://doi.org/10.1007/978-3-031-23724-9_34

the advancement in computer vision studies, scientists have found another way to improve the effectiveness of damage assessments [1]. Specifically, an image classification algorithm to distinguish damaged buildings and floodplains from undamaged buildings is applied.

The loss of life and property caused by a hurricane is countless. The images taken by the satellite help in addressing the issue of detecting the damaged structures [2]. The current ways of dealing with the damage detection is still under human control, making it more time consuming and unreliable. That is where computer vision comes into play. We aim to assess and detect damages done to buildings and roads due to hurricanes by studying the post-event satellite images using CNN.

Before the CNN era, methods for assessing flood risk were established, including precipitation analysis, catchment capacity, river network analysis, flood contour and depth generation based on topology data, and flood spread simulation. It takes advantage of the unique characteristics of each hazard and cannot be applied directly to damage assessment in post-hurricane images.

This work deals with detecting the damage caused by the hurricanes on buildings and roads with the help of CNN pre-trained models using the datasets Hurricane Harvey (2017) and a custom Dataset which contains the images of Hurricane Harvey and Hurricane Ida.

The impact a natural calamity can cause is very calamitous and becomes very difficult while assessing. Moreover, the nearby residents' lives are also at risk. Methods using the images before the damage occurred and the images after the damage will be useful.

In the following sections, we have included a literature review conducted on existing building and road damage detection research papers, the gaps or limitations that we observed through the literature review, the methodologies we propose to solve these gaps, a critical analysis based on the review, followed by a conclusion.

2   Background and Related Works

Damage detection is necessary for assessing the areas and degree of damage done by natural disasters for gauging the situation better. Typically an image classification algorithm is implemented to distinguish damaged buildings and floodplains from undamaged buildings. Results found from various classification algorithms carried out are then compared with results from land surveys for finding accuracy. Methods involving convolutional networks for image detection and further classification such as using Pytorch Models (Resnet50, Inceptionv3), Watershed Segmentation, GIS and more methods have been used for the research work. Damage caused to buildings and roads in particular has been carried out. Various datasets have been used for carrying out research, like, Quickbird, IKONOS, TerraSAR-X, GeoEye, etc. which include both optical as well as SAR images. Finds the radar characteristics like the correlation coefficient and the backscattering difference between two SAR images taken in different times and state their respective accuracies. The limitation in the method being the noise present in the radar system [3]. Follows a similar method based on morphological feature extraction, giving encouraging results. The limitation posed in the system being that when the building collapses on its base, the damaged building stays undetected. The dataset used is Ikonos Images [4].

A comparison between pixel-based approach and object-based approach has been done and their user and producer's accuracy have been obtained and compared. The object based method's accuracy is 50%. The further improvements in the models bring better detection in edges and shapes for improving the accuracy [5]. Post-event IKONOS and QB images were employed in an automated damage detection method and the resultant damaged areas from the IKONOS and QB images agreed reasonably well with the visual inspection results and the field survey data. The results for the moderately damaged and partially collapsed are not distinguished. The dataset used is Ikonos and Quickbird [6]. Uses texture features of pre- and post-earthquake SAR images based on watershed segmentation. The accuracy obtained from the method is 80.63%. The algorithm may not always detect the edges of the building from shadows. The dataset used is GCM, Turkey [7]. Using the suggested GIS for choosing a route to deal with emergency situations, by using weighted-cost distance function. The accuracy was 66–68%. The accuracy obtained from the hilly areas was less and missed detection pixels were many in number. The dataset used is NDVI from SPOT [8]. Using the image analysis and mapping techniques, the authors proposed to expand a capability for understanding the impact of tsunami affected area to be used for emergency and disaster relief activities, combined with tsunami numerical models. The accuracy for water segment is 78%, for soil segment is 83%, for debris 76%, 97% for vegetation, 74% for building and 75% for road. The dataset used is Quickbird [9]. Utilisation in using multi- temporal and mono-temporal techniques that evaluate the changes between the before and data which interpret only the after-event data were applied in. This paper has combined different datasets and carried out damage detection using methodologies on all the datasets that include SAR, optical, LiDAR images, making it very practical [10]. Extracts road damage from remote sensing images, road features and their changes after earthquakes using edge and line detection. The overall accuracy is 86%. The improvements include the use of geometric features rather than spectral features for improvement in accuracy [11]. Remote Sensing Data and Image-Based Analysis, pixel based analysis, visual analysis, crowd sourced analysis. The results showed that when integrated with the results of predictive modelling and RS data, an increase in average accuracy levels occurred both by applying CS as a direct value and within 270-m buffers around the elicited data points. There is a limited correspondence between RS and CS Dataset has caused a decrease in the accuracy. The accuracy in the model is 48.55%. The dataset used is Quickbird [12]. Multiscale segmentation wavelet transform is evaluated on terrains such as roads and the output of the objects of the two images are differentiated. Further improvements include adding shadow images as well as other radiometric measurements. The KNN model gives 78% accuracy for Haiti region and 91% for Bourmedes. The dataset used is Geoeyes [13]. An fuzzy methodology using an flexible network system model was designed to analyse and evaluate the damage caused to the buildings. The limitation include over segmentation. The use of spatial neighbourhood information to improve the detection of the building. The overall accuracy is 82%. The dataset used is Quickbird [14]. Given a pair of imagestrips, the researchers extracted features of the building's overlapping windows, which were then used to learn a shared sub-space. Based on the changes detected, the results were shown to a set of human- observers to obtain feedback from them. Using this feedback in a supervised setting to learn a damage detection classifier. The dataset used is DigitalGlobe. The accuracy is 88% [15]. Applies an improved method for classifying better building damage evaluation with the help of images which happened before the damage and after the damage has occurred. The limitation being the model is very time-consuming. The dataset used is Quickbird. The mean accuracy is 84.5% [16]. Implementation of IDEAS, which is an image- based disaster damage assessment system, to evaluate seismic damages done inside buildings. The paper further discusses how IDEAS quickly and automatically assesses the damage immediately after an earthquake happens even if there are hundreds or thousands of video cameras equipped. The accuracy in the paper is 97.6% [17]. Normalized Digital Surface Models (nDSM) were generated by subtracting the pre and post event Digital Elevation Model (DEM) and Digital Surface Model (DSM) for the years 2010 and 2011. The automatic building extraction using nDSM differences with RS and Information Technologies integration was revealed as an efficient and time saving method for detecting damaged buildings after an earthquake. The overall accuracy is 96.54 % for region-1 and 90.72% for region-2 [18].

3   Proposed Methodology

For this task of damage detection post-Hurricane, 11 Pre-trained models and a Custom model are used for the implementation. The 11 pre-trained models considered are VGG-16, Resnet50, Alexnet, Densenet, Inception V3, Mobilenet, Wide Resnet, Resnext, Shufflenet, Squeezenet, GoogleNet. The proposed approach is to classify the images as damaged and not damaged. The 11 Pretrained models are utilised with the help of transfer learning. In transfer learning, the pretrained models have been trained on a larger dataset such as Imagenet. The knowledge the model gets from the larger datasets can then be transferred to any dataset. The custom model is created with 8 convolutional layers. Using the dot product operation between the input data and the receptive field of the neuron, the output of each neuron gets calculated. To prevent overfitting in the model, Max-pool layer and Avg-Pool layer have been added. The pretrained models and the custom model are then added with a classifier and an optimizer. The classifiers include the relu activation function, and the optimizer includes Adam optimizer. To prevent overfitting and loss, the cross entropy loss function and dropout function has been added with the classifiers. The dataset used for this approach is DigitalGlobe's Open Data Program for post-Hurricane Harvey

(In Texas). It consists of pre and post event Imagery over affected areas. The pre-events cover images from the year 2016 to the day Hurricane Harvey first occurred. The post-event images have data of around a week after Hurricane Harvey hit Texas. The aim for using the dataset is to understand which regions are damaged by floods. The good quality of images and high resolution makes it ideal for us. A custom dataset is generated using the images of the Hurricane Harvey dataset and added images of hurricane Ida which took place in 2021 [19]. Programming Language used is Python. Figure 1 contains the sample images from Hurricane Harvey Dataset and Fig. 2 contains the images from the Custom Dataset.

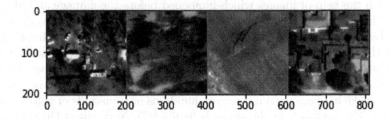

Fig. 1. Images from Hurricane Harvey Dataset

Fig. 2. Images from Custom Dataset

4   Dataset

The dataset used for this approach is DigitalGlobe's Open Data Program for post-Hurricane Harvey (In Texas). It consists of pre and post event Imagery over affected areas. The pre- events cover images from the year 2016 to the day Hurricane Harvey first occurred. A custom dataset was also created which consists of images of the Hurricane Harvey (2017) and Hurricane Ida (2021) dataset. There are certain images which are blurry due to illumination, fog, dust which can hamper the performance and can reduce the accuracy.

5   Implementation and Results

GPU used is NVIDIA TESLA P100 GPU (Kaggle), NVIDIA Tesla K80 GPU (Google Colab). From the literature survey conducted, the following models were selected: VGG-16 [20], Resnet-50 [21], Inceptionv3 [22], Densenet [23], Alexnet [24], Googlenet [25], Resnext [26], Wide Resnet [27], Shufflenet [28], Squeezenet [29], Mobilenet-v3 [30]. Activation function and Dropout Function include Relu and Dropout which helps in being an effective technique for regularisation and prevents the co-adaptation of neurons. To minimise overfitting, Adam Optimizer and Cross Entropy loss as a criterion is used. The learning rate for Adam Optimizer is 0.0002. Images from the dataset are given as an input for the models. The Dataset contains 3 categories: training, testing, validation images. All the models are trained for 185 epochs. The output of the model consists of the predicted labels. The labels are computed by using the argmax function which returns the max value. In the argmax function, logits are taken as input parameters. The predicted labels return either 0 indicating not damaged or 1 indicating damaged. The method is to classify the buildings as damaged and not damaged. These are the following classes: Damaged and Not Damaged class. Figure 3, 4 shows the images of the Damaged and Not Damaged class.

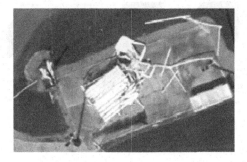

Fig. 3. Damaged building

Fig. 4. Not Damaged building

5.1   Fine-Tuning the Model

A sequential container is used. In a sequential container, various functions are added in an order. The functions added in the sequential container are: linear function, which linearizes the transformation and the dropout value is set to 0.2. Activation function used is Relu as it converges better compared to the other activation functions and improves the training of the models and helps to lower overfitting. A 2d convolution is applied over the input. The params.grad function for these models have been set to True to ensure the weights are efficiently distributed. By setting it to true, it helps in assigning the weights better which can then be efficiently distributed using backpropagation. The optimiser used is Adam optimiser, and assigned a learning rate of 0.0002. CrossEntropyloss function ensures the weights are assigned properly, so as to prevent the loss. These methods were utilised to prevent the overfitting and to increase the accuracy in the models.

5.2   Custom Model

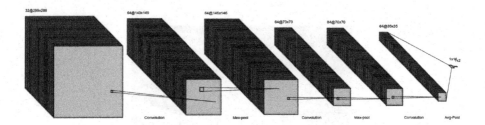

Fig. 5. Custom model

Model Architecture. The custom model (as shown Fig. 5) has 8 layers. The network is divided in 3 phases: Input layer, Feature extraction and Classification. The input image size is 299×299. For the feature extraction phase, max-pool and convolution layers have been used. Using the dot product operation between the weight of the neuron and a receptive field in the input to which they are attached, the output of the neuron is computed. Pooling layers consist of 2 major layers which are Max-Pool layer and Avg-Pool layer. The two max-pool layers are placed between the convolution layers. Its objective is to help in reducing overfitting. It takes the maximum of the region from the input that the kernel has covered. Avg-Pool Layer and Max-pool Layer are similar except that Avg-pool Layer takes the average of the region and consists of ReLU activation Batch Normalization layer. The activation function layer helps in learning the function maps between inputs and output data. Batch normalisation helps a layer to learn independently of the other layers present in the model. It's used to normalise the output of the previous layers and prevent the model from overfitting. The HyperParameters like Batch Size and Learning Rate are also adjusted. For the optimization, we choose Adam Optimizer as the model optimizer which has a learning rate of 0.0002 and CrossEntropyLoss as the function loss.

6 Performance Metrics

The following performance metrics were calculated for each model for both the datasets.

TP- True Positive
FP - False Positive
TN - True Negative
TP - True Positive
P - True Positive + False Positive
N - True Negative + False Negative.

$$Recall = TP/(TP + FN) \tag{1}$$

$$Accuracy = (TP + TN)/(P + N) \tag{2}$$

$$F1 - Score = 2TP/(2TP + FP + FN) \tag{3}$$

$$Precision = TP/(TP + FP). \tag{4}$$

6.1 Loss Comparison Plot

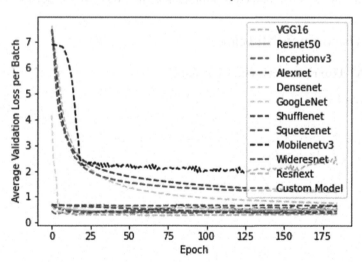

Fig. 6. Loss comparison based on Custom Dataset

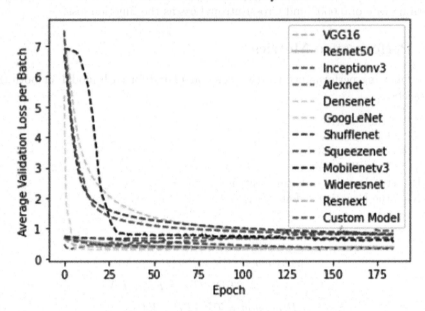

Fig. 7. Loss comparison based on Hurricane Harvey Dataset

In Fig. 6 and 7, the average validation loss is decreasing with the increase in the number of the epochs. Using functions such as Dropout, Adam optimizer and Cross Entropy loss has helped in minimising the overfitting problem.

7   Performance Metrics

7.1   (A) Hurricane Harvey Dataset

(See Table 1).

Table 1. Performance metrics for Hurricane Harvey Dataset

Model name	Accuracy	Precision	Recall	F1-score
VGG-16	0.8977	0.9183	0.9649	0.9410
Resnet-50	0.9356	0.9530	0.9739	0.9634
Inception_v3	0.8938	0.9593	0.9241	0.9414
Alexnet	0.8963	0.9058	0.9759	0.9395
Densenet	0.9350	0.9500	0.9762	0.9629
GoogleNet	0.9103	0.9402	0.9581	0.9491
Shufflenet	0.8796	0.9127	0.9491	0.9305
Squeezenet	0.9108	0.9296	0.9687	0.9488
Wideresnet	0.8735	0.8836	0.9712	0.9253
Resnext	0.8921	0.9304	0.9473	0.9388
Mobilenet-v3	0.7407	0.7548	0.9420	0.8380
Custom model	0.9144	0.9293	0.9733	0.9508

7.2   (B) Custom Dataset

(See Table 2).

Table 2. Performance metrics for Custom Dataset

Model name	Accuracy	Precision	Recall	F1-score
VGG-16	0.8708	0.8812	0.9708	0.9238
Resnet-50	0.8909	0.9058	0.9695	0.9366
Inception_v3	0.7947	0.7842	0.9811	0.8717
Alexnet	0.8688	0.8718	0.9783	0.9220
Densenet	0.8940	0.8913	0.9884	0.9373
GoogleNet	0.9065	0.9158	0.9775	0.9456
Shufflenet	0.8250	0.8993	0.8881	0.8936
Squeezenet	0.8914	0.8982	0.9779	0.9363
Wideresnet	0.8029	0.7873	0.9871	0.8760
Resnext	0.8877	0.8835	0.9890	0.9333
Mobilenet-v3	0.7479	0.7532	0.9534	0.8416
Custom model	0.9017	0.9042	0.9840	0.9424

8   Result Analysis

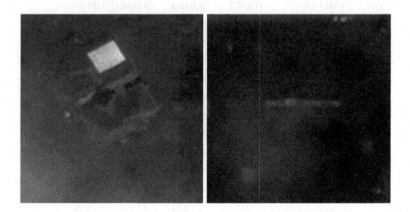

Fig. 8. Blur images

At times the angle at which image is taken, can result in the image to be blurred, shadows can make it difficult to identify the building. Depending on the illumination, being too bright or too dark can influence as the building may start blending with the surroundings. To tackle overfitting, Adam optimizer has helped to minimise the issue, and to tackle the vanishing gradient problem, we have used the CrossEntropyLoss function. Figure 8 shows images in the dataset where the clarity is not clear due to illumination, fog, dust etc.

9   Conclusion

In this paper, a thorough literature review and implementation of - 'Damage Detection of buildings and roads using Satellite Images' has been carried out. Many existing research works show errors while detection due to an over- fitting problem, thereby misclassifying damaged structures as not damaged. This paper tries to minimize the overfitting issues by combining two different datasets with two different orientations obtaining the accuracy of 91.44% and 90.17% for the hurricane Harvey Dataset and Custom Dataset respectively for the Custom Model. Furthermore, one of the most significant difficulties of object detection using satellite imagery is that an object viewed from different angles may look completely different and this is the future scope that needs to be considered.

References

1. Cao, Q., Choe, Y.: Building damage annotation on post-hurricane satellite imagery based on convolutional neural networks (2021)

2. Kaur, S., Gupta, S., Singh, S., Koundal, D., Zaguia, A.: Convolutional neural network based hurricane damage detection using satellite images (2021). https://assets.researchsquare.com/files/rs-934531/v1/61a71f08-c163-442b-a62e-1af4cdc8708d.pdf?c=1632928070

3. Shinozuka, M., Ghanem, R., Houshmand, B., Mansouri, B.: Damage detection in urban areas by SAR imagery. J. Eng. Mech. **126**(7), 769–777 (2000). https://doi.org/10.1061/(asce)0733-9399(2000)126:7(769)

4. Andre, G., Chiroiu, L., Mering, C., Chopin, F.: Building destruction and damage assessment after earthquake using high resolution optical sensors. The case of the Gujarat earthquake of January 26, 2001. In: IGARSS 2003. Proceedings of the 2003 IEEE International Geoscience and Remote Sensing Symposium (IEEE Cat. No.03CH37477). IEEE (2003). https://doi.org/10.1109/IGARSS.2003.1294454

5. Yamazaki, F.: Damage detection based on object-based segmentation and classification from high-resolution satellite images for the 2003 Boumerdes, Algeria earthquake (2005)

6. Yamazaki, F., Yano, Y., Matsuoka, M.: Damage detection in earthquake disasters using high-resolution satellite images (2005)

7. Turker, M., Sumer, E.: Building-based damage detection due to earthquake using the watershed segmentation of the post-event aerial images. Int. J. Remote Sens. **29**, 3073–3089 (2008). https://doi.org/10.1080/01431160701442096

8. Geshi, S.: Disaster damage detection and its recovery support system of road and railroad using satellite images (2010)

9. Koshimura, S., Kayaba, S., Gokon, H.: Object-based image analysis of post-tsunami high-resolution satellite images for mapping the impact of tsunami disaster. In: 2011 IEEE International Geoscience and Remote Sensing Symposium, pp. 1993–1996 (2011). https://doi.org/10.1109/IGARSS.2011.6049519

10. Dong, L., Shan, J.: A comprehensive review of earthquake-induced building damage detection with remote sensing techniques. ISPRS J. Photogramm. Remote. Sens. **84**, 85–99 (2013). https://doi.org/10.1016/j.isprsjprs.2013.06.011

11. Ma, H., Lu, N., Ge, L., Li, Q., You, X., Li, X.: Automatic road damage detection using high-resolution satellite images and road maps. In: 2013 IEEE International Geoscience and Remote Sensing Symposium - IGARSS 2013, pp. 3718–3721 (2013). https://doi.org/10.1109/IGARSS.2013.6723638

12. Hassanzadeh, R., Nedovic-Budic, Z.: Assessment of the contribution of crowd sourced data to post-earthquake building damage detection. Int. J. Inf. Syst. Crisis Response Manag. **6**, 1–37 (2014). https://doi.org/10.4018/ijiscram.2014010101

13. Sghaier, M.O., Lepage, R.: Road damage detection from VHR remote sensing images based on multiscale texture analysis and dempster shafer theory. In: 2015 IEEE International Geoscience and Remote Sensing Symposium (IGARSS), pp. 4224–4227 (2015). https://doi.org/10.1109/IGARSS.2015.7326758

14. Janalipour, M., Mohammadzadeh, A.: Building damage detection using object based image analysis and ANFIS from high resolution image (case study: BAM earthquake, Iran). IEEE J. Sel. Top. Appl. Earth Observ. Remote Sens. **9**, 1–9 (2015). https://doi.org/10.1109/JSTARS.2015.2458582

15. Gueguen, L., Hamid, R.: Large-scale damage detection using satellite imagery. In: 2015 IEEE Conference on Computer Vision and Pattern Recognition (CVPR), pp. 1321–1328 (2015). https://doi.org/10.1109/CVPR.2015.7298737

16. Dubois, D., Lepage, R.: Ensemble classifiers for building damage detection. In: IEEE International Geoscience and Remote Sensing Symposium (IGARSS), pp. 2715–2718 (2015). https://doi.org/10.1109/IGARSS.2015.7326374

17. Chu, E.T.-H., Wu, C.-C.: An image-based seismic damage assessment system. Multimed. Tools Appl. **75**(3), 1721–1743 (2015). https://doi.org/10.1007/s11042-015-2602-9

18. Menderes, A., Erener, A., Sarp, G.: Automatic detection of damaged buildings after earthquake hazard by using remote sensing and information technologies. Proc. Earth Planetary Sci. **15**, 257–262 (2015). https://doi.org/10.1016/j.proeps.2015.08.063

19. Hurricane Ida. https://en.wikipedia.org/wiki/Hurricane_Ida

20. Simonya, K., Zisserman, A.: Very deep convolutional networks for large-scale image recognition (2014). https://arxiv.org/pdf/1409.1556.pdf

21. He, K., Zhang, X., Ren, S., Sun, J.: Deep residual learning for image recognition (2016). https://arxiv.org/abs/1512.03385

22. Shlens, J., Ioffe, S., Vanhoucke, V., Szegedy, C., Wojna, Z.: Rethinking the inception architecture for computer vision (2016). https://arxiv.org/pdf/1512.00567.pdf

23. Huang, G., Liu, Z., van der Maaten, L., Weinberger, K.Q.: Densely connected convolutional networks (2017). https://arxiv.org/abs/1608.06993

24. Alom, M.Z., et al.: The history began from AlexNet: a comprehensive survey on deep learning approaches (2018). https://arxiv.org/pdf/1803.01164.pdf

25. Szegedy, C., et al.: Going deeper with convolutions. https://arxiv.org/pdf/1409.4842.pdf

26. Xie, S., Girshick, R., Dollár, P., Tu, Z., He, K.: Aggregated residual transformations for deep neural networks. https://arxiv.org/abs/1611.05431

27. Zagoruyko, S., Komodakis, N.: Wide residual networks (2016). https://arxiv.org/abs/1605.07146

28. Zhang, X., Zhou, X., Lin, M., Sun, J.: ShuffleNet: an extremely efficient convolutional neural network for mobile devices (2017). https://arxiv.org/abs/1707.01083

29. Iandola, F.N., Han, S., Moskewicz, M.W., Ashraf, K., Dally, W.J., Keutzer, K.: SqueezeNet: AlexNet-level accuracy with 50x fewer parameters and <0.5MB model size (2016). https://arxiv.org/abs/1602.07360

30. Howard, A.G., et al.: MobileNets: efficient convolutional neural networks for mobile vision applications (2017). https://arxiv.org/abs/1704.04861

Integration of Machine Learning in the Spatio-Temporal Analysis of Mangrove Forest

Praneetha Bonala[✉] ⑩, Suraj Sawant⑩, Amit Joshi⑩, and Mahesh Shindikar⑩

Department of Computer Engineering and IT, College of Engineering, Pune, Maharashtra, India
pranee221196@gmail.com, {sts.comp,adj.comp,
smh.appsci}@coep.ac.in

Abstract. Mangroves are an intricate part of the coastal areas (inter-tidal zone). Many biotic and abiotic factors have an impact on the status, health, and functioning of the mangrove ecosystem. Spatial-temporal analysis of these dynamic systems would be significant in the conservation and efficient management of its fragile ecosystem. This paper brings forward two objectives: (1) the use of Machine Learning algorithm to determine the Spatio-temporal characteristics of the mangrove forests over a period of four years, with temporal data collected after every two to four months based on certain factors such as cloud cover, at Thane Creek and Vasai Creek in Mumbai, Maharashtra, India. For this study, data is collected from Landsat-8 and Sentinel-2A satellites. These images were classified using Random Forest algorithm. The results, in regard to mangrove forest cover, were compared, showing Sentinel-2A providing more acceptable and accurate data, thus proving by indicating a stronger ability to extract features of land use classes. This showed an overall accuracy ranging from 91% to 99% in classification. (2) for the study of Land Use Land Cover maps for 5 years between 2001 and 2021, Landsat-7 and Landsat-8 data were acquired and classified using a decision tree algorithm, CART. This showed an overall accuracy from 92% to 99% for the cover maps. Other accuracy measures such as Overall Accuracy, Producers Accuracy, Kappa Coefficient, and Matthew's Correlation Coefficient were also computed to determine the correctness of the classified trained samples and its results. The result of this study provides an allusion for the direction that is needed to be administered for the protection of mangroves. All the image data were collected from Google Earth Engine, which is a powerful cloud computing platform.

Keywords: Mangrove forest · Machine learning algorithms · Land use land cover · Google earth engine · Thane and Vasai creek

1 Introduction

Mangroves are the essential features of our coastal ecosystems which strive in saltwater, throughout the tropics and subtropics zones of the globe. They live in the coastal inter-tidal zone along shores, rivers, and estuaries. These trees grow in less oxygen

V. Sugumaran et al. (Eds.): AIR 2022, CCIS 1738, pp. 375–388, 2022.
https://doi.org/10.1007/978-3-031-23724-9_35

soil areas, where steady waters permit these fine sediments to settle, thus reducing erosion from storm and tides [1]. Various kinds of flora and fauna are found within the mangrove ecosystem. They provide ecological benefits such as giving food, extending breeding areas and nursing grounds for several faunas, thus storing carbon, reducing pollution and protecting the coastlines [2]. Safekeeping these forests, opens to many socio-economic benefits and independent businesses [3]. These mangroves benefit the environment thus providing higher socio-economic value, such as: (1) Protecting coasts from winds, waves, and water currents; (2) Forestalling soil disintegration and siltation; (3) Safeguarding coral reefs, seagrass, and transportation lanes; (4) Providing wood and other forest products; (5) Providing habitats and nutrients for a spread of organisms; (6) Supporting coastal fishing and other vocations [4].

Regardless of their diverse value, global mangrove loss is widespread. Over the most recent twenty years of the twentieth century, the mangrove cover reduced by 35% on a global scale. Although there are many ways to ensure its safety, adequate measures need to be followed to help us understand the trends in this ecosystem [5].

Remote sensing is the most advantageous way of understanding the mangrove patterns, such as providing coverage, free low-cost data. Remote sensing with the help of Geographic Information System (GIS) tools, can to a great extent supplement field examinations in the vast swamps of mangrove forests and by also studying its various species in the region of interest [6–8].

Many GIS techniques, over the years, have performed change detection of the growth of mangroves, and these images were given to train with various machine learning algorithms, mainly for supervised and unsupervised classification models [9–11]. Studies also show the use of the post-classification change detection technique which provided a better accuracy when compared with the Principal Component Analysis (PCA) [12]. The use of vector change analysis showed satisfactory results for change detection compared to other methods [13]. A substitute methodology was proposed to check the mangrove forests by utilizing Remote Sensing using the GIS information and a Machine Learning procedure, Decision Tree Learning. In this, multi-temporal Landsat Thematic (TM) data has been used to acquire bits of knowledge regarding mangroves. Decision Tree was used as an ideal solution to help classify the various spectral behaviours by significantly following three rules. These rules have been made based on the calculations of Digital Elevation Models (DEM) [14], TM band values (majorly TM5,6), and Normalized difference vegetation index (NDVI) [15], which helped acquire information related to its change detection over the years, and results gained, showed an accuracy rate going from 81–87% and Kappa Coefficient going from 0.74–0.81 precision [16]. Researchers have also provided a comparative approach on the usage of classification algorithms, mainly Random Forest (RF) and Support Vector Machine (SVM) were used for mangrove change detection and proved that the Random Forest technique provides satisfactory results [17–19].

The objective of this paper is (1) to provide a comparative analysis for the use of Sentinel-2 and Landsat-8 satellite imagery by evaluating the change in the area of mangrove cover for years 2018 to 2021, with a temporal difference of images collected after every 2–4 months, depending on the climatic conditions; and (2) to provide a Land Use Land Cover (LULC) maps for years 2001, 2002, 2019, 2020 and 2021, showing the spectral changes it resonated over a period of 20 years.

2 Proposed Methodology

2.1 Study Area and Data

Mumbai City is the capital of Maharashtra state in India. Being one of the biggest cities of Maharashtra, it has the largest population. Found at 19.0760° N and 72.8777° E coordinates, it has a coastline that stretches for about 150 km, where 60% of the coastline is covered with mangroves. The spread of mangroves along the coast lines presents remarkable differences, which will further be discussed in our Region of Interest, being Thane Creek, found in Thane near Mumbai, and Vasai Creek, Gorai Creek, and Malad Creek found in Mira Bayankar region, in the North of Mumbai.

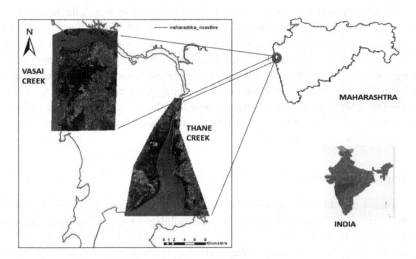

Fig. 1. Study area

Available research papers for this study area, shows how tidal dynamics affects the mangrove cover [20], with classification of mangrove specie shows 66% accuracy, and Wide Dynamic Range Index (WDRI) and Normalized Difference Water Index (NDWI) is used for mapping the mangrove species, by distinguishing between healthy and infected specie, using the Remote Sensing Tool, Arc GIS software [21].

To understand the patterns of the mangrove forest cover, various multi-temporal data from the year 2018 to 2021 from every two to four months were collected for our study region, Thane Creek. Our second study region, Vasai Creek, it is found to be often cloudy, thus making it challenging to acquire a cloud-free Landsat-8 and Sentinel-2 Images, using Google Earth Engine. Here, the data was acquired for January and May from 2018 to 2021.Hence the study area is shown in Fig. 1.

The Landsat-8 images has a resolution of 30 m, while the Sentinel-2 images has a resolution of 10 m. Only four bands, namely Blue, Green, Red, and Near-Infrared bands, were selected from each satellite to provide analysis.

Additionally, Landsat 7 and Landsat 8 data consider six spectrum bands, being Blue, Green, Red, Near Infrared, Short-wave Infrared 1, and Short-wave Infrared 2 for years 2001, 2002, 2019, 2020, 2021 respectively, were collected. These yearly data were layered further to provide optimal analysis for LULC stretched over 20 years.

These images were collected from Google Earth Engine (GEE), which helps and stores large datasets [22]. This data was further used to validate classification accuracy yearly for the months mentioned above.

2.2 Image Preprocessing

First, for the comparative analysis between Sentinel-2 and Landsat-8, the images having the least cloud cover for our study months were selected. Equally scattered ground control points (GCPs) were chosen with the reference maps shown in 2016 [23]. These images were further clipped, to extricate small areas for the coastal regions where the mangroves forest grows. Second, for the LULC analysis, multiple images were layered together to provide study analysis on cloud-free images for major classification classes found in the study regions. This process worked on the productivity of the analysis by eluding irrelevant calculations hence improving the classification accuracy by lowering disturbance from nearby areas.

2.3 Image Classification

Different land-use classes being considered is regarding the actual conditions of the study area and other facets identified using the high-resolution images which are available on Google Earth [24].

For our comparative analysis, three land cover types were defined: (1) Mangroves, (2) Water, (3) Other (e.g., Built-up, nearby hilly regions, mudflats). These ground control training points were merged and trained using the Random Forest machine learning algorithm. This algorithm has proven to be effective for mangrove classification [17]. Among all the accessible characterization strategies, Random Forest shows better accuracy. The random forest technique can likewise deal with enormous information with various factors. It can automatically evaluate the training dataset when a class is more inconsistent than different classes in the information.

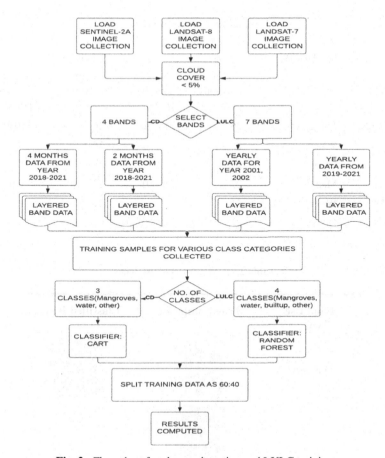

Fig. 2. Flow chart for change detection and LULC training

Important steps for the classification for Change Detection (CD) and Land Use Land Cover (LULC) is shown in Fig. 2. Table 1 and Table 2 show the review of land use classes and no. of training samples collected for our study purpose, respectively.

Table 1. Training samples

	Land use type	Landsat-8		Sentinel-2A	
		No. of polygons	No. of training points	No. of polygons	No. of training points
Thane Creek	Mangrove	26	15030	26	15030
	Water	25		25	
	Other	25		25	
Mira Bayankar-Vasai	Mangrove	27	13691	27	13691
	Water	21		21	
	Other	21		21	

Table 2. Review of land use types

Land Use Type	True Composite	Classified Image
Mangrove		
Water		
Built-up		
Other		

2.4 Accuracy and Validation

After classifying the study regions for our land-use classes, a more significant part of the investigation was carried out, and further altering was performed to remove conspicuous errors. The fidelity of the classification results were validated. To quantify the nature of the characterization, few precision measures were utilized in this study.

Usually, these measures are validated with the on-site ground evaluations, which is considered the most prominent way of assuring the accuracy of the training data samples and results. Also, a confusion matrix is beneficial to determine the overall accuracy of the implementation. The Overall Accuracy (OA), producer Accuracy (PA) can be obtained from the confusion matrix. Although these values do not explain how each class performs, Kappa Coefficient (K) and Matthew's correlation coefficient (MCC) can give more valuable information on the classification of the model selected. The kappa measurement is a proportion of how intently the cases ordered by the machine learning classifier matches the information named as ground truth, controlling for the precision of a random classifier as estimated by the normal exactness [20]. It is equivalent to 1 method shows perfect acceptance where as a value near zero implies that the acceptance is nothing but accepted by coincidence. According to [25], usage of Kappa measurement is broadly referred in Remote Sensing. MCC values are generally found between −1 to 1, which shows the rate of agreement of the classified points, with the training samples [26, 27].

It can be calculated as:

$$MCC = \frac{TP*TN - FP*FN}{(TP + FP)(TP + FN)(TN + FP)(TN + FN)} \tag{1}$$

Ground survey analysis and high-resolution images that are available on Google Earth are found to be most effective for evaluating the classification results [28].

3 Results and Discussion

The classification of the satellite images into mangroves forests and other land-use classes were derived from Sentinel-2A and Landsat-8 images, training them by using Random Forest Classifier, with number of trees set to 50. A comparative analysis of both satellite sources and Study Regions were considered for the years 2018–2021 was compared.

3.1 Comparison Results

For Thane Creek region, Sentinel-2A and Landsat-8 data were collected for months January, May, October and December, starting from year 2018- December to 2021- December, where for Landsat-8, no data was found for the month of May for year 2020 and 2021.

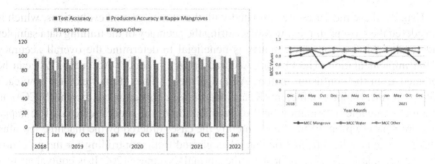

Fig. 3. Accuracy and MCC results for Thane Creek using Sentinel-2A

In Fig. 3, the graph on left shows OA and PA showing average accuracy of 96.13% and 92.48% respectively, whereas K values for mangroves, water and other showed an average percent of 67.55, 98.87 and 98.78 respectively. MCC values computed and shown on the right in Fig. 4, show average values for the aforementioned classes as 0.75, 0.98 and 0.91 respectively.

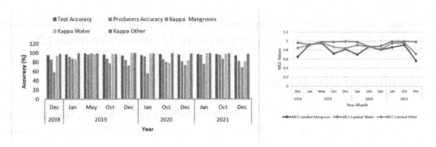

Fig. 4. Accuracy and MCC results for Thane Creek using Landsat-8

Using Landsat-8, Fig. 5 shows the accuracy percent graphs on left with OA, PA, K for land use classes as 96.62%, 89.514%, 76.18%, 91.93% and 99.29% respectively. MCC Values, for each class, showed average values as 0.80, 0.95 and 0.87 respectively.

Comparison of these above results were plainly done based on mangrove forest area cover. The mangrove cover stretches in the study regions, for the year 2021, were compared with the Ground analysis and showed that Sentinel-2A data showed closest area calculation, than that of Landsat-8.

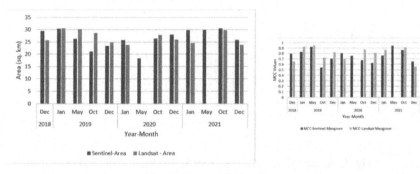

Fig. 5. Comparative analysis

Figure 6 Comparative analysis of Sentinel-2A and Landsat-8 in terms of area (left) and MCC Mangrove Results (right) for Thane Creek

In Fig. 7, irregularities in the mangrove cover area for Thane Creek, can be seen covering from December 2018 to December 2021, from 29.485 sq km to 25.815 sq km for Sentinel-2A and 25.67 sq km to 23.78 sq km for Landsat-8, respectively. Also, the MCC values for both the sources were showing greater than 0.5, indicating good, classified results.

For Vasai Creek region, Sentinel-2A and Landsat-8 data were collected for months January, May starting from year 2019-January to 2021-January. This was due to difficulty of finding images with less cloud cover.

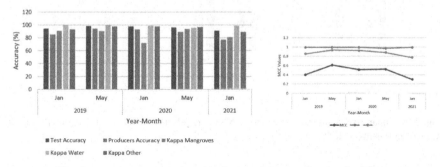

Fig. 6. Accuracy and MCC results for Vasai Creek using Sentinel-2A

In Fig. 7, the graph on left shows OA and PA showing average accuracy of 95.11% and 86.95% respectively, whereas K values for mangroves, water and other showed an average percent of 84.08, 98.51 and 94.43 respectively. MCC values computed and shown on the right in Fig. 7, show average values for the aforementioned classes as 0.5, 0.98 and 0.87 respectively.

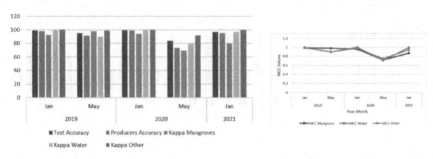

Fig. 7. Accuracy and MCC results for Vasai Creek using Landsat-8

Using Landsat-8, Fig. 8 shows the accuracy percent graphs on left with OA, PA, K for land use classes as 94.82%, 91.23%, 86.7%, 93.22% and 98.16% respectively. MCC Values, for each class, showed average values as 0.904, 0.91 and 0.91 respectively.

In Fig. 8 irregularities in the mangrove cover area for Vasai Creek, can be seen covering from January 2019 to January 2021, from 19.709 sq km to 23.544 sq km for Sentinel-2A and 17.825 sq km to 23.498 sq km for Landsat-8, respectively. Also, the MCC values for both the sources were showing greater than 0.3, indicating satisfactory classified results.

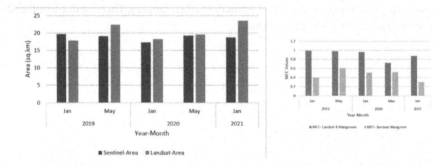

Fig. 8. Comparative analysis of Sentinel-2A and Landsat-8 in terms of area(left) and MCC Mangrove Results(right) for Vasai Creek

3.2 LULC Results

For LULC Map generation, yearly stacked images, of 6 Bands, of Landsat 7 and Landsat 8 were generated. They were categorized into four land cover classification were defined: (1) Mangroves, (2) Water, (3) Built-up, (4) Other (e.g. nearby hilly regions, mudflats). The training points were combined and trained using a decision-tree method, CART to get information related to mangrove distribution [29]. One benefit of this strategy is that it can join different sources of information to characterize the order rules.

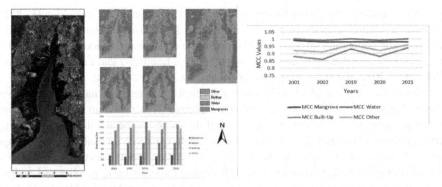

Fig. 9. LULC Maps for Thane Creek for years 2001, 2002, 2019, 2020, 2021 (left); MCC values for each Land-Use Class

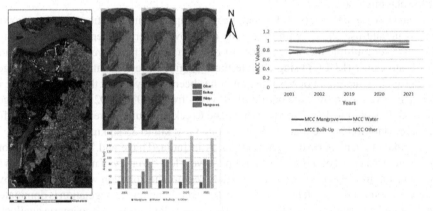

Fig. 10. LULC Maps for Vasai Creek for years 2001, 2002, 2019, 2020, 2021 (left); MCC values for each Land-Use Class

Figure 9 and Fig. 10 shows a brief description in the overall LULC maps generated for four land-use classes, for the study areas Thane Creek and Vasai Creek, respectively, from 2001 to 2021. The area covered the mentioned classes (shown in left), show an irregular pattern in the mangrove area cover, for Thane Creek, showing an overall increase in mangrove area, from 34.56 sq km to 35.91 sq km with MCC values averaging to 0.99 for mangrove class and, for Vasai Creek, with area varying from 23.45 sq km to 19.67 sq km, showed an overall decrease in the cover from 2001 to 2021, with MCC value averaging to 0.9. An overall average accuracy of 98.784% and 95.154% is achieved for the LULC maps were achieved respectively.

3.3 Discussions

Present study is an attempt to provide change detection analysis for the past 20 years from 2001 to 2021, using Remote Sensing and suitable algorithms. For the same, various datasets have been used. In Landsat-7, which had data available for the past 20 years, was not considered due to the failure of Scan Line Corrector (SLC) from May31, 2003. Thus, a comparative analysis was provided using Landsat-8 and Sentinel-2A satellite imagery and depending on it availability, change analysis was provided from year 2018 to 2021. However, for LULC, multi-temporal data of Landsat-7 and Landsat-8 for years 2001,2002,2019,2020 and 2021 were collected, for further analysis.

Out of the available Machine learning algorithms, to detect the changes in mangrove cover, Random Forest Algorithm found to be effective. This algorithm helps in gathering more accurate pixels as mangrove cover, and the same has been validated by making frequent visits of the study area. Thus, it provides better analysis for evaluating the change cover. In this study, we find that Sentinel-2A showed an average accuracy of 96.187% and 95.118%, with MCC values being >0.5 for both the study regions, whereas Landsat-8 showed an average accuracy of 96.68% and 94.822% with MCC values being >0.3 for the same. As compared with the ground truthing has highest confirmation in terms of mangrove area cover with Seninel-2A. It provides the agreement (i.e., the MCC values) of the classified points.

Land Use Land Cover (LULC) maps provide important information regarding growth or loss in land-use classes with vegetation cover over a period. Hence, giving effective insights over multiple factors. Majority of research papers that have implemented Land Use Land Cover (LULC) using Google Earth Engine have recommended CART algorithm for classification. For Vasai region, it has been observed that there is a decrease in the mangrove cover, over the period of 20 years from 2001 to 2021, showing changes from 23.45 sq km to 19.67 sq km. For Thane Creek, irregular pattern was observed for the same duration, in the mangrove area from 34 sq km to 35 sq km.

Unlike other mangrove vegetation places in India, Thane and Vasai Creek region, along the West Coast of India, shows comparatively less diversity of mangroves. This was proved from the ground surveys. In the study region, the zonation within the mangrove forests, remains far from delineation. Here, the overall mangrove vegetation is dominated by Avicennia marina, Sonneratia apetala, Bruguira cylindrica and Excoercaria agallocha species. Avicennia marina is found to be very resilient to different stresses like organic pollution, chemical effluents and it can also sustain very high salinity. This specie also shows remarkable copacing capacity. Thus, the entire mangrove forests, reflects uniform spectral signature.

4 Conclusion

In this study, the spatio-temporal analysis of the various land use classes of Thane and Vasai Creek complex were conducted, and based on its distribution and variation pattern, analysis was carried out. Sentinel-2A showed better area calculations in terms of accuracy's and MCC value, for this satellite imagery than that of Landsat-8, using Random Forest algorithm. Thus, can be determined that Sentinel-2A, having resolution of 10m, gives better results than that of Landsat-8, which has a resolution of 30m. LULC showed an overall increase for mangrove cover area, in Thane Creek region and a decrease in the cover for Vasai Creek. Thus, accurate and timely changes of land use land cover elements is critical for understanding the relationships and interactions among human and natural phenomenon to make better decisions for its prosperity and sustainability. Land-cover data on the other hand provides essential information for sustainable management of natural resources. Thus, the present work provides a baseline replicable data for mangrove cover management of the study area. In future, the same study can be carried out by using Deep Neural Networks.

References

1. Lugo, A.E., Snedaker, S.C.: The ecology of mangroves. Annu. Rev. Ecol. System. 39–64 (1974)
2. Duke, N., Nagelkerken, I., Agardy, T., Wells, S., Van Lavieren, H.: The importance of mangroves to people: a call to action. United Nations Environment Programme World Conservation Monitoring Centre (UNEP-WCMC) (2014)
3. Goa, S. I.: Conservation and management of mangroves in India, with special reference to the State of Goa and the Middle Andaman Islands (2000)
4. Kathiresan, K.: Importance of mangrove ecosystem. Int. J. Mar. Sci. **2**(10) (2012)
5. Valiela, I., Bowen, J.L., York, J.K.: Mangrove forests: one of the world's threatened major tropical environments: at least 35% of the area of mangrove forests has been lost in the past two decades, losses that exceed those for tropical rain forests and coral reefs, two other well-known threatened environments. Bioscience **51**(10), 807–815 (2001)
6. Kuenzer, C., Bluemel, A., Gebhardt, S., Quoc, T.V., Dech, S.: Remote sensing of mangrove ecosystems: a review. Remote Sens. **3**(5), 878–928 (2011)
7. Fu, W., Wu, Y.: Estimation of aboveground biomass of different mangrove trees based on canopy diameter and tree height. Procedia Environ. Sci. **10**, 2189–2194 (2011)
8. Zahed, M.A., Rouhani, F., Mohajeri, S., Bateni, F., Mohajeri, L.: An overview of Iranian mangrove ecosystems, northern part of the Persian Gulf and Oman Sea. Acta Ecol. Sin. **30**(4), 240–244 (2010)
9. Sremongkontip, S., Hussin, Y.A., Groenindijk, L.: Detecting changes in the mangrove forests of southern Thailand using remotely sensed data and GIS. Int. Arch. Photogramm. Remote Sens. **33**(1), 567–574 (2000)
10. Ma, C., Ai, B., Zhao, J., Xu, X., Huang, W.: Change detection of mangrove forests in coastal Guangdong during the past three decades based on remote sensing data. Remote Sens. **11**(8), 921 (2019)
11. Altaei, M.S.M., Mhaimeed, A.D.: Satellite image classification using image encoding and artificial neural network. Int. Res. J. Adv. Eng. Sci. **3**(2), 149–154 (2017)
12. Afify, H.A.: Evaluation of change detection techniques for monitoring land-cover changes: a case study in new Burg El-Arab area. Alex. Eng. J. **50**(2), 187–195 (2011)
13. Kotkar, S.R., Jadhav, B.D.: Analysis of various change detection techniques using satellite images. In: 2015 International Conference on Information Processing (ICIP), pp. 664–668. IEEE (2015)
14. Balasubramanian, A.: Digital elevation model (DEM) in GIS. University of Mysore (2017)
15. Gandhi, G.M., Parthiban, B.S., Thummalu, N., Christy, A.: NDVI: vegetation change detection using remote sensing and GIS–a case study of Vellore District. Procedia Comput. Sci. **57**, 1199–1210 (2015)
16. Liu, K., Li, X., Shi, X., Wang, S.: Monitoring mangrove forest changes using remote sensing and GIS data with decision-tree learning. Wetlands **28**(2), 336–346 (2008). https://doi.org/10.1672/06-91.1
17. Campomanes, F., Pada, A.V., Silapan, J.: Mangrove classification using support vector machines and random forest algorithm: a comparative study (2016)

18. Thomas, N., Bunting, P., Lucas, R., Hardy, A., Rosenqvist, A., Fatoyinbo, T.: Mapping mangrove extent and change: a globally applicable approach. Remote Sens. **10**(9), 1466 (2018)
19. Chen, B., et al.: A mangrove forest map of China in 2015: analysis of time series Landsat 7/8 and Sentinel-1A imagery in Google Earth Engine cloud computing platform. ISPRS J. Photogramm. Remote Sens. **131**, 104–120 (2017)
20. Azeez, A., et al.: Multi-decadal changes of mangrove forest and its response to the tidal dynamics of thane creek, Mumbai. J. Sea Res. **180**, 102162 (2022)
21. Zurmure, N., Sawant, S., Shindikar, M., Lele, N.: Mapping the spatiotemporal changes in mangrove vegetation along thane creek, India. In: 2021 IEEE International Geoscience and Remote Sensing Symposium IGARSS, pp. 7557–7560. IEEE (2021)
22. Mutanga, O., Kumar, L.: Google earth engine applications. Remote Sens. **11**(5), 591 (2019)
23. Global mangrove watch (2016). https://www.globalmangrovewatch.org
24. Li, M.S., Mao, L.J., Shen, W.J., Liu, S.Q., Wei, A.S.: Change and fragmentation trends of Zhanjiang mangrove forests in Southern China using multi-temporal Landsat imagery (1977–2010). Estuar. Coast. Shelf Sci. **130**, 111–120 (2013)
25. Landis, J.R., Koch, G.G.: A one-way components of variance model for categorical data. Biometrics 671–679 (1977)
26. Chicco, D., Jurman, G.: The advantages of the Matthews correlation coefficient (MCC) over F1 score and accuracy in binary classification evaluation. BMC Genomics **21**(1), 1–13 (2020). https://doi.org/10.1186/s12864-019-6413-7
27. Yao, J., Shepperd, M.: Assessing software defection prediction performance: why using the Matthews correlation coefficient matters. In: Proceedings of the Evaluation and Assessment in Software Engineering, pp. 120–129 (2020)
28. Estoque, R.C., et al.: Assessing environmental impacts and change in Myanmar's mangrove ecosystem service value due to deforestation (2000–2014). Glob. Change Biol. **24**(11), 5391–5410 (2018)
29. Giri, C., et al.: Distribution and dynamics of mangrove forests of south asia. J. Environ. Manag. **148**, 101–111 (2015)

Detecting Diseases in Jasmine Plants Using Proposed Image Pre-processing Algorithm

D. Padmapriya$^{(\boxtimes)}$ (iD) and A. Prema (iD)

Department of Computer Science, VELS Institute of Science Technology and Advanced Studies (VISTAS), Pallavaram, Chennai, India
tpadmapriya08@gmail.com, prema.scs@velsuniv.ac.in

Abstract. It is common knowledge that India's economy depends heavily on agriculture. Agriculture productivity is the source of economic growth in India. However, plant diseases can directly affect the yields in agriculture and timely detection of diseases is a most difficult challenge for researchers due to the lack of specific techniques in detecting diseases of plants. Since the Jasmine crop is one of the fastest-growing crops in Tamil Nadu state India. This study examines the use of an Image Processing-based Machine Learning (ML) technique, which has five main phases, to identify diseases in jasmine plants. Image acquisition, input image pre-processing, segmentation of the pre-processed images, feature extraction from the segmented images, and disease classification are the phases. Generally, Jasmine plants are affected by many diseases caused by bacterial, viral, and fungi. Among many diseases in Jasmine plants, this research focuses on detecting four types of common diseases, namely leaf spot, rust, powdery mildew, and turning yellow that occur on Jasmine plants. However pre-processing tasks can affect the performance of classification of diseases, there is a need for an efficient pre-processing technique which leads to better accuracy in detecting Jasmine plant diseases. Hence it is significant that the image data is pre-processed before the segmentation task for cleaning to overcome issues related to image data. And to avoid these issues, this paper focuses on image resizing, changing the color space of the images, etc. The image acquisition phase is carried out in real-time image sets which are collected from different Jasmine plant cultivation. Input images of Jasmine leaf with diseases are captured from the normal Android mobile camera or Android tab. The median filter is applied to the input images followed by bilateral filtering is implemented for contrast enhancement. The pre-processed images are taken to the segmentation and feature extraction process for identifying diseases in Jasmine plants. The objective is to develop effective preprocessing techniques for getting better accuracy in detecting diseases of Jasmine plants. This article proposes a hybrid pre-processing methodology for reducing noise in the image and for resizing an image.

Keywords: Image processing · Machine learning · Jasmine plant · Diseases · Median filter · Pre-processing

1 Introduction

In India, there are broad varieties of crops available on agricultural farms. Farming of crops needed monitoring diseases that can affect the production quality. Though the

V. Sugumaran et al. (Eds.): AIR 2022, CCIS 1738, pp. 389–399, 2022.
https://doi.org/10.1007/978-3-031-23724-9_36

diagnosis of earlier symptoms is microscopic, it is difficult to detect diseases in plants manually and is also a time-consuming process. There is a need for AI to automatically detect diseases in plants and classify them with their symptoms [1]. It is very essential to identify plant disease at its beginning stage to maximize the production that will gain the returns in agriculture. Leaf spots are the essential symptoms that can be used to determine plant diseases [2]. Plant diseases are also identified by classifying the quality of leaf images like a normal leaf or a lesion leaf. This process includes retrieving features from the leaf images and extracting features that are fed into the classifier [3]. An automatic diagnosis of diseases in plants helps to monitor large fields of agricultural land [4].

The images in training dataset had differing in size, background effect, and side effects related to lighting conditions and shadow in the image as theses input images are captured using normal Android mobile or tab. The important image pre-processing tasks are image resizing, image filtering, and image enhancement. Using the image filtering techniques, image smoothing is done. To increase the contrast of the image enhancement is used. The color conversion is used to grey images from RGB images [5, 12]. As the median filter wipes out salt and pepper noise and other noises in the image, it is applied to the Jasmine leaf images [6]. When building machine learning models, the common issues associated with image data are complexity, inadequacy, and inaccuracy [7].

The purpose of image pre-processing is to reduce the complexity of the images for further processing. Since The task of image pre- processing is to remove noise in the input images and to enhance the images for further processing. Image pre-processing is a crucial step in building a machine learning model.

This work implemented proposed pre-processing techniques that described in this paper. And achieved better accuracy in classifying diseases of Jasmine plant. This paper discussed basic diseases of plants in Sect. 2 and major diseases of Jasmine plant in Sect. 3. And related works are described in Sect. 4, the proposed system are explained in Sect. 5 and experimental results are shown in Sect. 6.

2   Diseases in Plants

The diseases in the plant are largely responsible for national economic losses that lead to decreases in the production of agriculture [10, 11]. These diseases are categorized and caused by pathogens (living agents) such as Bacterial, Viral and Fungi.

- Bacterial Diseases-As its name describes, this type of disease is caused by bacteria and is shown as yellowish green lesions at the beginning and then grows into dark, twisted and water-soaked [11]. The common bacterial diseases are:

  - Rust
  - Mildew
  - Rots
  - Cankers
  - Spots
  - Wilts

- Viral Diseases-This type of disease is caused by a virus spread by wind and water on parts of the plant. Once the plant is affected from viral diseases, their leaves become curled and wrinkled [13]. Some of viral diseases are

  – Soft Spot
  – Spot
  – Wilt

- Fungal Diseases-Once the plant is affected by the fungi, the leaves of it are shown as gray spot and become water-soaked. This disease is white in color and is seen on both the upper and under surface of the leaves [10].

3 Major Diseases in Jasmine Plants

Among several types of diseases in Jasmine plants, this research concentrates on the following 4 major diseases that occur mostly in Jasmine plants.

- Turning Yellow- This disease in Jasmine leaf manifest itself as an early symptom with the leaf color changing to yellow. Some leaves turn from green to yellow at the intermediate stage [8].
- Powdery Mildew- This is a type of fungi disease which occur on both dry and fresh Jasmine leaves. Once affected the leaves of Jasmine plant coated with powdery and spreading to stems in a short while [4, 9].
- Rust- Once Jasmine plant is affected by Rust disease, the green color of the leaf becomes brown in color. Then this brown color becomes dark, while the final symptom is when the leaf becomes dry [7, 13].
- Bacterial- Bacterial disease in Jasmine plants can be seen as reddish color at the early stage and change into brown color spots at the intermediary stage. This disease becomes black spot at the final stage & the leaf becomes dry. This type of disease can damage the plants from its growth [4, 11].

4 Related Work

An automatic illness detection framework using image processing techniques in MATLAB is proposed by [1]. The process of their system consists of image loading, pre-processing, segmentation, feature extraction, and classification. They used techniques like k-means for segmentation process, GLCM for feature extraction and Random Forest for classification of diseases in rice plant [1].

A comparison of two classification techniques Support Vector Machine (SVM) and K- Nearest Neighbor (K-NN) for classification of diseases founded on different types of plants is done in [2]. They used sample images from CLAES (Central Lab of Agriculture and Expert System). Their comparison results showed that SVM performance better than K-NN in terms of accuracy of SVM 88.17% over K-NN 85.16% [2].

Authors in [3], developed a system for disease detection in five types of plants which includes Neem, Eucalyptus, Indian beech, Lemon and Mango. They used the k-means technique for segmentation; the SURF (Speeded up Robust Features) technique for feature extraction, and the SVM technique for classifier. They implemented a method called Bag of Visual Words in their system for better identification of diseases in plants [3].

In [4], authors proposed a method for Plant Health Monitoring using image processing techniques. Their proposed work focused on detection of diseases on sugarcane plant leaf using Android mobiles. They used SVM and KNN techniques for their work to give effective results [4].

In [5], Authors recommended a method for detection of plant leaf diseases using image processing techniques in detecting four types of diseases like Rust, Bacterial Blight, Cercospora Leaf Spot and Powdery Mildew. Their system consists of available techniques like K-means, Local Binary Pattern (LBP), and SVM. They experimented with more than 500 images and got an accuracy of 98.2% in identifying diseases in plants [5].

Authors recommended a method for fault detection in plants in [6]. Their proposed method includes techniques for pre-processing, segmentation, and histogram equalization. Their algorithm steps include RGB image acquisition, k-means clustering, masking green pixels, removing masked pixels, and plotting histograms [6].

In [8], authors established spectral disease indices for detection of wheat leaf rust. They generated an index to accurately estimate disease severity on Wheat leaf. Their generated index required to be tested on various sensors and these indices are based on spectral variations for other types of vegetation diseases in wheat leaf [8].

In [9], authors proposed a powdery mildew detection Machine Vision system for automatic detection of mildew type diseases in Greenhouse of Tomato plants. They used L*a*b color space, Sobel operator and histogram of gradients and then Random Forest classifier in the detection process. Their system reduced processing time by taking advantage of GPU (Graphics Processing Unit) and multicore processors. They proposed Hough Forest algorithm for detection of powdery mildew in tomato plants [9].

In [10], authors proposed a method for detection of bacterial disease in Tomato and Crape Jasmine leaves. Their work comprised of six steps which consisted of image acquisition, color transformation, filtering, segmentation, feature extraction, and classification. They used techniques like YIQ color space, median filter, Otsu's threshold, and Haralick texture features for their work [10].

In [11], authors experimented with various methods for classifying disease in Citrus plants. They discussed diseases of citrus plants, pre-processing techniques, methods of image enhancement, color-based transformation methods, segmentation methods, feature extraction techniques, and methods for classification for identification of plant diseases. They also compared a few existing techniques in terms of their advantages and disadvantages. They concluded that the techniques k-means, SVM and NN are the most prominent techniques to implement automatic systems [11].

Authors presented a method to classify leaf diseases using Gist and LBP techniques in [14]. They extracted features from pre-processed leaf images. The features extracted from Gist and LBP are concatenated and processed using various classifier techniques [14].

5   Proposed System

In this research work, the proposed works consists of number of phases or steps. Figure 1 represents the brief architecture of the proposed system. This architecture diagram depicts the flow between various phases and description of task.

Architecture Diagram

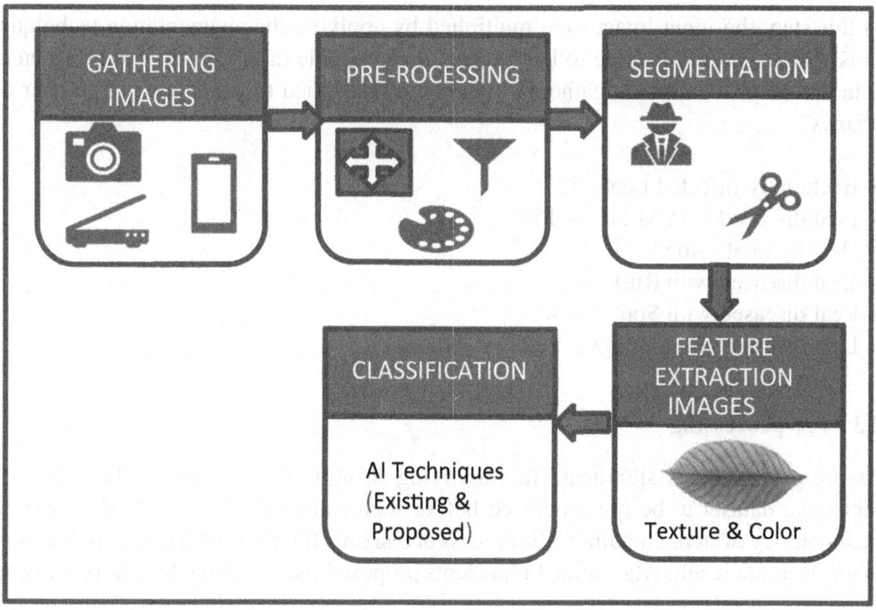

Fig. 1. Architecture diagram for proposed system

The proposed system architecture consists of the following Phases:

- Gathering images
- Augmentation
- Pre-processing
- Segmentation
- Feature extraction
- Classification

5.1   Gathering Images

Collecting data is the first and foremost step in this research. The data collection in this study is the collection of raw images of Jasmine leaf. For training purpose, this research gathered number of Jasmine leaf images as follows:

- Bacterially Infected Leaf -14

- Leaf diseased with Mildew -6
- Healthy Leaf -18
- Leaf diseased with Rust - 29
- Leaf diseased with Spot - 29
- Leaf diseased with Yellow – 5

5.2 Augmentation

In this step, the input images are multiplied by applying the augmentation technique. This will also help Machine to learn more. It can handle data scarcity and insufficient data diversity. As a result, gathered images are multiplied to get following number of images

- Bacterially Infected Leaf - 727
- Leaf diseased with Mildew - 153
- Healthy Leaf - 465
- Leaf diseased with Rust - 491
- Leaf diseased with Spot - 563
- Leaf diseased with Yellow – 262

5.3 Pre-processing

As pre-processing is significant in classifying Jasmine Plant diseases, there is need for image dataset to be pre-processed before segmentation task. This work proposed methodology of steps containing the process of resizing, filtering and image enhancement to get accurate result. Algorithm 1 represents proposed methodology for pre-processing steps.

Resizing of the Images. All the gathered images are resized to 256 px × 256 px. Images of bigger size are reduced and images of smaller size are enlarged. Thus, the size of the image data set is normalized for further processing. Care is taken to avoid distortion of images while resizing the images.

Filtering. Of all the techniques used, the "MEDIAN BLURRING" algorithm is more effective in arresting salt and pepper noise and hence it is used in this research.

Median Blur Algorithm. In this algorithm, the median of all the pixels in the image under the active kernel area and central element is replaced with the median value. In this median blurring algorithm, the central element is replaced with some pixel value in the image. The only constraint in this algorithm is that the kernel image size should be a positive odd integer.

Algorithm 1: Pre-processing Images
Input: Leaf Image
Output: Pre-processed Image

1	Read the Input Image
2	Apply Image Transformation Techniques
3	Resize the Image into 256 **X** 256
4	Convert RGB image to Gray Image
5	Filter Image using Median Filter 6 Display pre-processed Image

5.4 Segmentation

The aim of segmentation is to find the Region of Interest (RoI) from the pre-processed images. With respect to the RoI, this process is used to divide the images into various parts based on predefined criteria. There are various segmentation techniques available such as Otsu's threshold, edge detection, k-means clustering, etc., [9].

In this research, the pre-processed images are divided into two parts, namely the leaf margin and its background at the first stage, and then background parts are removed by making its pixel values as zero i.e. black color. At the second stage, the green pixels are removed to get the diseased part, which is RoI.

5.5 Feature Extraction

This is the process of describing an image for classification purposes. There are many techniques available for feature extraction which have been used by researchers [13].

The common feature extraction methods are based on color, shape, and texture features of an image. This research concentrates on extracting color and texture features for classifying Jasmine plant diseases.

Among the various feature extraction methods, this research used color histograms for extracting color features and Local Binary Patterns for extracting texture features from the diseased part of the Jasmine leaf image.

5.6 Classification

Classification is a technique for recognizing, understanding, and grouping concepts and objects into pre-set labels. With pre-set training image sets, machine learning algorithms utilize a lot of methods to predict future image sets into corresponding labels. There are lot of classification algorithms in Artificial Intelligence field. Among numerous classification algorithms, Support Vector Machine, Logistic Regression, Decision Tree, Random Forest, Naïve Bayes, and etc., [15].

An SVM uses step-by step procedures to train and classify data by finding a hyper-plane in an n-dimensional space. Based on the number of features from the dataset, the hyper-plane is drawn as a line between the various categories of data [16].

The aim of classification in this research was to find the disease of a given image leaf into the type from which it belongs. The disease types are denoted as labels with the SVM classifier to classify the diseases of Jasmine plants.

6   Experimental Results

6.1   Initial and Augmented Images

Initially, collected original images are processed for augmentation to obtain more number of training set of images. Figure 2 depicts the actual number of images of Jasmine leaves collected and Fig. 3 depicts the increased number of images of Jasmine Leaves after augmented processing of collected images.

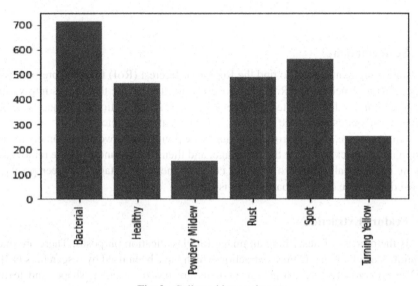

Fig. 2. Collected image dataset

6.2   Pre-processed Images

In this step, at first the images are resized to a fixed size of 256 × 256. Resized images are processed using a filtering technique to remove unwanted noises in the images.

Figure 4 represents resized images of Jasmine Leaf and Fig. 5 depicts filtered images of Jasmine Leaf.

6.3   Images in Different Color Spaces

In this step, re-sized and filtered images are transformed to different color spaces, namely, RGB, Lab, and HSV for further processing. Here Fig. 6 represents HSV of Jasmine Leaf images.

The above diagram Fig. 7 represents RGB color space of Jasmine Leaf images.

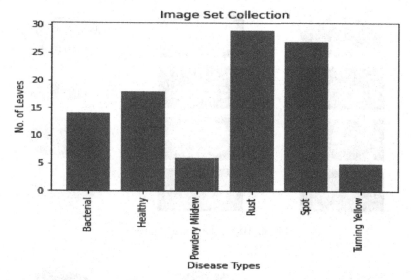

Fig. 3. Augmented image dataset

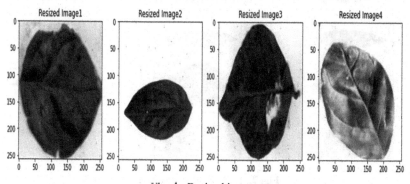

Fig. 4. Resized images

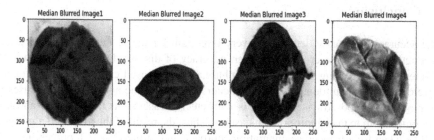

Fig. 5. Images after filtering techniques applied

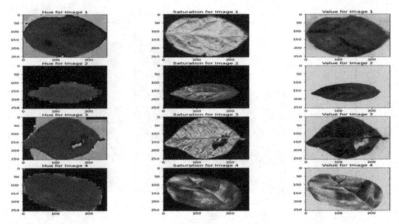

Fig. 6. HSV color space of images

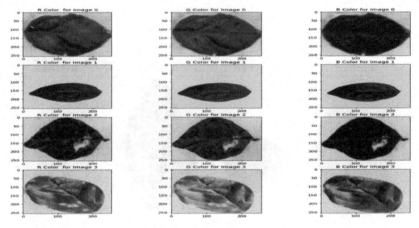

Fig. 7. RGB channel of images

7 Conclusion

The accuracy of disease detection is very important for the successful cultivation and production of Jasmine crops. Moreover, accuracy of disease detection is depends on efficient pre-processing used in earlier phase. This proposed can be extended for the development of an automatic, efficient, accurate, and fast method to detect diseases in the plant. The proposed system can be used to detect diseases in the Jasmine plant and also recognize them to take appropriate measures. Thus, the result of the proposed algorithm will be taken for advanced segmentation approach and further research processing.

References

1. Devaraj, A., Rathan, K., Jaahnavi, S., Indira, K.: Identification of plant disease using image processing technique. In: 2019 International Conference on Communication and Signal Processing (ICCSP) (2019). https://doi.org/10.1109/iccsp.2019.8698056
2. Saadoon, S., Adel, A.: A comparison between SVM and K-NN for classification of plant diseases. Diyala J. Pure Sci. **14**, 94–105 (2018). https://doi.org/10.24237/djps.1402.383b
3. Singh, D.A.A.G., Leavline, E.J., Abirami, A.K., Dhivya, M.: Plant disease detection system using bag of visual words. Int. J. Inf. Technol. Comput. Sci. **10**, 57–63 (2018). https://doi.org/10.5815/ijitcs.2018.09.07
4. Dhandapani, V., Remya, S., Shanthi, T., Vidhy, R.: Plant health monitoring using image processing. Int. J. Eng. Res. Comput. Sci. Eng. **5**(3), 591–596 (2018)
5. Oo, Y.M., Htun, N.C.: Plant leaf disease detection and classification using image processing. Int. J. Res. Eng. **5**, 516–523 (2018). https://doi.org/10.21276/ijre.2018.5.9.4
6. Sarkar, B.S., Tapadar, A., Saha, P.: AI based fault detection on leaf and disease prediction using K-means clustering. Int. Res. J. Eng. Technol. **05**(03), 926–931 (2018)
7. What is Image Pre-processing Tool and How its Work? https://www.mygreatlearning.com/blog/introduction-to-image-pre-processing/. Accessed 15 Mar 2022
8. Ashourloo, D., Mobasheri, M., Huete, A.: Developing two spectral disease indices for detection of wheat leaf rust (Pucciniatriticina). Remote Sens. **6**, 4723–4740 (2014). https://doi.org/10.3390/rs6064723
9. Wspanialy, P., Moussa, M.: Early powdery mildew detection system for application in greenhouse automation. Comput. Electron. Agric. **127**, 487–494 (2016). https://doi.org/10.1016/j.compag.2016.06.027
10. Revathy, R., Roselin, R.: Digital image processing techniques for bacterial infection detection on Tomato **6**(6), 391–398 (2015)
11. Iqbal, Z., Khan, M.A., Sharif, M., Shah, J.H., ur Rehman, M.H., Javed, K.: An automated detection and classification of citrus plant diseases using image processing techniques: a review. Comput. Electron. Agric. **153**, 12–32 (2018). https://doi.org/10.1016/j.compag.2018.07.032
12. Chaitra, K.M., Faiza, A., Harshitha, I.P., Meghana, D.M., Rachitha, M.V.: Plant leaf disease identification system for Android. IJERCSE **5**(6), 48–53 (2018)
13. Saradhambal, G., Dhivya, R., Latha, S., Rajesh, R.: Plant disease detection and its solution using image classification. Int. J. Pure Appl. Math. **119**, 879–883 (2018)
14. Dhar, P., Rahman, M., Abedin, Z.: Classification of leaf disease using global and local features. Int. J. Inf. Technol. Comput. Sci. **14**, 43–57 (2022). https://doi.org/10.5815/ijitcs.2022.01.05
15. 5 Types of Classification Algorithms in Machine Learning. https://monkeylearn.com/blog/classification-algorithms/. Accessed 21 Apr 2022
16. Support Vector Machine Algorithm - GeeksforGeeks. https://www.geeksforgeeks.org/support-vector-machine-algorithm/. Accessed 21 Apr 2022

3D-Zeit: A Framework for Generating 3D Model as an AR Object Using Object Recognition

Rahul Kumar Choudhary, Ganesh Goel$^{(\boxtimes)}$ [ID], Mohammad Osama Akhtar, Sampada Suwal, and Tejaswi Khanna

Sharda University, Greater Noida, India
ganeshgoel29@gmail.com, tejaswi.khanna@sharda.ac.in

Abstract. Augmented reality integrates virtual and real worlds, providing users with new tools for efficiently transferring knowledge for a variety of operations in a variety of settings. Creating 3D models of an object or the surface requires complex tools and techniques. This work presents a model to generate a real time 3-Dimensional model using 2D images of objects. The 3D model is then rendered as an AR object, which can be experienced in real time. The objective is to create a system that takes a 2D image and recreates the image as a 3D structure and then visualize it in a real-time environment.

Keywords: Augmented reality · Artificial intelligence · 3D model

1 Introduction

AR is a variant of the well-known concept of Virtual Reality Technology (VR). Augmented reality abbreviated as AR is the experience that designers use to view the enhanced parts of the user's physical world with the computer's generated input. It is the platform where one can visualize the virtual environment and can interact with animated or virtual objects. 3D modeling and 3D scanning are two methodologies for building 3D objects of AR:

The process of creating a three-dimensional representation of an object using computer graphics is known as 3D modeling. When used to replicate tangible items, this technology is advantageous since "it doesn't need any physical connection with the object because everything is taken care of by the computer". As a result, 3D modeling is great for designing virtual items, scenes, and characters that don't exist in the actual world [1].

The generation of AR assets is based on 3D scanning of real-world objects and settings. The content developers don't have to create the model from the beginning with this strategy. Instead, they use one of two approaches to scan the object: photogrammetry or scanning with a 3D scanner device (LiDAR or similar) [1]. The objective is to create an end-to-end multi-level framework that displays object 3D geometry in a pixel-aligned manner at a resolution of 1K without the use of any post-processing while maintaining the characteristics of the original inputs. Our method, unlike coarse-to-fine

V. Sugumaran et al. (Eds.): AIR 2022, CCIS 1738, pp. 400–409, 2022.
https://doi.org/10.1007/978-3-031-23724-9_37

procedures, does not require an explicit geometric representation at the coarse level. Higher levels, on the other hand, acquire implicitly encoded geometrical background without having to make an explicit geometry decision too soon. Our technique is built on the Pixel-Aligned Implicit Function paradigm. We can combine holistic embedding obtained through coarse reasoning with picture features discovered from high-resolution input in a principled manner thanks to the representation's pixel-aligned structure. Only the top level makes the final geometric determination, as each level gradually adds extra information that was omitted in prior levels [2].

Finally, in order to complete the reconstruction, the algorithm needs to recover the backside, which is not visible in any single image. Missing information not expected from observable metrics, such as poor resolution input, will result in estimates that are overly smooth and foggy. The challenge is solved by employing image-to-image translation networks to generate backside normal. By ensuring that the visible and occluded regions have the same amount of detail, we may prevent ambiguity and improve the visual quality of our reconstructions by conditioning our multi-level pixel-aligned form inference with the inferred back-side surface normal.

1.1 Problem Statement

Nowadays, creating 3D models of objects with low-cost hardware and high performance is very important since it has vast applications in Aeronautical fields, Machinery Fields, Motor's manufacturing factories, etc. It is not an easy task to be applied and requires vast knowledge of complex tools. Augmented Reality is one of the finest techniques to take advantage of the real-world environment's hardware resources (AR).

Object recognition is utilized for simulating 3D modeling. You can identify objects in pictures and videos using object recognition, a type of computer vision. Everyone can quickly recognize people, objects, settings, and visual components when looking at an image or watching a movie.

These recognition techniques are computationally intensive and require huge resources. Hence, there is a need to create a system which enables developers and designers to simulate 3D models.

1.2 Objectives

The main objectives of the proposed work are

- **Studying the state of the art of Object Recognition for 3D modeling in real time environment:** This objective aims at studying how object recognition can be combined with the real world and what are the problems and how can those problems be solved using this technique.
- **Development of mobile applications for the generation of 3-D models using real time camera feed/input of the object:** This objective aims to create an application which will enable its users to create the 3D model of object in real time anywhere on their device without having any knowledge of programming.

- **Rendering 3D model in real time environment:** This objective aims at experiencing the created 3D model in real time and get an idea of how will it look after placing the object at the desired location.

2 Related Work

Table 1 below represents the review of similar works done in the past in chronological order. This review contains all their findings, drawbacks, and results.

Table 1. Chronological review of previous work

Ref	Result accuracy or any other parameter)	Finding/achievement	Drawback
[31] (2007)	Our approach relies heavily on camera motion tracking in conjunction with human interaction, as well as the utilisation of 2D images to create the illusion of 3D	A tracking technique that detects camera movement in all six degrees of freedom could improve usability on phones with enough processing power	However, owing to the restrictions of the mobile media API, only phone specific extensions can capture video quickly enough
[32] 2010	Consumers will be able to benefit from a modern form of personalised tailoring thanks to body scanners	– Mass-produced clothing will also be improved as a result of applying body scanning technology – 3D body scanning technology is future for clothing industry	The requirement to be scanned when wearing only a few layers of clothing can appear intrusive, and the scan posture is not natural in such situations
[33] 2010	Resulting is easy to use and cheap that it does not require expensive equipment	Adding depth in the 3D creation with low-cost goal and targeting professional 3D creators to implement modelling in AR environment improves precision	Navigation of coordinates are not clear enough to imply while projecting shadows in 3d models. FPS is very low from 10–18 ft/s^2

(continued)

Table 1. (*continued*)

Ref	Result accuracy or any other parameter)	Finding/achievement	Drawback
[28] 2014	–	The fact that we employed both the real space surrounding the physical object and the object itself as a display area at the same time distinguishes this approach from other three-dimensional visualization methods	The current system perfectly matches the physical object and 3D data, but the procedure is confined to a single viewer
[29] 2018	–	The selection of the "missing components" needs the study and investigation of models with similar features, according to art historical and archaeological research	The use of a VR viewer needs a dual rendering pipeline, needing the scene to be rendered twice: this could be a critical factor in the event of particularly complicated sceneries, forcing the destruction and reduction of the virtual model
[30] 2018	Pose matching Mechanism: Accuracy: 93.5% Learning time in sec: 120 s	In terms of frame level accuracy and cumulative learning time of the dance steps, the suggested method's effectiveness and efficiency are tested and evaluated	–
[34] 2018	Making 3D animation model on blender should be done with care for proper accuracy. Especially when it comes to marking the section of image objects, blender use must be done accurately	The application can improve the understanding of Animation model in a precise manner. The science behind concept of animation model and object recognition is clarified	Proper care of measurement should be done by section to section and inch by inch for precise output

(*continued*)

Table 1. (*continued*)

Ref	Result accuracy or any other parameter)	Finding/achievement	Drawback
[3] 2019	–	At the point of consumer integration, AR tools can be used. Concept testing and fit assessments, for example	Future research is needed to develop VR and AR goods that shorten the time it takes to launch a new product and improve consumer responsiveness
[35] 2021	–	–	Although the app allows users to inspect the product's physical qualities, it is not a complete "one-stop shop" platform. It merely provides a detailed description of the product and a 3D model of it, with no opportunity for the consumer to purchase it

3 Methodology

A multimodal interactive experience called augmented reality involves adding artificially created perceptual information to real-world objects, sometimes spanning multiple sensory modalities like vision and hearing. "The more AR becomes part of our lives, the higher the need for content to adapt to the 3D world" [1].

To combine diverse views and relate entire understandings of the consumer involved 3d modeling process, a mixed methods technique was used. A qualitative technique was employed to brainstorm the knowledge in order to gain profound insights on the 3D model and the potential for VR or AR technologies. For defining parameters and identifying variables while building models and simulation systems, qualitative approaches are preferable in the fields of operations management and industrial engineering. Virtual reality and augmented reality, however, are more recent technologies, so there isn't much knowledge about them to comment on them in-depth [3]. The essence of augmented reality is content. It guarantees that users have an incentive to return [1].

Perfect digital twins of the real world must be created using 3D models. When combined with other rendering elements (such as animation, music, and physics), they form the most common sort of AR content and give an extra layer of immersion to the user experience. Figure 1 below represents the basic process flow of the framework.

3.1 Creating 3D Objects from a 2D Image

This work has created 3D models from 2D images using Pixel-Aligned Implicit Function model [2]. Here, high definition (HD) image was uploaded of an object at runtime. Using

Fig. 1. Basic process flow of the framework

this image, an algorithm was created, which clears the background environment and other noise from the image and detects only the object in the image. After that it reconstructs the image back view and creates a completely constructed 3D object in the form of a wave front (.obj extension) along with a .png image which contains the object's front and back view together. Figure 2 represents different views of the 3d object along with its 2D image.

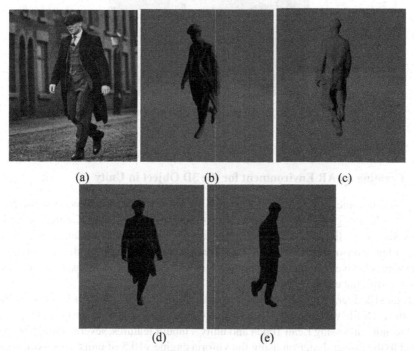

Fig. 2. (a) 2D image of an object. (b) Left Side view of the 3D object (c) Back view of the 3D object. (d) Front view of the 3D object (e) Right side view of the 3D object

You can see from the above Fig. 2, that our algorithm clears the background and only detects the object within the image.

3.2 Rendering the 3D Object in Blender

Animated films, visual effects, art, 3D printed models, motion graphics, interactive 3D apps, virtual reality, and computer games can all be produced using the 3D computer graphics software package Blender [4].

After creating the 3D object in the form of wave front, this 3D object is imported it into blender to get a better view of the 3D object and get it exported for later use in unity. Figure 3 represents the rendered 3d object in blender.

Fig. 3. 3D model rendered in blender

3.3 Creating an AR Environment for the 3D Object in Unity

Unity Technologies is a cross-platform game engine. It was first announced and offered as a Mac OS X-only game engine at Apple Inc.'s Worldwide Developers Conference in June 2005. Since then, the engine has been updated to support a variety of platforms, including PC, mobile, console, and virtual reality. Three-dimensional (3D) and two-dimensional (2D) games, as well as interactive simulations and other interactive experiences, are all possible with the engine [5].

Using Blender, 3D object is exported in the form of a FBX file (fbx extension). After that, the FBX file was imported in unity as a GameObject. Later on the GameObject was used in unity and using Lean Touch and unity's inbuilt features, several animations were added to the object. Later on using the vuforia engine v10.5 of unity, this work created an AR experience of the 3d object within unity. Later, deployed the AR application was deployed in an android device which takes real time video feed using the device's rear camera. This camera feed detects a plane where the 3d object can be placed in the desired location to get a real experience. Figure 4 represents the 3D object in the AR environment on the android device.

In Fig. 4, you can see the 3D object in real time environment on an android device.

(a)   (b)

Fig. 4. (a) 3D objects in real-time environment (b) 3D objects in real-time environment

4   Conclusion

This work has developed a basic, straightforward, and practical method for generating 3D objects in a real-time AR environment without the need for specialized hardware such as a LIDAR scanner, which collects data using a laser pulse. These are used to make 3D models of things and maps of environments. However, this work has used a simple camera from any device to capture an image of an object, and then utilize those images to create a 3-Dimensional object, which then can be exhibited in real time using unity and our algorithm. This work also includes an Android application being developed that allows users to observe the produced object in a three-dimensional environment without the need for any specific hardware or coding experience. This framework works best for High-Definition images with lesser number of features. However, when the images are of low-resolution, the 3D object might get distorted. This work has a lot to be improved in the future like maintaining the color texture of the 3D object, improving rendering quality of the 3D objects with images of low-resolution etc.

References

1. Paula: Creating immersive 3D content for augmented reality. https://www.wikitude.com/blog-3d-content-for-augmented-reality/. Accessed Mar 2022
2. Saito, S., Simon, T., Saragih, J., Joo, H.: PIFuHD: multi-level pixel-aligned implicit function for high-resolution 3D human digitization. In: 2020 IEEE/CVF Conference on Computer Vision and Pattern Recognition (CVPR) (2020). https://doi.org/10.1109/cvpr42600.2020.00016
3. De Silva, R.K.J., Rupasinghe, T.D., Apeagyei, P.: A collaborative apparel new product development process model using virtual reality and augmented reality technologies as enablers. Int. J. Fash. Des. Technol. Educ. **12**, 1–11 (2018). https://doi.org/10.1080/17543266.2018.1462858
4. Blender (Software) - Wikipedia. https://en.wikipedia.org/w/index.php?title=Blender_(software)&oldid=1079472778. Accessed Mar 2022

5. Unity (Game Engine) - Wikipedia. https://en.wikipedia.org/w/index.php?title=Unity_ (game_engine)&oldid=1079034864. Accessed Mar 2022

6. Brannon Barhorst, J., McLean, G., Shah, E., Mack, R.: Blending the real world and the virtual world: exploring the role of flow in augmented reality experiences. J. Bus. Res. **122**, 423–436 (2021). https://doi.org/10.1016/j.jbusres.2020.08.041

7. Alldieck, T., Magnor, M., Bhatnagar, B.L., Theobalt, C., Pons-Moll, G.: Learning to reconstruct people in clothing from a single RGB camera. In: 2019 IEEE/CVF Conference on Computer Vision and Pattern Recognition (CVPR) (2019). https://doi.org/10.1109/cvpr.2019.00127

8. Güler, R.A., Neverova, N., Kokkinos, I.: DensePose: Dense Human Pose Estimation in The Wild. ArXiv180200434 Cs, February 2018. Accessed 29 Mar 2022. http://arxiv.org/abs/1802.00434

9. Bhatnagar, B., Tiwari, G., Theobalt, C., Pons-Moll, G.: Multi-garment net: learning to dress 3D people from images. In: 2019 IEEE/CVF International Conference on Computer Vision (ICCV) (2019). https://doi.org/10.1109/iccv.2019.00552

10. Bogo, F., Kanazawa, A., Lassner, C., Gehler, P., Romero, J., Black, M.J.: Keep it SMPL: automatic estimation of 3D human pose and shape from a single image. In: Leibe, B., Matas, J., Sebe, N., Welling, M. (eds.) ECCV 2016. LNCS, vol. 9909, pp. 561–578. Springer, Cham (2016). https://doi.org/10.1007/978-3-319-46454-1_34

11. Chen, L.-C., Papandreou, G., Kokkinos, I., Murphy, K., Yuille, A.L.: DeepLab: semantic image segmentation with deep convolutional nets, atrous convolution, and fully connected CRFs. IEEE Trans. Pattern Anal. Mach. Intell. **40**, 834–848 (2018). https://doi.org/10.1109/tpami.2017.2699184

12. Chen, Z., Zhang, H.: Learning implicit fields for generative shape modeling. In: 2019 IEEE/CVF Conference on Computer Vision and Pattern Recognition (CVPR) (2019). https://doi.org/10.1109/cvpr.2019.00609

13. Gabeur, V., Franco, J.-S., Martin, X., Schmid, C., Rogez, G.: Moulding humans: nonparametric 3D human shape estimation from single images. In: 2019 IEEE/CVF International Conference on Computer Vision (ICCV) (2019). https://doi.org/10.1109/iccv.2019.00232

14. Li, R., Xiu, Y., Saito, S., Huang, Z., Olszewski, K., Li, H.: Monocular real-time volumetric performance capture. In: Vedaldi, A., Bischof, H., Brox, T., Frahm, J.-M. (eds.) ECCV 2020. LNCS, vol. 12368, pp. 49–67. Springer, Cham (2020). https://doi.org/10.1007/978-3-030-58592-1_4

15. He, K., Zhang, X., Ren, S., Sun, J.: Deep residual learning for image recognition. In: 2016 IEEE Conference on Computer Vision and Pattern Recognition (CVPR) (2016). https://doi.org/10.1109/cvpr.2016.90

16. Horn, B.K.P.: Shape from Shading: A Method for Obtaining the Shape of a Smooth Opaque Object From One View, p. 198

17. Jackson, A.S., Manafas, C., Tzimiropoulos, G.: 3D human body reconstruction from a single image via volumetric regression. In: Leal-Taixé, L., Roth, S. (eds.) ECCV 2018. LNCS, vol. 11132, pp. 64–77. Springer, Cham (2019). https://doi.org/10.1007/978-3-030-11018-5_6

18. Iizuka, S., Simo-Serra, E., Ishikawa, H.: Globally and locally consistent image completion. ACM Trans. Graph. **36**, 1–14 (2017). https://doi.org/10.1145/3072959.3073659

19. Johnson, J., Alahi, A., Fei-Fei, L.: Perceptual losses for real-time style transfer and super-resolution. In: Leibe, B., Matas, J., Sebe, N., Welling, M. (eds.) ECCV 2016. LNCS, vol. 9906, pp. 694–711. Springer, Cham (2016). https://doi.org/10.1007/978-3-319-46475-6_43

20. Joo, H., Simon, T., Sheikh, Y.: Total Capture: A 3D Deformation Model for Tracking Faces, Hands, and Bodies. ArXiv180101615 Cs, January 2018. Accessed 29 Mar 2022. http://arxiv.org/abs/1801.01615

21. Kanazawa, A., Black, M.J., Jacobs, D.W., Malik, J.: End-to-end recovery of human shape and pose. In: 2018 IEEE/CVF Conference on Computer Vision and Pattern Recognition (2018). https://doi.org/10.1109/cvpr.2018.00744

22. Karras, T., Aila, T., Laine, S., Lehtinen, J. : Progressive Growing of GANs for Improved Quality, Stability, and Variation. ArXiv171010196 Cs Stat, February 2018. Accessed 29 Mar 2022. http://arxiv.org/abs/1710.10196

23. Lassner, C., Romero, J., Kiefel, M., Bogo, F., Black, M.J., Gehler, P.V.: Unite the people: closing the loop between 3D and 2D human representations. In: 2017 IEEE Conference on Computer Vision and Pattern Recognition (CVPR) (2017). https://doi.org/10.1109/cvpr.2017.500

24. Lazova, V., Insafutdinov, E., Pons-Moll, G.: 360-degree textures of people in clothing from a single image. In: 2019 International Conference on 3D Vision (3DV) (2019). https://doi.org/.10.1109/3dv.2019.00076

25. Liu, S., Saito, S., Chen, W., Li, H.: Learning to Infer Implicit Surfaces without 3D Supervision. ArXiv191100767 Cs, November 2019. Accessed 29 Mar 2022. http://arxiv.org/abs/1911.00767

26. Lombardi, S., Saragih, J., Simon, T., Sheikh, Y.: Deep appearance models for face rendering. ACM Trans. Graph. **37**, 1–13 (2018). https://doi.org/10.1145/3197517.3201401

27. Kim, M., Lee, J., Whon, K.: SPAROGRAM: the spatial augmented reality holographic display for 3D visualization and exhibition. In: 2014 IEEE VIS International Workshop on 3DVis (3DVis) (2014). https://doi.org/10.1109/3dvis.2014.7160106

28. Gherardini, F., Santachiara, M., Leali, F.: 3D virtual reconstruction and augmented reality visualization of damaged stone sculptures. IOP Conf. Ser.: Mater. Sci. Eng. **364**, 012018 (2018). https://doi.org/10.1088/1757-899x/364/1/012018

29. Iqbal, J., Sidhu, M.S., Ariff, M.B.M.: AR oriented pose matching mechanism from motion capture data. Int. J. Eng. Technol. **7**, 294 (2018). https://doi.org/10.14419/ijet.v7i4.35.22749

30. Honkamaa, P., Jäppinen, J., Woodward, C.: A lightweight approach for augmented reality on camera phones using 2D images to simulate 3D. In: Proceedings of the 6th International Conference on Mobile and ubiquitous multimedia - MUM 2007 (2007). https://doi.org/10.1145/1329469.1329490

31. Apeagyei, P.R.: Application of 3D body scanning technology to human measurement for clothing fit. Int. J. Digit. Content Technol. Appl. **4**, 58–68 (2010). https://doi.org/10.4156/jdcta.vol4.issue7.6

32. Schlaug, F.: 3D Modeling in Augmented Reality. http://liu.diva-portal.org/smash/get/diva2:411715/FULLTEXT01.pdf

33. Hendajani, F., Hakim, A., Lusita, M.D., Saputra, G.E., Ramadhana, A.P.: 3D animation model with augmented reality for natural science learning in elementary school. J. Phys. Conf. Ser. **1013**, 012154 (2018). https://doi.org/10.1088/1742-6596/1013/1/012154

34. Shinde, P., Padwal, O., Pandhare, N., Mawal, A.: 3D modeling for advertisement using augmented reality and artificial intelligence **9**(6), 5 (2021)

Automatic Image Captioning Using Ensemble of Deep Learning Techniques

Rupendra Kumar Kaushik[✉] [iD] and Sushil Kumar Sharma

Institute of Technology and Management, Aligarh, India
rupendrakumarkaushik@gmail.com

Abstract. A picture can represent thousands of words. This proverb is indeed true. What can't be described in words can be conveyed by images almost effortlessly and effectively. This paper aims at providing a framework that can help generate descriptions of images. Automatically describing an image is a problem that falls under both the fields of computer vision and natural language processing. This problem applies to virtual assistants for indexing images, editing tools, and disabled people's support. Its difficulties stem from the ambiguity and diversity of possible descriptions of a picture because people can describe an image from various angles. We used deep learning techniques like Convolutional Neural Network combined with long short-term memory (LSTM). We have trained the model using the dataset Flicker8K and then evaluated our model using standard metrics, which are the BLEU-1 metric. The experimental results provide comparable results to the standard.

Keywords: Neural networks · Object detection · Image caption

1 Introduction

We, people, can see an image and afterward can depict it. Whatever is happening inside that image, humans can comprehend that, which allows us to perceive the world in a completely interactive way. If the same abilities were given to machines, it actually stays an errand to a considerable extent. This includes not just the ability to perceive what is inside our seeing reach, yet additionally creating the portrayal of it. Presently, producing portrayal appears to be practically normal to us. However, it regularly happens, so we people wind up depicting pictures in altogether different ways, each right in our own point of view. In this manner, creating a characteristic portrayal considering the articles and exercises in the picture actually stays a difficult errand.

Having the option to consequently portray a picture in syntactically right language and is similar to creating a subtitle for the description of the image, that should not just catch the items contained in the picture but in addition communicate how these articles are identified with one another in terms of their characteristics and the exercises which they are engaged with. Also, the semantic information must be communicated more in a characteristic language like English, which means required a language model too notwithstanding visual comprehension of picture.

V. Sugumaran et al. (Eds.): AIR 2022, CCIS 1738, pp. 410–418, 2022.
https://doi.org/10.1007/978-3-031-23724-9_38

One objective of picture handling ought to be to give the profound picture comprehension to machines for example understanding the total picture situation and exercises, not just the individual articles. Picture subtitling follows a similar way: by removing the total detail of individual article and their related relationship from a picture. At long last, the framework creates consequently the significant sentence to depict the picture.

two young girls are playing with lego toy.

boy is doing backflip on wakeboard.

Fig. 1. Motivation/Concept figure: "Two young girls are playing with Lego kits" and "Boy is doing a backward flip on wakeboard"

This issue is significant, just as troublesome on the grounds that it is associating two significant computerized reasoning fields: computer vision and natural language processing. How is this problem useful? Generation of depictions has huge loads of uses in the reality. It very well may be utilized as portraying pictures to practically weakened individuals. Most present day cell phones are currently ready to catch photos, and making it workable for the outwardly debilitated to make significant pictures of their environmental factors. These pictures can be utilized to create the inscriptions that could be recited so anyone can hear to give outwardly hindered individuals a superior comprehension of the environmental factors. Picture subtitle age could like-wise make the web more open to outwardly weakened individuals. Right now, picture subtitling is being utilized generally by Facebook Lite Messenger which depicts picture on the off chance that the web is delayed in downloading the picture. Also, nursery schools can utilize this sort of programming to show the children. The applications are versatile thus making this problem an important one.

This paper aims at providing a framework that can help generate descriptions of images. Automatically describing an image is a problem that falls under both the fields of computer vision and natural language processing. Its' challenges are because of the variability and ambiguity of possible descriptions of an image as people can describe an image from different perspectives in different manners. The experiment conducted in this work took use of a deep learning technique, Convolutional Neural Network combined with long short-term memory (LSTM). We trained the model using the dataset Flicker8K and then evaluated our model using standard metrics, which are the BLEU-1 metric. The experimental results provide comparable results to the standard.

The next section discusses some of the prior work on automatic image captioning. We examine approach and model building in Sect. 3 with its performance and experimental analysis in the Sect. 4. Section 5 discusses the results of the research. The conclusion and future scope are discussed in the final Sect. 6.

2 Literature Review

A caption creation framework that precisely produces sub-titles like how humans rely on the association between the significance of article in image and how they would be identified with one another items in image is called a caption creation framework that precisely produces sub-titles like how humans. Although an image could be depicted with more than one sentence, we only require a single sentence to effectively prepare the image inscribing model, which can be provided as a subtitle to the image. As a result, the challenge of text summarization in NLP arises. The recovery strategy and the generative technique are the two primary types of recovery strategies. A significant amount of work is completed as a result of this, in accordance with recovery-based techniques. The Im2Txt model [1] is one of the most effective models of retrieval-based methods. Vicente Ordonez, Girish Kulkarni, and Tamara L Berg were the ones that came up with the idea. In general, their approach may be broken into two parts: 1) image matching and 2) caption creation.

In generative models, the problem of recovery strategy limitations is addressed. We were able to create fresh sentences by utilising the generative models. The generative models can be divided into two types: pipeline-based models and start-to-finish models (Fig. 1). The Pipeline type models make use of two independent learning measures, one for language demonstration and another for picture acknowledgment, in order to maximise learning effectiveness. They begin by recognizing things in an image and then applying the resulting consequences to the goal of presenting words. We have combined the language demonstrating and picture acknowledgment models in one model [9], whereas in start to finish models, we have combined the two models into one model. In a start to finish framework, both models learn at the same time. They are created by the use of a combination of convolutional and long transient memory organisations. The "Show & Tell" model [10], is an end-to-end generative model of the generative type. For the image captioning challenge, the Show & Tell model makes use of current advances in image recognition and neural machine translation technology. The Inception-v3 model is used with LSTM cells [10] to get this result. The Inception-v3 model will be used to offer object identification capabilities, while the LSTM cell will be used to provide language modeling capabilities [5, 6] (Fig. 2).

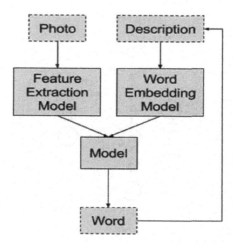

Fig. 2. Block diagram to generate word from a sequence

3 Proposed Model

3.1 Overview

The architecture used for the model in this paper is akin to practical approaches in statistical machine translation that have been studied previously. These models have taken in an expressive portrayal of a single sentence using an encoder RNN and alluded to another RNN to transform the portrayal into objective language by utilizing an encoder RNN. In addition to their ability to cope with successions of subjective length, RNN and model design have the additional benefit of increasing the joint likelihood of a unique and target sentence, which has been developed at the cutting edge and results in machine interpretation.

Although RNNs have been demonstrated effective on errands, for example, age of text and discourse acknowledgment [22, 23], it is troublesome to prepare them to learn long-haul elements. This issue is disappearing and detonating inclinations that could come about because of spreading angles through the various layers of the intermittent organizations. LSTM networks give an answer by fusing memory units that make the organizations realize when to fail to remember past concealed states and when to refresh shrouded states with new data.

3.2 CNN-Based Image Feature Extractor

A feedforward neural network is a convolutional neural network. This concept is to generate images by doing a two-dimensional convolution over each of the K color channels. We follow an affine convolutional layer with non-linearities in the context of neural networks. The most frequently encountered nonlinearity is the rectified linear unit (ReLU), which is just the hinge loss, $r(x) = \max(0; x)$ (Fig. 3).

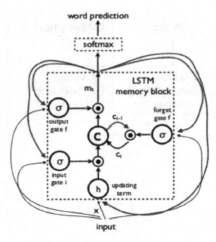

Fig. 3. LSTM unit and its gates

Where the maximum is determined element by element.

Thus, $h(x) = \max(0; \sum_{k=1}^{x} g_k(x + b_k))$ is the total unit of a convolutional neural network.

3.3 LSTM Caption Generator

In this work, we use a variation on the RNN thought called a Long Short-Term Memory (LSTM) unit. Given a state at time t, the LSTM update equations are:

$$i_t = \sigma(W_{ix}x_t + W_{im}m_{t-1})$$
$$f_t = \sigma(W_{fx}x_t + W_{fm}m_{t-1})$$
$$o_t = \sigma(W_{ox}x_t + W_{om}m_{t-1})$$
$$c_t = f_t \odot c_{t-1} + i_t \odot tanh(W_{cx}x_t + W_{cm}m_{t-1})$$
$$m_t = o_t \odot c_t$$
$$p_{t+1} = Softmax(m_t)$$

where σ denotes the sigmoid function, $\odot$ denotes element-wise multiplication, and tanh denotes the hyperbolic tangent.

4 Experiment

4.1 Datasets and Preprocessing

The datasets utilized for all analyses were the rendition of Flickr8K. This dataset has different pictures taken from Flickr, an assortment of everyday action pictures, joining five physically composed inscriptions for each picture. The datasets are split into a preparation, approval, and test set separately: Flickr8K - 6000, 1000, 1000. The images are then converted into 4096-element, which were trained for object recognition on the ImageNet dataset. These words are used as an input, which are embedded and fed to LSTM, and the outputs are assigned as probabilities by the softmax.

4.2 Hyperparameter Tuning

To achieve precise and solid results, it is necessary to discover the optimal hyper bound-aries for a design in order for it to be optimally adjusted and demonstrated optimally. All architectures shared the following hyper-parameters:

- Parameter optimization is carried out using the Adam algorithm with the following hyper-parameters: $\alpha = 0.001$, $\beta 1 = 0.9$, $\beta 2 = 0.999$, and $\varepsilon = 108$. We employed RM-SProp, which reduces the learning rate by a factor of 2–10. Nonetheless, we concluded that Adam outperforms the RMSProp.
- The cross-entropy of each word in each minibatch caption is the loss function's mean. Cross entropy $(P, I, C0...t1, Ct) = \log(P (Ct|C0...t1, I))$, where P is a trained network that predicts the following word in a caption prefix. I is the image that caption C depicts. The dropout rate for each application is 0.5.

The following hyperparameters which were fine-tuned:

- Whether opting for ReLU after the image projections.
- Whether to go for L2 weights regularization
- We used minibatches sizes (64, 128, 256) for the experiments.

4.3 Evaluation Metrics

After captions generations, our next task is to check for captions optimally. The basic technique used to get a human for caption evaluation. Presently, this is the most precise technique, yet human assessment for inscription creation is costly. Henceforth, we need an assessment technique that is quick, reasonable, and free of language and could connect with the inclusion of human assessment.

How should translation performance be quantified? Since there are many "perfect" translations of the source sentence, the idea is to use the BLEU metric. These translations vary in word choice and order, even when the exact words are used. The greater the number of matches, the more accurate the candidate translation. The most often used metric in picture description literature is the BLEU score, which requires access to ground truth, i.e., human-generated descriptions, and measures the word precision between generated and reference phrases (Table 1).

5 Results and Analysis

5.1 Quantitative Results

We report the performance of CNN-LSTM models on the Flickr8k test set, 1000 images. We include a few results from this field. Our model of CNN-LSTM gives BLEU- 1 score of 55.95. The limitations lead to limited usage of the available vocab and little variety in sentence generation. Due to computational restrictions, we were not able to train the model on larger datasets like Flickr-30k and MSCOCO.

Table 1. Results of our models on Flickr 8k dataset along with a comparison with other notable works

Model	B-1
CNN-LSTM	55.60
Show and Tell	62
Show attend and tell	66
Karpathy et al.	56.9

Fig. 4. Captions generated (CNN + LSTM model is marked in blue) (Color figure online)

5.2 Qualitative Results

The generated captions are shown in Fig. 4. The captions displayed in blue color are obtained by the proposed model (CNN-LSTM). The model is to identify people walking on a beach at sunset. So, it correctly identifies the weather and light conditions to determine that it's sunset. Similarly, for another example as well.

6   Conclusion and Future Work

We introduced this CNN-LSTM to perceive images naturally and generate a related representation in syntactically correct English. This model is based on convolutional neural organization, which converts a picture to a correct representation, followed by repetitive neural organization, which generates a corresponding sentence. The model has been trained to optimize the likelihood of a statement being associated with a picture. Experiment on Flickr-8k demonstrates the model's resilience by evaluating the quality of words using BLEU, a metric often used in machine translation. It is hypothesized that as the size of available picture description databases increases, so does performance. While the results are encouraging, the model does not perform well with images that contain complex items or images that contain simple objects but have complicated relationships.

In the future, we can be training the model on big image datasets such as Flick30K and MSCOCO, as well as increase the number of training epochs, which will aid in improving the model's performance on the photos and provides more accurate captions.

References

1. Anderson, P., et al.: Bottom-up and top-down attention for image captioning and visual question answering. In: 2018 IEEE/CVF Conference on Computer Vision and Pattern Recognition (2018). https://doi.org/10.1109/cvpr.2018.00636
2. Ordonez, V., Kulkarni, G., Berg., T. L.: Im2Text: describing images using 1 million captioned photographs. In: Proceedings of the 24th International Conference on Neural Information Processing Systems (NIPS 2011), pp. 1143–1151. Curran Associates Inc., Red Hook (2011)
3. Krizhevsky, A., Sutskever, I., Hinton, G.E.: ImageNet classification with deep convolutional neural networks. Commun. ACM **60**, 84–90 (2017). https://doi.org/10.1145/3065386
4. Simonyan, K., Andrew, Z.: Very deep convolutional networks for large-scale image recognition. arXiv preprint arXiv:1409.1556 (2014)
5. Szegedy, C., et al.: Going deeper with convolutions. In: 2015 IEEE Conference on Computer Vision and Pattern Recognition (CVPR) (2015). https://doi.org/10.1109/cvpr.2015.7298594
6. Szegedy, C., Vanhoucke, V., Ioffe, S., Shlens, J., Wojna, Z.: Rethinking the inception architecture for computer vision. In: 2016 IEEE Conference on Computer Vision and Pattern Recognition (CVPR) (2016). https://doi.org/10.1109/cvpr.2016.308
7. Karpathy, A., Joulin, A., Fei-Fei, L.: Deep fragment embeddings for bidirectional image sentence mapping. In: Proceedings of the 27th International Conference on Neural Information Processing Systems - Volume 2 (NIPS 2014), pp. 1889–1897. MIT Press, Cambridge (2014)
8. Hochreiter, S., Schmidhuber, J.: Long short-term memory. Neural Comput. **9**, 1735–1780 (1997). https://doi.org/10.1162/neco.1997.9.8.1735
9. Karpathy, A., Fei-Fei, L.: Deep visual-semantic alignments for generating image descriptions. In: 2015 IEEE Conference on Computer Vision and Pattern Recognition (CVPR) (2015). https://doi.org/10.1109/cvpr.2015.7298932
10. Vinyals, O., Toshev, A., Bengio, S., Erhan, D.: Show and tell: a neural image caption generator. In: 2015 IEEE Conference on Computer Vision and Pattern Recognition (CVPR) (2015). https://doi.org/10.1109/cvpr.2015.7298935
11. Xu, K., et al.: Show, attend and tell: neural image caption generation with visual attention. In: Proceedings of the 32nd International Conference on International Conference on Machine Learning - Volume 37 (ICML 2015), pp. 2048–2057. JMLR.org (2015)
12. Donahue, J., et al.: Long-term recurrent convolutional networks for visual recognition and description. IEEE Trans. Pattern Anal. Mach. Intell. **39**, 677–691 (2017). https://doi.org/10.1109/tpami.2016.2599174
13. Yao, T., Pan, Y., Li, Y., Qiu, Z., Mei, T.: Boosting image captioning with attributes. In: 2017 IEEE International Conference on Computer Vision (ICCV) (2017). https://doi.org/10.1109/iccv.2017.524
14. Liu, S., Zhu, Z., Ye, N., Guadarrama, S., Murphy, K.: Improved image captioning via policy gradient optimization of SPIDEr. In: 2017 IEEE International Conference on Computer Vision (ICCV) (2017). https://doi.org/10.1109/iccv.2017.100
15. Hessel, J., Savva, N., Wilber, M.: Image representations and new domains in neural image captioning. In: Proceedings of the Fourth Workshop on Vision and Language (2015). https://doi.org/10.18653/v1/w15-2807

16. Oruganti, R.M., Sah, S., Pillai, S., Ptucha, R.: Image description through fusion based recurrent multi-modal learning. In: 2016 IEEE International Conference on Image Processing (ICIP) (2016). https://doi.org/10.1109/icip.2016.7533033
17. Zhou, L., Xu, C., Koch, P.A., Corso, J.J.: Image Caption Generation with Text-Conditional Semantic Attention. ArXiv, abs/1606.04621 (2016)
18. Chen, X., Zitnick, C.L.: Learning a recurrent visual representation for image caption generation. ArXiv, abs/1411.5654 (2014)
19. Chen, X., Zitnick, C.L.: Mind's eye: a recurrent visual representation for image caption generation. In: 2015 IEEE Conference on Computer Vision and Pattern Recognition (CVPR) (2015). https://doi.org/10.1109/cvpr.2015.7298856
20. You, Q., Jin, H., Wang, Z., Fang, C., Luo, J.: Image captioning with semantic attention. In: 2016 IEEE Conference on Computer Vision and Pattern Recognition (CVPR) (2016). https://doi.org/10.1109/cvpr.2016.503
21. Rennie, S.J., Marcheret, E., Mroueh, Y., Ross, J., Goel, V.: Self-critical sequence training for image captioning. In: 2017 IEEE Conference on Computer Vision and Pattern Recognition (CVPR) (2017). https://doi.org/10.1109/cvpr.2017.131
22. Graves, A.: Generating Sequences with Recurrent Neural Networks. ArXiv, abs/1308.0850 (2013)
23. Graves, A., Jaitly, N.: Towards end-to-end speech recognition with recurrent neural networks. In: Proceedings of the 31st International Conference on International Conference on Machine Learning - Volume 32 (ICML 2014), pp. 1764–1772. JMLR.org (2014)

Automated License Plate Detection and Recognition Using Deep Learning

Simar Vig, Archita Arora, and Greeshma Arya[(⊠)] [iD]

Indira Gandhi Delhi Technical University for Women, New Delhi, India
greeshmaarya@igdtuw.ac.in

Abstract. This paper aims to review the use of deep learning algorithms in Automatic Number Plate Recognition Systems, namely – Convolutional neural Network-Recurrent Neural Network (CNN-RNN), YOLO (You Only Look Once), and SSD (Single Shot Detector). These techniques have shown promising results in speed and accuracy for real-time detection of vehicular license plates. This paper discusses the advantages these algorithms bring to the table and their limitations. Furthermore, it talks about specific approaches that can be combined with the proposed deep learning models to increase the accuracy of ANPR systems. It also tries to comment on their application based on their appropriateness.

Keywords: Automatic Number Plate Recognition · OCR · SSD · YOLO · CNN-RNN · Deep learning · Neural networks · Object detection

1 Introduction

License plate detection and recognition models are beneficial and have been integrated into solutions to real-life problems. For example, Automatic Number Plate Recognition (ANPR) Systems can be used in investigating criminal activity as it provides a line of inquiry and evidence. It can also be incorporated into Parking Systems as an alternative to the manual process of noting down license plate numbers, which is still used to generate parking tickets. It also finds use as a crime deterrent, surveillance in traffic control systems, electronic toll collection systems, etc.

Several ANPR models use neural networks for license plate detection and recognition. These models use neural networks like CNN-RNN, Faster-CNN-RNN, YOLO, SSD, etc., because they boast higher speed and accuracy in detecting and recognizing number plates. Because of their high speed in processing the input that they receive in the form of a passing picture of a vehicle, these algorithms are great additions to real-time vehicular license plate detection systems. Much research exists that uses transfer learning on these deep learning models to achieve optimized results for license plate recognition. Though CNN-RNN and SSD models are really fast, they showcase lesser accuracy than YOLO, which surpasses its competition in terms of accurate results.

This paper aims to discuss popularly used deep learning models that are suited for object detection and are thereby used as part of automatic license plate detection systems. It also aims to discuss strategies that can be employed or neural networks that

V. Sugumaran et al. (Eds.): AIR 2022, CCIS 1738, pp. 419–431, 2022.
https://doi.org/10.1007/978-3-031-23724-9_39

can be used in combination with these deep learning models to increase accuracy and overcome the challenges faced by these models such as skewed or veiled input, error introduced by angular or tilted images, background noise, etc. The challenges necessitate the combination of other machine learning technologies into image classification and OCR, in order to ensure image rectification and more accurate character segmentation. Though, ANPR boasts of extensive research, it still demands more work in order to form a reliable and consistent part of intelligent traffic management systems and smart cities. The errors introduced by an unstructured dataset need to be combatted and an ANPR system that can be unfailingly used for license plate detection and recognition across the globe, overcoming the barriers of varied characters from different languages, forms the future scope of this paper.

2   CNN-RNN

License plate recognition (LPR) is the process of automatically recognizing or "reading" license plates. LPR is used in a variety of applications, including traffic surveillance, location tracking, and automated vehicle tracking. LPR systems use computer vision, data mining, and machine learning to identify vehicles and their contents [1]. They can be used for both police purposes, such as catching red light runners, and for commercial purposes, such as tracking vehicles at parking lots or toll booths.

Ordinary frameworks for license plate recognition include localization of license plate accompanied by OCR (Optical Character Recognition). Accurately predicting the bounding container of the license plate is the purpose of License Plate Localization. Most of the prevailing algorithms display good results only under managed situations or whilst using image capture systems with excessive complexity which include license plate of a specific colour, constant size or license plate of a specific country. Varying light situations, distortion and blurring of images make accurate localization of these license plates a hard mission [2].

Two intrinsic properties of a license plate can facilitate detection:

- license plates have characters of fixed-length, even from various countries having different sizes, fonts, colours, and distortions.
- All the characters in a license plate are placed sequentially and horizontally and each character occupies a fixed proportion [3].

The various patterns and model context properties of the license plate are handled simultaneously by a two-stage method based on CNN-RNN. This method involves unconstrained localization of the license plate and takes benefit of the high-level semantic feature representation of deep learning. Long Short Term Memory is used by the network for extracting contextual information. LSTM is combined with CNN to attain excellent results.

In the first stage, an anchor mechanism is used to find license plates by characters. All generic methods for object detection have an assumption that every object is having a well-defined and closed boundary. This may not be appropriate for characters having multiple strokes [3]. In addition, finding a clear border is even more difficult for pictures with low quality. Fine-scale proposals are introduced to address this issue. A part of the character is represented by each proposal [3].

The characters are not located precisely by conventional RPN. Thus, a vertical-anchor mechanism is developed for predicting the confidence of character and position of all fine-scale proposals in the y-axis. The license plate can be located accurately if we connect fine-scale proposals. Also, the search space and the computation can be decreased by using the fixed-width property (Fig. 1).

Fig. 1. RPN proposal and fine scale character proposals

The fine-scale proposals received by CNN-RNN are combined in the second stage. Each fine-scale proposal has a confidence score. The regions of the license plate are obtained by connecting the fine-scale proposals and considering the confidence score (Figs. 2 and 3).

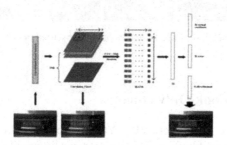

Fig. 2. Fine-scale character proposals generation.

Fig. 3. Fine-scale proposals are shown in the image on the left whereas the image on the right displays connecting filtered proposals.

This two-stage method overcomes the limitations of general detectors that are capable of locating only a class of license plates. This model can locate license plates of various countries. If the model includes only CNN and LSTM without fine-scale proposals, the performance of the model is affected. There is a significant degradation in the performance (Figs. 4 and 5).

Fig. 4. The images shows the various types of license plates - obscured and defaced which have been detected using the model.

Fig. 5. Detection of license plates having obscured or defaced edges.

3   YOLO - You Look Only Once

Another deep learning neural network – YOLO (You Only Look Once) has shown promising results in the field vehicle identification and license plate recognition. YOLO, much like Single Shot Detector (SSD), is a one stage detector, unlike CNN-RNN and Faster-CNN-RNN. A one stage detector consists of only one stage of detection, i.e., both region proposal and classification ensue concurrently. Hence, one stage detectors are generally faster as compared to their two stage counterparts in which region proposal occurs first, which is followed by classification.

You Only Look Once deep learning neural network has been applied in a manner that is quite alike to the human object detection and recognition system. The architecture of YOLO neural network can be understood as a customized version of GoogLeNet, which is a convolutional neural network (CNN) which has twenty-two layers. The forepart of the YOLO neural network is this tailored GoogleNet architecture (Fig. 6).

The loss function for YOLO can be given by the following equation:

$$loss = l_{box} + l_{cls} + l_{obj} \qquad (1)$$

where, lbox: bounding box regression loss function, lcls: classification loss function lobj: confidence loss function

Object detection typically entails localization and classification of objects within input images or input feed. Localization within an input image is achieved by bounding

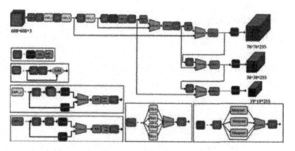

Fig. 6. Detailed architecture of YOLOv5

boxes. The aforementioned bounding box's prediction comes with a loss function which provides the error between the expected bounding box and the actual bounding box. The bounding box regression loss function is given by the following equation:

$$l_{box} = \lambda_{coord} \sum_{i=0}^{S^2}$$

$$\sum_{j=0}^{B} I_{i,j}^{ojb} bj(2 - w_i \tag{2}$$

$$\times h_i) \left[\left(x_i - \hat{x}_i^j \right)^2 + \left(y_i - \hat{y}_i^j \right)^2 + \left(w_i - \hat{w}_i^j \right)^2 + \left(h_i - \hat{h}_i^j \right)^2 \right].$$

It generally refers to cross entropy losses. As the predicted probability deviates from the actual label, so does the cross entropy loss. It may also refer to Hinge Loss/Multi-class Support Vector Machines Loss. Basically, the score of correct classification must be higher than sum score of all the inaccurate classifications by a large enough margin. The classification loss function is defined as follows:

$$l_{cls} = \lambda_{class} \sum_{i=0}^{S^2} \sum_{j=0}^{B} I_{i,j}^{obj} \sum_{C \in classes} p_i(c) \log(\hat{p}_l(c)). \tag{3}$$

The confidence loss function is defined as follows:

$$l_{obj} = \lambda_{noobj} \sum_{i=0}^{S^2} \sum_{j=0}^{B} I_{i,j}^{noobj} \left(c_i - \hat{c}_l \right)^2 + \lambda_{obj} \sum_{i=0}^{S^2} \sum_{j=0}^{B} I_{i,j}^{obj} \left(c_i - \hat{c}_l \right)^2, \tag{4}$$

where,

λcoord: position loss coefficient

λclass: classification loss coefficient

$\hat{x}$ and $\hat{y}$: actual target central coordinates

$\hat{w}$: width of the actual target

$\hat{h}$: height of the actual target

Considering that the anchor box at the coordinates (i, j) contains the true targets, Ii, jobj equals 1. Else, Ii, jobj equals 0.

pi(c): category probability of the target

p̂ l(c): true value of the category

Length of pi(c) and p̂ l(c) is equal to the overall sum of categories which is represented by C.

Following are the train logs for YOLO version 5 (Figs. 7, 8, 9, 10 and 11):

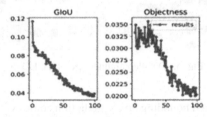

Fig. 7. GIoU and objectness.

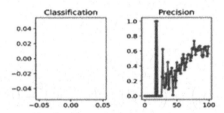

Fig. 8. Classification and precision.

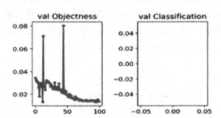

Fig. 9. val objectness and val classification.

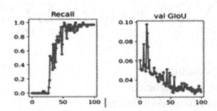

Fig. 10. Recall and val GIoU.

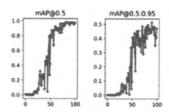

Fig. 11. Mean average precision.

The major problem that arises with using a deep learning neural network is the complexity that comes along with using a large number of parameters. With every additional layer that further improves the predictive accuracy of the network, the parameter values that must be established and the computations that come along-side them, also soars. This problem was solved by the introduction of Multi-Layer Perceptron to articulate the non-linear correlation of data, within the convolution process. YOLO employs the following steps in order to detect objects (license plates in this particular use case):

- The image that is fed into the deep learning neural network as input is initially split into S*S grids. This is done as part of the region proposal step (Fig. 12).

Fig. 12. The passing input image that is fed to the neural network is split into grid cells of equal dimensions.

- It predicts each grid region's bounding box (Attributes of a bounding box includes height, width, class and bounding box center) (Figs. 13 and 14).

Fig. 13. YOLO uses a single bounding box regression for the purpose of object detection and classification. Confidence score signifies what the likelihood of the bounding box containing a particular object.

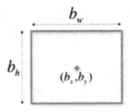

Fig. 14. Attributes of a bounding box includes height, width, class and bounding box center.

- You Only Look Once i.e., YOLO's algorithm makes use of a single bounding box regression. The single bounding box regression methodology serves the intent of predicting a particular object's class, height, width and center.
- YOLO's algorithm further makes use of an IOU or Intersection over union. This helps it to provide an output box which is a perfect fit for the particular object in terms of height and width. Each grid cell is entrusted with the responsibility of predicting the bounding boxes for the objects contained by the input image and calculating their corresponding confidence scores. If the bounding box predicted by the YOLO algorithm is accurately close to the real one, then, the IOU is equal to one. Otherwise, it is equal to zero. Therefore, IOU uses method of elimination to disregard bounding boxes that are not the same as the real boxes for the respective objects within the input image (Fig. 15).

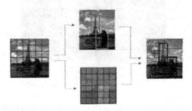

Fig. 15. The image depicts the various steps of image processing that YOLO employs to detect and classify objects.

Utilizing YOLO network offers the following advantages

- Accuracy: YOLO uses a methodology of predictive object detection that delivers accurate conclusions with marginal errors.
- Speed: This algorithm enables real time prediction of license plates because of enhanced detection speed.
- Learning capabilities: This deep learning has exceptional learning ability that enables it to learn the depictions of license plates or number plates and apply them for detection and classification of the same.

The very speed by the virtue of which, YOLO has found real time application, restricts the accuracy that the algorithm can achieve in terms of object detection and classification, especially when the size of the object that is required to be detected is small. This is true for license plate which covers a small area on the otherwise large vehicle [4]. This problem arises since the image which is being fed to the neural network as input is divided into 7*7 grid cells. The YOLO algorithm is so designed that detection is carried for each and every grid cell. YOLO uses the last-stage feature map, which has merely the coarse information as it passes across the deep learning neural network, the accuracy has certain constraints. [5] has tried to increase the algorithm's capability of generalization and accuracy by introducing an attribute for the inherent color of the motor vehicle's number-plate. Thus, the motor vehicle's number-plate is acquired from the motor vehicle's image. This is followed by the implementation of the Radon transform algorithm to rectify the tilted region of motor vehicle's number-plate, and to improve the accuracy of location of the target region through edge, color and additional physical attributes. Using the additional characteristics can aid in eliminating detections which are incorrect and also reduce to an extent, the interference caused by background noise. The effectiveness of this technique for the purpose of slant correction has previously been explored [6]. [7] used transfer learning on a YOLO detector. The license plates that were detected by this state-of-the-art deep learning neural network were classified into separate categories based on license-plate styles using a combination of Siamese neural network (SNN) and Multi-task learning (MTL). The research showed promising result and was able to achieve greater accuracy of 96.8% for non-standard license-plate style (license plate on which the design or the markings are requested by an applicant) and 99.2% for standard license-plate style.

4   SSD - Single Shot Detector

A Single Shot Detector (SSD) consists of two important elements:

- Backbone model – It is an image classifier which is pre-trained on a large, existing database. It serves the purpose of extracting feature maps.
- SSD head – It refers to the one or more convolutional layers which are affixed to the backbone architecture. It serves the purpose of applying convolution filters to detect and classify objects contained by the input image. The outputs of the backbone model are construed as the bounding boxes and classes of objects in the spatial location of the final layers activations [8] (Fig. 16).

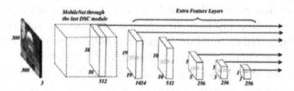

Fig. 16. A single shot detector with MobileNet architecture as the backbone model.

A Single Shot Detector operates by dividing the image fed into it as input into several grid cells. In the scenario where no object is detected, the class of the said object is taken to be the background class and the object location is disregarded. Every grid cell in the image may be allocated multiple pre-defined prior/anchor boxes. The suitable anchor box is mapped with the respective bounding boxes of each and every object within the input image fed to the deep learning architecture, as part of the matching phase. Matching phase occurs during the training period. Basically, the anchor box possessing the greatest measure of similarity with a particular object inside the image is held accountable for foretelling the said object's category and exact position inside the image. To exemplify, an image containing a picture of a flower and a house can be taken into consideration. The house may be denoted by a wider and taller anchor box, while the flower may be denoted by a smaller anchor box. Therefore, this particular characteristic is employed for the purpose assisting in the prediction of the class that the identified objects belong to and object locations after the object detection model is trained. All anchor boxes are defined by two properties - an aspect ratio and a zoom level.

Features at various layers correspond to various sizes of regions in the image fed as input to the neural network owing to the convolution operation. The size signified by a particular feature becomes larger, as we go further into the deeper layers of the deep learning model. This is called feature learning. It means that the deeper one goes, the smaller the size of the feature representation is, resulting in enhanced performance in the classifier. The number of parameters in the function also increases continuously at each layer. To simplify, let's consider a scenario wherein we begin with the bottommost layer i.e., the input layer, where one feature signifies a 5×5 region. Convolution operation is applied on this layer, and we get the resultant intermediate layer wherein each feature signifies a 3×3 region of the bottommost layer (input layer). The previous step is repeated i.e., convolution operation is applied to the intermediate layer. This step gives us the topmost layer wherein every feature represents a 7×7 region of the bottommost layer (input layer). The resultant 2-Dimensional arrays are called feature maps. When an identical feature extractor is applied at several locations of the input map, a collection of features is generated. This is achieved by applying the backbone model or the feature extractor on the input image in a form of a sliding window. The exact same Receptive Field is possessed by features that belong to the same feature map. Not only this, but they also observe the very same pattern although on varied locations [8].

A Single Shot Detector follows the aforementioned procedure but goes the extra mile by applying extra convolution layers to the feature map obtained as result. All of which subsequently yield their corresponding predictions. Since the prior convolutional layers supporting Receptive Field, which is smaller, can correspond to objects which are smaller in size, predictions from these prior convolutional layers aid in dealing with small objects. The added convolutional layers also help in generating better class scores which further help in improving the performance of the system [9].

Therefore, a Single Shot Detector operates by establishing a hierarchy amongst the grid cells. This facilitates in making more accurate predictions pertaining to the class and location of the objects that are detected within the input image. Hence, to optimize the performance of an SSD model, the number of classes, learning rate, width multiplier and the resolution multiplier need to be augmented.

Following is the output of an ANPR system that used MobileNet V2 as the backbone model, i.e., an image classifier which serves the purpose of extracting feature maps and an SSD head which applies convolutional layers to the existing backbone. The architecture of MobileNet is established on depthwise separable convolution and pointwise convolution (Fig. 17).

Fig. 17. Confidence scores for some input images.

The above architecture also includes an FPN (Feature Pyramid Network), which is nothing but a feature extractor. An FPN uses a single-scale input image. The input image is of a random dimension and the output is feature maps of proportional size. These appear at several levels in a convolutional manner. This process's a lot better at identifying smaller objects in the frame and is completely independent of the backbone model's convolutional architecture. Using MobileNet V2 definitely makes the model light and more appropriate to be used in mobile devices. However, accuracy takes the brunt of it. Such an application will be ideal for use in mobile devices because its lightweight and requires less processing power [9] (Fig. 18).

FPS describes how quickly the deep learning model can process the input that is fed to it as image or video and give the consequent result. The Mean Average Precision compares the ground-truth bounding box to the detected box and thereby yields a score, called the confidence score.

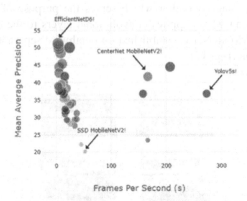

Fig. 18. Comparison of various object detection models for automatic license plate detection on the basis of Mean Average Precision (mAP) and Frames Per Second (FPS).

5   Conclusion

The use of deep learning models for license plate detection and recognition have shown great results. These models are trained on huge and varied datasets so that they yield the most accurate predictive output. The main object of this paper was to study the different object detection models and see how they fared in automatic license plate detection i.e., identify a vehicular license plate from an image frame and then separate the character on the number plate in order to identify the license plate number. The accuracy of such a model can be enhanced by the addition of a function that saves the license plate numbers of previously detected license plates on different motor vehicles. This will contribute towards the accuracy of the model's predictions in future. Furthermore, as discussed above, these traditional deep learning models can be used in conjunction with supporting neural networks to enhance the accuracy of the system. For example, FPN can be added to SSD to increase its accuracy. A 1-stage detector like SSD is fast and apt for real time use but its accuracy needs to be increased.

The latest version of YOLO has shown the most accurate results in terms of license plate detection. It was able to detect even small-sized objects. However, there still persist challenges that need to be tackled in this field. Not all deep learning models are appropriate to detect license plates and license plate numbers, that use different languages, specific to different regions. Character Segmentation, which is an essential step of Optical Character Recognition (OCR), is especially challenging because the model may confuse certain letters or numbers that look alike. Even after the application of several layers of feature extraction, the deep learning model may make false or incorrect conclusions. [10] ANPR/ALPR systems may use a combination of two or more of these deep learning object detection models to combat this. For example, a two stage YOLO model may be used or [11] SSD may be used in conjunction with Faster-RCNN, etc. It is very important, rather imperative to eliminate these cases of errors when such a model is being put to practical use in a crime deterrent or surveillance system. Detection of license plates from low-resolution images or videos, skewed or tilted images is tough.

Also, an effective image classifier mandates the use of a hugely diverse database for training purposes. The CNN-RNN method is highly effective even for detecting highly obscured or defaced license plates. However, the performance is degraded if the tilt angle becomes too large as a vertical anchor mechanism is being set depending on the characteristics of the license plate.

References

1. Cheang, T.K., Chong, Y.S., Tay, Y.H.: Segmentation-free vehicle license plate recognition using ConvNet-RNN. arXiv preprint arXiv:1701.06439 (2017)
2. Shivakumara, P., Tang, D., Asadzadehkaljahi, M., Lu, T., Pal, U., Hossein Anisi, M.: CNN-RNN based method for license plate recognition. CAAI Trans. Intell. Technol. **3**, 169–175 (2018). https://doi.org/10.1049/trit.2018.1015
3. Li, H., Wang, P., Shen, C.: Toward end-to-end car license plate detection and recognition with deep neural networks. IEEE Trans. Intell. Transp. Syst. **20**, 1126–1136 (2019). https://doi.org/10.1109/tits.2018.2847291
4. Kim, J., Sung, J.-Y., Park, S.: Comparison of faster-RCNN, YOLO, and SSD for real-time vehicle type recognition. In: 2020 IEEE International Conference on Consumer Electronics - Asia (ICCE-Asia) (2020). https://doi.org/10.1109/icce-asia49877.2020.9277040
5. Zhang, S., Chen, S., Li, J., Zhang, H.: An improved vehicle-license plate recognition based on color clues and coding rules. In: 2019 IEEE 4th International Conference on Image, Vision and Computing (ICIVC) (2019). https://doi.org/10.1109/icivc47709.2019.8981034
6. Modi, N.D., Paunwala, C.N., Modi, C.K., Patnaik, S.: Skew correction for vehicle license plates using principal component of Harris corner feature. In: 2011 International Conference on Communication Systems and Network Technologies (2011). https://doi.org/10.1109/csnt.2011.77
7. Elnashar, M., Hemayed, E.E., Fayek, M.B.: Automatic multi-style Egyptian license plate detection and classification using deep learning. In: 2020 16th International Computer Engineering Conference (ICENCO) (2020). https://doi.org/10.1109/icenco49778.2020.9357371
8. Liu, W., et al.: SSD: single shot multibox detector. In: Leibe, B., Matas, J., Sebe, N., Welling, M. (eds.) ECCV 2016. LNCS, vol. 9905, pp. 21–37. Springer, Cham (2016). https://doi.org/10.1007/978-3-319-46448-0_2
9. Wang, Q.: License plate recognition via convolutional neural networks. In: 2017 8th IEEE International Conference on Software Engineering and Service Science (ICSESS) (2017). https://doi.org/10.1109/icsess.2017.8343061
10. Yonetsu, S., Iwamoto, Y., Chen, Y.W.: Two-stage YOLOv2 for accurate license-plate detection in complex scenes. In: 2019 IEEE International Conference on Consumer Electronics (ICCE) (2019). https://doi.org/10.1109/icce.2019.8661944
11. Islam, T., Rasel, R.I.: Real-time Bangla license plate recognition system using faster R-CNN and SSD: a deep learning application. In: 2019 IEEE International Conference on Robotics, Automation, Artificial-Intelligence and Internet-of-Things (RAAICON) (2019). https://doi.org/10.1109/raaicon48939.2019.45

Challenges in Scene Understanding
for Autonomous Systems

Rishika Bhagwatkar$^{(\boxtimes)}$ ⓘ, Vinay Kumar ⓘ, Khursheed Munir Khan ⓘ,
Saurabh Kemekar ⓘ, and Anamika Singh ⓘ

Visvesvaraya National Institute of Technology, Nagpur, India
{rishijn04,vinaykumard1107,khurshh,saurabh.kemekar}@students.vnit.ac.in,
anamikasingh@ece.vnit.ac.in

Abstract. Autonomous robots and Machine Learning have played a
pivotal role in solving many real-world problems over the past decade. In
all applications of learning and exploration-based algorithms for robots,
one has to incorporate scene understanding to enable the robot to
be aware of the environment in which it is functioning. This imposes
inherent importance on the development of accurate and efficient scene
understanding algorithms. Although methods like semantic segmentation
deliver commendable performance in most settings, some noticeable set-
backs exist. In this work, we present various limitations and drawbacks
faced by current autonomous pipelines along with solutions to mitigate
the same.

Keywords: Machine learning · Autonomous systems · Scene
understanding

1 Introduction

Over the past decade, robot automation has shifted from traditional to learning-
based approaches. Learning-based approaches rely heavily on the type and
modality of data to be dealt with. Also, there has been extensive research in
deep learning towards developing foundational models for visual modalities like
images and videos. This coupled with the advent of portable and high accuracy
imaging cameras, has paved the way towards a new generation of automated
robots that rely on visual inputs for a majority of their state recognition and
decision processes. The most widely implemented example is that of self-driving
cars and self-aware systems. In such systems, accuracy and speed both hold
utmost importance and one cannot afford to compromise any of the two.

There exist a plethora of models for both semantic and syntactic understanding of images. However, one modeling paradigm that has played a pivotal role
in real-time accurate scene understanding is semantic segmentation. Semantic
segmentation, as the name suggests, is based on the idea of extracting different
semantic layers from an image. It is traditionally modeled as a supervised labeling task where each pixel of the input image is classified in one of C classes.

V. Sugumaran et al. (Eds.): AIR 2022, CCIS 1738, pp. 432–443, 2022.
https://doi.org/10.1007/978-3-031-23724-9_40

These classes are pre-determined and an image can have an arbitrary number of instances of each class. Since semantic segmentation leverages several layers of classification maps, it requires the model to learn very robust and noise-agnostic representations of the input.

The above-stated objectives often incur a large computational overhead and hence lead to significantly slower performance on onboard systems. Some onboard systems may even fail to host the bare minimum hardware required to instantiate such deep neural networks. Hence, there has been substantial work in reducing model sizes, i.e., knowledge distillations [1] and building lifelong learners using continual learning [2]. These paradigms focus on compressing larger, deep networks into smaller shallow networks while maintaining performance. These shallow networks require exponentially lesser computation and can run on onboard hardware with significantly higher speeds.

Finally, the most important aspect of training such systems is that the training data needs to be an accurate representation of the deployment scenario, i.e., the training and deployment data should originate from the same data distribution. There have been attempts to train models using techniques that mitigate the disparity between different domains and enable a model to transfer its knowledge from the source training domain to the target deployment domain [3]. However, these methods require the data to have corresponding entities in the source and target domain and often require large amounts of data augmentation.

Even though many models and techniques exist for visual scene understanding and interpretation, a few challenges have been omnipresent since the inception of these fields.

1. Understanding the scale at which useful information is encoded. The global vs. local feature trade-off.
2. Limited availability of reliably labeled, good quality data.
3. Lack of datasets across multiple domains to enable domain adaptation.
4. The task dependence of data augmentation techniques that highlight useful semantics and help generate artificial data.
5. Portability of semantic-segmentation and large-scale classification models.

In this work, we present a survey on our analysis of the above-mentioned problems and techniques to mitigate the same.

2   Local vs Global Feature Trade-off

An image contains features at several spatial scales. Features like the background and the colour of the sky are present in a significant part of the image and are called global features. However, features like pedestrians on a road and traffic signs occupy and interact only with a limited region of the image and hence are called local features. While designing scene understanding techniques, it is important to strike a balance between both local and global features. Although most models employ convolutional networks, only a few models explicitly segregate the local and global feature extraction pipelines [4].

One of the categories of contrastive learning, context-instance contrast or local-global contrast, mainly focuses on learning the familiarity between both types of representations, local and global. It is primarily exploited by two types of techniques

1. Predict Relative Position: The relative positions among the local components are learnt. For the prediction of relations between local components, the global context plays a vital role. For example, in an image of dog, the understanding of what a dog looks like is vital for the prediction of the distance between the local components such as the tail and the face [5].
2. Maximizing Mutual Information: It does not involve the prediction of relative positions of local components but instead focuses on maximizing the mutual information between the local and global context to understand the implicit relationships [6].

Another mechanism widely adopted in recent years is attention [7]. Attention was originally a technique proposed to enable neural networks to pay different amounts of attention to different parts of lingual inputs like sentences. However, this mechanism has been extended to images and has proven great success in improving scene understanding performance. Given n feature vectors, $x_i \in \mathbb{R}^d \forall i \in \{1, 2, \cdots, n\}$ their self-attention is given as

$$Attention(K, Q, V) = \left(\frac{QK^T}{\sqrt{d}}\right) V$$

where K, Q and V are called Keys, Queries and Values respectively. Where, $K = W_K X, Q = W_Q X$ and $V = W_V X$ where $W_K, W_Q, W_V \in \mathbb{R}^{d \times d}$ are weight matrices and $X \in \mathbb{R}^{n \times d}$ is a matrix of the feature vectors arranged along the rows. The output of the attention function is again a set of n vectors but now the ith vector represents a linear combination of all the vectors, where the coefficients of the linear combination are the attention scores. Since the weight matrices are learnable, it enables the model to adaptively change the attention coefficients in order to decide the amount of weight assigned to local and global features.

The adaptive nature of attention makes it almost scale agnostic while keeping the computational overhead relatively less. This is due to the fact that attention leverages a series of linear transforms to realize the cosine similarity between vectors and combines them accordingly. This makes attention-based models use significantly less compute as compared to convolutional models. These factors make attention-based models a worthy competitor for on-board deployment in robotics. However, owing to their simplicity, attention-based models require longer pre-training on images than on text.

3   Data Limitations

As deep learning models become more and more accurate, their complexity also scales proportionally. This induces an ever-growing dependence on data. State-of-the-art models require millions of data points for pre-training and hence require substantially large training times. However, the critical issue is the limited availability of human-annotated data. This limitation has induced a shift in learning paradigms from supervised to unsupervised learning methods.

Unsupervised or self-supervised learning involves techniques that enable models to learn data representations without the need for explicit human-annotated labels. Contrastive objectives like InfoXLM, MoCo, SimCLR, Barlow Twins and VICReg [8–12] have been successful in learning representations of data that deliver performance at par or even better than supervised models on tasks ranging from simple object classification to complex tasks like object detection, scene understanding and semantic segmentation.

Since these models do not require supervised data to train, they can benefit substantially from the large amounts of unlabelled data available. Continual learning is a technique that enables models to continually learn and adapt their weights over a prolonged period of time. Continual learning methods, coupled with self-supervised contrastive learning objectives can be employed to develop life-long learning models. These models can enable robots to autonomously function and learn from the collected data simultaneously. Since only a few data points are processed on each instant of time, these models can very easily be deployed on onboard hardware. Moreover, such models eradicate the requirement of repetitively training over the same data on the collection of new samples.

Most of these paradigms benefit from subtle augmentations introduced in the data during training and hence can be trained on augmented or synthetically generated data. Such models can be coupled with generative models like Generative Adversarial Networks (GANs) and Autoencoders that generate synthetic images, hence overcoming data scarcity while maintaining reliability and performance. However, as we explain in the next section, some limitations exist in transferring knowledge learnt from synthetic data to real-world data.

4 Domain Adaptation

Autonomous robots can be deployed in a wide range of environments, from controlled indoor settings to unexplored outdoor terrain. This demands robustness and adaptability. While both robustness and adaptability can be incorporated using the paradigms presented in Sect. 2 and Sect. 3, some aspects are domain-dependent. These paradigms fail to transfer knowledge when stark differences exist between the training (source) domain and deployment (target) domain. For example, an autonomous driving car trained on video game data may not be able to perform well in real-life settings. This calls for parallel datasets that enable models to learn corresponding features across different domains [14].

As the name suggests, domain adaptation involves learning features that (1) enable a robot or model to transfer its knowledge from one data domain to another while (2) maintaining limited but important knowledge about the domain-specific features in order to identify the domain correctly and adapt its

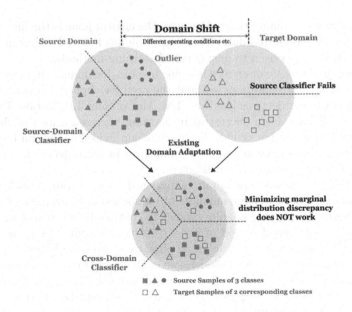

Fig. 1. An overview of Domain Adaptation [13].

actions accordingly. Here, as we can see from Fig. 1, the inter-class distance is increased while the intra-class distance is minimized across the domains.

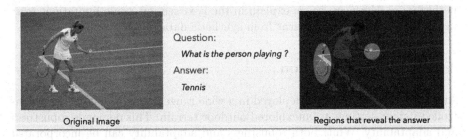

Fig. 2. An example to show how a mask is created in visual question answering systems [15].

4.1 Domain-Invariant Features

Domain-invariant features are features that are common across all domains. For example, avoiding pedestrians, vehicles and trees can be learnt very well in video game settings while maintaining performance on real-world test cases. Domain-invariant features usually transfer from one domain to another without requiring much change or adaptation. They are usually the passive, inherent features that are omnipresent across all domains.

Learning domain invariant features requires eradicating domain-specific information in order to pay more attention to domain agnostic information. Most works involve learning similarities between augmented views of images across different domains and some methods even rely on explicitly labeled domain-agnostic data.

Traditional approaches tend to minimize the distance between the representations of corresponding images across the domains using the generalised equation given below.

$$\mathcal{L} = \sum_{i=1}^{N} ||F(x_i^s), F(x_i^t)||_2 \tag{1}$$

where $F(.)$ is function that produces encoding of source domain images x_s and target domain images x_t. However, such entropy minimization techniques suffer from the problem of probability imbalance which implies that the models learn categories proportional to the number of samples in each category.

Recently, the maximum mean discrepancy (MMD) loss [16] was introduced to reduce the distribution differences between the domains to minimize the intra-class distance and maximize the inter-class discrepancies. It focuses on utilizing the distances between the mean embeddings of the features to represent distances between the source and target distributions. Given the source data distribution X_s and target distribution X_t over the set $\mathcal{X}$, the MMD is a feature map ϕ: $\mathcal{X} \rightarrow \mathcal{H}$ where $\mathcal{H}$ is the kernel that belongs to a Hilbert space. The MMD is defined as follows

$$\text{MMD}(X_s, X_t; \mathcal{H}) = sup_{||h|| \leq 1} E_{X_s}[h(X_s)] - E_{X_t}[h(X_t)] \tag{2}$$

Recent developments in contrastive methods such as MoCo [9] have also been used to learn domain agnostic features. Its loss function is given by

$$\mathcal{L}_c = \mathbb{E}_{w_q \sim \mathcal{D}_U^W} \left[\mathbb{E}_{w_k^+} [\Upsilon] \right] \tag{3}$$

where

$$\Upsilon = -\log \frac{\exp\left(\text{sim}\left(w_q, w_k^+\right)/\tau\right)}{\sum_{w_k \in N_k \cup \{w_k^+\}} \exp\left(\text{sim}\left(w_q, w_k\right)/\tau\right)} \tag{4}$$

where the similarity metric is defined as $\text{sim}(\boldsymbol{u}, \boldsymbol{v}) = \boldsymbol{u}^\top \boldsymbol{v}/\|\boldsymbol{u}\|\|\boldsymbol{v}\|$, w_q and w_k are query and key encodings respectively, while τ is a temperature hyper-parameter usually between 0 and 1.

However, the performance of such models is highly dependent on the types of augmentation techniques used. We explain the dependency of augmentations on the task to be performed in the Sect. 5.

4.2   Domain-Specific Features

Although domain-invariant features are more important in most deployment scenarios, domain-specific features enable robots to identify their current setting and adapt their actions accordingly. This is particularly useful in deployment scenarios that involve frequent indoor-outdoor transitions. For example, rescue robots often need to explore indoor caves, passages and debris while transitioning back to the outdoor settings once exploration is complete.

DSBN [17] presents a domain-specific batch normalization approach to describe domain discriminative representations explicitly. In convolutional neural networks, GDCAN [18] creates a domain conditional attention module that activates distinctly relevant channels for each domain. At higher layers, DWT [19] performs the domain-specific whitening operation. Further, recent state-of-the-art transformer paradigms have also been used to specifically learn source and target domain information. Two special tokens, [SRC] and [TRG], are used to learn mappings that contain domain-specific information of both domains. Also, masking the respective domain is taken care of to prevent mixing of domain information between both the domains [20].

5   Task Dependency of Augmentations

Augmentations play a vital role in increasing the complexity of the input and hence increasing the model's capacity. However, the utilization of different sets of augmentations is dependent on the task to be performed. In this section, we described the role played by augmentations in various tasks.

In supervised classification, the augmentations applied to the input data generally include rotations, random cropping and horizontal flips. These augmentations preserve the fundamental textures of categories and create a more complex input to enhance learning. Thus preventing overfitting on the training set and paving the way for better learning of features transferable to the test set. Without such augmentations, the learning would become very simple and would not result in good quality generalisable features of the trained categories.

In multimodal models such as Visual Question Answering (VQA) models, the input during augmentation (not training) is an image and the corresponding question-answer pair. In this setting, the images are often augmented by a mask which highlights the components in the image to be used in the answer. This enables one to leverage any type of attention mechanism between the highlighted portion of the image, question and the predicted answer. The attention mechanism improves the reasoning ability of the models and also helps in investigating biases in the dataset. For example, in Fig. 2, the input image displays a woman playing tennis. The associated question"what is the person playing?" and the answer "tennis" helps in making a mask that highlights the portion of the image associated with the answer. Hence, the mask only highlights the racket and ball. On the other hand, self-supervised contrastive methods such as SimCLR [10] utilize augmentations to make positive-negative pairs. The main objective of contrastive learning is to increase the contrast between the categories and decrease the contrast within the categories. However, here Siamese networks are used and hence 2 augmented views are required. The augmentations used include random cropping, Gaussian blur, solarization, grayscaling, horizontal flips, etc. It is proven in various studies [9–12] that the selection of augmentations in contrastive learning dramatically influences the performance of deep networks (Fig. 5).

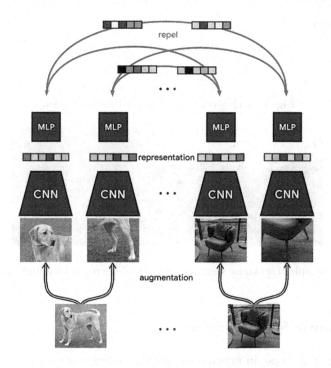

Fig. 3. SimCLR framework

From Fig. 3, we can observe that two different augmented views are obtained for each input. Since both of them belong to different categories, the embeddings obtained are repelled from each other using the InfoNCE loss function as given in Eq. 5.

$$l_{i,j} = -\log \frac{\exp\left(\text{sim}\left(z_i, z_j\right)/\tau\right)}{\sum_{k=1}^{2N} 1_{[k\neq i]} \exp\left(\text{sim}\left(z_i, z_k\right)/\tau\right)} \tag{5}$$

where $\text{sim}(u, v) = u^\top v/\|u\|\|v\|$ is the similarity metric, z_i, z_j represent the embeddings of the augmented views of an images and z_k represents the embeddings of the augmented view of an image from a different category. The loss brings z_i, z_j closer (by increasing their similarity) and pushes z_k away from both of them (by decreasing their similarity). Thus, the augmentations play a crucial role for the creation of positive-negative pairs in such models.

Hence, we can observe that the type and extent of the augmentations used rely heavily on the task to be performed.

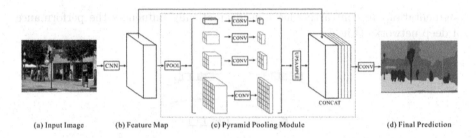

(a) Input Image   (b) Feature Map   (c) Pyramid Pooling Module   (d) Final Prediction

Fig. 4. Architectural diagram of PSPNet model.

Fig. 5. An example of semantic segmentation of real-life roads for autonomous vehicles.

6   Semantic Segmentation

The most popular task in urban scene understanding is semantic segmentation. The objective of this task is to classify each pixel in an input frame into one of the pre-determined classes or categories of objects. This enables models to develop masks that clearly demarcate objects like roads, pedestrians and other vehicles. This masking results in ease of extracting features and, hence, provides seamless integration with later components of a robot control pipeline.

However, the sizes of real-world datasets are very small (approximately 4000 images) and are not enough to learn high-quality features. The pixel-wise annotation for each image is highly laborious and takes a lot of time (approximately 90 min for each frame in the cityscapes dataset [21]). Hence, recent works focus on utilizing large-scale synthetic data such as GTA [22] and SYNTHIA [23] to train their models and further perform domain adaptation on the real-world data. Domain adaptation also enhances the adaptability with real-life scenarios such as different lighting conditions (day or night).

There are many works implementing such models that leverage a variety of techniques to learn features. The mechanisms can be broadly divided into the following categories

1. Self-supervised Learning
2. Adversarial Learning
3. Image Translation

Most of the works build upon plausible combinations of the aforementioned mechanisms to learn the domain-agnostic and domain-specific features.

The most common practice for performing semantic segmentation is using convolutional neural networks (ex. UNet [24]) to first encode the image and then further upsample the encoding to produce layer wise classification masks of size same as the input size. The skip connections between the encoder and the decoder help mitiagate information bottlenecks between the encoding and the upsampling operations. Recent models such as PSNet, as shown in Fig. 4 introduce a special pooling module that involves 4 different max pooling operations with different strides and window sizes [25].

Further, an ideal model should continually learn as new samples are collected. The requirement of repetitively training over the already available data is computationally inefficient and often infeasible owing to the limited computational capacity of onboard hardware systems.

7   Conclusion

In this work, we present various aspects of visual scene understanding and interpretation in detail. We first emphasise the importance of efficient and accurate visual scene understanding pipelines in modern autonomous systems. We then explain the problems faced by learning-based autonomous systems. We mainly focus on local vs. global feature learning, data limitations, domain adaptation and semantic segmentation for autonomous learning pipelines. We explore various suitable solutions for each of the problems in detail. This work will serve as a foundational overview for the development of various autonomous learning pipelines in the future.

References

1. Shu, C., Liu, Y., Gao, J., Yan, Z., Shen, C.: Channel-wise knowledge distillation for dense prediction. In: 2021 IEEE/CVF International Conference on Computer Vision (ICCV) (2021)
2. PLOP: learning without forgetting for continual semantic segmentation. In: Proceedings of the IEEE Conference on Computer Vision and Pattern Recognition (CVPR) (2021)
3. Besnier, V., Bursuc, A., Picard, D., Briot, A.: Triggering failures: out-of-distribution detection by learning from local adversarial attacks in semantic segmentation. In: Proceedings of the IEEE International Conference on Computer Vision (2021)
4. Lin, C.Y., Chiu, Y.C., Ng, H.F., Shih, T.K., Lin, K.H.: Global-and-local context network for semantic segmentation of street view images. Sensors 20(10), 2907 (2020)
5. Doersch, C., Gupta, A., Efros, A.A.: Unsupervised visual representation learning by context prediction. In: 2015 IEEE International Conference on Computer Vision (ICCV) (2015)

6. Bachman, P., Hjelm, R.D., Buchwalter, W.: Learning representations by maximizing mutual information across views. Red Hook, NY, USA (2019)

7. Vaswani, A., et al.: Attention is all you need. In: Proceedings of the 31st International Conference on Neural Information Processing Systems, Red Hook, NY, USA (2017)

8. Chi, Z., et al.: InfoXLM: an information-theoretic framework for cross-lingual language model pre-training. In: Proceedings of the 2021 Conference of the North American Chapter of the Association for Computational Linguistics: Human Language Technologies (2021)

9. He, K., Fan, H., Wu, Y., Xie, S., Girshick, R.: Momentum contrast for unsupervised visual representation learning. In: 2020 IEEE/CVF Conference on Computer Vision and Pattern Recognition (CVPR) (2020)

10. Chen, T., Kornblith, S., Norouzi, M., Hinton, G.: A simple framework for contrastive learning of visual representations. ArXiv (2020)

11. Zbontar, J., Jing, L., Misra, I., LeCun, Y., Deny, S.: Barlow twins: self-supervised learning via redundancy reduction. In: Proceedings of the 38th International Conference on Machine Learning, vol. 139 (2021)

12. Bardes, A., Ponce, J., LeCun, Y.: Variance-invariance-covariance regularization for self-supervised learning. In: ICLR, Vicreg (2022)

13. Li, X., Zhang, W., Ma, H., Luo, Z., Li, X.: Partial transfer learning in machinery cross-domain fault diagnostics using class-weighted adversarial networks. Neural Netw. **129**, 313–322 (2020)

14. Kundu, J.N., Kulkarni, A., Singh, A., Jampani, V., Babu, R.V.: Generalize then adapt: source-free domain adaptive semantic segmentation. In 2021 IEEE/CVF International Conference on Computer Vision (ICCV). IEEE (2021). https://doi.org/10.1109/iccv48922.2021.00696, https://doi.org/10.1109%2Ficcv48922.2021.00696

15. Visual question answering. https://blog.allenai.org/may-i-have-your-attention-please-eb6cfafce938

16. Wang, W., et al.: Rethinking maximum mean discrepancy for visual domain adaptation. IEEE Trans. Neural Networks Learn. Syst. (2021)

17. Chang, W.G., You, T., Seo, S., Kwak, S., Han, B.: Domain-specific batch normalization for unsupervised domain adaptation. In: 2019 IEEE/CVF Conference on Computer Vision and Pattern Recognition (CVPR) (2019)

18. Li, S., Xie, B., Lin, Q., Liu, C.H., Huang, G., Wang, G.: Generalized domain conditioned adaptation network. IEEE Trans. Pattern Anal. Mach. Intell. (2021)

19. Roy, S., Siarohin, A., Sangineto, E., Bulò, S.R., Sebe, N., Ricci, E.: Unsupervised domain adaptation using feature-whitening and consensus loss. In: 2019 IEEE/CVF Conference on Computer Vision and Pattern Recognition (CVPR) (2019)

20. Ma, W., Zhang, J., Li, S., Liu, C.H., Wang, Y., Li, W.: Exploiting both domain-specific and invariant knowledge via a win-win transformer for unsupervised domain adaptation (2021)

21. Cordts, M., et al.: The cityscapes dataset for semantic urban scene understanding. In Proceedings of the IEEE Conference on Computer Vision and Pattern Recognition (CVPR) (2016)

22. Richter, S.R., Vineet, V., Roth, S., Koltun, V.: Playing for data: ground truth from computer games. In: Leibe, B., Matas, J., Sebe, N., Welling, M. (eds.) ECCV 2016. LNCS, vol. 9906, pp. 102–118. Springer, Cham (2016). https://doi.org/10.1007/978-3-319-46475-6_7

23. Ros, G., Sellart, L., Materzynska, J., Vazquez, D., Lopez, A.M.: The synthia dataset: a large collection of synthetic images for semantic segmentation of urban scenes. In: 2016 IEEE Conference on Computer Vision and Pattern Recognition (CVPR) (2016)
24. Ronneberger, O., Fischer, P., Brox, T.: U-Net: convolutional networks for biomedical image segmentation. In: Navab, N., Hornegger, J., Wells, W.M., Frangi, A.F. (eds.) MICCAI 2015. LNCS, vol. 9351, pp. 234–241. Springer, Cham (2015). https://doi.org/10.1007/978-3-319-24574-4_28
25. Zhao, H., Shi, J., Qi, X., Wang, X., Jia, J.: Pyramid scene parsing network. In: 2017 IEEE Conference on Computer Vision and Pattern Recognition (CVPR) (2017)

An Effective Genetic Algorithm Based Multi-objective Optimization Approach for Coverage Path Planning of Mobile Robot

Monex Sharma$^{(\boxtimes)}$ (ID) and Hari Kumar Voruganti (ID)

National Institute of Technology, Warangal, Telangana 506004, India
msharma@student.nitw.ac.in, harikumar@nitw.ac.in

Abstract. Coverage path planning (CPP) is a subtopic of path planning problems in which it is required to visit free cells of the given area at least once by avoiding the obstacle(s) with minimum cost. CPP is one of the most crucial research areas for mobile robots. This research presents three different methods for solving CPP. The first method proposes an improved genetic algorithm to solve a single-objective optimization problem. The second and third methods employ an improved genetic algorithm to solve a multi-objective optimization problem. The second method involves constant weighting factors in the weighted sum method while the third method has taken optimized weighting factors. In this paper, the working environment is divided into a grid of squares where the side of the square is equal to the diameter of a robot. The main aim of the research is to minimize the completion time of the task to be performed by the robot. The paths generated by the methods are discussed. The objective functions are the distance traveled by the robot and the number of turns in the path. The two objective functions are then used to calculate the completion time. The results show that the completion time of the third method is minimum and the first method is maximum.

Keywords: Coverage path planning · Mobile robot · Genetic algorithm · Multi-objective optimization

1 Introduction

An important topic of study in the science of robotics is path planning (PP). Shortest path planning (SPP) and coverage path planning are two types of path planning (CPP). The shortest path planning of redundant manipulators moving along constrained paths while avoiding obstacles was explained by Chembuly et al. [1]. Salama et al. defined the shortest path planning of a mobile robot using the radial cell decomposition algorithm that can avoid the complex geometry of obstacles along its path [2]. There is an ample amount of work related to the shortest path planning of robotics. However, there are several research gaps in CPP as the area is newer compared to the SPP. The CPP problem is considered as the subtopic of a path planning problem in which it is necessary to visit or pass the entire given area at least once by avoiding the collision with any obstacle(s) with minimal cost [3]. Many CPP algorithms have been developed and applied to vacuum cleaning

© The Author(s), under exclusive license to Springer Nature Switzerland AG 2022
V. Sugumaran et al. (Eds.): AIR 2022, CCIS 1738, pp. 444–457, 2022.
https://doi.org/10.1007/978-3-031-23724-9_41

[4], window cleaners [5], robotic painting [6], automated vehicles for agriculture [7], lawnmowers [8], and many more. Particularly, in the pandemic situations like Covid-19, it is important to avoid direct contact with surfaces infected with the virus. An autonomous robot for cleaning is a viable solution for safety and also reduced human labor [9]. Minimum length of distance traveled, the minimum number of turns taken by a robot, minimum path overlapping, and maximum coverage area are some of the objective functions in the CPP optimization problem solved by many researchers [10–17].

Presently, many commercial robots use randomization techniques to solve the CPP problem. These methods are easy but inefficient as mobile robots consume more time to cover the workspace [20]. Different solutions to the CPP problem have been put up by researchers in recent years. In order to resolve the offline CPP problem with a barrier in a known environment, Gabriely et al. presented the Spanning Tree Coverage (STC) technique [10]. The program creates different-sized grids out of the environment. As the goal function, they minimize the number of times each path must be repeated. Distance transform (DT) was the method for CPP that Zelinsky et al. proposed [11]. The program creates grids out of the area and determines the CPP between the goal destination and the starting position. According to the placement and design of obstacles, Zhou et al. divided the working area into more manageable sub-regions using the boustrophedon exact decomposition method [12]. Then, they use dynamic programming to determine the ideal order to cover each sub-region. A solution to the CPP problem combining boustrophedon and a genetic algorithm (GA) was put out by Zhongmin et al. [13]. Boustrophedon divides the area into sub-regions and finds the optimized order to cover each sub-region using GA. Ryerson et al. used GA for CPP to guide autonomous agricultural equipment while avoiding obstacles [14]. Yakoubi et al. solved the online CPP of sensor-based autonomous mobile robots using GA [15]. They divided the entire area into grids that is equal to the size of the robot. The sensors create mini-paths randomly in the region of the sensor range and obtain a population of a generation. Rainer et al. proposed a method for CPP based on GA [16]. The authors discretized the environment into grids in which the side of each grid is the same as the robot's diameter. They consider straight, left, right, and U-turns as decision variables and minimize the energy generated by them. A chromosome is considered as a path and after the required iteration; the optimal solution is obtained with minimum energy. Shang et al. published work for multi-objective CPP based on improved GA [17]. They used the length of the driving path, elevation height, and the number of turns as the objectives of the problem. They turned the multi-objective problem into a single-objective problem using the weighted sum method, which produced the best result. The researchers select the weighting elements at random [17]. After the survey of the literature, there is a research gap in multi-objective optimization using GA and optimizing the weighting factors in the weighted sum method (WSM) to solve the CPP problem.

In this research, utilizing a genetic algorithm with improved single-point crossover and mutation, we provide a single objective offline CPP approach and two multi-objective offline CPP techniques to find the best solution for the known environment of a floor cleaning robot. The weighted sum method is used for multiple objective optimizations problem. Among the two multi-objective offline CPP approaches, in the first technique weighting factors are randomly chosen and kept constant in the entire program while in the second technique, weight factors are optimized to get the best solution. The given environment is discretized into grids according to the shape and size of the robot. It is considered that when a robot passes through a grid, the grid is fully covered by the robot. The rest of the paper is organized as follows: Environment modeling is presented in Sect. 2. In Sect. 3 proposed methods are presented, results and discussion are provided in Sect. 4. Finally, Sect. 5 presents the conclusions and future scope.

2 Environmental Modelling

This paper considers the 2D working environment of rectangular shapes and implements a grid method to represent the environment of a mobile robot as shown in Fig. 1. The length and width of the model are L and B respectively. The area covered by the robot is a circle of diameter (w). The mobile robot is allowed to move in 4 kinematic degrees of freedom: front, back, left, and right as shown in Fig. 2. The workspace is discretized into grid elements of square shape with its side (s) equal to the diameter of the mobile robot (w). Hence the working model can be discretized into s2 grid areas. The number of grids in the working model is $\frac{L \times B}{s^2}$. The grids which are occupied by the obstacles are called obstacle grids and are represented by black color on the grid map. While the grids which are free of obstacles are known as free grid and is represented by white color. It is assumed that when a robot passes through a free grid, the grid is completely covered by the robot. The mobile robot is required to pass through each free grid at least once to fulfill the complete coverage area.

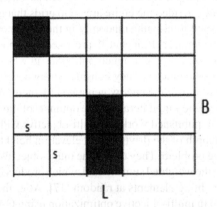

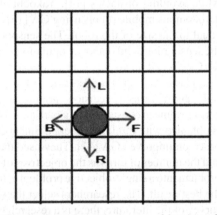

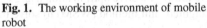

Fig. 1. The working environment of mobile robot

Fig. 2. Four kinematic degrees of freedom of the mobile robot

3 Proposed Method

The problem is formulated as an optimization problem and GA is chosen to solve the optimization problem. The GA is inspired by the theory of evolution [18]. It is based on the principle of survival of the fittest. GA begins with the initialization of the parent population. Parents are selected from the population using selection techniques. Offspring(s) are generated from the selected parents using operators (crossover and mutation) of a genetic algorithm. Then the total population (parent and operators population) of the current generation is sorted to obtain the fittest to get the parent population for the next generation. The flowchart of the genetic algorithm is given in Fig. 3. Figure 4 shows the parent population merged with the population obtained from operators and the merged population is sorted to get the fittest population for the next generation.

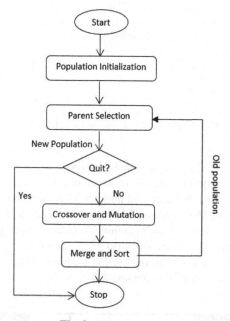

Fig. 3. Flowchart of GA

In this paper, the robot is allowed to move in four directions as shown in Fig. 2. Each grid in the working model has node number and (x, y) coordinates. GA uses the node of the grid as the decision variable of the problem. Hence, the number of decision variables depends on the size of the environment.

3.1 Initialization

In GA, the initialization of the population is important. Hence it is necessary to create a variety of paths in it. To execute this, different path orders are randomly generated. Initiating from the robot starting point, the robot selects a neighboring node with robot kinematic constraint motion randomly. The selected neighbor node is appended to the starting point and stored in the memory. The process is repeated till all the free grids in the working environment are saved in the memory and a solution (chromosome) is obtained for initialization. Further, the N number of chromosomes is created by repeating the same procedure to get the initial population. The robot might get stuck at a node (dead end) that is surrounded by visited nodes, boundaries, and/or obstacles. When the robot

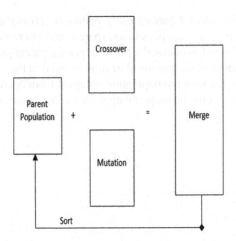

Fig. 4. Operators, merge and sort function

is at a dead end, it calls the shortest path planning function that allows the robot to travel to the nearest free grid at minimum cost as shown in Fig. 5. The red color line belongs to the path covered by the robot and grid number 35 is the robot's current location. It can be observed that grid 35 is surrounded by grid 36 (obstacle grid), grid 34, and grid 29 (occupied grids). The shortest path planning, rapidly exploring random tree (RRT) function is called to find the nearest free grid 18 as shown in Fig. 5 [19]. RRT creates branches of all possible moves from the current location of the robot for each motion and searches until the nearest goal is obtained.

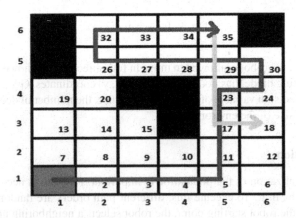

Fig. 5. Shortest path planning to avoid dead-end (Color figure online)

3.2 Fitness Evaluation

The task of the CPP problem is to minimize the completion time by optimizing the total distance traveled and the number of turns with complete coverage of the given area. In this research, three cases of CPP problems have been discussed. The decision variables are nodes of the working environment which is a discrete type optimization method.

Single Objective Optimization Problem using Improved GA: In this case, the objective function is the total distance traveled and the constraint is the number of turns. The constraint is the number of turns which is handled using the penalty approach. The optimization problem is stated as:

$$\text{Min}(z) = \text{total distance traveled by the robot}$$
$$\text{such that:}$$
$$g \leq n\_turns$$

Multi-objective Optimization Problem using GA and WSM: The total distance traveled ($z1$) and the number of turns taken by the robot ($z2$) is two objective functions. The two objective functions are converted into a single objective function using the WSM method. The optimization problem is stated as:

$$z_1 = \text{total distance travelled by robot.}$$
$$z_2 = \text{number of turns taken by robot.}$$
$$\text{Min}(z) = w_1 \times z_1 + w_2 \times z_2.$$

where w_1 and w_2 are weighting factors and $w_1 + w_2 = 1$.

In this case, the random weights are chosen to demonstrate the effectiveness of the algorithm. The weights are chosen according to the application [17].

Multi-objective Optimization Problem using GA and Improved WSM: This method is similar to the regular weighted sum method, however, it provides the optimized value of weighting factors w_1 and w_2. The range of w_1 value is given and the value of w_2 is found for every value of w_1 in the range. The result should be the combination of w_1 and w_2 that provides the minimum value of the objective function (z). Unlike the regular weighted sum method, w_1 and w_2 are not constant for the entire problem.

The completion time of the task in the working environment depends on the distance traveled by the robot. Due to the rapid acceleration and deceleration of the robot during turning, the robot would consume more time. Hence total completion time depends on the total distance traveled by the robot and the number of turns taken by the robot.

Total time taken for CPP by the robot is defined as:

$$t = t_s \times z_1 + t_t \times z_2$$

where: $t_s = \frac{d}{v}$

$$t_t = \frac{\Pi \times w}{2 \times v_t} + \frac{2 \times v}{a} + \frac{2 \times v_t}{a_c}$$

d = distance between two grids (m).
v = velocity of robot in straight motion (m/s).
v_t = turning velocity of robot (m/s).
w = distance between rear wheels of robot (m).
a = acceleration in straight motion (m/s²).
a_c = circular acceleration/deceleration (m/s²).

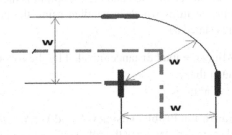

Fig. 6. Turning of robot (Color figure online)

In Fig. 6, the red color belongs to the robot wheels before the robot's turn while the blue color represents the robot wheels just after the turning.

3.3   Selection

There are N number of chromosomes in a population for each generation. A vector array is created which consists of randomly arranged integers from 1 to N (number of chromosomes). The first two indices of the vector array are selected. The integer value of the two indices is used to select the indices of two parents from the population.

3.4   Crossover

Crossover is a process of a combination of two-parent chromosomes and generating offspring(s). There are two basic crossover methods: one-point crossover and multiple point crossovers, in which the number of points of crossover decides the number of cutting points in the parent chromosome. In this research, an improved one-point crossover is used that takes two parents for crossover and provides one offspring. After the regular one-point crossover is completed and if the offspring generated is not able to provide complete coverage of free grids in the working environment, then an improved crossover method is applied to cover the entire free regions. All the genes of offspring after the crossover point are deleted and the current location of the robot is marked. A cell that is among the neighboring free cells of the current location of the robot is found, then the cell is appended to the modified offspring. The process is repeated until all the free cells are covered by the robot.

3.5 Mutation

An index (i) from the offspring is selected randomly. A mutated vector is created which consists of the genes from index 1 to index (i) of the offspring. A cell is selected which belongs to the neighboring free cells of the current location of the robot in the working environment. The selected cell is appended to the mutated vector. The process is repeated until the mutated vector has occupied all the free cells of the working environment.

4 Results and Discussion

The environment is rectangular and has a total of 64 grids including obstacles and free cells. The rectangular environment is 160 cm in length and 160 cm in breadth. The diameter of the robot and side of the square cell is taken as 20 cm. The working environment of the robot is shown in Fig. 7. The GA parameters are shown in Table 1. The initial position of the robot is in the down left corner (cell 1). The maximum number of turns allowed in the first method (single-objective optimization using GA) is 20. Weighting factors are $w1 = 0.75$ and $w2 = 0.25$ for the second method (multi-objective method using GA and WSM). In the third method (multi-objective method using optimized WSM), the weighting factor $w1$ has a range from 0.5 to 0.9, and the range of $w2$ is determined by using $w2 = 1 - w1$. The fitness value for each combination of weighting factors is generated to find the minimum of the fitness function.

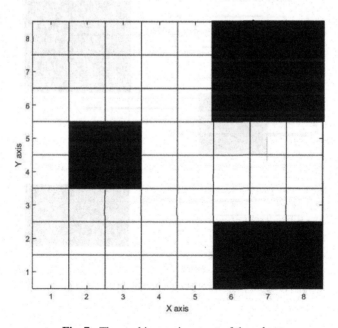

Fig. 7. The working environment of the robot

The chosen environment has 45 free cells and 19 obstacle cells. The graphical result of the path of the robot in the working environment and cost function – iteration of single-objective optimization (SOO) using GA is given in Figs. 8 and 9 respectively. The multi-objective optimization (MOO) using GA and WSM are given in Figs. 10 and 11 respectively. Figures 12 and 13 show, respectively, the multi-objective optimization (MOO) using GA and optimized WSM. It is assumed that the robot moves at an average speed of 0.1 m/s in a straight line and 0.05 m/s when turning. Acceleration in straight motion is 0.5 m/s2 and acceleration for circular motion is 0.1 m/s2. Total distance traveled, number of turns, and total time taken by robot for three methods are shown in Table 2.

Table 1. GA parameters

GA parameters	Value
Number of the population (N)	30
Number of generations (MaxIt)	50
Crossover probability (pC)	0.8
Number of crossovers (nC)	24

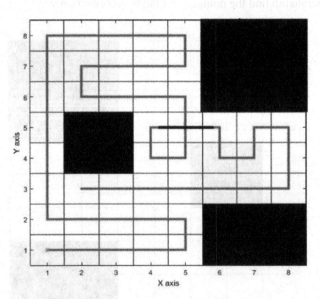

Fig. 8. Path of robot obtained by SOO using GA

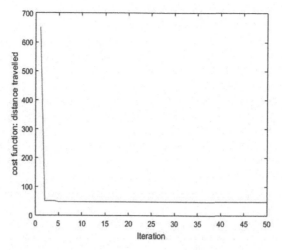

Fig. 9. Cost function – iteration of SOO using GA

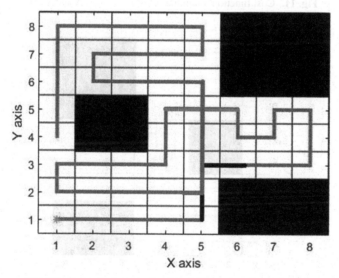

Fig. 10. Path of robot obtained by MOO using GA and WSM

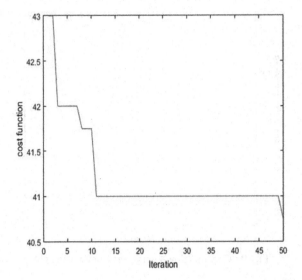

Fig. 11. Cost function – iteration of SOO using GA and WSM

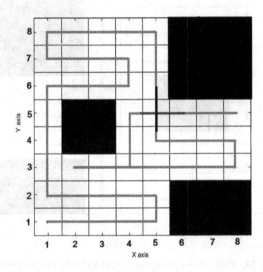

Fig. 12. Path of robot obtained by MOO using GA and optimized WSM

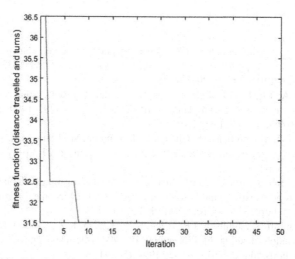

Fig. 13. Cost function – iteration of SOO using GA and optimized WSM

Table 2. Comparison of results of different methods

Methods	Distance traveled (z_1)	Number of turns (z_2)	Completion time (t) in seconds
SOO using GA	46	18	**230.24**
MOO using GA and WSM	40.75	19	**227.42**
MOO using GA and optimized WSM	31.5	15	**178.2**

5   Conclusion and Future Work

Three methods of CPP problem using GA and a comparison of results among them is presented. It shows the fitness function(s) of the GA algorithm is directly related to the completion time of the task. The research gives the guarantee of 100% coverage of free grids in the working environment using all three methods. The results show the completion time of the task is minimum with MOO using GA and the optimized weighting factor. In the future, the values of fitness function can be considered experimentally for completion time and the electrical energy consumption using a real robot. The experimental validation can be performed with a real robot in a real environment. Moreover, this research can be extended to different shapes and sizes of environments like non-rectilinear and larger environments.

References

1. Chembuly, V.V.M.J.S., Voruganti, H.K.: Trajectory planning of redundant manipulators moving along constrained path and avoiding obstacles. Proc. Comput. Sci. **133**, 627–634 (2018). https://doi.org/10.1016/j.procs.2018.07.094
2. Salama, O.A.A., Eltaib, M.E.H., Mohamed, H.A., Salah, O.: RCD: radial cell decomposition algorithm for mobile robot path planning. IEEE Access **9**, 149982–149992 (2021). https://doi.org/10.1109/access.2021.3125105
3. Pathmakumar, T., Rayguru, M.M., Ghanta, S., Kalimuthu, M., Elara, M.R.: An optimal footprint based coverage planning for hydro blasting robots. Sensors **21**, 1194 (2021). https://doi.org/10.3390/s21041194
4. Nasirian, B., Mehrandezh, M., Janabi-Sharifi, F.: Efficient coverage path planning for mobile disinfecting robots using graph-based representation of environment. Front. Robot. AI **8**, 624333 (2021). https://doi.org/10.3389/frobt.2021.624333
5. Farsi, M., Ratcliff, K., Johnson, J.P., Allen, C.R., Karam, K.Z., Pawson, R.: Robot control system for window cleaning. In: Proceedings of 1994 American Control Conference - ACC 1994 (1994). https://doi.org/10.1109/acc.1994.751894
6. Atkar, P.N., Greenfield, A., Conner, D.C., Choset, H., Rizzi, A.A.: Uniform coverage of automotive surface patches. Int. J. Robot. Res. **24**, 883–898 (2005). https://doi.org/10.1177/0278364905059058
7. Ollis, M., Stentz, A.: First results in vision-based crop line tracking. In: Proceedings of IEEE International Conference on Robotics and Automation (1996). https://doi.org/10.1109/robot.1996.503895
8. Bosse, M., Nourani-Vatani, N., Roberts, J.: Coverage algorithms for an under-actuated car-like vehicle in an uncertain environment. In: Proceedings 2007 IEEE International Conference on Robotics and Automation (2007). https://doi.org/10.1109/robot.2007.363068
9. Banjanovic-Mehmedovic, L., Karabegovic, I., Jahic, J., Omercic, M.: Optimal path planning of a disinfection mobile robot against COVID-19 in a ROS-based research platform. Adv. Prod. Eng. Manag. **16**, 405–417 (2021). https://doi.org/10.14743/apem2021.4.409
10. Gabriely, Y., Rimon, E.: Spanning-tree based coverage of continuous areas by a mobile robot. In: Proceedings 2001 ICRA. IEEE International Conference on Robotics and Automation (Cat. No. 01CH37164) (2001). https://doi.org/10.1109/robot.2001.932890
11. Alexander, Z., et al.: Planning paths of complete coverage of an unstructured environment by a mobile robot. In: Proceedings of International Conference on Advanced Robotics, vol. 13 (1993)
12. Zhou, P., Wang, Z., Li, Z., Li, Y.: Complete coverage path planning of mobile robot based on dynamic programming algorithm. In: Proceedings of the 2nd International Conference on Electronic and Mechanical Engineering and Information Technology (2012). https://doi.org/10.2991/emeit.2012.407
13. Wang, Z., Zhu, B.: Coverage path planning for mobile robot based on genetic algorithm. In: 2014 IEEE Workshop on Electronics, Computer and Applications (2014). https://doi.org/10.1109/iweca.2014.6845726
14. Ryerson, A.E.F., Zhang, Q.: Vehicle path planning for complete field coverage using genetic algorithms (2021). https://doi.org/10.32920/ryerson.14640621.v1
15. Yakoubi, M.A., Laskri, M.T.: The path planning of cleaner robot for coverage region using Genetic Algorithms. J. Innov. Digit. Ecosyst. **3**, 37–43 (2016). https://doi.org/10.1016/j.jides.2016.05.004
16. Schafle, T.R., Mohamed, S., Uchiyama, N., Sawodny, O.: Coverage path planning for mobile robots using genetic algorithm with energy optimization. In: 2016 International Electronics Symposium (IES) (2016). https://doi.org/10.1109/elecsym.2016.7860983

17. Shang, G., Gang, L., Peng, Z., Jiangyi, H.: Complete coverage path planning for horticultural electric tractors based on an improved genetic algorithm. J. Appl. Sci. Eng. **24**(3), 447–456 (2021)
18. Eiben, A.E., Rudolph, G.: Theory of evolutionary algorithms: a bird's eye view. Theoret. Comput. Sci. **229**, 3–9 (1999). https://doi.org/10.1016/s0304-3975(99)00089-4
19. Zhang, H., Wang, Y., Zheng, J., Yu, J.: Path planning of industrial robot based on improved RRT algorithm in complex environments. IEEE Access **6**, 53296–53306 (2018). https://doi.org/10.1109/access.2018.2871222
20. Habib, M.A., Alam, M.S., Siddique, N.H.: Optimizing coverage performance of multiple random path-planning robots. Paladyn J. Behav. Robot. **3**, 11–22 (2012). https://doi.org/10.2478/s13230-012-0012-5

Trending Technologies: Frameworks and Applications Focusing Real Life Issues

Smart Monitoring System for Waste Management Using IoT

Balaji Morasa$^{(\boxtimes)}$ ⓘ, Yasmine Begum Anwaraly ⓘ, Jayasaradhi Reddy Chennuru,
Charunya Devara, and Mahesh Gavvalla

Sree Vidyanikethan Engineering College, Tirupati, A.P., India
balajim@vidyanikethan.edu

Abstract. In the past three decades, the population has increased tremendously; as a result, the generated garbage has increased uncontrollably. Today waste management became very harder. This paper presents internet-based Garbage Management and Monitoring System that checks the bin level and the methane concentration over the dustbins by using sensors. This system employed with a microcontroller that acts as an interface between the Sensors and system and Control unit. Based on the waste level in garbage bins, the necessary action takes place. The sensed data is uploaded into the Thing speak cloud for further analysis. By using the tools in Thing Speak, we can determine those which areas the bins are filling fast. Therefore, the bins in the areas that are filling very slowly, moved to the areas where the bins are filling fast The Node MCU, Methane sensor, Ultrasonic distance sensor is hardware part for measuring the status of the garbage bin. ThingSpeak and Blynk are software part. Blynk is used to get notification. Therefore, the system achieves effective usage of bins and hardware optimization. Moreover, the fuel consumption reduces.

Keywords: Node MCU · Blynk · ThingSpeak · Ultrasonic distance sensor · Methane sensor

1 Introduction

The unwanted material, which is leftover in the cities, public places, colleges, schools, restaurants, water bodies and houses, creates garbage. For a smart and healthy lifestyle, the necessity is cleanliness. This System helps to lessen the waste management problem. The IoT (Internet of Things) in which the things in daily life packed with a microcontroller for processing, antenna for communication, and protocols make them communicate with each other and with the users. Therefore, the Internet of Things became a part of the Internet and human life. The project "Smart Monitoring System for Waste Management using IoT" is an ingenious system that helps to keep public places clean [1]. This technology continuously monitors the bins and sends notifications to a mobile application about the amount of garbage collected in the bins. To achieve this, the system uses ultrasonic distance sensors and methane sensors placed over the bins to detect the garbage level. The result compared with pre-defined thresholds and suitable decision is

V. Sugumaran et al. (Eds.): AIR 2022, CCIS 1738, pp. 461–470, 2022.
https://doi.org/10.1007/978-3-031-23724-9_42

taken. If the result crosses the threshold level, a notification will be sent to the Control unit. The system uses Node MCU, a Wi-Fi modem, to transmit sensed data and a 9V battery powers the system. The ThingSpeak cloud used to analyze and visualize the data from the bins. By using ThingSpeak cloud, the efficient placing of bins at different locations can achieved. Finally, this system keeps the public places clean by clearing the garbage from the bins by providing a pictorial view of the bin level through the mobile application [2].

In the paper "Smart Dustbin-An Efficient Garbage Monitoring System," [3] has proposed a system that relates existing garbage bins and their count. The garbage bins are filled with wastes, which leads to pollution to environment. In the paper "IoT based Smart Bin" [4] the authors proposed that when the bin reaches 70% of bin a notification is sent through IFFTTT webhook software. Thus, the waste management becomes easy.

In the paper "Smart Garbage Monitoring System using Internet of Things (IOT)" [5] proposed a system which employed microcontroller to transfer the data to control unit through Node MCU and control unit sends a message to the vehicle through a GSM module.

2 Proposed System

The proposed system uses gas sensor and ultrasonic sensor to give an accurate indication of the garbage level in the bin at any time. Using the data from the sensors, the waste collection routes get optimized, and it reduces fuel consumption. It permits the garbage collectors to schedule their daily or weekly collections and reduces the overhead. An ultrasonic distance sensor measures if the bin is entirely or partially filled with waste. Here, ultrasonic sensor is placed at the top of the bin which measures the distance of garbage from the top of the bin. The threshold value is fixed irrespective of the size of the bin. The bin is full of garbage if the sensed distance is less than the threshold value. The system notifies with the message "Collect the GARBAGE" or if the methane concentration is more than the threshold value, then also it notifies with a message "Collect the GARBAGE".

The proposed system architecture is shown in Fig. 1. This system employed with Node MCU powered with a battery. Two sensors namely ultrasonic distance Sensor and Methane Sensor are attached to Node MCU [6]. The Methane Sensor monitors the concentration of methane in the garbage bin, while the Ultrasonic Distance Sensor calculates the distance to the object. The microcontroller present in the Node MCU processes the sensed data. If the sensed data crosses the threshold levels, then a notification is sent as "Collect the GARBAGE". The total sensed data is uploaded into ThingSpeak cloud. By using the data, we can able, to determine the places in which the garbage bins are filling very fast. Therefore, the effective placing of garbage bins is achieved [7]. The control unit takes care about to which vehicle the notification has to send and to rest no. The vehicle that received the notification collects the waste in the garbage bin. Thus, the goal is achieved [8]. The Fig. 2 shows the flow diagram of garbage bin. The complete sensed data is uploaded to ThingSpeak cloud for analysis purpose. The notification is sent to vehicle from control unit through Blynk when garbage bin crosses the threshold level [9].

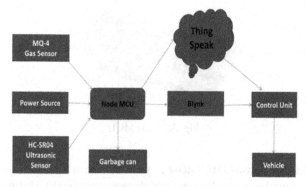

Fig. 1. Architecture of proposed system

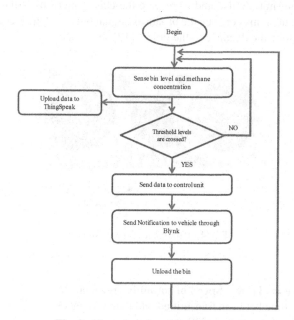

Fig. 2. Flow chart for proposed system

3   System Requirements

3.1   Hardware

Node MCU/ESP 8266. Expressive Systems created the Node MCU/ESP 8266, an open-source Wi-Fi SoC. ESP 8266 is an integrated chip that provides internet connectivity to the Microcontroller. It has totally 30 pins in which, nine are digital pins and one is an analog pin. It has a microcontroller and makes use of a built-in Wi-Fi module. Through the 2.4 GHz antenna, it transmits the monitored sensor data to web pages, clouds, and mobile interfaces [10, 11] (Fig. 3).

Fig. 3. Node MCU

Ultrasonic Distance Sensor (HC-SR04). An ultrasonic distance sensor is an electrical device that uses sound waves to determine the distance to an object. Distinct echo patterns generated from the surfaces by the reflection of high frequency waves. It contains a transducer to transmit a pulse and to receive the echo pattern from the surface of the object. The time intervals between the broadcast signal pulse and the received echo pulse are used to compute the distance to the object [12] (Fig. 4).

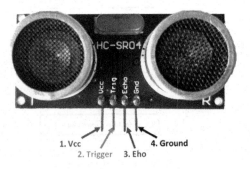

Fig. 4. Ultrasonic distance sensor

Actual Distance = (Time * Speed of sound in free space)/2
Where, Time = time between transmitted and received pulse.
Speed of sound in free space = 340 m/s.

Methane Sensor (MQ-4). MQ4 Sensor tells us the methane gas concentration in the air. Methane sensor can able to sense in the range of (200–10,000) ppm. The sensor can operate at temperatures from −12 to 55 °C. It is very power efficient [13] (Fig. 5).

Fig. 5. Methane sensor

LM7805 (+5 V Positive Voltage Regulator). LM 7805 is a +5 V Positive Voltage Regulator that has maximum input voltage of 30 V, operating current (IQ) is 5 mA and output current up to 100 mA. It also has short circuit current limiting protection and internal Thermal Overload protection [14] (Fig. 6).

Fig. 6. LM7805 voltage regulator

3.2 Software

Blynk Mobile Application. Blynk is a mobile application and a works on both IOS and Android operating system. This app can control boards such as Arduino, Teensy 3, MSP's, ESP8266, Raspberry Pi boards and the liked over the Internet. By simply dragging and dropping widgets in the workspace, we may create a graphical interface for a project. It controls hardware remotely, it displays real time sensor data, it can store and visualize the data [15, 16] (Fig. 7).

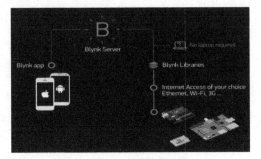

Fig. 7. Blynk mobile application

Thing Speak. Thing Speak is an Internet of Things analytics platform service given by Math Works. It visualizes, and analyses the data in the database i.e., cloud. ThingSpeak gets the data from the devices through virtual channels by API keys. Using this platform visualization of live data is created in the form of charts and graphs, and it is informed to the user. ThingSpeak works with Arduino, MSP'S, Teensy 3, Nanode, Raspberry Pi boards etc., and MATLAB [17, 18] (Fig. 8).

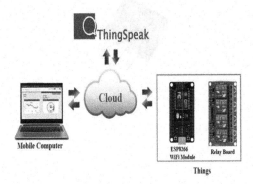

Fig. 8. ThingSpeak IoT platform for smart monitoring system

Arduino IDE. Arduino is Integrated Development Environment software that allows us to write the code in C/C++. The code written in Arduino called as Sketch. This IDE consists text editor to write the code. Every code has two functions namely setup and loop. The setup function executed only once, here the declarations and baud rate are set upped. In loop function, main code is written which executes over infinite times [19] (Fig. 9).

Fig. 9. Arduino IDE

4 Results and Discussion

The prototype model for the proposed system is as shown in Fig. 10. It has an ultrasonic sensor and methane sensor placed over the lid to measure the distance and methane concentration respectively. The node MCU processes the data, transfers it to the ThingSpeak, and alerts through mobile application Blynk. Node MCU powered with a battery source.

Fig. 10. Prototype model of smart garbage system

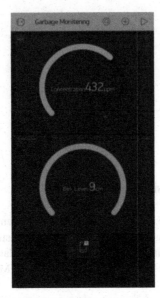

Fig. 11. Status of the bin when it was empty

The Blynk platform is used to monitor the status of the bin as shown in Fig. 11. It shows the sensed data of sensors. The Fig. 11, shows the readings of the garbage bin when it is empty.

Fig. 12. Blynk notification when bin crosses threshold levels

The system has two threshold levels. When any one of the threshold levels is crossed then the notification is sent to vehicle through Blynk mobile application. The notification in Blynk mobile application when the status of the bin crosses the threshold levels is as shown in Fig. 12.

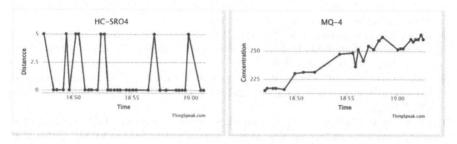

Fig. 13. Field charts displaying the sensed data form ThingSpeak

Sensed data of ultrasonic distance sensor and methane sensor is shown in Fig. 13. The field chart on the left side shows ultrasonic sensor reading and field chart on right side shows methane sensor reading. By using this data, we can create a MATLAB visualization.

5 Conclusion

The problem of the waste management in the public places is eliminated in this system. It avoids the spillover of waste from the garbage bins. It continuously monitors the bin status and updates the status of bins. By using the status of the bins, the control unit takes the decision accordingly. The components ESP 8266 Wi-Fi, Ultrasonic distance sensor, Methane sensor, Blynk mobile application, and Thing Speak are more enough to implement the proposed system practically. Therefore, the effective placement of garbage bins is achieved. Moreover, the system reveals the total waste generated in a particular place in a day/week/month.

References

1. Srinivasan, P., Thiyaneswaran, B., Jaya Priya, P., Dharani, B., Kiruthigaa, V.: IOT based "smart dustbin." Int. J. Adv. Eng. Res. Dev. **4** (2017). https://doi.org/10.21090/ijaerd.it011
2. Chaware, S.M., Dighe, S., Joshi, A., Bajare, N., Korke, R.: Smart garbage monitoring system using Internet of Things (IOT). IJIREEICE **5**, 74–77 (2017). https://doi.org/10.17148/ijiree ice.2017.5115
3. Monika, K.A., Rao, N., Prapulla, S.B.: Smart dustbin-an efficient garbage monitoring system. Int. J. Sci. Eng. Res. **6**(9), 7113–7115 (2016)
4. Shafee, S.S., Rawate, A.M., Sumera, A.: IoT based garbage bin monitoring system. J. Xidian Univ. **14** (2020). https://doi.org/10.37896/jxu14.9/033
5. Lakshmi Devi, P., Chandan, B.R.: IOT based waste management system for smart city. IAETSD J. Adv. Res. Appl. Sci. **4**(7), 8 (2017)
6. Chowdhury, P., Sen, R., Ray, D., Roy, P., Sarkar, S.: Garbage monitoring and disposal system for smart city using IoT. In: 2018 Second International Conference on Green Computing and Internet of Things (ICGCIoT) (2018). https://doi.org/10.1109/icgciot.2018.8753060

7. Sinha, T., Kumar, M., Saisharan, P.: Smart dustbin. Int. J. Ind. Electron. Electr. Eng. **3**(5), 101–104 (2015)
8. Abba, S., Light, C.I.: IoT-based framework for smart waste monitoring and control system: a case study for smart cities. In: 7th International Electronic Conference on Sensors and Applications (2020). https://doi.org/10.3390/ecsa-7-08224
9. Kumar, N.S., Vuayalakshmi, B., Prarthana, R.J., Shankar, A.: IOT based smart garbage alert system using Arduino UNO. In: 2016 IEEE Region 10 Conference (TENCON) (2016). https://doi.org/10.1109/tencon.2016.7848162
10. Gaddam, M., Dileep Thatha, V., Ravi Kavuluri, S., Krishna Popuri, G.: Smart garbage collection management system. Int. J. Eng. Technol. **7**, 193 (2018). https://doi.org/10.14419/ijet.v7i2.7.10291
11. Enam, Md.A., Khan, S., Singh, B., Kumari, N.: Smart dustbins with GSM and ARDUINO module. Int. J. Latest Technol. Eng. Manag. Appl. Sci. (IJLTEMAS) **VI**(XII) (2017). ISSN 2278-2540
12. Kiran, S.C.V.S.L.S.R., Kumar, B., Umar, M., Krishna, V., Karthik, K.: IJARCCE implementation of smart garbage monitoring system using IoT. Int. J. Adv. Res. (2019). https://doi.org/10.17148/IJARCCE.2019.8124
13. Arebey, M., Hannan, M.A., Basri, H., Abdullah, H.: Solid waste monitoring and management using RFID, GIS and GSM. In: 2009 IEEE Student Conference on Research and Development (SCOReD) (2009). https://doi.org/10.1109/scored.2009.5443382
14. Yasmine Begum, A., Balaji, M., Satyanarayana, V.: Quantum dot cellular automata using a one-bit comparator for QCA gates. Mater. Today: Proc. **66**, 3539–3546 (2022). https://doi.org/10.1016/j.matpr.2022.06.416
15. Saranya, L., Rajeshwari, P., Pradeep, G., Priyadharshini, M., Praveenkumar, S.S.: Garbage management system for smart city using IOT. Int. J. Pure Appl. Math. **118**, 597–601 (2018). ISSN:1311-8080
16. Yasmine Begum, A., Balaji, M., Vishnuvardhan, G., Harshavardhan, G., Lazer Mathew, T.: Development of animal collar for state of health determination of livestock. J. Inf. Optim. Sci. **41**, 489–497 (2020). https://doi.org/10.1080/02522667.2020.1724613
17. Bhalerao, P.S., Jadhav, M.R., Nikam, S.S., Khamkhedkar, S.K., Dhagate, D.R.: Microcontroller based smart dustbin with GSM module. Int. J. Adv. Res. Sci. Eng. **7**(7), 170–176 (2018)
18. Morasa, B., Nimmagadda, P.: Low power residue number system using lookup table decomposition and finite state machine based post computation. Indonesian J. Electr. Eng. Comput. Sci. **26**, 127 (2022). https://doi.org/10.11591/ijeecs.v26.i1.pp127-134
19. Mohd Yusof, N., Jidin, A.Z., Rahim, M.I.: Smart garbage monitoring system for waste management. MATEC Web Conf. **97**, 01098 (2017). https://doi.org/10.1051/matecconf/201797 01098

Implementation of LiDAR Based Self Driving Car Using Raspberry Pi 3

V. Jyothi[1]([⊠]), Gunti Manideep[1], Pyata Deekshitha Reddy[1], and M. V. Subramanyam[2]

[1] Department of ECE, Vardhaman College of Engineering, Affiliated to JNTU, Shamshabad, Hyderabad, India
jyothinaikv@gmail.com
[2] Department of ECE, Santhiram Engineering College, Affiliated to JNTUA, Nandyal, Andhra Pradesh, India

Abstract. Time and automation play a central role in our lives and the advancement in technology is proportionate with time, so self-driving cars have been introduced with the main objective of saving time. It helps in performing other work (for ex. office work, etc.) while traveling, rather than getting engaged in driving the car. This car is competent at identifying the surroundings, traversing, and satisfying the transportation capabilities without any human input. The device LiDAR aids in viewing other vehicles, therefore acting as an eye for self-driving cars. It provides a complete picture of the surroundings, ensuring a safe drive. The bright side of autonomous cars is that they result in fewer road fatalities and increased credibility. Its other benefits include space-saving in parking and also, driverless cars will result in less breaking and accelerating and therefore less gridlock on highways.

Keywords: Automation robot · Power steering motor · Main motor ultrasonic sensor · Light Detection, and Ranging (LiDAR)

1 Introduction

According to the reports, an average of 3,700 people per day die due to vehicle crashes globally. The main intention of the autonomous car is to reduce the deaths that occur due to improper driving. A self-driving car, favored by ADAS (advanced driver assistant system), is referred to as an unmanned car that guides itself towards the journey's end without any human interference. Cars utilizing this technology will have their own set of advantages. It can cut fuel usage and pollution caused by carbon emissions dramatically. An Autonomous Vehicle steers to the final destination given by the user, based on multiple sensors (Radar, Lidar, Camera, ultrasonic Sensors). Lidar is abbreviated as Light Detection and Ranging or laser imaging, Detection and Ranging in the name itself, the operation of it can be outlined. LiDAR sensor is being introduced as peripheral tracking to facilitate the reduction of road fatalities that occur due to human error. The sensor prototype was introduced in the year 1961 for the space program shortly after LASER (Light Amplification for stimulated emission of radiation) was introduced.

© The Author(s), under exclusive license to Springer Nature Switzerland AG 2022
V. Sugumaran et al. (Eds.): AIR 2022, CCIS 1738, pp. 471–478, 2022.
https://doi.org/10.1007/978-3-031-23724-9_43

2 Related Work

A vehicle that travels from an initial point to the desired point automatically can provide a plethora of benefits, such as transferring goods or gathering important data in adverse conditions that humans cannot handle. Many researchers have provided an overview of the subject, and a few have made recommendations [1–4]. In recent years, the growth and upgrading of existing technology and software have as facilitated this. Even though some of these technologies are cutting edge, they come with significant disadvantages including high energy expenses and computing costs. These shortcomings prevent them from being used in embedded systems.

A 2D LIDAR-based approach was proposed by Yan Peng et al. [6], which they evaluated using a MATLAB simulation. The key idea is to go through three processes before deciding if a barrier is real and how to go over it. Filtering, pre-processing, and clustering are the three procedures. The vehicle's turn angle is estimated by the obstacle avoidance algorithm as it continues to gather data. The MATLAB simulation makes the expensive LIDAR SICK LMS511 that was used unsuitable for use in practical situations. In comparison to the aforementioned writers, we employ a far less expensive and compact LIDAR setup, as well as a tiny integrated net that consumes little resources.

[8] describes a surveillance robot built using a Raspberry Pi and three ultrasonic sensors for measuring distance. A backpropagation neural network is used in the obstacle avoidance approach, which uses a gradient descent technique brings the network closer to very less error for every transition. Initially, there was a gap in coverage in ultrasonic sensors between what was available and what was available compared to LIDAR, which offers 360° of coverage. Furthermore, the robot's training in this approach is incredibly slow, resulting in the robot malfunctioning early in the execution. According to the preceding sources, there are a variety of ways available, ranging from low-cost to high-cost hardware. They are often costly to implement and are not suitable for usage in tiny embedded devices. We pair a reliable piece of hardware with a powerful algorithm in our proposed implementation.

3 Progression of Self-driving Cars

From level 0 to level 5, a vehicle can be categorized into six driving levels: Level 0: A vehicle is entirely operated by hand. They have no robocar features at all, and all risks of driving should be handled by the person in the driving seat. They should respond promptly before the situation goes out of control. Level 1: It is highly popular across the world. It implies that automobiles are built with features that allow both the driver and the vehicle to engage in vehicle control. Because the user must still pay attention to steering and other controls, adaptive cruise control, which maintains speed by establishing limits and also allows for a safe following distance, is a perfect example. Level 2: vehicles feature a well-designed internal system that allows for autonomous steering, braking, and acceleration. However, the user must always be aware of his or her surroundings and act on the wheels. Level 3: Automobiles are referred to be automated since the driver has little or no control over the vehicle. The user is free to conduct other work or relax, however napping is not suggested because they must be fully aware of the car's actions on motorways and in traffic jams. Level 4: Cars are also automatic and allow users to even have a nap or deep sleep by not at all focusing on driving. If the situation cannot be handled by the user, the car can be well managed. However, there are a few restrictions that prevent them from being called self-driving cars. Level 5: A car is also referred to as self-driving cars. It doesn't require any communication with the user at all in controlling and taking up decisions, but it still takes time to bring these level 5 cars into mass production to the market.

4 Phases of Working

The main purpose of self-driving cars is mentioned in this chapter. (a) Perception: The vehicle can determine its near vicinity. This will aid the vehicle in avoiding collisions with other cars as well as keeping an eye on any barriers that may appear along its route. Many technological devices are now accessible in stores that can be used for this purpose. One such example is LIDAR.

Monovision cameras are another common perception device used in self-driving automobiles. Monovision cameras have only a single light source. Monovision cameras are quite basic, and the video signal is typically utilized for sensing basic surroundings such as road markers, speed limitation boards, and other stiff infrastructure. The hardware is low-cost and straightforward. Automobile monovision cameras are simpler and have a lower pixel density than mobile phone cameras. (b) Motion Planning: Motion planning entails doing low-level actions to achieve high-level goals. It's difficult to plan an automobile's route in a changing environment, especially when the automobile must employ its whole capability. There has been recent improvement in processing power, both in terms of hardware and communication topologies, which can help us develop a self-navigating automobile that is error-free. To avoid any form of disaster, motion planning includes route variables that must be supervised. These are the path variables:

(c) Navigation: For localization, the Global Positioning System (GPS) is employed. The GPS antenna is positioned on the vehicle's roof, and it receives signals from orbiting satellites to calculate their worldwide coordinates. Using these coordinates, the car may locate itself on a map of the road network and go to its destination. GPS will be combined with inertial navigation systems (INS), which are comprised of the equipment required to determine the vehicle's location, orientation, and velocity without the need for external devices.

(d) Overtaking: Overtaking, which is known to be the leading cause of accidents throughout the world, is of much more concern in the case of self-driving cars. The car must safely cross another vehicle while keeping an eye out for a car approaching from behind. This ensures that overtaking is done safely. In self-driving cars, algorithms are used to do the overtaking. The vehicle will be fitted with the appropriate electrical gadgets to fulfill the mission, which will be based on the logic in the algorithm. With the use of a sensor, the source car measures the distance between it and the automobile in front of it and then estimates the relative speed required to surpass it.

5 Designing of Proposed System

Our autonomous vehicle implementation uses the Raspberry Pi 3B and the RP Lidar A2 as its two main pieces of hardware (Fig. 1). We employed a Light Detection and Ranging module to find obstructions (LIDAR). LIDAR is a surveying tool that pulses light in all directions (360°) and uses a sensor to calculate the signals that are reflected at any angle. The distance to the nearest barrier was calculated using the time and wavelength of the acquired pulse. Processing of both of these measurements is necessary for navigation and hazard detection. A Raspberry Pi 3 computer is used to process this data. The Raspberry Pi 3's 40 General Purpose Input Output (GPIO) pins make it a small, effective, and inexpensive single board computer (SBC). The Raspberry Pi is the ideal candidate because to its low power consumption and absorption. Our comprehensive design also includes a small engine-powered vehicle, a motor driver (L293D), a lithium-polymer battery, and a USB power bank. Since Direct Current motors use a lot of energy, we purposely selected separate power sources for the Raspberry Pi and the Direct Current motors. In this method, we can communicate with the Raspberry Pi 3 and find its location even if the Lithium-Polymer battery is entirely depleted, as well as get measurements of the surrounding environment. The average power consumption of each component when in use is 850 mA for the Direct Current motors, 1.0 A for the LIDAR module, and 0.55 A for the Raspberry Pi 3. During normal operation, each component uses an average of 850 mA for the Direct Current motors, 1.0 A for the LIDAR module, and 0.55 A for the Raspberry Pi 3.

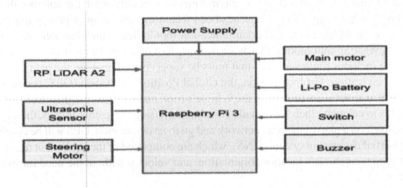

Fig. 1. Block diagram of autonomous vehicle using Raspberry Pi 3

The proposed work diagram consists of the following modules:

- **Power Supply:** The detailed diagram of the power supply is shown in Fig. 2.

REGULATED POWER SUPPLY

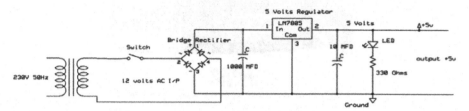

Fig. 2. Regulated power supply

- **Raspberry Pi 3-model B:** In this project, a raspberry pi that is connected to a computer was used. A conventional keyboard and mouse and a low-cost, credit-card-sized computer called the Raspberry Pi are both used (Fig. 3). The Raspberry Pi is a tiny CPU with a lot of functionality, including a 64-bit processor, 1 GB of RAM, and compatibility for the UART, I2C, and SPI protocols. The Raspberry Pi is connected to Bluetooth via UART protocol receiver and transmitter pins, LCD via SCL & SDA pins, IR via digital GPIO pins, and motors via relay via digital GPIO pins. The Raspberry Pi module requires 5 V and 2 A of power.

Fig. 3. Raspberry Pi 3 board with two USB ports

RP LiDAR A2 Sensor: Robotic Navigation Using 2D LIDAR Sensor 360° Scanning Radius LIDAR Sensor Scanner for Obstacle Avoidance (Fig. 4). The improved 2D laser range scanner is called the RP LiDAR A2M5/A2M6. Within an 18-m radius, the system can do a 2D 360° scan. Maps, localisation, and object/environment modeling can all be done using the resulting 2D point cloud data. A pulsed laser is used in the remote sensing technique known as LIDAR to measure distances to the earth. To perform a 360° omnidirectional laser range scan for its surrounding environment, RPLIDAR A2's core rotates clockwise.

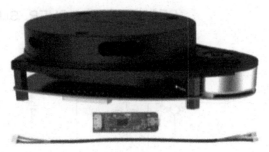

Fig. 4. RP LiDAR A2 sensor

Ultrasonic Sensor: An ultrasonic sensor is a device that uses ultrasonic sound waves to calculate a distance to an item. A piezoelectric crystal is used by the transmitter to produce the ultrasonic sound waves for Ln, the ultrasonic sensor. A transducer that produces an ultrasonic sound and another that hears its echo make up ultrasonic sensors.

6   Challenges with Autonomous Cars

The unemployment issue also arises from the generalization of autonomous cars, as the people who serve as drivers will be no longer required. Many who make a living as licensed drivers would lose their jobs. Another big issue is protection and confidentiality, as these cars would be connected to GPS, allowing someone to obtain and exploit the vehicle's location. Terror organizations may also use these trucks to carry out their crimes. Another major impediment to the adoption of these vehicles is that many countries' road infrastructure is inadequate to accommodate this innovation. To fully depend on these vehicles, comprehensive testing and analysis are needed, which may take up to 10–15 years.

7   Results

In the lab at our college, we conducted a number of studies to ascertain the vehicle's functionality. The research space was 5 m × 14 m and had a surface area of 70 m^2. There were a total of six BS mounted, two at the starting and finishing points as well as two more strategically placed to guarantee that the entire area was covered. The terrain was littered with numerous obstructions of varied sizes in various places. The car reached the GP from the SP in 5 min and 31 s. The average speed of the vehicle was 0.31 m/s. The installed Direct Current motors used 7.31 W, while the Raspberry Pi3 and LIDAR used an average of 9.5 W. With its numerous exposed interfaces and potent CPU, the Raspberry Pi offers a versatile base platform for testing sensor devices, gathering data, and computing prototype applications. It typically needs 4 min and 41 s to reach its destination. The side and top view of the car is presented in Fig. 5, the mapping environment is presented in Fig. 6.

Fig. 5. Side and top view of self-driving car

Fig. 6. LiDAR mapping environment

Figure 7, shows the location around the lidar and its perception It is represented using two coordinates x and y respectively.

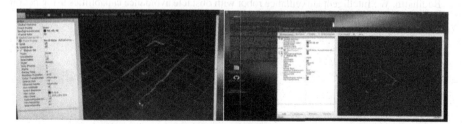

Fig. 7. Location perception

8 Conclusion and Future Scope

An autonomous vehicle built with a Raspberry Pi and LIDAR is demonstrated in this paper. The vehicle can use existing wi-fi networks to find out where it is precisely in the area and to travel with safety safely travel from one location to another while avoiding obstacles. Implementing a mapping function to create an image of the environment might help us improve our work even further.

References

1. Bimbraw, K.: Autonomous cars: past, present and future a review of the developments in the last century, the present scenario and the expected future of autonomous vehicle technology. In: 2015 12th International Conference on Informatics in Control, Automation and Robotics (ICINCO), pp. 191–198 (2015)
2. Memon, Q., Ahmed, M., Ali, S., Memon, A.R., Shah, W.: Self-driving and driver relaxing vehicle. In: 2016 2nd International Conference on Robotics and Artificial Intelligence (ICRAI) (2016). https://doi.org/10.1109/icrai.2016.7791248
3. Flämig, H.: Autonomous vehicles and autonomous driving in freight transport. In: Maurer, M., Gerdes, J.C., Lenz, B., Winner, H. (eds.) Autonomous Driving, pp. 365–385. Springer, Heidelberg (2016). https://doi.org/10.1007/978-3-662-48847-8_18
4. Blaga, B.-C.-Z., Deac, M.-A., Al-doori, R.W.Y., Negru, M., Danescu, R.: Miniature autonomous vehicle development on Raspberry Pi. In: 2018 IEEE 14th International Conference on Intelligent Computer Communication and Processing (ICCP) (2018). https://doi.org/10.1109/iccp.2018.8516589
5. Pire, T., Cristoforis, P.D., Nitsche, M., Jacobo Berlles, J.: Stereo vision obstacle avoidance using depth and elevation maps. In: IEEE RAS Summer School on "Robot Vision and Applications". VI Latin American Summer School on Robotics, Santiago, Chile At: Santiago, Chile (2012)
6. Peng, Y., Qu, D., Zhong, Y., Xie, S., Luo, J., Gu, J.: The obstacle detection and obstacle avoidance algorithm based on 2-D lidar. In: 2015 IEEE International Conference on Information and Automation (2015). https://doi.org/10.1109/icinfa.2015.7279550
7. Takahashi, M., Kobayashi, K., Watanabe, K., Kinoshita, T.: Development of prediction based emergency obstacle avoidance module by using LIDAR for mobile robot. In: 2014 Joint 7th International Conference on Soft Computing and Intelligent Systems (SCIS) and 15th International Symposium on Advanced Intelligent Systems (ISIS) (2014). https://doi.org/10.1109/scis-isis.2014.7044725
8. Budiharto, W.: Intelligent surveillance robot with obstacle avoidance capabilities using neural network. Comput. Intell. Neurosci. **2015**, 1–5 (2015). https://doi.org/10.1155/2015/745823

Fast Implementation of AES Modes Based on Turing Architecture

Garvit Chugh[1]([⊠]) [iD], Samanyu A. Saji[1], and Nitesh Singh Bhati[2]

[1] Indian Institute of Technology, Jodhpur, India
{chugh.2,saji.2}@iitj.ac.in
[2] Delhi Technical Campus, GGSIPU, Greater Noida, Delhi, India

Abstract. With high-level computing facilities starting to become more affordable, there is a notable rise in the use of Graphics Processing Unit (GPU) for applications in general. A GPU is and has always been considered a co-processor and hardware with high cost-performance. It has also been seen that FPGA implementation of encryption is slower than GPGPU implementation. Therefore, the implementation of various cryptographic modules on GPU is becoming more and more popular among researchers. This paper aims to propose and test a fast implementation of AES, and its multiple modes like ECB, CBC, CTR on the latest Turing Architecture based GPUs and compare its performance with its predecessor Pascal Architecture based GPUs. The results gathered from the experiments show that the output comparisons of ECB and CTR mode make it clear that the ability to parallelize directly affects the throughput. The Turing architecture has undoubtedly provided a tremendous amount of hardware acceleration and provided high results on even a medium-range GPU like the 1650.

Keywords: AES · Turing · GPU · ECB · CBC · CTR · Encryption

1 Introduction

With the rise of IoT and Cloud computing service technology, the amount of user data and file data that needs to be managed and transmitted has risen significantly. To keep people's personal information safe, it is important to encrypt it in a way that is both safe and quick. Because servers that handle a lot of clients or IoT devices need to encrypt a lot of data quickly without sacrificing service quality, Graphic Processing Units (GPUs) have been thought of as a good candidate for a crypto accelerator in this case. This is because GPUs can handle a lot of data quickly without sacrificing service quality.

New graphic hardware technologies are allowing Graphics Processing Unit (GPU) to allow more computations at a faster speed of processing. For instance, it can process floating point operations at a faster rate than a Central Processing Unit (CPU). Also, it is able to offload some of the intensive code onto itself from the CPU and provides extra support to the CPU, and accelerates the process. GPGPU (general-purpose computation on GPUs) initiated the area of research for GPU-based encryption as it led to a new

© The Author(s), under exclusive license to Springer Nature Switzerland AG 2022
V. Sugumaran et al. (Eds.): AIR 2022, CCIS 1738, pp. 479–489, 2022.
https://doi.org/10.1007/978-3-031-23724-9_44

shift in the paradigm where the CPUs are not heavily dependent on every non-graphic application. Some of the work could be offloaded to the GPUs.

Modern GPUs are nowadays even more effective than general CPUs due to the parallel-based structure and usage of hundreds of small cores as compared to a few cores in a CPU. Also, memory bandwidth is an essential factor, as the processing speed of many applications is based on how fast the data can be transferred from the memory to the processor, and GPUs have been operating at a memory bandwidth approximately six times higher than that of the CPUs. Older GPUs like the GeForce 8800 GTX has been working at 85 GB/s and moving to a more recent GPU like GTX680, and it operates with speed up to 200 GB/s.

In this paper, we will look at the most recent architecture for the GPUs provided by NVIDIA, which is the Turing Architecture. The aim of building such an architecture was to provide the world with real-time rasterization of graphics for improved ray tracing and deep learning. The new Turing based GPUs provide fundamental advancements such as improved efficiency in streaming multiprocessors, a tensor core for AI needs, and an RT core for ray tracing purposes. This is possible due to the fact that the Turing architecture consists of 18.6 billion transistors in a 12-nm process, including several thousand programmable processing elements, industry-first support for GDDR6 memory, and high-bandwidth NVLink for multi-GPU connectivity.

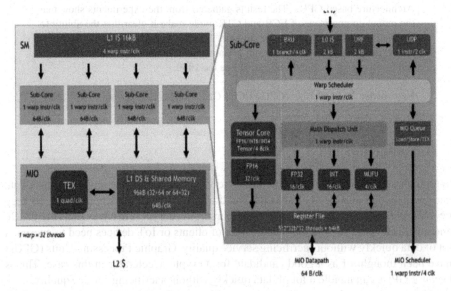

Fig. 1. Turing GPU architecture

As shown in Fig. 1, the Turing GPU SM comprises four sub-cores and a memory interface (MIO). Math throughput, memory bandwidth, L1 data cache topology, register file, cache capacity, and a new uniform data path. These were all de-signed or modified to increase processor efficiency over the previous generation. These features help improve the high-performance computing capabilities of the GPU; these are further explained below [1].

1.1 Enhanced L1 Data Cache

Turing Architecture has incorporated twice the number of instruction schedulers, providing a simplified issue logic and creating a low latency-based, large, and fast L1 cache. It can be seen in the left part of Fig. 1 [2].

1.2 Execution of Floating Point and Integer in a Concurrent Manner

The register file capacity has been doubled in this new architecture inside each of the four sub-cores, and a fast FP16 Math module has been introduced. With these advancements, 36 integer instructions can co execute with every 100 floating-point instructions [2].

1.3 Uniform Datapath and Uniform Register File

In Turing, the control flow resides in each SIMT thread. In contrast, in comparison to the older chips, the control flow lives in the scalar thread, and it depends on the developer to write the code in such a way that promotes parallelism and uniformity [2].

This work presents an improved implementation of The Advanced Encryption Standard (AES) and its various modes on a GPU and the comparison of its improvement on the Turing Architecture based GPUs as compared to the previous generation's, i.e., Pascal-based GPUs.

The more popular and widely adopted symmetric encryption algorithm likely to be encountered nowadays is the Advanced Encryption Standard (AES). It is a Symmetric-key symmetric block cipher, and it is found at least six times faster than triple DES, which was designed to overcome vulnerability against exhaustive key search attack, but it was found slow. AES is an iterative rather than a Feistel cipher. It is based on a 'substitution–permutation network.' It comprises a series of linked operations, some involving replacing inputs with specific outputs (substitutions), and others include shuffling bits around (permutations).

Interestingly, AES performs all its computations on bytes rather than bits. Hence, AES treats the 128 bits of a plaintext block as 16 bytes. These 16 bytes are arranged in four columns and four rows for processing as a matrix.

The performance of AES can be mainly attributed to the mode being used. If a mode does not depend on the previous cipher text and each plaintext block is run in parallel with different threads, there is a chance of producing a better result. Another important dependency is its key and the tables; however, you cannot exactly change much of it. Therefore, in order to improve AES performance, it is seen that table values, plain text, and key values are imported to the shared memory area, which reduces the data fetching time, and moving it to the registers may further improve the performance. Still, the size of the data is more than the typical size of registers, so it is not possible in a single go.

Since the only possibility of improving the speed of the AES technique is through modes, this work is based on the three modes of AES, namely Electronic Code Book, Cipher Block Chaining, Counter.

1.4 Electronic Code Block (ECB)

ECB is a quite simple mode of encryption in which one has a 16-byte block of data, and the electronic codebook will just encrypt those 16 bytes. It is a more straightforward mode in the sense that there's no initialization vector or counter involved, so it's a simple operation and very easy to implement. ECB is an excellent mode for working with raw chunks of data. It does have some limitations in database applications; for instance, if you have a database application that is using small amounts of data, maybe a four-byte pin code or something relatively small, and you need to encrypt it. Generally, you would not use ECB mode to do that encryption; you would like to use a mode that uses an initialization vector or a counter to generate some additional variance in the encrypted values.

1.5 Cipher Block Chaining (CBC)

This is a mode that is very commonly used in database encryption. It takes a 16-byte block of data and applies an encryption key to it but in CBC mode also uses an initialization vector, and then the encryption happens, and you get an encrypted block of data which is good in database applications because we're getting some variance through the initialization vector so even if one tried to encrypt the same credit card number for example twice with CBC mode it'd get a different result. Therefore, the security in a database application is more robust when one uses a CBC mode, and for that very reason, it's very commonly used in applications that are encrypting a data-base, for instance, Microsoft sequel server or Oracle or db2 or MySQL databases.

1.6 Counter (CTR)

Counter mode or CTR mode, in some respects, is like the cipher block chaining in the sense that we have a chunk of data and we have an encryption key. We have an initialization vector, but, in this case, we call it a counter, and we combine those to encrypt our data. In order to perform decryption, the counter mode operates on each 16-byte block of data and produces the outputs that are not typically chained together. The initialization vector in this mode, as its name implies, is usually a counter starting with 0 or 1 and then 2, then 3, then four, and so it increments like that. A nice thing about the counter mode is that it's one of the modes of encryption that allows truncation, so if you have your 4-byte pin code and you want to encrypt that and store it as 4 bits, counter mode gives you the ability to do that.

The remaining section of this research work has been organized as follows. Section 2 explains the literature review of various experiments conducted on different GPU architectures with the same AES modes; Sect. 3 describes brief information regarding applied approaches and the proposed methodology; Sect. 4 presents the comparative study of the results; and Sect. 5 provides the conclusion and future work.

2   Related Work

Many researchers have extensively explored various characteristics of GPU and various encryption schemes on it. Using GPUs instead of CPUs or with an alliance of both, many encryption algorithms have seen a faster implementation. In this section, those works will be reviewed, followed by an analysis of the same.

Hon-Sang and Wai-Kong [3] performed a similar experiment on the grounds of implementing a faster version of block ciphers on the GPU; they used the Kepler Architecture of the GPU to conduct their investigation. They achieved encryption throughput of 90.3 Gbps, 50.82 Gbps, and 83.71 Gbps for IDEA, Blowfish, and Threefish, respectively.

Barlas et al. [4] conducted an experiment on their proposed framework, which can help optimally consolidate CPU and GPU resources for the encryption or decryption of block ciphers such as the AES. Their framework, based on the results of their experiment, proved to be a better dynamic load balancer.

Che et al. [5] performed an experiment aiming to test the potential of CUDA in terms of performance when compared with single-threaded and OpenMP-based multi-threaded CPU computation. The results of their investigation show how developers are currently being forced to fine-tune their code in accordance with the CPU and its shortcomings.

Lee et al. [6] presented techniques to accelerate block ciphers such as the AES. They performed their experiment on the Maxwell architecture-based GPUs. Their proposed techniques consist of new methods of placement of the encryption keys and TBox in the memory. Their techniques provided improved parallel granularity be-tween the CPU and GPU as well. Their experiments fetched results such as high encryption speed with 149 Gbps (AES-128), 143 Gbps (CAST-128), 124 Gbps (Camelia), 112 Gbps (SEED), 149 Gbps (IDEA), 111 Gbps (Blowfish), and 197 Gbps (Threefish).

Nishikawa et al. [7] performed a similar experiment to Che et al. [3] as they performed a series of investigations on various encryption techniques such as the AES, Camellia, CIPHERUNICORN-A, and Hierocrypt-3 and tested their performance on the CUDA architecture-based CPU. The results of their experiments showed that the Fermi architecture provides more suitable and practical use for cryptographic accelerators than conventional GT200 architectures.

Le et al. [8] proposed that the current implementations of AES and DES are suffering from CPU resource consumption, and it does not provide very high throughput. Therefore, their experiments are based on a new AES implementation that is based on the parallel capabilities of the more unique GPU architectures. The results of their experiments show that using a GPU accelerates the process of AES.

Abdelrahman et al. [9] proposed an experiment that tries to improve the condition between the CPU and GPU data transfer overhead using the Pascal Architecture of the current GPUs. Their investigation is based on two different techniques, namely the streaming technique and the unified memory technique. Their results fetched speeds of 80 Gbps using the streaming technique. Also, they achieved 280 Gbps Kernel throughput using 32bytes/thread granularity and shared memory key storage.

Mei et al. [10] presented an alternate way of arranging the memory spaces in the CUDA architecture in order to overcome the extra communication delay of the architecture. This additional modification allowed the GPU to overcome the limitations of working only with highly intensive applications and incorporate lite applications as well. The CUDA architecture can act as an accelerator for even more applications.

Biryukov and Großschädl [11] performed cryptanalysis on the usage of GPU for encryption techniques such as the AES. Their experiment showed that in the current scenario, a throughput of 1012 AES operations per second could be reached. If any organization wants to break this AES, they would have to make a supercomputer based on a similar processor architecture, then using RKC, they can break the system, but it would take a lot of time, for instance, a full year.

An and Seo [12] performed a similar experiment to ours, but they performed extra steps to optimize memory and kernel parallelism and CUDA stream. Their main focus was to improve the functioning of the core implementation of all the AES modes. Their investigation on the RTX 2070 GPU provided results like 10% to 67% improvement in the throughput.

3 Proposed Methodology

The major focus of this work is to test the proposed methodology of various modes of AES on the Turing architecture-based GPUs and compare the results with its predecessor, the Pascal architecture.

The focus is given to the AES-256 implementation due to the consideration of the security point of view, as lower key size can directly affect security. The initial part of this analysis mainly focused on implementing a simple, single-threaded implementation, in order to get a clear picture about the AES algorithm and to check for its correctness. This simple adaptation of textbook AES showed the inefficiency of running a large-sized input, and the issue with the ECB mode of operation. An increase in the size of data to be encrypted led to longer waiting times for encryption. Also, we tried recreating a famous example showcasing the vulnerability of the ECB mode, where we encrypt an image of Tux, the penguin (Fig. 2), using ECB and CBC modes. This proves to be an excellent example in showing the issue with independent block operations.

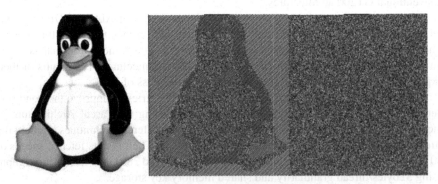

Fig. 2. Tux the penguin, encrypted using ECB and CBC modes respectively

However, it is evident that ECB is capable of supporting parallelization, whereas CBC is not able to do so for encryption. The parallel execution ability of the CPU was tested next, when we tried to run the same code using multi-threading. Two approaches were followed for multi-threading; pthread and openMP. Both produced better timings compared to the initial naive implementation for ECB. However, pthread was seen to take more time for the completion of execution compared to openMP. OpenMP was also cleaner to implement due its simple code syntax. Multi-threading was not an option for CBC encryption due to its serial behaviour. However, parallelization was possible for decryption. CBC Decryption was seen to give a throughput similar to the parallel ECB.

In order to better understand the GPU performance, it is necessary to have a better context about the working of both CPUs and GPUs. The most important difference between them is their design goal itself. CPUs were designed to manage heterogeneous tasks as quickly as possible, and are limited by the amount of concurrency that they can provide. GPUs were designed by keeping concurrency in mind. It usually has hundreds of cores, which can run concurrently. They are more concentrated in improving performance for parallel, computation-intensive applications. CPUs are more versatile in nature, with elaborate ISAs, and the ability to handle multiple tasks like I/O. The parallel performing ability of GPUs makes them a favourite for both graphical and non-graphical applications like high-resolution video-image renderings, ML and AI, and cryptocurrency-based applications.

The first important task to be implemented in the GPU was the naive algorithm. Initially, all the works were carried out using ECB implementation, because of its simplicity. All the sub-functions used were directly converted into CUDA based code here. Every important AES algorithm functions, like SubstituteBytes(), AddRoundKey(), ShiftRows(), MixColumns(), and their corresponding inverses were declared as '__device__'. This essentially means that these computations have to be done in the GPU device itself. Yet another special keyword is '__global__', to notify that this function could be run on the device and called from the host code itself. So, __global__ acts as an interface to __device__ functions. This initial implementation on GPU was direct, with it making use of thousands of cores of the GPU. We see an immediate difference in the overall performance of the output as the size of input data increases. We see that at a point of above 14 KB, the GPU overtakes CPU in terms of performance throughput, and increases the margin in an exponential fashion.

More improvements were added to this basic implementation. We have gone with the idea of allocating a single block, that is, 16 bytes to a single thread. This model of execution is seen as very efficient for parallelizable modes (ECB and CTR). As soon as the thread is allocated to a particular block, we will be able to move the block contents to the register and do the execution privately. This however, is not suitable for the other modes like CBC, specifically in the encryption point of view. So, in order to make that possible, we had tried to share the data between threads and achieve synchronization. However, this didn't provide correct results, and we were forced to use CPU for the encryption part. This significantly reduces the throughput. However, the decryption could be done in parallel, and hence its throughput is in similar ranges with CTR/ECB modes.

An obvious improvement is the addition of the t-tables. Bringing in T-tables can significantly bring down computation requirements. Hence it is added to the constant memory of the GPU for quicker access. Another extensively used item as far as AES is concerned, are the round keys for encryption and decryption. Since they don't change constantly, one of the first things that can be done during execution is to expand and store the keys in the constant memory. These improvements result in the final output of the implementation.

4 Comparison and Analysis

On paper, the Turing architecture has the following differences when compared to the Pascal architecture:

- Twice the register file capacity.
- Improved SIMT model and branch unit.
- Concurrent Floating Point and Int instructions.
- Uniform Registers and Datapath.
- New Tensor Core.
- Fast FP16 Math core.

We conducted our experiment on the Ubuntu operating system for all the architectures, rest of the details are mentioned in the Table 1. The results for the schemes implemented are mentioned below in Tables 2, 3, 4 and 5 respectively.

Table 1. System configurations

S. No.	Architecture	Configuration
1.	Pascal	CPU: Core i5-7200U processor, 2.50GHz*4 GPU: NVIDIA Geforce 940MX Graphics GDDR5 VRAM Memory: 8GiB OS: Pop_OS 20.10, 64 bits V11.0.221
2.	Turing	CPU: AMD Ryzen 7 4800HS @ 2.9GHz × 16 GPU: GeForce GTX 1650 Ti Memory: 16GiB OS: Pop_OS 20.10, 64 bits V11.0.221

Table 2. Results based on Pascal architecture for encryption

MODE	ECB		CTR		CBC	
Size (bytes)	Time (s)	Throughput (in Gbps)	Time (s)	Throughput (in Gbps)	Time (s)	Throughput (in Gbps)
1202	0.154655	0.006320	0.152444	0.000356	0.001253	0.000251
4652	0.156666	0.007555	0.145636	0.001120	0.001354	0.005643
9302	0.156963	0.086552	0.154236	0.013655	0.001698	0.009145
18602	0.158001	0.095222	0.156003	0.056465	0.002365	0.012644
37202	0.158005	0.155422	0.156895	0.954410	0.002954	0.064848
74402	0.163212	0.198433	0.159254	0.987999	0.005621	0.094122
148802	0.163333	0.436217	0.163544	0.999788	0.008952	0.112145
297602	0.212544	1.036520	0.165445	1.123335	0.035611	0.125440
595202	0.221532	1.254602	0.212333	1.365421	0.046211	0.135410
1190402	0.245645	2.365412	0.245888	1.958752	0.076599	0.087845
94371750	0.313564	2.899945	0.325444	3.564211	3.698745	0.114455
188743501	0.623644	3.215554	0.598788	5.369987	6.398745	0.102365

Table 3. Results based on Pascal architecture for decryption

MODE	ECB		CTR		CBC	
Size (bytes)	Time (s)	Throughput (in Gbps)	Time (s)	Throughput (in Gbps)	Time (s)	Throughput (in Gbps)
1202	0.002321	0.006354	0.002321	0.002112	0.001425	0.003411
4652	0.002455	0.006988	0.002541	0.002345	0.003651	0.003478
9302	0.002547	0.016541	0.002799	0.006441	0.003689	0.006987
18602	0.003651	0.135887	0.003621	0.012523	0.014981	0.011811
37202	0.004522	0.198745	0.006545	0.023541	0.019841	0.026144
74402	0.004769	0.365412	0.007566	0.095412	0.051431	0.131119
148802	0.004968	0.456223	0.009864	0.132454	0.098746	0.269874
297602	0.005465	0.765321	0.009978	0.564122	0.098991	0.798474
595202	0.009987	1.123564	0.012541	0.987121	0.122114	1.123989
1190402	0.012562	1.987452	0.016879	1.378111	0.165771	1.698799
94371750	0.265422	2.598744	0.076954	2.634577	0.219711	3.246987
188743501	0.465221	4.125451	0.135412	4.325122	0.498754	4.369874

Table 4. Results based on Turing architecture for encryption

MODE	ECB		CTR		CBC	
Size (bytes)	Time (s)	Throughput (in Gbps)	Time (s)	Throughput (in Gbps)	Time (s)	Throughput (in Gbps)
1202	0.000547	0.017609	0.001020	0.009443	0.000069	0.139362
4652	0.000710	0.052552	0.000724	0.051536	0.000333	0.111760
9302	0.000682	0.109185	0.000856	0.086991	0.000513	0.145060
18602	0.000540	0.275733	0.000733	0.203132	0.001033	0.144062
37202	0.000873	0.340930	0.000495	0.601277	0.002059	0.144544
74402	0.000855	0.696178	0.000812	0.733044	0.004198	0.141786
148802	0.000856	1.390692	0.000855	1.392318	0.004576	0.260143
297602	0.001135	2.097649	0.001455	1.636311	0.015914	0.149605
595202	0.001365	3.488375	0.001661	2.866726	0.034444	0.138242
1190402	0.001719	5.539984	0.002637	3.611389	0.060242	0.158083
94371750	0.155665	4.849992	0.118392	6.316770	2.932362	0.257463
188743501	0.313270	4.819958	0.240282	6.284067	5.832434	0.258892

In Table 4, we can see that the multithreaded CPU's performance varies in between .11 Gbps and .18 Gbps. Very large size of inputs like that above 50 MB was seen to increase the throughput above 0.25 Gbps. It maintained a range of values between 0.2 Gbps and 0.27 Gbps.

Table 5. Results based on Turing architecture for decryption

MODE	ECB		CTR		CBC	
Size (bytes)	Time (s)	Throughput (in Gbps)	Time (s)	Throughput (in Gbps)	Time (s)	Throughput (in Gbps)
1202	0.000898	0.010726	0.000753	0.012792	0.000914	0.010538
4652	0.000694	0.053784	0.000376	0.098449	0.000333	0.116600
9302	0.000734	0.101450	0.000612	0.121673	0.000717	0.103855
18602	0.000357	0.417076	0.001109	0.134261	0.000647	0.230133
37202	0.000702	0.423977	0.000807	0.368813	0.000743	0.400581
74402	0.000855	0.626560	0.000864	0.688926	0.000795	0.748719
148802	0.000649	1.834256	0.000929	1.281412	0.000904	1.316850
297602	0.001451	1.640822	0.001455	1.636311	0.001124	2.118178
595202	0.001594	2.987222	0.001835	2.594895	0.001815	2.623489
1190402	0.002514	3.788080	0.002925	3.838465	0.002431	3.917413
94371750	0.125035	6.038102	0.118392	6.376901	0.103977	6.017360
188743501	0.249472	6.052575	0.238630	6.327570	0.208918	6.115998

5 Conclusion

In this paper, a benchmarking approach has been proposed for AES implementation tailor made for the Turing architecture-based GPUs. The various modes of AES, namely ECB, CTR and CBC have been tested in this experiment, for both, encryption and decryption. The results and the work provided will help readers to get a clear understanding of the usage of GPU in an overall system apart from the AES implementation on the same. The results of the experiment show that even though the CBC mode was not used in a parallel mode here, the output comparisons of ECB and CTR makes it clear that the ability to parallelize has a direct effect on the throughput. Hence, CTR mode can be easily considered as an alternative to ECB mode, whereas CBC's support for parallel decryption still makes it a worthy candidate for the same. Also, the Turing architecture has surely provided a tremendous amount of hardware acceleration and provided high results on even a medium range GPU like the 1650.

We looked into how to make block cypher algorithms run faster on different types of GPUs. In the future, we will try to improve public-key algorithms in the GPU environment. As a result, it can be thought of as being useful in places like cloud computing services and IoT edge computing services, etc.

References

1. Burgess, J.: RTX on – the NVIDIA Turing GPU. In: 2019 IEEE Hot Chips 31 Symposium (HCS) (2019). https://doi.org/10.1109/hotchips.2019.8875651
2. Burgess, J.: RTX on—The NVIDIA Turing GPU. IEEE Micro **40**, 36–44 (2020). https://doi.org/10.1109/mm.2020.2971677
3. Cheong, H.-S., Lee, W.-K.: Fast implementation of block ciphers and PRNGs for Kepler GPU architecture. In: 2015 5th International Conference on IT Convergence and Security (ICITCS) (2015). https://doi.org/10.1109/icitcs.2015.7292982
4. Barlas, G., Hassan, A., Jundi, Y.A.: An analytical approach to the design of parallel block cipher encryption/decryption: a CPU/GPU case study. In: 2011 19th International Euromicro Conference on Parallel, Distributed and Network-Based Processing (2011). https://doi.org/10.1109/pdp.2011.51
5. Che, S., Boyer, M., Meng, J., Tarjan, D., Sheaffer, J.W., Skadron, K.: A performance study of general-purpose applications on graphics processors using CUDA. J. Parallel Distrib. Comput. **68**, 1370–1380 (2008). https://doi.org/10.1016/j.jpdc.2008.05.014

6. Lee, W.-K., Cheong, H.-S., Phan, R.-W., Goi, B.-M.: Fast implementation of block ciphers and PRNGs in Maxwell GPU architecture. Clust. Comput. **19**, 335–347 (2016). https://doi.org/10.1007/s10586-016-0536-2

7. Nishikawa, N., Iwai, K., Kurokawa, T.: High-performance symmetric block ciphers on CUDA. In: 2011 Second International Conference on Networking and Computing (2011). https://doi.org/10.1109/icnc.2011.40

8. Le, D., Chang, J., Gou, X., Zhang, A., Lu, C.: Parallel AES algorithm for fast data encryption on GPU. In: 2010 2nd International Conference on Computer Engineering and Technology (2010). https://doi.org/10.1109/iccet.2010.5486259

9. Abdelrahman, A.A., Dahshan, H., Salama, G.I.: Enhancing the actual throughput of the AES algorithm on the Pascal GPU architecture. In: 2018 3rd International Conference on System Reliability and Safety (ICSRS) (2018). https://doi.org/10.1109/icsrs.2018.8688724

10. Mei, C., Jiang, H., Jenness, J.: CUDA-based AES parallelization with fine-tuned GPU memory utilization. In: 2010 IEEE International Symposium on Parallel & Distributed Processing, Workshops and Ph.D. Forum (IPDPSW) (2010). https://doi.org/10.1109/ipdpsw.2010.5470766

11. Biryukov, A., Großschädl, J.: Cryptanalysis of the full AES using GPU-like special-purpose hardware. Fund. Inform. **114**, 221–237 (2012). https://doi.org/10.3233/fi-2012-626

12. An, S., Seo, S.C.: Highly efficient implementation of block ciphers on graphic processing units for massively large data. Appl. Sci. **10**, 3711 (2020). https://doi.org/10.3390/app10113711

N-Dimensional Structure: A Data Structure with Fast Access and Sorting of Integers

Harshit Gupta[1], Shruti Gupta[1]([⊠]) [iD], and Akash Punhani[2]

[1] ABES Engineering College, Ghaziabad, India
shrutigupta.it@gmail.com

[2] SRM Institute of Science and Technology, Modinagar, Ghaziabad, U.P., India

Abstract. Various Data Structures have been introduced till date that aim at either to improve them in terms of time or space complexity or they are particularly designed for some special applications. This work aims at developing a new data structure that takes the idea of plotting each digit to another dimension and thereby reducing the access time for keys stored in it. In order to make it practical to implement, a tree-based approach has been used to store it in the memory. The asymptotic time complexity is $O(nu)$ for extracting the keys in sorted order where u is the size of universe. In practical testing, the procedure took much less time to complete as compared to Merge Sort which is the best Comparison based Sorting Technique in terms of worst-case time complexity. This work discusses the concept, implementation and algorithms associated with the data structure. Then it evaluates it against various test scenarios with other sorting techniques.

Keywords: Data structure · Algorithm · Sorting · Efficiency · Fast access · Time complexity · Optimization

1 Introduction

Data structures have been in use since the beginning of the era of computers. There have been various advancements in the field since then which continue till date. The aim is either to improve them in terms of time or space complexity or they are particularly designed for some special applications with pre implemented methods that makes it easy to use and prevents the user from getting deep inside the complexities of implementation of methods. Unlike most algorithmic issues, "linear time" is too slow; we can't afford to scan the complete data structure to answer a single query—and the goal is usually logarithmic or even constant query time. Also, because the data corpus is usually huge, space becomes a pressing concern, and you don't generally want a data structure that is larger than the data. However, these days, storage is becoming cheaper on the other hand we want to answer queries at a fast rate.

This work proposes a new data structure which can be used to sort numbers or retrieve sorted list of numbers from it in less or at least similar asymptotic time as compared to pre-existing sorting techniques including algorithms and data structures with pre implemented extract procedures and search time which is independent of number of

© The Author(s), under exclusive license to Springer Nature Switzerland AG 2022
V. Sugumaran et al. (Eds.): AIR 2022, CCIS 1738, pp. 490–509, 2022.
https://doi.org/10.1007/978-3-031-23724-9_45

elements present in the data structure in terms of time complexity which is definitely much less than "linear time" in practical implementation.

This paper is organized into the following manner:

First, it discusses the concept and idea behind this data structure and plotting of numbers in a space and the basic idea to store it in memory using a direct intuitive array based implementation of the data structure.

We propose the tree base implementation of the data structure along with all the methods associated with it for insertion, deletion and search of elements, and then finally the extract sorted method for sorting numbers using the data structure.

Then, we evaluate our methods against benchmarks. Experimental Results show that proposed structure outperforms many pre-existing algorithms for the purpose of searching.

2   Literature Review

Tries were proposed in 1960 [1] that are used for storing alphabetical words in a corpus with an efficient search complexity. Bitwise Tries have also been used since a long time. Individual bits are utilized to traverse what basically becomes a sort of binary tree in bitwise attempts, which are similar to character-based trie. Although this procedure appears to be slow, it is cache-local and extremely parallelizable due to the lack of register dependencies, and as a result, it performs quite well on recent out-of-order execution CPUs. In [2], Huang et al. proposed a multi-block bitwise trie structure for exact r-neighbour search in hamming space. Bucket sort is another sorting technique being used for optimal sorting but it is not suitable everywhere. Bucket sort divides the data pieces to be sorted into buckets, which are subsequently sorted individually using any other sorting approach or by recursive application of the bucket sort technique itself. The difficulty of a bucket sort is determined by the number of buckets utilised, the technique used to sort each bucket, and the uniformity of the data items' distribution. A stable sorting technique was introduced in [3] which a novel technique for sorting large scale data. Its primary aim was to check sorted big numbers however it performed better than quick sort and similar sorting techniques for sorted numbers. Apart from Merge Sort itself, tim sort was introduced which has been analysed in [4] which improves over merge sort modifying its performance in terms of time complexity in some scenarios.

Keshav Bajpai in [5] proposed an efficient version of counting sort that reduced the sorting time to half from counting sort for an array of 10,000 integers. In 2002, a new randomized sorting algorithm [6] was proposed sorting n integers in O(n/spl radic/(log log n)) expected time and linear space. Another algorithm for integer sorting was proposed in 2001, which claimed to sort n integers in linear space in O(n log log n log log log n) time. Under certain conditions, it claimed to have a time complexity of O(n log log n) [7].

Apart from the various proposed algorithms, only few get used frequently considering there practical limitations and performance. Timsort is a modified version of merge sort that is used internally by Java and Python for there default sorting algorithm. It has the best case complexity of O(n) and a worst case time complexity of O(log n). Its complexity analysis has been done in this paper [8].

In [9], Kumar et al. proposed a new sorting algorithm called recombination Sort which is derived from the recombination of cardinal principles from a number of different sorting methods. Radix sort's ability to deal with each digit of a number separately, counting sort's concept of counting the number of occurrences of elements, bucketing from bucket sort, and hashing a number to a multidimensional space are all combined to form a single sorting algorithm that outperforms its parent algorithms. For the best, average, and worst situations, the time complexity of the proposed Recombinant Sort was expected to be $O(n + k)$. In the worst-case situation, the k in $O(n + k)$ will become n, but n's order will never approach two, i.e., k will never approach n^2.

Moving on from sorting algorithms and looking at some data structures, Burst tries [10] were proposed in 2002 which claimed to be fast and efficient data structure for string keys. However, integers can be converted to strings and stored in the same. Self balancing trees like AVL, Red Black Tree, B Trees [11] have been used in database systems for indexing keys which have search complexity in the order of $O(\log n)$ and insert complexity $O(\log n)$. Numbers can be retrieved from the data structure in $O(n)$. So, they have an $O(\log n)$ time complexity for sorting numbers. There detailed evaluation has been done in this article [12]. A workshop proceeding [13] proposed various efficient data structures for storing partitions of n integer, however the best time complexity for them was $O(n^2)$. A dynamic integer set [14] was proposed in 2014 which had $O(n)$ space complexity and $O(\log n)$ time complexity for main set operations like insertion, deletion, predecessor/In 2019, FASTSET [15] was proposed which claimed to have optimal performance for most of the commonly used set operations claiming that previously existing sets had at least one non-optimal operation. The author also, compared it with the inbuilt set of Java collections implementation. In 2021, new data structures were proposed for orthogonal range reporting and range minimum queries in [16]. It proposed a data structure that can be used for 2-D orthogonal range minima queries in $O(n)$ and and $O(\log \epsilon n)$ time, where number of points is represented by n in the data structure and ϵ is an arbitrarily small positive constant. A sorting algorithm was also proposed in 2021 in [17] which proposed a parallel multi-deque sorting algorithm. In 2017, A paper introduced an implementation and statistical comparison of different edge detection techniques like Prewitt, Sobel and Robert [18]. It was developed on the top of Multi-Stack Sort enhancing the performance while getting rid of the weakness of MSP Sort. It was primarily for multi-core CPUs and GPUs. In 2021, an energy efficient enhancement for prediction-base scheduling was proposed which helps in the network lifetime improvement in WSNs [19]. In 2019, another efficient sorting algorithm was introduced for non-volatile memory which claimed to outperform many other sorting algorithms in terms of execution time and non-volatile memory writes [20].

There have been various sorting algorithms introduced till date that have various properties associated with themselves namely Bubble Sort, Quick Sort, Heap Sort, Insertion Sort, Merge Sort, etc. Though, this paper doesn't propose exactly a sorting algorithm, but a data structure that can be used to sort numbers. Just like heap sort (analysed in the cited paper) [21] uses heap data structure to extract numbers in a sorted manner.

3 Methodology

3.1 U-Dimensional Space

The idea behind this new data structure is to plot numbers in a u dimensional space which we like to call a Universe. For a u-dimensional universe, we can plot numbers from 0 to 10^{u-1}. We can think of it as a cartesian u dimensional space where each integer can be represented as a point in the space.

For example, if we take a 3-dimensional space, we can plot numbers from 0–99. We reserve one dimension for storing value 0. Which means each number has value zero in the zeroth dimension. We can say 0 is 000, 1 is 001, 2 is 002, 10 is 010, and 99 is 099. We won't be able to plot 100 in this space because we want the zeroth dimension to be zero always. This might not make sense now but will help us in the implementation phase. Let us now take this 3-d space and plot some numbers. We will only look at the non-zero dimensions here, i.e. first and second dimension here. Let us take some numbers. We will then break them down to dimensions and plot them as given in Table 1.

These numbers plotted in a 3D space while only looking at the non zero dimensions looks like the space as shown in Fig. 1.

3.2 Array Based Implementation

If we try to implement this in a machine, we can use a 2-D array to do this, which is very intuitive. However, this approach is just for a better understating of how the tree-based implementation was derived and to get the intuition behind it. It will look like a table given below. In the array, the first dimension will represent the first non-zero dimension and the second similarly will represent the second non-zero dimension. Hence, we can locate each number in the array using these two dimensions.

Table 1. 3-D equivalent for numbers

Serial number	Integer	Equivalent	Point in 3-dimensions
1	4	004	(0, 0, 4)
2	7	007	(0, 0, 7)
3	12	012	(0, 1, 2)
4	34	034	(0, 3, 4)
5	68	068	(0, 6, 8)
6	91	091	(0, 9, 1)

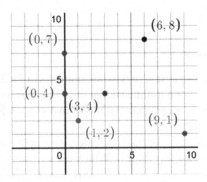

Fig. 1. Numbers plotted in a space

For example, 4 will be found in the array a at a[0][4], 7 will be found in the array a at a[0][7], 34 will be found in the array a at a[3][4], 68 will be found in the array a at a[6][8], 91 will be found in the array a at a[9][1] and so on.

It will be a binary n-dimensional array where it will hold value 1 when the number is present and 0 elsewhere. For holding multiple elements of same number we can instead use it as a counter.

Like if there are multiple copies of 4 say there are 2 4's in the universe, one can set a[0][4] to 2 for this. The sample array for the forementioned numbers is given in Table 2. In the other method, we can use a separate kind of terminal array where it will have a list of elements. It will look like [4, 4] at a [0][4]. The same approach has been implemented in the algorithm section in this report.

Table 2. Array representation of numbers for a u-d space

[x] [y]	[x] [0]	[x] [1]	[x] [2]	[x] [3]	[x] [4]	[x] [5]	[x] [6]	[x] [7]	[x] [8]	[x] [9]
[0] [y]	0	0	0	0	1 (0, 4)	0	0	1 (0, 7)	0	0
[1] [y]	0	0	1 (1, 2)	0	0	0	0	0	0	0
[2] [y]	0	0	0	0	0	0	0	0	0	0
[3] [y]	0	0	0	0	1 (3, 4)	0	0	0	0	0
[4] [y]	0	0	0	0	0	0	0	0	0	0
[5] [y]	0	0	0	0	0	0	0	0	0	0
[6] [y]	0	0	0	0	0	0	0	0	1 (6, 8)	0
[7] [y]	0	0	0	0	0	0	0	0	0	0
[8] [y]	0	0	0	0	0	0	0	0	0	0
[9] [y]	0	1 (9, 1)	0	0	0	0	0	0	0	0

A similar approach can be used to represent any set of numbers and we can generate the array for the same. If we wish to perform various operations in this array say search, insert, delete by key, one can easily do that by accessing the particular dimensions in the increasing order according to the values it should hold. If we want to get a sorted list of all the numbers, we can do so by starting with an empty array, iterating through the dimensions of the u-d array one by one and keep adding to the array whenever we find non zero value in the u-d array.

3.3 Tree Based Implementation

While exploring any non-zero dimension n, the value can be only be an integer in the range of 0 to 9. And if we access next dimension $n + 1$ for any of the value from 0–9, there might be elements only in some of the values for the specific dimension.

For example, in the previous example, there were no elements present for 1st non zero dimension at [2][y], [4][y], [5][y], [7][y], [8][y]. So, we don't need the $n + 1$ and following dimensions where $n = 2, 4, 5, 7, 8$. This fact can be used in saving storage. Though, we will have to change the implementation and use an abstract way to represent the u-d array.

If we treat each dimension as an array of 0–9 of itself and at each of these values, we point them to the next dimension as presented in Tables 3, 4, 5, 6 and 7, then we only need to keep those arrays that have points present in the dimension. Let's say for first dimension we have a 1-d array as given below. At each position in the array we only store one address of the array for the next dimension for the current value of current dimension.

Table 3. Array for first non-zero dimension

[0]	[1]	[2]	[3]	[4]	[5]	[6]	[7]	[8]	[9]
add0	add1	NULL	add3	NULL	NULL	add6	NULL	NULL	add9

Table 4. Array at add0 for value 1 in second non-zero dimension

[0]	[1]	[2]	[3]	[4]	[5]	[6]	[7]	[8]	[9]
0	0	0	0	1	0	0	1	0	0

Table 5. Array at add3 for value 3 in second non-zero dimension

[0]	[1]	[2]	[3]	[4]	[5]	[6]	[7]	[8]	[9]
0	0	0	0	1	0	0	0	0	0

Table 6. Array at add6 for value 6 in second non-zero dimension

[0]	[1]	[2]	[3]	[4]	[5]	[6]	[7]	[8]	[9]
0	0	0	0	0	0	0	0	1	0

Table 7. Array at add9 for value 9 in second non-zero dimension

[0]	[1]	[2]	[3]	[4]	[5]	[6]	[7]	[8]	[9]
0	1	0	0	0	0	0	0	0	0

This way, we didn't have to store empty arrays for 2, 4, 5, 7, 8.

In a similar way, it can be implemented for any number of dimensions. This will ensure memory efficiency and thereby reduce the time complexity of extracting sorted elements from the data structure.

If we look at it, then the structure it represents is sort of a tree, where each tree can have at max 10 children. Because each element of the array points to another array of the next dimension. Each array used in this representation is a node of the tree.

There will be two types of arrays, the ones which are not of the last dimension, and the ones of last dimension. The intermediate dimension nodes will have values of addresses. The terminal or last dimension nodes will store the count of elements present for that number in the particular space or universe.

3.4   Algorithms

In the tree implementation, an object-oriented approach is used. So, in place of directly considering nodes as arrays, objects will be created which will along with the address or count array, will also store the current dimension number and current dimension value. The class diagram for the representation of nodes is given below. Only Universe is the class which is exposed to the user. One can initialize the data structure by initializing the Universe class by selecting the suitable number of dimensions he/she wants. The other too classes are internally initialized by the universe class itself directly or indirectly by Dimension class. The user has access to AddToUniverse(), SearchInUniverse(), DeleteFromUniverse() and ExtractSorted() methods of the Universe class (Fig. 2).

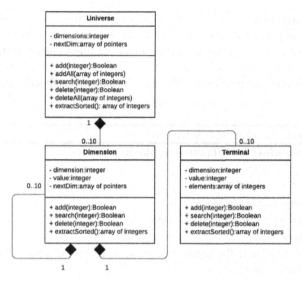

Fig. 2. Class diagram for tree based implementation

Algorithm 1: Add number to Universe

function ADDTOUNIVERSE (universe, num):

1. *numString* ← *string(num)*

2. *numLen* ← *length(numString)*

3. **if** *numLen>universe.dimensions*-1 **do**

4.   **return** False

5. Add to *numString* in the beginning a string with every character '0' of size (*universe.dimensions - numLen*-1)

6. *numValue* ← *numString*

7. *value* ← *int(numValue*[0])

8. **if** *universe.nextDim*[*value*] = NULL **do**

9.   *universe.nextDim*[*value*] ← *Dimension*(1,*value*)

10. **if** *length(numValue*[1:]) = 1 **do**

11.   **return**
    ADDTOTERMINAL(*universe.nextDim*[*value*],*numString*,*numValue*[1:])

12. **else do**

13.   **return**
    ADDTODIMENSION(*universe.nextDim*[*value*],*numString*,*numValue*[1:])

The above Algorithm 1 will be exposed as a member function of the Universe class (the only class exposed to the user). It will take up a number to be inserted into the universe, convert it into a string, add zeroes in the starting to make the length equal to size of the universe. Then, it will extract the first digit from the left and find the next dimension or terminal where it needs to be inserted and give it a function call for addition.

Algorithm 2: Search number in Universe

function SEARCHINUNIVERSE(universe, num):

1. *numString* ← *string(num)*
2. *numLen* ← *length(numString)*
3. **if** *numLen* > *universe.dimensions*-1 **do**
4.   **return** False
5. Add to *numString* in the beginning a string with every character '0' of size (*universe.dimensions- numLen*-1)
6. *numValue* ← *numString*
7. *value* ← *int(numValue[0])*
8. **if** *universe.nextDim[value]*=NULL **do**
9.   **return** False
10. **if** *length(numValue[1:]) = 1* **do**
11.   **return**
         SEARCHINTERMINAL(*universe.nextDim[value],numString,numValue[1:]*)
12. **else do**
13.   **return**
         SEARCHINDIMENSION(*universe.nextDim[value],numString,numValue[1:]*)

The Algorithm 2 will be exposed as a member function of the Universe class. It will take up a number to be inserted into the universe, convert it into a string, add zeroes in the starting to make the length equal to size of the universe. Then, it will extract the first digit from the left and find the next dimension or terminal where it needs to be searched and give it a function call for search.

Algorithm 3: Delete number from Universe

function DELETEFROMUNIVERSE(universe, num):

1. *numString ← string(num)*
2. *numLen ← length*(numString)
3. **if** *numLen>universe.dimensions*-1 **do**
4.   **return** False
5. Add to *numString* in the beginning a string with every character '0' of size (*universe.dimensions- numLen*-1)
6. *numValue ← numString*
7. *value = int(numValue[0])*
8. **if** *universe.nextDim[value]*=NULL **do**
9.   **return** False
10. **if** *length(numValue[1:])* = 1 **do**
11.   **return**
    DELETEFROMTERMINAL(*universe.nextDim[value],numString,numValue[1:]*)
12. **else do**
13.   **return**
    DELETEFROMDIMENSION(*universe.nextDim[value],numString,numValue[1:]*)

The Algorithm 3 will be exposed as a member function of the Universe class. It will take up a number to be inserted into the universe, convert it into a string, add zeroes in the starting to make the length equal to size of the universe. Then, it will extract the first digit from the left and find the next dimension or terminal from where it needs to be deleted and give it a function call for delete.

Algorithm 4: Extract Sorted Numbers from Universe or Dimension

function EXTRACTSORTED (a):

1. *extractSorted ← empty array*
2. **for each** *dimension* **in** *a.nextDim* **do**
3.   **if** *dim* not = NULL **do**
4.   *extractSorted.append(dim.extractSorted())*
5. **return** *extractSorted*

Algorithm 4 will be exposed as a member function of the Universe class. It will iteratively give call to all the next dimensions [0..9] and will keep on appending the results to an array which be initialized beforehand. Finally, this array will be returned.

Algorithm 5: Add number to Dimension

---

function ADDTODIMENSION(dimension, numString, numValue):

1. $value \leftarrow int(numValue[0])$
2. **if** $dimension.nextDim[value]$= NULL **do**
3.   **if** length($numValue$) not =1 **do**
4. $dimension.nextDim[value]$ =   **Dimension**($dimension.dimension$+1,$value$)
5.   **else do**
6. $dimension.nextDim[value]$ =**Terminal**($dimension.dimension$+1,$value$)
7. **if** $length(numValue[1:]) = 1$ **do**
8.   **return**
    ADDTOTERMINAL($universe.nextDim[value]$,$numString$,$numValue[1:]$)
9. **else do**
10.   **return**
    ADDTODIMENSION($universe.nextDim[value]$,$numString$,$numValue[1:]$)

In Algorithm 5 function extracts the first digit from the left from the number and iteratively calls itself for the next dimension for that digit and finally, when only one digit is left, it calls the AddToTerminal function. If there is no next dimension present for some digit, it initializes one.

Algorithm 6: Search number in Dimension

---

function SEARCHINDIMENSION(dimension, numString, numValue):
1. $value \leftarrow int(numValue[0])$
2. **if** $dimension.nextDim[value] = $ NULL **do**
3.   **return** False
4. **if** $length(numValue[1:]) = 1$ **do**
5.   **return**
    SEARCHINTERMINAL($universe.nextDim[value]$,$numString$,$numValue[1:]$)
6. **else do**
7.   **return**
    SEARCHINDIMENSION($universe.nextDim[value]$,$numString$,$numValue[1:]$)

In Algorithm 6 the function extracts the first digit from the left from the number and iteratively calls itself for the next dimension for that digit and finally, when only one digit is left, it calls the SearchInTerminal function.

Algorithm 7: Delete number from Dimension

---

function DELETEFROMDIMENSION(dimension, numString, numValue):
1. *value* ← *int(numValue[0])*
2. **if** *dimension.nextDim[value]* = NULL:
3.   **return** False
4. **if** *length(numValue[1:])* = 1 **do**
5.   **return**
    DELETEFROMTERMINAL(*universe.nextDim[value],numString,numValue[1:]*)
6. **else do**
7.   **return**
    DELETEFROMDIMENSION(*universe.nextDim[value],numString,numValue[1:]*)

In Algorithm 7, the function extracts the first digit from the left from the number and iteratively calls itself for the next dimension for that digit and finally, when only one digit is left, it calls the DeleteFromTerminal function.

Algorithm 8: Add number to terminal

---

function ADDTOTERMINAL(terminal, numString, numValue):
1. *terminal.elements.append(int(numString))*
2. **return** True

In Algorithm 8, the function simply appends the integer value of the number to the member list of the terminal.

Algorithm 9: Search number in terminal

---

function SEARCHINTERMINAL(terminal, numString, numValue):
1. **if** *int(numString)* in *terminal.elements* **do**
2.   **return** *self.elements.search(int(numString))*
3. **else**
4.   **return** False

In Algorithm 9, the described function returns true if the integer value of the number is present in the member list of the terminal.

Algorithm 10: Delete number from terminal

---

function DELETEFROMTERMINAL(terminal, numString, numValue):
1.   **if** *int(numString)* **in** *terminal.elements* **do**
2.   **return** *self.elements.delete(int(numString))*
3.   **else**
4.   **return** False

In Algorithm 10, the function deletes and returns true if the integer value of the number is present in the member list of the terminal otherwise it returns false.

Algorithm 11: Extract sorted numbers from terminal

---

function EXTRACTSORTEDFROMTERMINAL(terminal):
1.   **return** *terminal.elements*

In Algorithm 11, the function returns the array of member elements present in the terminal.

3.5   Theoretical Analysis

The time complexity analysis of various operations performed on the data structure are given in Table 8.

Table 8. Asymptotic time complexity analysis for various operations supported by the proposed data structure

S.No.	Operation	Best case	Average case	Worst case
1	Insert	$\Omega(u)$	$\theta(u)$	$O(u)$
2	Delete	$\Omega(u)$	$\theta(u)$	$O(u)$
3	Search	$\Omega(u)$	$\theta(u)$	$O(u)$
4	Extract sorted numbers	$\Omega(nu)$	$\theta(nu)$	$O(nu)$

The theoretical time complexity analysis of the data structure has been compared for various operations in this section. The X-axis denotes the number of elements present in the data structure. As we move with the X-Axis, the size of the data structure increases. The Y-Axis is a theoretical order denotation of the worst-case time complexity for the specific operation as presented in Fig. 3.

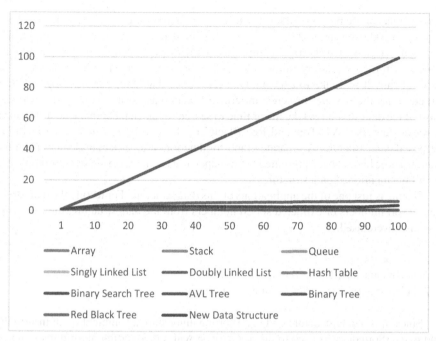

Fig. 3. Time complexity comparison of various data structure for insert operation

The graph in Fig. 4 shows the time complexity analysis for various commonly used data structures for the insertion operation. The Y-Axis here represents the value in which the order of time it will take to execute. As we can see, for some of the data structures, the insertion time complexity goes in linear time while for some, it is very less and we

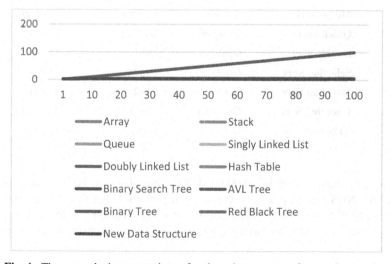

Fig. 4. Time complexity comparison of various data structure for search operation

can see that for the proposed data structure, it lies in the lower level. The size has been kept up to 100 to ensure that the reader can distinguish between the lines in the graph.

Figure 4 presented the time complexity analysis for various commonly used data structures for the search operation. The Y-Axis here represents the value in which the order of time it will take to execute. One can notice that here, that the proposed data structure has the best performance in terms of worst-case search complexity whereas most of the data structures take linear time to search for an element in the data structure. However few like AVL Tree and Red Black Tree have search complexity near to the proposed data structure. A separate graph for deletion of a particular element from the data structure has not been presented in this paper as it is same as to the search complexity for all the mentioned data structures.

Sorting is just one of the applications of this data structure. For testing the data structure to sort numbers or extracted sorted numbers from the data structure, the following test cases were used.

- All elements zero
- All elements sorted from 0 to n − 1
- All elements reverse sorted from n − 1 to 0.

Since, it is a data structure and not a sorting algorithm, a combination of insertAll() and extractSorted() was used to do comparison with other sorting algorithms in terms of time complexity and space complexity. The asymptomatic complexity of both the algorithms is presented in Table 9. Here n is the number of elements present and u is the number of dimensions for the data structure.

Table 9. Asymptotic time complexity analysis for sorting algorithms

S.No.	Algorithm	Best case	Average case	Worst case
1	**Merge Sort**	$\Omega(nlogn)$	$\theta(nlogn)$	$O(nlogn)$
2	**Quick Sort**	$\Omega(nlogn)$	$\theta(nlogn)$	$O(n2)$
3	**Bubble Sort**	$\Omega(n)$	$O(n2)$	$O(n2)$
4	**Selection Sort**	$O(n2)$	$O(n2)$	$O(n2)$
5	**Insertion Sort**	$\Omega(n)$	$O(n2)$	$O(n2)$
6	**Counting Sort**	$\Omega(n+k)$	$\Omega(n+k)$	$\Omega(n+k)$
7	**NDS Sort**	$\Omega(nu)$	$\theta(nu)$	$O(nu)$

If we take numbers up to 10,000,000 the value of u will be 8. Hence for time complexity, NDS Sort in practical scenario will perform better than Merge Sort. This is because NDS Sort is not a comparison-based sorting algorithm. Table 10 shows the space complexity for various sorting algorithms and the u-dimensional data structure.

Table 10. Asymptotic space complexity analysis for sorting algorithms

S.No.	Algorithm	Best case	Average case	Worst case
1	**Merge Sort**	$\Omega(n)$	$\theta(n)$	$O(n)$
2	**Quick Sort**	$\Omega(\log n)$	$\Omega(\log n)$	$O(n)$
3	**Bubble Sort**	$O(1)$	$O(1)$	$O(1)$
4	**Selection Sort**	$O(1)$	$O(1)$	$O(1)$
5	**Insertion Sort**	$O(1)$	$O(1)$	$O(1)$
6	**Counting Sort**	$\Omega(k)$	$\Omega(k)$	$\Omega(k)$
7	**NDS Sort**	$\Omega(n)$	$\theta(nu)$	$O(nu)$

In the best case, all the elements will belong to only one dimension, let's say, there is only one element repeated. In that case, the space complexity will be linear.

In the worst case, if elements belong to all different dimensions at all level, in the last dimension, there will be at max n children, reducing by the factor of 10 in each dimension as we move up the tree implementation. Since, the dimensions are u the space complexity will be in the order of nu.

4   Results and Discussion

The testing of sorting numbers with the proposed data structure and Merge Sort was done on Google Colab which uses a Virtual Machine with Intel(R) Xeon(R) CPU @ 2.20 GHz, RAM of 13 GB and a HDD Size of 110 GB approx. The observed time taken by the algorithms is given in Table 11. The column names specify the number of elements taken. The range taken was 0 to n − 1, n − 1 to 0 and all elements 0. Each cell represents the time taken by algorithm in seconds. Time Complexity is presented in Figs. 5, 6 and 7.

Table 11. Time taken by system in sec to execute NDS Sort and other sorting algorithms using Python on Google Colab

Algorithm	Input	10	100	1000	10,000	100,000	1,000,000	10,000,000
Merge Sort	0 to n-1	0.0001	0.0003	0.004	0.0514	0.6884	7.6915	89.4555
	n-1 to 0	4.1962E-05	0.000387	0.00605011	0.052137	0.636338	7.418624	86.438826
	All 0	6.84E-05	0.000546	0.00457239	0.057035	0.737706	7.427241	85.912622
Quick Sort	0 to n-1	0.00174332	0.001148	0.05484915	5.037439	Crashed	Crashed	Crashed
	n-1 to 0	4.3869E-05	0.001741	0.07280445	8.614189	Crashed	Crashed	Crashed
	All 0	3.5286E-05	0.001638	0.21693325	23.6059	Crashed	Crashed	Crashed
Bubble Sort	0 to n-1	0.00016713	0.000635	0.06683016	6.313508	Crashed	Crashed	Crashed
	n-1 to 0	3.2902E-05	0.00242	0.15939116	17.38576	Crashed	Crashed	Crashed
	All 0	2.3603E-05	0.000927	0.06036782	6.286249	Crashed	Crashed	Crashed
Selection Sort	0 to n-1	8.4639E-05	0.000704	0.05371523	4.918	489.1333	Crashed	Crashed
	n-1 to 0	2.5749E-05	0.000838	0.05344391	5.174935	Crashed	Crashed	Crashed
	All 0	1.4544E-05	0.000751	0.04826069	4.75796	Crashed	Crashed	Crashed
Insertion Sort	0 to n-1	0.00000083	0.000056	0.00052929	0.005517	0.033569	0.335155	3.4667594
	n-1 to 0	1.7166E-05	0.00092	0.10612702	10.77562	Crashed	Crashed	Crashed
	All 0	8.3447E-06	3.46E-05	0.00031519	0.0029	0.03819	0.305743	3.0626819
Counting Sort	0 to n-1	2.3603E-05	0.000134	0.00172091	0.008509	0.086685	0.867572	8.5488007
	n-1 to 0	2.718E-05	0.000135	0.00148439	0.008563	0.082525	0.85849	8.4852989
	All 0	2.5511E-05	0.000132	0.00106096	0.011068	0.0807	0.83579	6.6027911
NDS Sort	0 to n-1	0.0001	0.0003	0.0029	0.0365	0.4191	4.7976	55.8676
	n-1 to 0	7.1287E-05	0.000255	0.00345135	0.033077	0.401883	4.661522	53.242062
	All 0	0.00017571	0.000271	0.00270486	0.034662	0.400066	4.643523	51.733629

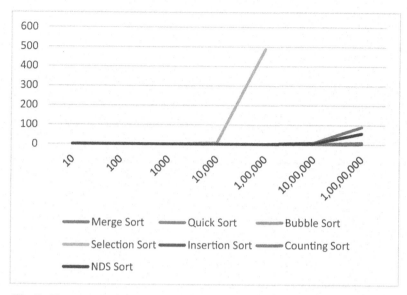

Fig. 5. Time complexity comparison of sorting algorithms for numbers 0 to n − 1

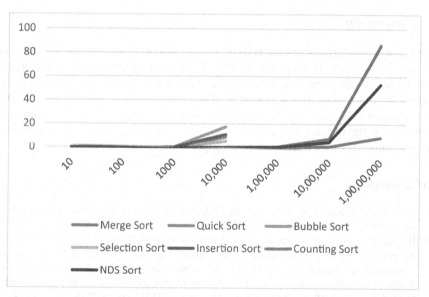

Fig. 6. Time complexity comparison of sorting algorithms for numbers from n − 1 to 0 (reverse sorted order)

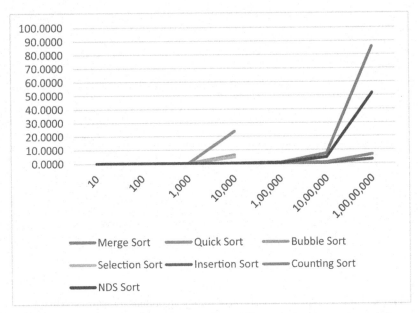

Fig. 7. Time complexity comparison of sorting algorithms for all elements 0

5 Conclusion

The data structure has efficient methods for adding, searching and deletion of numbers in the data structure with time complexity of each operation independent from the number of elements present in the data structure. The NDS Sort, proposed in the paper which is nothing but utilizing the ExtractSorted Method of the data structure. The NDS Sort, is more efficient than many sorting algorithms for positive integers. Extensive evaluation shows that it significantly outperforms Merge Sort and other sorting techniques over several testing scenarios mentioned in the paper in previous sections.

References

1. Fredkin, E.: Trie memory. Commun. ACM **3**, 490–499 (1960). https://doi.org/10.1145/367 390.367400
2. Huang, Y., Duan, L.-Y., Wang, Z., Lin, J., Chandrasekhar, V., Huang, T.: A multi-block N-ary trie structure for exact r-neighbour search in hamming space. In: 2017 IEEE International Conference on Image Processing (ICIP) (2017). https://doi.org/10.1109/icip.2017.8296455
3. Shabaz, M., Kumar, A.: SA sorting: a novel sorting technique for large-scale data. J. Comput. Netw. Commun. **2019**, 1–7 (2019). https://doi.org/10.1155/2019/3027578
4. Nicolas, A., Cyril, N., Carine, P.: Merge Strategies: from Merge Sort to TimSort (2015). ⟨hal-01212839v2⟩
5. Bajpai, K., Kots, A.: Implementing and analyzing an efficient version of counting sort (E-counting sort). Int. J. Comput. Appl. **98**, 1–2 (2014). https://doi.org/10.5120/17208-7427
6. Han, Y., Thorup, M.: Integer sorting in O(n√(log log n)) expected time and linear space. In: Proceedings of the 43rd Annual IEEE Symposium on Foundations of Computer Science (2002). https://doi.org/10.1109/sfcs.2002.1181890

7. Han, Y.: Improved fast integer sorting in linear space. Inf. Comput. **170**, 81–94 (2001). https://doi.org/10.1006/inco.2001.3053

8. Nicolas, A., Vincent, J., Cyril, N., Carine, P.: On the worst-case complexity of TimSort. In: 26th Annual European Symposium on Algorithms (ESA 2018), August 2018, Helsinki, Finland, pp. 4:1–4:13 (2018). https://doi.org/10.4230/LIPIcs.ESA.2018.4. ⟨hal-01798381⟩

9. Kumar, P., Gangal, A., Kumari, S.: Recombinant sort: N-dimensional cartesian spaced algorithm designed from synergetic combination of hashing, bucket, counting and radix sort. Ingénierie des systèmes d information **25**, 655–668 (2020). https://doi.org/10.18280/isi.250513

10. Heinz, S., Zobel, J., Williams, H.E.: Burst tries. ACM Trans. Inf. Syst. **20**, 192–223 (2002). https://doi.org/10.1145/506309.506312

11. Bayer, R., McCreight, E.: Organization and maintenance of large ordered indices. In: Proceedings of the 1970 ACM SIGFIDET (now SIGMOD) Workshop on Data Description, Access and Control - SIGFIDET 1970 (1970). https://doi.org/10.1145/1734663.1734671

12. Bell, J., Gupta, G.: An evaluation of self-adjusting binary search tree techniques. Softw.: Pract. Exp. **23**, 369–382 (1993). https://doi.org/10.1002/spe.4380230403

13. Lin, R.-B.: Efficient data structures for storing the partitions of integers (2005). https://www.yumpu.com/en/document/read/52473115/efficient-data-structures-for-storing-partitions-of-integers

14. Patrascu, M., Thorup, M.: Dynamic integer sets with optimal rank, select, and predecessor search. In: 2014 IEEE 55th Annual Symposium on Foundations of Computer Science (2014). https://doi.org/10.1109/focs.2014.26

15. Lancia, G., Dalpasso, M.: FASTSET: a fast data structure for the representation of sets of integers. Algorithms **12**, 91 (2019). https://doi.org/10.3390/a12050091

16. Nekrich, Y.: New data structures for orthogonal range reporting and range minima queries. In: Proceedings of the 2021 ACM-SIAM Symposium on Discrete Algorithms (SODA), pp. 1191–1205 (2021). https://doi.org/10.1137/1.9781611976465.73

17. Kittitornkun, S., Rattanatranurak, A.: A parallel multi-deque sorting algorithm. In: 2021 25th International Computer Science and Engineering Conference (ICSEC) (2021). https://doi.org/10.1109/icsec53205.2021.9684620

18. Srivastava, D., Kohli, R., Gupta, S.: Implementation and statistical comparison of different edge detection techniques. In: Bhatia, S.K., Mishra, K.K., Tiwari, S., Singh, V.K. (eds.) Advances in Computer and Computational Sciences. AISC, vol. 553, pp. 211–228. Springer, Singapore (2017). https://doi.org/10.1007/978-981-10-3770-2_20

19. Mohiddin, Md.K., Kohli, R., Dutt, V.B.S.S.I., Dixit, P., Michal, G.: Energy-efficient enhancement for the prediction-based scheduling algorithm for the improvement of network lifetime in WSNs. Wirel. Commun. Mob. Comput. **2021**, 1–12 (2021). https://doi.org/10.1155/2021/9601078

20. Chu, Z., Luo, Y., Jin, P.: An efficient sorting algorithm for non-volatile memory. Int. J. Softw. Eng. Knowl. Eng. **31**, 1603–1621 (2021). https://doi.org/10.1142/s0218194021400143

21. Schaffer, R., Sedgewick, R.: The analysis of heapsort. J. Algorithms **15**, 76–100 (1993). https://doi.org/10.1006/jagm.1993.1031

Spatial Variation of Air Quality in Delhi During Diwali: A Case Study of Covid-19 Period

Vijay Pal$^{(\boxtimes)}$ (iD), Surinder Deswal, and Mahesh Pal

Department of Civil Engineering, NIT Kurukshetra, Kurukshetra, Haryana, India
vijaypal.mahariya088@gmail.com, {sdeswal,
mahesh.pal}@nitkkr.ac.in

Abstract. The current study compared air pollution levels during the Covid-19 pandemic years (14 Nov. 2020, 04 Nov. 2021) and the previous year's Diwali celebrations (19 October 2017, 07 November 2018, 27 October 2019) in Delhi. $PM_{2.5}$, NH_3, SO_2, PM_{10}, NO_2, CO, and O_3 concentrations were substantially higher in 2020 Diwali than in 2017, 2018, 2019, and 2021 Diwali. $PM_{2.5}$, PM_{10}, and CO concentrations were always above the permissible limits (**Very poor and Sever AQI Category**); however, except on Diwali days, NO_2 concentrations were within allowable limit (**Good and Satisfactory AQI Category**), and other pollutants such as SO_2, NH_3, and O_3 concentrations were determined to be within permissible limits (**Good AQI Category**) throughout the year in Delhi. This data suggests that during the pandemic, people were following the guideline given by honorable Supreme Court of India and use less amount of firecrackers than in previous years. But the stubble burning contribution in 2020 was higher than last year and the meteorological condition was also unfavorable in that year.

Keywords: Diwali · Covid-19 · Spatial analysis · Firecrackers · Air pollution

1 Introduction

Air pollution is the world's most critical issue brought about by humans induced activities releasing chemicals and other pollutants into the atmosphere [1]. Pollutants in the air are hazardous to both the environment and our health. From respiratory disease to climate Change, air pollution has a wide range of health and environmental issues [2]. Understanding causes and impacts of air pollution is essential in improving the environment. The entire world is facing significant challenges in terms of degraded air quality due to a significant increase in anthropogenic emissions and a lack of adequate awareness of environmental health [3]. Air quality in metropolitan areas and other population centers has become a severe health concern due to excessive pollution concentrations and health hazards. It estimated that only air pollution is responsible for 40% of the patients suffering from heart and breathing problems [4, 5].

The outbreak of novel Corona virus since December 2019 is posing a threat to humanity across the globe. Outbreaks of this virus resulted in about 6 million official casualties globally, with many more unaccounted for. According to several recent researches, air

V. Sugumaran et al. (Eds.): AIR 2022, CCIS 1738, pp. 510–517, 2022.
https://doi.org/10.1007/978-3-031-23724-9_46

pollution aggravates the Covid-19, resulting in higher fatalities [6]. Diwali is a light festival celebrated in India during the post-monsoon months of Oct. or Nov. [4]. The festival's date varies from year to year and symbolizes the spiritual triumph of light over darkness. In spite of it being a festival of lights, people celebrate it by burning firecrackers in huge quantities. Excessive use of firecrackers during this period leads to that is harming to the environment and mankind by increasing the air pollution [7]. The purpose of this study is to examine existing patterns of air pollution distribution throughout Diwali celebrations during the pandemic of Covid-19 and the previous year. And their effect on human health in Delhi and by the spatial analysis we identified the area of high concentration of air pollution in Delhi during Diwali period and by this study we found out percentage of population impacted by negative effect.

2 Literature Review

A study conducted during the Pre-Diwali, Diwali, and Post-Diwali days of October and November for two consecutive years, 2018 and 2019, found that fireworks during the festival had a negative impact on ambient air quality owing to the emission and build-up of PM2.5, PM10, SO2, and NO2. Because of the washing off of contaminants by rain water, the effect was determined to be smaller in 2019 than in 2018 [1]. A study conducted during the first three weeks of November 2020 revealed extremely low AQI levels between 8:00 p.m. and 10:00 p.m. on Diwali day. A short-term change in AQI was seen throughout the night, and a modest positive correlation was found between AQI and temperature, whereas humidity was shown to have a negative association [4]. Previous studies have been done on three megacities namely Mumbai, Delhi and Kolkata and it was concluded that the highest concentration was observed in Delhi. The analysis was carried out by Arc GIS during Diwali festival season [5].

2.1 Factor Affecting Air Pollution

The number and type of pollutants emitted into the air have a significant effect in establishing the degree of air pollution in a given location [8]. However, other variables are mostly at work;

- Topography, such as mountains valleys;
- The physical and chemical property of pollutants; and
- Wind speed, temperature, air turbulence, rainfall, air pressure, and cloud cover are all examples of weather.

2.2 Health Effects of Firecrackers

The firecrackers pollute environmental air by dust fumes and the heavy metals, which pollute ground also. Firecrackers generally contain 10% Sulfur, 15% carbon, 70% potassium nitrate and small 1% of toxic heavy metals like cadmium, copper, barium, rubidium, lead, zinc, barium, lithium, titanium, etc. Some highly toxic heavy metals like cadmium, manganese, lead copper, zinc, and potassium release from "phuljhari" and "anar" [9]. In many firecrackers colors display occurs due to the presence of toxic metals. The blazing red color is produced by lithium strontium; blue is produced by copper compounds whereas bright green is produced by Barium [10]. After Diwali period each year, a significant change in asthmatic patients due to excessive particulate matter in air is reported in Delhi [11].

3   Methodology

The flow chart of Methodology of this study to achieve the objective is shown in Fig. 1. Delhi, India's national capital, has a population of 16.7 million people and is located in the northern section of the country at longitude 28.61 °N and latitude 77.23 °E. The city is bounded on the west, north, and south by the state of Haryana, and on the east by the state of Uttar Pradesh. The Delhi ridge and Yamuna flood plains are two notable aspects of Delhi's geography (Fig. 2).

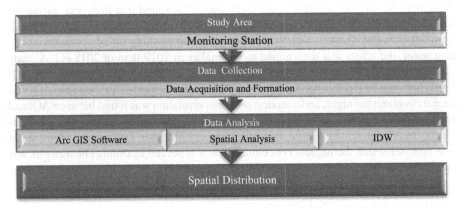

Fig. 1. Flow chart showing spatial distribution methodology

3.1   Data Acquisition and Analysis

The ambient air quality data acquired from the CPCB was utilised in this study to analyse the change in air quality caused by the bursting of crackers in Delhi on the occasion of Diwali. The information was gathered during a five-year period (2017–2021) [12].

The 12 monitoring station were Anand Vihar, NSIT Dwarka, IGI Airport, RK Puram, ShadiPur, Ashok Vihar, DTU, IHBAS, CRRI, Siri Fort, Punjabi Bagh, Mandir Marg, Round-the-clock air quality data from 7 days before Diwali and 7 days after Diwali were utilized as a comparison.

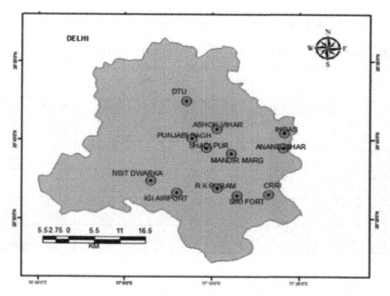

Fig. 2. Study area map showing the location of monitoring stations

3.2 Arc GIS

Using the ESRI Arc GIS 10.5 Platform, we examined the spatial variation in pollutants of air within each year of all stations. The interpolation technique used was a deterministic approach based on the linear combination and Inverse Distance Weighting interpolator to calculate the value on those stations where values were not measured based on the values measured station [5].

4 Results and Discussion

As fire crackers contain several chemicals and other material which produces air pollution, the concentration of various gaseous vapors (NO_2, SO_2 etc.) and particulate matter (PM_{10}, $PM_{2.5}$) were used for comparison during the study period [7]. The 24 h average concentration of PM_{10}, $PM_{2.5}$, NO_2, SO_2, NH_3 and 8 h average concentration of CO and O_3 in Ambient air during Diwali days from year 2017 to 2021 in Delhi are plotted in Fig. 3 and Fig. 4. In general, out of all pollutants, PM_{10} and $PM_{2.5}$ have highest concentration on days other than Diwali day. The particulate concentration level was found significantly higher than the permissible limit (Table 1).

Table 1. AQI scale 0–500 (units: $\mu g/m^3$ unless mentioned otherwise) [13].

AQI Category (Range)	PM$_{10}$ 24-hr	PM$_{2.5}$ 24-hr	NO$_2$ 24-hr	O$_3$ 8-hr	CO 8-hr (mg/m^3)	SO$_2$ 24-hr	NH$_3$ 24-hr	Pb 24-hr
Good (0-50)	0-50	0-30	0-40	0-50	0-1.0	0-40	0-200	0-0.5
Satisfactory (51-100)	51-100	31-60	41-80	51-100	1.1-2.0	41-80	201-400	0.6 – 1.0
Moderate (101-200)	101-250	61-90	81-180	101-168	2.1-10	81-380	401-800	1.1-2.0
Poor (201-300)	251-350	91-120	181-280	169-208	10.1-17	381-800	801-1200	2.1-3.0
Very poor (301-400)	351-430	121-250	281-400	209-748*	17.1-34	801-1600	1201-1800	3.1-3.5
Severe (401-500)	430 +	250+	400+	748+*	34+	1600+	1800+	3.5+

The Table 2 provides standard color coding for severity of pollution level by the central pollution control board. In the present study different color coding is used while showing spatial distribution of various pollutants in GIS because of the reason that in case of very poor and severe conditions the recognition of color gets difficult and same for good and satisfactory conditions. Different colors used in this study to define the severity of pollutants are as:-

Table 2. Showing color coding as per AQI category

AQI category	Color
Good	Green
Satisfactory	Yellow
Moderate	Orange
Poor	Red
Very poor	Purple
Severe	Maroon

The concentration of air quality also depends on meteorological conditions. Keeping in view of this; last five-year meteorological data is given in Table 3.

The 24 h average concentration of PM10, PM2.5, SO2, NO2, NH3 and 8 h average concentration of CO, O3 in Ambient air on Diwali day for year 2017 to 2021. By and large all the air quality parameters have highest concentration level on the Diwali day of 2020 (14 November) and 2021 (04 November) at all monitoring station. The possible reason was adverse meteorological condition due to decreasing in 24-h average temperatures wind speed and mixing height in November as compare to October. And another possible

Table 3. Metrological condition during Diwali days [14].

Year	Episode	Monitoring date	Temp (°C)	PPT (MM/D)	W.S. (M/S)
2017	Pre Diwali	18/10/2017	15.39	0	3.77
	Diwali	19/10/2017	16.89	0	1.69
	Post Diwali	20/10/2017	13.85	0	2.24
2018	Pre Diwali	06/11/2018	16.12	0	3.33
	Diwali	07/11/2018	18.75	0	2.7
	Post Diwali	08/11/2018	13.23	0	1.28
2019	Pre Diwali	26/10/2019	13	0	2.88
	Diwali	27/10/2019	14.38	0	3.23
	Post Diwali	28/10/2019	14.08	0	2.38
2020	Pre Diwali	13/11/2020	14.12	0	1.21
	Diwali	14/11/2020	12.99	0	2.73
	Post Diwali	15/11/2020	13.97	3.65	3.84
2021	Pre Diwali	03/11/2021	14.13	0.01	3.57
	Diwali	04/11/2021	10.98	0	1.3
	Post Diwali	05/11/2021	10.17	0	1.61

was stubble burning, Stubble burning contributed 32% during 2020 Diwali season and 12% during 2019 Diwali season (Source: SAFAR, IITM). PM2.5, PM10, and CO were always in Very poor and Severe AQI Category, but the NO2 concentration was in Good and Satisfactory AQI Category, Diwali days, the other pollutant like SO2 NH3 and O3 concentration were found Good AQI Category in Delhi throughout last five years.

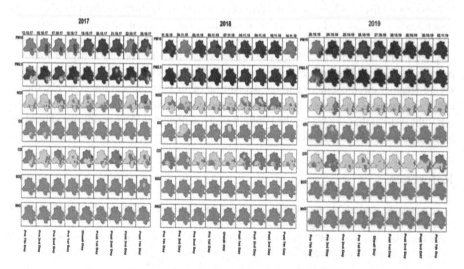

Fig. 3. Showing analysis 2017, 2018 & 2019

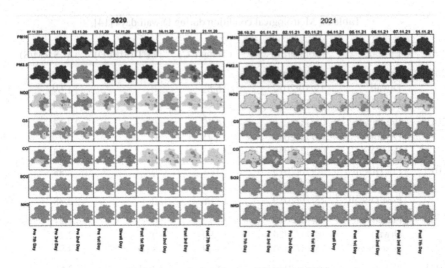

Fig. 4. Showing analysis of 2020 and 2021

The above Fig. 3 and Fig. 4 shows the spatial distribution of Air Quality during Diwali season of last five-year 2017, 2018, 2019, 2020, and 2021 respectively.

5 Conclusion

The current study examined Delhi's air pollution levels for non-pandemic years (2017, 2018 and 2019) and pandemic-stricken years (2020 and 2021) during Diwali. The impact of bursting of fire crackers is significant on ambient air quality during Diwali season which leads to health and environmental hazards. The concentration of SO_2, NH_3, O_3 and NO_2 are mostly within the permissible limit (**Good AQI Category**) on Diwali Day but Particulate Matter (PM_{10}, $PM_{2.5}$) level was found to be much higher than the permissible limits (**Very poor and Severe AQI Category**) during Diwali days. Due to severe weather circumstances and the deposition of air pollutants at lower levels, the air quality worsens as the Diwali festival falls in the winter. We must remember that Diwali is a light festival that celebrates the triumph of good over evil. As a result, we should try to make Diwali as eco-friendly as possible.

References

1. Chandu, K., Dasari. M.: A case study on air pollution during Diwali festival at Visakhapatnam, India. Eco. Env. Cons. **26**(4), 1754–1759 (2020)
2. Chatterjee, A., Sarkar, C., Adak, A., Mukherjee, U., Ghosh, S.K., Raha, S.: Ambient air quality during Diwali festival over Kolkata - a mega-city in India. Aerosol Air Qual. Res. **13**, 1133–1144 (2013). https://doi.org/10.4209/aaqr.2012.03.0062
3. Thakur, B., Chakraborty, S., Debsarkar, A.: Air pollution from fireworks during festival of lights (Deepawali) in Howrah India - a case study. Atmósfera **23**, 347–365 (2010)

4. Lawrence, A.J., Abraham, A., Ali, F.: Air Quality in six northern Indian cities during Diwali 2020: the real tragedy in disguise. Asian J. Chem. **33**, 909–918 (2021)
5. Mandal, J., Chanda, A., Samanta, S.: Effects of COVID-19 pandemic on the air quality of three megacities in India. Atmos. Res. **259**, 105659 (2021)
6. World meter. https://www.worldometers.info/coronavirus. Accessed 20 Mar 2022
7. Sati, A.P., Mohan, M.: Analysis of air pollution during a severe smog episode of November 2012 and the Diwali Festival over Delhi, India. Int. J. Remote Sens. **35**, 6940–6954 (2014). https://doi.org/10.1080/01431161.2014.960618
8. Saxena, P., Srivastava, A., Verma, S., Shweta Singh, L., Sonwani, S.: Analysis of atmospheric pollutants during fireworks festival 'Diwali' at a residential site Delhi in India. In: Energy, Environment, and Sustainability, pp. 91–105 (2019). https://doi.org/10.1007/978-981-15-054 0-9_4
9. Deswal, S.: Environmental pollution during Deepawali: a case study of Delhi (2011)
10. Deswal, S.: A case study of noise and air quality of Delhi (2008)
11. Pratap, V., Saha, U., Kumar, A., Singh, A.K.: Analysis of air pollution in the atmosphere due to firecrackers in the Diwali period over an urban Indian region. Adv. Space Res. **68**, 3327–3341 (2021). https://doi.org/10.1016/j.asr.2021.06.031
12. CPCB. http://www.cpcbenvis.nic.in. Accessed 30 May 2022
13. CPCB: National Air Quality Index, Ministry of Environment, Forests & Climate Change (2014)
14. Power LARC NASA. https://power.larc.nasa.gov/data-access-viewer/. Accessed 09 Mar 2022

Shop-Easy: An Online Shopping Framework Emphasizing Vocal for Local Using Location and Review Based Services

Aviral Jain, Divyaman Tyagi, and Shanu Sharma[(✉)] [iD]

Department of Computer Science and Engineering, ABES Engineering College, Ghaziabad,
India
shanu.sharma16@gmail.com

Abstract. Nowadays the trend of online shopping is increasing day by day. A huge transformation and usage of online applications for shopping day-to-day essential items have been experienced during Covid-era. To further facilitate the online shopping industries, the local shopkeepers, and the customers, in this paper an efficient and organized online shopping platform is presented, which can be used by local shopkeepers to showcase their products digitally and by customers to easily manage and organize their day-to-day shopping-related tasks. With this proposed platform, the local regional shopkeepers can introduce their shops and products to nearby residents from time to time which makes their shop to be known by everyone, selling their products in an easier way and helps them in maintaining their ledger on a daily basis. Further, the proposed system will assist the customers by helping them in keeping track of their shopping lists timely and by choosing the best shop according to the location, item, and review-based notifications and reminders.

Keywords: Shopping · Online · Recommendation · Product · Location-based services · Notification

1 Introduction

In today's era, the trend of online shopping is increasing day by day. A lot of online shopping applications can be seen on the internet for various shopping-related tasks. Nowadays big companies and startups are moving towards instant delivery of essential and daily usage items to customers. One can see a huge transformation and usage of shopping applications for essential and daily usage items also in Covid-era. Due to this increase in the trend of online shopping, there is a significant loss of small shopkeepers who are unable to give facilities to customers as big giants. Due to a lack of resources and lack of money, they are unable to advertise themselves which led them backward day by day. The users also in online shopping usually experience a lot of issues such as searching or getting the correct product, as it is not possible for everyone to choose the best or required product among the enormous variety of available products on the internet. Moreover, it is not possible for everyone to use an online shopping platform

V. Sugumaran et al. (Eds.): AIR 2022, CCIS 1738, pp. 518–530, 2022.
https://doi.org/10.1007/978-3-031-23724-9_47

effectively due to a lack of technical knowledge. Still, a lot of people prefer their nearby stores for day-to-day items purchasing but, in some cases, they face an issue if the locality is new to them.

Today in the busy schedule users usually maintain a shopping list and then forget to even look at it and this will make it of no use. Secondly, when people move to a new city, they rarely know the locality, it took time and sometimes money to understand the best shop near them. Moreover, for shopkeepers also setting up a shop is a difficult and time-consuming task because it requires understanding the customers and their needs. Keeping these things in mind we came up with a digital approach to solve these problems. Although a large range of shopping applications are available in the market, with the power of advanced technologies there is always a scope for improvement.

In this paper, a user-friendly online platform for both customers and shopkeepers is proposed that emphasizes on "Vocal For Local" initiative also which was started by the government of India. With this proposed framework, the local shopkeepers of any particular area can introduce their product digitally and can also provide a detailed overview of the product also such as selling price, GST, profit in an organized manner. The shopkeeper can update the price or the product list any time and any number of times and also provide the shopkeepers the details of highly demanding products in their locality, moreover making the billing easy for them. On another side, the proposed system can generate notifications to customers to remind them about the correct time to buy the goods on the basis of the surroundings of their mobile phone, further, this application will provide a review of the shops and the product to the user. Moreover, the user will know is there any offer by any nearby shop and there will be a better recommendation system and product searching system near to their home or location.

With the aim of proposing a better platform for shopkeepers and customers, the work related to the proposed system is structured as the discussion on the existing platforms related to the proposed work is presented in Sect. 2. The functionalities of the proposed system, design, and implementation details along with the various interfaces of the proposed application are presented and explained are discussed in Sect. 3. The paper is concluded by presenting the discussion on the work in Sect. 4.

2   Background and Related Work

In our daily life, people generally face the issue of forgetfulness, like sometimes they forget their tasks like shopping or doing some other activity due to a hectic schedule or engagement in other tasks. This gives them a guilty feeling of being unable to do their tasks timely and wasting their time also. Users usually maintain a shopping list and then forget to even look at it and this will make it of no use. Nowadays various mobile-based applications and stand-alone devices are present in the market such as Apple Reminders, Alexa which can perform various tasks for users. Such application provides many features like voice interaction, setting alarms, music playback, playing audiobooks, making to-do lists, providing weather, latest news, sports news, and many other things. Apple Reminder provides the feature of creating a list and setting up the notifications which can be location-based also to the users. These platforms are provided with a user-friendly interface so that they can be used more easily. These platforms are consisted of voice interaction, setting alarms, making To-do lists, and many other things. Most of these types of applications are very general which can be used as maintaining the shopping list effectively. The description of some of the devices and applications is presented in Table 1.

Table 1. Analysis of existing related applications

Apps/Devices	Description
Amazon's Alexa [7]	It is a virtual assistant technology which mostly based on a polish speech synthesizer (lvona) that provides many features like voice interaction, setting alarms, music playback, playing audiobooks, making todo lists, providing weather, latest news, sports news, and many other things if a person not having these echo dots they can use their mobile application on their phone.
Apple's Reminder loco [8]	It's a software which comes preinstalled on iOS devices like macOS, watchOS. It provides the feature of creating a list and setting up the notifications which can be location-based also. In this application, you can modify the position radius also for customizing location-based services.
Google's Nest Mini [9]	Google Nest, previously named Google Home, is a line of smart speakers developed by Google under the Google Nest brand. The devices enable users to speak voice commands to interact with services through Google Assistant. Both in-house and third-party services are integrated, allowing users to listen to music, control the playback of videos or photos, or receive news updates entirely by voice.
To-Do List App [10]	To-Do List is a software that provides a platform to add your task easily, it provides voice based interaction to maintain the list (e.g. for instruction "buy milk Monday", the task "buy milk" will be added on the coming Monday as your due date). You can put new tasks in your Inbox and then move them to relevant projects; you can also set due dates
Tick Tick [11]	Tick Tick is time tracking software operated by Higher Pixels (former The Molehill), that offers online time tracking and reporting services through their website along with mobile and desktop applications. Tick tick tracks time based on clients, projects and tasks, either through a timer or through manual entry.

As mentioned in Table 1, the existing applications and devices can be used effectively to maintain the shopping list and setting reminders also, whereas the real-time applicability of these applications to provide location-based services is still not functional.

Further, when a person moved to a new city, they rarely know the locality, it took time and sometimes money to understand the best shop near them. And as a consumer when someone changes their locality or goes to an unknown place it becomes a challenging task for them to search for their required product or to find a good shop in that locality.

Considering the point of local shopkeepers in a specific society, the setting up of a shop is a very difficult and time-consuming task because it requires a proper understanding of the customers and their needs. Also, with the increasing trend of online shopping, small shopkeepers face a backlash from the big giants of the digital market who captured the market through the means of smartphones and the internet by providing the customers with a variety of products at home and it becomes exceedingly difficult for shopkeepers who have no access to such platform to reach their customer in a smart and advanced way to sell out their goods so they can earn their living. Thus, it takes too much time for them to establish their shop to spread it to every person in the nearby locality. Local shopkeepers also face difficulties to introduce new schemes and offer on their products to their nearby customers.

As the online shopping platforms gained huge popularity among customers so it is the need of the hour to introduce small shopkeepers' products on the online platforms, thus with this paper a user-friendly Shop-Easy Online framework is proposed to local shopkeepers and customers to provide a location and review-based shopping experience to both customers and shopkeepers.

3 Shop-Easy: Proposed Shopping Framework

The development of an efficient shopping application always being a challenging task for developers, as shopping includes a lot of subjective features such as the brand of product, its price, and preferred choice. But with the development of innovative technologies, there is always an option of developing a better and optimized platform. Thus, here an online shopping framework is presented considering local shopkeepers and users in mind. The various functionalities, design, and implementation approach is discussed in further subsections.

3.1 Proposed System Functionalities

The proposed shopping platform "Shop-Easy" is designed with the help of novel technologies to provide both consumers and shopkeepers a stage to perform their tasks more effectively and easily with a better user interface and databases for storing their data securely and systematically. Features of the proposed system are described in Table 2.

Through Shop-Easy, the user will have the feature to schedule their tasks smartly and get notification of that task according to the location or time. The customer will be able to view the shop according to their location. Further, the user will be able to provide a review of the shop as well as the product. The products will also be recommended to the customers according to their offers and promotion through the proposed portal. On the other side, the shopkeeper can introduce their product digitally and can assess the market in their benefits. The portal also provides the feature of maintaining their ledgers effectively. They can assign the offer on particular products through portal to attract customers. Using recommendation and review system shopkeepers can assess the market and the customers can also choose the best option among the given options present on the platform. Further, the customers can customize their portal by adjusting the threshold distance according to their comfort so that when you cross that value you will be easily notified by the app to buy your product or to complete that task.

Table 2. Proposed functionalities of shop-easy platform

Functionalities to shopkeepers	Functionalities to customers
Location and distance-based addition of shop in "Shop Easy" portal	Portal to know about the location based local shops and their products
Digital showcasing of the product on the portal	Maintenance of shopping lists smartly on the portal
Real-time display of offers to customers	Location and product based notification to customers
Maintenance of ledger at the portal	Offer based product recommendation notification to customers
Reviews and promotion of shop to nearby societies	Product comparison to get the best deal

3.2 Proposed System Functionalities

The proposed system is designed to provide two types of interfaces to users, one for the consumers and another one is for shopkeepers. For the consumers, the system is designed to provide a location and time-based notifications of nearby shops. The proposed system is designed to provide two types of interfaces to users, one for the consumers and another one is for shopkeepers. For the consumers, the system is designed to provide a location and time-based notification of nearby shops. An easy interface is designed to maintain the shopping list effectively. On the other hand, Shopkeepers can register their shops and add/update their products on the application and can advertise any kind of sale in the neighborhood to attract new customers. Moreover, Shopkeepers will get full monitoring of their monthly, and yearly sales and can invest smartly. The working of the proposed system is depicted in Fig. 1 and is described below:

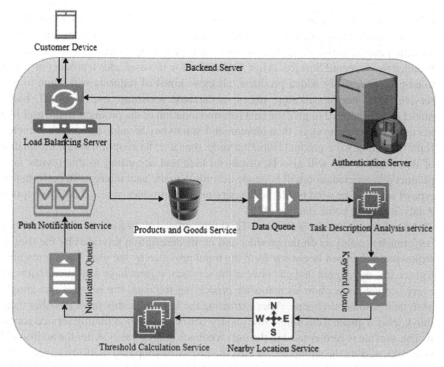

Fig. 1. System design flow diagram

As presented in Fig. 1, different types of servers and services have been used for implementing the Shop-Easy Platform, which are further discussed below:

- Load Balancing Server balances the load of the whole platform so that there should not be any delay due to load on any other services of the system. Basically, a Load Balancer is a reverse proxy as the user does not know how many services are running behind the load balancer. It helps in horizontal scaling of the system if there is too much load on one service then there can be many replicas of that service to fulfill all the requests in no time. For selecting replicas it uses consistent hashing. In the Shop-Easy platform, Load Balancer is used for path-based service selection. Like if a user is Logging-in or Signing-in then this type of request should assign to the Authentication Server. It balances the load if multiple users need to get access to the shopping platform for their smooth processing of different requests. Users will get the login into the platform through the means of some credential used for authentication here authentication server will come into the effect,
- Authentication Server has an internal database to store the user information and the login credentials. All this information is taken at the time of signing-in. And login credentials are used in a log-in process to authenticate the user. If the credentials are correct a token is generated and given to the user for a particular amount of time to prove his/her identity. And there is a cache that stores these tokens to verify the logged-in user identity in no time. After a regular interval, the server renews the token

to avoid any kind of misuse. After the authentication gets done, the user can sign in into its account where different actions like adding the task, making the record related operation can be performed which is done using product/goods record service.

- Product/goods record Service- After Authentication if a user adds a product or wants to edit the previously added products, all these kinds of requests will come to this service. This service will store data in a database for future use. Here ML based model is incorporated to give the best recommendation of the products to the user like if a user is purchasing eggs, then recommend him to buy bread to make bread omelet. If the user bought the product from that shop, then user have option to rate the quality of that product that will also be displayed here and according to this review next product recommendation will be made according to the user interest. To perform this type of activity one need to fill the description of its product, where Task Description Analysis service come into the effect

- Task Description Analysis Service- To get the related shop for the user, this service performs text analysis on the product and on its description provided by the user. It strikes out the related keywords form the input provided by the user. For maintaining a glitch free movement of data between the services, system have data queue between every service connection so that after processing the data, the services can simply push their results into queue. After extracting the keywords, this service pushes them into keyword queue from where low latency best shop location finding service access it. This service is further used in the user feedback analysis also. After the addition of tasks like, adding the shopping list etc., the proposed shopping platform suggests the shops related to the shopping list along with the location of the shop using the Nearby Location Service.

- Nearby Location Service plays the main role in the functioning of the whole proposed system. This service has maximum load and complex calculations due to the constant stream of user's GPS coordinates, thus its replicas are used for better performance. The service picks the keyword from the keyword queue and check-in its database to find the best shop for the user. Shops will be ranked according to the review provided by the previous customers of that shop and also the smallest Euclidian distance from the user's location. The two types of scenarios can occur in this case, one when the shop is previously registered with the shopping platform, and another one is when shops are not registered. The Google Maps Nearby API is used to find the best nearby shops for the user, which further uses the Threshold Calculation Service to get the best shop for a particular product.

- Threshold Calculation Service: This service picks the list provided by the Nearby Location Service, and using user's speed it sets the threshold range for the user, e.g., if the user is walking then the threshold can be set up to 100–250 m but if a user is in the car, then 1–5 km threshold can be set. Finally, the shops, which will be selected after the threshold calculation service, will be notified to the user using the push-notification service.

- Push Notification Service: In laymen's term the job of this service is to send the push notification to the user which is not an easy task because the system has to maintain a stream of notifications with the user as there can be many products notification to be sent to the user simultaneously. This service is based on the pub-sub model where there are three entities namely publisher, topic, and subscriber. In the proposed Shop-Easy system the publisher is the threshold calculation service, i.e., the service that publishes the data. Topics are the related data box-like groceries can be one topic, stationary can be one topic so publisher add data to that related topic. Subscriber are the end-user who subscribes to their selective topic. This model is very helpful because there can be many users in the same locality who need the same product. So, they can simply subscribe to a topic and then the load on the system will be much less.

Customer Side Designing. As mentioned above, the Shop-Easy platform for the customer's side is implemented, where the user can use the platform in the following way:

- User installs the Shop-Easy application and all the requests from the application will go to the server and the requests related to sign-up and login will go to the Authentication Server.
- Once the Authorization will be done, a reply will be sent back to the system.
- User can add the tasks using Add Task Page.
- All the tasks listed with the user's current GPS location will be sent to the server.
- Load Balancer server will then distribute the request to the Product/goods record service.
- Via Data Queue, Product/goods record service server will forward this request to the Task Description Analysis service.
- Task Description Analysis service will put product-related keywords to the keyword queue.
- Nearby Location Service will pick the keyword from the queue and find the shops near the user and forward them to the Threshold Calculation Service.
- In Threshold Calculation Service User and shop relative distance will be calculated and if that distance is within the threshold then a request will be forwarded to the Notification service.
- Notification Service will send the notification to the user.

Shopkeeper Side Designing. Similar to Customer side designing, the signup and login process is same for shopkeepers on the Shop-Easy platform. The flow of shopkeeper side designing will be as:

- Shopkeeper can register their shop by providing shop name and by providing access to GPS location.
- Shopkeeper can give a short description about the shop.
- Can list all categories of products available in his shop on Shop-Easy Platform.
- Can also update any special offer or any important notification as a banner
- This banner will be visible on the map information like special discount or non-availability of some product.

3.3 Results and Discussion

The various results generated during development of the Shop-Easy online shopping platform are discussed below. The system is developed by considering some assumptions and dependencies such as:

- User should add at least five products
- GPS should be turned on while using Shop-Easy system on user's mobile phone.
- Customer should have an active internet connection.
- Shop-Easy mobile application requires many supports from mobile application like permission to use GPS, Camera, Internet, File Storage.
- User should allow the application to use all these mobile features for the working of the application.

As explained in the previous sections Shop Easy will be a user-friendly platform that will make the user shopping experience more familiar. Some of the results of Shop-Easy platform are presented as Fig. 2 shows the entities of the Shop Easy user along with their data type in the form of which data is stored. Figure 3 presents the different functionalities performed by the user along with the activities performed by the server in the Shop Easy to fulfill the User request. When the user adds some task in the form of data then this data is encapsulated by the platform and sent to the server where different processes are performed on it like the recording of task, text/speech analysis, product-oriented keywords to fulfill the user's request.

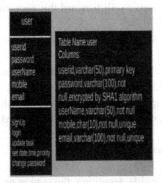
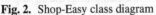

Fig. 2. Shop-Easy class diagram

Fig. 3. Customer side designing

Figure 4 represents the initial screen of the Shop-Easy Platform, where user can register or log in in the system as presented in Fig. 5 and 6 respectively. After the user gets registered then he/she will be able to see the login page as shown in Fig. 7, where currently no task is added.

Fig. 4. Shop-Easy initial screen

Fig. 5. Sign up screen

Fig. 6. Login screen

Fig. 7. Home screen

The user can also maintain their profile by updating person details on Shop-Easy platform as shown in Fig. 8.

Fig. 8. User profile page

Fig. 9. Add task page

Further, the user can maintain the shopping list by adding products using add task page in the proposed system as shown in Fig. 9 and 10 respectively. The user can add different categories of tasks which can be seen in Fig. 11.

Fig. 10. Creation of tasks list

Fig. 11. Different categories of tasks in Shop-Easy platform

Now according to the maintained list, the Shop-Easy platform recommends the location and review based best shops to user as shown in Fig. 12 and 13.

Fig. 12. Discount and location based shop recommendation through Shop-Easy platform

Fig. 13. Recommended shop along with a description provided by shop keepers

4   Comparative Analysis of Features of Proposed System

To check the novelty and efficacy of the proposed online shopping platform, a comparative analysis of features of the proposed system is done with some of the existing applications which are summarized in Table 3. As claimed by the authors in this paper, the proposed Shop-Easy platform is providing some required features which can provide the more friendly and easy shopping experience to both local customers and shopkeepers.

Table 3. Comparative analysis of features of Shop-Easy shopping platform

Features available	Time base reminders	Location base reminder	Notification of nearby shops	Review system	Ledger for shopkeepers	Customer rating system
Jio Mart [12]	No	No	No	Yes	No	Yes
Meesho [13]	No	No	No	Yes	No	Yes
Tick [11]	Yes	No	No	No	No	No
To-Do: List [10]	Yes	No	No	No	No	No
Shop Easy	Yes	Yes	Yes	Yes	Yes	Yes

5   Conclusion

In this paper, a Shop-Easy Online framework is proposed with the aim of providing an efficient environment for customers and local shopkeepers for maintaining their tasks smartly. In comparison to existing systems, the proposed system includes features that target mostly local shopkeepers and customers to provide them with location-based services. The system can be used effectively to increase the sale and popularity of the local shopkeepers in nearby localities. The rating and review feature of the system can also provide more visibility to shops in nearby localities. Further, the location and time-based notification facility to customers will be proved as a time-saving solution to customers. For future additions, the WhatsApp Bot can be incorporated into the system to make its operation more swiftly. With the increasing online shopping trends, the proposed system can be proved to be a money-saving and time-saving platform for both shopkeepers and consumers.

References

1. Eisenman, B.: Learning React Native, 1st edition. O'Reilly, USA (2015)
2. Crockford, D.: JavaScript: The Good Parts. O'Reilly, USA (2008)
3. React Native - A JavaScript library for building user interfaces. https://en.wikipedia.org/wiki/React_(JavaScript_library). Accessed 07 Dec 2021

4. React Native: The Virtual DOM. https://www.codecademy.com/article/react-virtual-dom. Accessed 08 Dec 2021
5. Article on nodejs/node. https://github.com/nodejs/node. Accessed 02 Nov 2021
6. The MIT License. https://en.wikipedia.org/wiki/MIT_License. Accessed 02 Nov 2021
7. Amazon Alexa. https://en.wikipedia.org/wiki/Amazon_Alexa. Accessed 12 Dec 2021
8. Apple Reminder Loco. https://en.wikipedia.org/wiki/Reminders_(Apple). Accessed 14 Dec 2021
9. Google Nest Mini. https://en.wikipedia.org/wiki/Google_Nest_(smart_speakers). Accessed 20 Dec 2021
10. To-Do List. https://en.wikipedia.org/wiki/Wikipedia:To-do_list. Accessed 20 Dec 2021
11. Tick Tick. https://en.wikipedia.org/wiki/Tick_(software). Accessed 21 Dec 2021
12. Jio Mart. https://en.wikipedia.org/wiki/JioMart. Accessed 27 Dec 2021
13. Meesho. https://everipedia.org/wiki/lang_en/meesho. Accessed 27 Dec 2021

Women Assault Detection and Providing Help Using Pitch

Rachakonda Hrithik Sagar$^{(\boxtimes)}$ (iD), L. Krishna Sai Raj Goud, Aastha Sharma, Tuiba Ashraf, and Arun Prakash Agrawal

Department of Computer Science and Engineering, School of Engineering and Technology, Sharda University, Greater Noida, India
hrithiksagar36@gmail.com, 2018005582.aastha@ug.sharda.ac.in, arun.agrawal@sharda.ac.in

Abstract. Women's safety has ever been a serious concern. Even after several initiatives taken by governments all over the world, viz installation of CCTV cameras, panic buttons on mobile phones, deployment of security personnel, etc., there are still some challenges to be addressed. Women are still susceptible to acid attacks, molestation, eve-teasing, and sexual harassment. Solutions offered so far are constrained by the cost and feasibility of application depending upon the geographical region. For example, CCTV cameras seem to be a good solution but are costly and at times cannot be installed in rural areas due to electricity constraints and privacy constraints. Keeping this in view, the authors in this paper propose an economically viable solution for women's safety by intercepting the pitch of female voices using sensors. Sensors are economic, affordable, portable, and easy to install even on trees in rural areas. They also do not require too much electricity to keep them operational. Motivated by the advantages offered by sensors, authors have proposed a novel economic solution for women's safety. The proposed solution was implemented using sound frequency sensors, GSM GPRS Module, Arduino, and raspberry pi.

Keywords: Women safety · Arduino · Sensors · High pitch · Pitch detector

1 Introduction

According to IPC (Indian Penal Code) or SLL (Special Local Laws) in the year 2020, there were 3,71,503 crimes against women in India as per National Crime Record Bureau [2], in the year 2019, the number is 4,05,326, and year 2018 it went up to 3,78,236. Where Delhi alone contributes 12000 cases on average, Uttar Pradesh contributes around 50000 cases per year, Telangana 20000, Rajasthan 35000.... These numbers go very high. These numbers are of just 1 year or a couple of years and not at all low. These are just regular crimes but when we come under the rape category, it is to be analyzed that major cases were under 18 years to 30 years aged women, 63% of the cases were of this age, and the rest 37% of cases were registered under below 6 years, 6 years to 12 years, 12 years to 16 years, 16 years to 18 years, 30 years to 45 years, 45 years to 60 years of ages [1]. Out of 18–30-year aged women 17500 cases were registered under this age group and numerous unregistered cases, and in total 25500 cases were registered in the year 2020 as per the Indian Government, in which highest numbers were registered in these cities, Rajasthan, Uttar Pradesh, Odisha, Madhya Pradesh, Maharashtra, Andhra Pradesh, Assam, West Bengal. Which contributes to about 2000 cases on average. These seem like small numbers, but when seen from the point of view of friends and family they seem very huge. Moreover, this is just one category, then went in-depth there are many more categories and their total cases constitute to, where Table 1 shows the records of the crimes that involved women in India in the year 2020 [6]:

Table 1. Records of crimes in the year 2020 in India [6].

"Police disposal of crime against women cases (crime head-wise) - 2020"	4,83,284
"Police disposal of crime against women cases (states/UT-wise) - 2020"	5,73,049
"Court disposal of crime against women cases (crime head-wise) - 2020"	16,27,099
"Court disposal of crime against women cases (states/UT-wise) - 2020"	17,89,601
"Disposal of persons arrested for crime against women (crime head-wise) - 2020"	4,07,975

If we analyze Table 1, just 20% of registered cases get justice, and the rest are free and still roaming out as free birds. Total types of crimes against women include Rape, insult, Kidnapping, cruelty, domestic violence, asexual assault, trafficking, deaths due to dowry, murders, abduction, acid throwing, forced marriages, child marriages, honor killings, sex-selective abortions, and so on. The major contribution of this paper is as follows:

- Detecting High pitch of females such as screams, help words.
- Tracking the location
- Contacting emergency contacts in emergencies.

The main purpose of this research and implementation is to help in decreasing as many as possible crimes against women in places where CCTVs (closed-circuit television) can't be installed, or in villages. Isolated places. For example, in the year 2020, there were 62,000 kidnappings and abductions, 35,000 rapes and attempts to rape, and 86,000 assaults, we aim to decrease the number as much as possible.

1.1 Input

The input of this model can be sound sources such as humans' voices, screams, frequencies such as frequencies of screaming of saving words which we categorized in each Indian Languages for example in Hindi, "Bachao", in English "Help, Save, police", in Telugu "Kapadandi", "Madad" in Gujarati, "Udhavi" in Tamil, "Mai kar madath" in the Kashmiri Language… etc. Screams in the sense, the screaming tone of women when they get scared or getting assaulted.

1.2 Error Handling

Major errors that can occur in our model are fake encountering of the input and outputs others can be power discharging issues, and errors in the working model we provided a solution to solve these problems in the proposed system section of this document. Apart from practical problems, errors for coding are handled by using "Try-Catch" methods of the programming language which allows programmers to understand questions like what's happening in the code, what is causing an error and to rectify it, and to help run other parts of the program.

2 Background

As we all are aware the most likely scenarios where harmful situations for women arise can be:

- Isolated places at night-time, where there is no surveillance either by humans or technologically.
- Different types of harassment are:
- Rape, Domestic Violence, and Harassment.
- This can occur on lowkey Streets when women stay alone at their own houses, office basements or apartments basements, Parks, city outskirts, public transport generally at night times and low public spots, in developed/semi-developed states such as Indian metro states there exists lots of nightclubs, which acts as the base for most of the crimes that occur at women's, area around the clubs when people are drunk and not in their proper state.
- Considering the above point, while further understanding the problem, we concluded that, as the technology and culture are drastically upgrading year by year hence the party culture is widespread throughout the world, which is leading to many loopholes where women and men are getting pickpocketed, killed, raped, harassed...etc. going home after partying is one of the major issues, where people need to trust other people who provide their service to them such as cab drivers, people who give lifts, and people that are met at the same party.
- Areas nearby the women's Colleges and hostels are the main hotspots, moreover, areas, where construction works are being done as the laborers who work in those sites, are also at risk of attacks on women.
- One more unspoken truth of the world is Human Trafficking, Where most girls and women are trafficked for economical and sexual misuse, specifically prostitution, forced labor, pornography... was officially stated by United Nations Office on Drugs and Crime (UNODC) that the most common form of human trafficking is sexual exploitation which is around 79%, 2nd most common is forced labor, around 18%, moreover, they reported that around 20% of the trafficked humans are children and in places like Africa 100% of them are Children.

Hence, considering all the above-mentioned problems and facts, we came forward to help every innocent woman and child who might be in the mentioned scenarios, with all love and concern we would never want to repeat all these to any one person in our presence and came up with this idea of women safety without disturbing humans privacy as it is the most valuable thing [5].

3 Literature Review

One of the most convenient tools in the world right now for women's safety is CCTV Cameras. They have their demerits such as privacy issues, they cost a lot, can't be installed in every part of the area this gets complicated when it comes to every piece of land such as a district consists of an area and a state consists of a district hence considering this way it costs a lot to plant CCTV in every instance, these are very sensitive and can break, thus neglecting the main objective of capturing every detail of a crime incident i.e. they are vulnerable [1, 7]; CCTV can't stop the crime, be smart, and report the incident. In a nutshell, cameras act as the front-line system of police when police aren't there. When it comes to evening and nighttime, most of the CCTV cameras don't work properly at night and need infrared night vision and night cameras which increase the complexity and cost of the products all over the country when taken country-wise [2, 5]. These have a blind spot too, it's not mandatory that even after the country has enough CCTVs after spending a lot on these, there is still a chance of frailty. After All these reasons there still exists many more reasons for CCTVs being misused such as, as mentioned, people's privacy gets disturbed and in such cases, they are recorded and being misused as "Caught in Act" format videos which can be uploaded on the internet and make humans lose their privacy [1, 10]. Other is, CCTV spread discrimination and prejudice, such as regional, sexual, age, class, race. Etc. When the videos get leaked or the operators spread the word [8]. No government has made a law to protect humans from getting caught on camera.

4 Dataset

The Dataset for this kind of approach is not much explored. Hence, the Authors came up with a solution to develop their dataset which can be useful with numerous applications in the field. Where the parameters they decided to consider were, as follows:

"**Vocal type**", which describes the mode of the speech, and voice. Which Sub divides into the given following list:

Modal Speech, Aggressive Speech, Fear Speech, Aggressive Roar, Fear Scream, Pain Mild, Pain Moderate, and Pain Intense. These values are denoted with 0 to 7 where 0 starts from Modal Speech and leads to 7 as Pain Intense.

Other parameters are categorized as **Acoustic Variables**, which in general means temperature, pressure, particle motion, or Density, and are subs categorized into the following mentioned entities:

- Duration is denoted as dur.
- Mean F0 (Frequency) in Hz, denoted as mF0
- Mean F0 in ERB, denoted as F0erb
- Maximum F0 (Hz), denoted as maxF0
- Minimum F0 (Hz), denoted as minF0
- Standard deviation in F0 (Hz), denoted as F0sd

- Coefficient of variation denoted as F0CV.

The third category is named **Vocaliser Sex**, which can be: M, which stands for Male, F, which stands for Female. Hence, the final dataset is described as an excel sheet or statistical data, and of which columns are described in Table 2.

Table 2. Description of dataset columns

Vocaliser_ID	Vocal type label: vocal type is defined as (modal speech – pain intense)	VC_0_F0sd
Sex: denoted as vocaliser sex (M or F)	F0erb	VC_0_F0CV
Age: denoted as numerical value	VC_0to7_mF0	VC_1_dur
Height: denoted in terms of centimetre	VC_0_dur	VC_1_mF0
Handgrip	VC_0_mF0	VC_1_F0erb
Chest: size of the chest	VC_0_F0erb	VC_1_maxF0
Bicep: size of the bicep	VC_0_maxF0	VC_1_minF0
Vocal type code: vocal type defined value (0–7)	VC_0_minF0	VC_1_F0sd VC_1_F0CV

And so on till VC_7. Where VC is Vocal Type, which consists of values in terms of the mentioned units, Hz or ERB, and one can download the dataset and modify it from this link

5   Proposed Approach

5.1   Research Used

Screams represented the overall utmost values of F0 (Frequency) (Fig. 1) and in turn the highest degree of variability, among vocal types; both between and within the genders. For instance, [9, 11]; the average F0s values of the scream of the women ranged between 484 and 1981 Hz, which is demonstrating a variance of nearly 1500 Hz between the lowest-pitched and highest-pitched women [12, 13]. And the fearful speech is relatively much more bridled, with mean F0s ranging between 307 and 570 Hz in women. Figure 1 displays the waves generated when the higher degree of an intraindividual variance in F0 by various vocal types produced by an individual adult female.

The distance between two sensors: Hollering can usually be heard maximum [6]; 3 to 5 miles or 4–8 km in the echoing place. But we will keep our several sensors at a distance of every 1 km consecutively at the blind spot for the perfect surveillance.

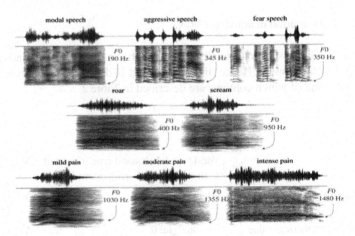

Fig. 1. Waveforms demonstrate a higher degree of intra-individual variance in F0 by various vocal types produced by an individual adult female [14].

5.2 Hardware Necessities for Our Product Development

Hardware necessities for the development of the product are mentioned below.

Arduino. Arduino is a device with an open-source software and hardware organization that manufactures single-board microcontrollers and microcontroller kits for building various projects Fig. 2 shows the Arduino Uno board.

Fig. 2. Arduino (Source: Arduino. cc)

The Arduino board has different sets of pins such as digital input/Output pi and analog Input/Output pins. These pins will be connected to many different breadboards, other different circuits, and other sensors. The boards feature periodical communications interfaces, together with connections on some models, which can also be used for loading the programs.

Raspberry Pi. RPi is a mini-computer that is so small that it can fit in our hands. The most important thing is a camera and a camera for user integration called DSI in its terms [3]. It runs on a software called Raspbian, it works on the Linux version. We can install it using a micro Sd card. This, when combined with a GSM module, is used to give the location of the model.

GSM Module. GSM module means "Global System for Mobile Communication" Sometimes it is even called a GPRS module. It is used to inaugurate conveyance between an IoT device such as a raspberry pi along with a mobile or laptop or any transmissible device. In devices such as us women's safety or any security devices, this module is used to provide alert messages in any kind of the emergency reach of the victim which is already saved in the modem and attached to the device, and then it can send messages during the emergency state. Some of the GSM modules functions are: Send an SMS, read an SMS, Delete an SMS and Observe the strength of the signal, where Fig. 3 shows what a GSM module looks like, it consists of an Antenna, SIM Card slot, and GPS tracker.

Fig. 3. GSM module (Source: Arduino. cc)

Sound Frequency Sensor. The sound sensor is the sensor that detects the intensity of sound waves in the surroundings. It is also present in mobile phones (microphones). This sensor plays a major role in the proposed model and looks as shown in Fig. 4 containing 3 pins and a microphone for capturing sound frequencies.

Fig. 4. Sound frequency sensor (Source: Arduino. cc)

Like ears, the sound sensor works the same. Like a diaphragm, the sound sensor has a microphone, amplifier, and peak detector which makes the sensor similar to the ear. Sound sensor processes and digitalizes the capacitance change made by the sound waves propagating from the surroundings. Sound sensors are simple and easy to use. This gives analog output to us which is later converted into digital input in the microcontroller board. LM393 Audio Amplifier is the sound sensor that costs a low, low-powered, and powerful amplifier that suits our project. It has 3 pin signals (output pin), +5 v, and GND (ground pin).

Jumper Wire. To make a project we need to connect one device to another device. These devices and sensors use a wire called jumper wire to make connections. Jumper wires connect pins at each end to different/same devices. This wire makes the connection to pins such as ground, power, and input/output pins on a device to other devices.

5.3 Software Specifications

Arduino IDE. Arduino IDE is Arduino's software; it is a text editor like a notepad with different features. It is used for writing code, compiling the code to check if any errors are there, and uploading the code to the Arduino.

5.4 Frequencies of Different Sounds

In general, the real-time difference btw the voice range we have found after calculating from various research sources (everywhere it is written different): Woman: 150 to 270 Hz and Man: 60 to 160 Hz.

- Types of speech with their threshold frequency in females considering lower pitch females:

  - Modal speech: 148 Hz
  - Aggressive speech: 345 Hz
  - Fear Speech: 307 Hz
  - Roar: 400 Hz
  - Scream: 484 Hz
  - Mild pain: 1030 Hz
  - Moderate pain: 1355 Hz
  - Intense pain: 1480 Hz

- Types of speech with their threshold frequency in males:

  - Modal speech: 81 Hz
  - Aggressive: 300 Hz
  - Fear Speech: 289 Hz
  - Roar: 379 Hz

- Scream: 467 Hz
- Mild pain: 271 Hz
- Moderate pain: 340 Hz
- Intense pain: 441 Hz.

5.5 Working

The authors in this research paper have summed up the methodology as follows: A woman speaks at a higher pitch i.e. about an octave higher than a man. The average pitch range of an adult woman is from "165 to 255 Hz", whereas a man is between "85 to 155 Hz" [4]. So, the authors proposed a solution to build a sensor, where a particular threshold value of the certain hertz is fixed, above which will be the range of screaming pitch of females. This sensor will be connected to the emergency helpline numbers. Several sensors will be kept at a distance from other sensors consecutively within the blind spot area for perfect surveillance. If a woman will scream at the time of harassment around the sensor, then the pitch will surpass the threshold value and it will start beeping loudly and give direct calls to emergency numbers.

5.6 Cost Estimation

Estimates for the cost of the prototype and the comparisons with the competitors are given in Table 2 which compares the costs of the prototype if it is built using the premium high-quality product and built using locally available products in the states of India (Table 3).

Table 3. Cost estimation of the prototype (INR)

Model	Cost (Rupees)	High-quality cost (Rupees) (est)
Sound sensor	100	250
Arduino UNO	700	1500
Buzzer	30	100
GPRS/GPS module	500	900
12V Dc battery	350	400
Total	1700	3150

So, these costs sum up to 1700 Indian Rupees and the original costs turn out to be 3150 Indian Rupees. The point to be noted is that these prices are made for a prototype but then the cost for building a bulk product decreases up to 30% which is one of the good advantages of the Indian market.

5.7 Cost Comparison with CCTV

The average cost of a CCTV without any implementation is a minimum of 1,000–2,000 per piece just for a camera and the high-quality ones will range up to 23,000 [6, 11]. As per, "The Wire", states that "CCTV Surveillance is rising in India, but crime rates remain unaffected". It even says that cities with more cameras have more number of crimes, which allows us to assume that, Government requires a second level of protection along with the CCTVs, as the assaulters are required to be tracked out at the time of assault not after they are done with it and followed thereafter, the authors in this paper are trying to do the same thing and the block diagram is shown in Fig. 5 of the proposed model [15].

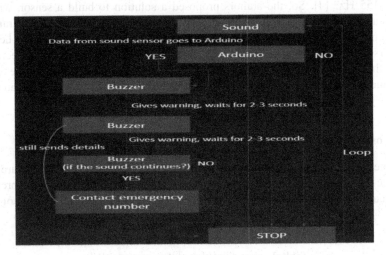

Fig. 5. Working on the proposed model

5.8 Process Flow of the Solution

The very first step is to detect the screams of women, through the help of a sensor known as a sound sensor. After which a deep distortion sounds are released as a warning which scares the weak-hearted culprit, as per human psychology, when people get to know someone is watching their actions they tend to get away from it and this helps by reducing 50% of the assaults. Even after trying to stop these assaults there still exist people who do not mind those alarms or warnings and continue to do so. Hence for such cases, the authors in this paper suggest, sharing the immediate current location to the nearby emergency centers such as law enforcement agents or security forces, but after confirming the assault, for which they have assigned a team called as "Response Team", whose task is to check the location for fake alarm or fake assault creation, in case it is fake, they report to the team that it is fake and close the case, in case it is real, nearby devices get connected using IoT to track the location of the culprits and which provides work of the Response Team easy by letting them know the details of the culprit in Realtime which is being lacked by CCTVs.

Locations, where this device can be planted, are on trees, electric polls where regular people cannot reach out due to fear of electric shock, places that are not visible to the naked eye at the first or second glance, but there exists the notice board such as CCTV boards which says "You are under CCTV surveillance" similarly for their device, "You are under influence of scream detection region". These devices are located in important places which we have categorized as 2 parts, likely Primary Locations and Secondary locations. Primary locations include very important and crime-prone areas such as Places where there don't exist CCTV Cameras where are needed, isolated places, and Deadly streets in Villages, Mountains, and Valleys, Places with a high rate of crime against women, empty roads. Secondary locations include Places like cities, lanes, construction places, party locations, and general locations where CCTV does not exist. The authors in this paper are planning to integrate with the state government and the central government to take their help to implement the initiative along with the communities like National Commission for Women, and SHE Teams. Storing of the data will be done only when the model recognizes any situation as an assault until the verification team investigates and provides a report. This data is strictly prohibited for 3rd party access and will not be used for any other purpose.

Advantages of this technology can be that this works without service of any internet using its own GPS/GPRS modules which is the major positive aspect of the device and thus can be used in remote locations which tick the box of primary locations category, detects screams of only girls. Authors have decided to include only girls' screams because the main aspect of this device is to reduce the crime rate against women and to track the assaulter's location. Where Fig. 6 denotes the demonstration of violin plots with the mean F0 as full distribution for each gender and vocal type.

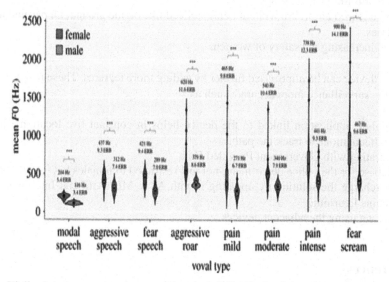

Fig. 6. Violin plots demonstrate the mean F0 as the full distribution for each vocal type and gender [14]

6   Results and Discussion

The goal of developing a women's safety device is to take appropriate action at the perfect time which requires detecting first and taking an action. This paper consists of 6 chapters, where the introduction consists of a detailed intro of the problem authors have dealt with. Then there's Background, which includes the motivation for the solution. Literature Review has some summaries of similar technologies in the field. Dataset Chapter describes the dataset and how they created it. The proposed Approach has a detailed description of the solution, experiments they've performed, and justification for the work is given here, where they discussed hardware, software, Input, and process flow of the solution. In the conclusion, the authors have mentioned some limitations and the future scope of the solution.

Currently, in the world, we have CCTV cameras as security for humans and females included but these do have a blind spot and can't recognize the situation and call for help at the same time hence making the situation no help but our product have a lot of advantages such as

- The use of Beep sound: If they hear an alarming beep sound at the time of the abuse, it's more likely they get scared and run away and thus, decreasing the cases of harassment.
- The use of emergency numbers: to get immediate help for the victim.
- We can put this technology on different streets to identify if there is any unwanted situation.
- It can be used even at night-time.
- Can be used in blind spots which lack electricity and light.
- Can be used in rural areas.
- Easily affordable technology.
- Can be placed anywhere without being noticed like on the ground, on barren land, or on trees.
- Thus, increasing the safety of women.

The device can be improvised further by adding more features. These features could make the surveillance more accurate such as

- A mobile application linked to the device helps in constant live location while in assault situations to track the path.
- Integrating with Government Provided Data.
- Database for the police department, not just restricted to females but for all genders.
- Supercharge the solution by updating it with AI & ML (Artificial Intelligence and Machine Learning)
- Tracking using the adjacent devices.

References

1. Tanwar, D., Nijhawan, V., Sinha, P., Gupta, R.: Design of low-cost women safety system using GPS and GSM. In: 2021 8th International Conference on Computing for Sustainable Global Development (INDIACom), pp. 827–831 (2021)

2. Jatti, A., Kannan, M., Alisha, R.M., Vijayalakshmi, P., Sinha, S.: Design and development of an IOT based wearable device for the safety and security of women and girl children. In: 2016 IEEE International Conference on Recent Trends in Electronics, Information & Communication Technology (RTEICT) (2016). https://doi.org/10.1109/rteict.2016.7808003

3. Toney, G., Jabeen, F., Puneeth S: Design and implementation of safety armband for women and children using ARM7. In: 2015 International Conference on Power and Advanced Control Engineering (ICPACE) (2015). https://doi.org/10.1109/icpace.2015.7274962

4. Seelam, K., Prasanti, K.: A novel approach to provide protection for women by using smart security device. In: 2018 2nd International Conference on Inventive Systems and Control (ICISC) (2018). https://doi.org/10.1109/icisc.2018.8399093

5. Helen, A., Fathila, M.F., Rijwana, R., Kalaiselvi V.K.G.: A smart watch for women security based on IoT concept 'watch me.' In: 2017 2nd International Conference on Computing and Communications Technologies (ICCCT) (2017). https://doi.org/10.1109/iccct2.2017.797 2266

6. Sheikh, J.A., Fayyaz, Z.: #MeToo: an app to enhancing women safety. In: Ahram, T.Z., Falcão, C. (eds.) AHFE 2018. AISC, vol. 794, pp. 546–553. Springer, Cham (2019). https://doi.org/10.1007/978-3-319-94947-5_55

7. Velayutham, R., Sabari, M., Rajeswari, M.S.: An innovative approach for women and children's security based location tracking system. In: 2016 International Conference on Circuit, Power and Computing Technologies (ICCPCT) (2016). https://doi.org/10.1109/iccpct.2016.7530325

8. Monisha, D.G., Monisha, M., Pavithra, G., Subhashini, R.: Women safety device and application-FEMME. Ind. J. Sci. Technol. 9, 1–6 (2016). https://doi.org/10.17485/ijst/2016/v9i10/88898

9. Pantelopoulos, A., Bourbakis, N.G.: A survey on wearable sensor-based systems for health monitoring and prognosis. IEEE Trans. Syst. Man Cybern. Part C (Appl. Rev.) 40, 1–12 (2010). https://doi.org/10.1109/tsmcc.2009.2032660

10. Vigneshwari, S., Aramudhan, M.: Social information retrieval based on semantic annotation and hashing upon the multiple ontologies. Ind. J. Sci. Technol. 8, 103 (2015). https://doi.org/10.17485/ijst/2015/v8i2/57771

11. Sethuraman, R., Sasiprabha, T., Sandhya, A.: An effective QoS based web service composition algorithm for integration of travel & tourism resources. Procedia Comput. Sci. 48, 541–547 (2015). https://doi.org/10.1016/j.procs.2015.04.133

12. George, R., Cherian, V.A., Antony, A., Sebastian, H., Antony, R.M.: An intelligent security system for violence against women in public places. Int. J. Eng. Adv. Technol. 3(4), 64–68 (2014)

13. Owren, M.J.: Human voice in evolutionary perspective. Acoust. Today 7, 24–33 (2011)

14. Lavan, N., Burton, A., Scott, S.K., McGettigan, C.: Flexible voices: Identity perception from variable vocal signals. Psychon. Bull. Rev. 26(1), 90–102 (2018). https://doi.org/10.3758/s13423-018-1497-7

15. CCTV Surveillance is Rising in India, World, but Crime Rates Remain Unaffected. https://thewire.in/rights/cctv-surveillance-is-rising-in-india-world-but-crime-rates-remain-unaffected. Accessed 12 Jan 2022

Cognitive Workload Estimation Using Eye Tracking: A Review

Annu Pradhan[✉] [iD] and Ela Kumar

Indira Gandhi Delhi Technical University for Women, Delhi, India
annupradhan26@gmail.com, ela_kumar@igdtuw.ac.in

Abstract. Eye tracking is the process of gathering hidden information present in the eye. To specifically understand visual attention and workload, eye tracking data can be of immense help. Eye tracking technology can help us to understand where the eyes are currently focused at, for how long this focus is. Cognitive workload can be estimated by analysing eye tracking data, Human behaviour can be studied with eye tracking metrics. The principal objective of the paper is to give a review of workload estimation through eye tracking metrics via statistical and machine learning approaches. Eye Tracking parameters are used for calculating cognitive workload and to understand the in-depth process behind decision making.

Keywords: Fixation · Saccades · Machine learning · Eye tracking · NASA-TLX · Pupil dilation · Fixation duration

1 Introduction

Cognitive workload can be defined as the ability of mental resources required by an individual at any instant of time. It influences the cognitive process required to respond to the environment and make decisions. Workload is a quantifiable mental effort put forth by an individual in response to a cognitive task.

Eye tracking elucidate the procedure of computing gaze. These computations are performed by an eye tracker that records eye location and eye motion. The working of eye tracker is defined as following: (1) Heat radiation is pointed on the way to pupil, giving rise to noticeable mirroring between pupil and optic. (2) These reflections are traced by a thermal camera.

An approach is proposed for the assessment of cognitive workload by analysing the dissimilarity in pupil diameter and various facets of eye movements at different levels of mental workload. During the experiment [3], these facets were measured with eye trackers to see if they were actually indicators of mental stress. In general, the pupil diameter and fixation time increase significantly as the mental load increases, whereas the distance and speed of the saccade do not show much difference. This mental load assessment can serve as a stimulus to assist information systems operators in meeting their operational requirements. The study [4] result shows that the interaction with the secondary operation leads to a decrease in driving speed by a significant amount. Secondary tasks have harmful consequences on the driving performance. Drivers reported

V. Sugumaran et al. (Eds.): AIR 2022, CCIS 1738, pp. 544–552, 2022.
https://doi.org/10.1007/978-3-031-23724-9_49

that interacting with multiple vehicle systems significantly increased subject mental load more than a single trivial task or normal driving. Pupil diameter is contemplated as a significant index of cognitive load. Tiny but ubiquitous alteration forms the basis of cognitive pupillary measurements which provide unique psychological indicators of the brain's dynamic activity in human cognition [5]. The Index of Cognitive Activity is a signal processing technique that uses varied involuntary characteristics to isolate the result of lighting and cognitive load on pupil size [6, 17]. Eye tracking parameters provide significant information about a subject's cognitive workload classification [8]. In [10], bivariate analysis methods were employed for summarizing the relationship between two variables where the analysis between NASA-Task Load Index (NASA-TLX) and performance scores is summarized.

The principal objective of this study is to provide a review for determining the relationship between cognitive workload and different eye tracking metrics via descriptive statistical methods and machine learning methods. The flow of this work is as follows: A brief discussion about cognitive workload and eye tracking metrics is presented in Sect. 2, while the research procedure describing the generally used hardware and workload assessment tool is discussed in Sect. 3. In Sect. 4 cognitive load estimation methods based on statistical and machine learning approaches is presented followed by conclusion in Sect. 5.

2 Background

Cognitive workload can be defined as the amount of mental labour required by an individual in regards to cognitive task. It is typically scrutinized as the asset of a subject rather than its cognitive task [10]. The manifold intricacies of mental task need contrasting levels of attentiveness. The acumen and attention are seriously distorted in response to mental fatigue. Mental load is basically the consequence of reciprocity between task demands and subjects' personification, individually neither the task demands nor the subject can elucidate mental workload. It is basically an aggregation of mental resources required to attain a distinct level of task performance. According to [17], different types of eye tracking metrics such as pupil diameter, fixation duration, saccadic duration and many others are significant contributors for determining cognitive workload. A brief discussion about different eye tracking metrics is mentioned beneath.

2.1 Gaze Points

Gaze points are the individual points obtained on the screen when the eyes are focused on a particular area. It gives information about where our eyes are looking at a particular instant.

2.2 Fixation

Eyes fixated at particular locale for a short period induce a fixation. Fixation has two important properties: (1) Multiple gaze points constitute a fixation. (2) Fixation have time duration along with structural coordinates. They are not actual since they are constructions and resultants of arithmetic computations which renders a sequence of gaze points into sequence of fixations.

2.3 Saccade

A saccade is the quick movement of eyes from one locale to another locale. It can be defined as general eye movement between fixations.

2.4 Velocity Classification

According to [20], one of the useful aspects of the Tobii Pro software is the classification of gaze data according to relative speed. By default, a certain speed threshold is set, which is the neutral point, where speed points above this neutral point are classified as saccade, and points below this neutral point are classified as a fixation. Fixation is useful because it refers to a normally stationary eye movement that forces the subject to keep their gaze in a relatively constant position. Although saccades are usually associated with rapid eye movements, it should be understood that short saccades, called micro-saccades, may be the result of spontaneous noises from eyelashes but the ambient data may still be useful with the Tobii Pro Velocity Classification System making it easy to implement output and metric classification methods that use fixed points as valid data points for further analysis. In [18], author proposed a new taxonomy for fixation identification. It classifies algorithm on the foundation of space and time-based criterion. The space-based criterion divides the algorithm into conditions to use information about speed, distribution of data and location of interest. Time based standardization differentiates the algorithm according to time usage and local context. Author emphasizes the fact that in speed-based algorithms fixation points have low speed and saccade points have high speed. Distribution based algorithms use the intermediate range of fixation points under the assumption that fixations data points usually occur next to each other. Area-based algorithm identifies areas that depict accurate visual representations.

2.5 Fixation Duration

Fixation duration is the average time spent on all fixations [12, 13]. This duration length usually varies from 150–300 ms. It can be both shorter and longer. It is roughly defined as the time period between the termination of one saccade and the onset of next saccade. The amount of involvement increases with fixation duration.

2.6 Pupil Dilation

Iris controls the pupil size depending upon the amount of light present in the surrounding. Pupils dilate to get more light in the eye, in contrast to the contraction in bright light. According to [14], pupil inflation is a common characteristic when workload increases in performance-based activities. Pupillary dilation is known to respond rapidly to changes in the brightness of the field of view and a person's cognitive load while performing visual tasks [15]. The study results emphasized that pupil inflation is an authentic index of cognitive workload estimation. Both authors have created a neural network-based calibration interface for eye tracking system that eliminates individual pupil size impairments.

2.7 Gaze Entropy

Gaze entropy is the average amount of information required for specifying the distribution of eye fixation [16]. It describes entropy to be a quantitative process that gauges the ocular skimming behaviour during the cognitive workload process. To compute the central uncertainty for a series of fixations produced in a given time period, Shannon entropy's equation is applied for the probability distribution of fixation points. In [10], the entropy was calculated on the basis of Shannon's entropy. The reason behind is that the probe pattern becomes arbitrary to a greater extent when workload shoots up. The results indicated that gaze entropy is appreciably associated with NASA-TLX rating (rm = .51, p < .001).

2.8 Saccadic Intrusion (SI)

Saccadic intrusion (SI) is a one of the distinct types of eye manoeuvre. An interlude of SI is generally a round trip from a gaze-based fixation coordinate. The gaze of the subject moves away very fast from one fixation point and returns back to the original fixation point. In [19], it is asserted that SI is very closely related to mental activity. SI are independent of changes in brightness, so SI was used as an indicator of cognitive workload [19].

3 Procedure

Cognitive workload estimation procedure initiates with experimental setup. A wearable eye tracking system is then used to extract eye monitoring metrics. Custom MATLAB and Python programming language programs can be used to analyze data from an eye tracking system. Eye tracking measures can also be used for exploratory data analysis. Figure 1 displays the approach's flowchart. Below, the components of the research process are addressed.

3.1 Participants

In order to estimate workload using eye tracking based system, participants are required to be a part of the experiment while it is being performed. For ensuring safe driving experience, pinning down fatigue and workload is crucial. Twenty healthy participants (10 men and 10 women) with central age distribution of 22.8 (normal deviation of 1.89 years) participated in the study [10]. Every partaker had driving experience of at least one year of driving experience. The agenda and research strategy of the test was elucidated to the candidates in advance. People in the study [8] are not trained surgeons to participate in robot skills training i.e., the participants have limited past robotic experience). Eight surgeons from a large medical school were hired voluntarily. (±standard deviation) age was 26 years (±1.6). No one had previous experience of clinical robots.

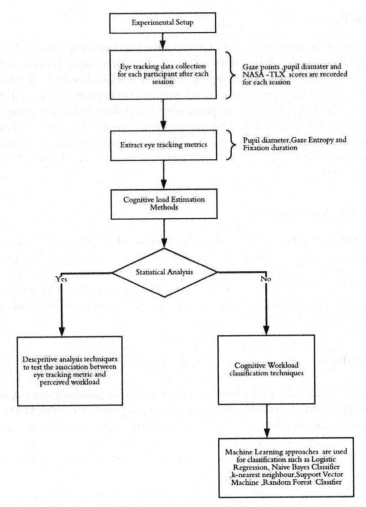

Fig. 1. Cognitive workload analysis workflow

3.2 Instruments

- **Simulation Software**

  The system consists of a surgical console with robotic controls (pedals, main controls and controls for positioning) and a robot-based arm for remote surgery [10]. The console comprises of a popular simulation software provided by the da Vinci manufacturer, allowing trainees to do simulated movements without actually touching the robotic arm. This study used both console and software. A simulator model for performing driving activity, number GDS SEDAN-2014-D developed at by Grid space. Co. Ltd. was used in the study [8]. This simulator provides realistic driving conditions and can be used to teach real driving.

- **Eye Tracker**
  Tobii Pro Glasses 2 is a wearable eye tracker, used to record driver appearance. The glasses elucidate exact information on what a particular participant is viewing [8, 10].
- **Cognitive Workload Assessment Tool**
  The NASA Task Load Index (NASA-TLX) is used in a comprehensive scale. It is a rational, multi-dimensional assessment tool that estimates the amount of mental workload required to assess workload. NASA-TLX, the total cognitive workload is a combination of 6 scales namely: Cognitive Need, Physical Need, Temporary Need, Performance, Effort, Disappointment/Frustration. Each of these small scales has a meaning and a specific standardized scale is also provided for the participant to rate. In [1], the suitability of using blink frequency and duration of blink is used as a method to evaluate a surgeon's cognitive workload. The correlation was performed between eye blinks and NASA TLX. The principal objective of the paper [2] is to probe the impact and relevance of road conditions and driving information on the subjects psychological functioning. Drivers found that the feeling of frustration, business, and mental illness dominated the impact of high-level load. Highway conditions provide an average of 62 overall performance points better compared to city and rural roads. Repeated measure correlations were used to examine the relationship between the workload (NASA-TLX rating) and task outcome. NASA-TLX compatibility performance and task outcome for all tests was .55 (p < .001), indicating that if the workload is high, performance is not good [10].

4   Cognitive Load Estimation Methods

4.1   Statistical Analysis

Correlation is a statistic that estimates the extent to which two variables change in context of one another. It indicates the strength of association between two variables and is expressed as a numerical correlation coefficient. Repeated Measures Correlation (rmcorr) accounts for the non-independence between observations using Analysis of Covariance, (ANCOVA), for statistical adjustments for interpersonal variability [11]. Rmcorr provides the best linear fits for each participant using parallel regression lines, i.e., with identical slopes and distinct intercepts, by reducing the variances measured between individuals. A descriptive analysis of the eye blink data is performed [1]. Moderate blinking is used to divide surgeons into unusual and normal blink groups. Author compared activity performance (work time, instrument trajectory distance, and error rate) and NASATLX performance between the two groups. The surgeon's blink rate and blink duration were compared with results from the NASA TLX report using Pearson's correlation test.

4.2   Machine Learning Based Classification Methods

- **Logistic Regression**
  To classify high and low levels of workload by eye-tracking metric, logistic regression is performed using IBM SPSS Statistics version 25 software, and each NASATLX

dimension was individually examined to understand its relationship to gaze points [8]. It is found that logistic regression model performed best in terms of accuracy and coefficient of determination (R2). Logistic regression is typically used in applications that require a deep understanding of the reasons for decisions made by a model.

Logistic Regression is used to figure out the probability of a certain class such has high/low. A logistic function is used to model a binary variable in the fundamental form of the statistical model known as logistic regression. Hence here logistic model was used to classify eye tracking metrics into high/low workload. It's an S – shaped curve that converts a real number into a quantity between 0 and 1, but not exactly at 0 and 1.

- **Naïve Bayes Classifier**
  A supervised machine learning algorithm based on the Bayes Theorem is called the naive Bayes classifier. The fact that each feature in the naive bayes classifier is independent of the others is one of its distinctive features. [7]. The Bayes theorem is used to calculate the likelihood of a hypothesis given the available data. The conditional probability determines this. The Bayes theorem offers a method to review previous predictions because conditional probability is the probability that an outcome will occur based on previous outcomes that occurred under similar conditions.

- **K-Nearest Neighbour Algorithm**
  K-nearest neighbour is a machine learning algorithm that works on the main principle of similarity between a new data point and old data points available in the corpora. A new data is categorized into a distinct category using the KNN algorithm. The classifier model indicates that the nearest neighbor hyperparameter number is 5 for KNN [9].

- **Support Vector Machine (SVM)**
  Support vector machine is widely used for classification problem but it can also be used for a regression problem. Its main objective is to find a hyperplane in an N expanse space that classifies the input data records in a well-defined manner. Here hyperplanes are ruling based parameters that help to separate data points. Data records falling on both sides of the hyperplane can be classified in distinct classes. A line is just present when the no of data records is two, it transforms into a two-dimensional plane when the no of data records is three. In [9], author used SVM with a linear kernel and logistic regression and multilayer perceptron (MLP) to achieve the best classification quality. These models required 5, 5, and 4 features per class, respectively.

- **Random Forest Classifier**
  An example of supervised machine learning is the Random Forest classifier. It is centered on the concept of group learning. The practice of combining many classifiers to tackle complicated issues and enhance model performance is known as ensemble learning. It is a decision tree (CART) mod-el bootstrapping algorithm. A model composed of several decision trees. This approach gets its term "random" from two fundamental ideas that make it successful. First, when creating trees, random sampling of training data points Second, while dividing nodes, random subsets of features are taken into account. The random forest's hyperparameters, with a tree count of 100, were specified in the classifier model [9].

5 Conclusion

We came across different eye tracking metrics used in eye tracking based methods. From the review we identified that fixation duration, pupil dilation, saccadic intrusion and gaze entropy are prominent contributors of workload estimation. Statistical methods were used for finding correlation between individual eye tracking based metrics and cognitive workload. Different classification-based machine learning approaches were used for accurately classifying cognitive workload using NASA-TLX based scores.

References

1. Zheng, B., Jiang, X., Tien, G., Meneghetti, A., Panton, O.N.M., Atkins, M.S.: Workload assessment of surgeons: correlation between NASA TLX and blinks. Surg. Endosc. **26**, 2746–2750 (2012). https://doi.org/10.1007/s00464-012-2268-6
2. Sugiono, S., Widhayanuriyawan, D., Andriani, D.P.: Investigating the impact of road condition complexity on driving workload based on subjective measurement using NASA TLX. In: MATEC Web of Conferences, vol. 136, p. 02007 (2017). https://doi.org/10.1051/matecconf/201713602007
3. de Greef, T., Lafeber, H., van Oostendorp, H., Lindenberg, J.: Eye movement as indicators of mental workload to trigger adaptive automation. In: Schmorrow, D.D., Estabrooke, I.V., Grootjen, M. (eds.) FAC 2009. LNCS (LNAI), vol. 5638, pp. 219–228. Springer, Heidelberg (2009). https://doi.org/10.1007/978-3-642-02812-0_26
4. Lansdown, T.C., Brook-Carter, N., Kersloot, T.: Distraction from multiple in-vehicle secondary tasks: vehicle performance and mental workload implications. Ergonomics **47**, 91–104 (2004). https://doi.org/10.1080/00140130310001629775
5. Beatty, J., Lucero-Wagoner, B.: The pupillary system. In: Cacioppo, J.T., Tassinary, L.G., Berntson, G.G. (eds.) Handbook of Psychophysiology, pp. 142–162. Cambridge University Press (2000)
6. Marshall, S.P.: Method and apparatus for Eye Tracking and Monitoring Pupil Dilation to Evaluate Cognitive Activity. National Center for Biotechnology Information. PubChem Patent Summary for US-6090051-A. https://pubchem.ncbi.nlm.nih.gov/patent/US-6090051-A. Accessed 12 Nov 2021
7. Friedman, N., Geiger, D., Goldszmidt, M.: Bayesian network classifiers. Mach. Learn. **29**, 131–163 (1997). https://doi.org/10.1023/A:1007465528199
8. Bitkina, O.V., Park, J., Kim, H.K.: The ability of eye-tracking metrics to classify and predict the perceived driving workload. Int. J. Ind. Ergon. **86**, 103193 (2021). https://doi.org/10.1016/j.ergon.2021.103193
9. Kaczorowska, M., Plechawska-Wójcik, M., Tokovarov, M.: Interpretable machine learning models for three-way classification of cognitive workload levels for eye-tracking features. Brain Sci. **11**, 210 (2021). https://doi.org/10.3390/brainsci11020210
10. Wu, C., et al.: Eye-tracking metrics predict perceived workload in robotic surgical skills training. Hum. Factors: J. Hum. Factors Ergon. Soc. **62**, 1365–1386 (2019). https://doi.org/10.1177/0018720819874544
11. Bakdash, J.Z., Marusich, L.R.: Repeated measures correlation. Front. Psychol. **8**, 456 (2017). https://doi.org/10.3389/fpsyg.2017.00456
12. Hofmann, M.J., Biemann, C., Remus, S.: Benchmarking n-grams, topic models and recurrent neural networks by cloze completions, EEGs and eye movements. In: Cognitive Approach to Natural Language Processing, pp. 197–215 (2017). https://doi.org/10.1016/b978-1-78548-253-3.50010-x

13. Nuthmann, A.: Fixation durations in scene viewing: modeling the effects of local image features, oculomotor parameters, and task. Psychon. Bull. Rev. **24**(2), 370–392 (2016). https://doi.org/10.3758/s13423-016-1124-4. https://www.researchgate.net/publication/279961525_Fixation_durations_-_why_are_they_so_highly_variable

14. Batmaz, I., Ozturk, M.: Using pupil diameter changes for measuring mental workload under mental processing. J. Appl. Sci. **8**, 68–76 (2007). https://doi.org/10.3923/jas.2008.68.76

15. Harris, D., Duffy, V., Smith, M., Stephanidis, C. (eds.): Human-Centered Computing (2019). https://doi.org/10.1201/9780367813369. https://www.taylorfrancis.com/chapters/edit/10.1201/9780367813369-108/pupil-dilation-indicator-cognitive-workload-human-computer-interaction-marc-pomplun-sindhura-sunkara

16. Shiferaw, B.A., et al.: Stationary gaze entropy predicts lane departure events in sleep-deprived drivers. Sci. Rep. **8**, 1–10 (2018). https://doi.org/10.1038/s41598-018-20588-7

17. Marquart, G., Cabrall, C., de Winter, J.: Review of eye-related measures of drivers' mental workload. Procedia Manuf. **3**, 2854–2861 (2015). https://doi.org/10.1016/j.promfg.2015.07.783

18. Salvucci, D.D., Goldberg, J.H.: Identifying fixations and saccades in eye-tracking protocols. In: Proceedings of the Symposium on Eye Tracking Research & Applications - ETRA 2000 (2000). https://doi.org/10.1145/355017.355028

19. Tokuda, S., Obinata, G., Palmer, E., Chaparro, A.: Estimation of mental workload using saccadic eye movements in a free-viewing task. In: 2011 Annual International Conference of the IEEE Engineering in Medicine and Biology Society (2011). https://doi.org/10.1109/iembs.2011.6091121

20. Beauchamp: Tobii – OpenWetWare. https://openwetware.org/wiki/Beauchamp:Tobii. Accessed 12 Nov 2021

Author Index

Printed in the United States
by Baker & Taylor Publisher Services